Sixth Edition

Play at the Center of the Curriculum

Judith Van Hoorn
University of the Pacific

Patricia Monighan Nourot
Late of Sonoma State University

Barbara Scales
University of California, Berkeley

Keith Rodriguez Alward

PEARSON

Boston   Columbus   Indianapolis   New York   San Francisco   Upper Saddle River
Amsterdam   Cape Town   Dubai   London   Madrid   Milan   Munich   Paris   Montreal   Toronto
Delhi   Mexico City   São Paulo   Sydney   Hong Kong   Seoul   Singapore   Taipei   Tokyo

This book is dedicated to Millie Almy, beloved mentor to our study of children's play, and to Patricia Monighan Nourot, our beloved co-author, whose life and scholarship were testaments to the power and joy of play.

Vice President and Editorial Director: Jeffery W. Johnston
Senior Acquisitions Editor: Julie Peters
Editorial Assistant: Andrea Hall
Vice President, Director of Marketing: Margaret Waples
Senior Marketing Manager: Krista Clark
Production Project Manager: Jennifer Gessner
Procurement Specialist: Michelle Klein
Senior Art Director: Jayne Conte
Cover Designer: John Christiana

Cover Photo: © Agnieszka Kirinicjanow/E+/Getty Images
Media Project Manager: Noelle Chun
Full-Service Project Management: Aptara®, Inc.
Composition: Aptara®, Inc.
Printer/Binder: Courier Westford
Cover Printer: Courier Westford
Text Font: ITC New Baskerville Std

Credits and acknowledgments for material borrowed from other sources and reproduced, with permission, in this textbook appear on the appropriate page within the text.

Every effort has been made to provide accurate and current Internet information in this book. However, the Internet and information posted on it are constantly changing, so it is inevitable that some of the Internet addresses listed in this textbook will change.

Photo Credits: Judith Van Hoorn, pp. 1, 248, 338; Annie Fuller/Merrill Education/Pearson Education, pp. 5, 51, 70, 79, 82, 89, 124, 205, 208, 240, 269, 302, 312, 318, 350, 367, 399, 410; Scott Cunningham/Merrill Education/Pearson Education, pp. 16, 235; David Kostelnik/Pearson Education, pp. 23, 198, 218; Miredi/Fotolia, p. 32; Pressmaster/Fotolia, pp. 37, 106, 386; Benjamin LaFramboise/Pearson Education, pp. 41, 171, 186, 294; Todd Yarrington/Merrill Education/Pearson Education, pp. 46, 373; Stockbyte/Getty Images, pp. 57, 59; Andrey Stratilatov/Shutterstock, p. 63; Krista Greco/Merrill Education/Pearson Education, pp. 95, 300; Barbara Schwartz/Merrill Education/Pearson Education, pp. 120, 224; Anne Vega/Merrill Education/Pearson Education, pp. 129, 152, 162, 335; Monkey Business/Fotolia, p. 136; Merrill Education/Pearson Education, p. 142; Sergiyn/Fotolia, p. 176; Barbara Schwartz/Merrill Education/Pearson Education, p. 224; David Nourot, p. 255; Kate_sept2004/E+/Getty Images, p. 266; Laura Bolesta/Merrill Education/Pearson Education, p. 274; Diego Cervo/Fotolia, p. 332; Corbis, p. 390; Anthony Magnacca/Merrill Education/Pearson Education, p. 402; Carla Mestas/Pearson Education, p. 419

Library of Congress Cataloging-in-Publication Data was not available at the time of publication. Available upon request.

10 9 8 7 6 5 4 3 2 1

ISBN 10:   0-13-346175-0
ISBN 13: 978-0-13-346175-6

PREFACE

In this sixth edition of *Play at the Center of the Curriculum,* we reaffirm our commitment to play in the early childhood classroom. This is an important time and opportunity for informed innovations in the way we educate young children. And early childhood is an important time in the lives of our future citizens. The stakes are enormous.

Today, children have fewer opportunities to play in schools and communities. At the same time, the natural link between play and development is becoming increasingly recognized. This is a time to reconcile early childhood education practices with developmental theory, research, and the wisdom of practitioners. Developmental theory shows that play is critical to the development of intelligence, personality, competencies, a sense of self, and social awareness. Research evidence shows that play supports learning across all domains of children's development.

Therefore, we believe that a developmentally appropriate, holistic, and integrated early childhood curriculum has play at its center. We demonstrate how play can be drawn on to improve developmentally based early childhood education. We propose that play is a critical dimension to children's learning and development throughout the preschool, kindergarten, and primary-grade years.

We believe that an ideal early childhood classroom is characterized by an abundance of play. Our experience tells us that teachers can learn to structure the early childhood classroom environment and to sequence classroom routines so that the learning expectations for children are embedded in spontaneous and guided play activity.

It has always been important that educators assure the community that its youth will receive the necessary abilities and skills to be productive citizens. In many schools, the articulation of academic expectations and standards represents an attempt to meet this responsibility. In this edition, we pay particular attention to demonstrating how developmentally appropriate standards can be met in a play-centered curriculum.

> . . . [A]lmost all children can play well . . . [P]lay teaches children how to be sociable and channels cognitive development . . . These capacities serve people lifelong once they go to work (Sennet, 2008, p. 268).

Play at the Center of the Curriculum carefully blends theory and practice. As seasoned teachers, we demonstrate how to draw both the methods and the content of a successful curriculum from children's play. We interweave vignettes of children's play, theories of play and development, and instructional strategies and guidelines that place play at the center of the curriculum.

By combining sound theory and research with practical illustrations, *Play at the Center of the Curriculum* achieves a solid argument for play. Teachers and students in

iii

the field of early childhood education will find this book to be a valuable resource. This is not merely a "how-to" book, nor is it simply a "thought" book. Rather, it is a blending of each, serving the reader in a number of ways.

Play at the Center of the Curriculum is a resource for those who want to engage children in a developmental zone where children and teachers are learning from and with each other. Current and future teachers are guided in methods of supporting children's progress through play. The teacher becomes the architect of the learning environment, using play and development as the blueprint.

NEW TO THIS EDITION

- This sixth edition is updated to include discussions of current topics in early childhood education that relate to play in early childhood practice and policy. New vignettes from classrooms link current best practices with theory and empirical research. Scores of new resources are cited throughout.

- The new chapter feature *Family Diversity* illustrates the many ways that the play-centered curriculum provides an inclusive, welcoming program for all children and families. We expand our emphasis on diversity in this new edition. Chapters provide more discussion and examples of how educators build on the children's strengths and meet the needs of children with special needs as well as children from diverse backgrounds and cultures, including children who are dual language learners.

- Each chapter has been organized with new pedagogical features to enhance students' learning: *Learning Outcomes, Summaries,* and *Applying Your Knowledge.* Chapters begin with a list of key learning outcomes to give readers an overview of the focus of the chapter. Chapter summaries highlight key concepts and review main points. The feature Applying Your Knowledge concludes each chapter so readers can assess their understandings of key concepts and consider practical applications in programs for young children.

- This sixth edition introduces the new focus on *advocating for play*. Early childhood professionals are advocates for play practices and policies that benefit children. In the first chapter we describe the many ways that early childhood educators and students can become informed advocates for play at multiple levels, from daily acts of advocacy with children, families, and colleagues to working together to affect public policy. Several chapters throughout the text include a new feature called *Advocacy in Action.* Case studies and vignettes portray teachers advocating for play as they develop environments and experiences for children's play, promote families' understanding of the importance of play, and advocate successfully for policies that make a difference in children's lives. The last chapter concludes with resources that educators can use to advocate for play with links to online resources.

- The mathematics and science chapters (Chapters 7 and 9, respectively) have been thoroughly revised and reorganized based on current frameworks and standards. Core concepts and processes are included. The science chapter reflects the inclusion of engineering and technology in the science framework and standards. We underscore that engineering and technology are important dimensions of traditional early childhood programs that provide opportunities for children's constructive play.

- There is increased emphasis on promoting children's health, well-being, and safety. The revised chapter on outdoor play (Chapter 12) features numerous practical strategies and resources for teachers and further emphasizes the contributions of outdoor play to children's healthy development and growth. We include an expanded section that clearly defines rough and tumble play and discusses its importance in development. The revised chapter on toys and technology (Chapter 13) considers the benefits and risks of new media technology and recommends guidelines for using screen technology in ways that support children's health, well-being, and developing competencies.

ORGANIZATION AND STRUCTURE

This text has been written for students with varying experience and knowledge. Chapters 1 through 6 are designed to form foundational concepts and principles. We recommend that these be read first.

Chapter 1 presents a rationale and framework for play at the center of a balanced, developmentally based curriculum. Numerous examples illustrate how teachers balance spontaneous and guided play with teacher-planned activities to support children's learning and meet program expectations.

Chapters 2 and 3 introduce theory and research that support our understanding of play and development. The reader is introduced to the ideas of major figures in developmental theory—Piaget, Vygotsky, Erikson, and Mead—as well as to the work of contemporary researchers. We provide perspectives on how play supports the development of children's symbolic thought, language and literacy, logical–mathematical thinking, problem solving, imagination, and creativity.

Chapters 4 and 5 bring this developmental focus back to the reality of the classroom. We explore the teacher's role in setting the stage, actively guiding, and orchestrating play. These chapters show the many factors regarding intervention strategies, environments, materials, and timing that educators consider in program implementation. The issue of how teachers might respond to violent and aggressive play is addressed through vignettes and practical strategies.

Chapter 6 looks at the many ways that play can be used to assess children's developmental progress and describes play-centered approaches to authentic assessment. Included are many examples of play that embed state and national curriculum standards.

Chapters 7 through 11 explore curriculum areas that are of interest to contemporary early childhood education: mathematics, language and literacy, science, the arts, and socialization. Each content area chapter begins with a vignette that focuses on how the curriculum is embedded in the children's spontaneous play. The chapters describe how spontaneous and guided play provide balance to teacher-planned activities. The reader will find a rich palette of practical ideas for the articulation of the play-centered curriculum. Throughout these chapters, we discuss how teachers respond to the challenge of our ever-more ethnically and culturally diverse classrooms as well as meeting expectations and standards in a developmentally appropriate manner.

Chapter 12 advocates for the importance of outdoor play to promote children's health and well-being. Outdoor play involves children in physical activity, engagement with nature, as well as opportunities for self-initiated play and inquiry. The place for children's rough and tumble play in school settings is discussed extensively. This chapter presents best practices in planning, observing, interpreting, and assessing young children's outdoor play.

The chapters on science and outdoor play develop the text's emphasis on the importance of developing children's connection with nature and the environment. New curriculum has been added to the art chapter foregrounding novel ways to enhance children's engagement with natural materials.

Chapter 13 looks at ways in which play, toys, and media technology interact to affect the young child's life. We present many ideas and observations useful to teachers and families on the roles of toys and games. We recommend guidelines for the use of media technology to support children's health and developing competencies.

Depending on the background of students, instructors can vary the order of these chapters and draw on some of the suggested resources to extend students' understanding. Chapters 7 through 13 can be assigned in an order that is compatible with the instructor's course structure.

Chapter 14 extends understandings of developmental theory and play, expanding on the constructivist views presented by Piaget and Vygotsky in Chapters 2 and 3. The role of play in developing intelligence, personality, competency, and sense of self is explored. We pay particular attention to the role of work and autonomy in the early childhood years as they relate to the broader goals of education. This chapter will be more meaningful after reading the more experience-focused chapters that have preceded it.

KEY FEATURES OF THIS TEXT

Appropriate Practice for All Children: An Integrated Approach

An inclusive, play-based curriculum recognizes the individual and cultural differences of all children not as "add-ons" but as an integral way to enrich the curriculum. Play-centered curricula build on the strengths as well as the challenges of children with special needs. Throughout this book we discuss how a play-centered curriculum incorporates children's diverse heritages, cultures, languages, and family backgrounds.

Vignettes

Each chapter anchors its focus in the world of children by beginning with a vignette related to play and education. Numerous additional classroom vignettes are provided throughout each chapter. These practical observations ground the reader in day-to-day educational experiences.

Learning Outcomes, Summary, and Applying Your Knowledge

Each chapter begins with a list of the most important learning outcomes to give readers an overview of the focus of the chapter. Chapter summaries highlight key concepts and review main points. The feature Applying Your Knowledge concludes each chapter so readers can assess their understandings of key concepts and consider practical applications in programs for young children.

Play Advocacy

In this text we emphasize advocacy as a dimension of professional practice. Chapter sections and special features on play advocacy support readers in becoming informed and effective advocates for play. We recognize multiple ways that early childhood educators advocate for play in schools and communities as well as at the state and national levels. Teachers promote play through "daily acts of advocacy" by maintaining nurturing, appropriate environments and experiences for children as they learn and grow. They advocate for play as they show families and colleagues how play supports children's development and learning. Early childhood educators work together as informed, persistent advocates for public policies that promote play and benefit children. Case studies of successful play advocacy efforts empower future teachers to participate in a community of change. Recommended books, resources, and links to professional organizations that promote play advocacy are included.

INSTRUCTOR RESOURCES

Online Instructor's Resource Manual

This manual is written for instructors teaching courses at the undergraduate and graduate levels. It includes suggested approaches for using this text as well as chapter-by-chapter guides, ideas for projects—both in and out of class—and suggested resources for further study.

Online Test Bank

The Test Bank includes a variety of test items, including essay, multiple-choice, and short-answer questions.

ACKNOWLEDGMENTS

From the very first edition, this book has been a co-authored, collaborative venture. For this sixth edition, we thank Sandra-Waite Stupiansky for joining our cooperative work and co-authoring the mathematics chapter. We thank Jane P. Perry for her excellent revision of her superb outdoor play chapter (Chapter 12).

We gratefully acknowledge the many early childhood educators who have shared their experiences, ideas, critical reviews, exemplary references, and examples from their own practice with us: Melinda Bachman, Lyda Beardsley, Libby Byers, Greta Campbell, Shirley Cheal, Suzanne DiLillo, Randi Dingman, Heather Dunlap, Sandra Easley, Johanna Filp-Hanke, Patricia Fluetsch, Buffy Frick, Anita Gensler, Janet Gonzalez-Mena, Suzanne Gray, Cynthia Halewood, Bonnie Hester, Kristin Hope, Jackie Imbimbo, Rochelle Jacobs, Robin Johnson, Richard Karsch, Marjorie Keegan, Susan Kyle, Rose Laugtug, Janet Lederman, Theresa Lozac'h, Kim Lovsey, Christa McCoy, Gail Mon Pere, Virginia Quock, Margaret Potts, Ada Rappeport, Kitty Ritz, Shane Rojo, Kathy Rosebrook, Ann Siefert, Dorothy Stewart, Lisa Tabachnick, Lia Thompson-Clark, Lea Waters, Maureen Wieser, and Professors Millie Almy, Jennie Cook-Gumperz, Ann Dyson, Celia Genishi, Ageliki Nicolopoulou, and Diane Levin, as well as Vivian Paley. Their contributions have been inspiring, practical, and have enriched our text.

We acknowledge the special contributions of Leni von Blanckensee, a specialist in educational technology as well as an experienced teacher, who contributed to our understanding of young children and technology.

We thank the University of the Pacific for the McDaniel Grant and the Merck Foundation Grant, which provided support for developing Chapters 7 and 9. Thanks to Marcy McGaugh and Genoa Starr for their excellent work preparing the manuscript.

We are especially grateful to our wise and wonderful editor, Julie Peters, for her counsel and encouragement on this sixth edition and two previous editions. Andrea Hall, Jennifer Gessner, Jane Miller, Karen Jones, and Leanne Rancourt served as managers and editors for this sixth edition. We appreciate their technical expertise as well as their support at each stage of the production process. We also wish to thank the following reviewers of the manuscript, who provided valuable comments and suggestions: Antonio Gonzalez, University of Texas, El Paso; Dennis Kirchen, Dominican University; and Hollie H. Queen. Above all, thanks to the children and their teachers who brought life to our presentation of the play-centered curriculum.

CONTENTS

6   Play as a Tool for Assessment   136

9   Science in the Play-Centered Curriculum   235

10   The Arts in the Play-Centered Curriculum   266

11   Play and Socialization   300

12   Outdoor Play   332

Authored by Jane P. Perry, University of California

13 Toys and Technology as Tools for Play   367

CHAPTER 1

Looking at Play Through Teachers' Eyes

LEARNING OUTCOMES

- Write a rationale for placing play at the center of the early childhood curriculum.
- Describe a model and important considerations for implementing a play-centered curriculum. Define spontaneous play, guided play, and teacher-directed play.
- Summarize the main points discussed by each of four teachers who were interviewed.
- Explain how the NAEYC's position on developmentally appropriate practice relates to spontaneous or guided play.
- Discuss challenges and opportunities related to the development and implementation of standards for young children's learning and development.
- Explain why the teacher's role is critical to the quality of a play-centered curriculum.
- Describe several things teachers can do to become more informed advocates for play.

With dramatic gestures, Brandon loudly sings, "Can you milk my cow?" After he and his kindergarten classmates finish the song with a rousing, "Yes, ma'am!" their teacher, Anna, calls on Becky and Tino to figure out the date and count the number of days the children have been to school. (This is the 26th day.) As other children join in the counting, Brandon takes a toy car out of his pocket. He spins the wheels, turns around, and shows it to Chris. After a moment, he reaches out to touch Kara's shoelaces, whispering, "I have snaps." Then he opens and refastens the Velcro snaps on his shoes.

Anna announces that it's choice time and calls on children to leave the circle and go to the activities of their choice. Brandon sits up straight, wanting to be called on and ready to start. The moment his name is called, he heads to the housekeeping area, where Chris and Andy are opening some cupboards. Brandon announces: "I'll make breakfast." (He picks up the coffeepot.) "Here's coffee." (He pretends to pour a cup and gives it to Chris.)

Mary, a new student in the class, wanders into the housekeeping area holding the pet rat. Brandon interrupts his breakfast preparation and says to Mary, "You can't bring Fluffy in here. You have to keep her near her cage."

Within a few minutes, the theme of the children's play turns from eating to firefighting. Brandon and Andy go to the block area to get some long block "hoses." They spend a few minutes there pretending to hose down several block construction "fires." Brandon knocks one down, to the angry cries of the builders, Valerie and Paul. He then transforms the block hose into a gun, which he uses to shoot at them.

As he and Andy stomp about the block area, Brandon passes Mary, still holding the rat, and says to her, "That's too tight. See, like this." He takes the rat from her, cradles it, looks it in the eyes, and pats it. "Fluffy was at my house during vacation. I got to feed her. See, she remembers me."

Brandon, Andy, and Mary spend the next 10 minutes building a house and a maze for Fluffy. Brandon has chosen to play in the block area each day for more than a month. The children gather five arches for a roof, partially covering a rectangular enclosure they have made by stacking blocks horizontally using long blocks and, when none are left, two shorter blocks placed side by side.

After building the "roof," Brandon rushes to a nearby table, where Rotha and Kai are chatting and drawing. He grabs a piece of paper and hastily scribbles on the middle of it, knocking off a few templates and scissors in the process. "This is my map. This is my map for the maze," he says. Brandon then goes to his teacher for some tape to put on the maze. He points to a figure on the paper where two lines intersect and says, "See my X? That's where Fluffy gets out." ∅

Every observation of children's play illustrates its multidimensional qualities. By observing Brandon's play for just a short time, we can learn about the way he is developing socially. For example, we see that Brandon is able to join Chris and Andy in their play in the housekeeping area by introducing an appropriate topic, offering to make breakfast. This observation also informs us about Brandon's developing cognitive abilities. In his play, he uses a block to symbolically represent first a hose and then a gun. While building the house for Fluffy, Brandon demonstrates practical knowledge of mathematical equivalencies when he uses two short blocks to equal the length of one longer block. By observing Brandon's play, we witness how he applies his developing abilities in real situations.

This observation also raises some of the many questions that teachers ask about children's play. How should a teacher respond when a child plays during group instruction? How can a teacher balance children's spontaneous play with more teacher-planned activities? Should teachers redirect children when they select the same play materials or themes day after day? Should gun play be allowed? How can play help us understand and assess children's cognitive, linguistic, social, emotional, and physical development? How can we be sure we are creating an inclusive curriculum that promotes equity and school success for all? How can a play-centered curriculum address mandated frameworks and standards?

Observing Brandon leads us to the central issue this book addresses: Why should play be at the center of the curriculum in early childhood programs?

PLAY AT THE CENTER OF A DEVELOPMENTALLY BASED CURRICULUM

What is the specific rationale for making play the center of the curriculum? The premise of this book is that play-based early childhood programs place the developmental characteristics of the young child—the learner—at the center of the curriculum. This book draws on evidence that play is a fundamental activity of early childhood and a central force in young children's development. During early childhood, play is essential and drives young children's development.

The Power of Play in Development

As we describe in the chapters that follow, play is simultaneously a facet of development and the source of energy for development. Play is an expression of the child's developing personality, sense of self, intellect, social capacity, and physicality. At the same time, through their play children direct their energy toward activities of their own choice, which stimulate further development.

Play is essential for optimal development and learning in young children. The match between the characteristics of play and the characteristics of the young child provides a synergy that drives development as no teacher-directed activity can.

However, a play-centered curriculum is not a laissez-faire curriculum in which anything goes. It is a curriculum that uses the power of play to foster children's development. Play fosters all aspects of young children's development from birth through age 8: emotional, social, intellectual, linguistic, and physical. It involves the integration of what children have learned. It is a curriculum in which teachers take an active role in balancing spontaneous play, guided play, teacher-directed play, and teacher-planned activities. Play-centered curricula support children's development and learning in all settings and contexts, both indoors and outside.

In honoring the child's play, we honor the "whole child." We think of the child as a developing "whole" human being in whom the processes of development are integrated. This view contrasts with the ideas that early childhood development involves the linear acquisition of separate skills or that kindergarten and primary-grade children have outgrown the developmental benefits of rich play experiences. These views are not supported by research.

In promoting a play-centered curriculum, we make short- and long-term investments in children's development. In the short term, play creates a classroom atmosphere of cooperation, initiative, and intellectual challenge. If we look at long-term consequences, we find that play supports children's growth in broad, inclusive competencies such as self-direction and industry. These are competencies valued by both parents and educators, and ones that children will need to develop to function as adults in our society.

Throughout this book, we emphasize how curricula in particular areas such as mathematics, language and literacy, science, art, socialization, and technology support and enrich young children's play. This idea contrasts with the widespread notion that play serves merely to support subject-matter competencies. Our view also contrasts with the idea of play traditionally found in the intermediate grades—play as a reward for finishing work.

This does not mean that all play is equal in our eyes. Play is fun, but it is more than fun. Play-centered curricula are not opportunities for teachers to stand aside, but require highly competent, involved, and purposeful teachers. The critical dimension

Play involves interest, motivation, and active engagement.

is to provide conditions that foster children's development using their own sources of energy. In the following chapters we articulate how a play-based curriculum supports children's own developmental forces.

Play as a Fundamental Human Activity

Play is a human phenomenon that occurs across the life span and across cultures. Parents in Mexico teach their babies the clapping game "tortillas," while older children and adults play Loteria. South Asian adolescents play soccer, while younger children play hopping games accompanied by singing. Chinese toddlers clap to a verse celebrating their grandmothers, "banging the gong merrily to accompany me home," while the grandmothers, in their old age, play mahjong. As humans, we not only enjoy our own engagement in play but are also fascinated with the play of others. The entertainment and sports industries reflect the popularity of observing others at play.

Grounding Practice in Theory, Research, and the Wisdom of Practitioners

The idea of play at the center of the early childhood curriculum is grounded in work from four early childhood traditions: (a) early childhood practitioners, (b) theorists and researchers who study play, (c) researchers and theorists in the field of development and learning, and (d) educational historians. These four traditions inform our ideas of play-based practice.

Play and the Wisdom of Practitioners Historically, play has been at the center of early childhood programs. A kindergarten student playing with blocks might spend an hour focused intently on this task, but might squirm when asked to sit down for 10 minutes to practice writing letters of the alphabet. Early childhood educators have observed and emphasized that young children bring an energy and enthusiasm to their play that not only seems to drive development, but also seems to be an inseparable part of development (e.g., Paley, 2004, 2010).

The Characteristics of Play   Theorists who study play suggest possible reasons for its importance in the development of young children when they describe the characteristics of play. According to theorists, play is characterized by one or more of these features: (a) active engagement, (b) intrinsic motivation, (c) attention to means rather than ends, (d) nonliteral behavior, and (e) freedom from external rules.

When young children are actively engaged, we observe their zest and their focused attention. Adults often marvel at children's unwillingness to be distracted from play that interests them. Brandon, for example, shows his genuine desire to be doing what he does, without encouragement from Anna. This is what we mean by **intrinsic motivation**—the desire to engage in an activity arises from within the child. When children are actively engaged and intrinsically motivated, they demonstrate their abilities to use language to communicate with others, solve problems, draw, run and climb, and so on. Children's sense of autonomy, initiative, and industry are rooted in intrinsic motivation and active engagement.

When children pay attention to means rather than ends, we notice that they are less involved with achieving a goal or outcome than with the activity itself and the enjoyment of it. Young children are well aware of the grown-up things they cannot yet do. Even the competencies that are expected of them are often frustrating, such as waiting for a snack, sharing, cutting with scissors, and (in the primary years) learning to read, add and subtract, and carry out simple household chores. In contrast, in their play, children can change the goals and the ways to achieve the goals.

We often sense children's exhilaration as we observe them shifting means and goals as they figure out new ways to solve problems. These open-ended explorations involve opportunities for creative thinking that are lacking in curricula designed for children to arrive at a single, "correct" response (Monighan-Nourot, Scales, Van Hoorn, with Almy, 1987).

Young children's play is often nonliteral pretend play that is not bound by external rules. How is such fantasy play useful to a young child who is learning to function in the real world? Children's symbolic development is fostered through the creation and use of symbols in pretend play as well as in hypothetical, "as if" situations. Through play, children develop boundaries of the real and the imagined and also visions of the possible—the drive that turns the wheels of invention.

Practice, Research, and Theory   Early childhood educators have always been guided by theory and research in psychology, anthropology, and sociology as well as education. Support for placing play at the center of the curriculum comes from the work of theorists and researchers from many disciplines who examine the role of play in development and learning.

For more than a century, theorists have explored these links. Their theories and writings reflect the time in which these theorists lived. Therefore, we discuss these theories from current viewpoints that reflect today's concerns and understandings of development. In the chapters that follow, we turn to the work of Piaget and Vygotsky for understanding the importance of play in cognitive development. We turn to Erikson and Mead to understand the role of play in the child's developing sense of self and ability to establish social relationships, and to Vygotsky and Erikson to understand how play might reflect issues of culture and society.

In the 21st century, we find research on young children's play is flourishing. Thirty years ago, there were comparatively few books on children's play, and searches of journals turned up few articles. In the first edition of this text, published in 1993, we pointed out that the literature in the field of children's play had been growing. As we review the research for this sixth edition, we find that empirical research and writing in the field of young children's play is burgeoning—there are hundreds of recent articles in international journals and scores of recent books (e.g., Cohen & Waite-Stupiansky, 2011; Elkind, 2007; Fromberg & Bergen, 2006; Hirsh-Pasek, Golinkoff, Berk, & Singer, 2009). In addition, throughout this edition we discuss recent critical thinking that addresses challenges in early childhood education to promote inclusive, multicultural, and peaceful classrooms (e.g., Falk, 2012; Fennimore & Goodwin, 2011; Levin, 2003, 2013).

Play and Traditions of Schooling   Writings on the history of schooling also lead us to place play at the center of the early childhood education curriculum. Historians have examined issues such as "What is worth learning?" and, importantly, "Who should learn?" as well as the ways in which formal schools differ from informal apprenticeship structures found in less industrialized, traditional societies (Dewey, 1915).

Early schools in the Middle East and Europe evolved with specific purposes and expectations, such as training scribes who could write official documents. Only select groups of boys attended school during middle childhood and adolescence. Later, as formal schools spread geographically, the reasons for schooling as well as the expectations of what should be learned changed. Several centuries ago, schools often prepared students for particular professions. The number of students attending schools began to grow, and the diversity of students began to increase. The rationale and expectations for schooling continued to change.

During the late 1800s, a greater number of adults needed to have basic competencies in numeracy and literacy, whereas a more elite group of adults needed more technical competencies. It was also during this period and the early 1900s that girls and boys younger than 7 or 8 years of age entered "school-like" settings. For the children of factory workers, these settings were child-care institutions designed to keep children out of harm's way. In contrast, for the children from more affluent families, the settings were nursery schools and kindergarten classes that aimed to support the development of the child. Play comprised a large part of these programs.

By the mid-1950s, the gradual blending of the goals of child care, preschool, kindergarten, and the primary grades frequently led to increased pressure for highly structured curricula and programs that stressed "academic" skills (Nourot, 2005). Trends in the history of formal schooling as well as current practices lead us to articulate our position that play should be at the center of the early childhood curriculum.

PLAY AT THE CENTER OF THE EARLY CHILDHOOD CURRICULUM: A MODEL FOR PRACTICE

We consider this a pivotal moment for early childhood educators. We cannot continue educational practices that are failing so many of our youngest students. Young children have fewer rich opportunities for play not only in schools but also at homes and community settings, both indoors and out.

This is also a time rich in possibilities. Researchers and practitioners are learning more about the central role of play in all interrelated facets of development: social–emotional, cognitive, linguistic, and physical. The evidence-based early childhood literature demonstrates the important role of play. This is the time to place play at the center of the curriculum and reconcile program practices with the wisdom of practitioners, theorists, and research.

Play-centered programs promote equity because they are built around the strengths of young children rather than their weaknesses. To meet the needs of all children, we recommend preschool–kindergarten programs that are firmly play centered yet complemented by **daily life activities** and some teacher-directed activities. We see first and second grades as transitional years, with play and daily life activities complemented with increased time for teacher-planned activities. In the primary grades, play and work are merged into increasingly complex and extended projects, further integrating play and areas of academic learning.

In our view, education for children from preschool through the primary grades should promote the development of both the competent young child and the competent future adult. This is best accomplished by means of a balanced, play-centered program in which neither spontaneous play nor teacher-planned activities are the only mode. As Figure 1.1 illustrates, play is at the center of a balanced curriculum.

In the play-centered curricula described throughout this book, a constant flow occurs among these three strata. We show how children repeat daily life and teacher-directed activities in their play, how teachers plan daily life activities so that they draw on the power of play, how teachers can develop effective assessment strategies, and how teachers integrate children's play into the curriculum. We illustrate how daily life activities include preschoolers setting the table, kindergartners planting a garden, first graders writing and mailing their first letters, and second graders learning to tell time. We examine how teacher-planned activities include projects and thematic units as well as subject area units.

In contrast to the common emphasis on **instrumental play** (that is, play used to support subject-matter objectives), we emphasize how curricula in content areas can enrich and support good play. By changing our focus from play to daily life activities to

Figure 1.1
Play at the Center of a
Balanced Curriculum

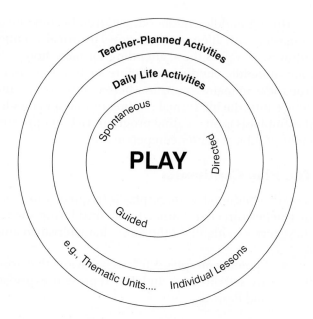

teacher-planned activities (and always back to play), our view becomes the opposite
of the traditional view. When children play, they are intrinsically motivated and
engrossed in what interests them most. They are also practicing and developing competencies at the edge of their potential. In play, self-directed learning engages and
focuses attention and provides numerous opportunities for all children to develop
self-regulation and to practice self-control.

When children are involved in such daily life activities as writing a letter, sending an e-mail message, cleaning up, or learning to tie their shoes, they are engaged
in what is important in the lives of the adults around them. The purpose of daily life
activities is readily apparent. There are procedures to learn and social rules to obey.
This is not necessarily true of play. For example, when a child like Brandon pretends
to make coffee for breakfast, he does not have to adhere to the sequence of how an
adult makes coffee. He can choose to turn the cup of coffee into a glass of orange
juice or a cup of ice cream if he wants to. Play also has rules, but children have more
power to determine them.

Children's involvement in play, daily life activities, and teacher-planned activities differs when we compare the rationale for children's activity. Children play
because of their own intrinsic interests. In play, no "one task" is imposed on the
child by adults. The child does not need to use a sense of will or purposeful intention to meet adult expectations. A sense of will is needed to accomplish tasks or daily
life activities that are not of one's choosing. This is self-regulation. Unless teacher-
planned activities are developmentally attuned to the children's level, it is difficult
for the children to adhere to the task. Prior to middle childhood, most children
have difficulty maintaining sufficient willpower to learn such adult competencies as
reading or writing.

During middle childhood, children become increasingly interested in and able to master daily life competencies. Historically, children living in more traditional cultures, as well as those attending formal school, were 7 or 8 years old—the beginning of middle childhood—before such tasks were expected of them. This remains true today in many countries where educators wait until children are 7 or 8 years old before introducing formal reading or mathematics lessons. Until middle childhood, the emphasis is on creating programs rich in opportunities for the informal development of subject-matter competencies.

The Play Continuum

In early childhood settings, play is frequently described as "spontaneous," "guided," or teacher directed. Rather than considering them as different categories, we use these terms to highlight the most characteristic feature of the play.

- **Spontaneous play** refers to behaviors that arise from intrinsic motivation, that are self-directed, and that represent expressions of children's own interests and desires.

   Four-year-olds Grace and Sophia stroll over to the maple trees at the border of the yard. It's late October, and leaves cover the ground. Sophia kicks at the leaves. When Grace begins to pick them up, Sophia joins her. The children spend several minutes gathering the red, orange, and gold leaves. Sophia drops one, and they watch it flutter to the ground. They scatter the leaves, then pick up more. As a large golden leaf twirls to the ground, Grace exclaims gleefully: "They're helicopters!" ✇

   The characteristics of play are most visible in spontaneous play. This vignette reflects all of these characteristics: intrinsic motivation, active engagement, attention to means rather than ends, freedom from external rules, and nonliteral behavior.

- **Guided play** refers to children's play that is influenced in an intentional manner by adults. As an educational term, to guide means to influence someone's thinking or activity. In this example, the children are actively engaged. Though they choose to participate, Roseann both initiates and guides their activity.

   Five kindergartners gather around the large table, constructing a collage that represents the ocean and hilly shoreline. Roseann, their teacher, makes a simple sketch on butcher paper and sets out colored paper and a collection of small objects, including dried flowers, feathers, and shells. She also puts out sheets of brightly colored construction paper, scissors, and glue sticks. She anticipates that the children will create collages using these materials as well as others that are always available on a nearby shelf. As she plans the activity and selects materials, Roseann keeps in mind that Logan, a child with attention deficit disorder, loves to glue and paste materials that are bright and tactile. Logan carefully selects several opalescent shells and pastes them onto a wave. Roseann notices that Jayden has been observing Logan for several minutes. He hesitates as he examines the materials, moving his hand across a few of the shells. Quietly, Roseann leans toward him and asks: "Which shell do you want to paste first?" ✄

■ **Teacher-directed play** refers to children's play that is organized and, literally, directed or controlled by an adult, such as singing a song. Teachers' intentions are clear and specific, even when expressed in a soft tone or even when several choices are provided. Despite the teacher's instructions or directions, the characteristic of the activity may still be defined as play. Inasmuch as the activity is goal directed by adults, it is guided or directed play rather than spontaneous play. The following is a clear example of directed play:

It looks like all the children in the second-grade class that Molly teaches are giggling. So is Molly and Mrs. Kim, Yae Suk's mother. Last week Mrs. Kim made chop chae with the children and provided chopsticks. Though several children ate the clear rice noodles, vegetables, and beans with ease, most children—and Molly—found it challenging. After class, Mrs. Kim had volunteered to return to teach the children to use Korean-style chopsticks, which are thinner and shorter than most. Today she's returned with dried kidney beans. Molly sets up individual trays so the beans don't fly across the room. Mrs. Kim shows the children how to hold the chopsticks and pick up beans one at a time. She demonstrates, picking up one, then two at a time, then three. What a challenge for hand–eye and small muscle coordination. Though only a few children use the chopsticks with ease, all the children are attentive and involved. Ethan finds that he can pick up one at a time, then two at a time, then three at a time! Others are fascinated with his skill. Mrs. Kim starts chanting: "*hana, dhul, seht*" (one, two, three) as Ethan picks up one, then two, then three beans at a time. Pretty soon everyone is chanting, "*hana, dhul, seht,*" and starts giggling. ✄

The concepts of spontaneous play, guided play, and teacher-directed play may first appear to distinguish three separate domains of play. However, we conceptualize them as occurring along a continuum that goes from play that children initiate to play that teachers initiate, as shown in Figure 1.2.

Figure 1.2
The Play Continuum

Spontaneous Play	Guided Play	Teacher-Directed Play

Child Initiated ◄– – – – – – –► Teacher Initiated

In practice, these three contexts rarely remain separate. For example, we often see how children integrate mathematical aspects of their daily lives in their spontaneous play. Likewise, teachers often plan activities to extend children's understandings of these very same concepts. Observations of early childhood programs show that play generates teacher-planned activities and, conversely, that teacher-planned activities frequently lead to play.

Throughout this book, we emphasize that the balance among the three types of play—spontaneous play, guided play, and teacher-directed play—depends on many factors, such as the developmental level and interests of the children, the cultures of the families, and the culture of the school. Early childhood educators balance play with appropriate teacher-directed strategies as they address the needs of all children. For example, an older first grader who continues to struggle with letter–sound relationships or basic number concepts may need both more direct adult-guided instruction as well as more opportunities to integrate developing understandings within the context of spontaneous play.

Children's school curricula must be viewed in the context of their lives. The child who goes from child care to school to an evening at home watching TV has a different need for play than the child who attends nursery school 2 days per week and plays outside most of the time.

HOW TEACHERS OF YOUNG CHILDREN VIEW PLAY

In the following discussion, we return to the vignette of Brandon and the interview with his teacher, Anna. We also draw from interviews with other preschool and primary teachers who spoke about their implementation of a play-centered curriculum.

Play Through the Eyes of Brandon's Teacher

Brandon's teacher, Anna, uses her observations of his play to gain insight into his growth and development:

> Play gives Brandon opportunities to select activities of his own choosing. I am learning a lot about Brandon by watching him play. He tends to visit several areas during this 30- to 40-minute period, but I've noticed that he often sustains a dramatic theme such as firefighting for a fairly long time or returns to the same theme at several points during the day. He shows much more focused attention during this time than he does when I'm presenting a more structured lesson, like today, for example, in circle time when I introduced counting skills.
>
> He's definitely one of the more verbal children in our group. His social skills are improving, and he often demonstrates a caring attitude toward the other children. I noticed he was also very nurturing toward Fluffy today. He loves to help care for her. I feel this is a wonderful opportunity for him to

develop his sense of responsibility, though he has been a bit possessive about her since he took her home. He's really attached to her. He's interested in learning more about rats and brought in a book from the library and copied a picture. Choice time gives him and the other children more of a chance to develop their individual interests.

He generally gets along with the other children, but he can be aggressive at times—for instance, when he knocked down someone's blocks. This year he rarely gets into direct physical confrontations as he did last year in preschool. I've been keeping observational records of this, and it seems that these aggressive acts tend to happen when he's rushed or has too many people around him. Today's episode involving using the blocks as guns certainly raised my classic question about war play: "Should I stop it?" I'm often uncertain about what to do, especially when it is such a momentary theme as it was today. ✆

Anna continues:

Along with my written records, I've been trying to decide what else to include in his portfolio. Today I thought about keeping the map. He was so eager to take it home that I decided to make a copy of it to save.

I'm experimenting a lot with play. It's been a gradual process. Observing the children's behavior, I feel that I'm on the right track. It's hard to believe how different my program is from the way it was only 3 or 4 years ago. I had a desk for each child and all of my "inside" time was teacher directed, either whole-class activities or centers. My program is definitely play centered. I include materials that foster literacy, math, art, and social development, including some materials that I use in more directed activities. Now we have worktables and a lot more open space. The first thing I did was order blocks. We haven't had blocks in a kindergarten at this school for as long as I've been here and that's 12 years. The kindergarten teacher who has been here the longest said that her old set of blocks was probably still in a district storehouse somewhere.

I also expanded the housekeeping area. In the beginning, I had a very small one, but I never really thought about it as more than a special area where kids could go when they were finished with something else. Now I see how important the playhouse is. I have had a lot of fun making it more attractive to the children who are immigrants. I included more photos of their families, pictures from ethnic calendars showing places and people from different cultures, dolls with ethnically diverse clothing, and objects the children are familiar with from their own backgrounds, like rice bowls and chopsticks. The children seem to feel more at home in my classroom and can play out what they know.

Anyway, I think my kids are a lot more creative and thoughtful than when my program was more teacher dominated. For example, I see this in their stories and journals. Half of the students who were in my class last year are in

Kristin's class now. She told me last week that she noticed a difference. The children who were in my class are particularly eager to initiate projects, and they tend to stay engrossed longer. She also sees a difference in the way they cooperate with everyone, not just their good friends, and the way they respect each others' work. ✆

Anna mentioned that Sarah's mother noticed a difference, too. Several years ago, Anna followed a very structured reading program with prereaders and worksheets. This year the children began their own journals on the first day of school. She put pads of paper and pencils in many places in the classroom to encourage writing. Although Anna still attends to teaching phonemic awareness, she now uses a greater repertoire of strategies.

Sarah's mother told Anna that she was very happy that Anna was finally teaching reading. Indeed, Sarah was reading and writing a lot at home as well. Anna remarked that Sarah's sister was in her class 5 years ago when she was only following formal reading lessons and having her students work in workbooks. Anna realized that this story of the two sisters didn't conclusively prove the point, but she thought that in general her students were now much more self-directed in reading and writing. Anna pointed out that during what she calls *choice time* (which she used to call *play time*), probably a third of the children are reading or writing at any given moment.

In this brief conversation, Brandon's teacher mentions issues vital to the play-centered curriculum—issues that we examine throughout this book. She discusses the development of her program in terms of carefully observing children to understand their interests and development. She uses written observations and photos of play as part of her assessment program and puts play-created products, such as Brandon's map, in her students' portfolios. Anna reflects carefully on the effects of her interventions in children's play, questioning, for example, "what to do about war play" and "how to help immigrant children feel more comfortable in the classroom." She also experiments with curricular ideas such as using play to support emerging literacy and conceptual mathematics development.

Across the country, preschool and primary teachers continue to examine the role of play in their programs. Teachers are trying to make programs more empowering for all—that is, embracing the full range of diversity of children and their families and meeting the developmental needs of children. As we wrote this sixth edition of this book, we visited and spoke to the teachers and administrators at numerous schools to observe the variety of current practices and understandings about children's play. We highlight teacher conversations from Brandon's school purposely because the preschool, kindergarten, and primary-grade teachers at that school represent a broad spectrum, from those who follow teacher-directed, skill-based programs to teachers who implement play-centered curricula, such as Randi, Pat, and Kristin. Our conversations with these teachers exemplify some of the typical yet important ideas and concerns educators raise as they implement more play-centered curricula.

Randi, a preschool teacher, emphasizes the role of play in meeting the social and emotional needs of individual children. Pat, a kindergarten teacher, raises the question, "What is good play?" and the issue of assessment. Kristin, a first-grade teacher in her second year of teaching, focuses on the importance of choice in children's development. She also discusses how the play curriculum challenges students to use their developing academic skills in a comfortable environment.

Randi: Meeting the Needs of Individual Children in Preschool

I think that play gives children a chance to make their own choices, their own decisions. The chances it provides for socialization also are very important. As they play, children communicate their feelings and ideas. This is especially important in my program, where almost all my children have special needs. For many, English is a second language. Play gives them a chance to express themselves in a less formal and more comfortable situation than circle time, for example. Play also provides opportunities for children to use their own language fluently and to express ideas in nonverbal ways. It's important for developing their sense of self-worth.

Among the questions I have are "Am I doing the best I can for my students who are learning English as a second language?" It's hard for me when I can't follow the dialogue of their dramatic play. When I think about children like Brandon, I find I have questions about how to handle aggressive play. ✆

Pat: From Worksheets and Desks to Blocks and Bubbles in Kindergarten

I consider play anything children decide to do that's not adult directed, like reading by themselves. If the choice is theirs, logically, they should enjoy it. Play gives young children the time to develop language skills, get along with their peers, make choices, and be responsible. It gives me the chance to learn more about the children, see what they do, and discover what they're really interested in doing. It also gives me time to interact with each child personally.

What I want to happen, what I consider "good play," depends on the child. Yesterday, I observed Marissa in what I consider good play for her. Marissa always seems to follow the other children. Yesterday, however, she was playing by herself with a small playhouse. She had selected what she herself wanted to do. She talked to herself a lot and stayed focused. This is a new behavior for her: selecting her own activity and staying with it.

I've made a commitment to write observations. I need to learn more about what to look for when I'm observing. Also, I want to ask questions to find out what children are really thinking, so they can respond without thinking "What's the right answer?" I feel as though I'm at a new stage in learning how to intervene. ✆

Kristin: Letting Children Develop at Their Own Pace in First Grade

During free-choice time, my children have access to blocks, Legos and other manipulatives, art materials like paint and markers, and the housekeeping corner. It's also a time when they can dictate a story to me or a parent volunteer, or get some help from their peers in inventing the spelling of words.

I think kids need to have time to work on concepts they are developing at their own pace and by their own choice. Right now, there's a lot of writing going on. Some write letters. Others write whole sentences. In language, as in other areas, there is a wide range of abilities. During free-choice time, children work at a level that's comfortable for them. During the past year, I've extended the amount of play time I provide. Now I plan for at least 30 to 40 minutes a day, usually in the early afternoon. When they've had enough time to make their own choices about learning, the children are much more able to focus on the social studies or science activities scheduled at the end of the day.

Another goal of mine is to discuss my program effectively with parents. Play has never been a traditional part of first-grade curriculum in our area. Parents often ask me whether we really have time to play if we are to get the children ready for second grade. ✍

During our visits to schools, we listened to the questions about play, children's development, education practices, and state standards. These visits were fun because teachers shared so many stories, and they were impressive because teachers revealed insights and raised issues. In this book we address these issues and share stories from

The child's development is tied to social life.

some of the teachers we talked to, as well as stories of our own. We create bridges between practice, research, and theory that deal with play in a playful way.

PLAY AND DEVELOPMENTALLY APPROPRIATE PRACTICE

Some teachers with whom we spoke told us that their program consists mainly of play—spontaneous, guided, as well as teacher-directed play. Others, like Kristin, are experimenting with including more play in the curriculum. Some teachers are wondering if play is appropriate, and if so what kinds and how much. All are trying to answer questions about the role of play in meeting the needs of the children they teach.

Developmentally appropriate practice (DAP) is the term used by the National Association for the Education of Young Children (NAEYC) to describe programs grounded in child development theory and research and designed to meet the developmental needs of children (Copple & Bredekamp, 2009). The NAEYC's most recent publication and the organization's position statement, *Developmentally Appropriate Practice in Early Childhood Programs: Serving Children from Birth Through Age 8*, places greater emphasis on the centrality of play in development and learning. Copple and Bredekamp explain that this most recent position statement reflects current knowledge from research and recognition of the importance of the broader social context, including the context of children's lives. The 2009 statement reflects one of the core values of early childhood educators: recognition that childhood is both a time for learning and for "laughter, love, play, and great fun" (p. x).

> Play is an important vehicle for developing self-regulation as well as for promoting language, cognition, and social competence. . . . High-level dramatic play produces documented cognitive, social and emotional benefits. However, with children spending more time in adult-directed activities and media use, forms of child play characterized by imagination and rich social interactions seem to be declining. . . . Rather than detracting from academic learning, play appears to support the abilities that underlie such learning and thus to promote school success. (pp. 14, 15)

Most of the teachers we talked to take these development and learning needs into account with regard to how their teaching practices meet the needs of diverse children and families. For example, in discussing her program, Rosemarie considers both typical development of 3- and 4-year-olds, as well as the particular needs of children who are dual language learners. Neil thinks about the needs of 6- and 7-year-olds, including the individual needs of children such as Robert, identified as having learning disabilities that affect his working memory. A play-centered curriculum provides the integrative context essential to support the growth of the whole child, particularly through the preschool years and during the primary grades. The feature below, *Family Diversity: Building Upon Children's Experiences to Promote Learning*, shows how children draw upon their experiences and backgrounds in their play as they build new friendships and solve problems.

FAMILY DIVERSITY

Building Upon Children's Experiences to Promote Learning

Lisa and Peter are working in the "post office," wrapping packages and sending them "to the Philippines."

Lisa: "Do we have enough paper to wrap this package (three books)? They're for my Grandma Venecia from Cebu." Peter picks up two sheets of newspaper.

Peter: "We're going to have to tape these together. Wait, here's the tape. I'll hold this." They tape the two sheets together by cutting and sticking two short pieces of tape horizontally from one newspaper sheet to the other. They then try to cut a long piece, but the tape gets twisted. Lisa cuts four short pieces and tapes the paper together.

Lisa: "OK, put the books down here." They wrap the books, trying to make the package smooth around the edges, a difficult task because the books are not the same size. "This is going to be expensive! I bet it weighs a ton." They put the package on a scale that has numbers to indicate ounces as well as a teacher-made, nonstandard measurement chart with three different colors indicating three different degrees of heaviness.

Peter: "See. It's green. That's heavy. It's going to be three dollars!" He takes the star stamps and pad and stamps three green stars at the top left of the package. "Wait. You need to put her address on it." Lisa picks up a thin blue marker and slowly writes GRUM VNSESSA 632 SEEBOO. Then she carefully selects a thick red marker and draws a heart with a butterfly to the left of the address. ✄

In this episode, Lisa initiates a play theme that connects her relationship with her beloved grandmother to her new classmates and school. At the beginning of the year, Lisa spoke comfortably and fluently with her family members in her native Visayan but was hesitant to speak English with the other children. Lisa's play informs us about her dramatic gains in speaking English, including mastery of the language as shown by increases in sentence length and complexity as well as vocabulary. She is now comfortable initiating and developing conversations in English with her peers.

Lisa and Peter demonstrate that they know some basic information about the applications of mathematics to everyday situations. They know that one weighs a package before sending it, and they have some beginning understandings of the concept of weight. Both Lisa and Peter demonstrate that they understand that the weight of the package relates to the price of mailing it. Lisa also demonstrates that she is aware that numerals are used to write an address. Lisa and Peter are also learning about geometry and spatial relationships when they estimate how much paper they need to wrap their parcel. At the post office, they are able to take information about weight, prices, addresses, and area; coordinate the information; and apply it.

As we watch Lisa and Peter, we notice that they are able to sustain their cooperative play for more than 20 minutes. During this time, they encounter several problems. For example, Peter notices that one piece of paper is not large enough to wrap the package. Lisa solves the problem with the tape. Each time, one or the other or both come up with a solution that the other accepts. Their play is complex, cooperative, imaginative, and joyful.

ADDRESSING STANDARDS IN THE PLAY-CENTERED CURRICULUM

What do we hope children will gain from participating in early childhood programs? Early childhood educators know that the early years are critical for development. Therefore, we have high expectations for our programs and for ourselves as educators as well as for each child in our care. How do early childhood educators determine expectations about students' development, dispositions, and learning? How do we make decisions about curricula to benefit all children and support all domains of their development?

Throughout the history of early childhood education and care, there have been different and sometimes competing expectations for young children's development and learning, different views about curricula, and different ways of assessing students' progress and achievement (Almy, 1975).

Meisels (2011) uses the metaphor of a road map when discussing Common Core State Standards. From an education perspective, the terms **expectations**, **standards**, and **benchmarks** are used to refer to the destination; we need to know our destination so that we can make decisions about the route and know how far we have to go and when we get there. The curriculum we implement is the route that children will take to get to the destination, and assessments provide evidence of where the students are along the route and when they have arrived (that is, "Are we there yet?").

Meisels's metaphor underscores the obvious need to link standards, curriculum, and assessment. Standards are attempts to answer the question, "What should students learn and when should they learn it?" The metaphor also helps us put today's controversies in historical perspective and understand the different perspectives of current standards held by various stakeholders, educators, families, professional educational organizations, and policymakers.

Early childhood educators who implement a play-centered curriculum work in varied settings. In some programs, teachers determine the expectations or benchmarks for student learning that they decide are appropriate for the children in their program. They then plan curricular activities and assessments based on these expectations. Educators in other programs are required to develop a program curriculum and assessment tools that address standards or expectations adopted by the state governments. In general, preschool educators follow some form of early learning standards. Educators who work with children in grades K–2 consider the K–12 Common Core State Standards for English language arts and mathematics in addition to their state's Early Learning Standards. Programs such as Head Start and HighScope have their own nationwide standards.

As early childhood educators who are advocates for young children, we need to be informed about standards whatever our personal perspective and whether or not we are mandated to implement standards. Therefore, in this book we discuss critical issues relating to the development and implementation of developmentally appropriate standards. In the chapters that follow we include vignettes that show how teachers address standards in a play-centered curriculum.

Principles for Developing Appropriate Standards for Young Children

The standards movement has roots in different philosophies of education and different political perspectives. Although the standards movement had a growing effect on K–12 programs beginning in the 1980s, it was not until 2000 that many national associations and state departments of education considered standards for preschool and kindergarten children. The 2001 No Child Left Behind Act and initiatives to develop standards for young children led to efforts to ensure that standards would benefit young children. In the joint 2002 position paper, "Early Learning Standards: Creating the Conditions for Success," the NAEYC and the National Association of Early Childhood Specialists in State Departments of Education (NAECS/SDE, 2002) discuss issues relating to the development and implementation of standards for young children. (All NAEYC position statements may be found at the NAEYC website, www.naeyc.org.) This key statement posits that early learning standards can lead to high-quality educational experiences that benefit young children, but only when the following four conditions are implemented:

1. The content and outcomes of early learning standards are developmentally appropriate to children's current developmental abilities as well as their life situations and experiences. (See pp. 4–5.)

2. Numerous stakeholders are engaged in developing and reviewing early childhood standards. Stakeholders include parents and other community representatives and early childhood educators, including early childhood special education specialists. (See p. 6.)

3. "Early learning standards gain their effectiveness through implementation and assessment practices that support all children's development in ethical, appropriate ways" (p. 6). This means that teaching practices promote social interactions and curricula promote engagement and depth of explorations.

    "Tools for assessing young children's progress must be clearly connected to important learning represented in the standards; must be technically, developmentally, and culturally valid; and must yield comprehensive, useful information." (p. 7).

4. Standards are accompanied by strong support for early childhood programs, including adequate support for professionals and professional development, and respectful support for families as partners in their children's education. (See pp. 7–8.)

Identifying the Most Important Early Learning Standards   For more than a decade, the NAEYC has worked with other national education associations to identify the "big ideas" and important processes that are developmentally appropriate for young children. Many national educational associations developed K–12 academic subject-oriented frameworks and standards. These include the International Reading Association (IRA), the National Council of Teachers of Mathematics (NCTM), the Consortium of National Arts Education Associations, the National Science Teachers Association (NSTA), the National Council for the Social Studies (NCSS), the National Association for Sport and Physical Education (NASPE), and the International Society for Technology in Education (ISTE).

The NAEYC has issued joint position papers with the International Reading Association as well as with the National Council of Teachers of Mathematics. Both underscore the importance of curricula that provide children with numerous opportunities to revisit these big ideas and processes—in their spontaneous play as well as in more teacher-directed activities. The statements endorse the four NAEYC conditions summarized above for the development and implementation of early learning standards. Content standards for children in preschool through primary grades must be meaningful and encourage children's active, engaged experiences. Standards should build upon children's prior experiences in their homes and communities as well as school. Standards should lead to more inclusive curricula that meet children's special needs and reflect the cultures and languages of children and their families. The NAEYC position papers support the type of curricula that we advocate throughout this book: in-depth, engaging curricula that provide children with opportunities to revisit these big ideas and processes—in child-initiated play as well as in more teacher-planned activities.

The Development and Implementation of Standards: Challenges and Possibilities

In the years since 2002, the adoption and implementation of K–12 and early learning standards led to widespread discussion within the early childhood education community. In our discussions with early childhood educators we have found that the concerns they raised often related to the NAEYC's four principles. For example, educators are concerned that standards do not reflect an adequate understanding of the integrated processes that characterize young children's development and learning as well as cultural and individual differences. Many teachers feel that they are being pushed toward more teacher-directed instruction and toward a curriculum with a narrow focus on English language arts and math.

Educators are deeply concerned that assessments they are required to use are often developmentally inappropriate, particularly the use of "high-stakes testing" to make "high-stakes" decisions, such as telling parents that their child is not ready for first grade. In fact, the NAEYC and NAECS/SDE joint position statement *Early Learning Standards: Creating the Conditions for Success* (2002) emphasizes that "such misuses of standards-related assessments violate professional codes of ethical conduct" (p. 7).

Among early childhood educators and researchers, the level of concern was heightened with the 2010 Common Core State Standards Initiative that included K–12 English language arts and mathematics. The stated purpose is to provide consistent expectations for learning in all 50 states and ensure that high school graduates succeed in college and in the workplace. In principle, Common Core State Standards were to be developed and implemented based on empirical evidence. Standards should identify what learning is most important and lead to students' attainment of higher-level cognitive abilities.

In a timely 2010 joint statement, the NAEYC and NAECS/SDE expressed concerns that the Common Core State Standards might lead to unintended consequences such as narrowing the scope of early childhood curriculum with its focus on the development of the whole child. Since 2010 there have been numerous critical analyses and responses to the Common Core State Standards that focus on the lack of empirical research as a base for the development and implementation process and the assessment methods that are used (e.g., Meisels, 2011; Miller & Carlsson-Paige, 2013). One of the most outspoken critics of Common Core State Standards is Diane Ravitch, former U.S. assistant secretary of education from 1991 to 1993 and one of the initial architects of the standards movement. For example, she points out that "(t)hey are being imposed on the children of this nation despite the fact that no one has any idea how they will affect students, teachers, or schools" (2013, n.p.).

Many critiques written by early childhood educators and researchers express concerns about reduced emphasis on play in early childhood programs. Gopnik (2011), a distinguished researcher and scholar, presents relevant research findings in her article "Why Preschool Shouldn't Be Like School: New Research Shows That Teaching Kids More and More, at Ever-Younger Ages, May Backfire."

As of 2013, the Common Core State Standards for mathematics and English language arts had been adopted by almost all 50 states, and in that same year the Next Generation Science Standards for K–12 were released for adoption. Increasingly, states have become engaged in plans to implement standards and the critical challenge of aligning curriculum and assessment.

The NAEYC's 2012 report *The Common Core State Standards: Caution and Opportunity for Early Childhood Education* was written to inform early childhood educators about the possible impacts of standards. The NAEYC's caution refers to "aspects of the Common Core that might pose threats to early childhood education" (p. 2). The NAEYC's discussion of opportunity points out that this is a critical time for early childhood educators to participate in state and local implementation processes. The NAEYC bases its analysis on the four necessary conditions for success identified in *Early Learning Standards: Creating the Conditions for Success* (NAECS/SDE, 2002). The 2012 report provides a systematic review of all four conditions and presents the NAEYC's serious concerns about each. The discussion of the third condition is particularly relevant to a balanced play-centered curriculum:

> Early learning standards gain their effectiveness through implementation and assessment practices that support children's development in ethical, appropriate ways. . . . Especially critical is maintaining methods of instruction that include a range of approaches— including the use of play as well as both small- and large-group instruction—that are considered to be developmentally appropriate for young children. (NAEYC, 2012a, n.p.)

We recommend that all those concerned with the education of young children read the entire NAEYC report as well as the "Joint Statement of Early Childhood Health and Education Professions on the Common Core Initiative" (Alliance for

Childhood, 2013). It is only through such careful analysis that teachers can advocate for appropriate policies that foster a balanced, integrated curriculum that uses the power of play. This is the approach that we take throughout this book to support all teachers working to implement a play-centered curriculum.

THE CRITICAL ROLE OF THE TEACHER

If play is at the center of the early childhood curriculum, how is the curriculum developed? The play-centered curriculum is a constantly evolving emergent curriculum. The teacher is the key to the play-centered curriculum. The knowledgeable teacher uses a wide repertoire of techniques to carefully orchestrate the flow from spontaneous play to guided and directed play to more subject-oriented instruction and back to play. This flow is in tune with and arises from the developmental needs of individual children in the class.

How might a teacher foster literacy, mathematical thinking, artistic expression, socialization, self-esteem, scientific thinking, and other concepts, dispositions, and skills valued in early education? How might a teacher address standards in an integrated and meaningful way? Let's look at an example:

> Scott introduced himself as a "third-grade teacher just promoted to kindergarten." This was the first year that he had tried to "incorporate any play . . . much less make play the major part of my program." With little opportunity to visit other programs, Scott started the year feeling that he was sinking as much as he was swimming. "In my sinking mode, I went for teacher-structured activities as life rafts. They felt safe. They were like the curriculum I knew."

A play-centered curriculum supports physical development.

It took Scott most of the year to set up an environment where his students could have choices and sustained time to play through activities. Scott needed to read enough to convince himself that play was truly the cornerstone of development for young children. Then he could begin to make changes based on that conviction.

He concluded: "This has become the most intellectually challenging year for me. I am learning how to plan for play and how to use play to assess students' growth. I like the concept of an evolving curriculum, but it takes patience as well as creativity to work it out each day. Things don't always work out as I had imagined."

"Because I'm an experienced teacher, I sometimes feel that I should be able to do this right away. But it doesn't work out that way. It involves a major shift in the way I'm thinking as well as in the way I structure the program: a paradigm shift."

Scott also mentioned how he felt at times when his colleagues from the "upper grades" come into his classroom. "I know they're thinking that I'm 'just' playing. I'm finally feeling that I can defend what I do, explain why play is so important."

"I've been joking that I want to 'up play' rather than 'down play' play! I want to show parents how it benefits their children. We had our first open house last week. I put together a Power Point with slides from last year and some slides from the first 2 weeks of school. It made a great difference for parents to see 'live' examples of how play is important. As I discussed the development of self-esteem, I showed several slides of Jimmy and Andrea building a tower taller than they are. (I wish I had had a video camera for that.)

The slides also gave me a chance to talk about play and social development. I purposely selected slides that included every student in my class so parents could get a personal message about how important play is to their own child's social development.

Of course, I also emphasized the ways in which children use what they've learned in academic areas and how much more they learn through play. I showed slides of the children building with blocks, pouring and measuring as they played 'making chili' at the sand table, and talked about their development of math concepts. I used slides of children writing in their journals, others scribbling on the chalkboard, and one reading to another as I talked about literacy development. The slides helped parents make the connections between play and their children's development in all areas.

I worked out a way to illustrate developmental progress. Four wonderful slides—if I may say so—show how Genette's block constructions became more complex over a 2-month period last year. ✄

As the examples throughout this book illustrate, a play-centered curriculum is orchestrated carefully by the teacher. It is not a step-by-step, teacher-proof didactic curriculum. Consequently, this is not a step-by-step curriculum guide. However, the play-centered curriculum we discuss is also very different from laissez-faire approaches to play such as recess time at many schools in which no one observes or intervenes. A play-centered curriculum involves teachers in careful planning and preparation, both inside and outside the classroom. A play-centered curriculum needs playful teachers who enjoy being spontaneous, involved, and creative as well as reflective and analytical.

In *From Play to Practice: Connecting Teachers' Play to Children's Learning*, authors Nell and Drew (2013) describe play workshops in which teachers play with engaging materials. Through joyful and creative experiences, teachers gain a deeper understanding and appreciation of a curriculum that has play at its center. Informed teachers who value play encourage playful and creative dispositions by being playful and imaginative themselves as they develop the curriculum.

ADVOCATING FOR PLAY

> *Advocate (verb).*   *Origin:*   *from the Latin* advocare *(to summon).*

People frequently think about being an advocate in a formal sense. The word *advocate* is used to describe formal roles in legislative and judicial proceedings. We hear the term used to describe high-level and highly public advocacy—for example, a national spokesperson before a crowd of reporters. Indeed, early childhood educators do advocate for play in highly public and publicized ways. But this is only a small part of the continuum of advocacy efforts.

The Advocacy Continuum

> *Advocate (verb).*   *Definition:*   *to support, promote, recommend*

Consider the many ways that early childhood educators advocate for play. Educators learn from and support each other in recognizing personal and public "daily acts of advocacy." There is a broad range or continuum of advocacy efforts, including advocacy at the interpersonal level, the program or school level, the community level, as well as the state, national, and international levels. In the vignettes in this chapter, we see each teacher promoting play. Sometimes it's a conversation we have with a co-teacher about promoting children's outdoor play. Advocacy might involve joining neighbors to urge the city to plant a shade tree in a local playground. Sometimes we advocate for play by sending a link to a video on play to another teacher across town, or by signing a statement circulated by a national play association, or by writing a letter to a newspaper or a response on a blog. Often we support play by keeping ourselves informed—and, always, by making sure we take the time to play!

Educators who implement a play-centered curriculum replay playful ideas for advocacy. We share and build on each other's ideas. Scott's ideas for an open house are not new, but he makes them his own and draws on his knowledge of the children and their families. What are some of the ways that he supports and promotes play? See what you find when you analyze these brief quotes from the vignette more closely. What does he do to make connections between play, joy, and learning more "real" to families?

> . . . I put together a slide show with slides from last year and some slides from the first 2 weeks of school.
>
> . . . The slides also gave me a chance to talk about play and social development. I purposely selected slides that included every student in my class so parents could get a personal message about how important play is to their own child's social development.
>
> . . . Of course, I also emphasized the ways in which children use what they've learned in academic areas and how much more they learn through play. I showed slides of the children building with blocks, pouring and measuring as they played "making chili" at the sand table, and talked about their development of math concepts. I used slides of children writing in their journals, others scribbling on the chalkboard, and one reading to another as I talked about literacy development. The slides helped parents make the connections between play and their children's development in all areas.
>
> . . . I worked out a way to illustrate developmental progress. Four wonderful slides—if I may say so—show how Genette's block constructions became more complex over a 2-month period last year. ✏

Becoming an Informed Advocate for Play

Throughout this book we advocate for the play-centered curriculum and for expanding all children's opportunities to play in their communities. The purpose of this book is to help readers become informed professionals. In each chapter you'll find examples of how teachers develop and advocate for play-centered programs as well as informative updated references.

Readers have varied backgrounds and experiences in working on behalf of children. Some of us are now more interested in or comfortable with working individually at the program level. Some of us prefer to participate in more public spheres. The following feature, *Becoming an Informed Advocate for Play: A Toolkit for Play Advocacy*, shows how to collect and develop the tools you need to become an effective and informed advocate for play.

Playing Around with Play

■ Play! Play is a fundamental human activity. Put theory into practice. All of us know that adults as well as children need to play. As you read this book, put your knowledge about the importance of play into practice. Take time to play. Why is play important to you? How do you choose to play?

■ What are your experiences and memories of play? Did you play as a child? Where did you play? What did you play and with whom? Create a virtual file

Becoming an Informed Advocate for Play

ADVOCACY IN ACTION: A TOOLKIT FOR PLAY ADVOCACY

"Start from where you are" is good advice when we think about becoming better advocates on behalf of young children. Whatever our experiences and the ways that we advocate for play, we need to be informed, persistent, professional, and committed.

In the past, our "toolkits" were portfolios or expandable files with resources on play and advocacy. There was so much stuff—so many fliers, catalogs, lists, handouts, and research and policy papers. We still recommend that your play toolkit include an actual portfolio or file box, but so many of our resources are now digital. That makes them easy to file and share—and sharing is advocacy.

A play toolkit for advocacy includes resources and information. It also includes the experiences and feelings that fuel our commitment and persistence. We become more informed advocates as we learn more about the role of play in children's healthy development and learning. We maintain our energy and drive by valuing and enjoying play in children's lives and in our own. We become more effective advocates by drawing upon our knowledge, our values, and our feelings when we advocate for play. The activities and resources below are some starters for a play toolkit for advocacy.

or scrapbook of memories and photos of your own play experiences from infancy up to the present day.

- Interview an older family member to find out what kinds of play or games were common or traditional in your family. Describe your family and cultural heritage of play. How might play reflect the area, background, culture, and language of your family?

- Create a play map. Print out a map and mark where the children and adults in your community play. Identity outdoor play space—safe open spaces, parks, and playgrounds. Identify what is private and what is public. Are there indoor play spaces such as children's museums, recreational centers, and gyms? What does your community need to support play?

- Learn more about the work of early childhood educators and the ways in which they advocate for play. Visit a play-centered early childhood program and write a detailed 10–20 minute observation of children playing. Carry out an informal interview with a teacher to learn about the opportunities and challenges for implementing a play-centered curriculum in that setting. As you read this book and become more informed, continue your observations and discussions. In what ways are these teachers and your colleagues advocating for play?

Resources for Informed Play Advocates: Getting Started

We start with this partial list of books and early childhood organizations that we've referred to or cited in this chapter. Many more excellent resources are included throughout the chapters that follow.

Several Books About Play and Early Childhood

- Elkind, D. (2007). *The power of play: Learning what comes naturally.* Philadelphia, PA: De Capo Press.
- Hirsh-Pasek, K., Golinkoff, R. M., Berk, L. E., & Singer, D. G. (2009). *A mandate for playful learning in preschool: Presenting the evidence.* New York, NY: Oxford University Press.
- Falk, B. (2012). *Defending childhood: Keeping the promise of early education.* New York, NY: Teachers College Press.
- Fennimore, B. S., & Goodwin, A. L. (2011). *Promoting social justice for young children.* New York, NY: Springer.
- Fromberg, D. P., & Bergen, D. (Eds.). (2006). *Play from birth to twelve: Contexts, perspectives, and meanings* (2nd ed.). New York, NY: Routledge.
- Levin, D. E. (2013). *Beyond remote-controlled childhood: Teaching young children in the media age.* Washington, DC: NAEYC.
- Paley, V. G. (2004). *A child's work: The importance of fantasy play.* Chicago, IL: University of Chicago Press.
- Paley, V. G. (2010). *The boy on the beach: Building community through play.* Chicago, IL: University of Chicago Press.

Some Organizations That Promote Play   The Alliance for Childhood is an advocacy organization of early childhood professionals that works to create conditions that foster young children's development and learning. The Alliance has a number of initiatives that focus on play. Resources on play are free and include excellent videos as well as summaries of research and implications for policy. (See the Alliance for Childhood website, www.allianceforchildhood.org.)

The Association for the Study of Play (TASP) is an interdisciplinary organization concerned with research about and theories of play across ages and around the world. Members represent disciplines such as education, folklore, psychology, anthropology, recreation, and the arts. (See The Association for the Study of Play website, www.tasplay.org.)

The National Association for the Education of Young Children (NAEYC) publishes many resources to help teachers implement play in early childhood education programs, including the recent books *From Play to Practice* and *Beyond Remote-Controlled Childhood* (see above). The NAEYC journals *Young Children, Early Learning Research Quarterly,* and *Teaching Young Children* feature articles on many facets of children's play. The *Play, Policy, and Practice (PPP) Interest Forum* is an active group of NAEYC members that sponsors programs and holds annual meetings at the NAEYC Conference. PPP addresses issues relating to practice, research, and current issues related to play and policy. (See the NAEYC website, www.naeyc.org.)

Expanding the Toolkit for Play Advocacy

This first chapter begins a conversation about advocacy for play. In the following weeks you'll have many opportunities to expand your toolkit for play advocacy by including your own observations in schools and communities, information you gather from readings and discussions, and online resources you bookmark. We hope that, week by week, as you broaden the way you define advocacy, you'll find more examples, add more resources to your toolkit, and find more opportunities for advocacy. Becoming an advocate takes time. Therefore, we conclude this advocacy discussion in the last chapter of this book with a focus on using tools and resources for effective play advocacy.

SUMMARY

- **Play at the center of a developmentally based curriculum.** The rationale for placing play at the center of the curriculum is that the developmental characteristics of the young child—the learner—should be at the core of the curriculum. This book is based on the evidence that play is a basic activity of early childhood and a central force in young children's development. Therefore, a developmentally based program is a play-centered program. Play is simultaneously a facet of development and a source of energy for development. Play is an expression of the child's developing personality, sense of self, intellect, social capacity, and physicality. At the same time, through their play children direct their energy toward activities of their own choice. These activities stimulate further development.

    - A play-centered curriculum is grounded in four early childhood traditions: the wisdom of early childhood practitioners, research and theory about children's play, research and theory in the area of development and learning, and the work of educational historians.

- **Play at the center of early childhood curriculum: A model for practice.** Educators develop a curriculum that includes play, daily life activities, and teacher-directed activities. Play includes spontaneous play, guided play, and teacher-directed play. In practice, however, these are not separate categories. In the play-centered curriculum the balance changes depending on the children's development and expectations for learning, interests, and strengths as well as their needs.

- **How teachers of young children view play.** In this section of the chapter we drew from interviews with four teachers who reflected on multiple aspects of implementing a play-centered curriculum. Anna discussed how she changed the room arrangement and included materials that reflected children's home cultures and fostered literacy, math, art, and social development. Randi, a preschool teacher, emphasized the role of play in meeting the social and emotional needs of individual children. Pat, a kindergarten teacher, discussed how the answer to the question "What is good play?" depends on the child or group of children. She also talked about assessment in a play-centered curriculum. Kristin, a first-grade teacher, focused on the importance of choices in children's development and how play also challenges children to use their developing academic skills in a comfortable environment.

- **Play and developmentally appropriate practice.** *Developmentally appropriate practice* (DAP) is the term used by the National Association for the Education of Young Children (NAEYC) to describe programs grounded in child development theory and research that are designed to meet the developmental needs of children (Copple & Bredekamp, 2009). The NAEYC's most recent publication and the organization's position statement, *Developmentally Appropriate Practice in Early Childhood Programs: Serving Children from Birth Through Age 8*, places greater emphasis on the centrality of play in development and learning. Copple and Bredekamp explain that this most recent position statement reflects current knowledge from research and a recognition of the importance of the broader social context, including the context of children's lives. The 2009 statement reflects one of the core values of early childhood educators: recognition that childhood is both a time for learning and for "laughter, love, play, and great fun" (p. x).

- **Addressing standards in the play-centered curriculum.** Current early learning and common core standards are attempts to answer the question "What should students learn and when should they learn it?" Many early childhood educators are required to address standards or expectations adopted by state governments and to link curricula and assessments to those standards. In this section of the chapter we discussed some of the main possibilities and key challenges relating to the development and implementation of early learning standards and common core standards.

- **The critical role of the teacher.** We contend that the teacher is the key to the play-centered curriculum. This is a curriculum in constant development—an emergent, evolving curriculum. The knowledgeable teacher uses a wide repertoire of techniques to carefully orchestrate the flow from spontaneous play to guided and directed play to more subject-oriented instruction and back to play. This flow is in tune with and arises from the developmental needs of children in the program.

- **Advocating for play.** Early childhood educators seek many avenues to advocate for play. The continuum of efforts includes advocacy at the interpersonal level, the program or school level, the community level, as well as the state, national, and international levels. We become more effective advocates by drawing upon our knowledge, values, and feelings when we advocate for play. This chapter recommended activities and listed resources for starting a toolkit for play advocacy.

APPLYING YOUR KNOWLEDGE

1. Write a rationale for placing play at the center of the early childhood curriculum.
   a. Illustrate with examples from a vignette in this chapter or your own observations.

2. Describe a model for implementing a play-centered curriculum.
   a. Define spontaneous play, guided play, and teacher-directed play.
   b. Discuss two issues teachers consider when balancing play, daily life activities, and teacher-planned activities.

3. Summarize the main points discussed by each of four teachers who were interviewed.
   a. Interview a teacher at the preschool through second-grade level about his or her use of play in the curriculum.
   b. Write your own interview (of yourself) stating why you think play should be at the center of the curriculum.

4. Explain how the NAEYC's position on developmentally appropriate practice relates to spontaneous or guided play.
   a. Read one of the references cited in this chapter and discuss how it contributes to your perspective on developmentally appropriate practice for young children.
   b. Observe a child with special needs at play in an early childhood setting. Relate your observations to the NAEYC's position.

5. Discuss challenges and opportunities related to the development and implementation of standards for young children's learning and development.
   a. Speak with two teachers who are implementing state early learning standards or common core standards about their perspectives on opportunities and challenges.
   b. Read and discuss one of the references about standards cited in this chapter. What further questions do you have?

6. Explain why the teacher's role is critical to the quality of a play-centered curriculum.
   a. Refer to two vignettes in this chapter or several of your own observations.

7. Describe several things that teachers can do to become more informed advocates for play
   a. Add to your play toolkit by carrying out and reflecting on one of the activities described in the section "Playing Around with Play."
   b. Add to your play toolkit by annotating the list of recommended books with descriptions from the publishers' websites.
   c. Write plans for two advocacy actions that you could begin this semester.

CHAPTER 2
Play and Development: Theory

LEARNING OUTCOMES

- Describe the "nature–nurture" debate and your understanding of how a constructivist view contributes to that debate.
- Explain the role of schemes and the dynamics of assimilation and accommodation in Jean Piaget's theory of development.
- Discuss your understanding of how social experience and play are central to Vygotsky's theory of development.
- Briefly describe George Mead's three stages in child development (the play stage, the game stage, and the generalized other stage) and give examples of how each relates to children's play.
- Discuss Erik Erikson's first four psychosocial stages and how children use play to support the strengths of each of these stages (trust, autonomy, initiative, and industry).

Five-year-old Sophie brings home a large painted butterfly with her own writing "B T R F Y" carefully drawn in the corner. Her parents approach her teacher, concerned that allowing her to spell words incorrectly will hinder her success when she begins kindergarten in the fall. ∅

The children in Roseanna's multiage primary class are deep into the third week of their project on restaurants. They've made paper and playdough pizzas, menus, uniforms for the waiters, and paper money for their transactions, and they have talked about a website for the restaurant. A group of children have finished making placemats and ads for the "Don't Forget the Olives" Pizza Parlor and are contemplating adding sushi to the menu. The school principal questions the value of this play-centered project and how it encompasses the district's academic standards. ∅

What answers can teachers give to questions about play in the classroom? Perhaps the most frequently quoted clichés are, "Play is the child's way of learning" or "Play is the child's work." But how does play contribute to development and learning? Is play related to work in some systematic manner, or is play simply evidence of the flights of fancy and freedom we associate with childhood?

To answer these and other questions we need to formulate our ideas about the nature of play and how it develops. Although other species engage in play, the range of play from motor play to pretend play to games with rules is a uniquely human capacity. The development of play through these stages forms the foundation for the development of intellect, creativity and imagination, a sense of self, and the capacity to interact with others in positive and morally sound ways. In this chapter and those that follow we discuss how play contributes to children's development and to the integration of physical, social–emotional, and cognitive competencies for the whole child. Many teachers find it challenging to explain the role of play in children's development and its place in the classroom, so exploring developmental theory will help meet this challenge (Sherwood & Reifel, 2013; Smith & Gosso, 2010; Trawick-Smith & Dziurgot, 2010; Wood, 2010; Broadhead & Wood, 2010; Howard, 2010; Jones & Reynolds, 2011; Kuschner, 2012).

While we focus primarily on the role of play in development, it is also important not to lose sight of that fact that play is a source of laughter and humor, of inventiveness and beauty. It allows us to entertain possibilities and to envision the future. It helps us persevere in our efforts and explore the full range of our emotions. It fosters the spontaneity and joy that make us truly human. Keeping this in mind, we invite you to consider how development itself contributes to play as an essential aspect of human existence.

In this chapter we look at major theories that address the development of play in childhood. In developing a theory of practice that is based in the daily lives of children and their teachers, we begin by discussing the more "classic" theorists in developmental psychology.

A CONSTRUCTIVIST VIEW OF PLAY AND DEVELOPMENT

Throughout history, people have tried to understand how humans develop from helpless infants to functional adults. In the West, this has given rise to the debate between "nature" and "nurture." The "nature" argument proposes that the form of adult capacities is contained in the seed of the infant and only needs to be nourished. The "nurture" argument holds that the adult is formed through experience and that the form of the adult reflects this experience. **Constructivism** concerns the interaction between "nature" and "nurture."

Constructivism emerged in the late 19th and early 20th centuries and is a belief that the developing child, in the context of the social and physical environment, explores and adapts to the environment by coping with everyday challenges. In addition, it recognizes the central role of play in young children's development. In this chapter, we explore four "classic" constructivist theorists and look at how they help early childhood educators understand and support children's development through the play-centered curriculum. These theorists are

- Jean Piaget (1896–1980)
- Lev Vygotsky (1896–1934)
- George Herbert Mead (1863–1931)
- Erik Erikson (1902–1994)

These theorists shared similar constructivist orientations. In fact, this similar orientation is reflected in the titles of their books: *Mind, Self, and Society* by Mead (1934), *Childhood and Society* by Erikson (1950/1985), *Mind in Society* by Vygotsky (published in English, 1978), and *Sociological Studies*, essays by Piaget (published in English, 1995). In many ways, the differences among their theories reflect the historical time and place in which they lived and their interests, background, and professional education (Beck, 2013). Perhaps most important, the theories reflect the specific questions these theorists asked about how humans develop.

PIAGET'S DEVELOPMENTAL THEORY AND PLAY

Though Jean Piaget was primarily focused on intellectual development, his work addresses social, moral, linguistic, and emotional development as well. Piaget viewed the development of knowledge as a gradual process of restructuring earlier ways of knowing into more adequate and generalized ways of knowing. He showed that children progressed through a universal series of stages in the development of their intelligence. The first 2 years encompasses the **sensorimotor period**, which is divided into six stages. During this period the child's understanding of the world is gradually constructed from a coordination of motor and sensory information, but the child lacks the representational capacity reflected in symbolic play and language.

The next major period is the **preoperational period**, which generally lasts between 2 and 7 years of age and is divided into three stages. The term *preoperational* refers to the lack of mental operations associated with logical thought. This period is sometimes called the **preconceptual stage** because children during this period are not able to form true concepts where classes and relations are reliably coordinated.

The third period is the **concrete-operational period**, which includes three stages generally lasting between 7 and 12 years of age. This period is marked by the development of what is typically recognized as rational and logically verifiable thought. However, thought is still tied to the appearances of reality and is closely tied to the characteristics of concrete objects.

This is followed by the formal operational period from early adolescence on and is divided into three stages. During this period, the child's thought is gradually freed from concrete reality and takes on hypothetical-deductive properties. Later in his career, Piaget was less tied to a formal definition of the various stages.

Piaget's theory places the child at the center of this construction with a heavy emphasis on the child's spontaneous, autonomous activities (Mooney, 2000; Saunders & Bingham-Newman, 1984). In the early childhood years this is always linked to play, both alone and with peers.

In Piaget's constructivist view, knowledge is not simply acquired by gathering information from the environment or copying the behavior of others, but is based on what the individual brings to each situation. The **schemes** or mental patterns that children have already constructed are modified and added to as children try to make sense of new experiences in light of what they already know.

Four-year-old Kim explains the word *invisible* to his friend Tony when the word comes up in a story read by a parent to the two boys. "It's like you go inside *visible,* and then no one can see you when you're in *visible!*" Kim asserts, and Tony nods his head in understanding. Kim bases his explanation on what he has experienced about not being seen in the game of hide and seek; if you hide inside something, then you can't be seen. ✇

According to Piaget, the means of organization is intelligent **adaptation**, where humans modify their means of interacting with the environment to fit their personal needs (see Piaget, 1962, 1963, 1947/2003).

Piaget proposed an interactive process between two aspects of adaptation that he called **assimilation** and **accommodation**. This interaction is the source of development and learning. In assimilation, new experiences are incorporated into and interpreted by existing structures of thought. Most important, elements of experiences are not simply added to the thoughts already there, like items tacked onto a grocery list. Instead, elements are transformed to fit into the structure or "template" of that individual's thinking. An example is the assimilative pattern developed in playing with playdough or clay. Claylike substances can be pinched, patted, molded, and rolled using patterns from previous experiences:

> What happens when Kaya encounters "oublek," a substance made of cornstarch and water that has some of the properties of clay, but also some different ones? Perhaps she is surprised that the new material oozes through her fingers rather than molding into a form. Kaya's efforts to accommodate to the differences that the new material offers cause a change in the assimilative structure that Kaya will apply to claylike substances in the future. ⌀

In Piaget's theory, accommodation is a complement to assimilation. Accommodation allows the structure of our thinking to change in adapting to new experiences. Accommodation is the process through which new schemes or mental patterns for potential behavior are created—existing patterns are modified to incorporate new information. Accommodation allows us to meet challenges presented by the environment, such as resolving the cognitive surprise generated by playing with oublek when playdough was expected.

Assimilation allows us to make sense of our experiences in light of what we already know. It allows us to consolidate, generalize, and apply our current structures of thinking to new situations. Accommodation challenges us to change and adapt to new information.

According to Piaget, there is constant interaction between these processes that create alternating states of tension and balance concerning what "fits" into our schemes and what doesn't fit. Awareness that a new idea or perception does not fit into our structure of thinking calls for a change in our mental models and results in the continuing development of thought. Through the interaction of assimilation and accommodation, children balance their internal states and meet their personal needs for intelligent adaptation.

In the early childhood years, assimilative and accommodative processes are constantly fluctuating. First, the mental patterns fit the new situation. Then new elements are introduced that contradict. Mental structures then change to accommodate these new elements. This process of construction and expansion marks the development of children's early thinking from personal ideas and concepts about the way the world works to more stable and predictable relationships between internal mental models and the external world that are coordinated with the views of others.

Because a young child's understanding of the world is closely tied to immediate contexts and lacks the stability of adult thought, his or her behavior is largely governed by play, and reality is assimilated to the immediate needs and perspective of the child. Through play and assimilation, young children bend their view of reality to their own immediate needs and wants.

Three Types of Knowledge

Piaget outlined three major types of knowledge: physical, logical–mathematical, and social. In play, children develop all three. **Physical knowledge** derives from activities with objects that allow children to make generalizations about the physical properties of objects. For example, through physical manipulation in play, children may discover that rocks sink and corks float, blocks stacked too high may fall, and sand and water may be used to mold forms.

Symbolic thought develops through make believe.

Logical–mathematical knowledge is constructed as children reflect on the relationships between actions on objects, for instance by comparing the sizes of two balls or the relative lengths of blocks. In logical–mathematical knowledge, the concepts used by the child do not come from the objects themselves but from the relationship invented by the child. These two types of knowledge, physical and logical–mathematical, are constructed through the child's own experiences, and play is critical to the development of both.

In contrast, **social knowledge** is knowledge imparted by other people and includes names for things as well as social conventions such as proper behavior at snack or group time. This type of knowledge falls closer to the accommodative end of the continuum, relying on imitation and memorization for its acquisition. However, social knowledge also depends on the mental structures created through logical–mathematical knowledge for its application. As Kamii (1982) pointed out, categories such as "good words" and "bad words" are derived from social experiences, but it is the logical–mathematical capacity for classification that enables children to decide when a word might meet with the disapproval of adults.

In practice, physical, logical–mathematical, and social knowledge are closely connected in any situation involving the education of young children, as we see in this example:

> Four-year-old Enid helps Madeline, the assistant teacher, bring food to the snack table. "We need one cracker for each place," Madeline coaches. Enid takes the crackers from the box, places one on each plate, and looks expectantly at her teacher. "There," Madeline says. "Let's count these together—1, 2, 3, 4, 5, 6, 7." Enid counts with her teacher. "Now let's count the crackers—1, 2, 3, 4, 5, 6, 7." They count together again. Madeline asks, "How many cups will we need if we have one for every person?"
>
> Enid carefully takes one cup at a time from the stack and places each next to a plate with a cracker on it. Two of the cups tip over as she sets them down, and as she replaces them upright, Enid looks intently at the uneven places in the tabletop that have pushed the empty cups off balance. She runs her hand over the table next to the remaining plates to find a smooth spot before she sets down the next cup.
>
> Enid looks expectantly at Madeline, pointing her finger at the first cup. "1, 2, 3," Enid begins, then hesitates. Madeline joins her by counting "4, 5, 6, 7," and they finish the sequence of numbers. "Seven plates, seven crackers, and seven cups," summarizes her teacher, and Enid beams at her accomplishment. "Would you like to ring the bell for snack?" Madeline asks. Enid nods and goes off to ring the bell. ✍

In this example, we see Enid constructing physical knowledge about strategies for placing crackers and cups on the snack table. She learns something about balance on even and uneven surfaces. Enid also constructs logical–mathematical knowledge about the relationship of cups to surfaces and about one-to-one correspondence.

Madeline helps her count using one-to-one correspondence and presents the idea of equivalent sets for the seven plates, seven crackers, and seven cups. Madeline also helps her to learn social conventional knowledge about the names and sequence of numbers in English, as well as the position of cups in relation to plates. Enid uses her knowledge of the purpose of the snack bell to call her classmates to enjoy her handiwork. Teachers' abilities to understand and support children's learning depend on their skill in identifying the types of knowledge being constructed by the child and finding strategies to enhance that construction. Teachers are challenged to provide opportunities for children to construct their own learning and apply what they have learned from others through playful activity.

Piaget: The Development of Play

Piaget's theory is intimately tied to the study of play. Many of his important works are filled with observations of his own three children at play during their first 2 years of life and of other children he observed in preschool settings in Geneva, Switzerland.

His important work, *Play, Dreams and Imitation in Childhood* (1962), made play a central part of his theory. He showed how children develop the ability to represent their world through a series of stages in which assimilation and accommodation are increasingly better coordinated with each other. Children's ability to represent their inner concerns and understandings is revealed in their play, which progresses through a series of stages. As each new stage develops, it incorporates the possibilities for play of all the previous stages (Figure 2.1). In the following sections, we present a brief description of these stages.

Practice or Functional Play   The first stage is termed practice or **functional play** and is a major characteristic of the stage of **sensorimotor intelligence**. Practice or functional play is what Piaget (1962) called "a happy display of known actions" in which children repeatedly practice their schemes for actions with objects or their own bodies. It is demonstrated by the play of the infant—the grasping and pulling, kicking, and propelling of arms and legs that infants engage in for the pleasure of mastering the movement. It continues as children take part in activities such as

Figure 2.1
Piaget's Stages of the
Development of Play

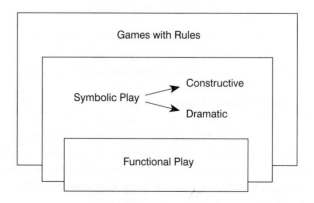

splashing water or sifting sand, honking a horn, or riding a bike. Practice or functional play remains a major form of activity throughout childhood and adulthood. How many adults doodle while talking on the phone or enjoy the exhilaration of jogging or moving to music? Opportunities for practice play remain an important source of development and pleasure throughout life and provide an essential feature of school curriculum, as we illustrate in subsequent chapters.

Symbolic Play   The second stage, **symbolic play**, begins at about 18 months of age and is a major characteristic of the stage of **preoperational intelligence**. Symbolic play involves the use of **mental representation** to pretend that one object stands for another or to take on a make-believe role. It forms a foundation of future abstract thinking and the ability to organize both work and play experiences as human beings develop. Three major forms of symbolic play are described by Piaget: constructive, dramatic, and games with rules, which coincide with the beginnings of conceptual thought.

The first, **constructive play**, provides a natural link between practice or functional play and more sophisticated forms of symbolic play. In constructive play, the child uses concrete objects to create a representation of an object: blocks or playdough manipulated to represent a house are typical examples. The intent in constructive play is to approach one's mental representation of the symbolized object as closely as possible.

> Three-year-old Sandy searches for just the right size and number of sticks to make five candles on her birthday cake. ∅

Following closely on the heels of constructive play, and often overlapping it, comes **dramatic play**. This play involves the creation of imaginary roles and situations and frequently accompanies the construction of pretend objects, but the representation is more abstract. Instead of simple object symbols, children use gesture and language to create imaginary roles and situations with complex themes, characters, and scripts. Sometimes this play is sociodramatic in nature, involving the negotiation of roles and pretend themes with others. At other times the play may be solitary, with characters, themes, and situations enacted by a single player.

> As Josh finishes his garage of blocks and parks a toy car in it, he pretends that an imaginary family piles into the car for a trip to the beach. ∅

> Sandy invites several children to play the part of guests at the birthday party as she enacts the role of the birthday girl. She "blows out" the stick candles, and the group shares her sand birthday cake. ∅

Both stages of symbolic play, constructive and dramatic, are intellectually and socially complicated. Their mastery sets the stage for playing games with rules, which appears around the age of 6 or 7 and continues as the predominant form of overt play throughout middle childhood, adolescence, and adulthood. Overt play is an important concept because older children and adults continue to engage in constructive and dramatic play long after early childhood, but in a more covert manner.

Realistic toys support and motivate play.

Dramatic and constructive play take the form of private fantasy and **hypothetical-deductive thinking** and accompany the daily internal lives of adults in many of the same ways that overt dramatic play enriches the lives of young children.

Games with Rules

The **games with rules** stage involves adherence to an external set of social rules that governs play. This type of play marks the transition from preoperational to **concrete operational thought** in Piaget's theory. In this play, rules may be negotiated and agreed on by the players before the game begins or negotiated on the spot as children spontaneously invent a game. The ability to negotiate and adhere to mutually agreed-on rules has its roots in the ad hoc negotiation of rules common to sociodramatic play at earlier stages of development (see Piaget, 1965c).

Piaget (1962) also theorized about the emotional nature of symbolic play, discussing the cathartic or "liquidating combinations" in play that allow children to discharge emotions associated with disturbing experiences. He also discussed the compensatory function of symbolic play that provides opportunities to "correct" reality that is confusing or unpleasant. So, for example, a child spanking a baby doll might discharge anger about his or her own punishment. Replaying a situation in which the child was not allowed to stay out after dark might prompt a dramatic play sequence of hunting monsters all night in the forest.

VYGOTSKY: DEVELOPMENT AND PLAY

Lev Vygotsky was a constructivist theorist primarily concerned with how development and learning takes place through social interactions within historical and cultural contexts. The English title of his major work, *Mind in Society*, conveys that the mind can never be considered or discussed as separate from the social, cultural, and historical context.

The influence of Vygotsky's work continues to grow in early childhood education practice and research. Vygotsky believed that conflict and problem solving in social situations are essential features of child development, as are make believe and play (Berk, 1994). In this chapter we discuss four important social–cognitive processes that are central to his theory: the zone of proximal development, the movement from interpersonal to intrapersonal knowledge, the acquisition of mental tools, and the transition from implicit rules to explicit rules.

The Zone of Proximal Development

Vygotsky coined the term **zone of proximal development** (ZPD) to refer to the context in which the child's understanding is furthered as a result of social interactions. He wrote that children perform beyond their usual level of functioning when engaged in the social and cognitive collaborations that create this zone. Vygotsky explained that play was essential to development and, in fact, the source of it: "Play is the source of development and creates the zone of proximal development" (1967, p. 16).

By observing children's symbolic play, teachers discover how new concepts, skills, and competencies emerge in the play of each child in relationship to others.

> Steven and Anthony are playing near the tunnel in the outdoor play yard. Steven, lying on his stomach with a face full of mock agony, moans, "Pretend you gave me medicine." Anthony pretends to feed him medicine, and Steven leaps up, announcing, "All better." Then Anthony becomes the patient, and Steven feeds him pretend medicine. They each take two turns. Then Anthony says, "I'm hungry," and they rush inside to get their lunch boxes, returning to the outdoor play area with a snack of pretzels. Steven holds up a pretzel and asks, "What letter?" "No letter," responds Anthony, and Steven takes a bite. "Now it's a B," shouts Anthony, and he bites his pretzel. "What letter?" "An O," shouts Steven. The final bite is eaten. "Now what letter?" asks Steven, holding out his empty hand. "No letter!" shouts Anthony delightedly, and they both fall on the ground laughing. ✆

Anthony and Steven have created a ZPD where their understanding of letters is further developed. In viewing play as the source of the ZPD, we focus on the **co-construction**, that is, the joint construction, of a pretend reality that is invented by the players and sustained by the rules they negotiate. Because relationships are of primary importance to young children, their desire to participate in imaginary worlds shared with others leads them to accept and invent new symbolic meanings, regulate their own impulses, and collaboratively construct pretend realities. As this vignette illustrates, children's co-construction of knowledge can be observed across a wide range of early childhood settings.

FAMILY DIVERSITY

A Mother Plays with Her Child in Her Native Language

Mrs. P. plays a tickle game in a Filipino dialect with her son, who is 18 months old. As she holds him with her left arm, she moves her right hand high above his head:

"*Banog-banong sa Cagon.*"   (Kite, kite of Cagon.)

He watches intently as she moves it toward him, her voice growing more and more dramatic.

"*Asa matagdon?*"   (Where will it alight?)

She moves her hand downward, tickles his chest, and they both laugh.

"*Dinhi-Dinhi!*"   (Here! Here!)

Interpersonal to Intrapersonal Processes in Learning

Another of Vygotsky's important contributions to understanding play and development is his assertion that every function in development occurs first at the social or **interpersonal** level and later at the individual or **intrapersonal** level (Vygotsky, 1978). In this view, social activities between children and adults or among peers promote development and are of primary importance.

In most cultures, this includes lullabies and baby games. Infants hear patterns of communication, not only the structure of language but also rhythm and intonation. The feature above, *Family Diversity: A Mother Plays with Her Child in Her Native Language*, illustrates this in further detail.

Young children frequently learn a new concept or skill with others, such as Amy learning to use a funnel to try to fill a water balloon with her playmates at the water table. She then tries her new concepts and skill in the bathtub at home. In schools, children learn from adults and from other children in both formal and informal activities. In this way, they develop understandings of activities and adult roles that are time and culturally specific.

At her retirement dinner, Leni is asked how things have changed in the 30-plus years since she started teaching:

Things are the same when I think about painting and drawing activities. But it's different for writing and even pretending to write. I started teaching before there were computers. Back in the '80s when they played office, the kids pretended to type using the old upright typewriter we had. Now kids use computers—and not only for pretend play, but to write and send class e-mails. And, I remember, when I was in second grade I was taught to write with a fountain pen and we had bottles of ink on our desks.

When I started teaching, this area was agricultural. When the kids played outside, they pretended to drive tractors and trucks. They'd "pick" food to "cook." Sometimes they'd set up fruit stands. Now the kids in my class pretend to go to the megastore—and they drive vans and SUVs and "commute to work."

Part of the difference reflects what the children bring to school. But I think a large part of the difference stems from the differences in what I do.

I always purposely set up the environment and plan the curriculum to reflect the lives of the families. If you walked in my classroom this year you'd know there are families from many cultures and different countries. We've always used simple phrases from each child's home language. And the languages have changed in the last decades. I've spoken Spanish for many years and now I'm learning Mandarin as well. ✄

Acquiring Mental Tools

Vygotsky (1978) explained that humans use tools to make activities possible and easier. Some tools are concrete objects, like levers and wheels, that make physical work easier. Levers and wheels are simple tools; other tools are complicated and often combine a number of simple tools (e.g., a car motor).

<u>Mental tools</u> have been essential to human evolution and cultural development. Mental tools are sometimes referred to as "tools of the mind" (Bodrova & Leong, 2007). Mental tools often make cognitive as well as physical activities possible and easier. For example, the use of language, whether spoken or signed, is a mental tool central to communication, particularly the communication of more abstract ideas and concepts. Technology, such as tablets, computers, and social media, are other examples of mental tools. Children from all cultures and all times learn to use mental tools from others—peers as well as adults. Teachers know that some mental tools may seem quite simple to adults but are challenging to young children. The chapters that follow provide numerous examples of the acquisition of mental tools and their application in areas related to language, technology, science, mathematics, and the arts.

In the following vignette, use of a metacognitive strategy is a mental tool. Elijah chants, "Over one, under two" to make sure that he follows the pattern he is weaving.

Sam and Elijah go to the same afterschool child-care program. This afternoon Sam (age 5) watches Elijah (age 8) weave on a handloom.

Elijah:	Do you want to try?
Sam:	I don't know how. How do you know what to do next?
Elijah:	Here. See. I'm making this design. I put this yarn over one, under two. See, it goes over one, under two. Try.
Sam:	Over one. Ok, under. This isn't right.

Elijah:	Help me do this row. Hold down that one (green). Now I go over (the green). OK. Now pick up those two—the red and orange—and I go under (the red and the orange). Remember, over one, under two. Over one, under two. Just say it with me, "Over one. Under two."
Sam:	That's too complicated.
Elijah:	Maybe next time. ✆

Understanding Rules

Vygotsky clarified how children develop their understanding of rules. He asserted that all play has rules and that with new levels of development, these rules become more explicit. In this way dramatic (pretend) play, where rules are implicit, forms the foundation for games, where rules are explicit. Rules in dramatic play govern the organization of roles and behavior in play and events. For example, "Daddies shake hands like this" and "Firefighters have to hook up their hoses first." Yet following these rules is largely taken for granted during children's dramatic play until conflict among players occurs when their expectations differ. Then children assert their versions of the rules governing characters' behavior and hypothetical events.

As children begin to articulate their ideas about rules that govern social behavior from their experiences and their family and cultural backgrounds, they also confront the ideas of their peers and the adults around them. They develop the capacity to negotiate rules of play that are set forth before play begins, such as a game of checkers or four square. Negotiating rules of play can be particularly challenging for children with developmental delays, children with emotional challenges, or children from families in which the expectations from home and those from school are mismatched. Yet basic to a play-centered curriculum are mutual understandings of social rules, for example, that throwing blocks or sand might hurt other children. In this way, children begin to understand why agreed-on rules are essential to the functioning of society.

Vygotsky's Levels of Symbolic Play

Vygotsky also contributed to our understanding of how play relates to levels in the development of symbolic thinking. He observed that very young children merged the meaning of objects with the objects themselves and thus could not think abstractly. In symbolic play, children use objects to represent ideas, situations, and other objects. Objects that represent other objects are called **pivots**. Children use pivots to anchor their mental representations of the meanings of words. For example, when Sam selects a book to represent a taco in his kitchen play, he anchors his concept of "taco-ness" with an object that opens and closes, and thus resembles a real taco. When children's representational competence grows, pivots become less necessary, and meaning may be carried completely in the mind, for instance, through the use of an imaginary object. For Vygotsky, the use of objects in play as

For Vygotsky, the use of objects in play marks a key stage in the development of thought.

support for the development of meaning-in-the-mind marks a key stage in the development of thought (see Vygotsky, 1967, 1978).

MEAD: PLAY AND THE DEVELOPING SENSE OF SELF

In all early childhood settings, teachers attempt to understand and support children's developing sense of self. In *Mind, Self, and Society*, George Herbert Mead (1934) described the relationship of play to the development of a stable sense of self.

For Mead, play is the major vehicle for young children to learn to differentiate their own perspectives from those of others in their social worlds. As children take on pretend roles of others and coordinate those roles with the roles taken by their playmates, they come to view their own behavior from the perspectives of other people.

> Robert is playing at being a waiter in a restaurant. He incorporates the perspectives of his "customers" when he asks them if they are ready to order. He then communicates with his "cook" in the kitchen and tells his customers: "It will take a long time to get a burger here. Better go to McDonald's." ⌀

This negotiation between the self and others also takes place outside play scripts, as we see when Robert, his cook, and his customers have to figure out how they will put away the props and furniture for their restaurant when the teacher announces that it's cleanup time.

The Play Stage

According to Mead, the preschool and primary-grade years provide the impetus and context for children to see themselves as unique human beings within the community of others. In Mead's theory, the young preschool child operates in the play stage of the development of the self. This is the stage in which a child can accomplish simple role transformations from self to others. This is what Smilansky (1968) described as the beginning stages of role-play. The child simply becomes a tiger, or an astronaut, or a veterinarian, and then returns to being the self with limited expansion of the components or complementary roles involved in the transformations.

> Three-year-old Jed announces "I'm a fireman! RRRRRRR!" and races around waving an imaginary hose. Five minutes later he becomes a puppy, barking and crawling on all fours. ✆

In Mead's terms the child is just beginning to differentiate the "I," or spontaneous aspect of the self, from the "me," or the sense of the self as a social object. In transforming himself into a puppy, for example, Jed is beginning to figure out how others might view him from their perspectives. This is the stage in which children often create imaginary companions, representing the companion's viewpoint as well as that of the self. Children at this stage form the rudiments of a sense of self that include their own perspectives as well as representations of how others view them. Emphases may differ according to culture; for example, cultural values and interpretations of children's behavior within an individualistic cultural orientation may be different from those with a collective or mutual interdependence cultural orientation.

The Game Stage

As role-playing becomes more complex, children enter into what Mead called the game stage of the development of the self. As the following vignette about Cindy shows, the child can coordinate the "I" aspect of herself with complex representations of the viewpoints of others about the "I."

> Five-year-old Cindy simultaneously plays the role of mother to her child, who is eating breakfast, wife to her husband, who is on his way to work, and ballerina to her coach, who has just called her on the phone in a typical "morning in the playhouse" enactment. ✆

Not only does Cindy need to adjust her voice tone, gesture, and language to what she believes is appropriate for each role, but she must also imagine the complementary roles of others to each of her roles and coordinate them. All the while she uses cardboard chips to represent scrambled eggs and pours milk from a wooden block.

At this point, the child in the game stage of development is learning to coordinate her representation of herself with the multiple perspectives that others might take. She can think about the various aspects of her "pretend selves" in relation to the other players. She shifts fluidly from the "I" to the "me" and considers herself a social object as well as an actor in her play.

The Generalized Other Stage

The third stage of the self that Mead describes is that of the generalized other. In this stage the child not only coordinates the "I" of the self with multiple "me's" but also adopts a **metacognitive** stance regarding the framework within which action takes place. For example, Cindy might begin to comment on the rules of her culture that define authentic roles of mother or ballerina or spouse. Early childhood educators frequently see children in this stage discuss their roles with comments such as, "Doctors talk like this" or "Babies walk this way."

Initially, such negotiations may be particularly challenging for children who are bicultural and bilingual. However, it is precisely these very capabilities that can support children's abilities to take the perspectives of others.

> In the dramatic play area, Eun Mi and Hyun Jae are engrossed in cooking, speaking in Korean as they prepare the pretend food.

Eun Mi: This special rice and kimchee is for grandfather.

Hyun Jae: And bring one rice bowl for grandmother! And this is for our "brother" Chung Shik. ⌀

By speaking Korean, they can express nuances of perspective taking, relationships, and customs that are hard to translate into English. For example, with this short, two-sentence exchange, they have indicated that they honor their grandparents not only by their terms for grandparents but also when Eun Mi uses the honorific term for rice. Hyun Jae uses the term for brother that communicates that their pretend brother Chung Shik is older than she. She has also shown that she is aware of the two different counting systems and has used the correct system for counting bowls. In these sentences, both children use verb forms that show they know they are talking to peers.

The generalized other stage is one in which games with rules become of interest as children coordinate the perspectives of players with their understanding of the framework that governs the rule structure of the game. Mead emphasized the importance of the social context in which children learn a game. This behavior reflects the understandings children have about the social rules of our culture, as expressed in both their role behavior within the play and in their negotiations about roles outside the play. This development takes time. Older preschoolers and kindergartners may follow game rules presented and played out in a rigid manner. Teachers find that children delight in creating their own games or devising their own rules for such games as Candy Land or Chutes and Ladders (Monighan-Nourot, Scales, Van Hoorn, with Almy, 1987).

> Sally, 4½ years old, has been playing Candy Land intently, by herself, for 30 minutes. She began by sitting on the floor and placing all the cards in front of her in straight rows—face up. She then carefully opens the board and puts all the markers on Start. She selects one marker. At that moment, she notices Pat, her teacher, observing her and invites her to sit and play.

> *Sally explains:*   "First, you have to pick a bunny or something to be your marker thing. Then you look at the board and see where you want to go, and pick the card that matches it!" ✄

Pat explains that Sally invented her own version of this game with rules. She delights in this game that reverses the rules so that they match her desires: She first decides where she wants to go, then picks the card.

ERIKSON: PLAY AND MASTERY IN THE INNER WORLD OF CHILDHOOD

Erik Erikson wrote extensively about the importance of play for young children's emotional development (see Erikson 1950/1985, 1977). When naming his theoretical orientation, he combined "psycho" and "social" to emphasize that the individual's inner psychological state is inseparable from the social context.

Psychosocial theory continues to influence early childhood education practice for several reasons. Teachers are concerned with supporting children's emotional and social well-being. Teachers turn to psychosocial theory in their efforts to foster children's mental health. Erikson described the development of the healthy personality from infancy through old age. In numerous writings, he theorized about how children's social and emotional development relates to their families, school, and the cultural contexts in which they live. Psychosocial theory, as Erikson explained, extends Freud's psychoanalytic theory by considering both the inner psychological dimensions and the outer social and cultural dimensions of children's developing identity (Erikson, 1950/1985).

Erikson described eight major stages of psychosocial development that build on previous stages (Erikson, 1950/1985). The first four stages describe development from infancy through early childhood. Rather than being stages that individuals "pass through," Erikson stressed that although the healthy personality exhibits the strength of a particular stage (e.g., trust), healthy individuals continue to rework the balance of the strength of the stage and its antithesis (e.g., mistrust) throughout their lives. For example, it is adaptable for healthy individuals of all ages to exhibit mistrust in situations where it is dangerous to be too trusting, such as being challenged to jump from a high wall.

Infancy: Trust and Mistrust

During the first year of life, infants are totally dependent on their caregivers. The caregiver's sensitivity and consistency in care lead not only to the infant's attachment to that caregiver, but also to the infant developing a sense of trust in his or herself and the outer world. The emotionally healthy infant's basic sense of trust is central to the toddler's development of autonomy.

> Akinyi rides comfortably on her mother's hip as they walk to the early morning market. She is turned sideways and sees her mother greeting several women that Akinyi sees every day. One of the women smiles, reaches over, and rubs Akinyi's back. Akinyi can feel her mother laughing softly. As her mother bends to choose vegetables for the afternoon meal, Akinyi rocks gently to one side, tied securely to her mother. ✆

Toddlerhood: Autonomy, Shame, and Doubt

During their second and third years of life, children's growing motor and cognitive competencies contribute to their psychosocial development. This is a time when children develop a sense of their own power, a sense of "I can do it." Children's developing sense of autonomy is shaped by their schools, families, and society. Erikson emphasized that we examine what young children are allowed or expected to do and how adults set limits or boundaries on children's behavior, so that a sense of autonomy is the outcome overall rather than children's sense of shame and doubt.

FAMILY DIVERSITY

A Special Education Specialist Visits the Home

Ethan, 2 years old, has delayed gross motor development. Nadia, a special education specialist, has visited Ethan's home several times each month since he was born. She watches on as Ethan and his mother play one of his favorite games, "Can you get me?" Ethan's mom gets down on her hands and knees. She makes a quick move toward him as she looks Ethan in the eye and, in a playful, higher voice says, "Can you get me?" She turns around and starts crawling away, with Ethan crawling after her. She takes quick backward glances to make sure that he's able to stay close enough behind her as she modifies her speed. Faster and slower. Faster and slower. Ethan is never more than a foot or two away. "Oh, Ethan, you're getting me! You got me!" She slows just enough so that he catches her as he crawls along at his full speed.

Later, as his mom talks with Nadia, Ethan continues to crawl around the furniture. At one point, he remains behind the couch for several minutes. Nadia calls, "Ethan, where are you? Are you hiding?" Ethan emerges with a wide grin.

Play links imagination with social life.

Even for the child who is developing a healthy sense of autonomy, teachers find that the balance between autonomy, shame, and doubt shifts from month to month and even from activity to activity within each day.

> William has made a high pile of plates, forks, and spoons and begins to set the table. He brushes against a chair, and forks and spoons fall everywhere. His teacher, Ron, notes that this usually self-sufficient, confident child looks doubtful of his ability and turns to Ron as if for reassurance. Ron stays where he is and responds in a quiet voice, "Go ahead. You'll fix it." ✆

Early Childhood and the Play Stage: Initiative and Guilt

Erikson called the next stage, usually from about 4 to 6 years of age, "the play stage." This is the stage of initiative and guilt. The sense of autonomy seen in younger children's activities slowly develops into more sustained, complex initiatives. Guilt arises when initiative is inappropriate or overreaching. For example, despite her aunt's admonition to watch out for her baby cousin, Breann attempts to leap from one post to the other, misses, and falls on Duane, who wails in protest.

As they develop, children's greater motor, cognitive, and social capabilities mean that they are able to initiate complex play with others and sustain play for a longer time. As a toddler, Ethan's hide-and-seek play is complemented by his mother's efforts to support his growing autonomy. Older preschool children and kindergartners enjoy related but greatly extended games of hide-and-seek.

Children's sense of initiative is supported by their increased small and large motor coordination and strength, as well as their developing cognitive abilities.

> Matthew, age 5, sits on the rug next to the puzzle rack. He selects a challenging puzzle with more than 30 pieces and a rather abstract picture. He starts with one edge of the puzzle, speaking to himself quietly, "Is this one it? This one? There, I got you!" ✆

For Erikson, this is the stage where imagination holds sway as children create their own "microreality" (Erikson, 1977). He described how, at this stage, children express their initiative in play by developing complex plots with conflicting turns and twists and a wide range of characters.

Children at this stage initiate play to work through past failures and present contradictions. Conflicts between archetypes of good and evil expressed in power roles such as superheroes and space aliens are common themes. Conflicts between child initiative and adult prohibitions are also expressed through **fantasy play**, such as the "naughty baby." In dramatic play, children enter into fantasies that allow them to explore their concepts of initiative and independence. Play themes that portray children as orphaned or separated from their parents, having to fend for themselves in the woods or at sea, are common in preschool and kindergarten.

Play-centered curricula support children's exploration of the psychosocial issues of taking initiative and feeling guilt over violating adult prohibitions. In contrast, curricula that emphasize learning by imitating models may undermine the development of initiative. In every teacher-initiated curriculum, judgments of right or wrong are consistently made by adults with regard to children's processes and products, and children learn to rely on adult judgment and approval rather than their own internal resources. For example:

> In completing a teacher-modeled project, Rebecca places the precut green strip of "grass" above her name on the page and then places the "trunk" of the tree at a right angle above it. She begins to tear pieces of tissue paper for her "fall leaves." As the teacher circulates about the classroom, she pauses and says, "You've done a good job on your tree trunk, Rebecca, but your grass needs to go along the bottom edge of the paper." The teacher removes the green paper strip of grass as well as the brown trunk, placing them to match her own model. Rebecca puts her hands in her lap and stares randomly around the room, as the teacher moves on to guide another child's activity. ✆

Too much activity forced on the child by others, claim Katz and Chard (2000), leads to "damaged dispositions" of intrinsic motivation, concentration, initiative, confidence, and humor that are essential to the learning process throughout children's lives.

Adults can support children's play by providing a safe environment in which developmentally appropriate limits are set to support children's developing sense of initiative. The child who is supported in taking initiative during this stage of development forms a firm foundation for the sense of competence and purpose that develops during middle childhood in the stage of industry and inferiority.

Industry and Inferiority: Play and Work in Middle Childhood

The flexible goals of the initiative stage, where process takes precedence over product, evolve gradually into goal-oriented projects where children's "I can do it" attitude is expanded to include perseverance and self-evaluation.

> Several groups of children in Leslie's second-grade class are writing plays that they will act out in the two kindergarten classes. For the past week, Peter, Lisa, and Leah have discussed dozens of ideas of how to write and perform a play based on the story of Homer Price and the doughnut machine. They are writing the scene where the machine is making dozens and dozens of doughnuts and the three children helping at the store race around stacking the doughnuts everywhere. They draft, read aloud, and agree on each section, then work with their fourth-grade mentor to correct errors.
>
> Oh! More doughnuts!
> Wow! More and more doughnuts!
> Fast, catch that one!
>
> They stop and evaluate the script. "Let's use real doughnuts." "How can we show that there are so many?" "Can we make it look like they're coming faster and faster?" Next week the children will revise and rehearse. Next Friday is their opening day in the kindergarten classrooms. ✑

Erikson (1977) wrote that play remains important during middle childhood and throughout adulthood. In middle childhood, children also have the cognitive and motor competencies to participate more fully in the work that their culture values. Children construct their sense of industry or inferiority based on these cultural expectations. At this stage each culture provides some forms of formal education or training for adult roles (Erikson, 1950/1985). For example, children participate in chores at home, begin formal instruction in literacy and mathematics, or in some more traditional cultures they may apprentice to a local artisan.

SUMMARY

Teachers of young children gain support for their use of play in the classroom by understanding the role of play in the developmental theories of Piaget, Vygotsky, Mead, and Erikson. These theorists suggest that each child develops through a constructive process that is shaped by family and community values and histories. In early childhood programs, these processes result in a peer culture of play that reflects the children's collective and individual understandings of the world. By learning as much as one can about the sociocultural factors children bring with them to school, and by observing and listening with care and understanding, teachers can enhance the learning and development of children in their care.

By placing play at the center of the curriculum, we make an investment to protect both the short-term and long-term futures of our children and our society. Play supports the development of intellect and all its manifestations. It also supports more general qualities related to emotional development, personality, socialization, imagination, and flexibility of mind that help to ensure a legacy of adaptation to change and freedom to make choices.

Although not all play may be seen as furthering children's development, in our view play is the necessary core to curriculum for young children. Play provides the teacher with cues and vehicles for assessing children and implementing curriculum goals. Most important, it allows children to develop to their fullest potential intellectually, socially, morally, physically, and emotionally as they learn to negotiate their developing sense of self with the demands of the group. Awareness of the possibilities inherent in play for understanding each child in the classroom opens many new doors for teachers. This awareness enhances both the professional knowledge and artistry that make teaching preschool and primary-grade children a fulfilling and important profession.

- **A constructivist view of play and development.** In the nature–nurture view of development, "nature" provides the biological givens of the child and "nurture" provides the environmental factors that determine how the biological givens unfold. The constructivist view adds the child as an active force in constructing themselves and thereby influencing and modifying both the nature and nurture dimensions of development.

- **Piaget's developmental theory and play.** In Piaget's constructivist theory of development, the ability of the child to effectively function in the world is entirely dependent on what the child can do. Behind all of the child's actions are biological or psychological schemes. Assimilating the world to the child's schemes makes it possible to function in the world. However, when schemes are not well suited to the goals of the child, the schemes undergo an accommodation to reality. The dynamics of assimilation and accommodation is tied to the child's development of play, which goes through a number of stages from functional play to symbolic play to games with rules.

- **Vygotsky: Development and play.** Whereas Piaget focused on the sensory motor and representational aspects of development, Vygotsky focused on the cultural–historic and social aspects of development. There are four central aspects of Vygotsky's writing:

  a. All conceptual learning first occurs in social interactions and later becomes internalized.

  b. All learning occurs in a social zone of proximal development (ZPD,) where the content of the social interactions are developmentally challenging, but attainable.

    c. The culture contains "mental tools" that, like all tools, extend the capacity to interact in the world. Development partially requires the acquisition of these tools.

    d. Society and culture provide rules that govern activity. These rules are first understood by the child implicitly, then through development and interaction they become explicitly understood.

For Vygotsky, as is the case for Piaget, play is an essential and critical aspect of all development.

■ **Mead: Play and the developing sense of self.** Sociologist George H. Mead wrote about the child's evolving sense of self, starting with an undifferentiated view where the sense of self is merged with the sense of others that eventually leads to a fully differentiated view in which the child is one social object among others. Mead's work is based on an understanding of how play affects a child's developing sense of self.

■ **Erikson: Play and mastery in the inner world of childhood.** Erikson described eight major stages of psychosocial development that build on previous stages (Erikson, 1950/1985). The first four stages describe development from infancy through early childhood: trust and mistrust, autonomy and shame and doubt, initiative and guilt, industry and inferiority. Rather than being stages that individuals "pass through," Erikson stressed that although the healthy personality exhibits the strength of a particular stage (e.g., trust), healthy individuals continue to rework the balance of the strength of the stage and its antithesis (e.g., mistrust) throughout their lives. Erikson emphasized the role of play at each childhood stage of development.

APPLYING YOUR KNOWLEDGE

  1. Describe the "nature–nurture" debate and your understanding of how a constructivist view contributes to that debate.
    a. Explain a core aspect of all constructivist views of development.
    b. In your own words, explain how play relates to a constructivist view of development.

  2. Explain the role of schemes and the dynamics of assimilation and accommodation in Jean Piaget's theory of development.
    a. List three types of knowledge discussed by Piaget and give examples of each.
    b. Describe three stages of play in Piaget's theory and give examples of each.

  3. Discuss your understanding of how social experience and play are central to Vygotsky's theory of development.
    a. List four key concepts in Vygotsky's theory and relate each to children's play.

   b. Give your understanding of the meaning of "pivots" in children's symbolic play.

4. Briefly describe George Mead's three stages in child development (the play stage, the game stage, and the generalized other stage) and give examples of how each relates to children's play.

   a. Discuss Mead's idea that children progress from an undifferentiated sense of self to an understanding that they are social objects among others.

   b. List three stages of play in Mead's writings and give examples of each.

5. Discuss Erik Erikson's first four psychosocial stages and how children use play to support the strengths of each of these stages (trust, autonomy, initiative, and industry).

   a. Erikson proposed eight stages of development, each with a characteristic psychosocial strength and antithesis. The first four stages relate to infancy, toddlerhood, early childhood, and middle childhood. Pair these with each of the following strengths of a stage and its antithesis: industry and inferiority, autonomy and shame and doubt, trust and mistrust, initiative and guilt.

   b. Give your own ideas about how play might help children develop strengths relating to trust and mistrust, autonomy and shame and doubt, initiative and guilt, industry and inferiority.

CHAPTER 3

Play as the Cornerstone of Development: The Literature

LEARNING OUTCOMES

- Discuss how children develop symbolic thought, language, and literacy skills; logical–mathematical thinking; and problem-solving ability through play.
- List three aspects of imagination and fantasy and describe how they are related to children's play.
- Explain how social–moral development relates to issues of autonomy and heteronomy.
- Discuss how Piaget, Erikson, and Vygotsky viewed the role of play in emotional development.

In this chapter we examine the literature on how play influences various aspects of child development, beginning with intellectual development and followed by a look at its effects on creativity and imagination, its influences on **socialization** and **moral development**, and its relationship to emotional development. In doing so, we also illustrate how the play-centered curriculum can meet standards for early education.

Historically, early childhood teachers believed that childhood play was valuable in and of itself (Bergen & Fromberg, 2006; Elkind, 2007; Nourot, 2005; Singer & Singer, 2005; Wolfe, 2002). As early childhood educators became more focused on specific outcomes of educational practice, the role of play became instrumental to curriculum goals for young children. Many advocates of children's play asked, "What aspects of desirable academic and social knowledge are constructed through play in early childhood?"

Much of the recent research has followed this instrumental focus and argues for the central role of play in constructing and consolidating particular knowledge, skills, and competencies in preschool and the primary grades, or "educational play" (see, for example, Fromberg & Bergen, 2006; Hirsh-Pasek, Golinkoff, Berk, & Singer, 2009). We take a slightly different stance and suggest that play itself is vital to childhood and that we can achieve educational goals by understanding and incorporating play into the classroom curriculum.

PLAY AND INTELLECTUAL DEVELOPMENT

For both Jean Piaget and Lev Vygotsky, play is intimately linked to representation— that is, how in symbolic play and **symbolic role-playing** the child expresses ideas, feelings, and needs. Additional elements of intellectual development include how children come to understand the perspectives of others, how children invent strategies for play with others (as in games with rules), and how children solve problems. We will round out our focus on intellectual development with a look at language and literacy, and logical–mathematical thought.

Play and the Development of Symbolic Thought

Symbolic thought is an important component of representational intelligence and underlies the pretense we associate with the play of preschool and primary-age children. It forms the foundation on which children construct their abilities to engage in abstract thinking in literacy, mathematical reasoning, and problem solving. Symbolic activities entail creating meaning and expressing that meaning through gesture (driving a pretend car), language, intonation ("OK, honey, it's bedtime"), and objects (using sand and rocks to make a birthday cake). The development of symbolic behavior has been frequently studied (Bergen, 2002; Fromberg, 2002; Honig, 2007; Johnson, 2006; McCune, 1985; Rubin, Fein, & Vandenberg, 1983).

> Sally picks up a wooden block and holds it to her ear. She makes pushing button motions with her fingers and says, "Hello, is Mickey Mouse there?"

Beginning at about 18 months, symbolic thought becomes possible, evidenced by the use of language and **pretend play**. From this point on, the ability to transform objects or situations, through the use of imagination, into meanings that are different from the original object or situation forms the foundation for intellectual development and communication (Piaget, 1962; Vygotsky, 1976).

Symbolic Play with Objects   Building on Vygotsky's notion that concrete objects serve as pivots to "anchor" children's imagination and pretense, researchers have studied young children's play with objects. They have discovered that, as children's play develops, they seem able to use objects that are increasingly different

Play with concrete materials supports children's imagination and pretense.

from the object represented in play, building the foundation for abstract thinking (Nourot, 2006).

This ability to abstract the essential features of an object and to mentally represent those features rests on the notion of symbolic distancing. Sigel (1993) coined the term **symbolic distancing** to mean the degree to which an object looks like what it is intended to symbolize. For example, to represent a car, a particular block might serve better than another because of its shape and size. A child's ability to use an object that looks different from what it is used to symbolize develops with age and is largely constructed through play (Fein, 1981; Scarlett, Naudeau, Salonius-Pasternak, & Ponte, 2005).

Symbolic Role-Play   Children also make symbolic transformations in their role-play. Research indicates that as children's capacities for representing ideas develop, they increasingly create pretend roles and situations without the use of costumes or props, using more subtle behaviors such as gesture and intonation to mark their transformation into make-believe roles in play. Teachers may note the subtle markers, such as a tone of voice, a walk, or a gesture that children use to enter make believe (Fromberg, 2002; Henderson & Jones, 2002; Morgenthaler, 2006; Nicolopolou, 2007; Smilansky, 1968, 1990).

Supporting Symbolic Play for Children with Special Needs   The concept of symbolic distancing is particularly useful when working with young children and children with developmental delays. Some children with **special needs** have difficulty in separating reality from fantasy (Bergen, 2003; Mindes, 2006; Odom, 2002; Preissler, 2006). When symbolic distancing is a challenge, most would select an object that is a replica or closely resembles the actual object in appearance and function. Teachers can support the success of children with special needs in integrated classrooms by including a range of play materials. Wolfberg (1999) reports her research on the scaffolding of imagination and pretense in the play of children with autism. She contends that both teachers and peers can support children's use of increasingly abstract symbolic representations through modeling and play orchestration.

Four-year-old Edna and 5-year-old Jonah, both children with autism in a full-inclusion preschool class, are involved in parallel play in the dramatic play area. Edna drives the grocery cart around the classroom, returning in a ritual fashion to tap the toy cash register on each round. Jonah is also in the pretend store, packing and unpacking toy plastic food in shopping bags repeatedly. Their teacher takes the role of cashier and orchestrates some cooperative play between Edna and Jonah by modeling and coaching how Jonah might load the groceries into Edna's cart and help her to her "car" in the block area. The teacher gradually reduces her coaching role from direct modeling to verbal prompts to observation as the two children master the sequence of pretend. ✍

Taking the Perspectives of Others   Playing with peers requires perspectivism, or the ability to mentally represent the viewpoint of others to negotiate group play situations.

> Both Samantha and Estelle want to play the part of the princess for the castle they have built of blocks. Play cannot continue until a compromise is reached. Their teacher suggests that one princess has a cousin who visits from another kingdom, and the girls promptly begin discussing how the two princesses' clothing and crowns might look different and talking about the carriage that they could build to make the journey between the two castles. ✍

The continuity and stability of the players' joint creation depends on their abilities to mentally represent and consider the perspectives of others in negotiating their roles and the plot of their play (Ariel, 2002; Curran, 1999; Sluss & Stremmel, 2004). Although young children with cognitive and emotional developmental delays can be observed playing with their peers in integrated classrooms, they may have particular difficulties taking the perspectives of their peers. For example, many have difficulty evaluating how their behavior affects others. Many children with social and emotional special needs are **egocentric**. Such children might fail to greet peers but might become upset if peers failed to greet them. Play-centered curricula provide all children with numerous opportunities to engage in behaviors such as compromising and negotiating that foster the development of social competence and friendships (Anderson & Robinson, 2006; Bergen, 2003; Buchannan & Johnson, 2009; Coplan, Rubin, & Findley, 2006; Dunn, 2003; Kemple, 2004; McCay & Keyes, 2001; Mindes, 2006; Odom, 2002; Panksepp, 2008).

Weighing the Demands of Play   Children who are new to the group or who may be having difficulties in social negotiations with peers may need the comfort and security of a fantasy script that is not too different from what they know. Almost everyone knows the script for playing house or blocks and trucks or riding trikes. The less demanding the symbolic distancing requirements of the play scenarios, the more attention children can devote to social negotiation with peers. This may be a particularly important issue for children with developmental delays who may have difficulties with the distancing demands of the play as well as challenges entering the play setting. It is also a consideration for teachers of children with difficulty in self-regulation, or children who are fearful and anxious and may respond aggressively to such frustrations (Ariel, 2002; Göncü, 1993; Green, 2006; Haight, Black, Ostler, & Sheridan, 2006; Scarlett et al., 2005).

Cultural and Linguistic Contexts for Symbolic Play   Weighing the social and cognitive demands of play situations also has implications for assessing and supporting the development of children from all cultural and linguistic backgrounds as well as those with special needs. Early childhood programs can empower children and families from diverse cultural and linguistic backgrounds (Brown & Conroy, 2011;

Bruder, 2010; Gray, 2011; Guralnick, 2010; Kirmani, 2007). All children need the support of familiar play accessories. Children who are dual language learners and those from all cultural backgrounds benefit from scripts and play accessories that are familiar as well as those that offer opportunities for both repetition and expansion (Burton & Edwards, 2006; Espinosa, 2010; Göncü, Jain, & Tuermer, 2007; Reynolds, 2002). Depending on temperament or family expectations, some children will naturally engage in more solitary play or parallel play as a way of meeting their own needs. When children come from family or cultural contexts in which play in school is not valued or encouraged, it is important that their teachers be sensitive to these concerns (Cooney, 2004; Hughes, 2003; Joshi, 2005; Roopnarine, Shin, Donovan, & Suppal, 2000).

Inventing Strategies   The most complex level of play, games with rules, requires players to reflect on the relationship of all the players within the framework of the rules. For example, a Monopoly player might want to figure out who is playing fairly according to the rules and who is not, or even whom she might make an alliance with to borrow from the bank. These and similar metacognitive demands on the skilled game player require advances in mental development to view both social and symbolic behavior from an objective stance—and then use that information to formulate a strategy (DeVries, 2006; DeVries, Zan, Hildebrandt, Edmiaston, & Sales, 2002; Kamii & Kato, 2006).

This kind of strategy-taking does not often appear until children are 6 or 7 years old. As an example, when 3-year-olds play Duck, Duck, Goose, after the goose is tapped and named, all the children get up and run. They understand the basic rule of the game, but cannot coordinate the perspectives of different players with their own. Four-year-olds understand that only the "goose" and "it" run and that the goose must chase and catch "it." But the players chase each other around the circle and the "goose" inevitably fails to tag "it." At 5 or 6 years of age, children begin to employ a strategy with "the goose," often circling in the opposite direction to tag "it" before "it" can manage to run back to the empty spot.

When children begin to spontaneously invent strategies and discuss and negotiate rules before games begin, games with rules become an appropriate addition to the school curriculum. Game materials and boards may be available, but children should be encouraged to invent and negotiate their own rules. In the primary grades, the playing and inventing of games with rules becomes a major component of play. Children use this newly emerging stage of play development to consolidate their understanding of rules and strategies and as an opportunity to display and elaborate on their new cognitive accomplishments.

Play and the Development of Language and Literacy

Much of the research on children's use of symbols has linked play to language and literacy development. Some researchers have focused on parallels between early language development and the use of symbols in play (Bergen & Mauer, 2000; Christie, 2006; Pellegrini & Galda, 1993; Uttal et al., 1998). Others have studied the ways in

Everyday objects scaffold children's symbolic play.

which children play with the elements of language, such as with sounds or meanings. Children's exploration of sounds, arrangements of words, and meanings of words form the context for children to invent unique forms of language and to master new forms as they are acquired. This play with language and sound also forms the basis for phonemic and **phonological awareness**. Language play is everywhere in classrooms with young children and often occurs in the most mundane of circumstances.

> It's juice time in a preschool setting, and James and Eva begin to giggle as they wait for their turns to pour juice. "You're juicy-goosey," contributes James. "You're juicely-goosely-foosley," chortles Eva, and they both dissolve in laughter. ✆

Yopp (1995) and Wasik (2001) report ways in which play with the sounds of language contributes to the development of phonemic awareness. **Phonemic awareness** includes the ability to recognize and manipulate individual sounds of words. It involves insights about the sounds of oral language and the segmentation of sounds used in speech communication.

The spontaneous play in the juicy-goosey example might be supplemented by teachers of young children with songs that play with sounds of language like "Apples and Bananas" or rhyming in "Down by the Bay"; nursery rhymes such as "One two, buckle my shoe"; and children's books like *The Cat in the Hat, Chicka Chicka Boom Boom,* or *Barnyard Dance.* The key to playing with sounds is to truly focus on listening and speaking the sounds rather than to focus on print.

As illustrated by the following examples, standards for planning curriculum for early literacy include such concepts as narrative and story comprehension as well as the phonemic and phonological awareness needed to decode sounds and symbols. When Tyler makes a road sign while playing with toy cars, he is making letter–sound correspondences. When Isabella sings "Down by the Bay," she recognizes and generates rhymes through songs and stories. When Kylie copies names from cubbies to send a letter in the play post office, she demonstrates growing awareness of beginning, ending, and medial sounds of words.

Literacy in Play: Decoding the Symbols   Research in the field of emergent literacy has looked at how children incorporate literacy play into their make-believe activities. Such play incorporates the social functions of literacy into pretend play scripts and addresses the early literacy academic standards related to concepts of print and early writing (Christie, 2006; Davidson, 2006; Einarsdottir, 2000; Neves & Riefel, 2002; Roskos, 2000; Roskos & Christie, 2000a, 2004; Singer & Lythcott, 2004).

> In one kindergarten classroom, children set up a bank, a store, and a restaurant, all built with blocks. To obtain money from the bank to spend elsewhere, "tellers" in the bank asked their "customers" to pick one of the blank books from the library corner and write their names on it. After counting out paper to represent money, the teller wrote CRTO ("credit to") in the book, and stamped it with a rubber stamp. ✄

In addition to understanding the social functions of print, children's schooling in the written symbols of language and mathematics requires the ability to perform symbolic transformations. For example, the ability to understand that _H_ and _K, bat_ and _14,_ are combinations of lines that represent sounds, words, and numbers is similar to the capacity to use a block to represent a truck or a telephone.

Children who become skilled at symbolic transformations in their play are also preparing conceptually to understand some of the subtleties of culturally shared symbolic systems used in written language—aspects that adults take for granted but that children find confusing (Dickinson & Tabors, 2002; Mayer, 2007; Opitz, 2000; Weitzman & Greenberg, 2002). For example, children are frequently bewildered by the arbitrary meaning assigned to symbols that look the same. The letter _C_ is sometimes pronounced as a _K_, such as in the word _cake_, sometimes as an _S_ as in _city_, and sometimes as a new sound, _CH_ as in _chicken_. This inconsistency among assigned meanings for symbols that do not change in appearance can be very confusing to children who have not developed the concept of _multiple transformations_ in their pretend play. For example, the idea that a rectangular block can be a car, a person, or a sandwich, depending on the child's imagination, prepares children to understand these differences when they begin to operate with our system of written signs and symbols. In both symbolic play and phonetic decoding, the concept that one object (that continues to look the same) may be transformed by the mind into several different meanings is essential.

A related concept is the idea that several objects that look different may be symbolically transformed to carry the same meaning. In play, for example, you might see Jennie use a block, a Lego, or a toy car to represent a walkie-talkie on a spaceship. These choices depend in part on what is available and also on the child's ability to abstract relevant features of objects to use them as symbols for alternative meanings. This concept is called on when children learn to identify symbols of written language, for example, in understanding that *A* and *a* both represent the same sound in our alphabet.

These competencies are closely related to academic standards for print and early writing. Here are some examples: When Kira says, "K starts my name," as she surveys the labeled photos at the sign-in table, she understands that letters make up words and distinguishes between print and pictures. When Michael pretends to read to the teddy bear in the book area, turning pages and orienting the book with pictures on top and text below, he handles books appropriately and respectfully. When Alysha uses a note pad and pencil to take Riordan's order in the classroom restaurant, she uses symbols and forms of early writing to create more complex play. When Emily makes a sign to lean against her completed block tower, "Du not dstrub!" she uses letters and/or phonetically spelled words and basic punctuation.

The Development of Narrative   The capacity to enter the "as if" or hypothetical world in which animals talk, such as that created by E. B. White in *Charlotte's Web*, or the ability to create such a frame oneself in telling or writing a story, rests on understandings constructed in dramatic play (Kalmart, 2008; McVicker, 2007; Riojas-Cortez, 2001). The ability to negotiate multiple roles and hypothetical situations in housekeeping play or to dictate and enact an episode of a superhero's adventure calls on the same capacities in young children's symbolic thought as those needed to write a poem or a narrative of one's own.

Taking on the roles of different characters and sequencing events to tell a story form the foundation for the important aspect of literacy learning called *narrative*. Reading comprehension, particularly with characters, motives, and plots, also rests on alternative perspectives and sequencing events to create and interpret meaning (Bruner, 1986; Fein, Ardeila-Ray, & Groth, 2000; Fromberg, 2002; Gallas, 2003; Nel, 2000; Nicolopolou, 2007; Roskos & Christie, 2000a). This ability to demonstrate a concept of story also appears in early education standards for literacy development.

These and other aspects of play and literacy relate to academic standards in a variety of ways. For example, when Ethan says, "Let's read the frog book first, it's my favorite," he chooses to read books for enjoyment. At circle time, Noah dramatizes the Scarecrow's walk from the *Wizard of Oz* seen the week before. In doing so, he retells, reenacts, or dramatizes stories. When Emma, while listening to *Charlotte's Web* at story time, predicts that Charlotte will go to the fair with Wilbur, she reads or listens to a story and predicts what will happen next.

Play and Logical–Mathematical Thinking

Another relationship between play and development is the construction of logical–mathematical knowledge. One expression of this is seen in children's construction of **cause-and-effect relationships** through physical activities. Block building, bike riding, and sand and water play all foster the construction of spatial relationships and an understanding of gravity and other concepts of physics. These real-life experiences are essential to children's future understanding and abilities to solve problems, and they form the foundation for learning science concepts as children develop (Bodrova & Leong, 2007; Chalufour & Worth, 2004, 2006; DeVries et al., 2002; Forman, 2005; Hamlin & Wisneski, 2012; Kamii & DeVries, 1993; Kamii, Miyakawa, & Kato, 2004; Seo, 2003).

Play activities easily relate to early science academic standards. When Jeffrey finds an equivalent block for a racing track construction, he is engaging in play as a means to develop questioning and problem solving. When Megan weighs her baby doll at the pretend hospital, she is beginning to use scientific tools and methods to learn about the world. When Matthew and Renee mix playdough to make their farm animals just the right color, they are learning that properties of substances can change when mixed, cooled, or heated. When Adrian uses straw and clay to make adobe bricks, he is learning that earth is made of materials that have distinct properties and provide resources for human activities.

In the development of logical–mathematical thinking, children construct their own schemes or mental patterns for organizing and interpreting meaning in the environment. In doing so, they develop the ability to classify and put objects and ideas into relationships with each other (e.g., ordering objects from least to most). Play provides children with a wide array of opportunities to construct concepts at their own pace.

> For the past two weeks Marie has been playing almost daily with a set of thick crayons, eight colors. Today there is something new. She chooses a large box of thin crayons, a total of 40 colors. She picks out all the crayons that have a red color and arranges them separately from crayons of orange and pink shades. As she colors a piece of scrap wood with multiple shades of red, she comments, "This is for my mom." Lily sits down next to her. Marie turns, offering a crayon. "There's more reds over here." ✍

In this example, Marie is coordinating relationships of "more than" and "less than" and "similar" and "different." The coordination of these relationships is the beginning of logical reasoning. Intellectual development leads to more mature play in preschoolers.

Dramatic play can also contribute to the development of classification and relational concepts in another way. In the following example, David identifies similar characteristics of familiar objects as he decides what to use as a prop. Before choosing the cookbook, presumably because of its qualities of opening and enclosing that are compatible with his idea of a hot dog, he scans the area, rejecting the pencil and a tennis ball in favor of the book. He later uses the pencil to represent the mustard bottle. This selective attention to similar characteristics of objects is another concept essential to the development of classification abilities.

> Six-year-old David is fixing dinner for his "son" Peter. Peter says, "But I want a hot dog for dinner!" "OK. I can make good hot dogs," notes David as he scans the playhouse area for a prop that exemplifies "hot dog-ness" for

him. He selects a paperback cookbook from the shelf, opens it, and "stuffs" it with a plastic marker. "Do you want mustard?" he asks. Peter nods emphatically and David shakes a pencil over the "hot dog," pretending that it is a bottle of mustard. ✆

Another relationship between play and logical–mathematical thinking rests on the symbolic transformations inherent in role-play. The child who transforms himself or herself into a veterinarian, a puppy, or an astronaut, and each time returns to the mental concept of self, is beginning to show evidence of **reversibility**, a feature of thinking that accompanies the development of logical thought in middle childhood and is important in competencies such as basic addition and subtraction. Some researchers have hypothesized that mental transformations in pretend play form the foundation for the Piagetian notion of conservation (Golomb, Gowing, & Friedman, 1982). Conservation involves the understanding that quantity does not decrease or increase with a change in its position or form, just as role-play involves understanding that the identity of a person remains the same when a role is taken (Forman & Kaden, 1987).

> Four-year-old Cassie asks as the family leaves a performance of *Seussical,* "Those people don't really look like that, do they? I mean they had to be real people in costumes?" Her parents went over the program with her and noted the names of the actors who had played particular roles. The next week, Cassie dressed her stuffed animals and dolls in feathers and bits of cloth and yarn, creating "weird animal" costumes, and confirming her concepts of how identities change. ✆

All aspects of logical–mathematical thinking show up in children's play. Everyday examples of ordering, classifying, quantifying/measuring, and comparing can be seen throughout children's play and can be related to early math and science academic standards. For example, when Naomi counts aloud to time the baking of pretend cookies in the oven, she is counting by rote memorization. When Elliot asks for more red paint at the easel, he is appropriately using comparative words. When Quinn counts out six coins to pay for ice cream at the pretend restaurant, he understands numbers and simple operations and uses coins in daily activities. When Tyson lines up the toy dinosaurs from smallest to largest, he is seriating and ordering.

Play and Problem Solving

The flexibility in thinking that allows one to solve a problem from a fresh perspective or use a tool in a unique way is part of critical thinking. Play contributes by allowing children to play through their ideas in the same way that adults talk through alternatives to problems they face and imagine consequences from varying perspectives. This process also leads to the discovery of new problems or new questions to be asked as children play and think more deeply about their experience (Chalufour & Worth, 2006; Holmes & Geiger, 2002; Levin, 2013; Segatti, Brown-DuPaul, & Keyes, 2003; Wolfe, Cummins, & Myers, 2006).

This playing through of alternatives may be nonverbal, as in the first example below, or it may include verbal communication, as in the second example of negotiating with peers.

> Second-graders Chrissie and Jake are making a sand mountain with a road around it designed for a ball to roll down. The moist sand is beginning to dry in the hot sun, and pieces of the road are crumbling. They first try a "patching" job with more sand, but it is too dry to stick. When that doesn't work, they dig under the dry sand to find more of the damp sand they originally used. ∅

Research on children who are popular with peers indicates that children who are flexible in their thinking frequently come up with unique alternatives for resolving disputes and suggesting compromise (Howes, 1992).

> Four-year-old Erica and 3-year-old Melissa are playing with a hospital bed, medical props, and two dolls. They agree to have their "patients" share the toy bed, but there is only one pillow. Erica takes a blanket and folds it several times, placing it under the head of her doll. "Now we both have pillows," she concludes, and the play continues, uninterrupted by disputes. ∅

Researchers who have studied children's play speculate that the conflicts and subsequent negotiations that occur as children shift from actors "in play" to directors "out of" play force children to consider the perspectives of their playmates. In play, children enact roles and move the story line forward with action and dialogue. Out of play, children step out of make-believe roles to negotiate new roles, behavior appropriate to roles, and ideas for the plot of their play. If one wants play to continue, then compromises must be made (Fromberg, 2002; Göncü, 1993; Reifel, Hoke, Pape, & Wisneski, 2004; Reifel & Yeatman, 1993; Sheldon, 1992).

All of the standards for early education that we reviewed include the ability to negotiate and resolve social problems, empathize with others, and try hard to be successful. These competencies and dispositions occur in everyday play. For example, Garrett and Lilly play space ship and negotiate the roles of pilot and copilot, thereby negotiating with peers to resolve social conflicts and cooperation in play. Mischa falls and hurts her knee. While the teacher is coming from across the yard, Jack hugs her and says, "You'll be OK!" thereby expressing empathy or caring for others. Shawn and Heather set up paint cups for Josa and tilt her easel so she can reach it from her wheelchair, thereby demonstrating respect for differences in interaction with others from diverse backgrounds and with different abilities. For 3 days in a row, Emily returns to the road project, adding new signs and persisting at building a bridge with buttresses, thereby "demonstrating persistence in play and projects."

Play and Children with Special Needs

Play-centered curricula can be beneficial for children who are often unable to resolve problems when they arise. This includes many children with social and emotional disabilities and children with developmental delays (Bergen, 2003; Buchannan & Johnson, 2009; Koplow, 1996; Odom, 2002; Wolfberg, 1999; O'Neill, 2013). Flexibility is an important dimension of problem solving (Holmes & Geiger, 2002). Because of the links between flexibility, language, and cognition, certain children with special needs lack this flexibility and react to the environment in a rigid manner. Extended opportunities to interact with peers in play can support the development of problem-solving skills.

> In a second-grade integrated classroom, Joe and Harold are playing with small racecars. Joe has a learning disability, which includes challenges with visual processing and visual discrimination. As Joe pushes his car on the carpet, he says, "I want my car to go faster." Harold looks around the classroom, spots a table and says, "We can use a table 'cause it's smooth." Joe then looks around the room and exclaims, "Let's go over there," and points to an area of the classroom that is covered in shiny tile. The children take their cars to the slick surface of the tile floor and begin racing them. ✇

Although some of the research and writing in the field of special education suggests that children with special needs are unable to solve problems, this example of Joe's success in problem solving in collaboration with Harold demonstrates that it is important to observe each child's abilities in different contexts.

A related issue is the role of the teacher. Genishi and DiPaolo (1982) and Pellegrini (1984) suggest that the teacher's presence during peer play negotiations may inhibit children from solving their interpersonal problems on their own. On the other hand, researchers such as Smilansky (1968, 1990) discuss the ways that the teacher's presence may support children's ability to work out solutions to disagreements during play. Teachers may find the issues of roles and timing especially challenging when working with children who have cognitive, social, or emotional delays or who are overly aggressive when others do not play according to their wishes.

In these and all interventions in play, the teacher's sensitivity and support for children's capabilities and patience for their intended meanings is paramount (Bergen, 2003; Brown & Marchant, 2002; Clark, 2007; Fromberg, 2002; Mindes, 2006; Wolfberg, 1999; Fiorelli & Russ, 2012; Leong & Bodrova, 2012; Spivak & Howes, 2011).

The idea that play promotes children's development is a major feature of Vygotsky's notion of the zone of proximal development (Vygotsky, 1967, 1978). He set forth the idea that children function above their normal level of ability when challenged by peers in their play. Children's desire to maintain social interaction and to encounter and coordinate perspectives other than their own contributes to the developmental stretch evident in play. Researchers studying children's play in mixed-age groups or classrooms with mainstreamed children report that younger or less sophisticated players play at higher levels of complexity when playing with older or more expert peers (Connery, John-Stgeiner, & Marjanovic-Shane, 2010; Katz, Evangelou, & Hartman, 1990). Children who are imaginative in their symbolic play transformations and flexible in their negotiations with peers are building concepts essential to critical-thinking expertise and social problem solving.

PLAY, IMAGINATION, AND CREATIVITY

Imagination and creativity are qualities that are sometimes taken for granted when reviewing the value of play in development. Much has been written concerning the curriculum appropriate for the 21st century (Almy, 2000; Galinsky, 2010). Bruner (1976) perhaps stated this dilemma best by asking, "How can a system that prepares the immature for entry into the society deal with a future that is increasingly difficult to predict within a single lifetime?"

One possibility is to foster adaptive, flexible, and creative thinking. These qualities are essential because "whenever the environment is changing, it selects for playful individuals" (Ellis, 1988, p. 24). Concerns about the effects of didactic teaching and skills-based curricula have led to research and writing urging educators to more carefully consider the need to foster imaginative and flexible minds and to provide rich and varied opportunities in the visual and performing arts (Brown, 2009; Elkind, 2003, 2007; Gallas, 2003; Holmes & Geiger, 2002; Isenberg & Jalongo, 2001; McGhee, 2005; Power, 2011; Prairie, 2013; Robson, 2010; Singer & Lythcott, 2004; Singer & Singer, 1990, 2006; VanderVen, 2006).

Standards for the arts are met in numerous ways in everyday play, as these examples show. When Robin appropriates scarves from the dress up box and creates a dance on the stage built in the block area, she is developing self-expression through

Solitary play fosters concentration and imagination.

visual arts, dance, music, and drama. When Patty becomes the wicked queen, snarling and lowering her voice to threaten the sad princess, she is showing an appreciation, interest, and knowledge of the arts. Likewise, when Leslie says, "I'll use collage like Steve does" as she cuts parts for a tree and flowers, she is also developing an appreciation, interest, and knowledge of the arts.

Singer and Singer have written extensively about the contribution of play to the imaginative thinking of children (see Singer, 2006; Singer & Singer, 1990, 2005, 2006). In the Singers' view, make-believe play is essential to the development of the capacity for internal imagery. It contributes to the development of creativity by opening children to experiences involving curiosity and the exploration of alternative situations and combinations. In addition, their research emphasizes the psychosocial benefits of imaginative play: Children who engage in lots of make-believe play are likely to be happier and more flexible when they encounter new situations.

Three Aspects of Imagination and Fantasy

Egan (1988) further developed Vygotsky's claim that play leads development in early childhood. He claimed that fantasy and imagination are the appropriate content of early childhood curriculum because they highlight for teachers the passionate concerns of young children. Egan's work emphasized three major aspects of imagination and fantasy in early childhood: (a) the oral nature of the peer culture in the early years, (b) the importance of binary opposites in creating dramatic tension in play themes, and (c) the sense of wonder, magic, and joy inherent in pretend play.

The Oral Culture of Early Childhood   Egan (1988) found the seeds of the ability to create a story in the orally expressed fantasy of early childhood. As each aspect of a story told in the fantasy play unfolds, its meaning is clarified and extended in relation to other aspects of the play. In solitary dramatic play, fantasy stories are told to the self, and in sociodramatic play the play's meanings are communicated and negotiated within the peer culture of the classroom (Ariel, 2002; Dyson, 1997, 2003; Fromberg, 2002; Katch, 2001; McEwan & Egan, 1995; Nicolopoulou, Scales, & Weintraub, 1994; Paley, 1981, 1994, 1995; Perry, 2001).

The accompanying ability to extend knowledge of characters, situations, and events from the everyday into the realm of the improbable or impossible is a primary form of logic that encompasses ambiguity and paradox and merges thought and feelings. This ability to make meaning through narrative forms is one of the first examples of the ordering and classification of human experience (Bruner, 1986, 1990). This early use of contradictory forms of logic in play is what Egan (1988) calls "mythic thinking," and it is seen in both the fantastic series of events that children may imagine in play and in role-play. For example, when 4-year-old Erin pretends that she is an undersea monster, she knows that she simultaneously is and is not the role that she plays. This early embrace of paradox lays the foundation for noncontradictory forms of logic that emerge in middle childhood. Egan believes that one must create and entertain a variety of possibilities before narrowing them down through logical thought. Young children's grasp of reality begins by stretching the borders of the known world into new dimensions and possibilities in play (Nourot, 2005).

Bipolar Opposites in Play   Children's play is often structured around binary opposition themes such as love/hate, danger/rescue, the permissible/the forbidden, big/little, good guy/bad guy, death/rebirth, and lost/found (Bettelheim, 1989; Corsaro, 1985; Egan, 1988; Garvey, 1977/1990; Katch, 2001; Paley, 1988). These oppositional tensions help children discriminate features of their physical and social worlds and to define themselves within those worlds. The unity of thought and emotion animates their abilities to make sense of life through the stories told in dramatic play. The following vignette shows how children move flexibly between sense and nonsense, the physically possible and impossible, the mundane and the exotic, the safe and the threatening, and, for some, the permissible and the forbidden.

> Dolly and Ruth are pretending to be witches and pretend they are taking blood from their playmates by touching their arms with a spoon, and then running back to the pot on the stove in the housekeeping area to add the imaginary blood of each victim, cackling as they stir the brew. Quincy is a witch, too, wearing a sparkling cape and carrying a cup with a plastic lemon in it. "This drink has poison and fingernails in it," he announces.
>
> Later Quincy holds up his cup. "But if you drink this magic potion, you can come alive again," and he offers some to John, who has just joined the play. "Can I play?" John asks. "Yes," agrees Dolly, "but you have to be a witch, like us." John pretends to take blood from Ruth, imitating the high cackling laugh he has heard Dolly use. Then Quincy offers his cup to Ruth, "This will turn you from a witch into a princess." She pretends to drink the princess-making potion, and then the other witches try to turn her back into a witch. "No, no, drink this one." The tension between the bad witches and the good witch Quincy with his magic potion continues a few more minutes until cleanup time is called. ✆

The framing of ideas for character, plot, and setting through bipolar oppositions, such as the good witch/bad witch/princess and the death/rebirth examples in the preceding vignette, also define these emerging aspects of story, even as it clarifies children's sense of themselves. Children want passionately for play to continue despite the potential pitfalls of differing ideas about characters or events in the play. The shared understanding that comes from framing play themes and characters in binary themes such as good guy/bad guy or danger/rescue supports the shared understanding and the subsequent negotiation that allows play to flourish (Nourot, 1997, 2006).

Wonder, Magic, and Joy   Although the development of logical thinking and the ability to negotiate meanings with others are important aspects of imaginative play in early childhood, the essence of play is captured in the magical and ecstatic experiences that define creative processes throughout life (Ariel, 2002; Brown, 2009;

Csikszentmihayli, 1993; Nachmanovitch, 1990). The joy and wonder encompassed in imaginative play are powerful links to others and an incentive to develop self-regulation. In addition, the desire for this sense of wonder and joy creates a powerful incentive for children to move beyond their own viewpoints to encompass the perspectives of others. In doing so, children experience the power of both friendship and fantasy in their play (Jones & Cooper, 2006; Jones & Reynolds, 2011; Reynolds & Jones, 1997).

PLAY AND SOCIAL–MORAL DEVELOPMENT

Every day in preschools, child-care centers, kindergartens, and primary-grade classrooms, differences in the nature of social interaction and the complexity of fantasy, constructive play, and games with rules are observed. These differences reflect aspects of children's cultural, familial, and individual styles as well as moral and social development. Teachers are better equipped to support play when they understand its developmental sequences and range of behaviors, as well as the social context of the children's families and culture as observed in the play (Bowman & Moore, 2006; Gaskins, Haight, & Lancy, 2007).

> In one kindergarten classroom, Jon and Rio were happily engaged in building a "ranch" out of blocks. Their intimacy was evident as they giggled and whispered to one another about their plans for the fantasy. "And then pretend the bad guys can get in here," one boy said to the other. Paul watched from the sidelines and finally began to build his own structure next to Rio and Jon. "But what about me?" Paul said plaintively, as the ranch builders began to expand their construction site. "I know," said Rio, "we'll make a line right here and you can build, too. We won't cross the line." ✐

In this example, we see Paul learning to assert his rights, and Jon and Rio learning to understand and accommodate the perspective of a third player, without giving up their investment in keeping their ranch to themselves.

DeVries and Zan (1994) and Kamii (1982, 1990) draw on Piaget's theories of moral development (Piaget, 1965c) when they discuss **autonomy** and **heteronomy** in classrooms for young children. Moral autonomy is characterized by being governed by oneself; moral heteronomy means being governed by others. Children who develop moral autonomy come to see moral values as internal guides, independent of whether they may be "caught" doing something inappropriate by a parent or a teacher. In a classroom that promotes moral autonomy, children construct beliefs about what is fair and unfair based on their experiences with their peers. Through social–moral dilemmas that involve **reciprocal interactions** with their playmates, children learn to make informed choices about their behavior and practice factoring in the perspectives of others (DeVries & Zan, 2005). In the preceding example, Jon and Rio were able to factor in Paul's desire to play with them and still preserve their own interactive play space. They compromised, treating one another with respect and consideration.

Parten's Research on Play and Social Participation

Parten (1932) studied the social behavior of children in a parent-cooperative preschool. Based on her observations, she hypothesized a continuum of social participation in play, ranging from onlooker behavior to solitary, parallel, and two forms of group play.

Onlooker Behavior   **Onlooker behavior** is when a child watches as others play, either because of reluctance to join or as a way of scanning for an opening. Less-sophisticated players may hang around the edge of a play scene to learn by observing and imitating others—at times they may be unsure how to enter a play episode. More sophisticated players use onlooker behavior to help them make choices, to decide which activity to select, or to ascertain the most effective strategy for gaining entrance into an already-established play episode. Sometimes onlookers are simply interested in the play or behavior of others. Sensitive teachers are aware of these possible functions of onlooking and use observation and intervention skillfully to determine what role, if any, they might take to help children make choices about their play activities. Onlooker behavior is not simply immature behavior, but in fact represents time for children to contemplate their actions.

Solitary Play   **Solitary play** is defined as playing alone, without overt interaction with peers.

> Four-year-old Amani carefully paints a heart shape at the easel and fills it in with bright pink. She stops to contemplate her painting briefly, then adds arms and legs. "There!" she says softly. "It's a heart person!" 🖉

Parten found solitary play to be typical of the youngest children in her group, but more recent research has shown solitary play performs several functions depending on the age of the child and the context of play. For example, solitary play may provide the context for complex dramatic play, such as enacting a family drama with toy dinosaurs, or it may provide an occasion for needed respite from the demands of negotiating with others, such as solitary play with pegboards. Sensitive teachers are aware that children need opportunities for privacy and solitary play as well as opportunities for sharing and group play in the classroom. For some children who have been traumatized by violence and loss, the need to play alone is paramount (Scarlett et al., 2005).

Parallel Play   **Parallel play** is defined as play with shared materials or physical proximity without attempts to coordinate play. Nonverbal negotiation of materials may occur, but joint play themes or constructions are not elaborated. For example, Juliann and Helen are playing parallel to one another with small wooden blocks and a large dollhouse. They each carry on quiet dialogues animating their characters. As one child puts down a block or a piece of dollhouse furniture, the other may pick it up, but they do not overtly acknowledge each other's play. This type of play is thought to represent the earliest, undifferentiated form of **group play**, and teachers may often see it as a prelude to full-blown group play as children test the waters with their peers and gradually begin cooperative efforts.

Group Play Parten differentiated two forms of group play. The first, associative play, is seen when children share and coordinate materials and space in proximity to one another but lack true cooperation. It is similar to parallel play in its form but includes some of the elements of group cooperative play as well. For example, Frank and Sandra are playing with Lego blocks at a small table. They negotiate with one another over the number of wheels they may each use out of the basket of parts, but they each continue to work on their own projects rather than focus on a joint project.

The second form of group play, cooperative play, involves sophisticated efforts to negotiate joint play themes and constructions with peers and is characterized by children stepping into and out of their play to establish roles or events. For example, three children playing restaurant may alternate their roles in the play as customer, cook, and waiter/waitress with comments about the plot made from outside the play, such as "Pretend the hamburger got burned."

PLAY AND EMOTIONAL DEVELOPMENT

The sense of connection and joy that children experience in play is closely related to emotional development (Thompson, 2013). Children's **emotional development** refers to their capacity to feel or experience a wide range of emotions, such as happiness, sadness, anger, jealousy, excitement, wonder, and fear. Emotional development also involves children's capacity to manage or regulate their emotions and their expression. Piaget, Vygotsky, and Erikson wrote about the importance of play in emotional development.

Dramatic play themes that portray children as orphaned or separated from their parents, having to fend for themselves in the woods or at sea, are common in preschool and kindergarten. Other common themes involve life and death. At times, conflicts between child initiative and adult prohibitions are expressed in the classroom through fantasy play, such as the "naughty baby."

Erikson's (1950/1985, 1977) research and writing shows that, through their sociodramatic and pretend block constructions, children respond emotionally to the major life themes that their new cognitive capabilities present. Themes such as death and life, love and hate, care and jealousy occur frequently in the play of young children. Erikson wrote, "The play age . . . offers the child a micro-reality in which he can use toys (put at his disposal by those who sanction his play) in order to relive, correct, and re-create past experiences . . ." (Erikson, 1977, p. 99).

In their play, children reassure or frighten themselves, often at the same time. Erikson also reminds us that children further develop their sense of purpose in play. In dramatic play, children enter into fantasies that allow them to explore their concepts of initiative and independence.

Bebbie, Betty, and Helen are playing in the sand area. They have constructed a volcano and invented a danger and rescue plot for their characters. Bebbie and Betty laugh with delight as the water cascades over their wet sand volcano. They use their voices to protest when Helen begins to stomp on the sand. Later in the play, the three children express conflicts between archetypes of good and evil in their superhero rescue roles. ✆

Piaget (1962) also wrote about play as a cornerstone of emotional development. Like Erikson, he described the **liquidating function** of play that allows children to neutralize powerful emotions and release them by reliving them through make believe. He also described the **compensatory function** of fantasy play that helps children rewrite events in which their feelings of helplessness or fear are overwhelming. Similarly, Vygotsky (1976, 1978) discussed play as the primary matrix for children to develop **self-regulation** of their behavior and emotions in early childhood.

Contemporary theorists and writers emphasize the importance of emotional development. Entry into school presents additional challenges to emotional development centered on the home and family. With school comes the advent of social comparisons and the need to come to terms with challenges such as insecurity, envy, humiliation, pride, and confidence. Learning to interact with others in a responsible manner, to wait for one's turn, and to regulate one's own emotions presents major milestones in the development of emotional competence. Gardner (1993) wrote that "interpersonal and intrapersonal intelligence" is characterized by the ability to accurately read and respond to the feelings, motivations, and desires of others and access one's own feelings and use them to guide behavior. Similarly, Goleman (1995) explained that emotional intelligence is characterized by empathy and self-regulation, a construct that he and Lantieri have developed for educators and families in their book *Building Emotional Intelligence: Techniques to Cultivate Inner Strength in Children* (2008). Indeed, a growing trend in the early childhood research and literature is the emphasis on the importance of young children's play in emotional development (Bodrova & Leong, 2007; Bowman & Moore, 2006; English & Stengel, 2010; Honig, 2007; Hyson, 2004; Jones & Cooper, 2006; Landreth, Homeyer, & Morrison, 2006; Nissen & Hawkins, 2010; Soundy & Stout, 2002).

Play and the Harsh Realities of Some Children's Lives

The degree to which contemporary play invites realities that are both incomprehensible and frightening to children remains a thorny issue for both teachers of young children and researchers of play (Ariel, 2002; Farish, 2001; Katch, 2001; Lancy, 2002; Levin, 2003b, 2013; Waniganayake, 2001). Much of the play that teachers see as risky or full of violence and aggression may stem from children's need to repeat and revise frightening or confusing experiences through imagination in much the same way that adults talk through emotional distresses (see Clark, 2007; Haight et al., 2006; Katch, 2001).

Jason's teacher, in the Diversity box below, understands that "righting" the imbalance in a world in which community violence is common and the evening news shows vivid and repetitive images of catastrophe and violence is an important aspect of play in schools. These children are all playing through a disturbing event in their community, and their active collaboration with Jason contributes to his healing.

Children also try to make sense of frightening images and scripts from the national media. For example, in the aftermath of September 11, 2001, teachers from across the nation reported children repeatedly crashing toy planes into buildings in their play and expressing confusion about the continual replay of the images on television.

FAMILY DIVERSITY
A Child Copes with the Death of an Aunt

Six-year-old Jason organizes his classmates to pick dandelions from the school lawn at recess time. They create bouquets and stash them in their cubbies when they return to their first-grade classroom. At their play and project time later in the day, the children construct a pretend casket from blocks complete with handles for pallbearers and enact a pretend funeral with Jason coaching them on the prayers and songs. Other children join, and the bouquets of dandelions are shared and thrown on the "casket" as it is lowered into the grave site marked by tape on the classroom rug. Jason's 19-year-old aunt was killed in a drive-by shooting the previous Saturday.

Children often play out frightening themes and challenge school-based rules regarding weapon play, violence, or use of language in efforts to create meaning for themselves. These emotional roots of play and the possibilities for healing they present must be carefully interpreted by teachers (Katch, 2001; Koplow, 1996; Levin, 2013; Levin & Carlsson-Paige, 2006).

But sometimes stress levels are too high for children to use play to cope with their emotions. It is important that teachers seek professional resources when children's play takes forms that are disruptive or upsetting to the other children or to the teachers themselves. School counselors and psychologists have long explored the ways in which children struggle to make sense of frightening or confusing events (Axline, 1969; Erikson, 1950/1985, 1977; Landreth, Homeyer, & Morrison, 2006; Winnicott, 1971). Erikson wrote about "play disruption" in children as they reached levels of stress and anxiety that were high enough to curtail play. Children who have been severely traumatized may not be able to use play to represent and work through stress and conflict in more typical ways. These children may require sensitive and careful orchestration from specialists as well as teachers in school and in therapeutic settings (Koplow, 1996; Scarlett et al., 2005).

SUMMARY

Play has a critical role in all facets of children's development. In this chapter we examined the research and literature on the many ways play influences development and learning, and how play provides experiences that relate to academic standards.

- **Play and intellectual development.** Ample research shows that play is critical to children's development of symbolic thought, language and literacy, logical–mathematical thinking, and problem solving.

- **Play, imagination, and creativity.** There is much evidence that play promotes imagination and creativity and that this is an important and sometimes overlooked component of the curriculum.
- **Play and social–moral development.** Children go through a number of stages in their moral development and in their ability to coordinate social actions with others. Play is an important context for this development.
- **Play and emotional development.** The emotional development of children is a vitally important consideration in early childhood education. There is a vast amount of research and theoretical literature on the importance of play in emotional development.

APPLYING YOUR KNOWLEDGE

1. Discuss how children develop symbolic thought, language, and literacy skills; logical–mathematical thinking; and problem-solving ability through play.
   a. Give examples of symbolic play with objects and symbolic role-playing.
   b. Give your own understanding of what is means to take the perspective of others. Why is this skill important, and how is its development related to play?
   c. Describe how literacy and development of narrative may be enhanced in children's play.
   d. Discuss how play contributes to the development of logical–mathematical thinking. Give examples.
   e. In your own words, how do you define problem solving, and how is this ability fostered in play?
2. List three aspects of imagination and fantasy and describe how they are related to children's play.
3. Explain how social–moral development relates to issues of autonomy and heteronomy.
   a. Give examples of onlooker behavior, solitary play, parallel play, and group play.
4. Discuss how Piaget, Erikson, and Vygotsky viewed the role of play in emotional development.
   a. Give an example of how a child might use play to deal with an emotional problem.

CHAPTER 4

Orchestrating Children's Play: Setting the Stage

LEARNING OUTCOMES

■ Describe four principles that guide how teachers can support play.

■ Identify four indirect strategies drawn from the continuum of play orchestration strategies that teachers can use to support play.

■ Explain how careful planning of a program's setting, routines, and daily schedule can optimize and balance both playtime and play choices for children.

■ Contrast two extensions for play in the curriculum and explain how they differ.

In Ann's K–1 combination classroom, the environment invites play. The housekeeping area includes kitchen furniture and accessories, a small couch, and a rocking chair. A girl doll with Asian features and two boy dolls, one with African American and one with Caucasian features, rest in two small beds near the rocker. The children have made a DVD and a television screen from different-size cardboard boxes. Hats and costumes are stored on shelves and hooks, and doll clothes in drawers. An accessory box with props for hospital play sits open on a shelf adjacent to the house, along with the ever-useful blank clipboards with paper and pencils attached. Ann considers these staples of her play environment. She explains that a local pediatrician had visited the class the day before and introduced terms and medical tools that she hoped would be recast in today's play.

Outdoors, the three-level climbing structure invites children to create their own degree of challenge. Soft rubber matting provides a cushion below, and ramps lead to the slide. There is ample space for Angie, who uses a wheelchair, to get out of her chair and maneuver onto the slide. Pathways around the structure are constructed so that the wheelchair can be easily moved for entering and exiting the play structure. There is a small wheelchair accessible garden area, with benches and a table for potting plants. Drawing and painting supplies are stored in a small cart, as many children like to draw and paint representations of the plants and rabbits housed in the outdoor yard. ✍

For a play curriculum to be effective, the teacher must orchestrate the dynamic flow of its elements by matching play to the child's developmental level and by providing opportunities for stretch and growth to occur for each child and for the group as a whole. Skilled teachers employ myriad strategies for "upping the ante" to encourage developmental stretch, as they foster children's feelings of trust and safety within play contexts (Barnes & Lehr, 2005; Bowman, 2005; Clawson, 2002; Derman-Sparks & Ramsey, 2005; Joshi, 2005; Piaget, 1977; Singer, Golinkoff, & Hirsh-Pasek, 2006; Singer & Singer, 2005; Swick, 2002).

A major step in setting the stage for play is to link expectations based on knowledge and understanding of development and learning with practical strategies for supporting play in settings for young children. These strategies can be explained by an approach to teaching where teacher's view children's behavior within the context in which it occurs, noticing the history of the children's past play themes and social hierarchy of the group. They are alert to a change in the dynamics of the play of the group when some factor changes, such as the entry of a newcomer, a child with special needs, or a child who is a **dual language learner**. Teachers draw on their knowledge of multiple theories of development and learning to interpret what they observe (Corsaro, 2011; Henderson & Jones, 2002; Hughes, 2003; Paley, 1999; Reynolds, 2002).

A play-centered curriculum is not made of fixed components but finds its direction in the themes and concepts children generate in their play.

PRINCIPLES GUIDING PLAY ORCHESTRATION

Four general principles guide our thinking about the ways teachers may support play across contexts that involve spontaneous play and contexts that involve guided or directed play:

1. Taking the child's view
2. Being a keen observer
3. Seeing meaning as it is constructed
4. Being a stage manager

In the examples that follow, we describe how these principles are applied for different ages of young children and in classrooms that include children with special needs and children from a variety of cultural, socioeconomic, and linguistic backgrounds.

Taking the Child's View

The first principle involves the teacher taking the child's view of experiences and materials in the classroom. Developmentally appropriate practice (DAP), a term coined by the National Association for the Education of Young Children (NAEYC), involves understanding age-appropriate development in young children (Bredekamp, 2004; Copple & Bredekamp, 2009; Sylva, Siraj-Blatchford, & Taggert, 2010). It also involves understanding the individual development of each child and the cultural context in which development occurs.

What does Raul bring to school from his home that is unique and different from the concepts and attitudes brought by Miko or Frances? How does the impending divorce of Jo Ann's parents affect her development and behavior? What special accommodations does Brian, who has spina bifida, need to have access to the slide or have an opportunity to swing? In taking the child's viewpoint, teachers work with aspects of developmentally appropriate practice: understanding both the normal development of a particular age group and the life experiences in and out of school

Teachers can create bridges from teacher-planned activities to spontaneous play.

that shape meaning for each child. For example, what does Emil's preoccupation with gunplay and soldiers mean in light of his family's recent immigration to the United States from a war-torn country? Will the addition of a private, small space outdoors, along with a few of the miniature ponies, encourage Fran and Celine to interact rather than merely watch others play?

Teacher as Keen Observer

The second principle of orchestrating play in the curriculum involves the teacher being a keen observer of children's behavior. His or her observation skills are supported by planning specific times to circulate through the classroom, to jot anecdotal notes on peel-off labels, or to sit and observe for a longer period in a specific area of the indoor or outdoor classroom. The teacher also uses observational strategies when working with a small group of children on a focused activity and takes time to write down children's observations, questions, experiments, and hypotheses as they work and play.

Seeing Meaning as It Is Constructed

Based on this third principle, the sensitive teacher recognizes that children construct meaning or their own understanding through many aspects of their experience. Sometimes meaning emerges as playmates suggest a new block to support a building or offer a costume for a role. Sometimes meaning emerges as the teacher and child sit together to figure out the spelling of a new word. Knowledge that is derived from children's interactions with adults and other children and is relevant to the context in which occurs is important. Knowing what is relevant by observing children's play enables teachers to intervene skillfully in ways that fall along a continuum of subtle to active participation in play. Such knowledge may enable teachers to decide to step back and give children the independence to resolve their own challenges or conflicts, or it may help them decide if it is necessary to more actively guide or redirect play.

Teacher as Stage Manager

The fourth principle involves the teacher's skill in organizing the environment. The teacher plans experiences or projects for children, anticipating needed spatial arrangements, basic materials, accessories, and time frames to enable children to construct knowledge through their play. In this role, the teacher supports play by indirectly orchestrating both the social and ecological (or physical) aspects of the environment, including the amount of time for children's self-directed play (Corsaro, 2012; Cryer, Harms, & Riley, 2006; Curtis & Carter, 2003; Greenman, 2005; Hand & Nourot, 1999; Katz & Chard, 2000).

A CONTINUUM OF PLAY ORCHESTRATION STRATEGIES

The model we present in Figure 4.1 represents a continuum of play orchestration strategies, ranging from very indirect to very direct roles on the part of the adult. The most indirect of these strategies involves arranging and accessorizing the physical

Figure 4.1
Continuum of Play
Orchestration Strategies

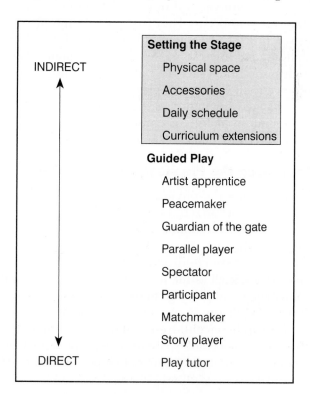

INDIRECT

Setting the Stage

Physical space

Accessories

Daily schedule

Curriculum extensions

Guided Play

Artist apprentice

Peacemaker

Guardian of the gate

Parallel player

Spectator

Participant

Matchmaker

Story player

DIRECT   Play tutor

environment for play and then planning curriculum based on observation and recording children's play. In Chapter 5 we describe increasingly directive techniques for guided play orchestration. Although arranging the environment and direct teacher intervention are presented as separate play orchestration strategies, skilled and observant teachers frequently use several strategies in supporting children's play. They often begin with more indirect strategies, perhaps moving to more directive ones and then, as they fine-tune adult involvement, returning to a less-directive role.

SETTING THE STAGE FOR PLAY

As adults, we look at an office, a restaurant, or an outdoor barbecue and know what kinds of activities and behaviors are expected. As children play in different areas of both the indoor and outdoor classroom, they learn the implicit and explicit rules about what is expected and, in effect, come to read the social and physical cues of that particular area. The environment, then, is "responsive," but children also shape its meaning by recalling what they may have done before in the area and by bringing their own knowledge of their cultures, situations, events, and people to bear on their understanding of what may be expected of them (Cook-Gumperz, & Corsaro, 1977; Corsaro, 2012; Qvortrup, Corsaro, & Sebastian-Honig, 2011).

At the indirect end of the continuum, teachers orchestrate play by setting the stage for it to occur. They first provide the physical space conducive to children's play, a process that reflects their respect for children's development, needs, special abilities, and interests as well as their families and communities. Teachers also use their professional skills to elaborate on and extend curriculum based on what they observe in the children's play and how it develops and evolves. Accessories for play are changed frequently as the teacher responds to children's advancing needs or are readily available for children to use on their own (Chalufour & Worth, 2004; Curtis & Carter, 2003; Reynolds, 2002).

Preparing the Physical Space for Play

In structuring the physical environment for play, questions to consider are, How is the space arranged, both indoors and outdoors? Is there a place to safely engage in **rough and tumble play**, an area to vigorously run and jump and chase? Are there clearly marked areas with **soft spaces**, such as soft chairs or a small grassy area outdoors, where children can find privacy? Are there other areas that have clear boundaries, such as the housekeeping, reading, and block areas? All these features contribute to supporting children's play complexity by fostering autonomous choices and the familiarity of ongoing play episodes.

Research on children's play environments indicates that between 30 and 50 square feet of usable space per child represents an ideal size for indoor environments. Spaces with less than 25 square feet per child may lead to increases in aggression and unfocused behavior for children (Smith & Connolly, 1980). For teachers, crowded physical spaces promote more directive teaching and limit opportunities for social interaction among children. Outdoors, a variety of choices and natural environments that include trees and grassy areas have been found to increase participation in play and reduce aggressive play (Moore & Wong, 1997).

In thinking about environments, teachers should consider both units (the spaces arranged for children's play) and the surrounding space (the area around a unit needed for people to move about). Space invites children to pause and attend, to play alone or with others, to move randomly or purposefully, and to combine materials or separate them. Space generally shapes the flow of play and communication in the classroom or outdoors (Clayton & Forton, 2001; Curtis & Carter, 2003; Hand & Nourot, 1999; Kostelnik, Onaga, Rohde, & Whiren, 2002; Kritchevsky, Prescott, & Walling, 1977; Rui Olds, 2001; Trawick-Smith, 1992, 2010). Figures 4.2, 4.3, and 4.4 show indoor and outdoor plans that support play-centered curricula.

Adapting Spaces for Children with Special Needs

Considerations of the physical space are extremely important when integrating children with special needs into the classroom. Educators cannot assume that children with special needs will be socially integrated merely by placing them in **inclusive** classrooms (McEvoy, Shores, Wehby, Johnson, & Fox, 1990). It is imperative for teachers to be aware of the particular alternative learning strategies of each child (Barnes & Lehr, 2005; Erwin, 1993). In some cases, adaptive equipment for children who cannot stand for long periods of time, such as a tabletop easel or exercise ball placed at a regular easel, may be needed to promote active engagement (Hanline & Fox, 1993; Sandall, 2003; Thomas, 2005). Based on this awareness, teachers can then plan environments that support the child's development of self-initiated solitary play as well as play with peers. Less may be more for children in wheelchairs, like Jake, whose wide, rigid leg braces make movement around the classroom a challenge. Teachers and children may need to think about what furniture or materials could be left out of the room or put in storage to provide more access or movement.

Outdoor environments that provide linkages among play areas, such as platforms, slides, or tires and nets, are most conducive to sustained play. Multiple levels of challenge and diverse materials help children make choices. Pathways should accommodate wheelchairs and other mobility aids. Ramps, decks, and stationary bridges are useful for parking wheelchairs so that children may access climbing areas (Burkhour, 2005; Frost, Wortham, & Reifel, 2012).

Paths and Boundaries

Research on children's environments suggests that clear boundaries between interest areas and clear paths of movement between them help children focus on their play and support their protection of **interactive space** (Corsaro, 2003; Perry, 2001; Ramsey & Reid, 1988). Boundaries must be low enough, however, for children to view available possibilities in the environment and for adults to observe children. Low adult–child ratios also contribute to the maintenance of

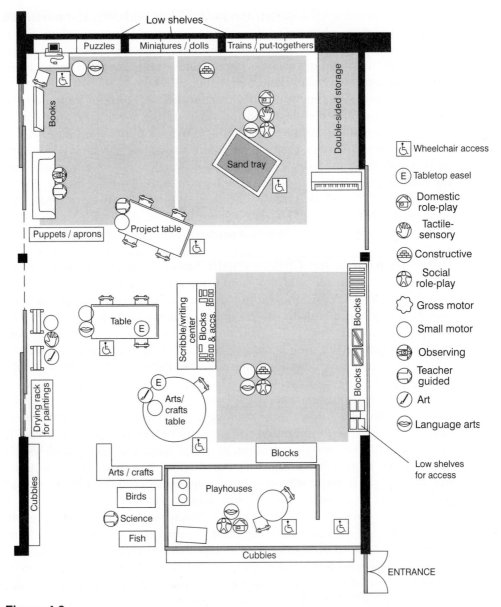

Figure 4.2
Preschool and Kindergarten Setting

play themes. Merely having an adult nearby can act as a buffer against interlopers or distractions, lending indirect support to established play interactions.

John and Sara are playing airport in the block corner. They have just painstakingly completed a control tower and runway when Andrew and Colin

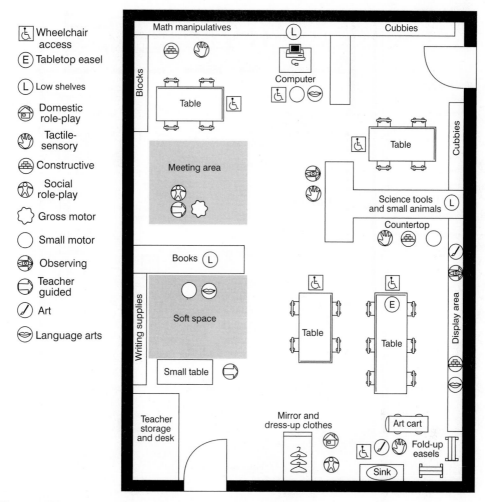

Figure 4.3
Primary Grade Setting

chase through the block area on their way outdoors to try out the magic capes they have made from yarn and paper. The block structures fall, and there are angry tears and accusations. If the pathway from the art area to the outdoors was rerouted around the block area, such events would be less likely. ✂

Quiet and Noisy Areas Another set-up strategy involves separating quiet and noisy or private and group activities in different areas. Activities likely to foster social interaction and busy noise are blocks, dramatic play, reading and writing corners, number activities, and climbing structures. Sandboxes, water tables, art activities, and computers are variable—in some situations with some children they may be conducive to social interaction; in others they may promote more parallel and solitary

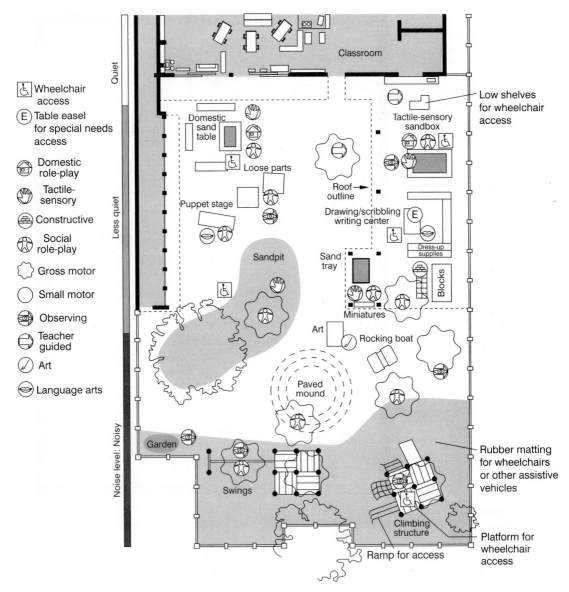

Figure 4.4
Outdoor Setting—Preschool and Primary Grade

play than cooperative play (Curtis & Carter, 2003; Ramsey & Reid, 1988). In general, activities that encourage gross motor play, such as tricycles and outdoor climbing structures, foster more social interaction than those that encourage small motor skills, such as puzzles, table toys, miniatures, or Montessori materials and, in fact, may support more **sociodramatic play**. Teachers may find that small motor toys promote more solitary and parallel play (Hendrickson, Strain, Trembley, & Shores, 1981).

Teachers express their own playfulness while orchestrating children's play.

Activity units that offer children privacy for playing alone or with one or two friends are created by furniture that defines the space. These "hidey-holes" for children to find respite from the group seem particularly important for children who may spend eight to ten hours a day in group settings.

Including Children with Special Needs   Areas that support social activities are critical in classrooms practicing inclusion. Many children with special needs are challenged by the social skills necessary for appropriate development, and it is important that teachers do not make assumptions about these social skills and, instead, carefully observe and support children's efforts, even if they appear to be characteristic of much younger children (Creasey, Jurvis, & Berk, 1998; DEC/NAEYC, 2009; Kostelnik, Onaga, Rohde, & Whiren, 2002; Odom, 2002; Sheridan, Foley, & Radlinski, 1995). Beckman and Kohl found that providing interactive toys leads to increased social interactions among both children with disabilities and those without (as cited in McEvoy et al., 1990). Similarly, Horner found that children with disabilities were able to adapt their social skills more readily when increased numbers of toys were added to a free-choice setting (as cited in McEvoy et al., 1990).

Children with health impairments may benefit from play spaces that foster less physically demanding play while also allowing them to be part of the group and to make choices about when to observe and when to join play (Burkhour, 2005; Frost et al., 2012). Quiet places are particularly important for some children who are easily distracted or frustrated (Bronson, 2000; Kostelnik et al., 2002; Kranor & Kuschner, 1996; Odom, 2002).

Hannah was diagnosed as having ADHD and language delays. With the supportive teamwork of her parents, the school psychologist, and the special education teacher, Hannah has been fully integrated into Pam's first-grade class. Pam finds that Hannah frequently has difficulty sustaining interactions with the other children. As part of Hannah's **Individualized Education Plan (IEP)**, Pam and the school psychologist are attempting to assess and support her progress in social activities with peers.

In addition to interacting with peers in Pam's class, Hannah's participation in afterschool child care means that she is with large groups of children for 10 hours each day, from 7:30 a.m. to 5:30 p.m. Pam observes that Hannah spends quiet time each day by herself in the classroom's reading loft, looking at picture books or talking quietly to the stuffed animals. When Hannah becomes frustrated, Pam finds that she can help Hannah **self-monitor** her behavior by suggesting that she go to the loft or another quiet place. ∅

Soft Spaces Children also benefit from soft areas in the classroom that provide privacy and refuge. The cozy nature of a corner with pillows, a rocker, carpeting, and materials that invite sensory exploration, such as sand or clay, evoke comfort, collaboration, and friendship in the environment. When children become angry or frustrated, teachers can give them a chance to retreat by themselves to a quiet, soft space, a place with no hard objects to throw or hurt themselves. Adults may need to accompany children who are, at that moment, very aggressive or have behavioral disabilities.

> The book corner is in a central area of the room. It is carpeted in a warm-toned tweed, which was selected both for its sturdiness and softness. The rug is bounded on one side by a piano that faces a low couch. Several thin, rectangular pillows, covered in a washable velour, are available for sitting on or leaning against the piano legs during circle time. At the wall end of the rug, each of two birch book display stands put five rows of picture books within easy reach of rug sitters. (Beardsley, 1991, p. 52)

Some of the outdoor spaces may be soft as well. A tree for shade, a grassy carpet to just sit on and watch or read or play alone or with a friend—these provide havens from the frequently active pace of outdoor play.

> In the outdoor garden area, Josh and Taylor sit with their backs against a row of hay bales, quietly looking at picture books. They're propped on the edge of the planter box that holds the newly blooming daffodils and crocuses planted by the children the previous fall. ∅

Friedrich Froebel (1782–1852) wrote about the importance of nature and forms of life and beauty as elements in a kindergarten or "garden of childhood." Providing materials that invite real-life experiences with plants and small animals, such as gardens and terrariums, and opportunities to care for these living things is essential. Activities such as gardening or woodworking, or washing dishes or furniture, give children a sense of competence as they use real tools. Forms of life also include culturally diverse objects and representations of experiences from children's lives, such as photographs and music.

Patterns, color, light, and visual and auditory harmony are all aspects of forms of beauty in the environment. The use of texture, paintings, color on walls or floors, music, and plants convey a feeling of respect and care for the environment and for children themselves in aesthetically pleasing forms. Access to water and to natural environments outdoors are also important aspects of forms of beauty (Hand & Nourot, 1999; Wolfe, 2002). For a contemporary extension of this approach, see Alice Waters' (2008) *Edible Schoolyard: A Universal Idea.*

Outdoor Play Spaces Although much of what we have discussed as important in play environments applies to both indoor and outdoor spaces, outdoor play environments offer unique opportunities for learning and development. Outdoor play offers choices to children in the use of natural materials like sand, water, and plant life, which are constrained indoors. Outdoor play offers opportunities for children to develop the naturalistic intelligence that Gardner (1999) described and to reap the benefits of fresh air, live plants, and perhaps the care of small animals, to which many children have little access. Opportunities for fine and gross motor play abound. Natural materials, such as pebbles, leaves, sticks, flowers, and feathers, find their way into children's dramatic play. These materials become treasures to sort, to touch, and to use in creating art pieces (Topal, 2005; Torquati & Barber, 2005). In Berkeley, California, an asphalt playground was replaced with soft spaces, a grassy field, small garden areas, and trees. The outcomes were reduced rates of accidents and aggressive behavior (Moore & Wong, 1997).

In early research on the effects of outdoor playgrounds on peer relationships among children with physical disabilities and typically developing peers, it was found that outdoor playgrounds that offered more clearly defined options, such as the ones in Figure 4.4 in this chapter, fostered more integration of children with physical limitations in play with typically developing peers. Fisman (2001), who studied children's responses to actual and ideal playgrounds, discovered that children expressed a desire for many more choices, flexible use areas, and soft private spaces for their outdoor play.

In another urban school setting, a working farm is located at the school site. Teachers in this district often take their classes there in the fall, winter, and spring to observe the changes in the seasons. Gardens, ducks, chickens, rabbits, goats, two horses, and a pig offer opportunities for children to observe and care for plants and animals, and teachers at the school use the farm as part of their planned curriculum (Waters, 2008). ✆

Unfortunately, in the rush to promote academic achievement in the early years, some educators have begun to limit access to outdoor play for children, especially in elementary school settings. However, there is growing research indicating that this is counterproductive (Jarrett & Waite-Stupiansky, 2009; National Association of Early Childhood Specialists in State Departments of Education, 2002; Walker & Berthelesen, 2008).

When Space Is Limited   In classrooms where space is at a premium, often in public school primary-grade settings, teachers may be creative in the use of portable accessories or "Murphy space." For example, in one first-grade classroom, where desks grouped as tables occupy a large part of the classroom, the teacher constructed easels that fold into the wall, much like a Murphy bed, that can be pulled out and set up during free play time. He complemented this with a rolling cart that includes art and carpentry materials that may be transported outdoors or to a table area.

Other teachers have decided that table space for all children to sit down at one time is not necessary in a classroom where the play goes on in specific areas. Freeing the room of large tables has enabled one teacher to rotate the use of center areas according to the play experiences he has planned and has left open space in the room for block play and a large dramatic play area.

Adjacent Areas   When setting up, teachers might also think about the effects of placing activity areas adjacent to one another to invite opportunities for the cross-fertilization of ideas of children engaged in play, even when the play areas remain distinct. For example, in one first-grade classroom ongoing play at the carpentry table adjacent to the block area prompted the construction of airplanes and helicopters to be housed at the block area airport. In a second-grade classroom, a post office created to encourage letter writing soon expanded to a bank and an office on either side, where children integrated literacy and mathematics concepts.

To encourage the cross-fertilization of ideas in **activity areas**, Griffin (1998) recommends that teachers keep a box of game parts, puzzle pieces, rocks, and miscellaneous small objects that children can use in their dramatic play. In this way, the puzzle pieces and objects associated with more structured activities are more likely to remain in their respective areas; also, children are allowed to appropriate flexible materials for their own uses.

Accessories for Play   The provision of accessories in the environment relates to symbolic distancing. For sociodramatic play, younger or less sophisticated players

FAMILY DIVERSITY
Family Factors and Clean-Up

Cultural and family factors may affect children's understanding of the school culture's conventions for returning objects to their original storage places. For example, a child who lives in a trailer or a crowded home may have learned to store toys out of view rather than display them on a shelf. Conversely, children who come from families where the adults do the cleanup may have no rationale for the expectation that they put classroom materials away.

need more realistic props to support or **scaffold** their play themes and roles. Their symbolic distancing skills are not well enough developed to appropriate a block or an imaginary gesture when a real-looking prop, such as a toy telephone, is not available. Generally, younger children (ages 2–3) prefer to have several sets of realistic props to use in their dramatic play. Multiple sets of brooms and phones, toy food and dishes, fire trucks, and toy animals are necessary elements to scaffold their dramatic play. If these are not available, play fantasies may give way to object disputes, and the symbolic distancing of roles and situations has little chance to get underway.

On the other hand, sophisticated dramatic players like to have lots of unstructured props—that is, props with limited specific use of their own—available for their dramatic play. Cardboard packing, rocks, sticks, and blocks are examples of unstructured props. Such nonrealistic props give the child leeway to make successive transformations—for instance, by using pebbles as money, food, buried treasure, and circus tickets—all in the course of a single play episode.

Primary-grade children enjoy having hats and scarves available for more formal play and dramatic enactments and will generally use both unstructured props and imaginary ones in such activities (Heathcote & Bolton, 1995). They also use miniatures, models, and games with rules as accessories to their fantasy play. Many children in this age group also enjoy collections and are supported by trays or boxes with compartments for organizing their collections.

> Randall and Amber have been making a volcano scene in a cardboard box for several days. After constructing the volcano from playdough, they use red and orange tissue paper to represent flames from the volcano and toothpicks and paper to make trees and homes on the sides of the volcano. They spend time coloring branches of their trees to represent ash and burned wood and discuss the escape and rescue operations of the people and animals who lived in the houses. ✻

Timing in the introduction of props is important. Replicas of real objects and props that relate to familiar scripts are appropriate at the beginning of the year, as children get to know one another. **Accessory boxes** that augment the familiar scripts of housekeeping or cars and trucks in preschool and kindergarten classes may be introduced later in the year. Many teachers have a large selection of accessory boxes built around themes, such as restaurant, office, beach trip, and camping, which they introduce to correlate with curriculum themes or have available on request by children. Accessory or prop boxes may be made from cardboard boxes, ice cream containers, or plastic bins (Desjean-Perotta & Barbour, 2001; Myhre, 1993). Figure 4.5 provides suggestions for themes and contents for prop boxes. Some teachers offer a rotating variety of theme boxes in a designated area of the room; others periodically replace or augment equipment in the housekeeping area or outdoor climbing structure. In the primary grades, these accessory boxes are valuable as prompts for enacted plays and story writing.

Office
stapler
tape
old adding machine or fax
   machine
copier made from cardboard
   box
telephones
computer keyboard
computer monitor made from box

Paint Store
painter's hat
bucket
brushes, scrapers
paper color chips in
   graded colors
cash register and "money"
order pads and pencils
home improvement catalogs
telephone

Flower and/or Fruit Stand
plastic flowers, fruits,
   vegetables
boxes or crates, tables
   for display
cash register and "money"
chalkboard for prices

Bakery
Play Doh, paper confetti
cookie sheets, tubes for
   decorating
oven
telephone
labels or chalkboard for prices
cash register and "money"
blocks for display cases
cookbooks

Gas Station
trikes, wagons
large boxes for pumps
plastic hoses

cash register and "money" or
   "credit cards"
window-washing supplies
   (spray bottles, squeegies)
large box for car wash

Restaurant
aprons
chef's hat
menus
tablecloths
silverware
dishes
play food
chalkboard and chalk for
   "specials"
order pads and pencils
cash register and "money"
telephone

Bank
tellers' windows
cash boxes
bank books
office supplies
play money

Shoe Store
shoes and boxes
foot measure, tape, ruler
socks
telephone
receipt book
price labels
cash register and "money"

Camping Out
sleeping bags
tent
camp cookware
flashlight
backpacks

Travel and Passport Office
computer keyboard, box for
   monitor

toy camera
drawing and writing supplies
blank books
travel brochures

Hospital or Doctor's Office
bandages
toy medical tools (e.g., blood
   pressure cuff, syringe)
cots or mats
waiting room with magazines
white coats
medical hats
rubber gloves
files, clipboards, and paper for
   patient information
telephone
computer keyboard, box for
   monitor

Pet Shop
toy animals
boxes for cages, aquariums
cash register, receipts, "money"
materials to make collars, pet
   toys, and animal food

Laundromat
washers and dryers made from
   cardboard cartons
plastic or straw baskets
clothing to "wash," sort, and
   fold
toy iron and ironing board
clothes rack and hangers
cash register or change
   machine
bulletin board and notices
magazines

Figure 4.5
Some Suggested Accessory Box Themes and Contents

Teachers help children sustain their play by sensitively entering into their activities.

Play Materials for Children with Special Needs   Older children with special needs characterized by autism, some speech disabilities, or developmental language delays may benefit from having multiple realistic or replica play accessories to support their fantasy play. Such costumes and props for pretend play enable children who are challenged to communicate their ideas with language to more fully participate in pretend play roles and situations (Cate, Diefendorf, McCullough, Peters, & Whaley, 2010; Marvin & Hunt-Berg, 1996; Wolfberg, 1999). Adaptive toys with technological features, such as a battery-operated bubble blower or electric dice roller, enable some children with physical disabilities to participate more easily in play (Locke & Levin, 1998; Stone & Stagstetter, 1998).

Familiarity Balanced with Novelty   Children need a balance of the familiar and the novel. In addition to the traditional housekeeping props, the teacher must consider the cultural backgrounds of the students. Does the family eat with chopsticks and cook in a wok? Does the family use a barbecue? Might cherry-picking baskets, beads and yarn, western hats or coal miners' hats be familiar objects in some children's homes? If we want all children to find a familiar script in the classroom, we must scaffold their symbolic behavior on what is comfortable and homelike to them (Derman-Sparks & Ramsey, 2005; Derman-Sparks & Edwards, 2010; Genishi & Dyson, 2009; Genishi, Huang, & Glupczynski, 2005; Hughes, 2003; Reynolds, 2002).

Areas where materials for art and music are available open up opportunities for new accessories or modifications of old ones (Bronson, 1995). In one classroom, small cans filled with rice, beans, or pebbles and then taped closed were placed next to the xylophone and rhythm instruments, with materials for creating individual shakers set out nearby. In another setting, a discussion of a Pisarro painting prompted the teacher to mix muted pastel colors and thicken the paints so that children might try the "painting in pokes" that they had noticed in the print borrowed from the public library (Beardsley, 1991).

Play Materials That Offer Alternatives   Teachers may set up environments that encourage a particular kind of play by combining or rearranging materials. For example, setting out toothpicks with clay may encourage more social interaction than clay alone; as children link structures, they build or construct birthday cakes or bridges in play that involves others.

Quiet and private materials offer children opportunities for exploration before they begin to play. In initial exploration, the focus is on "What can this object (or material) do?" After time to explore the material at hand, children begin to truly play, when the implicit question becomes, "What can I do with this object or material?" (Hutt, 1971; Wohlwill, 1984).

> Sandy approaches the used adding machine that another child has just left. She pushes keys and watches the numbers print for about 10 minutes. The next day she returns and continues her exploration, systematically trying each key to note the number it produces on the tape. On the third day she invites Mark to play. "Come to my store. You can buy cookies," and she rings up a pretend purchase. ✇

Materials that offer opportunities for **exploratory and self-correcting activity** include pegboards, form boards, miniatures, and picture lotto. These activities give children a relaxed time away from the mental effort of negotiating with their peers and help them restore a sense of order and control to their lives. Materials that support solitary play may also provide important relief from the pressures of social interaction for children learning English as a second language or those with language disabilities (Clawson, 2002). This function seems to be age related. McLloyd (1983) found that 3-year-olds used these materials in more solitary ways. While 5-year-olds more frequently engaged in cooperative play, they also sometimes chose solitary play, regardless of the structure of the materials. Their greater communicative competence allowed them to verbalize the need for privacy or collaboration when they desired it.

Play Safety

One of the most important issues related to play environments for young children involves the safety of toys and play environments. Each year, hundreds of children are injured while playing with commercial toys, and many of these injuries occur in school settings. Therefore, teachers must be knowledgeable and observant.

Government regulation of toy safety standards increased with the Hazardous Substances Act of 1973, the Consumer Product Safety Act of 1978, as amended August 12, 2011, and the Consumer Product Safety Improvement Act of 2008. These standards include the important requirement that toy manufacturers clearly label products with age appropriateness. For example, toys containing tiny pieces or sharp edges must be clearly labeled to warn adults that they are not designed for children under the age of 3. Toys that are electrical in nature, and thus present a potential hazard of burning children, must be labeled as hazardous for children age 8 and younger. Parents and teachers should be aware that some toys that have been imported may use paints containing lead.

Consumer publications inform teachers and parents about toy safety issues. The Consumer Product Safety Commission offers resources, such as "For Kids' Sake: Think Toy Safety" (2005) and "Shop CPSC Toy Safety Tips Before Shopping for Holiday Gifts" (2008), which are available online at no cost and are designed to help prevent toy and playground injuries. The American Academy of Pediatrics lists toy safety tips for the holidays, and the Toy Manufacturers of America, in conjunction with the Consumer Product Safety Commission (2012), has developed and published guidelines for guarding against potential accidents involving toys:

1. Select toys that are appropriate for children's interests and stages of development. This includes avoiding toys with long strings or small parts for infants and toddlers. "Choke tubes" are available to measure the size of pieces in toys that are suspected of being dangerous.

2. Read labels on packaging carefully and dispose of packing material (such as plastic wrappers) that might be dangerous to children and choose toys with nontoxic paints.

3. Keep toys clean and in good repair. Store toys designed for older children out of sight and reach from those at earlier developmental stages.

4. Supervise the play of children, particularly very young children, to see that they do not use toys in ways that are dangerous to their health or safety.

Not all products are screened under consumer safety guidelines. Parents, teachers, and other professionals who work with children and families must still be vigilant. Many products available from overseas do not meet these standards. Toys that children acquire from someone's attic could be in poor repair, have parts painted with lead-based paint, or have pieces missing that make them potentially hazardous.

Playground Safety   Another issue is playground safety. The NAEYC requires 75 square feet of play space outdoors per child as part of their accreditation criteria and recommends the following six elements of playground safety:

1. Careful supervision of children

2. Arrangement of space that protects against access to streets, standing water, and other hazards

3. Provision of sturdy and safe equipment designed for the physical and developmental level of children

4. Provision of resilient surfaces for landings
5. Provision of regularly scheduled maintenance and cleanup
6. A variety of choices for play

Jambor and Palmer (1991) offer general guidelines and specific criteria for playground safety in a checklist and discuss three general principles for school playground safety. First, enclosures that shelter play environments should have no visual barriers, so that children are supervised adequately and are protected from hazards outside the play area. Second, adequate space is needed to accommodate children safely using equipment on their own. Their recommendations include guidelines for space surrounding slides, swings, and climbing structures. Third, play surfaces must minimize the impact of children's falls. In general, Jambor and Palmer suggest that softer surfaces (such as grass or packed dirt), in contrast to cement or asphalt, are less likely to contribute to injury when children fall. Rui Olds (2001) also made helpful recommendations for installation of play structures.

Planning the Daily Schedule

Another element of the curriculum structure is the daily schedule of activities. The way teachers structure the day sends powerful messages to children about the value of their own choices and the activities they construct for themselves. This scheduling includes not only the content of the classroom, but also how much time is allotted for playful purposes (Cryer, Harms, & Riley, 2006; Hand & Nourot, 1999; Harms, Clifford, & Cryer, 1998; Trawick-Smith, 2010; Wasserman, 2000). The daily schedule is also an effective way to verify how much actual time is being made available for children's play. If an examination of the schedule indicates that most of the children's time is booked for circle, group, housekeeping, or other directed activities, there is probably too much "teacher choice and teacher voice" in the program. In full-day programs, 50 minutes of time for spontaneous play and self-directed choice time during the morning as well as the afternoon is ideal. (See Cryer, Harms, and Riley, 2006, for detailed examples.)

In the most free-flowing environments, the room is arranged with activities available for children to choose. Furniture and materials are flexible, and the teacher floats, interacting with small groups of children more often than with the entire class. The British Infant School, traditional nursery schools, and open classrooms are examples of this design. Teachers who use it in their classrooms have noted that lengthening the total time for free-choice activities and play increases children's focus and engagement in their chosen activities and also encourages them to try new experiences after they have touched base with their old favorites (Paley, 1984).

In other environments, more teacher direction and less child choice are evident. Small- and large-group direct instruction alternates with free-choice time. Teachers spend more time with designated groups and less time attending to the flow in the total classroom. The pitfall of this model is that what teachers perceive as play (e.g., building an airport with blocks) the children may perceive as labor, since their choice of activity rests with the teacher. Teachers may also miss out on important learning events when they attend to only one group.

The most structured environment leaves little time for free play. Play is regarded as recreational rather than as a vehicle for learning. Small- and large-group direct instruction characterize this design. Here the teacher's attention to children's play focuses primarily on concerns about safety rather than on aspects of social or intellectual development. Skills-based academic programs exemplify this model.

A play-centered curriculum that serves children's intellectual development and focuses on the construction of new and meaningful knowledge achieves a delicate and important balance between teacher-initiated or guided play and child-initiated play. Teachers who are sensitive to the distinction between labor required by others and playful work selected by children will note the importance of choices for children and allow ample time for children to elaborate on and complete activities they have begun. In any activity, teachers need to ask themselves, "How much of it is truly chosen by the child? Does the child have choices about where, when, how, and with whom she or he plays? How engaged are children in their play?" Assessing children's opportunities for spontaneous, self-directed play through examining the daily schedule is an effective reality check on how much time is actually being allocated for play.

EXTENSIONS FOR PLAY IN THE CURRICULUM

Setting the stage for play and curriculum planning go hand in hand. It represents the backstage versus the onstage aspect of teaching when we focus on play as the center of the curriculum.

Play-Generated Curriculum

Play-generated curriculum, or curriculum that emerges directly from the interests of the children, draws on teachers' observations of children's interests and themes in their play to provide opportunities to extend and elaborate on their learning.

In one first-grade classroom, several of the children had participated over the weekend in a community art fair called "Art in the Park." They had all contributed to a huge wall mural. On Monday, three of the children asked if they could have some large paper to show the other children "how you make a really big picture." The teacher set up large sheets of butcher paper. The children were provided with a complete palette of paints in multiple, small milk cartons, which were housed as a set in small tote boxes. Children experimented with recipes for making paint and mixing colors. Later in the week, the teacher brought in books from the library depicting murals in other communities around the world. In the following weeks, the teacher introduced new media, such as collage and group wood sculptures, for the children to try. ✆

Curriculum-Generated Play

This facet of curriculum planning involves a more direct role for the teacher. In planning **curriculum-generated play**, a teacher's observation of children's play leads her to include materials or techniques that she suspects will create a match with children's spontaneous interests (Bennett, Wood, & Rogers, 1997; Hand & Nourot, 1999; Stegelin, 2005). In this way, the teacher's knowledge of the content area, such as science, mathematics, art, or literacy, intersects with her sense of children's previous experiences and their current interests.

> The teacher of a second-grade science program noticed children's interests in the concept of water pressure as they experimented with dish soap bottles outdoors. She related these interests to requirements for physical science activities and the introduction of scientific terms in her Department of Education's science framework and state curriculum standards. The teacher placed holes in containers at different levels and set up plastic piping material with a water source, challenging the children to find out which arrangements would make the water squirt farther. She introduced terms like *pressure* in the context of their observations and introduced the term *hypothesis* in conjunction with the "guesses" that the children made about their experiments. ✇

> A kindergartner named Jennifer spent her choice time over several days creating a book she called "The Very Hungry Clowns," which consisted of clowns with butterflies in their tummies, a new one drawn for each day. Jennifer's merging of a phrase she had heard at home with the format and structure of Eric Carle's book *The Very Hungry Caterpillar*, read earlier in the week, were evident in her play creation. ✇

The technique of curriculum-generated play has elements in common with the thematic curriculum design seen in many programs for preschool and primary-grade children. We believe curriculum-generated play enhances the best of thematic curriculum. Some **thematic curriculum** is based on the teacher's interests, children's families, past experiences, and resources. Truly play-centered curriculum integrates teachers' interests and concerns with those observed in children as they play (Helm & Katz, 2010; Katz & Chard, 2000).

This continuity among families, community, and school curriculum is reflected strongly in the Reggio Emilia approach to early schooling (Edwards, Gandini, & Forman, 1993; Forman, 2005; Gandini, Hill, Cadwell, & Schwall, 2005; New, 2005; Wien, 2008; Wein, 2014). The contributions of families and community and the relationships and interaction among children as they construct knowledge in small groups are all highly valued aspects of this approach to curriculum planning. Also valued is time for themes, concepts, hypotheses, and multiple representations to emerge and evolve to completion.

The **spiral curriculum** approach, which revisits and revises representations of experience, is shared by both children and teachers. Bruner (1963) coined the term *spiral* *curriculum* to represent the idea that, at many stages of their development, children may grasp basic concepts, each time returning to the same ideas at a more sophisticated level of understanding. So, rather than focusing on the themes of curriculum, such as whales or dinosaurs, the teacher focuses on the concepts that might be revisited as children encounter those themes several times during their school experience.

Drawing on Experiences from a Variety of Cultures   One drawback of thematic curriculum that is not directly based in children's experiences is the unsatisfactory treatment of multicultural issues. Topics such as ethnicity and race, culture, and language may be overlooked or misrepresented. For example, teachers with good intentions may address cultural diversity in a manner that has come to be known as the tourist curriculum (Derman-Sparks & Edwards, 2010; Derman-Sparks & Ramsey, 2005). Using this approach, foods, festivals, and music from various cultures are introduced once a year, often in conjunction with a holiday. In addition, some teachers have fallen into the routine of presenting out-of-context knowledge of culture, such as depicting stereotypes of American Indians at Thanksgiving or Chinese culture at Chinese New Year, without addressing the real issues of cultural diversity in our daily lives. Instead, the antibias approach, advocated by Derman-Sparks and Edwards (2010) includes diversity as a regular aspect of the curriculum, where teachers foster children's positive attitudes toward the acceptance and celebration of differences among cultures. It is important that the environment reflect children's cultures and languages, and that the physical space and materials for play become vehicles for learning about our country's rich diversity (Gonzalez-Mena, 2008).

Consistent with this view, in a play-centered curriculum, aspects of the physical environment and accessories for play reflect cultural diversity. For example, in Janice's kindergarten room such items as the tortilla press, yogurt maker, seaweed toaster, rice bowls, and chopsticks are available alongside day-time planners and briefcases.

In a play-centered curriculum, art, music, literature, science, and mathematics experiences reflect cultural diversity in a manner that makes them part of everyday life in the classroom, not just an infrequent glimpse of fragmented information or a song or two.

In Consuelo's first-grade classroom, she observed the Southeast Asian children pretending to make rice and shrimp dishes in their sand and water play. She contacted one of the children's parents and included frequent cooking projects that introduced some of these foods and the techniques used to cook them to everyone in the class and offered them as part of the regular snack menu. ✍

In a second-grade classroom, the teacher incorporated literature describing the legends of several cultures into his curriculum on astronomy. He invited families of children to tell bedtime stories and family stories to the class and was pleasantly surprised when over half of the families participated. Family members, including parents and grandparents, aunts and uncles, even took time off work to come to school and share stories from their childhoods or family traditions and rituals. ✍

FAMILY DIVERSITY
Overcoming Objections to a Play-Centered Curriculum

The cultural values of some families may provide an additional challenge in advocating for play-centered curriculum. For example, Joshi (2005) described a common response of some parents to play at school, reflecting the belief in some cultures that education should be focused on learning correct behaviors and habits rather than playfulness and creativity. He recommended that teachers take the time to explain and describe how concepts, skills, and academic standards are embedded in play-centered curriculum at school and to respect the families' beliefs by offering suggestions for activities at home to enhance these academic goals. Documenting children's play and projects through photographs, visual arts, and writing can make the links between play and academic learning more evident to families.

Another curriculum strategy represents subtle orchestration on the part of the teacher and calls for finely tuned observation skills. In this strategy, the teacher provides opportunities and asks questions that encourage children to use newly constructed knowledge derived from the curriculum in their play. Because play is primarily assimilative in nature, it represents opportunities for children to consolidate and generalize their emerging mental concepts. This aspect of play is extremely important. The true test of whether teacher-planned experiences help children learn a specific concept or skill, such as counting money or using a calculator, is to see it "replayed" spontaneously by children in their play.

Integrating Academic Standards   Most states have adopted the Common Core State Standards for mathematics and English language arts. To align her curriculum to current standards, one first-grade classroom teacher complemented a mathematics unit on measurement with the creation of a shoe store in the dramatic play area. She was delighted to hear children use terms like "same size" and "half an inch shorter" as they used rulers, yardsticks, and shoe measurers in their play. In aligning her English language arts curriculum with the Standards, she facilitated children's abilities in making a shoe sale sign and sales receipt books and writing about shoes they loved to wear. The unit was expanded to include other stores that children knew about in their local shopping mall, and involved literacy, mathematics, art, and social studies concepts in the play. Table 4.1 illustrates some curriculum standards addressed by the shoe store project and the environmental supports provided for the children's play.

Table 4.1   Examples of Standards Addressed by the Shoe Store Project

Curriculum Standards	Play Example	Environmental Support Provided by Teacher
Phonemic and Phonological Awareness		
Makes letter-sound correspondences	Children make signs for shoe sale and labels for shelves	Supply blank signs and pens in block area
Demonstrates growing awareness of beginning, ending, medial sounds of words	Sandra writes receipts for shoe sales	Provide signs with words for sneakers, sandals, running shoes, dress-up shoes
Numeracy		
Uses comparative words appropriately, such as many–few, big–little, more–less, fast–slow	Discusses small, big, long, short in trying on shoes	Different size shoes are available as play props
Understands numbers and simple operations and uses math manipulatives, games, toys, coins in daily activities (adding, subtracting)	Counts out 6 coins to pay for shoes at pretend store	Pretend money and cash register
Measurement		
Uses measuring implements	Measures using foot measure	Yardstick and shoe measure from local shoe store
Estimates	"I need a smaller sandal"	
Ordering and Seriating		
Orders objects from smallest to largest	Lines up shoes on the shelf in order	Shoe rack and shelves with space for ordering pairs of shoes
Sorting and Classifying		
Describes how items are the same or different	"Those shoes have Velcro and these have buckles"	Shoes of similar kind (e.g., running shoes) but with different features

SUMMARY

Teachers use their experience in the classroom and knowledge of research and developmental theories when orchestrating children's play and setting the stage for a play-centered curriculum. Rather than following a fixed curriculum, the teacher guides orchestration by providing opportunities for development.

The following strategies and principles provide guidance to teachers as they plan and implement a play-based curriculum:

- **Principles Guiding Play Orchestration.** Teachers need to have an understanding of how to implement play-related principles. Guiding principles include (a) taking the child's view, (b) being a keen observer of children's behavior, (c) seeing meaning as it is constructed, (d) serving as stage manager to organize the environment, and (e) planning new curriculum.

- **A Continuum of Play Orchestration Strategies.** Teacher strategies designed to support play range from indirect to direct. Arranging the time, space, and materials for play is the most indirect strategy, while acting as a facilitator, participant, or tutor to influence children's play are the most direct.

- **Setting the Stage for Play.** There are many ways that teachers can create supportive and challenging play settings, both indoors and outside. A schedule of daily routines that allows ample time for play on a regular basis is a major aspect of the infrastructure. Pathways, boundaries, and adjacent areas as well as provision for quiet and noisy areas are necessary. Adaptations for children with special needs that foster less demanding play while still allowing children to be part of the group is an important consideration. Space should also accommodate vigorous play and engagement with natural materials. And of course, safety must be of paramount importance.

- **Extensions for Play in the Curriculum.** There are two principal ways that play can be extended to enhance curriculum goals. *Play-generated curriculum* emerges from the interests of children themselves and may arise from requests from children for accessories to support a theme they have invented. *Curriculum-generated play* involves a more direct role for the teacher and is based on observations of what children enjoy doing. For example, when a teacher observes children's interest in water pressure as they play with dish soap bottles outdoors, she can relate this interest to requirements for physical science activities. This can lead to a teacher-designed curriculum involving containers of water with holes at different levels as well as plastic piping material and a water source. The teacher can introduce terms such as hypothesis and pressure in the context of children's play and observations during the activity.

APPLYING YOUR KNOWLEDGE

1. Describe four principles that guide how teachers can support play.
   a. Write a newsletter to parents describing how taking the child's point of view enables teachers to implement the NAEYC's concept of developmentally appropriate practice in their classrooms.
   b. In an observation of your own or another program, include a description of features of the context, such as time of day, activity, site of activity,

number of children/teachers present, and other social and ecological elements you consider important.

   c. Examine the daily schedule of your own or another program to determine how much time is given to housekeeping and transitions versus self-directed play.

2. Identify four indirect strategies drawn from the continuum of play orchestration strategies that teachers can use to support play.

3. Explain how careful planning of a program's setting, routines, and daily schedule can optimize and balance playtime and play choices for children.

   a. List some of the reasons to establish a curriculum based on the infrastructure of the daily schedule of routines.

      i. Consider necessary routines for meal time, rest time, and personal care.

      ii. Allow ample time for self-selected play activities.

      iii. Consider a balance of guided and spontaneous play options.

4. Contrast two extensions for play in the curriculum and explain how they differ.

   a. Design two curriculum extensions that have a built-in self-directed play component.

   b. In an observation of your own or another classroom, identify some examples of curriculum extensions in children's play.

CHAPTER 5

Orchestrating Play: Interactions with Children

LEARNING OUTCOMES

- Discuss how observations of play and knowledge of children's development enable teachers to scaffold play in meaningful and relevant ways.

- Describe how the range of guided play strategies listed in the continuum of play orchestration strategies provides examples of how teachers can "learn to dance" with children as they facilitate play.

- Explain how observations of children's play enhances teachers' ability to effectively time and/or shift their strategies.

- Identify some differences between the peer culture and the school culture.

- Discuss the issues of exclusion and inclusion and their effect on developing a peaceful classroom.

Pam, a first-grade teacher, watches as three children begin to play a board game, counting out marbles as they move to designated spaces on the game board. Peter counts whatever numbers come to mind, although he uses **one-to-one correspondence** as he pulls them from the barrel (1, 2, 3, 4, 7, 10). Marcia counts hers quite precisely, using the conventional number sequence and one-to-one correspondence. Emily grabs a handful without counting, and Peter shouts, "You're cheating!" Pam asks if she may join the game and models counting in sequence and with correspondence when it is her turn. Soon Emily is imitating her strategy, and Peter is attempting to master the sequence for counting from 1 to 10. ✆

The 3- and 4-year-olds in Grace and Dorothy's classroom had just returned from a field trip to the outdoor farm at their local regional park as part of their project curriculum on the theme of mothers and babies. "Sophie," the mother pig at the farm, had four piglets. The children were excited about their opportunity to observe the piglets nursing and to watch them as they learned to move on their own. When the local news reported that the baby pigs at the regional park's farm had been stolen, the children were distressed and worried. They contributed their theories about what happened: "One day the baby pig woke up, and Tilden farm was gone," and "Maybe they just rolled down the hill," were two suggestions. After a phone call to the park ranger they had met during their visit, the news was not promising for the pigs' safe return. Grace and Dorothy supported the children's discussion and play, speculating about the pigs' fate for a few days. Then they turned the discussion from the fear and violence that first dominated to the ranger's plan that the park would build a pig-napping-proof pen and to feelings of empathy for Sophie and her babies. "She is missing her babies," went one dictated story. "The baby pigs are scared and sad without their mama," went another. The children set to work eagerly, using clay, blocks, sticks, and drawings to work on their designs for the "safe pigpen." They use the toy farm animals to test their designs and to play through their fears.

"Where did all my piggies go? Cow, will you help me find them?"

"Here we are—in the barn!"

"You scared me silly, babies! I couldn't see you. Remember, stay close to me!" (Stewart, 2001) ⌀

In each of these vignettes, we see how the teacher's ability to set up, observe, enter, and exit play with sensitivity and grace is crucial to successfully sustaining children's play. Each teacher does this by considering factors of age-appropriate activities and individual development. For example, Pam knows that 5- and 6-year-olds are just beginning to understand games with rules, and that children's emerging abilities to use both conventional numerical sequences and one-to-one correspondence in counting vary at this level of development. Grace and Dorothy understand the fears raised by the pig-napping at the local park, especially because the children had already begun to think about the mother pig–baby pig relationship they had observed firsthand. After supporting a discussion of their fears, Grace and Dorothy introduced ideas that shifted the children's thinking from fear and violence to empathy for the pigs and more positive alternatives, such as imagining ways to keep baby pigs safe.

A key role for the teacher lies in the ways he or she interacts with children as they play and think. The most important aspect of this role is the attitude that teachers maintain toward children's play. Teachers' respect for both individual and cultural variations in play themes and activities is essential, along with the cultivation of their own disposition of playfulness and humor (Bergen, 2002; Cooney, 2004; Lancy, 2002).

PLAY AND SCAFFOLDING

The notion of "scaffolding" was developed by researchers who studied the ways in which adults support and elaborate children's early language. Just as scaffolds on a building support the new construction, adults' interventions in play assist children's attempts at effective communication (Cazden, 1983; Ninio & Bruner, 1976).

Scaffolding includes the ways that teachers support and facilitate meaning making in children's play (Clay, 2005; Rowe, 1994; Simons & Klein, 2007; Wertsch & Stone, 1985). The environment also acts as a context for play at school. In the Reggio Emilia approach, the environment is seen as children's third teacher (Bodrova & Leong, 2007). Various environmental elements scaffold for certain kinds of play. For example, the housekeeping corner supports both constructive and dramatic play as well as the use of cooperative language; seriated cups, funnels, and pitchers in the water table suggest extensions for water play; small tables and chairs scaffold solitary or parallel play; rugs and cushions scaffold opportunities for cozy sharing or privacy (Beardsley, 1991; Henderson & Jones, 2002). In addition, environmental features provide scaffolding through the legacy of how children have previously played with various materials and at various sites in the classroom.

The impact that a teacher's presence has on children's play is an important aspect of scaffolding (Cook-Gumperz & Corsaro, 1977; Corsaro, 2011). In one classroom, interaction among children at a project table was considerably muted because much of the interaction was dominated by the teacher, who took over such tasks in conversation as initiating topics and controlling turn-taking. In a contrasting setting, teachers lingered close to children's play areas, doing productive work of their own, such as weeding the garden or untangling a ball of yarn, remaining available but unobtrusive as children sought to negotiate turns on a rope swing (Lederman, 1992).

Acquiring skills to negotiate their own interactions is basic to children's social and communicative competence, and it does not rest solely on adult modeling. Play provides occasions for children to corroborate, question, experiment, and stretch their understanding of the world and their places in it.

Other examples of scaffolding includes the use of music to encourage persistence at cleanup time or while on a hike. Along with scaffolding the group's efforts, songs with open-ended phrases also support children's developing abilities to hear and reproduce rhymes.

> Ted sings, "Exploring we will go, exploring we will go. We'll catch an ant and put him in our..." He pauses as Sarah and Luis complete the phrase with "pants." Nessa calls out "bants," and Anthony offers "shoe." More children join in as the singing continues, "And then we'll let him go!" (Beardsley, 1991, p. 115)

Scaffolding also supports children whose play reveals and expresses frightening or confusing experiences, such as some of the children in Grace and Dorothy's class. Scaffolding is also important for children who find constructing and negotiating a pretend reality challenging, such as children with autism or pervasive developmental delays (Clark, 2007; Griffin, 1998; Howard & Eisele, 2012; Koplow, 1996; Kostelnick, Onaga, Rohde, & Whiren, 2002; Phillips, 2002; Wolfberg, 1999, 2003). In the following example, two children with autism are supported in their efforts to engage in cooperative play.

> Jeremy enters the rug area where Todd is building with blocks. Jeremy watches and jumps up and down in place. The teacher suggests, "Jeremy, ask if you can help." Jeremy says tentatively, "Can I help?" as he looks at Todd. Todd nods his head, and Jeremy sits down. They begin to build a tower cooperatively. With a sudden kick, Todd knocks the tower down. They begin rebuilding the tower, and this time Jeremy kicks it down with his foot. Todd admonishes Jeremy, "No kicking!" as Jeremy jumps up and down in place. They rebuild the tower twice, taking turns knocking it down with their hands until it is time to clean up (Lovsey, 2002). ✆

Questions that arise for most teachers are, "How much scaffolding is helpful, what form should it take, and when should it be modified or removed?"

Teachers need to consider both the physical environment and the ways in which they intervene (or refrain from intervening) as integral elements of scaffolding. In the sand or water area, for example, the teacher might move an arrangement of water hoses with multiple outlets into the area, or by using a play voice direct attention to a "flood" or an "avalanche." Keen observational skills and a willingness to wait and watch as children construct their own meanings are key elements of successful scaffolding in play (Henderson & Jones, 2002; Jones & Cooper, 2006; Perry, 2001, 2003).

SPONTANEOUS, GUIDED, AND DIRECTED PLAY

Play orchestration is possible in three contexts of play among young children. In *spontaneous play*, the teacher's role is nearly invisible, just as setting the stage represents a prelude or backdrop to a drama. In *guided play*, the teacher's role is more directive, although these strategies, too, range along a continuum of less to more teacher direction. Guided play strategies differ depending on the nature of the materials and the content area of the curriculum. For example, art play and music play may call for more guidance when new materials and techniques are introduced. *Directed play* entails greater involvement by the teacher because the activity is introduced by the teacher and often has a preset goal and defined steps to achieve it, such as a pattern or template. The strategies listed in Figure 5.1 are

Figure 5.1
Continuum of Play
Orchestration Strategies

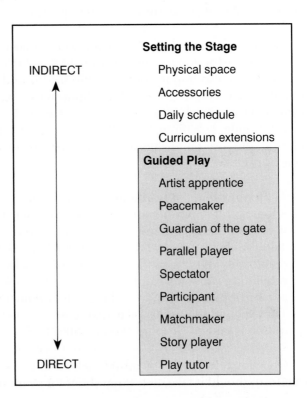

appropriate for orchestrating children's exploration and sociodramatic and constructive play in the classroom. Subsequent chapters delineate guided play strategies appropriate to specific content areas, such as language and literacy, science, and art.

In each case, the teacher orchestrates play in all its facets—intellectual, social, physical, and emotional—by being first and foremost a keen observer. In addition to possessing keen observational skills, the teacher who orchestrates children's play needs to learn to "dance" with the children as he or she facilitates their play. The first element of this dance is determining if and when to join the children (Roskos & Christie, 2001). First the teacher needs to ask, "Will the children benefit by my intervention, or shall I simply watch?"

Many teachers are uncomfortable with this notion of simple observation because it seems at odds with cultural stereotypes of teaching as an adult-directed activity (Henderson & Jones, 2002; Jablon, Dombro, & Dichtelmiller, 2007; Joshi, 2005; Yang & McMullen, 2003). One useful strategy to help teachers extend their observation skills and at the same time model representation, reflection, and recording is by taking the role of "scribe." In this role, the teacher draws or writes about children's play and then shares her recordings of her observations with the children (Jones & Reynolds, 2011; see also Jones & Cooper, 2006).

> In Gail's kindergarten classroom, as part of a thematic unit on airports, Tom and Alexis have built "a machine for seeing inside your suitcase" out of blocks, playdough, cardboard, and paper. Gail draws their constructions and then invites the children to label the parts and discuss their functions with their classmates at group time. Alexis points out that Gail has forgotten to draw an essential piece—a small ball of aluminum foil. "You forgot that important shiny part that makes the light go inside the suitcase," she says, and Gail adds it to the drawing, writing a label next to it. ✄

Vivian Paley (1981, 1984, 1992, 2004, 2010) is masterful at recording children's play and then using it as a frame for group discussion or as raw material for drama. Paley reports frequently asking children, "I noticed that you were playing." Remarking on an aspect of their play that she found interesting, Paley might ask, "Can you tell me more about it?" This form of **authentic questioning**, in which the teacher asks questions he or she does not already know how to answer, both acknowledges the children's play and adds to the teacher's information about them as individuals and as a group.

> Sally, a first-grade teacher who teaches in an ethnically diverse community with many dual language learners, frequently uses this technique in her classroom. For example, Sally took handwritten anecdotal records during the candy store sociodramatic play in her classroom. She noted that Javier modeled the invention and use of pretend money for Lee, who seemed at first confused, then enthusiastically began to count his change: "1, 2, 3, 4, 5—that

is five dollars!" Sally noted this in Lee's portfolio and then used the event to launch a discussion at group time about objects that could be used as pretend money.

"We could use those plastic buttons, because they're round," suggested Frank, representing in language his thinking about a perceptual feature of both money and buttons.

"Or shells," contributed Fran.

"Or make our own dollar bills with paper," shouted Emilia enthusiastically. A plan was made to extend their play by adding a bank the following day. ∅

What are some ways teachers can be more directly involved in children's play? Table 5.1 shows some orchestration roles that involve direct teacher intervention in children's play, ranging from the most subtle and indirect to the more active and direct.

TABLE 5.1 Spontaneous, Guided, and Directed Play

Curriculum Standard	Spontaneous Play	Guided Play	Directed Play
Demonstrates equivalency with blocks	Eric uses four triangular blocks to finish his yellow brick road of squares.	Teacher sets out tangram blocks and patterns; Sara and Ari negotiate the use of smaller rectangles to complete a house pattern.	Teacher sits with Matt and Brita and asks them to help her stack the blocks so they are all in squares.
Uses scientific tools and methods to learn about the world	Sandra uses a toy thermometer to take her doll's temperature. "Oh, it's 100. She needs to go to the doctor!"	Teacher sets out ice cubes and containers of warm and cold water and thermometers, asking the children, "What do you think will happen? How can you tell?"	Teacher directs a small group to measure temperatures of pans of water placed in the sun with varying numbers of ice cubes and to measure and mark the time for melting the ice.
Uses pictures and letters to express thoughts and ideas	Jeff answers the phone in the playhouse. "She's not here. Can I take a message? She will be glad you can come!" and scribbles on a notepad, using M for mom and drawing a smiley face.	Teacher sets up a card-making center with templates for Valentine hearts and paper letters to glue or copy.	Teacher directs children to make labels for their block structures, asking them to label parts of their constructions so they can photograph them.

The Artist Apprentice

The most subtle of the guided play strategies is what Griffin (1998) calls the **Artist Apprentice** role. In this role, the teacher helps to remove clutter in the physical space around an ongoing play episode or offers accessories for play, much like a set assistant in a theater.

> As Mark, Donelle, and Beth launch their spacecraft, land on a planet, and discover aliens, Ms. Toms, their teacher, helps to tidy the blocks when the spaceship "crashes," and the players move their play to the housekeeping corner. She provides a red scarf for their flag and a cardboard box for their control panel. ✆

In doing this, Ms. Toms helps the children maintain their thematic focus in play. If the blocks were to become scattered, the space travel might degenerate into block throwing. Alternately, the extended theme might become sidetracked in the search for appropriate accessories to represent the flags and the control panel. In the Artist Apprentice role, the teacher does not intervene with accessories or action unless she perceives that her action is helpful to sustaining the children's play.

Phillips (2002) described another example: Teddy, a 6-year-old with autism, repeatedly takes books from shelves and stacks them on the floor. The adult intervenes, first by clearing space for his purposeful play with books and then by using her words to give voice to his actions.

Another technique used by the Artist Apprentice is to physically protect an ongoing project and help others set up their own projects in adjacent spaces. In one preschool, a plastic hoop was used to designate "in-progress" constructions in the block area, so that new players would know that someone was saving the materials to play with later (Beardsley, 1991).

The Peacemaker

The next intervention role along the direct–indirect continuum is the **Peacemaker**, who may help children resolve conflicts that may occur in their play. First, the teacher may offer accessories that help to resolve disputes. For example, as 3-year-olds Mary and Jesse argue over a toy typewriter for their office play, the teacher might find another toy typewriter or help the children to imagine how they could use blocks to make another typewriter.

In terms of roles, teachers can help children resolve conflicts by suggesting related alternatives for disputed roles. In Chapter 3 we described a situation in a kindergarten classroom in which several children wanted to play the princess role in an ongoing dramatic play episode. The teacher asked if the princess might have a sister or some cousins who were not in the movie the children had seen, and the children agreed on new but related roles. These kinds of suggestions model for children the flexible thinking and problem solving that ideally occur in play and help them to generate solutions to role disputes on their own as teachers encourage them to invent their own alternatives.

Teachers also act in the role of the Peacemaker when they help children invent roles that stretch their thinking beyond the need to possess disputed materials.

> An observer to Mrs. Paley's classroom in Chicago noticed a child standing, arms flung across the front of the unit blocks. As a consequence, no one else was able to use the blocks. When the children complained to Mrs. Paley, who was seated at the story dictation table, she asked, "Ben, how can they get the blocks they need?" Ben replied (after a long pause), "They have to order them!" The other children immediately picked up blocks and "telephoned" their orders to Ben. ✆

Mrs. Paley remarked later that she could see that Ben "was a character in search of a part." Her one-line query to Ben provided the scaffold for successful negotiation and maintenance of the play episode by inviting the player to stretch himself and invent a part.

The teacher may serve as an interpreter of children's motives to their peers when conflicts occur, or when children disrupt the play of others. Some children slip easily into and out of play and learn to give their fellow players "meta-messages" about their intentions. Bateson (1976) coined the term **metacommunication** to describe the behaviors that people use to signal play. Such behaviors include winks or smiles, laughter, play voices, or exaggerated movements. Verbal markers may be as obvious as "Let's pretend that I'm the babysitter and you're the bad baby," or as subtle as the change in voice pitch to mark the role of the "Papa Bear."

Children whose play is characterized by imitation of content derived from media such as television or whose speech and language are delayed are frequently misunderstood by peers in their attempts to initiate and maintain play (Katch, 2001; Levin, 2003b; Ogakaki, Diamond, Kontos, & Hestenes, 1998; Ogakaki & Frensch, 1998; Wolfberg, 2003, 2009). These misunderstandings also occur in settings in which children speak different languages or dialects. In group settings, children develop their own ways of initiating and sustaining talk with others that are relevant to the local context of their classroom (Erickson & Shultz, 1982; Labov, 1972).

Teachers can help children interpret communicative cues and invent explicit strategies for finding out meanings of others when they feel confused. Such techniques may be particularly important in helping children interpret the cues of play fighting or rough and tumble play so that the play remains a healthy and safe exercise in physical challenge rather than an escalation into violent confrontation (Ariel, 2002; Blurton-Jones, 1972; Pellegrini 1998, 2002). For example, in a vignette in Chapter 11, the teacher intervenes directly for a child with a speech impairment by asking if he wishes to engage in the rough and tumble play fighting that his play partners have initiated, signaling to the children that rough and tumble is permissible only with consent of the parties, and then only if it seems safe (Carlson, 2011a, 2011b).

Guardian of the Gate

How can the sensitive teacher help a newcomer gain entry to ongoing play without disrupting an already-established episode or, alternatively, to judge when it may not be appropriate to interrupt?

Corsaro (1985, 2003, 2011) reports that in his observations, 75 percent of the time preschool children's initial bids to enter ongoing play episodes are rejected. Young children seem to intuitively protect their shared fantasies from interruption by interlopers. After two or three attempts at entry, 50 percent of children seeking to enter others' play are successful.

How can teachers help children develop effective strategies for entry and the confidence to try again if rejected at first? As **Guardian of the Gate**, intervention strategies on the part of the teacher to monitor the gates of play parallel those of the Peacemaker role.

One way teachers can encourage children is by introducing an accessory. Griffin (1998) told of a child who rode a trike every day around the periphery of other children's play, watching but never joining. She gave him an old camera, simply saying, "Take this with you on your travels." Other children soon noticed the camera and asked to be "photographed." Gradually, the child became included in playgroups and developed the confidence to play with others through the accessory that was uniquely his.

Sometimes teachers may suggest a new role. One teacher, seeking to help a child she had observed as an onlooker on the edge of play, asked her to help deliver a large package to the ongoing houseboat play. The "delivery people" were then invited to stay for lemonade, and the onlooker child became included in the play, with her teacher there as security. In another classroom, the teacher asked a group of children who were playing camping, "What could Carl be, a forest ranger?" In this way, the teacher opens up possibilities for the children to negotiate new roles within their play without interfering with the integrity of the ongoing episode.

Teachers also can interpret the social context of play. Schwartzman (1976) wrote that play offers teachers **sideways glances** at make believe. First, it reflects the social status of children in the group. Children with high status often play the most powerful roles and also assign roles to their peers. Children with lower status in the group may hold that status because of unskilled attempts to enter the play of others. Play also reflects children's understanding of the peer culture in the classroom. Teachers can explain children's motives to others in terms such as, "I see Sandy really wants to join your group. She is looking for a friend to play with. Would you like to be her friend?"

Orchestrating Play Entry for Children with Special Needs
Teachers may find that some children with special needs have less experience, confidence, or ability when engaging in play activities. Some consistently look to adults to help them enter the play of others. This is often true of children who are unable to clearly communicate their needs. Some children with special needs may have lower status than their nondisabled peers because of the difficulties they have in entering play. In the

role of **Guardian of the Gate**, teachers can provide the additional involvement that might be needed without increasing children's dependence on adults (Neeley, Neeley, Justen, & Tipton-Sumner, 2001). For example, a teacher might make a child's motives known to increase social interaction between disabled and nondisabled students (Allen & Brown, 2002; Bartolini & Lunn, 2002; Hanline & Fox, 1993).

> Emma, a kindergartner with delayed expressive language, loves to play catch and frequently approaches other children holding the ball and saying, "Emma, Emma," pointing to her chest. Her teacher has helped other children understand that Emma is asking them to play ball and prompts Emma to say "to me" as the ball play begins. ✆

Parallel Player

An even more active role for the teacher involves playing parallel to children. In this scenario, the teacher plays next to but not with the child, using similar materials but not interacting. The teacher might first imitate the child's behavior, such as pouring sand into a container, establishing a basis for reciprocity. Next, the teacher might introduce a variation in the play, such as using a funnel and watching to see if the child imitates the variation. In this way, reciprocity builds at a nonverbal level. In dramatic play, the teacher might use a prop in a new way, subtly extending the child's symbolic distancing, for example, by using a pretend gesture or an unstructured prop to make a telephone call within the child's view (Forman & Kuschner, 1977).

> In Jackie's multiage primary-grade class, Ted, Martha, Elisa, and Kim were calling themselves "ocean scientists" as they played on the carpet. They were sorting, ordering, and counting seashells, discussing their criteria for classification, and speculating about which was bigger: a large, flat, thin shell or a smaller, round, dense one. Periodically, one child would say, "We're scientists doing our work," and the others would nod in agreement. Jackie sat down on the carpet with the children, first manipulating shells and informally observing and joining their discussion. She then brought out a small plastic balance scale from the shelf and began to place large shells, one at a time, in one bin of the balance scale and count smaller shells into the other bin, watching until it balanced. The children began observing and commenting on Jackie's actions. Jackie then began to verbally describe her own hypotheses and behavior as she manipulated the shells and the balance scale. Soon another scale was produced, and the children began to play in pairs, returning to their original questions about which shells were bigger, now reframed as which ones weighed more. Jackie gradually withdrew from the play context, continuing to take anecdotal records for later inclusion in their portfolios and to support the class debriefing about choice time that would occur later in the day. ✆

Spectator

In the role of **spectator**, the teacher comments from outside the play about the themes and content of play. In this way, she indirectly coaches play from the sidelines by taking the role of an interested spectator or a peripheral participant. For example, as Maggie and Keisha approach their teacher carrying their suitcases, the teacher might ask about their imagined travel plans: "Have you bought your tickets yet? Do you have enough suitcases?" By referencing a present context and extending it to a future event, the teacher invites the children to elaborate their play to incorporate the teacher's comment. In this way, teachers validate children's dramatic play and may subtly suggest extensions.

As with all intervention strategies, particularly those that involve a more active role for the adult, teachers must be careful to gauge the situation and determine if comments, even from outside the **play frame**, might disrupt the flow of children's play or introduce elements incongruent with their intentions (Ghafouri & Wien, 2005). Williams (2002) suggests that this form of orchestration may be typical of some parents who, while valuing play, see it as a means of teaching cultural skills by directing play through their comments to children.

Griffin (1998) developed a scheme for analyzing strategies that children use to coordinate shared meaning in their make-believe play from both outside the play frame and as players inside the frame. For example, teachers, as spectators outside the pretend frame, can support children by implicit pretend elaboration, such as in the travel and suitcase example described earlier. In this role, the teacher is an implicit and undefined onlooker to play and may suggest extensions or clarifications that help move play forward.

Participant

In the next role the teacher moves from outside the pretend frame into an active role in the play as a participant, perhaps as a neighbor knocking on the door to borrow eggs, or as an ambulance driver bringing an injured person to the hospital. Once teachers are part of the enactment of a shared script, they can indirectly communicate actions, themes, and verbalizations in their role as participant.

> After the make-believe theme of an airplane trip had been established in Matt's kindergarten class, he noticed that children were boarding the pretend airplane and just sitting in the seats. He boarded as a passenger and asked Carlos, the flight attendant, what was on the menu for dinner. Carlos responded with, "You could have pizza or fried chicken," and then began to enact the rolling of a food cart down the aisle of the pretend plane. ∅

Another participant strategy that allows adults to enter the play space is the use of a direct or indirect comment to shift or extend the play in a particular way by interjecting high drama into the script. The teacher might report a warning or foretelling of an imaginary event as if it were real. "Quick, we need a nurse! Call 911," prompts Matt, as he enters his kindergartners' superhero play and encourages them to extend the make-believe play beyond the fight, die, and resurrect sequence he has observed in this play all week.

Through both dramatic underscoring and storytelling, teachers can interject verbal comments into the stream of play without disturbing the shared illusion of the pretend frame. In underscoring, the teacher might sing or use a sound effect to model the communication of pretend actions, roles, or objects.

> Matt speaks urgently to children playing firefighter, as they have arrived at the burning house with sirens blaring and limited action. "I'll turn on the hose—sh-sh-sh-sh" (making water sounds as he mimes turning on a faucet to douse a pretend fire). ✆

Storytelling is a verbal strategy that allows the player (adult or child) to communicate pretend transformations using narrative forms.

> First-grade teacher Sally shops at the pretend candy store in her classroom, elaborating the plot to extend children's problem solving as she tells her story. "It's my sister's birthday and she really likes gummy bears, do you have those? We are having a big party for 10 people and we need two bears for everyone. Can you sell me enough? Also, I need a birthday card. Do you have those?" ✆

As in the spectator intervention, the teacher must be sensitive to cues from children and not enter into play unless it is called for. If the teacher does enter the play as a participant, then he or she needs to play a supporting rather than a starring role. Many teachers of young children enjoy engaging in play as a participant and may have a tendency to control the flow of play without realizing they have usurped the power of the children. For example, in one preschool classroom, an overenthusiastic volunteer offered to play the injured party in hospital play. She ended up directing the entire play episode, assigning roles to children and suggesting what the doctor and nurse players should say and do.

Matchmaker

In the role of matchmaker, the teacher may deliberately set up pairs or groups of children to play with one another. He or she may, for example, pair a more sophisticated player with a less sophisticated player. As long as there is not too great a difference in their play styles and personalities, both children may benefit from this arrangement. Complementary emotional needs may also serve as a basis for matchmaking.

Wolfberg (1999) recounted her research in which she paired children with varying severity of autism with typically developing playmates in playgroups. Situations in which the child with more skilled play was able to bring his or her peer into a zone of proximal development in play abound in this interesting and valuable research.

FAMILY DIVERSITY

Matchmaking at Work

In one classroom, Sandy, whose parents were divorcing, sought out situations she felt she could control and in which she could feel power. Paul, on the other hand, was distressed over the birth of a baby sister and created a baby role for himself whenever possible. These two children were a perfect match in terms of their complementary emotional needs and spent long hours in house play with Sandy as a powerful and nurturing mother to the helpless baby, Paul.

Matchmaking may also be an effective strategy for orchestrating play with dual language learners. Children who are more proficient in English may be able to smooth communication among players with less fluency in English.

Story Player

Paley (1981, 1986, 1990, 1999) introduced the technique of story play for supporting children's play that structures its form but not its content. In her approach, children dictate stories to a teacher, who writes them out to be enacted by the class later in the school day (Cooper, 2009). The text is written down exactly as it is dictated and reread in the child's language. Each author selects who will take the parts to be enacted. The author serves as director as the teacher reads the story aloud. Elaborations of the plot are often enacted as the story unfolds in drama. Comments such as, "I forgot, the little bear does come home to his mom at the end," are sometimes added to the story's text. Props are not usually used to ensure that the children's imagination is exercised, although teachers may want to consider the developmental level of the child in making decisions about props.

Play Tutor

The teacher as play tutor takes on the most direct role of all by re-creating the emotional security of the caregiver–infant dyad, which is the source of human beings learning to play. In this context, the child feels safe and is able to take risks involved in using symbols and language to represent the meaning of the concrete. The teacher models and directs children's play in this role, supporting their efforts to symbolize and interact.

Researchers who study childhood play have been guided by the work of Smilansky (Smilansky, 1968; Smilansky & Shefatya, 1990) for many years. Smilansky focused on intervention with preschool children whose dramatic play lacked complexity. Direct tutoring may benefit those children whose play consists of repetitive one-liners

Playful interactions with adults are just as essential as those with peers.

imitated from television, or whose attempts to enter the play of others are awkward and intrusive (Bartolini & Lunn, 2002). Smilansky's strategies guide teachers in their attempts to help children elaborate their play through such elements as extended role-play, social interaction, verbalization, persistence, and **object transformations** in a process she calls **sociodramatic play training**.

Other researchers have employed a technique they call "thematic fantasy role-play" (Saltz & Johnson, 1974), in which the teacher assigns roles and directs the enactment of stories read aloud to the children. This technique assigns more control to the teacher than sociodramatic training, where children form their own story lines with teacher support. It also differs from Paley's story-playing approach in its emphasis on stories authored by adults and roles selected and directed by the teacher.

Another strategy involves both matchmaking and play tutoring. Teachers may ask children to serve as "play coaches" and help other children invent roles, pretend with objects, or join in a play episode. In many classrooms, children are given this role with regard to computer use, writing, or other activities in which the status of "expert" encourages children in particular roles to reflect on their own thinking and communicate it to others. It adds the dimension of expert–novice to the already powerful zone of proximal development created in pretend play. Smilansky (1990) found that the play coaches as well as their players benefit from this process.

Because play tutoring represents a very direct role for the adult, it must be used carefully (Trawick-Smith, 1998, 2010). Children who have difficulty with symbolic play distancing or social play negotiations might be better served by less direct teacher strategies. For example, a multiage setting often encourages more advanced play on the part of younger children and prosocial behavior on the part of older children, which may be a more desirable alternative than play tutoring.

CHOOSING A STRATEGY

Considerable skill and thought are required to determine which context, in combination with which child, calls for a given strategy. For example, the child who plays parallel functional play with blocks or sand is a likely candidate for the parallel player strategy. The child who hangs around the edges of playgroups might benefit from an accessory or entry strategy. As a general guideline, wise teachers intervene with the most indirect strategy possible. Many teachers begin by changing the setting for play, perhaps by adding new accessories. If that doesn't work, then the teacher proceeds to increasingly more direct strategies along the continuum.

Challenges in Play for Children with Special Needs

In intervening with all children in their play, there are several factors to consider. We believe it is essential for teachers to keep in touch with the power of the zone of proximal development created through play. All children, regardless of their current developmental capacities, stretch their competencies in play with others. For some children, playful interactions with adults are just as essential as those with peers. Smilansky's play tutoring approach and the overt modeling of pretense may be called for. For most children, however, the teacher in the role of matchmaker and stage manager serves to support play opportunities that are productive and engaging for all.

The matchmaking and tutoring roles present promising avenues for orchestrating pretend play with children with special needs (Bartolini & Lunn, 2002; Henderson & Jones, 2002; Kostelnik et al., 2002; Mindes, 2006; Odom, 2002; Phillips, 2002; Preissler, 2006). Wolfberg (1999) described an ongoing playgroup consisting of normally developing peers who were coached by the teacher to interpret, elaborate, and scaffold the play of autistic playmates.

One drawback of play in **inclusive environments** is that, although young children frequently empathize with their peers who have special needs, most young children are unable to take the perspective of another child and act altruistically on that understanding. For example, in one kindergarten classroom Pauline, a child with Down syndrome, was consistently manipulated by two of her peers into giving up her play materials in exchange for less desirable objects.

Another consideration is that children who are typically developing sometimes feel pressured to include peers who have special needs. They may subsequently comply with adult expectations by allowing the child with special needs in the play area and then ignore him or her (Trawick-Smith, 1994, 2010). Conversely, peers may overdo their helpfulness by treating special needs children in a patronizing manner or by doing too much for them. For example, in a preschool classroom, 4-year-olds Alicia and Emily consistently spoke for Theresa, a child with communicative delays. In doing so, they often squelched Theresa's efforts to communicate with others and her developing sense of initiative.

Challenges in Play for Children Who Are Dual Language Learners

Play with peers provides a safe context for negotiating turns, roles, and problems that arise in play. Linguistic skills are evident in these negotiations and in the enactment of play themes and entry into play. Given the importance of language for social competence and success in play interactions, dual language learners present some unique challenges to orchestration (Saracho, 2001).

One challenge is the observation made by many teachers that children prefer to play with peers who speak the same language (Clawson, 2002). Whether the groupings occur as a result of a shared language or dual language learners congregating together, the results call for sensitivity on the part of the teacher. Matchmaking children who are interested in similar things may be one approach. In this way, children who do not speak the same language begin to form a social history with one another as they play together (Orellana, 1994).

Other challenges call for different orchestration strategies. For example, a teacher may notice through observation that the onlooker behavior of a child masks a desire to join the play (Derman-Sparks & Edwards, 2010; Espinosa, 2010; Kirmani, 2007; Ramsey, 2006).

> Selena hovers at the edge of the restaurant area, watching as Mark and Cecilie cook a pretend dinner. Ann, their teacher, is a customer in their play restaurant. She comments from the participant role, "I'd like some cake after my dinner. Is it on the menu?" "Oh, I don't know if we have any," responds Mark. Ann asks Selena in Spanish if she knows how to make cake. Selena nods, and slowly begins to approach the pretend restaurant. "Selena knows how to make cake," Ann suggests to the two other players, and they hand her a bowl and spoon as she joins them in the kitchen. Selena begins to mix pretend cake ingredients and asks Ann in Spanish, *"Do you like chocolate?"* ✆

Timing Is Everything: Entering and Exiting Children's Play

When teachers enter and exit children's play or shift from one strategy to another, timing is crucial. Manning and Sharp (1977) and Jones and Reynolds (2011) recommended guidelines for entering play. First and foremost, teachers need to observe play long enough to see if any intervention is called for or if the children are best served by the teacher in a less direct role. As part of this observation phase, the teacher has an opportunity to ascertain the themes, characters, plot, and vocabulary negotiated by the children.

If teachers choose to enter the dance of interaction played out by the children, they must do it seamlessly, joining the flow of the play without disrupting its progress or integrity. Respect for children's ongoing, shared make believe is critical. Adult entry is more suitable at transition points during which children are "stepping out" of the play frame to negotiate rules about the play or ongoing themes or roles, rather than at the times when children are deeply engaged in pretend play (Bennett, Wood, & Rogers, 1997).

Leaving the play and returning control completely to the child players is just as important as a sensitive and flowing entry. Because the teacher's purpose is always to support children in their efforts to sustain and elaborate play on their own, the timing of exits is critical. Phasing out of play is one exit strategy that gradually returns the control of the play to children. As a participant within the play frame, a teacher might use storytelling to explain her departure or take a less active role.

> Karen enters the train play of a group of five preschool children with the intention of facilitating Heidi's entrance into the play. Karen sees that Heidi is now engaged with others eating "lunch" in the dining car. Karen announces, "Oh good. The next stop is mine, so I'll see you next Friday on the train." She says to the engineer, "I'll be getting off at the next station." ∅

Sometimes teachers may unobtrusively leave the area when children are very involved in play, as Jackie did when the children appropriated the seashell balancing activity. At other times, the teacher may speak from a different stance: "I promised some children in the block area I'd come visit their airport. I'll come back to watch you when I finish." This effectively places the teacher on the outskirts of play as a spectator and reminds the children of her real-life responsibilities as the teacher (Trawick-Smith, 1994, 2001, 2010).

PLAY AND THE CULTURE OF SCHOOL

Play always occurs within a social context and in relation to the various cultures that coexist within the classroom and the school. The **school culture** (Heath, 1983) represents the norms of school behavior commonly accepted in our society and shaped through teacher behavior. The **peer culture** represents an alternative and, to some degree, a complement to the school culture in the classroom.

Three types of play commonly occur in school settings: instrumental play, **recreational play**, and **illicit play**. Each is defined by the way in which the teacher responds to children's play and the context in which it occurs.

Instrumental play is sanctioned and often employed by the teacher to meet goals consistent with school curriculum. Examples include blocks, teacher-initiated games with rules that teach concepts or vocabulary, and dramatic play. In pretend play, teachers find that the negotiation of the features or implicit "rules" of adult roles provide fertile ground for children to test their mental concepts about gender and adult occupations with other children whose backgrounds may have created a

Children learn through guided play experiences.

different set of rules and expectations. In one preschool classroom, Nat and Katherine argue over who will make dinner, the mom or the dad. In Nat's home, his father is the primary caregiver and usually prepares the evening meal. In Katherine's home, her father commutes to work in a large city and her mother generally prepares meals.

Recreational play is sanctioned by the teacher as a means to let off steam. It often occurs outside the teacher's view. Playground play at recess and free play outdoors in some preschool and kindergarten settings are examples of this type of play.

Illicit play is not sanctioned by the teacher and, in fact, may be expressly forbidden. Children engage in illicit play either behind the teacher's back or as a direct challenge to the teacher's authority. Such play is thought to provide children with a sense of mastery and autonomy within the school setting that limits the range of acceptable behavior. Examples commonly seen in early childhood settings include transforming Tinkertoys into guns when such play is prohibited; "**group glee**" activities, such as coughing or snapping Velcro shoes; and passing secret notes or pictures (Corsaro, 2003; Sutton-Smith, 1997).

One aspect of illicit play that proves to be increasingly difficult for teachers is the consequences of outlawing weapon and violent play in the classroom (Katch, 2001, 2003; Levin & Carlsson-Paige, 2006). Strategies for coping with the behind-the-scenes tactics children use to circumvent teacher-made prohibitions about the content of play are addressed later in this chapter.

Scarlett, Naudeau, Salonius-Pasternak, and Ponte (2005) described other kinds of illicit play as "risky play," in which children endanger themselves and others, for example, by throwing sand or rocks. In this "mean-spirited play," characterized by teasing and bullying, and "mischievous play," such as rolling around on the carpet at circle time, children deliberately flaunt school rules. Scarlett et al. (2005) also described "ambiguous play," in which children seem to be using play as a means to master strong emotions, such as putting the baby doll in the oven (Ardley & Ericson, 2002) or tearing apart the housekeeping area as "naughty" kittens.

Although instrumental play in educational settings or, as Sutton-Smith (2001, 1997; Sutton-Smith, Meechling, Johnson, & McMahon, 1995) called it, "play in the rhetoric of progress" is sanctioned by educators, teachers should remember the importance of play that adults do not sanction. This mischievous or silly play represents another arena in which we find the social skills and concepts of young children developing.

Just as play serves an equilibrating or balancing force in our lives, by its paradoxical nature play also allows us to invert reality, to throw off balance what we know to be normal or sensible. This represents the power of both nonsense and festive play (Fromberg, 2002; Sutton-Smith, 2001, 1997; Sutton-Smith et al., 1995). One of the outcomes of play that is mischievous, rebellious, and nonsensical is the powerful social bonding that occurs among players as they jointly oppose traditional social norms and a sensible view of the world in a playful manner.

> David and Brad are playing with a squirrel doll in the playhouse. David squeaks the squirrel and taps it on Brad's shoe. Brad shouts "Stop, squirrel!" "I'm not a squirrel. I'm a squirmmy!" responds David in a high-pitched voice, hopping the squirrel doll up and down. He grabs a baby doll out of Brad's hand and makes a pouring motion over his head with it. "Sh-h-h." Brad questions, "Hot coffee?" "No, hot caw-caw," David responds, laughing loudly. "Hot caw-caw!" He and Brad fall together onto the floor, laughing hysterically. ✆

In their evolving peer culture, children confront the differing perspectives of one another and also that of the school culture represented by the teacher. As Corsaro (1985, 2003, 2011) advises, teachers must walk a fine line between respecting children's needs to ally themselves against the constraints of adult authority (to look the other way on occasion) and their own need to provide firm and consistent limits about what is acceptable in the school setting. "Adult ideas, materials, rules, and restrictions can be seen as frames or boundaries within which features of peer culture emerge and are played out" (Corsaro, 1985, p. 289). A relevant example of this dilemma is the ongoing debate in early childhood education about the use of toy and imaginary weapons and fantasies involving violence in preschool and primary-grade settings.

RESPONDING TO VIOLENT PLAY

Although pretend weapons and war play issues have plagued the curriculum and classroom culture decisions of teachers for decades, the increased numbers of children in schools whose lives are filled with violence and the increased access for all children to violent media imagery as seen on television and in computer games and video games have sharpened the debate. Educators and families can collaborate in early childhood programs to reduce aggression and violence. To begin this process, we as teachers must examine our own beliefs and experiences.

Many teachers of young children cope with frustration about violent play by outlawing toy weapons and violent themes, hence driving the play "underground" into the peer culture. Is it more effective to illuminate children's fears by openly discussing the violent content of play, or by creating more empathetic and rich contexts for play, than to ignore children's fears (Ardley & Ericson, 2002; Katch, 2001; Levin, 2003a, 2003b, 2006; Levin & Carlsson-Paige, 2006)?

When pretend play is largely an attempt to order what is confusing, chaotic, or frightening to children, then is it more important to consider the sources before invoking classroom rules about weapon play or violence? For example, in the days and weeks following the September 11, 2001, attacks in New York and Washington, and more recently following the Newtown massacre, many teachers believed that the block play, dramatic play, dictated stories, and story play enacting the violence may have been appropriate avenues for healing and making sense of fear. Similarly, Dorothy and Grace's children (in the chapter-opening vignette) needed to play out their fears regarding the lost baby pigs to move to a more empathetic stance. Does replay of violent imagery desensitize children, or offer them an avenue of control?

Ascertaining Children's Purposes in Play

When considering the motives for children's aggressive play, teachers should identify the sources of violent imagery. When does children's play reflect media violence that is pretend, and when does play reflect real-life violence? Many teachers report impatience, anger, and frustration with pretend media-based violent play. "How can their parents allow 5-year-olds to watch those teenage horror videos?" one teacher laments. On the other hand, teachers express empathy for children whose play includes violent images and themes that arise from violence in their home lives and experiences of their families.

A related question is one that calls on teachers to determine the purposes of the children's play and how development may relate to violent play. Young children are just learning to reliably negotiate the lines between reality and fantasy. Crossing those boundaries frequently in pretend play helps children clarify the meaning of violence in our contemporary culture. But how much of this play is too much? What are the fine lines between "playing through" confusing or frightening images or experiences and becoming obsessed with them?

Some war play or aggressive "good guy/bad guy" themes, such as that in superhero play, is often typical for many young children in our culture, though not in other cultures. The loud noises, fast pace, and especially the thrill of the chase that have been elements of diverse forms of sociodramatic play for decades often appeal to children. The themes of good versus evil, life and death, lost and found, and danger and rescue that occur in war play and other aggressive play give children opportunities to deal with these archetypal concerns.

FAMILY DIVERSITY

Real-Life Violence in Play

Tracy's home had been fire-bombed and her older brother injured. For several weeks her kindergarten peers, in their roles as paramedics and firefighters, carried the "injured" Tracy to hospitals they constructed in the block corner, under tables, and in the sandbox.

In considering that there are frequently multiple motives for children's aggressive play, teachers need to examine several issues. To what degree does the play reflect the desire to be powerful in the world? To what extent are the children playing out a script from violent media? To what degree does it reflect children trying to make sense of the real violence they have seen on the evening news or even in their own neighborhoods? Schwartzman (1976) pointed out that an important aspect of play is its inward perspective, or the process by which children repeat experiences that are puzzling, confusing, or disturbing to them.

One source of violent play that reflects real violence is the personal stories of children related to community violence, as shown in the *Family Diversity* feature.

A second source of such play is the violence of war. The meaning of war play is different for children whose families have directly experienced war. Millions of children are from refugee families who have fled the direct effects of war, either recently or in past generations. There is considerable literature on the effects of war on children and families (Van Hoorn & Levin, 2011).

Millions of children in the United States have direct experience with war when their parents or other relatives were deployed to Afghanistan or Iraq. As of 2010, more than 800,000 children have had a mother or father deployed in combat.

FAMILY DIVERSITY

War Games

Aashna's family are recent refugees who moved to a small American town directly from a refugee camp where his sister died. Deborah, the student teacher in the class, notices that Aashna startles frequently in response to sudden noises. During the past week, several children in the class have been initiating a war game. Each time, Aashna runs around the periphery of the group, then goes closer to the children, making rapid shooting sounds. Despite his limited English, he knows the script. Today, after a few minutes, Aashna is clearly agitated, repeating, "Garan, Garan," as he asks for his fourth-grade brother.

Researchers report that when their parents are deployed, preschoolers act out more and are more aggressive (see Chartrand, Frank, White, & Shope, 2008; Van Hoorn & Levin, 2011). Some of their teachers are unaware that these children have a parent deployed and therefore may not understand these changes in behaviors.

Looking at Pretense versus Reality in Violent Play   Teachers are concerned about violent pretend play suggested by media and toys. The explicit violent details of television, movies, and computer games, as well as the many toy weapons on the market today, seem to spur children on to greater heights of aggression, as we discuss further in a later chapter. In "firing" a toy gun, for example, children may lose sight of the story line of the pretend play and end up hurting one another through their aggression (Carlsson-Paige & Levin, 1990; Katch, 2001; Levin, 2003a; Levin & Carlsson-Paige, 2006). Children who are unduly repetitive in their imitation of characters' dialogue and scripts gleaned from television, movies, and video games need intervention from teachers to expand on their limited repertoires to more complex representations of characters, settings, and plots. Teachers struggle with alternatives to outright censorship to help children make sense of frightening and confusing images seen in the media, such as themes of bullying and violence that occur in the following example of Leo and Jeremy playing out an episode from the television series *Survivor:*

> Seven-year-old Jeremy and 6-year-old Leo are playing in the outdoor lawn area of their elementary school playground. "I'll make you eat these worms!" snarls Jeremy, attempting to stuff a handful of leaves and wood shavings into Leo's mouth. When Leo protests, Jeremy counters, "But that's how your team can win! You want us to win, don't you?" ∅

What can teachers do to mitigate the themes of violence in their classrooms? In what situations might children be playing out confusing and disturbing images from their own lives, rather than imitating scripts from television, movies, or even video games? These and other questions regarding violence and play have surfaced in our work with teachers, children, and families. Strategies to deal with violent play are discussed next.

Diffusing Violence in Play

When does the discharge of frightening feelings become obsessive? How can teachers and families work together to diffuse violence in children's play?

Observe Play Carefully   Many teachers report that they can follow the plot of the latest violent movies or the morning's TV cartoon shows by observing children's play. However, teachers can help children use the characters, play themes, and props derived from popular media in constructive ways.

Children engage in complex fantasy play that may involve danger and rescue themes.

By keeping informed about popular cartoons, videos, films, and television series, as well as toys that may be popular in the peer culture of the classroom, teachers are better able to understand the play they observe. Through close scrutiny of children's play, teachers can determine if some children are "stuck" in repetitive imitations of what they have viewed. Teachers may then orchestrate play to enable children to expand character roles, elaborate story lines, and transform themes (Carlsson-Paige & Levin, 1998; Levin, 2003b; Levin & Carlsson-Paige, 2006).

Look Beneath the Surface of Play   When teachers are sensitive to the underlying themes of play, they may suggest nonviolent alternatives that appeal to children. Good guy/bad guy play encompasses themes like danger and rescue, which are central to children's socioemotional development (Corsaro, 2003, 2011; Katch, 2001; Levin, 2006; Paley, 1990; Perry, 2011). Once the theme is identified, teachers may introduce literature with new characters and plots that elaborate on these themes in new ways.

In a preschool directed by one of the authors, teachers and parents embarked on an experiment to diminish the frequency of television-limited play that imitated cartoon violence. Noting that themes of good and evil, life and death, and lost and found dominated much of this play, the teachers and parents read various versions of *Peter Pan* and helped the children create and act out their interpretations of the characters and events in their play. Later in the year, *The Wizard of Oz* and *Peter and the Wolf* and other literary works were explored in similar ways. Children still used pretend weapons and fought and chased adversaries, but their repertoire of characters and actions for these themes was expanded. For example, after the *Peter Pan* theme was explored, one child noted that "turning bad guys into toads or rocks was better because if you shot them, they just came alive again." ☏

Set Limits   Teachers may also keep children "safe" by setting limits. For some children, the appeal of war play or media-derived play is especially irresistible when it is violent in nature. Because the script for war play or media play is usually simple and well known, children with limited social skills or language abilities are often drawn into the vortex. As the cast of the play grows, the level of aggression can get out of the children's control. By setting limits and carefully monitoring this play, teachers can help ensure that at-risk children are protected. It is also important for teachers to understand the circumstances in children's personal lives that might be leading to an overabundance of this type of play.

Several teachers we know set these limits by banning real-looking weapons from their schools while acknowledging children's need to do battle with imaginary ones. In this way, they avoid the phenomenon of children imitating action from television with single-use weapon toys. Other teachers make a point of talking to children about alternatives for their play plots when aggressive play gets out of control, perhaps suggesting strategies for tricking bad guys instead of shooting them. The following is one teacher's pragmatic approach to managing the problem of guns in her play yard:

> Out of concern for the lack of peacefulness in the play yard, the teacher asked the children at circle time to help her make a set of rules about gunplay, as she was worried because some children often wound up getting hurt. The teacher said she was also getting tired of trying to stop the gunplay and settle arguments all the time. She asked the children to vote on how many liked to have pretend shooting in the play yard. Most children, except for a small group of boys, voted against gunplay. The teacher wondered if it would be fair to those who wanted to engage in pretend gunplay to be prohibited from it. She thought perhaps they could work out some rules that would make others feel safe about people who wanted to pretend to use guns. She suggested that there be a place in the yard where people who wanted to pretend with guns could go and play in that way. A second rule would be that only people who consented to play this way could go there. A third rule was gun players could not point their guns at people who didn't want to play. They had to ask permission from the targeted person.
>
> The group then went on to discuss the best place for the gun-toting players. The large climber did not seem to be the fair choice because too many non–gun players wanted to use the climber for other games. The sand pit likewise. And the sand kitchen was obviously not a good place. Finally, it was

decided to move the blocks from under the semishelter to another location and designate this space with traffic cones as the gun players' area. The area had a small carpet that also helped define its area.

In using this strategy, the teacher did not prohibit gunplay directly, but instead limited its range to a space where it could be monitored effectively. If gun players left the pretend gunplay area and started shooting at someone who had not elected to play in this way, the teacher could ask the targeted child if he or she had chosen to be part of the gunplay game. If the targeted child said no—and usually did—the logic of pointing out the lack of agreement was obvious to all. If the child said yes, he or she would be directed to the gunplay area. In this way the teacher had the support of the group in limiting gunplay. After pursuing this approach for a week or so, the gun players became more and more isolated, and their numbers diminished greatly. Gunplay began to be less and less interesting as the majority of the children now had the space to peacefully pursue other more elaborate themes without interruption from gun players. ✆

A strategy such as this requires some courage on the part of the teacher, and watchful monitoring without giving gun players too much attention requires sensitivity. For those children who persist in gunplay, the teacher might work one on one with them to create drawings of their guns for a display of kinds of weaponry. This could lead to doing research on ancient weaponry or the invention of gunpowder and so on. While drawing with the gun players, she could learn more about the meaning that this play had for each child.

Addressing Exclusion—Supporting Inclusion

One compelling question that intersects with some of the thinking regarding violence in schools is the relationship of violence to exclusion, both for the child who is excluded and for those who are sought as play partners. Katch (2001) addresses these issues with her powerful insights into the hearts and minds of children whose violent imagery in play both attracts and repels others. Both the rejected children who retaliate with violence and the popular children who strike out in frustration at being continually solicited to play have feelings with similar roots.

Paley (1992) wrote eloquently on the problem, examining the tradition of early childhood educators to accept children's often painful rejection of one another in play as a natural part of growing up. In implementing a "You can't say you can't play" rule in her own classroom, she brought the issues of inclusion and exclusion and their accompanying social and emotional consequences to the forefront of the debate.

Building a Peaceful Classroom

In the preceding sections we focused on the multiple ways that teachers can respond to children's violent play, both directly and indirectly. We conclude this chapter by going beyond strategies for violence prevention to integrated strategies for peace promotion. Peace promotion is central to our ideas of a play-centered curriculum.

> In Dorothy and Grace's preschool classroom, the children began to consider remedies to the sadness of Sophie, the mother pig, on losing her children. They decided to paint a mural and to learn "Old MacDonald Had a Farm" on the bells. After weeks of mural construction and practice, the children went back to the farm to present Sophie with the mural and play their bell concert for her. ✆

In the classroom, just as at the international level, peace is more than the absence of violence. Violence is not only direct and clearly visible, but also can be insidious at a structural level. At the structural level, violence refers to inequalities—for example, racism, sexism, religion, nationality, and inequalities based on economic class—in schools, communities, and societies that disadvantage some and privilege others (Christie, 2011; Christie, Wagner, & Winter, 2001).

Peace educators and psychologists make the useful distinction between a negative peace and a positive peace. Teachers have seen many K–12 curricula that are promoted as violence-prevention programs, focusing on negative peace (i.e., stopping violence). Conflicts exist, but they are resolved or managed nonviolently.

A positive peace is marked not only by the absence of violence, but also by equity and opportunities to enhance growth for all. Peace education is truly an "umbrella concept" (Gustafson, 2000). Reviews of early education for peace and nonviolence theory, research, and practice show that traditional early childhood education has always been multifaceted in attempts to foster peaceful classrooms (Van Hoorn & McHargue, 1999).

In *Teaching Young Children in Violent Times: Building a Peaceable Classroom,* Levin (2003b) provided an example of a multifaceted play-based approach. She discussed and illustrated how teachers can build community, promote cooperation and peaceful conflict resolution, help children learn about and appreciate diversity, and help them deal with media-related violence as well as real violence in the news. Today, early childhood educators are finding a growing number of books and curriculum materials that describe play-centered approaches to promoting peaceful classrooms (Adams & Wittmer, 2001; Derman-Sparks & Edwards, 2010; Derman-Sparks & Ramsey, 2005; Jones & Cooper, 2006; Kreidler & Whittal, 1999).

SUMMARY

We think of this text as "play at the center of a curriculum for peace and nonviolence," for these are the values that are embedded in each chapter. Many of the classroom examples of play described in this book show children cooperating, considering the feelings of others, developing friendships, and playing with peers who speak different languages and come from diverse family configurations and ethnic backgrounds. These are all aspects of building a culture of peace.

Strategies discussed in this chapter for intervening in children's play promote children's linguistic and intellectual development as well as dispositions and behaviors inherent in a peaceful classroom: empathy, prosocial behavior, and cooperation.

The considerations for setting the stage discussed in Chapter 4 lead to more peaceful classrooms. There are subtle strategies as well as more visible ones. For example, teachers consciously set the stage so that children have sufficient space as well as materials that foster cooperation. Teachers plan a time schedule that balances activities so that children do not become overly tired, and they consider children's needs for private play. Environments welcome all children and their families and help all to learn about living in a diverse society.

How can newcomers to the United States find a place in the social group? What about children with physical limitations? When play is at the center of the curriculum, children are more autonomous and have multiple opportunities to develop social problem-solving abilities and to take the perspective of others.

Early childhood programs that promote peace are characterized by a pervasive culture marked by inclusiveness, empowerment of all, nonviolent conflict resolution, cooperation, and empathy. We firmly believe that the play-centered curriculum leads to a peaceful classroom and nurtures peaceful children.

- **Play and Scaffolding.** The impact of teacher's interventions is an important aspect of scaffolding. Various environmental elements scaffold for certain types of play; the housekeeping corner supports both constructive and dramatic play and promotes the use of cooperative language. Various accessories such as seriated cups, funnels, and pitchers in a water table suggest extensions for water play. Multiples of favored items assure children there is "one for them." Teachers must consider not only the arrangement of the physical environment, but also the ways they intervene (or do not intervene) as integral elements of scaffolding. When teachers take over too much of the talk at project or activity centers they hamper children's spontaneous language use.

- **Spontaneous, Guided, and Directed Play.** The continuum of play orchestration strategies, ranging from indirect to direct, provides a guide to teachers' decision making about how and when to intervene in children's play. It offers four options for indirect strategies, starting with setting the stage and continues with options for guided play that are on a continuum from the least direct role of Artist Apprentice to the most direct role as play tutor.

- **Choosing a Strategy.** In entering and exiting children's play, timing is everything and is contingent on teachers' careful observation of themes, characters, plot, and language used by children to negotiate their play scenarios. The matchmaking and tutoring roles offer primary avenues for orchestrating play with children with special needs.

- **Play and the Culture of School.** The "school culture" represents commonly accepted norms of behavior, and children's peer culture can be a complement or an alternative to it. Three types of play commonly occur in school settings: instrumental play, recreational play, and illicit play. Two of the three types of play are sanctioned by the school culture. They are instrumental play (such as blocks, teacher-initiated games with rules, and dramatic play) and recreational play (such as playground or outdoor play). Illicit play is not sanctioned by the teacher and usually is engaged in behind the teacher's back or as a direct challenge to the teacher's authority. Some forms of illicit play represent a challenge and pose a dilemma for teachers and is manifested in the controversy over the use of toy or imaginary guns or weapons in fantasy play.

■ **Responding to Violent Play.** Pretend weapons and war play are issues that have plagued the classroom culture for decades. It is important for teachers to consider the sources of such play and the motives behind it as they develop a strategy for intervening. Teachers and families may need to work together to diffuse violence in play. Three important issues are involved, first teachers need to observe play carefully to become aware of the source of the play fantasy. Looking below the surface may enable teachers to suggest nonviolent alternatives incorporating exciting elements such as danger and rescue that appeal to children. Teachers may set limits and monitor such play to be sure that at-risk children are protected. In building a peaceful classroom, teachers may also wish to develop strategies that address the issue of inclusion and exclusion in the classroom culture—who gets to play and who does not.

APPLYING YOUR KNOWLEDGE

1. Discuss how observations of play and knowledge of children's development enable teachers to scaffold play in meaningful and relevant ways.
    a. Create a hypothetical example or use an actual observation to illustrate why waiting and watching before deciding to intervene or scaffold children's play is important.
    b. Consider how this enabled scaffolding is thematically relevant.
    c. Draw a map of the activity centers in either your own or another classroom and indicate the kinds of play you expect to see at the various sites. Consider the effect of adjacent activity centers on one another. Consider the developmental level of anticipated play. Is there a balance between areas that support the play of younger versus older children?
2. Describe how the range of guided play strategies listed in the continuum of play orchestration strategies provides examples of how teachers can "learn to dance" with children as they facilitate play.
    a. List one strategy for each of the nine guided play interventions that best illustrates its approach.
    b. Draw a table like the one on page 112 using a standard taken from the Common Core Curriculum for either mathematics or literacy. Create a

mini-curriculum activity for a kindergarten class that involves (a) spontaneous play, (b) guided play, and (c) directed play.

3. Explain how observations of children's play enhance teachers' ability to effectively time and/or shift their strategies.
   a. Observe play behavior in a preschool or primary-grade setting. Analyze your observation and answer the following questions: How did children initiate play? How did children enter and exit play? How did they negotiate roles? How did adults support (or not support) play?
   b. What did you learn through your observation about how teachers can more effectively scaffold play?

5. Identify some differences between the peer culture and the school culture.
   a. Conduct several play observations in your own or another classroom. Identify features of the play you observe that illustrate the three types of play most commonly seen in school settings. In what ways did your play observations reveal the differences between the school culture and the peer culture?

6. Discuss the issues of exclusion and inclusion and their effect on the building of a peaceful classroom.
   a. Conduct three 20-minute observations of a preschool or primary-grade play yard. Analyze your observation to identify examples of exclusion and inclusion. Were teachers aware of exclusion? If so, how did they respond?
   b. Review Vivian Paley's book *You Can't Say You Can't Play*. How effective do you think this strategy would be in reducing exclusion in your school or one you have observed?

CHAPTER 6

Play as a Tool for Assessment

LEARNING OUTCOMES

- Discuss several key features of assessments of children's play and explain what is meant by the following terms: performance-based assessments, age-appropriate development, and individually appropriate development.

- Examine the purposes of assessment that are appropriate for early childhood education programs and the risks of high-stakes assessments.

- Discuss the benefits of using play-centered assessments with children from diverse families and backgrounds.

- Discuss the benefits of using play-centered assessments with children with special needs.

- Discuss how play-centered programs provide teachers with numerous opportunities to carry out authentic assessments of both age-appropriate and individual development.

- Explain why play can inform assessment and why it enhances the reliability and validity of assessments.

- Discuss several principles for implementing play-centered assessments.

- Discuss strategies teachers can use to organize and document information about young children's play.

- Describe how a teacher might use play-centered assessments to advocate for a play-centered curriculum.

In Kathy's kindergarten classroom, four children have set up a "bank." They have stacked two rows of large hollow wooden blocks to form a counter and built chairs for themselves out of small blocks. Additional smaller blocks on the countertop form windows and have the "teller's" name taped to each. Pat, an adult visitor to the classroom, walks up to a teller's window. Shawna, the teller, asks Pat if she brought her bank book. When Pat responds "No, I don't have one," Shawna directs Pat to the basket of small blank paper books that Kathy makes available in the classroom. "Write your name on it," Shawna tells Pat, and Pat prints her name on the front. "P-a-t," Shawna says as she touches each letter, and then remarks that her grandmother's name is Pat too. "Does she spell it like this?" Pat asks. "I don't know," replies Shawna, "I'll ask her."

Returning to her place behind the bank counter, Shawna takes the bank book and opens it to the first page. She carefully writes "CRTO," and then asks Pat how much money she wants. Pat says, "Fifty dollars." "I can't count that much, you know," says Shawna, "How about 10?" Pat agrees, and Shawna takes out a piece of 8×11 white paper, folds it in half and makes a series of horizontal cuts. She then cuts the paper down the middle and counts out 10 pieces of paper. She writes a "1" on each "bill" and counts them out carefully on the counter in front of Pat. "Here you go," Shawna says as she uses a rubber date stamp and a stamp pad to stamp the bank book. "Just come back when you run outta dollars." ✆

Later that day Kathy, the teacher, discusses the children's dramatic and constructive play with Pat, who teaches kindergarten in a neighboring school. They talk about how Shawna's play yields information about her social and emotional development and developing academic concepts and skills in literacy, mathematics, and social studies. More generally, they share examples of the ways in which their observations of children's play throughout the year give them deeper insights into children's interests, imagination, and dispositions, and how children's play reflects their experiences in their families and communities.

FEATURES OF ASSESSMENT OF CHILDREN'S PLAY

In the following discussion, notice the various ways that the teacher assesses the children's play, development, and learning.

Kathy has taken digital photographs of the bank in its various stages of construction over several days in order to assess "play as play." Both Pat and Kathy are impressed with the length of time the children have been engaged in play as well as the complexity of the block representation of the bank environment. Kathy's observational records indicate that the children who built the structure discussed and negotiated their experiences of how banks look, drawing on their personal experiences and the knowledge they bring to school. Their constructive play required spatial reasoning, including part–whole relationships, to select blocks for the counter and chairs, small blocks for the name plaques, and long rectangular blocks for the teller's windows. Kathy's notes indicate that Shawna was one of the children who persisted with this child-initiated project over several days' time while two other children lost interest after the first day. Shawna and her "new" best friend Emily continued the project and directed the creation of the tellers' roles that they were eager to play.

The tellers have each written their names and fastened them to the "name plaques," using a social form of literacy they have observed in banks and, at the same time, practicing their own renditions of their names. Kathy and Pat discuss the conversation about Pat's name and how Shawna spontaneously identified each letter. "Shawna is still working on the idea that some names are spelled the same way every time—probably because not all the adults who work in this classroom know how to spell her version of 'Shawna,'" Kathy informs Pat.

Another example of how Shawna is working on the consistency of letters to spell words is shown in her careful writing of "CRTO" in the bank book. There was quite a bit of negotiation when the bank "opened" before the children agreed on "the thing you hafta write in the book." Kathy points out that Emily's mother works in a bank and had apparently used the term "credit to" in talking about accounts. Emily was quite emphatic that this was the proper term and used her invented spelling concepts to create the notation "CRTO." The date stamp is another form of social literacy that children have observed in the real world. Kathy explains that she tried to support the children's play in an indirect, subtle way by moving the familiar rubber date stamp from the math center to a shelf of accessories near the emerging bank construction.

> "Shawna's awareness of the limitations of her counting amazed me," continues Pat. "I thought of offering to help her count to 50 and then realized she had already come up with her own, better alternative. I also wondered how she learned to cut paper that way." ✂

Kathy explains that weeks earlier they had experimented with paper folding and cutting to make shapes for valentines. Shawna was replaying this skill and applying it in a new situation. Kathy and Pat agree that Shawna's writing of a "1" on each bill and then counting them out carefully for the customer shows Shawna's counting skills. It also informally contributes to the concept of place value she will construct in the future.

Kathy's careful observations of this play sequence help her understand and appreciate Shawna's particular strengths and ways of thinking about the world. Indeed, play illuminates the development of each child. It allows teachers to notice and appreciate the interests and values that a child brings from home and the special kind of intelligence that he or she may use to express thoughts and feelings. Play allows us to see the cognitive as well as emotional aspects of every child's development and the ways in which they are interconnected.

Using Assessments of Children's Play as an Integrated Approach to Assessment

Play is a natural "piece" of the assessment pie because observations of play offer perspectives on children's progress in all areas of development as they are integrated into daily experiences. Ongoing observations of spontaneous play such as the "bank" are ideal complements to assessments made during guided and directed play in which teachers have specific goals for children or the more direct measures of children's achievement in teacher-planned, subject-centered curriculum.

In play, multiple facets of children's development are revealed. The vignette from Kathy's program is an example of kindergarten children's complex pretend play and, at the same time, their masterful constructive play with blocks. Kathy's observations provide empirical evidence of Shawna's and Emily's dispositions to learn, including self-regulation, and evidence that their development is age appropriate for 5- and 6-year-olds in the areas of emerging literacy and mathematics.

Gullo (2006) points out that when kindergarten teachers provide time and materials for children to engage in spontaneous play, teachers have "a unique opportunity to develop and engage in a regular, ongoing routine of informal assessment that looks at children's learning and development in multiple developmental ways in multiple contexts" (p. 142). Kathy's assessments of the children include written observations, photos, portfolios with samples of student work over time, developmental charts, and checklists that she organizes and updates regularly.

Play provides opportunities for **performance-based assessments** because they provide data on children's behaviors in engaging, familiar activities that take place in familiar environments. As the vignette from Kathy's kindergarten class shows, performance assessments can involve complex and ongoing measures that focus on children's individual styles and pace of learning. We see how assessments of play serve as means of learning and reflection for students when Shawna declares "I can't count that much, you know." Children need to develop this ability to reflect independently on their own developing concepts and take responsibility for their own learning. Such self-assessment is critical not only throughout the early years but throughout the life span.

Play is the window to view both **age-appropriate development** and **individually appropriate development**. In play, teachers can discern whether children's understandings of concepts fall within the range expected of a given age group. They may determine, for example, when some children in their group exhibit complex sociodramatic play. They consider how they might support other children by turning to play orchestration strategies, always beginning by trying less direct strategies.

Comprehensive assessments naturally include social–moral development in addition to the more traditional questions of cognition and attitudes toward learning. In a society that is increasingly diverse in its values and perspectives, it is essential that children develop the ability to understand the perspective of others, to communicate with people from other backgrounds, and to negotiate differences of opinions and behaviors. Assessments of play help educators shift their thinking to see social–moral development as having the same priority as cognition. Children's play provides a window to document progress and plan curriculum in these areas (e.g., DeVries & Zan, 2012; Leong & Bodrova, 2012; Levin, 2003b).

Communicating with Parents about Play and Assessment   Play is a particularly valuable tool that teachers use in communicating with families about their child's progress. Play illustrates the individual flavor of their child's expressions and humor, for example, how Shawna cheerily called to her customer, "Just come back when you run outta dollars." Parents appreciate hearing teachers' discussions of play observations and explanations of how their child is learning and developing through play.

Kathy also looks for ways in which children's play reflects their experiences at home, their styles of interaction, and the ways they represent ideas (Derman-Sparks & Edwards, 2010; Espinosa, 2010; Göncü, Jain, & Tuermer, 2007; Nieto, 2012). The trusting, reciprocal relationship that Kathy has established with Shawna's mother is an example of mutuality that allows both of them to support Shawna's development (Caspe, Seltzer, Kennedy, Cappio, & DeLorenzo, 2013; Copple & Bredekamp, 2009).

Kathy and Shawna's mother speculate that some of her interest in block building and her ability to assert herself with the boys in the classroom may come from her family experience as a younger sister living with two older teenage brothers. Kathy continues, "As a much younger sibling, her situation is somewhat similar to that of an only child in the family—Shawna seems to need a lot of time to play by herself. Although she has Emily and one other blossoming friendship in the room, she often will go to the library corner or the table toys and play alone. I also think her home situation has fostered her ability to assert herself with adults and talk easily with them. She often includes parents who visit the classroom in her play, just as she did with you today."

EXAMINING THE PURPOSES OF ASSESSMENT

Assessment of children's progress is a complicated and multifaceted issue in early childhood education. The overarching goal of assessment is to inform educators' professional judgment about curriculum to support the development of all children and benefit their lives.

Nearly two decades ago the National Early Childhood Assessment Panel, a policy group composed of respected early childhood educators, identified four major purposes of assessment for young children (Shepard, Kagan, & Wurtz, 1998a):

- Inform the teaching–learning process for children and their teachers.
- Identify children in need of special education services.
- Inform program evaluation and staff development.
- Focus on accountability for students, teachers, and schools.

The first three purposes are widely recognized as critical to quality programs for all young children (e.g., Copple & Bredekamp, 2009). These purposes provide a rationale and context for assessment in the play-centered curriculum. All children benefit when programs address their needs, abilities, and interests. The first two purposes focus on improving the teaching–learning process in the play-centered curriculum. The third purpose, serving program evaluation and staff development needs, also links to play, as does ongoing and purposeful teacher–family communications.

It is improbable that the way that accountability is being formulated will lead to the intended reforms. In an opinion piece in the *Washington Post*, Meisels, a leading scholar in the area of assessment, writes that though he strongly supports the development of goals and expectations for teaching, he does not support Common Core State Standards for K–2 that have set "sky high" expectations for young children with the probable result that many will be labeled "failures." Meisels explains that a major problem is that standards are not linked to assessments and curriculum. "If we have only standards, it's like having a list of destinations without a map" (Meisels, 2011). From Meisels's point of view, we are traveling down a road in which the curriculum and assessment measures are becoming more constrictive.

Indeed, accountability is often implemented by "high stakes standardized testing." These tests may appeal to some elected officials and school districts because they are simple to mandate, quickly implemented, and comparatively inexpensive (Miller, Linn, & Gronlund, 2013).

High-stakes testing is not a good fit for children ages 3 to 8, and it is never appropriate for early childhood play-centered curriculum and assessment. In fact, the National Early Childhood Assessment Panel recommended that the standardized tests that characterize such high-stakes assessment be postponed, preferably until fourth grade (Shepard et al., 1998a).

The NAEYC/NAECS/SDE position statement *Early Learning Standards: Creating the Conditions for Success* (2002) emphasizes, "Assessment and accountability systems should be used to improve practices and services, and should not be used to rank, sort, or penalize young children" (p. 7). Critical questions are raised regarding the implementation of high-stakes assessments (Seefeldt, 2005; Wien, 2004; Wortham, 2012). High-stakes standardized tests are encouraged by the No Child Left Behind Act of 2001 and, more recently, the funds for Race to the Top.

How have the results of high-stakes standardized assessments impacted children, families, teachers, and schools? Have young children benefitted? Some early childhood educators, family members, and community and professional organizations point out that high-stakes standardized assessments are, in fact, being used to rank and penalize young children (e.g., Meisels, 2011; Ravitch, 2010). Merrill, a second-grade teacher, expresses it this way:

> In my school, most of us are concerned that results from the mandated tests don't accurately reflect most of our students' capabilities. I know people are aware of how this problem impacts some of my students, including students identified with special needs and students who are dual language learners. But what about Madison and Amparo, who seem to have special needs but don't quite meet the criteria to get special services? . . . And

Play offers perspectives on children's progress in all areas of development.

probably another quarter of my class have stressful personal situations that I'm sure affect how they do on these tests. What about the student in my class whose mother has been unemployed for months? Or the one whose parents are separating? Or the girl who just transferred into my class because she was just placed with a new foster family? The whole school is gearing up for tests next month. I ask myself, "How can I add more stress to these kids' lives?" ✇

PLAY AND ASSESSMENT OF CHILDREN FROM DIVERSE CULTURES AND BACKGROUNDS

There is particular concern that assessment of children from diverse backgrounds remains fraught with bias. In too many instances assessments lead to overidentification and misdiagnosis of children from diverse cultures, languages, and backgrounds as having language or other developmental delays (Wortham, 2012).

Gullo is the author of numerous articles about the assessment of young children. He emphasizes that "(t)o obtain valid and reliable results, assessments must be free from linguistic or cultural biases. Assessment instruments and procedures must be chosen with care" (Gullo, 2006, p. 144).

The NAEYC's position statement "Screening and Assessment of Young English-Language Learners" (2005a) emphasizes that with all children the central purpose of assessment is to foster children's development and learning—that is, assessments need to benefit the child. The NAEYC's recommendations emphasize the need for educators and families to work closely together whenever assessments are conducted and interpreted, and ensure that results are implemented. Reciprocal and mutually valued partnerships of educators and families are needed.

> Pamela and Ben are kindergarten teachers in a rural school district that serves many dual language learners. The following interviews show how their play is an opportunity for formative assessment that leads to insightful curriculum decisions that are part of their conversations with parents.
>
> "We do more small-group directed play early in the day," explains Ben. "We focus on specific skills such as phonemic awareness using rhymes and songs, and letter and numeral formation using mazes and patterns, but we have 60 minutes of play time as well. Then the children are free to make choices about their learning, and we have many opportunities for block building, cooking, painting, clay, puppetry, and dramatic play that have always been the 'bread and butter' of good kindergarten programs. We also offer projects such as our Bubble Unit that integrate social studies, science, math, literacy, and the arts."
>
> Pam continues, "The combination of free-flowing play and small-group teaching and assessment gives us both very focused and spontaneous information about each child. It's a critical time of the day for our students who are dual language learners to develop both receptive and expressive language.

I also think kids will take more risks when they are creating and solving their own problems in play. For example, Gary loved our bubbles project. His enthusiasm inspired him to measure his bubbles every day for a week at home as well as school and to record their widths. A month ago he out and out refused to try to write any numerals—context is everything!" ✆

Nieto (2012) reminds us that childhood has always been a tough time for many children from diverse ethnic minority backgrounds and that, recently, childhood has become even more difficult because of inequities and discrimination in schools and communities. Fair assessment practices can begin with educators. How well do we know our students and their families? Nieto recommends that teachers begin with the simple but powerful act of learning each child's name and how to pronounce it. She urges educators to develop deeper relationships with families by taking the time to make home visits and participate in community events.

Nieto (2012) and Derman-Sparks and Edwards (2010) remind all of us that recognizing and confronting our own biases and stereotypes are lifelong processes. Not one of us is free from stereotypes. Based on their empirical research, Göncü, Jain, and Tuermer (2007) point out that a teacher's observations and interpretations are never bias free, but instead reflect the teacher's culture and class. Educators need to be self-reflective so that they do not use their power or status as a way to prove that theirs is the correct interpretation.

Hong (2011) draws on her classroom experiences to discuss education for dual language learners as a social justice issue. Hong personalizes the need for reflection and importance of teacher–parent partnerships by sharing her own experience as a parent of a toddler who is bilingual.

Hong's son speaks to his *Hami* (grandmother) and *Habi* (grandfather) in Korean. He speaks to his parents in English. Hong writes that he is a "confident language user, knowing when to code-switch easily" (p. 132). After he started school, his teacher (who didn't speak Korean) reported that he was making good progress in learning to speak English. Hong was shocked. Returning home, she asked her son about how he talked to his teacher. He told her that he spoke with his teacher exactly the same way he spoke in Korean with his *Hami* and *Habi*. When she asked why he didn't just talk to his teacher the same way he talked to her in English, he simply replied, "Because I didn't want to" (p. 132). ✆

Families and their young children differ in the challenges they face at home, in communities, and at school relating to poverty, language, immigration status, socioeconomic status, parental incarceration, and parental deployment in military service. For example, since 2001, almost 1 million fathers and mothers in the United States have been deployed in Iraq and Afghanistan. Many parents of young children have been killed, and many more have returned home injured. About 30% of returned combatants are in need of mental health services (Sammons & Batten, 2008).

The psychological effects of parental deployment on children are evident throughout the deployment cycle—predeployment, first month of deployment, sustained period of deployment, last month of deployment, and postdeployment/ reunion with family (see Pincus, Christensen, & Adler, 2005). As of 2008, approximately 20% of parents had been deployed at least two times, and about half of those had been deployed three or more times (Glod, 2008). In addition to assistance from the military, military families have organized self-support organizations that offer resource materials and advice. Some have written about the challenges they face.

In many instances, teachers are unaware that a child's parent has been deployed. The feature below, *Family Diversity: Young Children with Parents Deployed in Military Combat*, describes how Christina and Mya's mother Karen work together to support Mya at a time when her father is returning from Afghanistan.

FAMILY DIVERSITY

Young Children with Parents Deployed in Military Combat

All during April, 3-year-old Mya talks to her peers and teachers about how excited she is that her father is coming home. She shows everybody photos of her daddy. She draws pictures that show her, her mom, and her baby brother Sam next to a very large daddy figure covered in hearts. Her teacher Christina and her mother Karen talk almost daily.

Christina shares her delight in Mya's happy anticipation. Karen, however, cautions her that the last postdeployment time had not gone smoothly. She explains that what she and her family experienced is pretty common. She feels sad that she and Mya's father, Ron, bickered so frequently. She describes Mya's behavior: "At home, Mya swung from being withdrawn to being very clingy. Her teacher told me that Mya seemed angry and aggressive at school." She tells Christina that she is feeling anxious about the upcoming weeks and is particularly concerned about Mya's behavior.

The next day, Karen gives Christina copies of some materials written by military families and psychologists, including *The "So Far" Guide for Helping Children and Youth Cope with the Deployment and Return of a Parent in the National Guard* (Levin, Daynard, & Dexter, 2008). She also gives Christina a newspaper article written by the mother of a toddler, "One Husband, Two Kids, Three Deployments" by Seligman (2009), and explains that it pretty much tells Mya's story, too.

This is a whole new topic for Christina. She feels relieved that Karen thinks that their relationship is solid enough to share her concerns and alert her to watch Mya's behavior more closely. She feels awkward that she knows so little and is grateful for Karen's knowledge about the common ways that young children and their whole family may respond during deployment and reunions. Christina searches online using the key words "young" "children" "deployed parents" and "war" and finds several resources from educational and psychological organizations, which she shares with Karen.

At Karen's urging, they arrange for a school counselor to observe Mya twice and meet with the two of them prior to her dad's return. They will do more observations and meet again soon after her husband comes home. In the meantime, the school counselor and school psychologists will contact psychologists with more experience and expertise.

Now, after more than a decade of war, there are few empirical studies on the effects of parental deployment on U.S. young children's well-being (Van Hoorn & Levin, 2011). Tragically, the psychological and educational services provided on military bases are often unavailable to families living off the base on when the parent deployed is in the National Guard or Reserves.

PLAY AND ASSESSMENTS OF CHILDREN WITH SPECIAL NEEDS

Another purpose of assessment in programs for young children is identification and intervention for young children with disabilities. Acknowledgment of the limitations of many assessment instruments has led to an increased implementation of transdisciplinary, play-centered assessments in early childhood special education programs (see Kelly-Vance & Ryalls, 2005; Uren & Stagnitti, 2009). Assessments of children's play provide valuable information regarding all children's development and practical information on functional abilities that teachers find essential to making appropriate accommodations.

Eva is a kindergartner with an orthopedic disability. She has just returned to school after an operation to increase her stability. She will be using a wheelchair for the next few months. Several days prior to her return, Eva's teacher, Melinda, met with Eva, her mother and aunt, the school's special education specialist, as well as Eva's physical therapist (PT) and occupational therapist (OT), to make sure that accommodations were in place for a smooth transition back to the classroom.

Eva was excited for her PT and OT to meet her teacher and see her classroom. As she wheeled around the room, her mother emphasized to Melinda that Eva had become quite skilled: "She's pretty independent and very social. It's important that we encourage her and stand back as much as possible. That's really important to us." As Eva navigated easily between the tables, the occupational therapist pointed out accommodations that needed to be made. Several accommodations were one-time fixes, such as adjusting the height of several tables. Others involved ongoing checks, like making sure that pathways remained uncluttered. When Melinda discussed the varied activities, it became clear to everyone that although the tables were positioned to accommodate the wheelchair, there were not enough table blocks and not enough space around the easels.

Eva's aunt asked about time outdoors. Eva echoed her question; she missed playing outside with her friends. When they all went outside, Eva pointed with delight at the ramps. How welcoming! They'd already been thinking about her.

The special education specialist assured them that she would be there for Eva's first morning back. Next week, after Eva's first few days and ongoing observations, they would meet to identify goals and formulate a detailed plan. ✑

ASSESSING AGE-APPROPRIATE AND INDIVIDUALLY APPROPRIATE DEVELOPMENT

In a play-centered curriculum there are ongoing, multiple, and systematic ways of observing and assessing children's play to obtain empirical information on their age-appropriate development and highlight their individual strengths, competencies, and needs. The vignette of Kathy's kindergarten class illustrates how teachers carry out purposeful, systematic assessments that provide important information needed to benefit the development and learning of individual children, groups of children, and the class as a whole. Kathy employs **age-appropriate assessments** because they are carried out and interpreted in ways consistent with developmental theory, research, and practice regarding the characteristics and abilities of children of that age. Kathy also uses **individually appropriate assessments** because they are responsive to the child's culture, language, and family background and provide useful information on children's personal qualities such as talents, special needs, temperament, and interests. The National Association for the Education of Young Children recommends such practices as "sound assessment that is developmentally appropriate for children from birth through the primary grades" (Copple & Bredekamp, 2009, p. 22).

Kathy uses assessments that are "authentic" because both the content and the methods of collecting data on children's progress align with widely held expectations about the development of kindergarten children. **Authentic assessments** include the teacher's knowledge of the typical stages of development for children in a given age range, and the assessment process itself promotes learning and development (Shepard, Kagan, & Wurtz, 1998b). The criteria of authenticity in both content and assessment strategies is a key element in ascertaining the developmental appropriateness of assessment for children in preschool and primary grades (Copple & Bredekamp, 2009; Hyson, 2008; National Association for the Education of Young Children & National Association of Early Childhood Specialists in State Departments of Education, 1991).

Assessing Development of Concepts and Skills

For example, Kathy and Pat examined Shawna's assessment portfolio, which contained handwritten observational records of Shawna's spontaneous and guided play since the first week of school. They also compared Shawna's rendition of her name with well-formed letters and adequate spacing in March to the shakily written backwards "s" followed by a series of curved lines that Kathy had placed in Shawna's portfolio in early October.

Pat and Kathy looked at Shawna's early attempts at spelling words other than her name, beginning with the pictures and letters on a shopping list made in the playhouse in November, and then random letters in December and January. Her most recent writing, like the "CRTO" (Credit to) at the bank, showed attempts to use some beginning and ending consonant sounds. "I lk wtrmln" (I like watermelon) is Shawna's recent contribution to a class book about favorite letters of the alphabet.

TABLE 6.1   Record of Mathematics Concepts and Skills for Kathy's Kindergarten Class

Common Core State Standards	Play	Dates	Contexts
Know number names and count sequence.	S. and E. press leaf patterns into the sand, counting to 10 and laughing as they check results.	9/27	Outdoors—sand area
Count to tell the number of objects.	Sets table for stuffed animals, counts 1 to 4 to place cups and napkins.	11/6	Housekeeping area—play alone
Compare numbers	"I need more blocks; you have too many."	12/4	Block area—negotiates with boys; "Girls need blocks too!"
Understand addition	"I need 2 more to make 10 dollars."	3/27	Pretend bank—customer role

In the area of geometric and spatial reasoning, Kathy collected photos of Shawna's block structures, some built along with peers and others individually. Kathy also showed Pat an observation form on which she records anecdotal records of children's spontaneous and guided play (Table 6.1) and links them to the state academic standards for kindergarten.

Kathy also records notes from guided and directed play, as in this example from earlier months of the school year when she informally questioned Shawna regarding her understanding of number concepts:

> In the playhouse, Shawna was setting the table for "breakfast" for four stuffed animals. She had each animal sitting in a chair at the table and was passing out napkins. She took the napkins one at a time from the playhouse cupboard and placed each at an animal's place, walking across the playhouse each time. She went through the same process with spoons and cups until each diner had a place setting. After discussing Shawna's breakfast guests and the menu with her, Kathy asked Shawna how many of each—napkins, spoons, and cups—there were. Shawna counted each set aloud, "1-2-3-4." "Four and four and four," she said, smiling, "for my four friends." Kathy noted Shawna's competence with number concepts, including one-to-one correspondence in counting to four on the record of mathematics skills. ⌀

Later, in January, Kathy's observational records showed that Shawna had set the table for her snack group of six children. She had carefully counted the number of places aloud, then gathered sets of six napkins and six cups and placed one of each at each setting.

> "Sometime in those three months Shawna learned to count and mentally match equivalent sets. In October, when I discovered that many of the children were just beginning to construct the idea of one-to-one correspondence, I planned a series of guided play activities where I set up materials like straws and cups and brushes and paint boxes. I asked children to help me set the places for children to play and found out how they were thinking about counting. My observations of play helped me plan a curriculum that was a good match for children's needs and also see how successful my ideas were." ⌀

Development of Fine Motor Skills: Scissors Kindergarten is a critical time for the development of children's motor skills. Kathy's assessments of age-appropriate development include both fine and gross motor skill competencies. She collected samples of Shawna's cutting projects over the course of the school year. She recorded that when school started Shawna's attempts at using scissors were characterized by cutting straight short lines and then tearing the paper with the scissors the rest of the way. Kathy recalled guiding Shawna's hand to show her how to close the blades of the scissors on each cut, and how Shawna and a group of friends spent most of their time for nearly 2 weeks in November making collages for people from magazines and paper scraps. After that, Shawna's cutting showed smooth edges and control over different shapes. By February, she was cutting circles and hearts with ease and her subsequent use of folding to make multiple sets of a cut shape were a great advance from her cutting skills earlier in the year.

Documenting Age-Appropriate Social Development Up to this point, Kathy and Pat had discussed the aspects of Shawna's development seen in her portfolio and through observational records that reflected Shawna's progress in "age-appropriate development" in academic subject areas. Shawna's development of such concepts as the use of letters to represent spoken language, one-to-one correspondence, and spatial representation with blocks are aspects of development Kathy focused on in her observations. Skills such as counting in conventional order, using scissors, and writing her name also fell within the range of accomplishments Kathy expects of kindergarten children. More important, Shawna's records indicated growth in all areas from September to April.

Kathy's observational records and samples of Shawna's writing also document the development of Shawna's friendship with Emily. Although Shawna still chooses to spend part of each day in solitary play, Kathy was pleased to see the development of a close friendship with Emily because Kathy finds that, typically, kindergarten children can develop at least one friendship during the year. Her district has taken the lead among others in the state by incorporating standards of social and emotional development in their systematic assessment instruments. An example of standards is shown in Table 6.2.

TABLE 6.2   Curriculum Standards for Approaches to Learning and Social and Emotional Development for Kathy's Kindergarten Class

Date	Curriculum Standard	Play Observation	Notes
9/14	Children become more comfortable with taking risks and with generating their own ideas. Children are increasingly able to persist in and complete a variety of tasks, activities, projects, and experiences.	Sam finally joins the block play. "I can make good garages!"	B
11/7	Children show growing capacity to maintain concentration despite distractions and interruptions. Children use more and more complex scenarios in play. Children develop greater self-awareness and have positive feelings about their own gender, family, race, culture, and language. Children identify a variety of feelings and moods (in themselves and others).	Maddy and Joan continue to build their sand restaurant despite the noise and disruption from the nearby chase and rescue game.	C for M; O for J
2/27	Children increase their capacity to take another's perspective. Children show progress in developing and keeping friendships. Children manage transitions and follow routines most of the time. Children use materials purposefully, safely, and respectfully and take care of their own needs with the support of adults.	"I think she's sad because her dad went on a trip," comments Doug in response to Carrie's tears.	C

B = Beginning; O = Occasionally; C = Consistently

Kathy felt that Shawna's ability to negotiate with other children seemed to have been bolstered by the bond she formed with Emily. For example, Kathy believed that part of the reason Shawna was able to confront a group of children over taking more than their share of blocks was because she felt she was speaking for her friend as well as herself. Kathy also showed Pat samples of notes with pictures and Emily's name on them that Shawna had written. She recalled that Shawna had proudly written out Emily's house number when she drew a picture of Emily's house after visiting one day after school.

Assessing Individual Development

The second aspect of assessment that is of equal importance is that of individually appropriate development (Copple & Bredekamp, 2009). As discussed, this aspect takes into account children's talents and special needs; their cultural, linguistic, and family background; and their personal qualities, such as temperament and interests. Teachers often intuitively assess children's development with regard to individual personality and temperament and consider factors related to language, culture, and family background. Unfortunately, because these factors do not appear on report cards or find their way into "developmental norms" charts, these important individual aspects of development may not become part of written records, going by the wayside in favor of more academically oriented goals.

In her assessments, Kathy makes a point of including children's **dispositions for learning**, such as taking initiative, curiosity, and cooperation. These dispositions, or approaches to learning, are now more frequently included in state and national standards regarding appropriate assessment for children ages 3 to 8. Kathy also looks for ways in which children's play reflects their experiences at home, their styles of interaction, and ways of representing their ideas (Bodrova & Leong, 2007; Espinosa, 2010; Genishi, Dyson & Russo, 2011; Hughes, 2003; Leong & Bodrova, 2012; Wortham, 2012).

Intelligence Is Multifaceted

Howard Gardner (2011a, 2011b) extended the notion of "intelligence" beyond the paper-and-pencil language and math evaluations traditionally seen in school settings. He points out that abilities in music, spatial reasoning, and other aspects of personal expression are more often seen as special "gifts," rather than being integral to an individual's intelligence. Gardner reminds us that these multiple intelligences are present to some degree in all of us. Most of us have strengths in two or three intelligences that shape the unique way in which we see the world and express ourselves. Gardner believes that educators need to pay close attention to alternative avenues of expression as well as the traditional *linguistic* and *logical–mathematical* intelligences emphasized in schools and assessed on standardized tests.

Gardner has proposed other intelligences that operate in people's daily lives. One of these is *musical intelligence.* Musical intelligence is expressed as children hum and sing to themselves. They often find patterns of sounds in language such as alliteration and are interested in musical instruments, dance, and singing in the classroom. Another intelligence is *bodily kinesthetic intelligence.* Children who readily express this intelligence are very active, expressing their thoughts and feelings through bodily movement. They may dance or leap across the room, exhibit coordination beyond their years in large motor activities, and be particularly interested in and skilled at the mechanics of objects. *Visual–spatial intelligence* may be seen in children who are very interested and skilled in constructive play. Their block structures are very sophisticated in terms of design elements such as symmetry, color, and form, and their dramatic play is often characterized by elaborate use of objects to represent settings for their play. They may be very interested in art, using several different media to convey their ideas. In the example given earlier, Shawna exhibits several qualities associated with spatial intelligence. Gardner also posited a *naturalistic intelligence* that is characterized by particular sensitivity to the natural world. We see this in the child who loves to watch spiders spin a web, watch sowbugs move in the garden, and care for plants and animals.

Gardner (1993) also describes the personal intelligences that teachers see in young children. Children who express themselves through *interpersonal intelligence* are very interested in and savvy about other people's thoughts, feelings, and perspectives. They are often very social and well liked by other children and adults. Others may exhibit more *intrapersonal intelligence.* These children are very introspective, reflecting on their own thoughts and feelings, and are often able to discuss just how they solved a particular problem or how they felt in a certain situation. Interpersonal and intrapersonal intelligences are linked to the concept of "emotional literacy" proposed and described by Goleman (2011).

People construct their understandings in many different ways. Careful observation of children's play, in terms of both the process and content of their activities, offers teachers important clues about the individual development of each child within this framework of multiple ways of making meaning. Case studies, such as the information Kathy has collected on Shawna, are excellent examples of holistic assessment.

Children Need to Reflect on Their Own Learning   A major element of assessment approaches that provides multiple forms of representation is the provision of opportunities for children to reflect on their own learning and development.

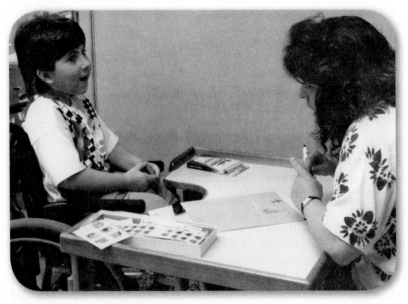

One-on-one interactions provide opportunities to assess children's skills.

NAEYC's 2009 position statement recognizes that this is a key element of developmentally appropriate assessment practice (Copple & Bredekamp, 2009, p. 22).

> As Shawna and Emily sorted through photos of the bank in its various stages of construction, Shawna remarked, "We got the name tags for the tellers, but next time we have to make a sign that shows people where to get in the line." ⌀

The many child-initiated projects described in this book, such as Kathy's "bank project" described at the beginning of this chapter and examples from other chapters such as the post office project and Sophie and the lost pigs project, illustrate how play and representations of play claim a central role in how children reflect on their own experiences and learning.

HOW PLAY INFORMS ASSESSMENTS

Play is the ultimate "integrated curriculum." Play offers teachers windows to view all aspects of children's development, including concepts, skills, dispositions, and feelings. All aspects of development, such as classification concepts or cooperative behavior, inform teachers about how to orchestrate more complex play.

Play occupies a privileged role in constructivist theories of learning and development. Therefore, it is the natural vehicle for assessing children's understanding of their experiences. Play also offers a multidimensional look at skills, concepts, and dispositions that are valued by teachers and appear in state and national curriculum standards. It helps teachers to see myriad different avenues for developing and expressing understanding of these concepts among individual children.

Because play is central to development, it is central to our efforts to assess and develop programs that serve the needs of all children. There has been widespread discussion in the early childhood community regarding the developmental appropriateness of many curriculum standards and benchmarks. Much of this discussion comes down to the means by which these competencies are assessed in addition to the standards themselves. In some instances, play-centered curriculum and assessments of play can enhance the developmental appropriateness of curriculum standards.

For example, one competency for understanding of numbers in kindergarten, "counts with one-to-one correspondence," is reflected in Kathy's goals. But each child approaches this concept in a slightly different way. Jonathan counts the number of blocks he needs to make the fence around his "lion cage" exactly the same on each side. Shawna sets the table in the housekeeping corner, and Emily arranges the paintbrushes and the cups in correspondence to one another as she mixes colors for the day's easel painting.

A play-centered curriculum provides an atmosphere for assessment that is both comfortable and challenging. Children have many opportunities to make choices regarding their modes of expression and their playmates. In a classroom well equipped for play, children will find familiar objects and means of expression that scaffold their activities and allow them to create and problem solve in ways most comfortable to them.

If assessments are to be useful to teachers' efforts to benefit children's development and learning, they must be valid and reliable. **Validity** refers to how well an assessment indeed measures what it proposes to measure. Children are best assessed by their performances in real contexts. For example, it makes sense to evaluate children's spatial reasoning while they are constructing with blocks or collage materials instead of administering a paper-and-pencil task.

Reliability refers to the degree to which the assessment's results are consistent. It is particularly difficult to assess young children's behaviors because they vary greatly day-to-day because of varying levels of energy, levels of self-regulation, focus, or interest. Play enhances reliability of assessments by ensuring that the results are based on many observations of the child at play with familiar materials and playmates. In this way, play-centered assessment differs from assessment that occurs only once or twice during a school year in which children are confronted with unfamiliar materials and intimidating contexts and are expected to perform to a standard of achievement.

> In Roseanna's K–2 multiage primary class in an ethnically diverse community, a pretend restaurant begins as the "Don't Forget the Olives Pizza Parlor" and evolves to include Chinese food. The first week, children labor over a large wall menu that depicts the food choices and combinations in both print and pictures. After making pretend pizzas with playdough made from a posted recipe, Matt and Sam introduce potstickers, rice, and noodles made from playdough as well. Celia, Mei Lin, and John write menus that show the pizza choices on one side, the Chinese food on the other, and drinks and desserts on the back. Their teacher helps them make copies to color and mount on colored paper for their customers as they enter the restaurant. "Then everyone can see what we have on the wall, and at their table!" exults Angie, as she dons her chef's hat. ✆

Embedded in these experiences, Roseanna plans to informally assess several curriculum standards:

- The English language arts kindergarten standard, "Determine or clarify the meaning of unknown and multiple-meaning words and phrases based on kindergarten reading and content," as illustrated in the signs and menus the children make for their restaurant.
- The kindergarten standard, "Identifying, sorting and classifying objects by attributes," as embedded in the arrangement of food on the serving trays and in grouping items for the menu.
- The first-grade standard, "Learning that properties of substances can change when mixed, cooled, or heated" as part of the physical science concept that

"matter comes in different forms," is evident in the playdough recipes that the children follow.

■ The kindergarten visual and performing arts standard, "Paint pictures expressing ideas about family and neighborhood," as addressed by painting pictures on placemats, tablecloths, menus, and advertisements.

■ The standards, "Understanding the concept of exchange and use of money to purchase foods and services" and "The specialized work that people do to manufacture, transport, and market goods," are economic concepts for first grade. They are exemplified in the children's study of ingredients for foods for the restaurant and the pricing and pretend sale of foods and drinks.

PRINCIPLES FOR IMPLEMENTING PLAY-CENTERED ASSESSMENTS

A major point of this book is that there is a reciprocal relationship between the development of play and the development of cognitive and social–emotional functioning in early childhood. Therefore, the development of play in a variety of contexts is of great importance to educators of young children.

A major challenge for the teacher in implementing assessments of play is the development of observation and questioning strategies that illuminate children's development while, at the same time, respect children's right to control their own play. Several teachers and researchers have proposed key principles that include carefully attending to the child by ascertaining the child's viewpoint; attending to the child's behaviors and verbalizations; respecting the child's intentions and autonomy by reflecting on whether a question empowers the child or fosters dependence on adult judgments; asking authentic questions; and respectfully challenging the child in his or her thinking.

Ascertaining the Child's Viewpoint

When Pat discovered Shawna could not yet count to 50, she might have asked Shawna how high she could count. Pat decided, however, that interrupting the flow of Shawna's play to do direct teaching or to ask her to perform a task was not appropriate in that context. Kathy's anecdotal record in which she questioned Shawna about the numbers of spoons, cups, and napkins demonstrated a situation in which questioning was not disruptive to the play. Shawna seemed pleased to explain to her teacher, "Four and four and four—for my four friends."

This judgment call on the part of teachers is one that requires sensitivity, thoughtfulness, and a repertoire of strategies for determining when to assess by careful observation and when to guide or directly question a child. As teachers use their careful observations of children's play, they grow in their understanding of how children think and feel. Through observations of children and ongoing conversations with families, teachers develop a deeper insight into children's purposes and conceptions concerning the world. Teachers also gain a greater appreciation of how the peer culture in the classroom influences learning.

As teachers gain an understanding of children's worlds, they become better able to plan curriculum that is relevant and appropriate to children's development. In guided play experiences, teachers have specific, intentional goals in mind. They may use these guided play contexts to assess children's progress in ways that pinpoint the questions they have about the development and learning of individual children and the group.

Attending Carefully to the Child's Behaviors and Verbalizations

A second key principle in formulating questions for children regarding their play is to carefully attend to the child's behavior and verbalizations (Wasserman, 2000). This may involve making eye contact or getting down to the child's level or moving close enough so the soft-spoken child may be heard. Attention also means looking for nuances of feeling in the child's behavior, voice pitch, or tone. For example, many young children talk as they play with objects, sometimes creating a running monologue about what they are doing.

Respecting the Child's Intentions and Autonomy   In the most fundamental way, this means not passing judgment on the child's play behavior or on the product of that play (Wasserman, 2000). Respect may take the form of the teacher's decision not to ask a question, but instead to subtly and quietly put forth a new object or material the child might choose to use, and see what he or she does with it. This is part of the Artist Apprentice strategy for orchestrating play that we discussed in Chapter 5.

Reflecting on Whether a Question Will Empower the Child or Foster Dependence on Adult Judgments

If the teacher does decide to ask a question after determining that it will not be too intrusive, then a third consideration arises: Does the adult's question empower the child, or does it foster dependence on adult judgment? For example, if Pat had offered to teach Shawna to count to 50, rather than accept the alternative of 10 dollars offered by Shawna, she might have conveyed that her adult knowledge was the only alternative in this situation. On the other hand, Pat might have felt that Shawna was eager to perform her counting skills and asked, "How high can you count?" In this way, she would have invited Shawna to show her rote counting skills. Instead, Pat chose to accept Shawna's suggestion of 10 dollars, believing that to do otherwise would have interrupted the flow of the play.

Asking Authentic Questions   Paley (1981) emphasizes that teachers' questions need to represent an authentic curiosity about how children are thinking about their experiences. She writes that she tries to never ask a question to which she already knows the answer. This is qualitatively quite different from finding out if the child knows what the teacher knows. The challenge is not to impart the teacher's knowledge to the child but to objectively and without judgment observe the process the child uses to interpret his or her environment. In addition, many educators have noted that children frequently bewildered by teachers asking questions to which there are obvious answers, such as "What color is the grass?" Genuine interest in children's own thoughts and perspectives is a more respectful and more meaningful approach to questioning.

Successful assessment of children's development in their play depends largely on keeping these principles in mind. Our viewpoints as teachers are transformed as we listen to children and open ourselves to children's purposes and meanings.

Respectfully Challenging Children's Thinking in Play   Other questioning strategies challenge children to analyze or generate hypotheses about their play. Asking children to predict, verbalize, or draw their plans for play or to explain how their ideas might be tested are all examples of questions that challenge children to stretch their thinking. Ask questions such as, "I wonder if there's another way to do that?" "What do you suppose the lion would do if you allowed him out of his cage?" "Do you think you could make that same color again with paints?"

Context is another dimension to assessing children's viewpoints as expressed in play. In an extension of the matchmaking strategy for orchestrating play described in Chapter 5, teachers wisely might consider structuring individual, small-group, and whole-group contexts for play. Teachers can use small-group projects and stable play groups to assess the development of children with special needs, as well as their typically developing peers.

STRATEGIES FOR COLLECTING AND ORGANIZING INFORMATION

In Kathy's classroom, several strategies for systematically collecting information about children's progress are evident.

Observational Records

The first and most essential strategy is the careful observation and recording of spontaneous and guided play. Kathy says that she identifies one or two children each day to observe during play and project time. She records her thoughts on Post-it Notes or on sticky mailing labels and then completes her notes after school. She says she finds that keeping observations to a maximum of three children a day makes the task easier to accomplish and that she can put together her notes on each child rather quickly. The dated observation then goes on the form. (See Table 6.1 and Table 6.3.)

Other teachers simply place their notes taken on Post-it Notes or mailing labels on a paper in the child's folder, but Kathy says she prefers to "log" the observations as she takes them. "Then I can see where a child is spending most of her time. I can also see if I am really getting a good picture of the child's activities or if some of my observations are too narrowly focused. For example, I looked at Mario's chart a few days ago and realized that nearly all my observations of him were taken on the outdoor climbing structure playing with the same group of boys. I have to make an effort to find him on his own and record his play."

Another strategy for collecting information about children's development is through observations of guided play experiences that teachers initiate. In her first-grade classroom, Anita frequently sets up a store as one of the centers. She is often a participant as well as an observer, focusing on children's counting and understanding of money. Setups that afford teachers opportunities to observe children's play and converse with them about their thinking include a center where leaves and rocks are available for classifying or one with a variety of objects and a tub of water.

Checklists

Yet another useful strategy in assessing development through play is a checklist. Checklists might include stages of early writing (Table 6.3) or stages of sociodramatic play, problem solving, block building, or cooperative group games. A comprehensive checklist for assessment of young children on many dimensions of development is the Work Sampling System developed by Meisels and colleagues (Meisels, Marsden, Jablon, & Dichtelmiller, 2013; Meisels, Xue, & Shamblott, 2008).

Checklists have the advantage of giving the teacher "quick glance" feedback regarding the stages of development of both individuals and the group. For example, if in looking at a class checklist for stages of block play a kindergarten teacher notices that many of the children are not yet constructing elaborated structures, she may want to consider some of the intervention strategies for play orchestration. Beginning first with the more indirect strategies, she may decide to introduce some accessory boxes for new play themes that might stretch children's block representations to more complex levels. Checklists also work to help summarize information from videoed sequences of children's play, guiding the teacher to organize a large quantity of information into a succinct form.

Many teachers combine checklists with portfolios of children's work and observations. Checklists have the disadvantage of giving the teacher too little information about the context or detail of children's play when the observations are made. Just marking the stage and date of the observation is useful as a broad measure of development but lacks the richness of detail provided by observations, videos, and portfolios.

In his first-grade classroom, Mark takes observations and materials from portfolios every 3 months and summarizes the stages of development they represent on a checklist of early writing. This way he gives himself a more detailed picture of individual children's progress, as well as the progress of the whole group and ensures that he has collected a representative sampling of each child's experiences in his classroom.

Portfolios

Teachers use portfolio assessment at all levels of education. Historically, teachers have gathered samples of children's "work" and collected them in files. But too often this work has represented a child's efforts to copy a set of sentences from the board, a teacher-modeled art project, or a set of math workbook computations.

TABLE 6.3   Checklist of Beginning Writing for Kathy's Kindergarten Class

Dates	Observed Behavior	Evaluation	Comments and Play Context
9/14	Uses scribble writing or approximations of letters	Beginning___ Consistently _X_	Kayla holds a pen and makes a row of circles. "This is my letter!"
	Tells about writing	Beginning___ Consistently___	
	Uses strings of letters	Beginning___ Consistently___	
12/5	Writes left to right	Beginning___ Consistently _X_	K. begins "Happy Birthday" at left side of card.
	Knows difference between writing and drawing	Beginning___ Consistently___	
	"Reads" pictures	Beginning___ Consistently___	
	"Reads" writing	Beginning___ Consistently___	
12/3	Dictates "art notes" to pictures	Beginning_X_ Consistently___	"And write sun here and then the moon, 'cause it's night" as K. points to images she has painted.
	Dictates stories	Beginning___ Consistently___	
	Copies name	Beginning___ Consistently___	
10/7	Writes first name, last name	Beginning___ Consistently _X_	K. writes first name with reversals.
	Copies words other than name	Beginning_X_ Consistently___	
12/5	Writes independently	Beginning___ Consistently _X_	K. begins "Happy Birthday" pretend writing of card.
2/18	Uses upper- and lowercase letters	Beginning_X_ Consistently___	"Does 'Mom' have a big M or little?" K. asks.
	Spaces writing	Beginning_X_ Consistently___	
	Uses begin/end consonants in writing	Beginning___ Consistently___	
	Invents spellings	Beginning___ Consistently___	
		Beginning___ Consistently___	

A preschool teacher holds a monthly art show. She asks children to pick out a piece of their art that they would like to be included in the show and their portfolios.

> Tommy's family hosted a Japanese exchange student in their home for the summer. Tommy's father is Chinese and Tommy has recently become interested in the written forms of both the Chinese and Japanese languages. Tommy was impressed by the Japanese writing on the boxes of Japanese toys he was given as gifts and by the student's translation of the symbols for him. Tommy's pretend writing "in Japanese" is clearly marked from the pretend writing he has also done "in English." His teacher has a short clip of him "reading" his writing to her. For the Japanese symbols, he makes sounds that he thinks are like the language he has heard. Then he translates it into English for his teacher. ∅

In this way, contemporary children's portfolios reflect much more of children's processes and self-evaluations (Laski, 2013; Smith, 2000; Strickland & Strickland, 2000; Wortham, 2012). For example, children select their own samples for a language and literacy portfolio and include drafts as well as their final writing and drawing projects.

Documentation Panels and Assessments

Teachers can also take photographs of projects in process. They and the children write captions and ongoing questions and insights. For example, in Greta's second-grade classroom, "project time" was the context for group projects that extended over several days or weeks.

> As part of a project in social studies focused on tools and inventions in the past, present, and future, one group designed a whole series of robots. They started with the "X-100 model" that could serve soft drinks, extending to the "X-500 model" that could clean the whole house. The children created a collection of promotional brochures for their robot series, and Greta helped them videotape their pretend television commercial showcasing their products. She documented their constructions as they developed and kept the drafts of their brochures and scripts for the television commercial. She kept notes on the development of their thinking as a group as well as their individual contributions to the project.
>
> Over time, it became clear that Sonia was the budding engineer of the group, suggesting additional functions and parts for the robots each day. Mauricio carefully wrote their scripts and illustrated the brochures. Lila, a child who recently moved from Mexico and who had been reluctant to speak English, starred in their commercial, which was presented in both English and Spanish. This project addressed Grade 2 social studies and technology for Greta's district as well as Common Core State Standards for English Language Arts. ∅

A key feature of documentation assessment is the opportunity for children to revisit their experiences and to elaborate their play in new ways. Documentation assessment also provides a powerful avenue for communicating with families about the play-centered curriculum and its outcomes for children.

Documentation assessment has been described in detail by early childhood educators at Reggio Emilia in Italy and many international educators who draw from that approach. Classic and more recent resources include work by such educators as Edwards and Rinaldi (2009), Edwards, Gandini, and Forman (1993), Gandini, Hill, Cadwell and Schwall (2005), Helm and Beneke (2003), Vecchi (2010), Wien (2008), and Wurm (2005).

Videos

Richard teaches a kindergarten–first-grade combination class in a rural area. Many of their parents work in the nearby electronics industry. The parent group at Richard's school purchased a camcorder a year ago. Richard videos children's open-choice playtime and, occasionally, their large-group-time discussions. Sometimes Richard sets the camera on a tripod in a given area of the classroom and lets it run. In this way, he sees what goes on over time with a play project.

He recalls two boys who came into his kindergarten class without preschool experiences or much contact with other children. Both boys were limited in their social negotiation strategies, and both chose to play in the block corner nearly every day. Richard videotaped their play periodically over 2 months, documenting on videotape their progress from grabbing blocks and shouting "Mine!" to cooperative constructive play projects.

Richard often tapes play in the housekeeping area as well. Several children in his classroom are dual language learners who speak Korean. Because Richard does not understand Korean, he is frequently at a loss to discover the content of some of the children's dramatic play sequences. With videotape as a tool, he is able to record sequences of play and then show them to a colleague who does speak Korean. She helps him to determine both the content and developmental level of the play he has taped.

"Letting the tape run" is also a strategy that Richard uses to assess what happens "on the periphery" of his classroom, and plan curriculum accordingly. He observes and reflects on what the camera picks up. He often invites the children to watch some of the tapes and solve the problems they reveal. For example, Richard noted that some of the block and manipulative accessories were not being used much by the children. Through the videotape, it was revealed that the children seemed to have difficulty taking out the materials and putting them away. The class watched the tape together, and some of the children explained their frustrations as they watched. They brainstormed a new way of storing the materials in the future. ⌀

Interviews of Children about Their Play

Another technique that Richard developed is interviewing children about their play. He circulates through the room with the camera, and children explain their constructive play projects, science experiments, or dramatic play.

During one play period, Juan described the three-story house he built with Cuisenaire rods while he and Richard conversed in Spanish. In the housekeeping area, a group of children had opened a restaurant and took Richard's order for spaghetti, writing his order on a clipboard and using invented spelling.

Richard checked in with children at various stages of their play. Richard's video showed that Amanda and Jerry persisted for 45 minutes in making "magic potions," proudly reciting their newest ingredients each time they were interviewed.

He recorded Juan and Marty arguing over their block play early in the hour, then returned much later to two smiling boys peeping out of a structure. "You wanted to build a firehouse and you wanted to build an office. What did you finally decide?" asked Richard. "A police," announced Marty, and they proudly showed off their telephone on the desk they built for "when people call 911." 🗗

Additional Models and Instruments for Assessing Play

In addition to the strategies discussed above, early childhood educators can become familiar with the many tools that have been developed to assess play. Some are

A teacher may assess dispositions to learn such as taking initiative, curiosity, and cooperation.

assessments that "stand alone," that is, they are unrelated to a particular curriculum. Other assessments were developed with the express purpose of helping teachers assess children's development and learning as part of the process of implementing an articulated early childhood curriculum.

It is helpful for all early childhood educators to become familiar with different assessments even if they are not implementing a particular model. We caution teachers not to adopt a "mix and match" approach. Curriculum models differ in their philosophy and goals and how children's development and learning is assessed. The different models for the education and care of young children are based on different beliefs about how children develop and how they learn as well as what they should learn. This leads to differences of the importance placed on play in the curriculum as well as the balance of spontaneous, guided, and teacher-directed play.

Play is central to many developmental early childhood curriculum models. Most models include opportunities for spontaneous play, guided play, and teacher-planned activities as well as time for direct instruction. Therefore, many program assessments are based on or include assessments of play.

Formal, standardized assessments of play stand in contrast to informal assessment methods appropriate for all programs and specific assessments developed for a particular curriculum. These formal instruments are designed to be administered by trained educators and psychologists in a standardized manner with specific populations of young children, and findings are interpreted and reported in specific ways.

The following examples illustrate the range of assessments used to assess pretend play:

- Smilansky (1968) developed a system for viewing children's sociodramatic play that is still used for assessing young children. Sociodramatic play appears in multiple contexts, such as the housekeeping area, around the climbing structure, in the sandbox, or with blocks. In all these contexts the features of sociodramatic play that mark social, linguistic, and cognitive complexity are the focus of assessment. The six components of Smilansky's system for evaluating play complexity relate to make-believe roles, make-believe props, make-believe episodes, persistence, social interaction, and verbal communication. Sophisticated sociodramatic play of preschool and primary-grade children includes all these elements in good measure. Children's developing complexity in their play may be traced through observational records or videos of dramatic play episodes.

- In their work on "master players," Reynolds and Jones (2011) present a useful scheme for assessing the sophistication of play. They report that children who were skilled at pretend play with others coped effectively with social constraints, showed mutuality in their interactions, added new elements to play, and were able to see patterns or to structure play for themselves and others.

- The Penn Interactive Peer Play Scale (PIPPS) is an instrument developed for teachers to assess children's interactive skill and social competence in play that is used internationally (Fantuzzo, Sutton-Smith, Coolahan, Manz, Canning, & Debnam, 1995). The PIPPS guides teachers in identifying techniques that children use to sustain play with one another. It includes descriptors for positive play interaction, such as sharing ideas, leadership, helping, and inclusive behaviors. Descriptors for negative play or disruption include starting fights or arguments, refusal to share or take turns, and physical and verbal aggression. A third factor labeled "disconnection" in play is characterized by behaviors that indicate nonparticipation in play such as aimless wandering or a refusal of invitations to play.

- Bodrova and Leong (Bodrova & Leong, 2007; Leong & Bodrova, 2012) propose that many children today from all backgrounds have not learned how to play. Therefore, play should be taught explicitly in early childhood programs. The curriculum they developed in *Tools of the Mind* emphasizes the importance of make-believe play in learning and development. Ongoing strategic assessment of children's pretend play focuses on how a child (a) plans for play, (b) plays for an extended time, (c) assumes pretend roles, (d) uses props, (e) uses language, and (f) provides evidence of his or her ability to maintain and contribute to the play theme over time.

USING PLAY-CENTERED ASSESSMENTS TO ADVOCATE FOR A PLAY-CENTERED CURRICULUM

Play-centered assessments provide **empirical evidence** of each child's development and learning. Observations and photos of children's play and samples of children's creations bring teachers and families together because these assessments "speak the language" that everyone understands. Assessments of children's play serve to advocate for the play-centered curriculum because families realize that teachers are truly interested in their children and are working to support their children's learning.

Parents are interested in learning about the growth and development of their child. Too often, however, they are put off or feel discounted by "teacher talk" in which assessments of children's learning is summed up in percentiles that are disconnected from real-world contexts. Even when parents realize that a teacher is truly dedicated to their child's well-being, this may create a gulf that is hard to bridge. Teachers report that families understand and support their child's play-centered curriculum when they can literally see their child's progress or difficulties.

Richard has found that video records of children's behavior have been very helpful in developing relationships of trust with parents and support for his play-based curriculum. In one instance, the parents of Maureen, a child whom Richard believed needed special help, refused to believe that their daughter needed to be referred for further assessment. Richard documented Maureen's behavior at group time where her need to be touching Richard at all times was evident. He documented Maureen's play with other children in which she would frequently lash out and hit others. Because Maureen was an only child and their home was at the outskirts of a rural community, she had few playmates. Consequently, her parents had little opportunity to compare their daughter's behavior with that of other children her age. The videos helped Richard and Maureen's parents work together with the school psychologist and agree on a plan for a special needs assessment for Maureen. Follow-up videos helped them plan strategies together that would smooth Maureen's relationships with others. ⌀

Teachers find that when families are involved in the assessment process, some children feel more comfortable and less hesitant. When they are an integral part of some assessments, family members can help elicit responses or contribute to physically supporting a child.

Play-centered assessments give family members an opportunity to observe not only their children in particular, but all the children and the whole curriculum.

Twice a year, Richard prepares a video with edited segments of children's activities and progress. At "Back to School Night" in the fall, he shows scenes from a typical day in his classroom, stopping the action to explain what can be learned about the children's development and learning. At "Open House" in the spring, Richard shows video clips of children's block constructions, dramatic play sequences, story plays, science experiments, and other events and projects that he has captured on tape, accompanied by an explanation of how the clip provides evidence of children's development. He creates a video "yearbook" for children and their families from clips of classroom life throughout the year so that children may keep a permanent record of their kindergarten experiences, development, and accomplishments. ⌀

Assessment is a purposeful dimension of the curriculum. The use of play-centered assessments helps create conditions for families to understand and advocate for play-centered programs.

As Richard's video yearbooks show, critical to all assessment issues is the notion of time. Children need time to inhabit their classrooms; develop relationships, competencies, and dispositions; as well as develop their concepts of themselves as learners and meaning makers—this is the missing element in the ubiquitous pressure to have children perform more and sooner. As Almy (2000) wisely advised, the adults in children's lives are the ones responsible. Working together they can ensure that children do indeed have time to play and to enjoy childhood in the 21st century.

SUMMARY

In this chapter we have looked at some of the ways that play episodes inform teachers in their efforts to assess children's progress. Play provides information to guide teachers' planning and serves as a means of evaluating the progress of groups of children as well as the progress of individuals. Play assessments are a means for teachers to evaluate the success of their curriculum planning to see if children replay the concepts and skills embedded in the curriculum and use them in their own play. Play-centered assessment is appropriate for use with all children. It may have special advantages for assessing the development of children with special needs and children who are dual language learners.

- **Features of assessment of children's play.** Play-centered assessment paints a portrait of the "whole child," as individuals who express their unique views of the world through play. The vignette "play at the bank" illustrates how a teacher's observations of a child's spontaneous play reveal multiple facets of development and learning.
  - A key feature of play-centered assessments is that they foster positive school–home connections. Play-centered assessments offer a supportive and clear format for teachers to communicate with families about their child's development.
  - Play-centered assessments provide information on children's age-appropriate development. Age-appropriate assessments are characterized by content and methods of collecting data on children's progress that align with widely held expectations about the typical children in a given age range with respect to their development and learning. The vignette "play at the bank" illustrates how teachers' records of children's play provide an ongoing, holistic record of a child's development of abilities, concepts, and skills (e.g., mathematics, fine motor skills, social and emotional development).
  - Another important aspect of assessment is that of individually appropriate development. This aspect takes into account children's talents and special needs; their cultural, linguistic, and family background; and their personal qualities such as dispositions for learning, temperament, interests, and the multiple intelligences each child brings to construct their understandings of the social and physical world.
- **Examining the purposes of assessment.** Assessment of children is a complicated and multifaceted issue in early childhood development. The goal of assessment in a play-centered curriculum is to support the development of all children from all backgrounds and all abilities and to inform educators' professional judgment to make educational decisions that benefit children's lives. Early childhood educators agree that multiple assessments over time are needed to
  - inform the teaching–learning process for children, their families, and their teachers,
  - identify and serve children in need of special education services and children from diverse cultures and backgrounds, and
  - inform program evaluation and staff development.

In addition, most early childhood educators and professional programs agree that the use of single, high-stakes assessments is not a good fit for children under 8 years of age and should not be used as the sole justification for making educational decisions.

Most early childhood programs are now required to assess children's learning with respect to state and national curriculum standards, including the Common Core State Standards for English Language Arts and Mathematics. We recommend that early childhood educators first assess whether a particular standard or learning expectation is age appropriate and individually appropriate for the children in their program. If so, we recommend that teachers use multiple play-centered assessments to enhance the developmental appropriateness, validity, and reliability of the standard.

- **Play and assessments of children from diverse cultures and backgrounds.** There is particular concern that assessment of children from diverse backgrounds remains fraught with bias.

  - In too many instances, assessments lead to overidentification and misdiagnosis of children from diverse cultures, languages, and backgrounds as having language or other developmental delays (Wortham, 2012). Therefore, it is essential that educators and adult family members work in partnership. When formal instruments and procedures are used, they must be selected with particular care to assure that the assessments will be valid.

  - Play-centered assessments are particularly appropriate for observations made of children who are engaged in activities of their own choosing and when the products of their activity are integral to assessment.

- **Play and assessments of children with special needs.** Another purpose of assessment in programs for young children is to identify and plan for young children with special needs. The limitations of many assessment instruments has led to an increased implementation of transdisciplinary, play-centered assessments in early childhood special education programs. Assessments of children's play provide valuable information regarding all children's development and practical information on functional abilities that teachers find essential to making appropriate accommodations.

- **Assessing age-appropriate and individually appropriate development.** Purposeful, systematic assessments provide important information needed to benefit the development and learning of individual children, groups of children, and the class as a whole. Assessments are age appropriate when they are carried out and interpreted in ways that are consistent with developmental theory, research, and practice regarding the characteristics and abilities of children of that age. They are individually appropriate when they are responsive to the child's culture, language, and family background and provide useful information on children's personal qualities such as talents, special needs, temperament, and interests.

■ **How play informs assessments.** Play occupies a privileged role in constructivist theories of learning and development. Therefore, it is the natural vehicle for assessing children's understanding of their experiences. Play also offers a multidimensional look at skills, concepts, and dispositions that are valued by teachers and included in curriculum standards. It helps teachers to see myriad different avenues for developing and expressing understanding of these concepts among individual children.

  ■ If assessments are to be useful they must be valid and reliable. Children are best assessed when they are active and engaged in a familiar environment, for example, using blocks to construct a space for play.

■ **Principles for implementing play-centered assessments.** A major challenge for early childhood educators is to implement assessments that illuminate children's progress and, at the same time, respect their right to control their own play. Key principles include the following:

  ■ Ascertaining the child's viewpoint
  ■ Attending carefully to the child's behaviors and vocalizations
  ■ Respecting the child's intention and autonomy
  ■ Considering whether the adult's question serves to empower the child or foster dependence on adults
  ■ Asking authentic questions (i.e., questions to which the adult does not already know the answer)
  ■ Challenging the children's thinking in their play so that they can show higher levels of cognition and creativity

■ **Strategies for collecting and organizing information.** We described multiple assessment strategies, including observational records, checklists, portfolios of children's work, documentation panels and assessments, videos, and interviews with children about their play. We also referred to tools designed specifically to assess play and models of assessments developed for the purpose of implementing a particular early childhood curriculum.

■ **Using play-centered assessments to advocate for a play-centered curriculum.** Assessments of children's play serve to advocate for the play-centered curriculum because families realize that teachers are truly interested in their children and are working to support their children's learning. Play-centered assessments provide empirical evidence of children's development and learning. Observations and photos of children's play and samples of children's creations bring teachers and families together because these assessments "speak the language" that everyone understands. Teachers report that families understand and support their child's play-centered curriculum when they can literally see their child's progress or difficulties.

Our view is that play-centered curriculum is the avenue that offers the opportunity for children to develop and learn in ways led by children's own strengths and interests as they enter school. Careful observation, orchestration, and documentation of children's play across a variety of contexts build the foundation for more formal instruction in traditional school subject areas such as mathematics, literacy, science, social studies, and the arts.

The use of standardized tests to assess young children is highly problematic. We contrast these assessments with the more spontaneous, contextualized assessment that play provides in classrooms for young children. Play-centered assessments inspire teachers to think beyond traditional means for assessing young children and to document children's interests and dispositions as well as competencies revealed in the full spectrum of children's behaviors, including play.

APPLYING YOUR KNOWLEDGE

1. Discuss several key features of assessments of children's play and explain what is meant by the following terms: performance-based assessments, age-appropriate development, and individually appropriate development.
   a. Write a detailed 15–30 minute observation of a child in an early childhood program setting.
   b. Describe how your written observation reveals multiple facets of the child's development. What additional questions would you have if you were the child's teacher, and what additional informal assessments would you plan?
   c. If you are unable to observe a child in an early childhood program setting, select the opening vignette from Chapter 1 or Chapter 12.

2. Examine the purposes of assessment that are appropriate for early childhood education programs and the risks of high-stakes assessments.
   a. Explain what is meant by high-stakes assessments and explain why it is inappropriate to make educational decisions based largely on single assessments.
   b. Interview a teacher in a local early childhood program and describe what assessments he or she uses when making decisions about working with individual children and the class as a whole.

3. Discuss the benefits of using play-centered assessments with children from diverse families and backgrounds.
   a. Write a 15–20 minute observation of the play of a child who is a dual language learner. Make sure that you do not include interpretations of behavior.
   b. Report on a book or journal article about the assessments of young children who are dual language learners or are immigrants to the United States.

4. Discuss the benefits of using play-centered assessments with children with special needs.
   a. Report on a journal article that describes a play-centered assessment appropriate for young children with special needs.

5. Discuss how play-centered programs provide teachers with numerous opportunities to carry out authentic assessments of both age-appropriate and individual development. Refer to multiple aspects of development (e.g., cognitive, linguistic, social–emotional, and physical domains, as well as dispositions for learning).
   a. What is the difference between age-appropriate development and individual development?
   b. Gardner expanded the concept of intelligence and emphasized that each person shows numerous forms of development. Consider the intelligences that Gardner describes and use yourself as an example. Reflect on your own play and discuss how play in your daily life reflects several intelligences.

6. Explain why play can inform assessment and why it enhances the reliability and validity of assessments.
   a. Explain how play informs assessment. Include examples.
   b. Explain why play enhances the reliability and validity of assessments of young children.

7. Discuss several principles for implementing play-centered assessments.
   a. What does it mean to ascertain the child's viewpoint and respect children's right to control their own play?
   b. Write a pretend dialogue between a child and a teacher in which the teacher asks an authentic question. Explain why Paley would consider this an example of an authentic question.

8. Discuss strategies teachers can use to organize and document information about young children's play.

9. Describe how a teacher might use play-centered assessments to advocate for a play-centered curriculum and provide at least two examples.

CHAPTER 7

Mathematics in the Play-Centered Curriculum

Co-authored by Sandra Waite-Stupiansky,
Edinboro University of Pennsylvania

LEARNING OUTCOMES

■ Discuss why mathematicians and educators describe the field of mathematics as creative and based on logical–mathematical thinking.

■ Describe the goals and foundations of early childhood mathematics education.

■ Explain how children's play supports their development of mathematical concepts and processes and provide examples.

■ Discuss ways in which the play-centered curriculum promotes the development of mathematical thinking for *all* children, including those from diverse backgrounds and children with special needs.

■ Summarize appropriate ways to assess young children's development of mathematical thought.

■ Discuss three contexts for developing logical–mathematical understandings for preschool, kindergarten, and primary-grade students.

Kierach and Omar, 5-year-olds in Sara's kindergarten classroom, excitedly ask Sara if they can go outside today for recess. Sara asks them if they think it's over 22 degrees, which is the threshold for going outdoors in the wintertime. They all scurry to the window thermometer and see that it hovers right between 20 and 25 degrees. "Yes," Sara exclaims, "recess is a go."

After bundling up in their winter gear, Sara and the 20 kindergartners head outdoors. She brings the wagon full of shovels, buckets, balls, and yardsticks. Today she even brings the roll-up and disc sleds since there is fresh snow on the ground.

Jocelyn and Reyna head for the sandbox, which today is a "snow box," with their arms overflowing with shovels and buckets. They immediately begin to make "birthday cakes" by filling the buckets of varying sizes with snow and stacking them in order from largest to smallest. They search around for twigs for birthday candles, making sure that they have six twigs for each cake since both of them are soon to be six. After they count the first six twigs in English, Reyna counts the second set in Spanish and Jocelyn echoes her.

Five other children use the roll-up and disc sleds to pull each other over the fresh snow. With Sara's encouragement they move to a little hill and take turns sliding down. They form an impromptu race between the circular discs and the rectangular roll-up sleds to see which one will slide faster and ask Sara to serve as the referee.

Charles and Kristina run over to Sara with plump, fluffy snowflakes on their mittens, excitedly showing her the visible crystals, which keep melting right before their eyes. Before the crystals melt, they rapidly count the flakes on their mittens.

Several children step into a snowbank at the edge of the play yard. The snow is as deep as their boot tops. Sara gets out the yardstick so that they can measure how deep the snow is—10 inches!

As Sara observes the children, she notes that all are active and engaged. These playful, snowy day activities involved all children in joint social interactions and meet their individual needs, including Reyna who is a dual language learner, and Kierach who has learning disabilities.

Sara takes note of all of the mathematics that is happening in the daily lives of children at recess on a snowy day. She sees geometry in the children's comparison of the shapes of the sleds and buckets of snow, measurement in the temperature and amount of snow, and number sense as the children's count the "candles," the points on a snowflake, and the number of pumps on the swings. The children may not realize that they are learning math, but Sara does because she has "mathematized" her indoor and outdoor classrooms. ∅

THE NATURE OF MATHEMATICS

When young children are free to explore the mathematical dimensions of their environments through play, they develop dispositions central to mathematical thinking such as curiosity, creativity, a desire to explore, and a drive to solve problems. At its core, children's mathematical play mirrors the creative work of adult mathematicians.

Holton and his colleagues write that "mathematical play...allow(s) complete freedom on the part of the solver to wander over the mathematical landscape" as well as opportunities for mathematicians to extend the boundaries of the ideas they pursue (Holton, Ahmed, Williams, & Hill, 2001, p. 403). In this playful spirit, mathematicians generate creative new ideas and solve challenging problems.

The basis of mathematics is logical–mathematical thought. Solutions to mathematical problems involve the logical relationships that our minds construct, rather than the information our senses observe (physical knowledge) or that we obtain from others (social knowledge). In childhood and later in adulthood, each of us constructs mathematical concepts over time. Logical relationships are at the heart of all mathematical thinking. Play provides the perfect context for young children to apply logic in its rudimentary forms within a nonthreatening, self-correcting environment.

Indeed, logical–mathematical thinking fosters our understanding of many everyday aspects of the physical world. How many floor tiles do we need to cover the kitchen floor? How many miles per gallon does our car get?

Children grapple with problems requiring logical–mathematical thought. How many large rectangular blocks do we need to build a ramp so the cars can get off the highway without falling over? How many forks do we need to set the table for four children? Logical relationships are at the heart of everyday problem solving.

Kamii (2013) explains that the problems children encounter in play, particularly in games and puzzles, are crucial to their development of logical thinking. When children play games such as Pick Up Sticks, they think about which stick to pick up without moving any other sticks. In doing so, they have to consider spatial relations (position of the stick) and temporal relations (which one to pick up first). Both these types of relationships, spatial and temporal, underlie much of mathematical thinking in geometry and measurement of time.

What do we mean by logical–mathematical thought? Sally is taller than Marie. Marie is taller than Melody. Although we've never seen Sally and Melody together, we know that Sally is taller than Melody. The relationship of Sally's height and Melody's height is a logical relationship that "must be." As adult thinkers, we are certain that Sally is taller than Melody without seeing the physical evidence; we do not have to see Sally, Marie, and Melody standing next to each other. Young children have not yet constructed this logical way of thinking about problems involving height, volume, or area, or even ideas that seem as simple to us as the idea of number.

Logical–mathematical thought does not emerge at once, like a butterfly emerging from a cocoon, but develops from infancy into adulthood. Like studying the metamorphosis of a butterfly within the cocoon, we can assess evidence of the many small changes in a child's development. Three- to 4-year-olds might delight in showing that they can arrange four "candles" in multiple ways on the "cake" they have made out of sand and know they still have four. Older children attain a more logical understanding when they realize, in this example, that no matter how large the number is, merely rearranging the "candles" does not alter the number. (See, for example, Baroody, 2000; Clements & Sarama, 2009; Cross, Woods, & Schweingruber, 2009; Kamii & Kato, 2006; Tyminski & Linder, 2012.)

THE GOALS AND FOUNDATIONS OF EARLY CHILDHOOD MATHEMATICS EDUCATION

The goal of early childhood mathematics education is to support young children's development of logical–mathematical thought. At the same time, this involves the acquisition of social knowledge and physical knowledge. Logical–mathematical thinking is not promoted by emphasizing skill and drill math lessons. The vignettes in this chapter show children immersed in problem solving and inquiry that involve "wandering over the mathematical landscape" as well as following a particular path to reach a specific solution. In the play-centered curriculum, children's spontaneous play and their participation in daily life activities are complemented by creative, articulated, teacher-planned mathematical activities.

The play-centered mathematics curriculum is based on the understanding of mathematics as well as the understanding of children's development and interests. Although adults may think about students' learning as occurring in separate subject areas, young children who participate in engaging, inclusive activities experience no such boundary. They don't think of themselves as being in "math land." Instead, they experience involvement in thought processes related to a variety of areas, such as the arts, science, and literacy, as well as social interactions with lively communication. Teaching for thinking is an important rationale for considering the full continuum of play when developing the math curriculum, from spontaneous play to teacher-planned activities.

> Throughout the early years of life, children notice and explore mathematical dimensions of their world. They compare quantities, find patterns, navigate in space, and grapple with real problems such as balancing a tall block building or sharing a bowl of crackers fairly with a playmate. Mathematics helps children make sense of their world outside of school and helps them construct a solid foundation for success in school. (NAEYC/NCTM, 2010, p. 1)

The National Association for the Education of Young Children (NAEYC) and the National Council of Teachers of Mathematics (NCTM) emphasize the importance of supporting children's interests and competencies in learning mathematics if we are to have successful mathematics programs. "Early Childhood Mathematics: Promoting Good Beginnings," a joint position statement of the NAEYC and NCTM (2010), quoted above, emphasizes that high-quality education programs for all young children build on their individual and cultural experiences and foster their interest in making sense of their world.

A second joint statement, "Where We Stand on Early Childhood Mathematics" (NAEYC & NCTM, 2009), includes the following recommendations:

- Enhance children's natural interest in mathematics and their disposition to use it to make sense of their physical and social worlds.

- Build on children's experience and knowledge, including their family, linguistic, cultural, and community backgrounds; their individual approaches to learning; and their informal knowledge.

- Base mathematics curriculum and teaching practices on knowledge of young children's cognitive, linguistic, physical, and social–emotional development.

- Provide ample time, materials, and teacher support for children to engage in play, a context in which they explore and manipulate mathematical ideas with keen interest.

- Integrate mathematics with other activities and other activities with mathematics (p. 1).

The Foundations of Early Childhood Education Programs

What should students learn? When should they learn it? Early childhood educators address these central questions when they determine which expectations for learning (also termed *standards* or *benchmarks*) are appropriate and relevant for the children's development. Then they plan curriculum that addresses these expectations and assesses children's learning. Expectations are linked to curriculum development and curriculum is linked to assessment. Assessment is never disconnected. A coherent and articulated early childhood education mathematics curriculum is based on two important dimensions: an understanding of mathematics and an understanding of children's development and interests.

Early childhood educators who implement a play-centered curriculum work in varied settings. In some, teachers determine the expectations or standards for students' learning that they decide are appropriate for the children in their program. They can then plan curricular activities and assessments based on these expectations. Educators in other programs are required to develop a program curriculum and assessment that address standards or expectations adopted by the federal or state government. In general, preschool educators in state-funded programs follow state early learning standards. Educators who work with children in grades K–2 consider the Common Core State Standards: Mathematics and, in some states, Early Learning Standards as well.

The questions "What should students learn?" and "When should they learn it?" lead to a third question: "What should teachers teach?" The NCTM proposes the following **focal points**, or "big ideas," to answer this question. The NCTM focal points for early childhood are **mathematical concepts** related to geometry, numbers and operations, and measurement. The NCTM proposes **mathematical processes** that describe how children develop their mathematical understandings such as problem solving, connecting, representing, reasoning and proof, and communicating.

In *Mathematics in Early Childhood Education, Paths toward Excellence and Equity*, Cross, Woods, and Schweingruber (2009) present an analysis of 20 years of research. They conclude that most children in the United States fail to realize their potential in mathematics. Their major recommendations are consistent with key standards and focal points: Mathematics for young children should focus on (a) number concepts and (b) spatial relationships, geometry, and measurement.

Knowledge of these focal points and mathematical processes can help all early childhood educators know what to look for and capitalize on "teachable moments" in children's play. Depending on the particular program, educators then decide to focus more on some concepts than others or include additional concepts or processes.

Mathematical knowledge is constructed by acting on objects.

THE DEVELOPMENT OF MATHEMATICAL UNDERSTANDINGS

Young children develop, consolidate, and extend their understanding of mathematical concepts and processes fundamental to mathematical understandings. Teachers notice children's engagement in every area of the environment and throughout the day, not only in math centers or during "math time."

For many years, teachers have been urged to **mathematize** the curriculum. Cross and colleagues (2009) define mathematizing as "making sense of abstract mathematics and for formulating real situations in mathematical terms [and state that children] need to connect ideas across different domains of mathematics (e.g., geometry and number) and across mathematics and other subjects (e.g., literacy) and aspects of everyday life" (p. 43). Similarly, Shillady (2012) recommends mathematizing the early childhood setting by "intentionally integrating math experiences into the daily curriculum and routines" (p. 34).

Based on numerous observations, we know that mathematizing the play-centered curriculum is an obvious and natural process for educators who understand the nature of mathematics, the developmental needs of children, and the tenets of a play-centered curriculum.

Play Supports the Development of Mathematical Concepts

In everyday spontaneous, guided, and teacher-directed play young children deepen their understandings of basic mathematical concepts such as geometry, number sense, and measurement.

> In a community near the ocean, 3-year-old Nicky and 2-year-old Schyler are playing outside in an old wooden boat. While Jo, their teacher, rocks their vessel, the children sing "Row, row, row your boat." They finish the song by counting, "one, two, three, we all fall out!" Laughing and tumbling out, they quickly board the ship to play again. A few minutes later Nick calls out, "Look, I caught two bluefish!" To which Schyler replies, "Look, I caught a triangle block fish!" ✇

The sections that follow emphasize in particular how spontaneous play supports children's development of concepts such as geometry and spatial relationships, number and operations, and measurement and patterns.

Geometry Young children's initial understandings of spatial relationships form a foundation from which more sophisticated geometric concepts develop as children grow. Young children explore and play with their spatial environment. As infants, they crawl around and over furniture. Later, they construct mazes with pillows or obstacle courses with chairs. They roll down hills, slick slides, and beanbag chairs. They play with their bodies' shapes as they dance, their round, fluid movements becoming linear and staccato. Perhaps this is the first awareness of spatial relationships—awareness of one's body and its environment. This fundamental exploration and play involves basic concepts of spatial relationships. All these concepts take time to develop, literally from infancy to adulthood.

Spatial relationships and basic geometric concepts are just as fundamental to children's understanding of the physical world as numerical concepts. As the following vignettes show, children's spontaneous play promotes understandings of spatial relationships.

> Four-year-old Janet paints a tree in close proximity to the house she has just finished painting. She paints grass around it so that the green fills in the space between the tree and the house. In one spot, the tree almost touches the house. Janet selects a narrower brush that her teacher has made available and carefully traces around the area between the house and the tree. ✆

> Three-year-old Tomás uses red and blue pegs to make four horizontal rows of alternating colors across the pegboard. He then constructs a brilliant strip of yellow pegs that runs vertically to the bottom of the pegboard. ✆

Their teacher notices the children's developing understandings of the mathematical concepts that are frequent elements of children's artwork. She sees that both children are deeply engaged and decides to weave terms such as horizontal and vertical into later conversations at a more appropriate moment.

> Together, 7-year-olds Nick and Emma stretch rubber bands across the pins of a geoboard, making hexagons and octagons. Observing their interest, their teacher, Eduardo, first informally introduces the terms *hexagon* and *octagon*. When the children show interest in these unusual words, he explains the derivation of *hex* (meaning six) and *oct* (meaning eight). He then introduces more advanced pattern cards for the geoboard and suggests that they try making their own cards as well. ✆

Children are intrigued with shapes. In this vignette, we see the children collaborating to develop a complex design with hexagons and octagons, and their teacher responding to the children's curiosity by introducing vocabulary so they can discuss their joint activity. Many classroom materials have regular Euclidean shapes such as triangles, circles, and squares.

Most objects, especially natural objects, have shapes that are irregular, such as a tree, a flower, or a puppy. Young children explore many irregular or non-Euclidean shapes. For example, 2-year-old Peggie delights in squeezing the light green playdough through her fingers. She then opens her hand and looks at the playdough form in her palm. It certainly is an irregular, though very interesting shape!

Numbers and Operations: Relationships Involving Amount and Quantity

The play-centered curriculum supports children's mathematical thinking, drawing upon their own interests and dispositions to roam freely about the mathematical landscapes of the play-centered curriculum. During the early years, children are able to construct relationships involving amount and quantity. Indeed, we see toddlers making judgments as to whether two quantities are equal or unequal or proudly holding up two fingers to sign that they are 2 years old.

Understanding Amount.   When young children describe aspects of the physical world, they often use concepts that indicate the amount.

> Three-year-old Steve takes big handfuls of playdough to make giant hamburgers. He rolls out two large, circular forms, and exclaims, "These buns are still too small," and places the hamburger inside. ⌀

Without adult prompting, young children exhibit keen interest in figuring out "how much" and "how many." Steve is judging "how much," that is, the amount of playdough in the giant hamburger relative to the amount in the bun. When children are learning to deal with quantities, initial concepts also include "some," "fewer," "all," "more," and "none." Indeed, some children seem to spend much of their time focused on whether they have the same quantity of whatever it is that their classmates have.

> *Steve:*   "You took more red [playdough] than me."
> *Karen:*   "Well, I'm the grandma so I get more." ⌀

Young children's ability to judge quantities as equal or unequal also relates to their ability to estimate number or amount.

> Four-year-old Sandra tells Melinda they need two big blocks. However, Melinda finds only small ones and returns to Sandra with an armful of five small blocks. ⌀

In a play-centered curriculum, young children have many daily opportunities to develop the ability to estimate "how much" and "how many." They will use **estimation** processes throughout their life as they make preliminary judgments and assess how reasonable an answer might be, for example, estimating that the block tower needs five more small blocks or estimating that the new kitchen floor needs five more tiles.

As we observe children's spontaneous play, we find that children also delight in ordering objects according to a common property such as color, shape, or size. We see this when children spontaneously line up cars, counters, or other objects by length, height, or even the shade of color, perhaps from light green to dark green. Mathematicians call this **seriation**.

> Holly, a second-grade teacher, initiates teacher-directed play in which children create flannel board cutouts of dolls of four different sizes, each having backpacks and objects of corresponding sizes that fit in the backpacks. Some children are intrigued by these multiple seriation problems and create one of their own by making cars of different sizes for the dolls to ride in. ⌀

A related but generally more difficult concept is **classification**. Objects are classified according to whether or not they have particular properties.

> As Samantha and Melissa play with the collection of animals in the block area, they first make separate enclosures in the barn for the sheep, horses, cows, dogs, and cats. Then they move all the horses to one side and make separate "stalls" for the "little ponies," the "riding horses," and the big "work horses." ⊘

Understanding Number Concepts   *"Five little monkeys jumping on the bed . . ."* How many monkeys were jumping? When people think about math, they generally think about relationships involving quantity. Children's construction of number concepts involving quantity develops throughout the early years. The concept of number is complicated and calls for integrating and coordinating related concepts that include one-to-one correspondence, number names, rote counting, and numerals.

> Craig and Atsmon place four horses on top of the four blocks in front of them. They demonstrate one-to-one correspondence by selecting a set of four horses with the same number of objects as their set of four blocks. ⊘

In fact, before children can perform operations with numbers such as addition and subtraction, they need to construct logical conceptual understandings. This is what mathematics educators describe as "number sense." It is more important than memorizing the numerals or number facts (NCTM, 2010). Numbers are the abstractions that can be applied to countless situations; they are a way of describing and communicating about the world. Children need to understand number concepts and learn the number words used in counting: one, two, three, and so on, not by rote memorization but through the multiple contexts of play, their daily lives, and teacher-planned activities.

Maria's teacher observes that she knows the number name for three in English and in Spanish. Concepts of number include concepts of the names we use to represent the number concepts.

> Maria tells Jason, "I got three, three buttons." Later, in playing in the housekeeping area, she talks to Rosa in Spanish, "*Tengo tres, tres botones.* ⊘"

As we see in the next vignette, constructing number concepts also involves the ability to count by rote. Indeed, young children begin by chanting number names out of order, "two, four, seven." They usually develop the skill to say the names of numbers in correct order before they fully understand the meaning of the number concepts, including the importance of the order.

> While filling a jar with cupfuls of water, 2-year-old Jeremy counts "five, six and seven, eight." (But the words do not correspond to the actions of either filling or pouring the cups.) ⊘

> Jeffrey sits outside next to the compact pile of weeds pulled from the garden. He bends a stem into different configurations, exclaiming, "It's a seven . . . Look, now I put a foot on it and it's a two!" ∅

Children need to be able to apply the numbers in a one-to-one manner to a set of objects. When they can count the number of objects in a set and describe the set according to its number of objects, they can answer the question, "How many are there?" One, two, three, four, five, and so on are *cardinal numbers* because we use them when we answer the question, "How much?" In contrast, first, second, third, fourth, and so on are *ordinal numbers* because we use them to indicate order and answer the question, "Which one?"

When children first start to count the numbers in a set and arrive at the total, if someone asks them what that total is they often have to go back and re-count the set to answer the question. Theorists hypothesize that the children need to be able to hold the number "in their head" or working memory long enough to answer. For many children, this does not occur until about kindergarten. Sets with fewer items such as three or four are much easier for children to count and compare than larger sets. Sets with more than 10 items can be difficult for young children to count, even in kindergarten, but provide the basis for future understanding of the base ten system of numbers used in most countries today. Integrating number concepts into play is a natural way for children to apply numbers in real-world, meaningful situations.

Numerals such as 7 and 2 refer to the notation or symbols we use to represent those number concepts. Different numerals have been used in different cultures, countries, and historical times. For example, today we can represent the same number concept by the numerals 15 (Arabic numerals) and XV (Roman numerals).

> One of the girls in Kristin's first-grade class is seated at a desk, working by herself. She draws a picture of a woman with a bubble caption above her head. In the bubble, she has printed the numerals in order from 1 to 21. When she notices Kristin looking at the picture, she explains, "She's counting in the picture." Then she begins to draw another picture of a counting lady. ∅

Measurement   In early childhood, children begin to develop an understanding of the many ways in which we take measure of our world. Young children begin by comparing the attributes or properties of objects such as size ("I want the bigger one"), height ("the snow is 10 inches deep"), and length ("my pencil is longer"). Kindergartners and primary-grade children are fascinated with measurements that use nonstandard units and enjoy making estimations and approximations:

> "The school is as long as . . ."
> "From my house to the school is as far as . . ."
> "That (block) tower is taller than our teacher!"

Standard measures are those that use conventional units of measure such as inches or centimeters, pounds or kilos, or quarts or liters. Children need to develop the ability to select and apply the appropriate "unit" of measure to apply standard units of measure successfully. They first need to distinguish which attribute they are measuring, such as length, volume, or weight. They then need to count the number of units that entails number sense, for example, "10 inches" or "3 cups." The cardinal numbers one, two, three, and so on describe how many objects there are in a group. We use cardinal numbers when we answer the question "How many?" Therefore, when we say that there are "five crayons" we are measuring the cardinality of the group. Teachers observe children starting with whole numbers then progressing over time to fractions of units (e.g., "a quarter inch," "a half cup"). Children require many experiences with a wide variety of materials to construct an understanding of which attribute to measure.

Sara knows that standard units are still difficult for her kindergartners. Throughout the year, Sara introduce tools for standard measures gradually and naturally as the children start to ask questions of their own that necessitate a standard unit of measure to answer, such as "How warm does it have to be for us to have outdoor recess?" Until then, how many buckets of snow and which is the fastest sled down the hill will help the children solve their measurement dilemmas using nonstandard measures. ✆

Sara and the other kindergarten teachers are knowledgeable about the Common Core State Standards: Mathematics (CCSS) (National Governors Association Center for Best Practices & Council of Chief State School Officers, 2010) since her school district has moved toward adopting them. As she reads through the section on "Measurement and Data," she finds that the standards require kindergartners to "describe measureable attributes of objects, such as length or weight" and "describe several measurable attributes of a single object" (2010, p. 12).

As she thinks about attributes that are measurable and used in the children's play, she considers different ways to address the standards in a natural and developmentally appropriate way, from spontaneous play to teacher-directed play to more teacher-planned activities. She challenges the children to use many nonstandard measures throughout their day by asking questions such as "How many buckets does it take to fill the wheelbarrow with snow?" or "Which sled gets down the hill faster, the circular disc or the rectangular sled?" She knows that with questions like these, the children have to figure out which attribute to compare (e.g., volume, speed). Learning which attribute to compare is one of the first steps in learning how to measure. Sara knows that her kindergartners are right where they need to be with the Common Core State Standards for mathematics.

Patterning   Early childhood educators know that being able to "see" patterns is a logical–mathematical competency that fascinates children and extends their reasoning. They also know that patterning is important for algebraic thinking (McGarvey, 2013).

We find patterns all around us. Patterns repeat themselves, progress on themselves, and move forward or backward in sequence. All of these aspects of patterning thrill and fascinate children when they start to discover them all around. There are patterns in music and dance, patterns in art, patterns in architecture and design. Most importantly, patterns are basic to mathematics and the number system.

Infants, toddlers, and preschool children delight in finding and following patterns. Creating their own patterns is exhilarating!

> Two-year-olds Marisol, Joey, and Luca clap out a pattern as they chant and clap in rhythm with their teacher, marking each syllable:
>
> "cabillito, cabillito" (1-2-3-4, 1-2-3-4)
>
> "horsey, horsey" (1-2, 1-2)
>
> "cabillito, cabillito" (1-2-3-4), etc. ✆

> Three-year-old Azlinda is stringing large translucent, shiny beads. She begins with a light blue one and a pink one, then a green one and a purple one, then without hesitation, blue, pink, green, and purple, repeated until the string is filled. Time to start again. ✆

Sara sees the kindergarten children using patterning daily in their play. They can be visual patterns such as Kierach's floor pattern or motorical like Kristina's hopscotch pattern that she uses with her feet:

> "Red, blue, red, blue," 5-year-old Kierach recites as he puts the color tiles on the floor of his block structure to make a checkerboard pattern like the one he has at home in his kitchen.

> "Two feet, one foot, two feet, one foot," says Kristina as she hops on the squares of the hopscotch frame she drew on the asphalt playground with chalk. ✆

Play and the Development of Mathematical Processes

Whether preschoolers or adults, mathematicians of all ages use mathematical processes to make sense of the mathematical problems they confront. Key processes that underlie mathematical thinking include problem solving, communicating, connecting, reasoning and proof, and representing (NCTM, 2006).

Problem Solving   The problems children face in their spontaneous play and everyday life situations are their own problems. Perhaps it is their ownership of these problems and the social nature of their play that contributes to the extraordinary competencies that Vygotsky observed in children's play that led him to hypothesize that play leads to development (Vygotsky, 1978).

> As Ricky and Christie build a symmetrical design with attribute blocks, they have to figure out what to add to the left side to match the green triangle. Ricky places a yellow hexagon on the right side. They both reach for another yellow block, then wonder what they will do now that they have two. ✆

Communicating

Three-year-old Penelope speaks Spanish and is learning English at a rapid pace since she joined Antonio's preschool class. As she counts her crackers at snack time, "*uno, dos, tres* . . ." the children sitting at her table do the same. Then Niko says, "Let's do it another way. One, two, three . . ." Penelope repeats Niko's words, laughing and eating the crackers after each number. Then they help themselves to three more crackers, with Niko and Penelope counting, "*uno, dos, tres* . . ." ✆

Antonio smiles as he eavesdrops on their conversation, knowing that the children are finding that they can communicate their math ideas in more than one language, which is a powerful mathematical tool for them to have.

As children share their ideas with each other and the adults in their lives, mathematical terms give them a powerful new vocabulary that allows them to describe qualities and quantities of their physical world. Mathematicians have precise definitions for the vocabulary they use. Learning to "talk the talk" of math is crucial for further development of mathematical thinking. Therefore, teachers need to use precise vocabulary when discussing mathematical ideas as Eduardo did when he explained the meaning of hexagon and octagon.

Eduardo, Antonio, and other early childhood educators know that it takes multiple introductions of a new word for a child to make the word his or her own. Children learn words best when used in real-life contexts such as play. They first learn a word as part of their receptive language, which means that they know its meaning when someone else uses the word. More difficult is making the new word part of their expressive language. This means that they use it to communicate their own ideas. At first they may use it incorrectly or mispronounce it. Eduardo knows that Nick and Emma must have many opportunities to use these mathematical terms and incorporate them into their own speech before they have really mastered them.

Connecting   As children play, they connect their mathematical concepts to the objects around them.

As they fill the buckets with snow, Jocelyn and Reyna make the connection between "snow cakes" and "birthday cakes," which share the same cylindrical shape. They connect the stacking of the cakes from the largest cylinder to the smaller cylinder to the block structures they make inside the classroom. ✆

Four-year-olds Joey and Krista sit across from each other at the snack table, Joey announces, "Hey, Krista, your shirt has the same stripe pattern as mine. Mine is red and white. Yours is blue and yellow." ✆

Thinking mathematically involves making connections as children find similarities and contrasts in their everyday lives. Teachers can provoke these connections by the questions they pose, the materials they provide, and the literature they read to the children.

> Margaret notices Alla's fascination with rulers, going around the classroom measuring everything and every one that she can. Margaret selects the well-loved children's book *Counting on Frank* to read to the whole class one day. As she reads the book about Frank measuring everything from how far a pencil will write to how many humpback whales would fit in his house, Alla exclaims, "Frank is just like me!" ∅

Representing   Whether using Piaget's concept of symbolic play or Vygotsky's concept of pivots, play is rich with opportunities for representation—using one thing to symbolize another. Children must be able to share or represent their imaginative ideas in some form if others are going to play with them. If a child picks up two cube blocks and wants to pretend that they are dice, she represents that idea in how she rolls the dice and pretends to "read" the number of dots. She symbolizes the dice through her actions with them. The blocks are the "pivots," or objects that symbolize dice.

Representation is a basic process underlying mathematical thinking from the time the child uses her first number words: "Mommy. Two shoes." As we've seen, numbers are representations of abstract ideas of quantity. Furthermore, numbers are represented by numerals. The child brings the meaning to the symbol representing "5," not the other way around. The numeral represents the abstract notion of "fiveness." Piaget contended that young children need multiple experiences with concrete objects before they can use symbolic representations for the objects without the objects themselves.

> It's Thomas' third birthday. He's celebrating with all his friends in a multi-age child-care program. The children are often particularly fascinated with the numbers that represent how old they are. Cooke, age 5, draws a big 3 on brown construction paper. He cuts three short straws as "candles" and hands them to Thomas. "Put them here on your birthday cake." Soon, other children want to make cakes to decorate with numerals and candles. ∅

Reasoning and Proof   Young children develop their ability to articulate their reasoning and show how they arrive at their conclusions as they solve problems in spontaneous and guided play as well as teacher-planned curricular activities.

> Four-year-olds Teresa and Jesse create a structure out of all of the large blocks from the wooden shelf of blocks. They come to a dilemma when there only remains a smaller shelf of small blocks. "Let's use these to make the second floor of our house. We can leave spaces for windows," suggests Teresa. "No, there's only that many," pointing to the smaller shelf of blocks. Teresa explains to Jesse, "There are enough. I know that there are lots because I lined them up yesterday and they went all the way 'cross the rug." ∅

Play with manipulatives can support mathematical thinking.

Teachers sometimes decide to guide children's play without being overly intrusive by modeling a curious disposition themselves and asking "How do you know that?" questions that promote logical–mathematical thinking.

Albert and Nelson, both 7, are intent as they play a board game, quickly taking turns throwing the dice and moving their pieces around the board. Nelson throws a 2 and a 6 and moves eight spaces.

Albert throws a 4 and a 6 and immediately calls out, "That's two more so I have 10."

"Two more . . ." echoes Nelson.

"Two more than your 2," explains Albert. ✌

THE PLAY-CENTERED CURRICULUM PROMOTES THE DEVELOPMENT OF MATHEMATICAL THINKING FOR ALL CHILDREN

The play-centered curriculum provides a rich context for all children to develop mathematical understandings in all areas of the environment and all times of the day. The vignettes discussed throughout this chapter illustrate that a carefully planned play-centered curriculum builds on each child's strengths and interests to meet individual needs.

If we we listen closely, much of the conversation in the dramatic play area involves math and relates to their experiences in home and other community settings. We see and hear children count as they set out plates for the table, sort out money at the store, seriate teddy bears by size, and measure cups of sand for a pretend soup. Art materials lend themselves to representations of familiar environments. Though teachers have often thought of mathematics as part of the "indoor" curriculum, teachers of young children can promote the playful development of mathematical concepts and processes outdoors as well.

Also reflected in children's play is their desire to learn about the adult world. We see this when they construct whole neighborhoods with blocks or use scales when playing store. Similarly, their interest in numbers is shown when they use yardsticks to measure a block structure, or phones and calculators when playing office, thus reflecting their lives in a number-literate environment. Young children also want to learn about serious issues in the adult world, many of which have an aspect that is mathematical in nature. Sometimes we hear children carrying out "adult conversations" about the cost of food, the price of gas, or rent increases.

A mathematics program centered on play and daily life situations provides numerous opportunities for strong partnerships with families. Family members recognize the importance of children's developing competencies in mathematics and want to support the development of their child's mathematical thinking at school and at home.

Orchestrating Play to Promote All Children's Understanding of Mathematics

Sustained efforts to promote equity lead teachers to continue to reexamine their programs to ensure that there are multiple possibilities for mathematical thinking. Early childhood educators orchestrate the play-centered curriculum to promote rich mathematical experiences that promote inclusiveness and equity. In doing so, they consider how they can employ different strategies in the contexts of play, daily life activities, and teacher-planned activities. The continuum of orchestration strategies discussed in the previous chapters ranges from the indirect strategies of setting the stage to more direct strategies of interacting with children as they play.

Setting the stage involves providing space, materials, and time so that children can become deeply engaged in activities that support mathematical thinking. How is the physical space arranged? Do the children have room to work on block constructions without constant interruptions from others in a crowded space? Should the small wooden table be located near the water table so children can have a place for their assortment of measuring cups and containers? What accommodations are needed so that children with physical disabilities can access the water table? Perhaps we need to consider placing a table at the math center to permit children to work in small groups and provide a consistent, defined space for teacher-planned mathematics activities.

Orchestration strategies include providing materials that increase creative possibilities. Are instruments for measuring, such as calculators, rulers, and scales, accessible to all children? Are materials such as blocks and manipulatives organized so that differences in size and shape are readily apparent? Are the numerals on the puzzles large enough for children with visual impairments to see clearly? Are there several kinds of table blocks available for children with different interests and abilities? Who plays with the pattern blocks, attribute blocks, Construx, and Lego blocks? Different types of clay provide opportunities for children to explore non-Euclidean shapes. Pattern boards, tangrams, and pattern blocks give children experiences with Euclidean shapes that they can also use to sort. The multitudes of peg-type manipulatives give children chances to think about quantity as well as patterns. Are the sandbox and the water table neglected areas stocked with cast-off materials and odd containers? Although it is useful to have containers of different shapes, it is also important to provide graduated sets. A measuring set with a quart pitcher, a pint pitcher, a cup pitcher, a half-cup pitcher, and measuring spoons of differing amounts gives children a chance to explore equivalencies.

Setting the stage is a playful activity for teachers as well as for children. All parts of the environment can be enriched further to stimulate mathematical thinking. This not only helps children acquire mathematical abilities within a meaningful context, but also helps them apply their abilities in numerous situations. What can we add to the housekeeping area? Are measuring spoons, food cans of different sizes, and silverware settings for six or eight available? Dramatic play accessory boxes can be assembled easily. What is needed to play store? Post office? Bank? Office? What can be added to support mathematics learning and foster social interactions in ways that support the inclusion of all children?

Time considerations are important. How long can children work uninterrupted? What are the rules about leaving a Lego construction overnight? Cindy is a student with special needs who tends to need close supervision after 15 minutes in the block area. How do we support Cindy's growth? And if Jonny has been working intently on his Lego construction for 20 minutes, must he stop because it is his turn to make an apple snack?

Teachers consider different strategies as they interact with children. Perhaps the teacher needs to take on the role of an Artist Apprentice or a Peacemaker or a Guardian of the Gate. Perhaps this is the moment to assume the role of a Spectator or a Matchmaker. Teachers use different strategies at different times.

> Sara observed that block play in her kindergarten class had settled into a routine five weeks into the school year. At the beginning, she enjoyed the great variety of construction. Now she wondered whether things had gotten into a rut. Day after day, block play involved building ramps and racing. The same boys tended to play in the same groups with the same repetitive themes. When car racing first came into vogue in the classroom several girls were involved and the ramps had become more complex each day. This was no longer the case.
>
> Rather than intervene directly through out-of-play suggestions or through entering and redirecting the play, Sara decided to experiment with accessories placed near the blocks. She placed a box of toy people and animals on the block shelves. This brought several children, including several girls, back to

the block area. New themes evolved. The castle-like structures that had been built during the first few days reemerged. The car races even seemed more complex, with drivers and teams. ∅

Supporting Children from All Cultures and Children Who Are Dual Language Learners

Today, as in the past, we see that the laws that ensure an appropriate and free education to all have not yet led to equal education (NAEYC/NCTM, 2010). National and state results from the 2011 National Assessment of Educational Progress still show that school success in mathematics is less typical of children who live in poverty and who are members of ethnic minority groups.

The joint statements of the NAEYC and NCTM (e.g., 2010) emphasize the important principle of building on the experiences and knowledge that children bring to school from their families and communities. Many educators, however, are unsure how to apply this principle to mathematics education.

Ensign (2003), a teacher in an urban school, developed the concept of culturally relevant mathematics to ensure that all children receive an appropriate and equitable education that supports their development of mathematical understanding. Similarly, Nieto points out that classrooms can mirror aspects of the community, but only when we learn more about the community and only when families feel welcome at school (Nieto, 2012).

In our discussions of assessment we point out the need for valid and reliable assessments. Informal as well as formal assessments of mathematics usually have a strong language component, which puts dual language learners at a disadvantage, even those gifted in mathematics.

> Marie, a dual language learner, plays with Laurie and Sandra, and her teacher observes the ease with which she participates with her peers who speak only English. They are examining and sorting a large collection of shells, a gift from Marie's cousins. Marie first makes two groups: larger shells and smaller shells. She sorts the shells in the group of large shells into what she calls "more shiny" and "not shiny." She sorts the small shells in the same way. ∅

Marie's teacher, Bas, takes photos and writes a detailed observation. Later in the day, he adds his comments. He notes that Marie demonstrates her understanding of relationships among the supraordinate classes of shells by pointing out to her friends the two groups that are "not shiny." Based on many observations of Marie's play, Bas recommends to the school psychologist that Marie be placed in the program for gifted students.

The feature below, *Family Diversity: Building Connections to Promote Children's Learning of Mathematics*, illustrates some of the ways that families and teachers partner to enrich the mathematics curriculum.

FAMILY DIVERSITY

Building Connections to Promote Children's Learning of Mathematics

Lisa teaches in a preschool located in one of the most culturally and linguistically diverse neighborhoods in her state. She speaks Spanish fluently and feels comfortable communicating with the family members who speak Spanish. Several volunteers work frequently in her program. Many more participate in special school events. Lisa is aware that she is less comfortable communicating with family members who speak languages other than English or Spanish. This year she has students who speak Chinese, Russian, Arabic, or Thai at home. She is concerned about how she'll go about involving their family members.

In October, Lisa begins home visits. She feels fortunate that she knows native speakers of each of these languages who will translate the initial letter home and communicate with relatives. She's also learned that when she makes communication with families less "language dependent" everyone feels more comfortable. Her computer tablet with its photo gallery is a huge help. She prepares photos of each child engrossed in several activities and as part of the class at a group time. She also has a set of photos that show the indoor and outdoor environments—including several that clearly relate to math. As she goes to each home, she stops to take a few photos of numbered street signs and neighborhood stores with ads that include numerals.

The photos are well received by every family. She explains that she uses the photos to help children learn mathematics and asks if a relative could translate a sign into their home language. She also invites them to the classroom. Within a few weeks, the classroom has a large and very colorful display of neighborhood photos and handmade signs printed in children's home languages that advertise, for example, *Lemones! $1 = 7 lemones!* One aunt brings in a book about shapes in Spanish. A grandfather from Thailand constructed a colorful poster with numerals in different languages, scripts, and sizes. Other relatives and Lisa work together so children who are dual language learners and all their classmates can turn to books relating to mathematics in the language spoken at home.

Supporting Children with Special Needs

It is critical for teachers to be skilled observers so that children's strengths, special needs, and individual interests in the area of mathematics can be identified during the early years. Inclusive mathematics curricula address the wide range of children's needs related to mathematics, including disabilities with calculations (*developmental dyscalculia*), those who understand mathematical concepts but have limited language ability, those with developmental delays, and children with auditory and visual impairments (Ginsburg, 2006; Smith, 2009). How can we address children's strengths and interests as well as their needs?

Eight-year-old Brendt has a keen eye for symmetry and yet experiences developmental delays in many areas. He has spent several days cutting squares and triangles of various colors and sizes using large, beginners' scissors. He carefully places them on the large mosaic he is constructing, exploring the relationships between shapes and sizes by superimposing the triangles on the squares. ✂

Kierach and Omar head for the swings, which are covered with snow. They push the snow off the seats of the swings and climb on. They challenge each other to count to 100 before jumping off the swings into the snowbank below. They count together to 39. Omar continues rapidly "40, 41, 42, 43, . . ." but noticing that Kierach hesitates, Omar shouts, "Let's jump!" and the two jump and roll in the snow. ✂

Sara reflects on how Kierach, who is not as fluent in his counting with double-digit numbers, is scaffolded by Omar, who is counting to 100 and beyond without errors. She marvels at how Kierach mimics Omar up through 39, then returns to the play on the swings without hesitation or fear of failure. He certainly is a "head taller" in his play than when asked to count in an academic setting.

THE ASSESSMENT OF CHILDREN'S MATHEMATICAL UNDERSTANDINGS

It is often difficult for early childhood educators to assess children's understanding of mathematical reasoning, both what they can do on their own and what they can do with the support of others. Promoting equity is an especially important consideration when assessing the mathematical understandings of children who are dual language learners and children with special needs. Teachers find that play-centered assessments provide insight into all children's use of mathematical reasoning in situations that are not stressful. In their series *Young Mathematicians at Work*, Fosnot and Dolk (2001) emphasize the importance of assessments that take place while children are actively engage in mathematical thinking. Play-centered assessments meet these criteria when children are actively engaged and know that they can work at their own pace without fear of failure. Teachers are then able to make curriculum decisions that are informed by more valid assessments.

Ongoing, formative, informal assessments, particularly observations of young children's play, provide teachers with empirical data and other information they need to plan for individual children and the group as a whole.

- *Careful observations and detailed records* of children's spontaneous and guided play are essential. Consider how Bas used his observations of Marie's play to assess her understanding of classification and how Sara observed Kierach's ability to count with support from a peer during spontaneous play in the snow.
- *Photos and videos* complement written records. They document the process as well as the products of children's play, for example, Jonny's Lego structure became not only larger but more complex over several days. A video of Albert and Nelson playing a board game would have caught that moment when

Albert explained that he figured out how many spaces to move by "adding on." It's useful for teachers to plan short times to document the play of particular children. Photos and videos complement but do not replace written records. An advantage of observational records is that we can take the child's viewpoint, ask authentic questions, and be more interactive in the process without being directive or obtrusive with a camera.

- *Portfolios* can include photos of three-dimensional products such as collages and block constructions as well as photos of products in progress and finished products. Portfolios are a powerful way to communicate with and involve families as partners in the assessment process. They are also excellent tools for promoting children's self-assessment. For example, children assess their own learning and progress as they select samples of patterns they have made across the year.

- *Checklists* help teachers maintain an overview of a single child's progress or the progress of all children in the class. For example, Sara uses a checklist to record whether a child has demonstrated that she can count to 100 by rote. Her checklist has three columns: one for the date, one for a brief description, and one that's further divided so she can indicate the child's level of proficiency (never, sometimes, often, always).

We recommend that a mix of all these approaches is the most useful strategy for both formative and summative assessment as well as useful communication with parents. The Work Sampling System (Meisels, Marsden, Jablon, & Dichtelmiller, 2013) is a model of such an approach that can be used to assess the development of children's mathematical understandings in a play-centered program.

Educators may decide that sometimes more formal assessments are appropriate to complement informal assessments, for example, when assessing a child's developing understanding of number. The ability to conserve is fundamental to a true understanding of number. When children develop the understanding that a given number of objects can be rearranged and that a change in the arrangement does not result in a change in number, the child is able to conserve number.

Amy is a 6-year-old student in Leni's first-grade class. She can draw the numeral 9 under the circle with nine ducks. When Leni asks her to show with her fingers "how many" nine is, Amy counts on her fingers from one to nine and holds up nine fingers. At first glance, it seems that "nineness" is a concept that Amy understands.

Leni models her assessment on one of Piaget's procedures (Piaget, 1965a). She places a pile of pennies on the table. She then selects nine pennies and places them in a row. Leni asks Amy to take pennies from the pile and make a new row that will have the same number of pennies as Leni's row. Amy does this easily. Next Leni moves the pennies so they are closer together than Amy's row. She asks Amy whether they now have the same number of pennies or whether she or Amy has more. Amy replies without hesitation: "I have more pennies because my row is longer."

Leni realizes that though Amy can count and recognize the numerals used in mathematical recording, she does not completely understand the concept of number.

Young children like Amy rely on their perceptions of how things look. Now that she's 6 years old, Amy might be able to tell us that when four pennies are rearranged, four pennies are still present. However, when the number is too large to grasp perceptually, she becomes confused. When nine pennies are rearranged, she looks at the two groups to determine which group looks bigger. Answers to problems involving logic are not "out there" in the physical world through better observation. Amy must use logic to construct the answer that rearranging the pennies does not change the total number of pennies.

Leni considers the expectations she has based on her knowledge of development and learning. She knows that children's abilities to understand these logical relationships between objects develop during preschool and throughout the primary grades. She uses information from the assessments in the days and weeks that follow to further develop the program's play-centered curriculum. ℘

Standards, Expectations, and Professional Expertise

More than a decade ago, the first national conference was held that addressed the issue of standards for prekindergarten and kindergarten mathematics education. The goal of the conference was to bring leaders in early childhood mathematics together "to help those responsible for framing and implementing early childhood mathematics standards" (Clements & Sarama, 2004, p. xi). An important outcome of the conference was a series of recommendations for early policymakers and leaders.

The first recommendation for the area of learning and teaching relates to the central role of play: "Mathematical experiences for very young children should build largely upon their play and the natural relationships between learning and life in their daily activities, interests, and questions" (Clements & Sarama, 2004, p. x).

The play-centered curriculum provides a conceptual perspective that helps educators consider mathematics curriculum focal points and standards in an integrated, developmentally appropriate manner. Table 7.1 highlights how vignettes from this chapter can address a state's early learning standards.

Common Core State Standards for mathematics were published in 2010 by the National Governors Association Center for Best Practices and the Council of Chief State School Officers as an attempt to coordinate the K–12 mathematics curriculum on a national level. The Common Core State Standards classify the K–2 standards into Measurement and Data, Geometry, and Numbers and Operations. Numbers and Operations is further divided into three distinct categories: Counting and Cardinality (kindergarten only), Operations and Algebraic Thinking, and Numbers and Operations in Base Ten. Table 7.2 illustrates how vignettes in this chapter address a number of Common Core State Standards in the play-centered kindergarten.

Table 7.1 Addressing Mathematics Standards in the Play-Centered PreK Curriculum

Examples of Content Standards*	Vignette
Computation and Estimation	
Solve problems using manipulatives to correspond to given number 1 to 6	Craig and Atsmon place four horses atop four blocks in the block center.
	Maria tells Jason that she has three buttons, then tells Rosa, "*tengo tres, tres butones*."
Geometry	
Identify and describe patterns; recognize and extend simple patterns	Tomas uses red and blue pegs to make alternating patterns on a pegboard.
	Peggie squeezes playdough through her fingers to make interesting three-dimensional shapes.
Measurement	
Practice using standard and nonstandard measures in everyday situations	Steve makes hamburgers from playdough, then declares that the buns are "too small."
Examples of Process Standards	
Problem Solving	Sandra and Melinda use five small blocks to replace larger blocks when they run out of the larger ones.
Communicating	Nicky and Schyler finish "Row, Row, Row Your Boat" by counting "1, 2, 3," then falling overboard.
	Penelope and Nico count their crackers at snack time in English and Spanish.
Reasoning and Proof	Teresa explains to Jesse that she "knows" that there are more small blocks than large ones because, "I lined them up yesterday."
Representing	Jeffrey makes a "7," then a "2" from the stem of a weed.
Connecting	Joey and Krista compare the stripes on their shirts.

*Examples of Early Learning Standards from Pennsylvania Department of Education. (2010). Pennsylvania Learning Standards for Early Childhood: Pre-Kindergarten (Revised 3rd ed.). Harrisburg, PA: PDE.

Table 7.2 Examples of Common Core State Standards: Mathematics in the Play-Centered Kindergarten

Examples of Common Core Standards	Vignette
Counting and Cardinality	
Know number names and the count sequence; count to tell the number of objects; compare numbers	Jocelyn and Reyna count "birthday candles" on their snow cakes in English and Spanish.
	Kierach and Omar recognize 22 degrees on the window thermometer.
Geometry	
Identify and describe shapes; analyze, compare, create, and compose shapes	Sara's students make three-dimensional snow forms from buckets and other containers.
Measurement and Data	
Describe and compare measurable attributes	Chhoun uses symmetry when building his block structure
Examples of Mathematical Practices	
Make sense of problems and persevere in solving them	Sara and her students conduct a series of experiments to determine if snow, water, or ice weighs the most based on the children's queries.
Reason abstractly and quantitatively	Alla reasons how her love of measuring is like Frank in *Counting on Frank*.
	Jocelyn and Reyna make birthday cakes out of graduated cylinders outside with snow, then inside with cylinder blocks.
Model with mathematics	Kierach makes a checkerboard pattern like his kitchen floor from color tiles.
	Ila and Erin take surveys of classmates' preferences using tally marks.

Sara volunteers to be part of a curriculum committee for her school district to rewrite the scope and sequence for mathematics (K–12). In preparation for the first meeting of the committee she rereads the NAEYC and NCTM joint position statement (2010). She reviews key points in the National Council of Teachers of Mathematics publications *Principles and Standards for School Mathematics* (2000) and *Curriculum Focal Points for Prekindergarten through Grade 8* (2006). She and the other kindergarten teachers meet to discuss these documents and study their state's standards for mathematics as well as the Common Core State Standards (CCSS) (National Governors Association Center for Best Practices, 2010).

Although she sees overlap and similarities, she finds differences in the wording and emphasis in the various standards. For example, the CCSS do not mention patterning specifically for the kindergarten level, although the NCTM focal points do. Sara knows that patterning is important for children's logical–mathematical reasoning, so she and the other members of the team decide to keep it in their curriculum. 𝒮

In speaking with teachers, we continue to hear concerns that a number of standards set expectations that are not developmentally appropriate. Most teachers are highly critical of the use of high-stakes tests as the primary mode of assessment and are concerned about the impact they have on how teachers teach. We agree. For example, in our examination of early learning standards, we found that problem-solving and computational skills as used in daily life were embedded in the written standards. Many schools and districts, however, encourage teachers to address math standards mainly through drill worksheets that are unrelated to the contexts of daily life. This is one illustration of how the implementation of standards, rather than the learning standards or curriculum focal points themselves, can be developmentally inappropriate.

What can teachers do? Early childhood educators who work with children 3–8 years of age have great expertise to contribute to the dialogue and decisions about developmentally appropriate practices in mathematics education. "Early Childhood Mathematics: Promoting Good Beginnings" (NAEYC & NCTM, 2010) emphasizes the importance of educators and families as key participants. It remains vital that all stakeholders understand that early childhood is a critical time for the development of children's mathematical understandings and that equitable resources are essential.

CONTEXTS FOR MATHEMATICS IN THE PLAY-CENTERED CURRICULUM

Early childhood educators orchestrate the play-centered curriculum to promote rich mathematical experiences for children throughout the day. Play is a natural context for developing an understanding of mathematics, and mathematics is a natural feature of children's play. Children's participation in daily life activities is a second natural context for mathematics. Basic mathematical competencies such as understanding number concepts and measurement are necessary for carrying out simple daily life activities in childhood as well as adulthood. Teacher-planned activities provide a third context for fostering mathematical understandings.

Throughout the early childhood years, play-centered mathematics programs include play, daily life activities, and teacher-planned activities, but during this time the balance changes. We recommend that play-centered mathematics programs for preschool and kindergarten students are firmly play centered but include many daily life activities and teacher-planned activities. We consider first grade as a transitional year with an increasingly greater complement of teacher-planned mathematics activities. In second grade, students are able to engage in more complex, long-term projects and activities. Mathematics is a central facet of projects in which play and daily life activities merge with teacher-planned activities.

Play: The First Context for Promoting Children's Understandings of Mathematics

Purposeful, intentional opportunities for spontaneous, guided, and teacher-directed play provide numerous possibilities for children to use their emerging logical–mathematical abilities. In play, we often see children's reconstructions of events in their daily lives: setting the table in the housekeeping area so that everyone will have one of each utensil or making playdough hamburgers that are "just as big" so everyone has enough.

Play has two characteristics not always found in everyday life situations that offer further advantages. First, play is flexible. Routines and problems encountered in everyday life usually have a desired outcome and sometimes have a single solution. Problems encountered in play more often have many possible solutions. They provide opportunities for children to "wander over the mathematical landscape." Second, play involves children in problems of their own choosing. In play, children explore mathematical ideas with the "keen interest" that the NAEYC and NCTM joint statement (2010) emphasizes as vital.

We contend that children's interests are heightened when they are encouraged to select the content as well as the level of difficulty of their activity. When children are engaged in problems of their own choosing it is more likely that they are working within their own zone of proximal development.

Throughout early childhood, play serves an instrumental purpose when it fosters competencies in mathematics. The vignettes in this chapter illustrate that play is vitally important in supporting, for example, children's understanding of number relationships and patterns. At the same time, the vignettes illustrate how the play-centered mathematics curriculum enriches and supports children's play.

> Chhoun, a 6-year-old in Virginia's kindergarten class, runs to the blocks purposefully. He builds a two-tiered structure and divides it into symmetrical sections. Several towers add an interesting touch of asymmetry. In front of the structure he builds four small, separate constructions that look like animals. He groups three to his right and a single one to his left. Leah and Becky work together to build a castle. It has a triangular base, so that one looks into the structure as if looking onto a stage. They also emphasize asymmetry by adding a second tier on one side. ⌀

Virginia was surprised at the children's skillfulness in block building and their sense of design. She wondered about their previous experiences with block building. When discussing their constructions, Virginia emphasized their use of balance and symmetry, and how they "decorated" the more regular, symmetrical structures with small shapes to make them a bit asymmetrical. She pointed out that the limited number of blocks available sometimes led to exchanges in which children discussed issues of fairness concerning the number of blocks each child could take. Children traded one longer block for two shorter blocks. They counted the total number of blocks different children had. They searched for particular triangular or cylindrical blocks to complete their structure or provide greater stability.

Many activities in everyday life require thinking about measurement.

Games with rules are a form of play that DeVries, Kamii, and others strongly recommend as experiences that encourage the use of logical–mathematical thinking. In *Young Children Reinvent Arithmetic*, Kamii (2000) provides an account of how, through collaborative research, she works with teachers to develop math curriculum based on group games and situations from everyday life. It includes a chapter by DeClark that chronicles her change from a teacher who relied on direct instruction and worksheets to one who advocates a game-centered curriculum. In *Developing Constructivist Early Childhood Curriculum*, Hildebrandt and Zan (DeVries, Zan, Hildebrandt, Edmaiston, & Sales, 2002) describe vividly how group games help children take the perspective of others because they must understand and play by rules others have proposed. Kamii (2013) and Alward (2012) argue that games and puzzles provide the context for logical-reasoning skills both for children and adults, particularly in social settings. Both of these theorists provide microanalyses of the thinking processes involved in specific games with manipulatives, numbers, and words.

Daily Life Situations: The Second Context for Promoting Children's Understandings of Mathematics

Daily life situations provide opportunities for children to make sense of their world and to develop mathematical understandings informally within the context of their own lives and the lives of people in their community. This now classic principle of John Dewey (1998) is emphasized by many math educators. As children encounter and try to solve problems in daily life that involve logical–mathematical thinking, they realize that as their understanding grows, they will become better at solving problems that matter to them, not simply problems on a worksheet.

The five children in Mireille's family child-care program, ranging from 2.5 to 5 years old, have gathered around the aquarium this morning to feed the fish. Mireille has shown them how to remove the lid, hold the can upright, and take just a tiny pinch of food. Today is Ted's turn. Ted, age 5, takes a pinch, then decides there are too many flakes. He moves several from his left palm to his right palm very slowly, flake by flake. Everyone, including Mireille, watch spellbound. Ted shakes these extra flakes back into the can. He turns and begins feeding the fish that have come to the surface before the first flake hits the water. ⌀

As children enter the kindergarten classroom each day, Sara places a survey at the front door, allowing children to "vote" on different classroom decisions for the day, like whether to have snack inside or out. A few weeks after this classroom routine had begun, Ila and Erin began taking "surveys" of their classmates' preferences, using classroom clipboards, scratch papers, and tally marks to query friends about their favorite color or their favorite place to play at school. ⌀

Teacher-Planned Activities: The Third Context for Promoting Children's Understandings of Mathematics

Mathematics in a play-centered curriculum includes teacher-planned activities as part of the continuum.

Pat plans a gas station project for her kindergartners that involves mathematics activities that she planned purposely as well as spontaneous play and daily life activities relating to math. In a corner of the yard, she sets up a gas station with two large cardboard boxes, an oilcan, and a pressure gauge. Immediately, children bring the trikes and wagon over and appropriate a piece of hose from the water table. Within a few days, the drivers are busy adding measured oil, checking tire pressure, and pumping gallons of gas.

Pat extends the gas station project to include her district's social studies curriculum "our neighbors." Pat is able to explain to parents and administrators how this project addresses standards because of her knowledge of the state's mathematics and social science frameworks and standards.

The children discuss their own experiences at gas stations. Many share vivid memories—cars breaking down and being fixed, getting stuck on the highway with a flat tire, tales of stolen cars, and accidents. These are important communications, and the storytellers receive serious attention and sympathy from their classmates. The children draw and write about these experiences in their journals. A trip to the school's library results in a great assortment of books about vehicles and transportation.

Pat arranges for a tour of the local gas station. The children gather around the mechanics as they point out where the big gas truck pumped the gas into the underground tanks. The kindergartners first estimate, then ask the truck driver at the pump how many gallons are in the tank. Then a garage mechanic shows them different tools. Many, like wrenches, came in graduated sizes. He demonstrates how he measures the oil and carefully uses a funnel to pour. ⌀

Teachers in some programs develop a special area designated for mathematics. Based on her observations in numerous classrooms, Scales (2000) noted that few preschool classrooms had areas designated for mathematics as they did for literacy and science. In such programs, teachers might not assess and consistently support the development of spatial reasoning and numeracy. In addition to an environment where math happens "everywhere," teachers can consider a designated "math happens here" area.

Play-Generated Curriculum and Curriculum-Generated Play: Integrating Contexts for Learning Mathematics

In play-centered programs, children's understanding of mathematics develops in the contexts of play, daily life activities, and teacher-planned activities. In practice, these three contexts rarely remain separate. For example, we often see how children integrate mathematical aspects of their daily lives in their spontaneous play. Likewise, teachers often plan activities to extend children's understandings of these very same concepts. Observations of early childhood programs show that play generates teacher-planned activities and, conversely, that teacher-planned activities frequently lead to children's spontaneous play.

Play-Generated Curriculum   Teachers often report that watching children's play in rich environments helps them generate creative ideas for innovative activities that are creative and challenging. Many preschool and primary standards and benchmarks include identifying and naming basic Euclidean shapes such as triangles, circles, squares, and rectangles. As imaginative block builders, sand castle designers, and artists, children have a need for the much more sophisticated mathematical vocabulary that teachers introduce.

Through careful observation and reflection on children's play, early childhood educators create numerous ways to extend play to teacher-planned mathematics activities related to their program's expectations, benchmarks, or standards. (See, for example, Copley, 2000; Drew, Christie, Johnson, Meckley, & Nell, 2008; Ginsburg, 2006; Murphey & Burns, 2002; Sarama & Clements, 2006; Seefeldt, Galper, & Stevenson-Garcia, 2012; Smith, 2009.)

> Sara notes the children's fascination with snow—how it floats slowly to the ground, melts on their tongues and warm hands, and blows in the wind. Kayle picks up some newly fallen snow in her hands. She asks Sara if the snow weighs less than water, to which Sara replies, "How can we find out?"
>
> With her encouragement, Sara's kindergartners fill a bowl with fresh snow, packed level with the top of the bowl. They tote them inside where Sara fills a matching bowl with water. They set the two bowls on the balance scale. The children gasp as the scale with the bowl of snow rises. Billy wonders, "What if we let the snow melt?"
>
> Thus, the series of experiments begins. They decide to freeze the bowl of water and see how much it weighs. Just before lunch, they place the bowl in the freezer. Sara helps them keep track of the time. When they return an hour

later they find that it hasn't frozen, and it still hasn't frozen two hours later when it's time to go home. When they return the next morning, everyone is eager to see what's happened. Everyone has a chance to touch the ice. It's definitely frozen solid, but is it heavier?

Sara sets up a chart that records their findings using rebus symbols for the bowl of snow, water, and ice. First the children predict the order from heaviest to lightest, then they test their predictions and correct their chart according to the findings. ✆

Here we see that, in play, Kayle formulated a mathematical problem. The children's sustained interest and the questions they raise inspire Sara to plan related activities. During these activities, children communicate their mathematical ideas in their own words, connect the weighing of snow and water to other experiences with measuring weight, represent their findings in a simple chart that Sara developed, and reason about and try to prove their hypotheses through careful observations.

Play-generated curriculum forges critical links between math, literacy, and science. The articles, "Reading in Math Class: Selecting and Using Picture Books for Math Investigations" (Thatcher, 2001) and "Books Count! Children's Books with Mathematics Themes" (Bohart, 2012) recommend that teachers select books that include meaningful math connections. It is our view that books that relate to the children's interests, as shown in their play, are particularly powerful.

Curriculum-Generated Play   We find curriculum-generated play when the formal math curricula that teachers implement in their districts flows back to guided and spontaneous play, then back to the development of math curricula activities related to play. Children consolidate and extend the experiences they have in their math education program through their spontaneous play.

Four-year-old Miriam discovered yesterday that she could make smaller triangles within the larger triangles she constructed on a geoboard. Today she is using colored rubber bands and four geoboards that combine to make a square. She is "going to town on triangles," Mrs. Ward, a participating parent, reports. Miriam's play with the geoboards illustrates how she integrates and extends her mathematical understanding through play. ✆

Teachers can consciously create bridges from mathematics programs that address standards when they provide and create environments that support playful activities.

Marilyn decides to turn the dramatic play area into a store. In addition to a balance scale, she is lucky to find an old hanging scale. She includes a Bates stamp with numbers that the children can rotate and change. She has several hand calculators and an old adding machine borrowed from a third-grade teacher. She also includes tubs of small objects, like Unifix cubes, that can be sold. She is delighted to find that she now has a use for out-of-date coupons and the weekly ads from local supermarkets. The pictures and the numbers make the messages understandable for kindergartners. The store is now open for business! On opening day, workers and customers discover that Marilyn has forgotten an important component: They need money. This leads to a group project of making bills and coins. ✆

When the mathematics curriculum involves children interacting with each other to address real problems, both children and adults find numerous bridges to play. (See, for example, Clements & Sarama, 2009; Copley, Jones, & Dighe, 2007; DeVries et al., 2002; Eisenhauer & Feikes, 2009; Ginsburg, 2006; Griffin, 2004; Kamii, 2000).

When providing an environment with the basics for rich play, accessories can be chosen that relate to specific aspects of math curriculum goals, including the focal points, standards, and benchmarks defined by the teacher, district, state department of education, or national organizations like the NCTM. As in all other subject areas, teachers can promote curriculum-generated play by ensuring that a wide selection of materials that promote mathematics activities is available during choice time.

After discovering that the "car racers" are fascinated with measuring, Sara develops a unit on measurement that addressed state curriculum benchmarks such as using nonstandard and standard units of measurement and mathematical processes such as communication and problem solving. Based on her observations of children's play and her knowledge of children's interests, she includes materials for activities that reflect the children's fascination with the minuscule and the gigantic, from tiny sprouting radish seeds to measuring the length of the playground. Many children spontaneously write about measuring in their journals, reflecting their interest in numeracy as well as literacy. Sara introduces a measured roadway for cars that she marks with colored paper. She then removes the paper and introduces nonstandard units such as Popsicle sticks, knots on a string, and Unifix cubes, along with standard measuring units such as rulers, yardsticks, and the popular tape measure. Sara's teacher-planned curriculum leads back to play. Sara takes photos and writes observations that show the children's use of standard and nonstandard units, one-to-one correspondence, the vocabulary they use to describe their mathematical investigations, and the creative problem-solving strategies of specific children. ✆

SUMMARY

Children think mathematically as they use their developing logical abilities to solve the real problems that confront them in play. In solving their own problems, children develop an appreciation for the usefulness of mathematics.

- **The nature of mathematics.** The basis of mathematical thinking is logical–mathematical thought. In mathematical play, children explore the mathematical dimensions of their environment and mirror the key aspects of the work of mathematicians. They develop dispositions central to mathematical thinking such as creativity and the drive to solve problems.

- **The goals and foundations of early childhood mathematics education.** The most important goal of mathematics education is to support children's development of logical–mathematical thought. Related goals include supporting children's development of social knowledge and physical knowledge. Successful mathematics programs support children's interests and build upon the knowledge and experiences children bring to school from their homes and communities. Early childhood educators determine the expectations for learning (also termed *standards* or *benchmarks*) that are appropriate and relevant for the children's development. Expectations for learning and curriculum are linked. The National Council of Teachers of Mathematics (NCTM, 2006) has proposed focal points as well as key processes that underlie mathematical thinking.

- **The development of mathematical understandings.** In balanced play-centered programs, young children develop, consolidate, and extend their understanding of mathematical concepts and processes fundamental to mathematical understandings. Teachers carefully mathematize the whole curriculum. They use a continuum of indirect and direct strategies to orchestrate mathematical play. Young children deepen their understandings of basic mathematical concepts such as geometry, number sense, and measurement. Children use mathematical processes to make sense of the mathematical problems they confront. Key processes that underlie mathematical thinking include problem solving, communicating, connecting, reasoning and proof, and representing (NCTM, 2006).

- **The play-centered curriculum promotes the development of mathematical thinking for all children.** The play-centered curriculum builds on each child's prior experiences, strengths, and interests. Sustained efforts to promote equity lead teachers to reexamine their programs to ensure the program meets the needs of all children and their families. In working toward a more inclusive program, educators consider how they can employ a wide range of strategies in the contexts of play, daily life activities, and teacher-planned activities.

- **The assessment of children's mathematical understandings.** In play-centered programs, assessments are purposeful. Assessments are always linked to program expectations and are used to inform curriculum and benefit children. Early childhood educators use multiple and ongoing informal assessments of children's play that include observational records, photos and videos, sometimes complemented with more formal assessments.

- **Contexts for mathematics in the play-centered curriculum.** Early childhood educators orchestrate the play-centered curriculum to promote rich mathematical experiences for children throughout the day. Play, daily life activities, and teacher-planned activities are natural contexts for mathematics in early childhood education.

In programs that provide a balanced continuum from child-initiated to teacher-planned activities, we find children who bring energy, joy, and imagination to their own relationships with mathematics.

APPLYING YOUR KNOWLEDGE

1. Describe the nature of mathematics.
   a. Use examples from the vignette on play in the snow to illustrate each aspect of your description.
   b. Write an observation of a child engaged in play that you think has mathematical dimensions. Explain how your observation relates to logical–mathematical thought, physical knowledge, and social knowledge.

2. Describe the goals and foundations of early childhood mathematics education.
   a. Summarize "Early Childhood Mathematics: Promoting Good Beginnings," the joint position statement of the NAEYC and the NCTM (2010).

3. Explain how children's play supports their development of mathematical concepts and processes and provide examples.
   a. Observe play in an early childhood education program. Discuss how the play you observed supported children's development of mathematical concepts and processes.
   b. Write a review of an article on play and the development of mathematical concepts and processes. Recommended sources include the NAEYC journal *Young Children* and the NCTM journal *Teaching Children Mathematics*.

4. Discuss ways in which the play-centered curriculum promotes the development of mathematical thinking for all children. Your discussion should include children from diverse backgrounds and children with special needs.
   a. Describe how you could adapt a play center to ensure that children of all ability levels can participate.
   b. Suggest accessories and vocabulary from diverse cultures and languages for two specific play centers (e.g., blocks, dramatic play center.)

5. Summarize three or four appropriate ways to assess young children's development of mathematical thought.
   a. Write a vignette based on a real or imagined spontaneous play episode that provides a window into the children's mathematical thinking.

6. Discuss three contexts for developing logical–mathematical understandings for preschool, kindergarten, and primary-grade students.
   a. Provide an example from a daily life context that provides opportunities for the development of a specific mathematical skill or process.
   b. Describe a teacher-planned activity for mathematical reasoning that emerged from a spontaneous play situation.

CHAPTER 8

Language, Literacy, and Play

LEARNING OUTCOMES

- Discuss some of the many ways that literacy includes more than "reading and writing."
- Discuss the role that communication in play has in the development of literacy and a sense of "topic" and "sequence."
- Describe some of the competencies that literacy activities can reveal.
- Identify the ways emergent literacy develops.
- Describe how many forms of "authoring," especially in children's own acts of writing, advance literacy in a primary-grade classroom.
- Discuss some ways that teachers can enhance literacy opportunities through guided play involving drama, story dictation, and story playing.
- Describe how a balance of time, space, materials, and guidance for literacy activities, on a continuum from guided to spontaneous play, can support children's literacy learning.
- Apply the expected competencies in reading and writing to develop some curriculum and environmental ideas for literacy learning in a preschool or kindergarten classroom.

At Patrick's school, "story playing" is a regular activity. Children have the option to dictate a **"story play"** to a teacher on a daily basis. Later, it is enacted by their friends during circle time. Three-year-old Patrick has attended his school for only two weeks. He has not yet made friends with anyone. He spends most of his time near his teachers, where he has observed the story play dictation frequently, but has not yet dictated a story of his own.

An important breakthrough happens when Patrick quietly tells the teacher he has a story to tell. His first story dictated, he is assured it will be enacted at circle time.

At circle time, Patrick is invited to the "stage" (a taped rectangle on the rug). He shyly steps forward. Patrick's story is "I have lots of friends." He picks himself to be one of his friends, along with Margaret and Barbara (two teachers). His teacher begins to read Patrick's story.

Teacher: Now, listen to what Patrick's story said. "I have THOSE friends."
            Who wants to be THOSE friends? If Patrick points to you, come
            right on the stage. All right, Patrick, pick someone who has a
            hand raised. All right, Sophia, you were picked. Who else?

With the teacher's active assistance, Patrick chooses Mary, Ian, and Catherine.

Teacher: Good! All right, now, those are THOSE friends. Now the last
            part of Patrick's story is "I have THESE friends." If you want to

be THESE friends, raise your hand and Patrick will pick. Patrick, would you like to pick Kelly? You want Felix to be one of THESE friends? All right, Felix, you're one of THESE friends.

Patrick then picks Nathan, who comes on stage, and then follows with Jessica and Sam.

Teacher: Now, Patrick, you've got THESE friends and THOSE friends. What would you like them to do?

Looking at the piano just outside the circle, Patrick says, "Play piano."

Teacher: Good, all Patrick's friends are piano players. ☞

What an important day for 3-year-old Patrick! Not only has his story launched him as a member of a community of "storytellers," but it has also established him as a person who, having started with only two friends, his teachers, now has new friends, his peers. For sure, Patrick will be chosen to have a part in the plays of others.

Patrick's story playing is guided play, in which the teacher's presence, comments, and questions serve to scaffold learning. Patrick's teacher has supported his first tentative effort to engage in a responsive dialogue with others. Participation in the story play activity leads children to an early awareness that language contains within it the expectations of a responsive "other." Patrick must tell his listeners what to do. With their responses, his own sense of self within a social world will grow (Bahktin, 2002; Richner & Nicolopoulou, 2001).

LITERACY BEGINS

While literacy in common terms is thought of as reading and writing, it also includes speaking and the many forms of communication. Current thinking has expanded this view to include a broader range of kinds of literacies, such as digital and visual literacy, as well as musical literacy, cultural literacy, and so on (Schickedanz & Collins, 2013; Wohlwend, 2013). The acquisition of literacy reflects family and cultural values and is affected by the context in which it emerges. Despite the ambiguity of its definition, literacy achievement is considered necessary not only for academic success, but also for the acquisition of what Bourdieu (2006) has referred to as **cultural capital**, which leads to economic well-being, status, and power in life. The view taken in this chapter is that literacy, particularly for young children, arises from the child's early and strong motivation to communicate to others their desires, needs, feelings, and what he or she is beginning to know about the world. Children, as well as adults, communicate in a variety of forms—verbal, nonverbal, gestural—that are shaped by cultural, ethnic, and family conventions and patterns (Cook-Gumperz, 1986; Erickson, 2004; Genishi & Dyson, 2009; Heath & Mangiola, 1991; Wohlwend, 2011).

Play provides the motivating context for the **literate behaviors** that precede the development of more specific literacy skills. Literate behaviors have numerous forms of expression, both verbal and nonverbal, that fulfill the fundamental purpose of communicating the child's needs, interests, and desires. For the young child, these larger purposes of language provide the motivation and framework for later literacy development (Heath & Mangiola, 1991). Taking a broad **sociocultural** perspective derived from Vygotsky (1962), we see language and literacy being constructed not solely in a dyadic mentoring relationship with the teacher, but also from the collective resources of families and the classroom (Heath & Mangiola, 1991; Wohlwend, 2011).

PLAY, LANGUAGE, AND LITERATE BEHAVIOR: A NATURAL PARTNERSHIP

In play-centered programs, communication through gesture, action, talk, and written symbols supports both play and literacy everywhere, from the library corner and the language arts center to the sand table and the dress-up corner. This opportunity to communicate allows children to establish a theme in play and a role for themselves in that play. Signs, even when not legible to everyone, can label things, allocate turns, and designate a territory (Schickedanz & Collins, 2013).

For example, children communicate through talking to themselves in solitary play and to their peers in social play. Noah is talking to himself at the easel—"Now there is blue, blue, and now white"—thus, schooling himself in the creation of a new color. Or, as Maria answers Juan, "I know what to do to help make a tunnel!

Many children spontaneously read in a print-rich environment.

You have to dig another hole." Children also create and share imaginary worlds and participate in the beginnings of narratives. Lizzy, whose mother is ill, wants to play hospital. She needs to communicate and use language to get the play going, attract other actors, and carry out the theme. Additionally, language makes such collaboration in play possible and facilitates the development of "friendship." Patrick had just two friends before he dictated his "I have lots of friends" story, but a whole classroom of buddies thereafter.

Collaborative activities with others enhance the complexity of play by deepening, lengthening, and diversifying play forms. For example, Lizzy's hospital starts with one ward, but it expands as the children pursue the theme to include everything from an operating room to an eye clinic, a pharmacy, and an ambulance unit.

The partnership of play and language also supports the development of children who are dual language learners. Through her interest in the class's story play activity, Russian-speaking Masha communicates her desire to play with others and rapidly acquires English skills in this motivating context. Finally, language in play enables children to share and exchange their knowledge about literacy skills. For example, in the social context of one first-grade classroom, children are encouraged to exchange ideas spontaneously and share what they know about writing during their regular "booklet writing time." In this way, not only the teacher, but also classmates, are resources for language learning.

Communication as a Prerequisite for Play with Others

In spontaneous play with peers, children recast their knowledge of the world in terms that are compatible with their interests, competencies, and levels of cognitive, social, and affective development. Play in the home corner is not simply a copy of what "mommies and daddies" do, nor is such play merely the children's attempt to repeat stories that have been read to them or that they have seen on television.

Spontaneously created play narratives are occasions for children to share and develop a sense of **topic and sequence**—the basic elements of written texts. In such collaborative literate behaviors, a topic and an ordered sequence are coordinated with play partners, thereby successfully maintaining the narrative thread of a cohesive interaction (Corsaro, 1997; Jaworski & Coupland, 2006).

> Jelani, playing at a sand tray, initiates the topic of "saving freezing bunnies" by hiding several miniature bunnies in a "safe sand mountain." Cody stays on topic by sprinkling dry sand over the mountain, exclaiming, "It's raining, it's raining." He has followed with an appropriate sequence of activity and expanded the initial topic as the two collaboratively construct a theme in their play discourse. ✆

In this vignette, Jelani and Cody verbally coordinated their constructive and dramatic play. Nonverbal expression, however, also contributes to and often provides the communication needed for shared spontaneous action sequences. Tag, chase, or superhero games immediately come to mind. One child sounds familiar superhero music, and others take up the theme. Soon a highly coordinated activity of swooping or "flying" gets underway.

Other nonverbal initiation of topic and sequencing actions occurs in such settings as the home play corner, where the function of the props is familiar to many of the children. For example, when Josh brought the laundry basket to Amanda, who had just picked up the iron and ironing board, he was on topic. When Ethan entered the play and began wielding a plastic carrot like a sword, he was clearly off topic and not in synchrony with the ongoing interaction.

Play as a Form of Communication

Long before acquiring verbal competency, young children are able to convey their needs and desires, likes and dislikes, competence, and knowledge in the language of their culture. They do this through gesture, expression, and choice of objects and activities, in solitary as well as interactive play. In dialogue, children express their unique personal identity and cultural heritage and learn to adapt to the communicative needs of others in the sociocultural diversity of the classroom (Corsaro, 2003; 2010; Dyson, 1997, 2003; Genishi, 2002; Genishi & Dyson, 2005, 2009; Hughes, 2003; Jaworski & Coupland, 2006; Reynolds, 2002). The wise teacher closely monitors the language of play, finding in it much of the source of a culturally and developmentally appropriate play-based curriculum and the grounding for an authentic assessment.

FOSTERING LITERATE BEHAVIORS

The natural processes of language learning are turned upside down when we attempt to teach isolated skills, such as letter formation and phonics rules, to children before they have shown interest and motivation in spontaneous efforts to dictate a text or write a letter themselves. Although they often play at letter formation, young children do not use or learn a word's component sounds before they articulate the word—they do not practice the "d," "o," and "g" sounds before saying "dog"—and they do not start with simpler sentences before expressing complex emotions or desires. It is through nonverbal communication—gesture, interaction, expression— that children initially communicate desire or pain. Only after using language in these ways do they come to consider adult norms (Heath & Mangiola, 1991; Schickedanz & Collins, 2013).

The Value of the Play-Based Curriculum

Contrary to traditional views, the rate and direction of the language learning process are not necessarily linear and progressive. Research tells us that for some children, the direction might be curvilinear or cyclical, and even sometimes regressive, only to spiral out again later (Heath & Mangiola, 1991). For example, in guided-play activities, Nathan dictated many stories, all of which revolved around tales about the Beatles that his father had read to him. His stories seemed to be attempts to mimic the adult fiction he had heard. As he became more integrated into the peer group culture of the school, his stories began to have greater personal meaning. At that point, teachers noted that his previously long-winded and convoluted narrative style seemed to shift to a more age-appropriate level. The urgency of Nathan's need to express something meaningful to his peers took precedence over seemingly advanced literacy skills that were not well established.

Learning for young children is determined largely by what they want to know and when they need to know it. To illustrate this point, we look at the development of an accurate concept of gender in children's storytelling efforts.

Early Story Constructions

Three-year-old children typically begin story constructions with fuzzy, gender-undifferentiated bunnies and cuddly creatures. Often, 4-year-old children, as they achieve greater narrative competence, may begin repetitively to relate gender-stereotypic stories derived from the media and peer culture, which marks their membership in the peer group (Nicolopoulou, 2001; Nicolopoulou, McDowell, & Brockmeyer, 2006; Nicolopoulou & Scales, 1990). It is followed, generally at about ages 5 and 6, by a spurt of more creative and elaborate narrative, encompassing and interweaving this same stereotypical material with material based on personal interests and family experiences and expectations (Nourot, Henry, & Scales, 1990).

As Dyson (1993, 1997, 2003), Paley (1995, 1997, 2004), Genishi and Dyson (2009), Tobin, Hsueh, & Karasawa (2011) and others (including Tobin, 2000) have noted, children's narratives are often centered around issues of power, fairness, gender, ethnicity, and culture. Dialogue about such issues not only provides a motivating context for the growth of language and literacy, but it can also provide the context for the construction of more accurate and more equitable notions of a social self within a social world.

When children have opportunities for spontaneous play and authoring in all its multiple forms, they integrate their experience and knowledge and generate a curriculum that is naturally relevant to their cultural and personal lives (Fein, Ardeila-Ray, & Groth, 2000; Genishi & Dyson, 2009)

Angela's Story   This is poignantly revealed in the case of Angela, who illustrated her traumatic story of poverty and homelessness, then dictated its text to a teacher she trusted. The words to Angela's story amplified her vivid illustrations and revealed much about life with her homeless mother. Here are her words:

> Once there was a lady who lived in a house and didn't have anything to eat.
>
> Once there was a woman dressed in blue and she wanted to go to the store, but she didn't have any money to buy anything.
>
> This is a lady who was afraid to go to the store because someone might kidnap her.
>
> This woman has a home and doesn't have any soap, so she had to buy some to wash her dress.

Once there was a little man who had nowhere to go and nowhere to stay because he had no house and the people he was with didn't want him there anymore.
Everything was stolen and there was nothing left.
The end.

Angela's words reveal not only the loss and sadness of her life outside school, but also her need to communicate her special story. It demonstrates the efficacy of the play-based curriculum to meet that need. Furthermore, the story's wording—"Once there was" and "The End"—reveals that Angela is beginning to grasp the social conventions surrounding the literate activity of storytelling. For homeless Angela, "school" learning is intertwined with other, more basic lessons in survival.

In preschool and kindergarten, drawing, along with scriptlike scribbling, is a form of early writing. It reveals much about the child's beginning knowledge of writing conventions and the function of texts. We find many correspondences to the competencies Angela has learned through play in the "Continuum of Children's Development in Early Reading and Writing," laid out in a joint position statement of the International Reading Association (IRA) and the National Association for the Education of Young Children (NAEYC) (1998) on appropriate standards for reading and writing and early indicators adopted by a number of states. For example:

- Angela uses illustrations or pictures to represent oral language.
- She describes people, places, and things in her story.
- She identifies the purpose of illustrations in a story.
- She includes a main idea in oral descriptions and drawings.
- She has dictated sentences.
- She has dictated the beginning, middle, and end of the story.
- She uses her illustrations and dictation to create a consistent writer's voice and tone (more advanced).
- She uses descriptive words and dictates a complete thought.
- She recounts experiences or presents the story in a logical sequence.
- When her story is bound and its pages stapled together like a book, she demonstrates the ability to use correct book handling skills (e.g., the book is right side up and the pages turn in the correct direction). (Scales, 2004)

How the Play-Based Literacy Curriculum Serves Children of All Cultures and Languages

Today's classroom is richly peopled with children of diverse backgrounds who bring to school markedly different cultures, languages, and ways of handling the English language (Genishi & Dyson, 2009). Traditionally, educators have attempted to ignore sociocultural differences in the classroom. In attempting to attain equity by neutralizing our classrooms, we fail to notice that children of different backgrounds bring rich variety to play patterns and language (Derman-Sparks & Ramsey, 2005; Genishi, 2002; Genishi & Dyson, 1984, 2005, 2009; Roopnarine & Johnson, 2013; Tobin, Hsueh, & Karasawa, 2011).

In one classroom, parents helped to create a print-rich environment by labeling the centers and materials in English, Russian, and Chinese, reflecting the various cultures and languages of the students. Some of the dual language learners in this classroom had younger siblings, parents, or other relatives who frequently visited or volunteered. Opportunities to use both their first language as well as English were, therefore, available. This created an atmosphere in which all cultures were recognized, accepted, and celebrated, and all children felt valued (Genishi, 2002).

Play-centered environments provide opportunities for second language acquisition. In contrast to classrooms where adults often control the language spoken, the play-based program exposes children to the full range of their peers' language abilities. Play encourages young dual language learners to develop their language competence for its strategic value in social relations. But it is also important to involve native speakers who can extend children's opportunities to use their primary language and to learn English as well. Books and recordings used in a classroom where there is a variety of languages, along with the presence of bilingual teachers, aides, parents, volunteers, and cross-age tutors, all support a program that is language-varied for all students (Genishi & Dyson, 2009; Genishi & Goodwin, 2008).

Dual Language Learners: Masha's Story

In the following, more lengthy vignette drawn from records of story plays created by an immigrant child, we document Masha's acquisition of a second language, as well as her integration into the play culture of an American preschool classroom (Scales, 1997).

> Having recently arrived from Russia, Masha spoke little or no English. She was very accomplished in arts activities and contented herself with these pursuits for most of the fall and winter, rarely going outside to the play yard. At circle time she was very attentive when children's story plays were enacted. Despite this interest, Masha had laboriously dictated only one story in October, near the beginning of the school year. This is what Masha dictated:
>
> "My head and my eye.
>
> My veil . . . white.
>
> And play veil.
>
> Someone pull my veil and play." ✇

In her beginning English, she has tried to recapture the excitement of whirling with colorful scarves in the language of dance with the other children.

After this first attempt, Masha did not dictate any stories for many months. But she had begun to make friends at the drawing table, where she was also near a teacher most of the school day. Finally, early in April, Masha rushed to Janet, her favorite teacher in the school, announcing urgently that she had a play to write, her first since October. It was a pivotal story that reflected her social development at the time. In her story, we hear a poised 4-year-old obliquely announcing that she is now ready to enter fully the world of her peers. She symbolically bids her teacher and mentor (and the drawing table as well) a gracious farewell. Tactfully, she honors her teacher by giving the only character in this play the teacher's name. Listen to Masha's story:

"Once upon a time, there was a little girl named Janet. And she so much liked to draw pictures, beautiful pictures. And she stopped drawing beautiful pictures and then she started to climb up the tree. And that's the end."

Masha furiously dictated 19 stories between April and the 1st of July. They vividly reflected her advancing development through the expression of her changing social motivations, her acquisition of greater and greater fluency in English, and her grasp of the peer culture. First to appear was the familiar character of Cinderella, which she also knew in Russian. Soon other Disney-inspired figures began to enter. She made sure that there were many roles so that all her new friends could participate; sometimes she multiplied the characters so that no one was left out. Some stories involved two Cinderellas and several others had multiple characters named Pocahontas, distinguished as "a big one" and "a little one." She wrote several stories about "Fly Horses" and, much to the teacher's consternation, many little horses began "flying" about the play yard daily as Masha's Fly Horse theme became more integrated into the peer culture. Masha, despite admonitions to slow down, kept flying. She had made the whole school her own, and she was not about to stop flying at this point. ℘

By June, a few months before kindergarten, Masha's stories began to express her growing awareness of herself as ultimately becoming independent not only from her teachers, but also from her parents. Listen to Masha reflect on growing up.

"Once upon a time, there was a little baby with her mother. And then the mother said to her little child, 'Look, child, there's your father who's coming.' The father, he come and he showed the little child a toy. And the little child grew up into a grown-up girl and that's the end." ℘

Masha's stories are a vivid record of one child's growth in language acquisition and social integration and reveal, in a minor way, how her personal play theme (Fly Horses) was integrated into the culture of her American classroom (Scales, 1997).

Seefeldt and Galper (2000) suggest that young dual language learners generally follow a pattern of second language acquisition that parallels the development of their first language (Otto, 2010). In Masha's example, we find the following:

- A silent period (throughout which Masha conversed in Russian with her mother and her bilingual cousin, Alex).
- A tentative use of new language (Masha's first story), marked by use of simple syntax and grammar and very short sentences.

- Complexity of language structures increases gradually (e.g., use of verb tenses includes past and future as well as present). (This was transitional for Masha at school's end.)
- Use of very short sentences.
- Moving from present verb/noun construction to past and future (transitional for Masha at school's end).

We see this pattern reflected clearly in the language Masha used to dictate her stories.

Variations in this pattern may, of course, occur, as is the case for Masha's younger cousin, Sonia, as seen in the feature *Family Diversity: One Size Does* Not *Fit All!*

This vignette certainly indicates the complex ways that second language learning may impact socioemotional development. It also illustrates the need to resist the notion of a "one size fits all" way of learning language or literacy. This vignette also demonstrates how difficult it is to be a young dual language learner in a classroom where English is the primary language spoken. It gives us a greater appreciation of the countless, sometimes unruly but always original, ways children learn (Dyson, 1997; Genishi, 2002; Genishi & Dyson, 2009; Genishi & Goodwin, 2008; Roopnarine & Johnson, 2013).

HONORING THE IMPORTANCE OF LITERATE BEHAVIORS

A group of fast-paced 4-year-old superheroes elaborated their play when their teacher suggested they draw pictures showing the features of their characters' costumes. The children excitedly drew their characters. The teacher then labeled each character's essential items of apparel—one character, for example, wore a special belt. As superhero experts, the children used their language skills to give the teacher the information

FAMILY DIVERSITY

A Closer Look: One Size Does *Not* Fit All

In the second month of school, after beginning to tentatively use English, Sonia acquired an English-speaking friend who began to "speak" for her. Sonia stopped using English in the preschool and did not speak in Russian while at school. No more of the "ABC" song was heard at naptime. Sonia and her new friend were inseparable, although their interactions did not involve speech. Teachers were alarmed and saw this as a possible indicator of a speech or emotional disorder. They consulted frequently with her parents, who reported that their child was becoming ever more fluent in English at home. Everyone doubted this until evidence of Sonia's bilingual competence finally arrived many months later in a tape recording Sonia's father shared with teachers. Sonia's English was more fluent than her parents'! However, Sonia continued to remain mute at school until she separated from her new friend on entering kindergarten.

she needed to label their characters accurately. Had the children been older, the teacher might have asked for their help in spelling, some of the children could have rendered their own labels, and language certainly would be used to verify and dispute the details of the pictures and the order of the story's sequences. Because they require consideration of a responsive other, all these types of communication—writing, drawing, oral expression, and the use of different media—serve as stepping stones to more developed literacy concepts.

Emergent Literacy

In examining children's early drawing, scribbling, and mark making, researchers note that children seem to know what writing is for before they learn the forms (Schickedanz & Collins, 2013). For example, Graves (1983) asserted

> Children want to write. They want to write the first day they attend school. This is no accident. Before they went to school they marked up walls, pavements, newspapers with crayons, chalk, pen or pencils, anything that makes a mark. The child's marks say "I am." (quoted in Morrow, 2009, p. 232)

Clay (1966) was the first to use the concept known as **emergent literacy**. The following is an adaptation of some of its key features:

- Literacy development begins early in life and is ongoing.
- There is a dynamic relationship between reading, writing, oral language, and literacy as each influences the other in the course of development.
- Development of literacy occurs in everyday contexts of home, community, and school.
- The settings for the acquisition of literacy are often social, often in collaboration with an adult or other children.
- Literacy activities are embedded in contexts such as art, music, play, social studies, and science, where purposeful meaning occurs.

Literacy development approached in this way accepts children at any level of development and provides a program for learning based on individual needs (Morrow, 2009).

As defined by Bergeron (1990), the whole language approach is similar to the emergent literacy perspective in that it embodies a philosophy of language development as well as an instructional approach. It is a concept that involves the use of real literature and writing in the context of meaningful experiences that engender motivation and intent in students.

Writing, Graphics, and Narrative Construction

Writing is critical in helping young children grasp the concept of "story" or "narrative" and the perspective this implies (see, for example, Dyson, 1989, 2003; Dyson

& Genishi, 1994; Genishi & Dyson, 2009). Writing, in turn, occurs as part of a so-cial context. It often emerges from the shared verbalizations surrounding scribbling, drawing, labeling, letter writing, or dictating that lead to an early understanding of the requirements of written communication. Whether the subject that is shared with friends is superhero lore or other fantasy creatures, children come to grasp the rela-tionships of an author to a text and a text to a reader.

Subsequently, children come to understand that stories follow specific narra-tive conventions characteristic of their cultures. Angela began her story by marking new episodes with "Once there was . . ." and closed with "The End," and marked sequences within her story with "and then." Later she linked events causally (using "because" and "so") as she encountered the need to explain her sequencing.

Opportunities for writing in the classroom should be abundant (Morrow, 2009). Children can be encouraged to send notes to each other by making a mailbox for intraclass mail from sturdy, 12-section beverage boxes. Bookmaking and publishing are encouraged by setting out a few pages of paper stapled together or with holes punched to receive yarn ties. In one class, an autograph book proved a successful activity for all when one child introduced the idea (Koons, 1991; Schickedanz & Collins, 2013). More high-tech activities for children in the primary grades can involve computer journals, PowerPoint presentations, e-mail, and speech-to-text programs (Schickedanz & Collins, 2013).

Another exciting possibility involves journal writing: The child creates a writ-ten and/or drawn record of his or her experiences. The child can do the writing independently, with the assistance of a speech-to-text program, or the journal can be dictated directly to the teacher. Journals can be prepared by adding pages to a construction paper cover or using binders with fairly sturdy paper—unlined for younger children, with lines for older beginning writers.

Awareness of Sounds and Patterns of Language

Letter–sound correspondences are arbitrary and must be taught. The more meaning-ful the context for introducing such correspondences, the more effective they are. An example of a meaningful context would be starting with a child's name. What is the sound of the letter that it begins with? What is the sound of the letter that it ends with? Patterns in the rhythm and structure of language, such as syllables, can be introduced by clapping on the accents in the child's name. In *Active Experiences for Active Children: Literacy Emerges*, Seefeldt and Galper (2000) suggest that phonemic awareness includes

- The ability to detect rhythm and alliteration
- **Phonological memory**
- The ability to break down and manipulate spoken words and isolated sounds in words

Although the terms sound similar, phonemic awareness and **phonics** are not one and the same (IRA/NAEYC, 1998). While phonemic awareness is a precursor to

Early literacy is enhanced with self-writing books.

understanding letter sounds in words, it is not the systematic presentation of letter sounds in words. Whatever the method used to teach reading (whole language, systematic phonics, or a combination of the two), children first need a strong basis in phonemic awareness (Schickedanz & Collins, 2013; Wasik, 2001).

Another key to developing phonemic awareness is in knowledge of *rimes* or *word families*. Whereas recognition of rhymes develops relatively early and easily, awareness of rime may require explicit instruction. With knowledge of **rimes** (the part of a syllable that consists of its vowel and any consonant sounds that come after it) along with **onsets** (the part of a syllable that precedes the vowel), such as the "w" in *will* or the "s" in *still*, children are able to decode words that are new to them. With knowledge of common and familiar rimes, such as *ack, ail, est, ice, ink,* and *ight,* children are able to read nearly 500 words typical to primary-level reading books (Seefeldt, 2005; Soderman, Clevenger, & Kent, 2013).

Teachers can introduce letter–sound correspondence with one of the most meaningful things children have—their names. For example, pronounce the initial consonant of a child's name; then ask, "Whose name am I thinking of?" (Seefeldt & Galper, 2000). Phonological units consist of syllables, rimes and onsets, and phonemes (Yopp & Yopp, 2009).

Changing the beginning letters of children's names to create a new variation is another game that draws attention to letter sounds and creates a hilarious response. Patterns in the sequence of sound in language can be foregrounded in a game that changes a vowel following a consonant in a little chant (e.g., "I Like Apples and Bananas"). Children delight in its silliness and quickly pick up the pattern by changing the vowels to "o" or "i" or "u" (Schickedanz & Collins, 2013).

LANGUAGE AND LITERACY LEARNING IN THE PRIMARY GRADES: THE MOTIVATING POWER OF PLAY

Erikson (1950/1985) noted that elementary school-age children become interested in mastery and the need to prove themselves competent in the activities that their culture values. For example, by first grade they are more ready to participate in the lives of adults and are coming to terms with social expectations of their teachers and parents in academic areas like literacy.

Parents of children involved in play-centered, emergent literacy programs sometimes question how children progress from drawing, scribbling, dictation, pretend writing, and invented spelling to the necessary formal conventions of literacy. Harriet, a primary-grade teacher, provides an answer. Having participated in workshops conducted by the Bay Area Writing Project (University of California, Berkeley), she views herself, her classroom environment, and her students as the major resources in a sociocultural context that enhances language and literacy learning (Scales, 1997). She believes in teaching specific skills (she gives spelling tests, for example). But, importantly, she is wise enough to provide ample time for children to integrate their emerging knowledge through playful engagement with the social resources of her classroom. The motivation and practice necessary to acquire skills in letter–sound recognition, rules for capitalization, punctuation, and dictionary spelling augmenting children's invented spelling are provided primarily through the children's spontaneous acts of writing about things that interest them, rather than through unrelated repetition.

A respect for "authoring" in many forms manifests itself in the centrality of a small-group activity called "booklet writing time," during which Harriet and trained parent volunteers support children in guided play surrounding writing and drawing. After booklet writing time, children are provided an opportunity to take the **author's chair** to read or tell the class about what they have written or drawn. Sometimes Harriet points out special features of children's stories, like, "Listen to Michelle's story, and when we get to the point where people are talking, put your hand up, and when they stop, put your hand down. That's called *dialogue.* Doesn't it make this piece of writing more interesting?" These intrinsically engaging activities not only involve children in learning about the function of language, but also offer the occasion for teaching necessary social knowledge, such as vocabulary, the structure of language, spelling, letter–sound correspondence, and phonemic awareness. Such social knowledge arises from the context of self-directed, developmentally appropriate activities.

After lunch, a period of spontaneous play again presents opportunities to write and draw, and children produce numerous pieces at this time. These can be as simple as a block builder's sign saying, "Don't shake the table," or a "Kwyot plas" sign, or as complex as the letter to the principal that two girls wrote, requesting better "pensiels."

Here is their letter to the principal, which displays the many literacy conventions they have learned as well as their creative adaptation of invented spelling to create the letters and sounds of the words whose correct spelling they do not yet know:

> **Dear M.r Boyan**
> the pensiels are bad. The
> blue Pensiels work
> betr than the red
> ones. Can you ordr sum
> blue pensiels for room 4?
>
> From Vanessa and Emilie

They address the principal as Mr., however they do not place the period correctly, indicating an abbreviation but writing it instead as 'M.r.' Harriet notices that their letters are well formed, although they do not always use a capital to begin a sentence. The beginning letter of each sentence is neatly placed just outside the left-hand margin. Later in conference with their teacher, the girls will review their work, and the teacher will help them if they wish to learn rules for capitalization and the dictionary spellings of some of their words.

During these spontaneous and guided play periods, the generative power of play motivates children's authoring. During this period, some groups may even create more extended pieces, such as a play or a class newspaper.

Like the ephemeral quality of play itself, the creative flow of writing is fleeting, not to be interrupted by premature corrections of "form." In this classroom, neither the teacher nor parent volunteers spell words for children; they encourage the children to try to figure out for themselves how words should look. Later, children are guided to learn correct form as individual development dictates. Here is an observation from this classroom:

> It is booklet writing time, and Jomar invites his teacher to look at his booklets. He has filled the pages of several. Each entry is dated, and he and his teacher start with the earliest. A vivid illustration accompanies this first story: "THiS Is MY SPASMANHEEIZFLIEEN."
>
> Pointing to the word *THIS*, Jomar's teacher, Harriet, comments, "I noticed you changed *THIS*. How did you know the dictionary spelling?"
>
> Jomar murmurs, "I learned it and I changed it."
>
> "It was a spelling word and you went back and fixed it," his teacher responds.

Carefully drawing a line with a ruler well below Jomar's writing and illustration, she says to Jomar, "Let's do some dictionary spelling because you already know a lot about dictionary spelling." She carefully copies the first word of Jomar's story and then comments enthusiastically that *Is* is spelled "just right too, except would we put an *I* like that there?" Jomar has used a capital *I*.

"No, we would dot it," Jomar replies. His teacher carefully writes *is* with a lowercase *I* after *This*. Harriet and Jomar read through his story and invite Jomar to point to the three words in his story that he would like to be able to spell the "dictionary" way.

Jomar points to SPASMANHEEISFLIEEN, and they discuss the "soft" sound of *c* in *spaceman*. Then his teacher invites Jomar to spell along with her as she writes the word *spaceman*. Later she comments, "You remember, we have just learned about 'ing' endings," and Jomar is guided in his dictionary spelling of the word *flying*. As they proceed through his story, she demonstrates that a "two finger space" is a good rule for separating words from each other (Morrison & Grossman, 1985). ✆

Jomar's teacher talks not about his most recent piece of writing, where he still may be integrating recently acquired knowledge, but about one of his earliest efforts. In this way, Jomar comfortably appropriates formal skills he has already nearly acquired in the context of his own writing. In the process of "proofing" his earliest efforts at "authoring," Jomar becomes what Harriet likes to call a witness to his own growth and development. As Michelle, one of Harriet's other students, reflects on her growth as an author, exclaims: "At first you couldn't even read what I wrote!" In this classroom, Michelle knew she was an author before she knew how to write (Morrison, 1985). The varied pieces of writing children produce in this first-grade classroom, as well as the story plays created by preschoolers, provide documents through which the children can observe their own personal progress as authors or playwrights.

Multimedia Extend Meanings of Literacy

The wealth of today's various media argues against narrowly defining literacy as the acquisition of specific reading skills. Consider the range of possibilities. Oral storytelling stimulates the listener's imagination and contributes to reading as a habit. Books, of course, contribute to knowledge of literature and, if illustrated, appreciation for art. Recordings and radio contribute strongly to imagination and can influence speech ability and comprehension. Movies, videos, television, computers, and today's principal storytellers, contribute to the child's imagination, speech, and ability to listen and comprehend, as well as to an appreciation of music and art. Interactive computers may make the broadest contribution across all areas, from imagination to potential for control of the medium and creativity in its use (Bellin & Singer, 2006; Brown, 1986; Christie & Roskos, 2006; Sarama & Clements, 2002; Schickedanz & Collins, 2013; Singer & Singer, 2005; Singer, Golinkoff, & Hirsh-Pasek, 2006; Singer & Lythcott, 2004; von Blanckensee, 1999; Wohlwend, 2011, 2013).

DYNAMIC APPROACHES TO PROMOTING LITERACY THROUGH PLAY

Young children spontaneously initiate sociodramatic play. Careful observation of the cadence of children's speech and gestures reveals (a) when sociodramatic play is co-ordinated and cohesive, (b) whether the children know who is taking part in it and who is not, and (c) what the play is about (Cook-Gumperz & Scales, 1982, 1996; Saw-yer, 2001; Scales & Cook-Gumperz, 1993). A well-coordinated play scenario is, in a sense, a story the children are telling with an agreed-on theme and cast of characters.

Sensitive teachers can enhance the development of this literate behavior by responding to or even helping establish sociodramatic play interactions by taking a participant role. They will want to avoid dominating the dramatic play with their power as grown-ups, but, on the other hand, letting go educative responsibility must also be avoided. In other words, a balance must be struck between spontaneous and guided play.

Using Drama Techniques to Enhance Sociodramatic Play

One way the teacher can support more complex sociodramatic play is to enter into what English drama educator Dorothy Heathcote called "**role**" within children's socio-dramatic play (Bolton, 2003; Heathcote & Bolton, 1995; Wagner, 1999). Heathcote developed an extensive repertoire of drama techniques for the classroom, emphasiz-ing strategies that enable children to create and elaborate on roles in spontaneously created dramas that center around historical, ecological, or social themes. One exam-ple of a drama that might be developed could center on caretaking in an animal habitat. Other scenarios she developed for elementary school-age children involved the impact of changes caused by technological advances: How does one fishing vil-lage confront the loss of its livelihood when a neighboring village upstream begins fishing with large nets instead of the old traditional ways (Heathcote, 1997)?

Drama themes are generated from the children's suggestions with minimal props and direction. Children playfully elaborate these dramas based on their own knowledge and understanding. These methods have been particularly successful with elementary school–age children. Heathcote suggested that in initial phases of a dramatic interaction (or a play interaction), the teacher's interventions must be subtle. By taking a role that enables the teacher to speak indirectly about the unfolding play or drama, its context can be supported and shaped.

By this indirect means, for example, one teacher was able to facilitate the expansion of a theme from random shooting play to more cohesive hospital play that involved many more players in meaningful roles. Indirectly invoking this prior play experience on a later occasion, the teacher enhanced the focus of chaotic play by merely giving each player an armband marked with a red cross. This new focus allowed less mature players to be included, and the older children assumed more complex roles in an elaborated play theme that entailed greater interactive challenge.

Later the teacher, in role, may shift responsibility for advancing the play to the children. The teacher, who in the earlier example is only a member of the "hospital governing board," may now appear to be "helpless" to know what to do next or who is in charge. In this way, the teacher can subtly shift her "teacher power" and authority to invent over to the children (Heathcote & Bolton, 1995; Heathcote & Herbert, 1985).

> Entering a hospital play scenario, the teacher addresses Jason as a colleague: "Jason, have you been 'certified' by the governing board of the hospital to serve as its 'director' of emergency units?" After assurances, the teacher retreats from the play to set up a "disaster control center equipped with cell phones." Jason and his friend, Juan, begin to man the dual steering wheels of the emergency truck and direct the flow of "casualties" to the "intensive care unit." ✆

Avoiding Some Pitfalls   The teacher in a "role" must not forget that it will be necessary to return to being the teacher—signaling this shift in relationships by a change of voice or posture—for it is inevitable that the children will have to go home, no matter how much fun they are having. Shoes, socks, jackets, and sweaters must be found, projects stored, and the school tidied for the following day. Hence, whatever part in the play teachers create for themselves, the roles must allow movement into and out of the play. Again, the teachers' roles should never be central ones; they should only allow the teachers to be available when needed to support, guide, and sustain the play, but never to direct or dominate.

Moreover, in assuming their "role" in play, teachers must communicate clearly that the drama is part of the world of pretend, in which things are only make believe. Otherwise, the children may become confused about the reality of their play.

Consider the teacher who failed to do this. After spending several days with a child constructing a robot out of cardboard boxes, tape, and wires, she was shocked when, on completion of the robot, her partner demanded that she "Plug it in!" It is impossible to describe the look of disappointment on the child's face when told, "It's only make believe." One can only speculate that the child's confusion arose because he thought he had entered the powerful world of adults, where things "really" happen, whereas the teacher felt she had entered the child's world of make believe, where all things are possible because they are only pretend. The teacher had much to learn from this episode.

Story Dictation and Story Playing

Do you remember 3-year-old Patrick, who dictated the story "I have lots of friends"? By encouraging a child to dictate stories to be acted out later by classmates, the teacher provides an outlet for the child's deeply felt needs—in Patrick's case, the need for friends. Furthermore, because of the urgency of the child's desire to communicate those needs, and because of the autonomy allowed by virtue of the child being the one to choose the subject, story, and players, the teacher establishes fertile ground for the development of literate behaviors.

The story dictation/story play curriculum, articulated largely by Paley (1981, 1986, 1992, 1999, 2004, 2010), recalls Ashton-Warner's (1963) discovery that reading is mastered easily if the words to be used are autonomously chosen (for these are the

Reading can be a social as well as solitary activity.

words that have personal and emotional impact for the child). It is a literacy and play curriculum that lends itself to applications in prekindergarten, kindergarten, and elementary classrooms, allowing opportunities for children to move from dictating story plays to eventually writing their own creative texts to be presented at a readers' theater or author's chair (Dyson, 1997, 2003; Owacki, 2001).

In the following section, we discuss stories dictated to teachers in one school over the course of several years. In this classroom, the story dictation and story play curriculum is quite simple. The opportunity to dictate a story is offered every day. A record of who has dictated and who has not is kept so that all may have a turn.

In some first- and many second-grade classrooms, children write their own stories and read them or enact them for their classmates (Dyson, 1997, 2003; Scales, 1997). Minimizing the addition of props to enhance children's use of their imagination, the child-authors and others whom they select act out the stories. For children who are not yet reading, the teacher can read the story, and the acting can spontaneously be performed with a bit of minimal direction from the child-author and the teacher. A record of these stories, along with field notes on the dramatization, is kept in each child's portfolio.

Laronda   Laronda comes from a large, hard-working, strict family where pretense is frowned on. She differs from her peers in class who are, for the most part, offspring of university-based, academically oriented families. She dictated a number of story plays during her second year at preschool when she was 4 years old. An enthusiastic storyteller, she quickly grasped the conventions of storytelling and story playing.

Laronda was popular with her classmates, and her stories mentioned many of her friends by name. In content, the stories were tied to themes and activities of a devoutly religious home life, the world of work, and the domestic comings and goings of an extended family. Laronda's stories rarely mentioned play as an activity and incorporated few fantasy elements. From her field notes, the teacher noted that other children frequently called on Laronda to play the role of "Queen" but never the "Princess." This, despite the fact that in some of her own stories Laronda created a "princess" role for herself, although one who "left because she had to cook." Apparently the children recognized something "adult" about Laronda's pragmatic world. There were few parties and no birthdays to celebrate there. There were domestic chores to be performed, and there was work to "go to" and "come home from."

Other children in this mostly middle-class group placed themselves at the center of the worlds they created, often being taken to the park to play, whereas the voice of Laronda was part of a choir of family voices. The teacher wondered about the impact of Laronda's group-oriented culture, which discouraged too much focus on the self, play, and imaginative expression. How much of Laronda's intellectual energy in future schooling would be spent in managing and bridging two disparate worlds in this cosmopolitan university community? (See Giddens, 2000; Gonzalez-Mena, 1998; Zapeda, Gonzalez-Mena, Rothstein-Fisch, & Trumbull, 2006.)

Jason   Jason, a kindergartner, is the only child of an adult-dominated household. His parents are adamantly opposed to gunplay and vigilantly monitor his television viewing to minimize his exposure to violence.

During the year, Jason cautiously attempted to establish himself as a member of the peer group, particularly with a group of the more vigorous boys in the class. The first of the last two stories he dictated shocked his parents:

> Once upon a time, there was a dragon and he went home. And he went to his friend's house. And then he went to another friend's house. And then he saw a horse. And then he saw another horse and killed the horses. And then he went back home. And then he saw ten hundred million horses and killed them. And then he saw some people and he killed them. And then he saw everything that's alive in the whole wide world and he saw all his friends and he killed them.

> Building the dramatic momentum of this chronicle of devastation, Jason's dragon went to "New York," where "he killed everything else." He then went to school and killed his teachers, all his friends, and the people at school, and "knocked down all the trees of the whole school."

> Finally ". . . he knocked down the whole world and the whole sky and every plant. The end." ✄

When Jason's alarmed mother queried him about this play, he turned to her with twinkling eyes and said, "I was a dragon, you know." This did not surprise the teacher, who had already seen in Jason's previous stories a little dragon shyly trying to show its face. She sensed that this story was Jason's declaration of independence. It unleashed the full power of his imagination, as well as his ability to express latent aggression in a literate, creative way.

Here is Jason's next (and final) story:

> Once upon a time, there was a Ghostbuster. And then the Ghostbuster went to his friend's house and instead of his friend there was a dragon. And then the dragon said, "Bye, bye. I don't want to play with you. I'm going to the park!" And the dragon went to the park and he got to the park and then when he was at the park he went on the swing. And then a girl came and she said, "What are you doing here?" And then the girl played on the slide. And then the dragon played on the slide. And the girl played on the swing. And then a spider came and then a spider found a web. And they both said, "How are you doing?" (Stage direction: One says it first and then the other.)
>
> And then the dragon went home and he drank some tea. And when he was done he went to bed. And the robbers came in and they looked around and then they went out. And then the little girl played a little more and went home and ate dinner and went to bed. And when she went to sleep some robbers came in, and they looked around, and they stole everything that she had. And they went out. And they all woke up in the morning and ate their breakfast. And they all went to the park and had a party. (Stage direction: All the characters hold hands and begin their singing.) The end. ✇

Here we see a competent and vigorous 6-year-old very much in command of the story writing conventions he has acquired. He uses a formulaic opening, "Once upon a time," and, although most of the occurrences are physical, one represents a mental event: Jason indicates expectation in the second sequence when he says, "instead of his friend there was a dragon." Jason supplies stage directions to clarify and expand the story and presents a mixture of popular media characters (Ghostbuster, robbers), fairy tale characters (dragon, spider), and others, all using direct speech and reciprocal conversation. Sentences are complex and include subordinate clauses, such as "when she went to sleep."

Using these conventions with style and poise, Jason constructs a story that successfully integrates the strands of his life (e.g., going to bed or to places like a friend's house or the park) and incorporates expectations derived from his family and teachers (you eat dinner, then go to bed; the girl and dragon take turns on the slide). In the style of many traditional tales, all of his characters, good and bad, end up as friends; they all go to the park and have a party. Furthermore, by including such details as Ghostbusters and robbers, Jason incorporates the demands of his peer culture. He now has established himself as not only his own "person," but as a full-fledged "member" of the group.

The story dictation activity of the preschool evolves naturally into journal and booklet writing activities in the later elementary years. The motivating power of this activity is augmented by the social opportunity to share stories from an "author's chair," as in a second-grade class mentioned earlier in the chapter, or in a third-grade classroom's **author's theatre** described so powerfully by Dyson (1995, 2003). Owacki (2001), also using drama in the classroom, devoted a chapter of her book to describing a primary-school curriculum called "Readers Theatre."

As children think and talk about their experiences, they learn that what they talk about can be written and what can be written can be read. In doing so, they begin to learn to listen, to speak to others, and thereby to learn the specifics of language and print conventions.

BALANCED OPPORTUNITIES FOR VARIED KINDS OF PLAY SUPPORT COMPETENCIES IN LANGUAGE AND LITERACY

Literate behaviors are best supported by a wide range of diverse classroom resources and activities that include story dictation and story acting and that are balanced on a continuum from spontaneous to guided play. Careful consideration of time, space, materials, and staff provides a planning context for achieving diversity and balance.

Time for Language and Literacy in Play

First, does the program permit sufficient time for literate behavior in play? The pattern of the day should allow for long, uninterrupted periods of spontaneous play in all centers. If children are rushed and the day is chopped up with teacher-planned "inside time," "group time," "sharing time," "snack time"—that is, with too much teacher choice and teacher voice—the children will have little opportunity to integrate and contextualize their play themes through literate behaviors.

Space for Language and Literacy Learning

Is sufficient space provided for literate behavior in play? Work tables, writing centers, and play areas should be spacious enough to accommodate communication and be set up in such a way that the children can establish face-to-face engagement and visually share materials (i.e., draw on materials, such as miniature toys, that serve as a source for topics) or comfortably share and exchange with one another their knowledge of language and literacy, as in Harriet's booklet writing time.

Materials for Language, Literacy, and Reading and Writing in Play

Materials for language and literacy play include all kinds of writing and printed materials, such as books, catalogs, tablets, clipboards, and sticky notes. Ample amounts of attractively displayed and maintained supplies of paper, crayons, and markers are needed. Books, paper, and writing materials should not only be in the reading or writing center, but also in the dress-up and home play corners, near the outdoor climber, in the block play area, and adjacent to the fishbowl (to record the daily development of the cluster of baby snails!). With the teacher's help, items can be labeled, directional arrows drawn, and symbols and signs made to identify activities and projects. A well-balanced collection of factual and fantasy books, biographies, poetry, and alphabet books is a valuable resource for both teachers and children. To enhance children's awareness of categories of literature, some books may be organized by topic in plastic bins or on shelves in a library area. Is informational material available at other sites in the classroom on such topics as animal habitats, animal babies, kinds of fish, and so on?

Common Core State Standards adopted by most states stress literacy and mathematics with an emphasis on informational reading. State standards for other disciplines (e.g., science, art, music, and social–emotional learning) can be addressed by a judicious choice of informational books and technologies for projects and students' independent research of a topic (Schickedanz & Collins, 2013).

In one second-grade classroom, after a trip to the zoo, children researched informational books about animals. They drew pictures of the elephant and identified its major attributes with labels like "large size," "trunk," and "large tusks."

Guidance for Literacy in Play

In promoting literate behaviors, the staff should know when and how to join imaginatively, but not take over, the children's play, and know when and how to withdraw. The need for guidance is suggested in some of the following issues that arise in classrooms.

Negative Talk   Social–emotional learning is enhanced when teachers help children turn negatives into positives through language. Concern is often expressed about negative ways children use language, such as name calling or disrespect for others. The worst is to say, "I'm not your friend." In one classroom, teachers thought children might be helped by being invited at circle or meeting time to create a chart with columns, with listed words written in the "happy" or "sad" columns. Teachers discussed how to change negative words to positive ones that make the classroom a happy place. Grown-ups call this *diplomacy*, a competency we need throughout our lives (Mitchell, 1993).

Relating to Children with Special Needs   These same teachers wondered how they could help children communicate in play with a child with a hearing impairment. Some suggested inviting someone fluent in signing to teach children to sing and sign. The teacher asked the children to place their hands over their ears and to try to communicate with each other. Wisely, the children themselves contributed nonverbal modes of communicating, such as suggestions to "look right at him" and "talk with your hands and eyes."

STANDARDS FOR LITERACY: CALLS FOR ACCOUNTABILITY

Many early childhood teachers are experiencing pressure to implement standards with emphasis on early literacy skills. These assessments are based on a range of standards that vary from state to state. In some cases these standards are in conflict with what teachers consider developmentally appropriate practice and may consequently narrow the efficacy of a play-centered program. Some teachers believe that too much testing could be detrimental to the emotional well-being of children and erode their sense of self-esteem (Fein, Ardeila-Ray, & Groth, 2000; Genishi & Dyson, 2009; Genishi & Goodwin, 2008; Wien, 2004). Many states have responded to current calls for greater consistency across states by adopting the Common Core State Standards and by using new and evolving assessment measures, which has opened a dialogue among early childhood professionals and educators. Under these new emerging standards, how can teachers be assured that all children in the play-centered classroom have equal opportunity to develop competencies in a broad range of literacy skills? (See Fein, Ardeila-Ray, & Groth, 2000; Roskos & Neuman, 1998; Seefeldt, 2005.)

Despite some educators' concerns about the evolving Common Core State Standards, it is fairly certain that testing will continue to be the primary method for evaluating the efficacy of educational practice for the foreseeable future. Guidelines in the "Continuum of Children's Development in Early Reading and Writing," the joint position statement of the IRA and the NAEYC (1998), provide helpful tools for implementing developmentally appropriate standards.

The many vignettes in this and other chapters illustrate how standards can be addressed in classrooms where the purposes of language are honored and supported by a language- and literacy-rich, play-centered environment. The motivating power of the story play curriculum for young dual language learner Masha comes to mind. Matthew, a child with special needs, struggles to use language to interact in fast-paced fantasy play with peers (Chapter 11). Three-year-old Patrick's introduction to early literacy with his "I Have Friends" story and Angela's compelling narrative reveal the agency and motivation in children's learning and demonstrate the acquisition of specific language and literacy competencies. In these vignettes, we witness an advance from the range of literacy learning displayed in the story play dictation of 3- and 4-year-olds like Patrick and Laronda to the more sophisticated story play productions of kindergarten-age children like Jason. In conferencing with Jomar's primary-school teacher, we observe Jomar integrate social knowledge about the conventions of writing as he "edits" his booklet writing. Emergent literacy is seen in Emilie and Vanessa's letter to their principal about the quality of the "pensiels" in their classroom. These vignettes reflect the role teachers play in supporting these children's advancing development. In large part, evaluation of children's progress in the early years has been based on compilations of documents the children produce and on systematic recording of teacher observations.

Teachers know that children of any age function at varying levels along a continuum of emerging competencies in reading and writing. In Table 8.1, phases of

TABLE 8.1   Expected Competencies in Reading and Writing

Expected Competencies	Examples	Teacher and Environmental Support
Phase 1: Awareness and exploration (goals for preschool). Children explore their environment and build the foundations for learning to read and write.	Children listen to stories and may pretend to read. They acquire book-handling skills. They engage in drawing and scribble writing as they develop competency in using writing tools. Many begin to write their names and attempt other favorite words such as *rainbow*, *I love you,* and *Dear Mommy* or *Daddy.* Children enjoy labeling their paintings, drawings, and many will want to dictate a narrative to go with their drawings.	Time, space, and materials for language and literacy are provided on a daily basis at multiple sites for storytelling and dictation. Many opportunities for spontaneous and guided exploration of book-handling skills, scribble writing, and spontaneous letter formation. Photographs of family and pets provided throughout the classroom.
Phonemic awareness developed through familiar songs, rhymes, and games.	Children begin to recognize written forms of favorite words.	Group activities emphasize phonemic awareness and beginning and ending letter sounds.
Phase 2: Experimental reading and writing (goals for kindergarten). Children develop basic concepts of print and begin to engage in and experiment with reading and writing while continuing to develop phonemic awareness as they engage in beginning reading. Children go from scribble writing to formal writing of words for notes, labels, and their own names.	May use invented spelling to enhance play, such as a "kwyot plas" sign.	Formation of upper- and lowercase letters is introduced through models and templates; appropriately ruled paper is available for spontaneous use in a print-rich environment. Clapping on the syllables of children's names develops awareness of phonemic units as well as of the beginnings and endings of words.
Phase 3: Early reading and writing (goals for first grade). Children begin to read simple stories and can write about a topic.	Children may read their own stories and story plays. Children begin to want to learn dictionary spelling of invented words, such as Jomar's "spasmanheeizflieeen."	Opportunities are provided for writing in journals and booklets on a daily basis. Writing materials are made available throughout the classroom to support children's spontaneous writing. Developmentally appropriate conventions of text construction, spelling, and writing are introduced in a small group or at circle time or to individual children in conference.

TABLE 8.1 (Continued)

Expected Competencies	Examples	Teacher and Environmental Support
Phase 4: Transitional reading and writing (goals for second grade). Children begin to read more fluently and write various text forms using simple and more complex sentences.	Children may begin to create writing tasks for themselves, such as a class newspaper or letters to parents or to others, such as Vanessa and Emilie's letter to the principal about the "bad pensiels" in their classroom.	Writing continues to occur on a daily basis; abundant books for independent and directed reading are available every day. Guidance in conventions of text construction, spelling, and writing is presented in whole or small groups and in conference. Features of a written text, such as dialogue, are considered in activities such as the "author's chair" or in reading and discussions of the writing styles of familiar authors.

Source: National Association for the Education of Young Children & International Reading Association (1998). Learning to Read and Write: Developmentally Appropriate Practices for Young Children. A joint position statement of the International Reading Association (IRA) and the National Association for the Education of Young Children (NAEYC). Washington, DC: National Association for the Education of Young Children.

development derived from the NAEYC and IRA's joint position statement (1998) provide an illustration of the range of expectations and suggested curriculum for young children.

SUMMARY

A play-centered language arts curriculum arises from a context that honors the purposes of children's communication and the responses they might evoke before it stresses isolated strategies for literacy learning, such as letter formation and phonics rules.

- **Literacy begins.** There are many ways that literacy includes more than reading and writing. Literacy encompasses the many forms of speaking and communication, both verbal and nonverbal, as well as interaction with the many new media and technologies.

- **Play, language, and literate behavior: A natural partnership.** Communication in play contributes to the development of literacy in many ways, occurring in the classroom, from the library corner and language arts center, to the sand table and the dress-up corner. Communication enables children to establish a role for themselves in the shared themes of play. They can create imaginary worlds, get a play theme going, and direct other actors. The partnership of play and language facilitates the language learning of dual language learners. It contributes to early story construction. Signs can label things, indicate turns for the swing, and designate a territory. Children can communicate even when talking to themselves. Even when communication is nonverbal, when gestures and props are shared in the home-play corner, synchrony of topic and sequence is clearly signaled; the laundry basket goes with the iron and ironing board, while a carrot wielded like a sword is off topic.

■ **Fostering literate behaviors.** Literate activity, like story dictation, can reveal the literacy conventions children are acquiring. In this chapter, literate behaviors, particularly in pretend and sociodramatic play and in storytelling, are seen as precursors to a grasp of the concept of "story" or "narrative" and the necessary perspective taking this implies. Such understanding emerges early in the child's life through play when children talk, draw, and share their early attempts at storytelling.

■ **Honoring the importance of literate behaviors.** Key features of literacy emerge early and are ongoing. They develop in everyday contexts of the home, community, and school that are often social in nature, occurring in collaboration with an adult or other children. There is a dynamic relationship between reading, writing, oral language, and literacy as each influences the other. Literacy activities are embedded in contexts such as art, music, play, social studies, and science where purposeful meaning occurs.

While much of literacy learning occurs in children's play communication with peers and others, letter–sound correspondence must be taught. Phonemic awareness is not the same as phonics and is distinguished by the ability to detect rhythm and alliteration, phonological memory, and the ability to break down and manipulate spoken words and isolated sounds in words and is best taught in meaningful contexts of games and songs. Phonemic awareness provides a sound basis for later understanding of letter sounds in words

■ **Language and literacy learning in the primary grades: The motivating power of play.** Through ample opportunities in guided and spontaneous play, children become participants in and authors and readers of their own stories. Reading widely and writing in many forms lead to an understanding of the many genres of authoring. Children become motivated to learn dictionary ways to spell words, develop phonemic awareness, recognize letter–sound correspondences, appropriately use upper- and lowercase letter forms, and master the rules for capitalization, punctuation, and other conventions of literacy.

■ **Dynamic approaches to promoting literacy through play.** Teachers can enhance literacy opportunities through guided play curriculum involving drama, story dictation, and story playing. When warranted by a problem in children's play, a sensitive teacher may enter the play event by taking a role that gives them the flexibility to leave when children are able to sustain the action themselves. Such problems may arise when a newcomer attempts to enter the play of others and the teacher may guide the newcomer's admission or redirection.

The story dictation and story play curriculum is a popular teacher-planned activity that supports children's developing ability to construct narratives in the motivating context of dictating a story to the teacher and inviting classmates to enact the roles in the narrative at circle time.

■ **Balanced opportunities for varied kinds of play support competencies in language and literacy.** A balance of time, space, materials, and guidance for literacy activities, on a continuum from guided to spontaneous play, supports children's literate behaviors. Although a classroom that is rich in language and literacy is a powerful resource for children, sources, agents, and settings for learning language are not limited to teachers and schools. In many contemporary classrooms, children's classmates and their worlds beyond school are also resources that provide a broad sociocultural context. Through a play-centered language arts curriculum, we tap into the richness of the full range of diverse cultures and language.

■ **Standards for literacy: Calls for accountability.** The NAEYC and IRA expected competencies in reading and writing can be applied to develop some curriculum and environmental support for literacy learning in a preschool or kindergarten classroom. With the adoption of the Common Core State Standards in many states, educators are now involved in a new dialogue about how to establish accountability to ensure all children have equal educational opportunities.

APPLYING YOUR KNOWLEDGE

1. Discuss some of the many ways that literacy includes more than "reading and writing."
   a. List some of the kinds of literacies besides reading and writing that are important for today's children.

2. Discuss the role that communication in play has in the development of literacy and a sense of "topic" and "sequence."
   a. Observe children in the home play center and note how language and gesture in interaction with playmates communicates topic and sequence in their ongoing play narratives.

3. Describe some of the competencies that literacy activities can reveal.
   a. Collect samples of children's dictated writing and identify some of the ways that children are acquiring a beginning knowledge of writing conventions and the function of texts.

4. Identify the ways that emergent literacy develops.
   a. Write a newsletter to parents summarizing the features of an emergent literacy concept. Suggest some playful activities that involve using

children's names to help them become aware of the patterns and structure of language.

5. Describe how many forms of "authoring," especially in children's own acts of writing, advance literacy in a primary-grade classroom.
   a. Examine a primary classroom environment, both indoors and outside, to discover where opportunities to use writing could be made available.

6. Discuss some ways that teachers can enhance literacy opportunities through guided play involving drama, story dictation, and story playing.
   a. With a partner, describe some of the benefits as well as the pitfalls teachers might encounter when they become directly involved in children's play.

7. Describe how a balance of time, space, materials, and guidance for literacy activities, on a continuum from guided to spontaneous play, can support children's literate behaviors.
   a. Using your own or a classroom you observe, examine the daily schedule of routines to determine the balance of options for kinds of play.
   b. Contrast the amount of time spent in housekeeping routines and circle time versus choice and free play.

8. Apply the expected competencies in reading and writing to develop some curriculum and environmental ideas for literacy learning in a preschool or kindergarten classroom.
   a. Create two circle time activities that use children's names to call attention to beginning consonants, syllables and phonemic units.

CHAPTER 9

Science in the Play-Centered Curriculum

LEARNING OUTCOMES

- Explain how spontaneous play deepens children's understandings of the physical world.
- Discuss two goals of a balanced early childhood science curriculum; include examples related to science and engineering.
- Define and provide an example for terms relating to the nature of science: *scientific practice, scientific concepts, crosscutting scientific concepts,* and *scientific content.*
- Explain how constructivist theories help us understand why young children do not carry out scientific and engineering practices the same way adults do.
- Describe ways that teachers can foster an appreciation for nature and the environment.
- Identify several ways that a teacher can build upon the strengths and address the needs of children who have special needs and children who are dual language learners.
- Explain and provide examples that illustrate how curriculum-generated play and play-generated curriculum foster children's scientific literacy.
- Provide two examples from your observations showing that an integrated science curriculum with play at its center can address science standards.
- Describe several strategies that help teachers gain confidence in teaching science.

> Rosa is playing with a boat at the water table under the shade tree. She slowly pushes the boat down and looks as the drops of water gradually fill it. She watches it sink, whispering, "Come up now!" She lifts it up. She collects small rocks and bark chips from the base of the tree and fills the boat with six large bark chips. "Here you go—Toot! Toot!" She adds three rocks and the boat slowly begins to take on water. Quickly, she piles on two more rocks and the boat sinks. The rocks go down with the ship but the bark chips come floating to the top. "Pop! Pop!" Rosa pushes one of the chips down again and watches as it pops up as soon as she lets it go. ✍

Let's take a brief look at Rosa's water play, a typical activity in early childhood education programs. How does Rosa's spontaneous play relate to science? Young children are involved in science as they seek answers to their own questions, even though this spontaneous play is not the formal, analytical process of the scientist or older student. When Rosa carefully pushes the boat down, we see her investigating what will happen. Scientists and engineers refer to their thought and behaviors as scientific practices. She observes the water entering the boat; observing is another basic scientific practice. Scientific practices (the things that scientists do) relate to Rosa's actions and developing understandings of the physical world. She is also extending her knowledge of important scientific concepts, in this case, cause and effect. She does not yet understand that objects that are heavier than their equal volume of water will sink and those that are lighter will float. However, through activities such as this, Rosa extends her beginning understandings of buoyancy. Rosa is also learning more about scientific content—sensory knowledge about the properties of the bark chips such as their specific color, shape, and size. Scientific practices, integrating concepts, and specific scientific content are key dimensions of an appropriate science curriculum for young children.

Why should early childhood education programs emphasize science? Young children need to learn about the physical as well as the social world and consider them both as being understandable. Science is a natural and necessary part of human development.

PLAY SUPPORTS THE DEVELOPMENT OF SCIENTIFIC UNDERSTANDINGS

Although science has always been an implicit part of the early childhood education curriculum that centers on play, many early childhood educators lack the background in science to make the connections to science explicit. In a rich, play-centered curriculum, thoughtful teachers balance play and teacher-planned curricular activities but clearly distinguish teacher-planned activities from child-initiated play.

The challenge for educators is to bridge the play-centered curriculum that emerges from the children's own interests with more formal teacher-organized and -directed science curriculum. In this chapter, we make explicit the connections between play and science. Many classroom teachers describe using in-depth investigative projects, themes, and units from resource books and science curriculum materials adopted by their districts. Although we agree that there are excellent science programs that promote guided discovery, such programs are not based on children's own expressed interests and initiative. In that sense, they represent only a small range of the early childhood science curriculum.

To design a program with play at the center, we highlight activities that children initiate through their own spontaneous play as well as guided and teacher-directed play. These vignettes demonstrate that science is already an integral part of the play-centered curriculum. Teachers can help parents, other staff, and administrators see how rich the traditional play curriculum is in the area of science. Another purpose is to point out how teachers can extend the play-based investigation of scientific ideas and practices that arise within the context of children's spontaneous play with guided and teacher-directed play (see Figure 1.2).

Young children's attempts to learn about the world and figure out how things work should be at the heart of their science curriculum. Science education has traditionally included the natural sciences: biology, chemistry, physics, earth and space sciences, and more recently environmental science. This has changed. In *A Framework for K–12 Science Education*, science education now includes engineering and technology as well as science (National Research Council, 2012, www.nationalacademies.org/nrc).

Engineering is not restricted just to what engineers do. Instead, in science education the term *engineering* is used much more broadly to encompass the systematic practices people engage in as they solve problems. Young children are engaged in engineering practices as they construct ramps so cars go faster. Similarly, they use engineering practices as they figure out how to swing higher or when they work together to design and build sand castles.

The term **technology** is also used in the framework in a broad sense to describe the particular systems and processes that result when people attempt to solve problems. The term technology is used more broadly than when we use technology in schools to refer to smart boards, computers, or mobile phones. Instead, technology refers to all tools people develop and use.

Early childhood is a time when young children learn to use many basic tools. Young children develop competencies in using the tools of their own culture, such as learning to eat with a fork or chopsticks. Indeed, early childhood educators spend much of their time supporting children's ability to use technologies: cutting with scissors, using a shovel to dig, or holding a pencil to write.

We welcome this change to broaden our ideas about science. Engineering and technology has always been an important yet unrecognized dimension of children's spontaneous play. Though the framework and standards do not apply to preschool children nor every student in K–12, all young children do engage in engineering and technology in play and in daily life activities. Moreover, when young children are playing, they don't make boundaries between science, engineering, and technology. When we observe children's spontaneous play in schools, homes, and community settings, we see many examples of engineering and technology and science practices.

The integrated play curriculum is the foundation for a developmentally appropriate science program for young children—science that encompasses the traditional natural sciences as well as engineering and technology. This chapter begins with a tour of the environment of an early childhood program, analyzing how different indoor and outdoor areas offer numerous opportunities for children to be involved in science.

Science and Spontaneous Play: Scientists Tour a Kindergarten Class

As all young children play, they are involved in activities that scientists would identify as "learning about science." This is what happened when several science professors toured a local kindergarten class. Marilyn is a biologist, Bob is a chemist, and Toni is a physicist.

Science and Spontaneous Outdoor Play.

Marilyn: I'm amazed at how much goes on in such a short time. I've seen a lot of activity related to the rain we had yesterday. Jerry was watching a snail move along the side of the sandbox. He observed and commented on the silvery trail the snail made and then discovered the many trails already made all over the wooden side of the sandbox. He and Alicia organized a "snail race" with three snails. The road was the slide. They were watching the different speeds the snails traveled. Observing and comparing are fundamental scientific practices. I was surprised that the children pointed out that the snails crawled up at an angle. Many adults wouldn't have discovered all that information about snail behavior.

Bob: Yes, I was also surprised at what I saw happening without any formal instruction. The sand in the sandbox is pretty wet, and several youngsters were making "cakes." There was a lot of investigating going on to find the best "batter," just the right amount of moisture to hold the shape in their cake pans. The kids had all kinds of ideas on how to improve the consistency, including adding more water and more coarse sand. Through the scientific practice of experimenting, they were learning about the properties of materials. Their attention span and absorption in their activity impressed me.

As the children continued to play, Marilyn, Bob, and Toni pointed out engagement with numerous science concepts, practices, and significant content. For example, Soshi was trying to pump on the swings. As she tried to figure out how the rhythmic rocking of her body would make the swing go higher, she was learning more about action and reaction. Lisa and Peter were "fishing" in a puddle and found a large worm with many rings that the children called "armor rings." Learning about the particular characteristics of living organisms is important content in biology. Jerry and Alicia's interest relates to ethology, the study of animal behavior. The children making sand cakes confronted an engineering problem: finding the right amount of liquid to add to the mix so that the cakes will hold their shape.

Science and Spontaneous Play in the Block Area.

Toni: This looks like "pre-architecture." I'm impressed with the children's understanding and use of shapes. This repetition of triangular blocks here and the interesting example of symmetry are important concepts in science, engineering, and mathematics.

Marilyn: Aren't these blocks fantastic! Look how the children are experimenting, trying to figure out if the longer block or the two shorter blocks will work better . . . and how they try again . . . and, of course, look at the fun they're having.

Toni: There are so many opportunities for questions for inquiry. I wonder if he will be able to figure out a way to make that block tower stand.

Marilyn: Yes, Luis just learned about the idea of buttressing . . . another important concept . . . and now, I bet, he's going to use it again over there.

They all fall silent for a moment, watching April and Tanisha build roads for small cars. The children use a block for an arch and several triangles to make a bridge. Tanisha puts a car at the top of the bridge and lets it roll down. April learns from her friend's solution and experiments by giving the car an extra push: "Sooo fast!" April, Tanisha, and Luis are engrossed in solving basic problems of engineering and technology. By extending our focus on science to include engineering and technology, we become more aware of young children's competencies and self-guided learning.

Science and Spontaneous Play in the Art Area.

Toni: There's a lot of play and science going on right here. Take a look at that clay table. What strikes me immediately is the way the children explore the properties of the materials. That "food" made out of playdough is not nearly as "good" as the food made out of plasticine. The kids have investigated the properties of these different kinds of clay and the limits of what one can do with the clay. Which clay is harder or softer? Which is smoother? I noticed one boy discover that the bridge he made with the playdough doesn't take much load. The plasticine had more of the tensile properties he needed in a building material.

Marilyn: I'm enjoying watching that girl, Marcia, mix finger paints. It seems like she's learning about concepts relating to shades of color. She's trying to engineer a shade of green that matches the color of the paper. And she's quite precise about it. Look how she adds such a small drop of white. She's involved in observing, comparing, and experimenting.

The visiting scientists observed as Soshi, Jerry, Alicia, and the other children followed their own interests. Through spontaneous play, these children are engrossed

Observing and describing are the foundations of science.

in science, engineering, and technology. In fact, in some of these activities, we see a curiosity about concepts that are milestones in the evolution of science itself: the principles of buoyancy, distance, and velocity, and the physics of the buttress.

Young children often embed their science investigations in fantasy play and imaginative narratives as they communicate with each other. This is a good thing! These interests and the activities they stimulate are common among children playing in environments that are rich in possibilities. How can our observations of young children's natural interests as expressed through play lead us to the formation of a coherent, effective science curriculum?

THE GOALS OF A BALANCED EARLY CHILDHOOD SCIENCE CURRICULUM

When we analyze the nature of science, we recognize that central to all scientific and engineering endeavors are dispositions such as curiosity, motivation to solve problems, and a desire to critically assess the results. We believe an essential goal of science education for early childhood education is to support and encourage these dispositions as children develop their relationship with the natural world.

Developmentally appropriate science programs are based on the similarities between actions of scientists involved in science and children involved in play—deep involvement and interest as well as the energy, knowledge, and abilities to pursue that interest, develop greater knowledge, and solve problems. In both science and play we find that the interest is often social—shared by others at home or at school or among teams of scientists and engineers.

This is our rationale for seeing play as the core of the early childhood science education program. Therefore, to infuse the early childhood program with science, we need to acknowledge the vitality of young children's scientific interests as demonstrated through their play. Young children's spontaneous play shows us the children's interests, what they are curious about, the questions they pose, and how they try to solve problems. We can then incorporate these interests and dispositions and the social energy that invigorates them into the curriculum.

A play-centered approach to early childhood science education addresses what we believe is the basic weakness of the traditional K–12 science curriculum. Our nation has contributed monumentally to the advancement of scientific knowledge and has prospered tremendously from its applications. Yet today many U.S. students graduate with a low level of science literacy that hampers future development of science, engineering, and technology (National Research Council, 2012). Most science courses are seriously flawed by their focus on science facts and rigid routines. What these curricula lack is that which is central to the scientific endeavor: the joy of discovery.

The child who wonders why certain yellow flowers appear in some places in a spring meadow but not in others is a young naturalist exercising inquiry. In contrast, the child who dutifully colors yellow in the outline of spring flowers on a coloring sheet is involved in activity unrelated to science. The first has put forward a problem to be solved that at its core is scientific; this child is acting like a scientist. The second child has engaged in an entirely different problem: how to respond to the teacher's challenge to color the flowers yellow.

In a play-centered curriculum, our youngest students are not simply studying facts but are pursuing problems of interest and judging the adequacy of their solutions. For children of all ages to develop the ability to engage in science, teachers must respect them as emergent scientists. In this way, we encourage all children to see themselves as members of the scientific community. If this sense of community with science is not established in the early years, the prospects of attracting these children to pursue science in adolescence and young adulthood are seriously diminished.

Scientific Literacy for All Children

For decades, the American Association for the Advancement of Science (AAAS) has supported Project 2061, an effort of scientists, science educators, and classroom teachers to ensure that all students have the opportunity to become literate in science, technology, engineering, and mathematics (STEM). Children are curious and eager to learn about the natural world. How is scientific literacy for children in kindergarten through the primary grades described?

The AAAS emphasizes that the most important goal is for young children to like science and become deeply engaged in the spirit of science. This is the time for children to ask "why" and "what" and to seek to answer to their own questions. It is a time for them to look carefully and talk about their observations, a time to make qualitative observations. It is a time for them to make collections and begin to count and measure. It is the AAAS's position that development of a more formal scientific worldview can wait until the later school years. This vision of the goals of science education is reflected in our descriptions of how young children develop understandings of the physical sciences, life sciences, earth and space sciences, and engineering and technology.

All national associations of scientists and science educators underscore the importance of both equity and excellence in science education. Early childhood educators play a critical role in providing equal, consistent support for girls and boys as well as for children from all cultures and backgrounds to define themselves as competent scientific investigators. (See, for example, the National Science Teachers Association position statements on multicultural education, gender equity, and science for English language learners, www.nsta.org/about/positions)

To develop an appropriate science curriculum, we need to draw on the nature of science as well as what we know about all children's development. When we analyze the scientists' comments as they observed the kindergarten program, we find that they discussed children's dispositions for learning science such as curiosity as well as scientific practices, content, and concepts.

As early childhood educators, we support equity and excellence when we analyze the scientific nature of every child's activities by asking ourselves, What scientific practices are they exercising? What scientific concepts are the children developing? What is the scientific content of their activity? How do children's experiences in school relate to their lives in their families and communities?

THE NATURE OF SCIENCE

The following is an out-of-date definition of the term *science*: "a study that deals with an area of facts or truths that are arranged systematically and demonstrate the operation of general natural laws." Many early childhood educators and parents of young children recall memorizing a definition such as this one.

Today's children are actively engaged in science. Young children think as scientists when they see science as part of their daily lives. One primary emphasis is on the importance of helping students develop their understanding of science by gaining competence in the practices or processes of science as well as acquiring scientific knowledge (explanations) and solving problems through participation in meaningful activities. Another primary emphasis is the long-term development of an understanding of key scientific concepts—the "big ideas" in science. Although scientific content knowledge, "the facts," remains integral to science education, merely learning scientific facts is no longer the primary goal of science education. Today's scientists and science educators view science as a social process in which knowledge is constructed through collaboration with colleagues.

Scientific and Engineering Practices

For clarity, we use both terms, **scientific practices** and **scientific processes**, during this transitional time when engineering and technology are being integrated into the K–12 science education curriculum. The term *practice* is used by scientists as well as engineers to emphasize active, cognitive engagement as well as the discipline of engaging in the enterprise of seeking understanding of the natural world. *Practice* is the term used throughout *A Framework for K–12 Science Education: Practices, Crosscutting Concepts, and Core Ideas* (National Research Council, 2012).

Young children naturally use scientific practices to seek answers to their questions. They observe, record, and analyze as they attempt to construct explanations to answer scientific questions. They design engineering solutions to problems they imagine or encounter. We watch them as they engage in observing, communicating with others, describing, comparing, questioning, collecting, organizing, analyzing and recording data, and interpreting results to reach conclusions.

In their spontaneous play in the yard, 6-year-old Mark and 7-year-old Gillian find earthworms in a pile of mulberry leaves near the fence. They observe that earthworms have rings and some of them are thicker at one end. They compare several earthworms and find that both small and large worms have a lot of rings, but that "only the bigger ones have a lump near the front." They want to find out what the lump is and if the older worms, like trees, have more rings. With their first-grade teacher's help, they find the answer to their question about the lump in a drawing of a worm found in a science resource book. No information is given about the number of rings, so they go back and count. They find they need a magnifying lens because one worm is tiny so it's difficult to count the rings. ⌀

Mark and Gillian collaborate in finding answers to their questions. This vignette shows their obvious delight in learning with and from each other and thereby illustrates their co-construction of knowledge as they answer their questions through this joint collaborative activity. As they draw pictures of the worm, they're involved in the scientific practice of recording information. By using common scientific tools such as a magnifying lens, they further develop science competencies. With further teacher guidance, young children can compare properties of objects, organize information, and record their data through drawings and technological tools such as photos or videos.

Scientific Concepts

Scientific concepts are organizing principles of "what we know." "Cylindrical," "green," "hard," and "life cycle" are examples of concepts that young children develop. Ibrahim knows that green is a property that can refer to different objects: the tomato leaf, the harder tomatoes, some of the crayons, and paint at the easel. Many basic concepts young children develop relate to the properties of objects and materials. They learn to describe objects in terms of such properties as color, shape, size, and weight. Teachers can model science conversations that acknowledge children's love of big, unusual, and descriptive words such as *transparent, minuscule,* and *chrysalis.* Using appropriate vocabulary is important in all areas of science.

As they grow older, children are better able to understand more abstract, relational concepts such as cause and effect, structure and function, and stability and change. The framework emphasizes **crosscutting concepts**, that is, concepts that cut across the arbitrary boundaries between the natural sciences and engineering. "Cylindrical," "green," "hard," and "life cycle" are examples of crosscutting concepts because they can be applied to varied content.

Young children learn such science concepts best when they encounter the same concept over time and in different science content areas. Duckworth (2001) reminds us that "we see how early experience, only partially understood, over time contributes to the construction of large ideas" (p. 185).

During their brief tour, the scientists observed that the children dealt with a great many scientific concepts through their spontaneous play. Tanisha and April were learning about concepts of distance and velocity. Like an engineer building a high tower, Luis was applying the concept of buttressing to add strength and stability.

Scientific Content

Scientific content refers to valid factual subject-matter information. It is important for children to have opportunities to return to favorite activities again and again. As children become deeply involved over an extended period, they enjoy their growing mastery of specialized science content.

Informative books related to science content areas abound. A book on insects might include sections with images and specific information about leafhoppers, aphids, dragonflies, mayflies, moths, and butterflies. It is vital that we provide ample opportunities for young children to explore a wide range of science areas to the depth they choose. In addition to books on life science, there are engaging books for young children with appropriate content in the physical, earth, and space sciences as well as engineering and technology.

In a balanced science curriculum, children learn science content within an organized framework of coherent scientific concepts and processes. In a play-centered science curriculum with sufficient time for spontaneous play, children's understanding of particular scientific content, concepts, and processes are expressions of their own curiosity, interest, and creativity. If we analyze the touring scientists' observations of the kindergarten class in terms of science content, we find that through spontaneous play some children were finding out about worms, some about sand, some about blocks, and some about different collage materials.

> Ibrahim's teacher has documented his involvement with guided play activities in the garden. He is one of several children who always returns to the school garden each day. At 4 years old, Ibrahim has learned a lot about the tomatoes in the small garden outside his child-care center. He knows that ripe tomatoes can be yellow as well as red, and he can identify several varieties of cherry tomatoes and beefsteak tomatoes. He can also distinguish a tomato leaf by its shape, texture, and fragrance. He knows when the tomatoes are ripe and how to pick them carefully.
>
> When Ibrahim's teacher shares her observations with his parents, she learns that his grandparents, who come from Oman, have several types of tomatoes growing in their garden. She explains to his parents how his playful gardening activities, at home as well as at school, relate to the science framework and specific state standards such as children's understandings of the attributes (properties) of objects such as smell, color, shape, and size; their understanding of the life cycles of plants; as well as their more general understanding of science as a personal and social endeavor connected to their everyday lives. ✆

SCIENCE, PLAY, AND CHILDREN'S DEVELOPMENT

In developmentally appropriate science education programs, teachers continually learn more about the development of each child they teach. What are the interests shown by 4-year-old Madison and 7-year-old Samuel? How can we describe their developmentally different way of understanding the physical world around them?

In developing an early childhood education science curriculum, teachers find constructivist theories helpful in looking at children's experiences in context and in interpreting children's interests and responses. The work of Piaget and contemporary cognitive scientists demonstrates that young children do not carry out scientific practices such as experimenting in the same way that adults do (Piaget, 1965a). For example, younger children might experiment with yellow and blue paint to create a particular shade of green, but their experimentation will not be systematic. Rather than adding a bit more blue and mixing it well, they might add different amounts of different colors, thus changing many variables. Similarly, young children might try different ways to use a set of weights to balance a balance beam, but their efforts are trial and error rather than planned and comprehensive.

A closer look at children's levels of cognitive development leads us to understand why young children will not be able to fully comprehend many scientific concepts in the way that adults do despite well-intentioned, diligent instruction. Although children's abilities vary considerably and are often underestimated, mature scientific thinking takes time. It involves such practices as the ability to analyze, to form propositions, and to make inferences and deductions. Young children are not able to do this in the way adults do. The deductions and inferences made by young children do not have the generalizable applications typically observed in the thought processes of most adolescents and adults. As shown in the previous examples, children's thinking is egocentric and perception bound; they are not yet able to understand all aspects of a sequence occurring over time.

To illustrate, Piaget (1965b) described his research on children's growing understanding of shadows in *The Child's Conception of Physical Causality*. He found that most of the young children believed that the objects themselves produced the shadows. When he asked very young children about shadows, they usually told him that the shadow next to a book was an actual substance coming from the book. The somewhat older children he spoke with had begun to understand the relationship between the shadow and the source of light. Yet not until most children were in middle childhood, however, did they explain to him that the shadow resulted from an absence of light because the physical object was blocking the light.

This does not mean that we should underestimate young children's abilities or ignore their interests and wait. Shadows illustrate this point well. Many young children demonstrate their fascination with shadows in their spontaneous play when they shake each other's "shadow hand" or play "shadow tag." Skillful teachers find guided play as well as teacher-planned activities that draw on children's interests expressed in their spontaneous play.

Science Learning and Social Contexts

Scientists as well as constructivist developmental theorists underscore the importance of historical, cultural, and social contexts, from the level of the child's family, school, and local community to the state, national, and global levels. The development of a child's science learning is inseparable from her or his social and cultural environments. Vygotsky (1978) emphasized that families, schools, and communities are integral to each child's development. In all cultures and settings, children have experiences that support the development of particular scientific processes, concepts, and content knowledge.

Parents and teachers in urban areas, for example, might focus on providing children with different types of building blocks. In Janet's urban kindergarten class, much of the children's spontaneous play relates to engineering practices. The children build cityscapes—apartment buildings, offices, malls, trains, and freeways. They ask numerous questions that reflect their understandings of engineering and technology as they watch the office building under construction a block away from their school. They draw pictures of cranes and scaffolds.

In contrast, children who live on farms about 50 miles away know a great deal about earth sciences and life sciences. Compared to urban children, they have more sophisticated concepts about life cycles and more differentiated knowledge about soil and weather.

We find that children's understandings usually develop faster in areas in which they have greater experience with the physical world and where important adults and peers share social knowledge with them. With time for further maturation and more interactions with the physical and social world, young children's manner of thinking changes. We need to build our science programs around children's preexisting knowledge and their present ways of thinking and provide experiences that will foster future development.

NATURE AND THE ENVIRONMENT: DEVELOPING A SENSE OF PLACE

Early childhood educators and naturalists express the concern that few of today's children have opportunities to develop a deep connection to the land, a sense of geographical place, through sustained opportunities to play outdoors in fields, woods, beaches, and even empty city lots. Around the world, more children are living in urban areas and spending more time indoors. The need for developing a sense of place is expressed beautifully by Nabhan and Trimble in their classic work *The Geography of Childhood: Why Children Need Wild Places* (1994).

Louv (2008) brought a sense of urgency about children's disconnection with the natural world to widespread attention with his bestselling book *Last Child in the Woods: Saving Our Children from Nature-Deficit Disorder*. He points out that most children now have a deficit of fundamental experiences in nature. Louv emphasizes that for children to develop emotionally, socially, and intellectually, they need unstructured, direct, and playful experiences with nature. Today, children around the world are growing up disconnected from themselves and from the natural world, at the very time that we recognize a need for all people to develop greater awareness, knowledge, and feelings about protecting the global environment.

Environmental education challenges all of us to slow down and do more. Sobel (2004) is a leading environmental educator who reminds us that developing a sense of place is a developmental process that requires more than a rigid "curriculum." In writings for educators such as *Children and Nature: Design Principles for Educators*

(2008) and *Place-Based Education: Connecting Classrooms and Communities* (2004), Sobel and his colleagues propose principles for teaching and learning. They point out that we must begin with the children's own immediate environments for them to engage emotionally as well as cognitively with the natural world. Young children need active time to play, to have outdoor adventures in schoolyards and neighborhoods, as well as quiet or solitary time to wonder and relax.

This is the approach taken by the North American Association for Environmental Education (NAAEE). In *Early Childhood Environmental Education Programs: Guidelines for Excellence,* the NAAEE explains that environmental education in early childhood promotes knowledge of the natural world and an emotional connection to nature as well as the growth of dispositions and acquisition of skills (NAAEE, 2010). The NAAEE guidelines underscore that young children need freedom to discover the natural world, to play and explore rather than following a more structured approach found in classes for older children and adolescents:

> Children are developing a relationship with the natural world. They are learning how to gently hold a worm, examine it then return it to its habitat. They are learning to appreciate all kinds of weather . . . Children are watching plants and animals change through their life cycles, and learning respect for the natural world and living things. Children who respect the environment feel an emotional attachment to the natural world, and deeply understand the link between themselves and nature, will become environmentally literate citizens. (pp. 3–4)

We find these guidelines for environmental education exemplary because their aspirational goals and principles and their guidelines for practice are congruent. For example, aspirational goals emphasize connecting with children's prior experiences

Observing plants and animals can lead to a curiosity about nature.

and promoting equity for all children. The corresponding guidelines suggest practical ways for educators to achieve these goals. The goals, principles, and guidelines reflect the authors' deep knowledge of children and extensive experiences in early childhood environmental programs.

Fortunately, in recent years there has been an enormous increase in environmental education resources with ideas for parents and educators of young children. Numerous books, journals, and articles suggest ways to engage children with the natural world (e.g., Arce, 2006; Benson & Miller, 2008; Campbell, 2009; Chalufour & Worth, 2004, 2006; Starbuck, Olthof, & Midden, 2002; Rivkin, 2006; Rosenow, 2008).

Helping Urban Children Develop a Sense of Place

Although play-centered curricula draw on and reflect children's social contexts, it is critical that we not limit our expectations and curricula to these contexts.

Melben (2000), a teacher in an urban elementary school, views urban children's lack of outdoor nature activities as an example of inequities. In an article in *Science and Children,* she presents examples of efforts to develop science projects that followed the children's own interests and drew from their experiences. Her descriptions of projects with rainwater and pigeons amply illustrate that children's understandings of ecology and sense of wonder can be promoted in urban as well as more rural settings.

This principle is particularly important in science. In cities and suburbs, and particularly in unsafe areas, we need to ask, How can we help urban children, their families, and ourselves develop a sense of place, an appreciation and ease with the outdoors, and a feeling of wonder?

As a preschool teacher in New York City, Butler realized that the children in her program had little knowledge about or appreciation for nature (Hachey & Butler, 2009). She wanted her students to have experiences with nature, to have time to listen to the calls of birds, hear the rustling of tree branches, and feel the texture of leaves. Her commitment to helping young urban children develop a love of nature and sense of place lead her to develop experiences that integrated nature-based play and gardening in the urban classroom.

These teachers in the United States are contributing to widespread global education efforts to enhance young children's connections with the natural world and their cultures. In South Korea, for example, an "eco-early childhood" curriculum promotes care for the local and global environment. This curriculum includes activities that promote habits like recycling and are integrated with Korean practices such as traditional exercises and meditation (Kim & Lim, 2007).

PROMOTING EQUITY AND EXCELLENCE FOR ALL

Observation of spontaneous play of individual as well as groups of children is central to discovering children's interests and promoting excellence for all children. Interests are the child's bridge between play and science and home and community. As teachers committed to equality of opportunity, it is particularly important for us to consider the ways in which honoring each child's interests leads to all children participating in science.

The urban children in Shelley's preschool program had been sloshing through the snow for weeks as they walked to school, delighting in falling snow, and sharing stories about snow adventures. Shelley first extended these activities by bringing snow and icicles inside in containers so that the children could have unhurried observations and chances to discuss the melting process. She then put water in an ice tray and took the tray out of the freezer throughout the morning so that the children could observe the changes. This led to a weeklong observation and exploration of the melting of a 50-pound block of ice that Shelley purchased from an ice company and placed in a baby bathtub positioned prominently in the classroom. ∅

Ferguson (2001) writes about Thomas, a 5-year-old in her class, sharing her concern that he appeared uninvolved with the other children as well as uninterested in the classroom curriculum. This changed dramatically when, during a class discussion about snakes, Thomas hesitantly shared that he knew all about snakes, that he "had almost 100 snakes in his basement" (p. 6). Of course, he received quite a response from his peers! Ferguson describes how she extended this teachable moment into a lengthy inquiry project, although she felt uncomfortable around snakes. Thomas and his Uncle Bob served as enthusiastic resource specialists to Ferguson and the other students. Uncle Bob brought in a large snakeskin. Thomas and several children took a trip to a pet store, where they saw a huge snake. This was followed with related classroom activities that reflected the children's interests, including a collection of plastic reptiles that Ferguson placed in the manipulative area. ∅

The feature *Family Diversity* describes how a teacher in a multiage child-care center incorporates the interests, talents, and knowledge of family members to enrich the program for all children.

Building on the Strengths and Needs of Children Who Are Dual Language Learners

From his first day at school, Carlos looked forward to experimenting at the water table. Initially, he spoke mostly with two other children who spoke Spanish as well as English. His teacher noted the complexity of Carlos' explorations during his spontaneous play. Recognizing his interests and level of ability, his teacher bought plastic tubing, funnels, and a series of graduated beakers so that Carlos and his friends would find many challenging problems to solve. ∅

FAMILY DIVERSITY

Interweaving Multicultural and Multigenerational Learning

Ryan, a teacher in a multiage childcare program (ages 3–8), knows that each year the children observe the life cycle of silkworms with great fascination. It's spring and the mulberry trees have just begun to leaf out. Ryan takes out the silkworm eggs he saved from last spring. He and the children go out to collect the smallest, most delicate leaves so the newly hatched, thread-like silkworms will have food when they hatch from eggs to larvae.

Bee loves to observe the tiny silkworm larvae and is always one of the children who participates daily in gathering leaves. With a few other children, she places them around the silkworm. What a voracious appetite they have and how quickly they grow! Bee is keeping a daily journal, measuring the silkworms with a twig and drawing pictures to record their enormous growth after just a few weeks of devouring leaves. As they spin their cocoon, Bee tells Ryan that her grandmother knows how to spin the silk from the cocoons into silk thread. Ryan knows that her grandmother comes from Laos and has seen a beautiful handmade traditional silk belt she made.

Ryan contacts Bee's mother, who says that she can bring her mother to school and serve as translator. Bee, her grandmother, Mrs. Xiang, and her mother work together with Ryan to plan two visits with activities that are multicultural, playful, and scientific. Before the activity, Mrs. Xiang will prepare the cocoon so she can pull out the fine silk threads. The children can then watch as she does so and makes them into thread. She will bring a small loom to show the children how she begins to weave, along with examples of handmade materials that show how she has dyed the silk threads and wove them using traditional patterns.

What an opportunity for extending the multicultural curriculum by literally weaving in science, engineering, and technology. Highlights of the school year always include family members coming to school to share their interests, talents, and knowledge. Ryan sends a note home inviting other parents to join them, and invites the other kindergarten class and the principal. What a wonderful way to advocate for play-centered science.

Alia, a kindergarten student who speaks Arabic, designed and built a treasure box. This is an example of a teacher-initiated carpentry project that requires little knowledge of English while promoting continuous, playful peer interactions. First, her teacher asked Alia and other interested children to make a drawing, like an architect's blueprint, to represent their design. With some adult help, Alia carefully cut out and traced the parts onto the wood, then cut the wood. She learned about sanding, first using coarse sandpaper then a finer grade. During subsequent days she nailed the sides of the box together. After she attached the top with a hinge, she decided to drill a hole in the top so that she could lift it more easily. This activity is part of an ongoing science and engineering program that builds on children's interests as demonstrated in their play and promotes equity for all children. ∅

These examples show how the play-centered science curriculum provides numerous opportunities for children to develop greater fluency in English as they explore the physical world and interact with their peers.

Teachers show that all children are welcomed by including known, familiar objects in the indoor and outdoor environment, particularly things children see at home. In this way, teachers reduce stressful situations and provide support for listening and speaking in relaxed and engaging situations. This encourages dual language learners, including children who are immigrants and refugees, to draw on familiar experiences and show their competencies. The NSTA position statement "Science for English Language Learners" urges teachers to build on children's funds of knowledge—that is, the knowledge that children gain from their family and cultural backgrounds (2009). Playful teachers consider the innumerable ways that dual language learners can relate science processes, concepts, and content to their everyday lives, families, and cultures.

Through science activities, teachers take advantage of the many ways that the development of a new language parallels that of the first language. Central to first language development is a supportive social and physical environment. Similarly, early childhood educators create environments in which children's learning of English can flourish (DeBey & Bombard, 2007; Genishi, 2002; Genishi, Dyson, & Russo, 2011; McDonnough & Cho, 2009). As children play and explore, they not only hear language but also wish to communicate their own observations, questions, and desires. Playful science experiences such as Alia's carpentry project and activities with blocks, plants, sand, and water provide daily opportunities for children's gestures to be understood in context. A single word or a two- or three-word phrase conveys ample meaning. Simple sentences contribute to conversations with peers and adults.

Developing Inclusive Science Curriculum for Children with Special Needs

Teachers plan play-centered science curricula that recognize the strengths and meet the needs of all young children. This includes children whose special needs have not yet been formally identified as well as those identified as qualified for receiving special services. The UN Convention on the Rights of the Child recognizes that all young children have the right to play. How can teachers ensure that children with special needs have numerous opportunities to engage in spontaneous and guided play related to science? Just as the scientists toured the kindergarten class with an eye toward opportunities for learning science, all teachers can tour their environment with an eye toward serving all students with special needs. Such informal tours are even more useful in the company of early childhood special educators, occupational therapists, and speech therapists.

Melva learned that in the following school year Aiden, a student with visual disabilities, would be a student in her second-grade class. To prepare, she wanted to learn more about his development and his interests, as well his specific visual abilities and challenges. During the last weeks of school, she met with family members, his current teacher, and the special education teacher.

As they walked through the classroom, his grandmother commented that he'd enjoy the math manipulatives and really like the terrarium with the desert lizard. Joy, the special education teacher, described a range of computer-assisted technologies including nature websites with special features to accommodate people with low vision.

Melva learned more by observing Aiden in his first-grade class. She saw firsthand that during spontaneous play, Aiden and several peers built with a set of table blocks and made structures with clay. Melva was surprised to confront her own stereotypes when she saw Aiden and a friend working on a large puzzle of a forest scene. ⍥

The following questions serve as an initial guide:

- Do all children have easy access to materials?
- Are particular accommodations necessary for a child to be able to see or hear or use tools such as scales, magnifying lenses, or scissors?
- Are there quiet corners for a single child to focus on a private exploration as well as open outdoor spaces for active social exploration, climbing, and swinging?
- Are spaces set up so that children can play alone or with one other child without the distraction of a larger group?
- What accommodations are needed so that the experiences of children with particular special needs are similar or nearly equivalent to those of peers?

The feature *Advocacy in Action: Make and Take Science Play Boxes* describes how a first-grade teacher supports children's natural scientific curiosity in a play-based way when they cannot attend school.

As they work with children with special needs, teachers remember that all children have particular strengths and interests. Pat shared one of her treasured memories of a kindergarten child with autism who loved to play with blocks. She honored his joy and involvement with blocks rather than insisting that he "go to another activity first." After many weeks, it was there in the block area that he first engaged in parallel play and later spoke his first word.

PLAY-GENERATED SCIENCE CURRICULUM AND SCIENCE CURRICULUM–GENERATED PLAY: MAKING CONNECTIONS

Recognizing the key role of play in development, we focus first on providing environments rich in possibilities for spontaneous play. This contrasts with science programs that typically begin with particular science content and then consider opportunities for children to explore it. Teachers use the framework of the play continuum as they plan play-centered curriculum. We begin with play-generated curriculum that emerges from children's own interests.

Becoming an Informed Advocate for Play

ADVOCACY IN ACTION: MAKE AND TAKE SCIENCE PLAY BOXES

Asthma has become a major public health concern. Kara teaches first grade in a school where the most common reason for absence is asthma. A fifth of the children in her class have already been diagnosed by age 6. In this school and across the country, an increasing number of children are spending more time in hospitals and at home because of this environmentally related illness. In the past when children were sequestered at home for more than a few days, Kara had mailed them schoolwork. She and several other primary-grade teachers discussed their concerns about the frequent absences of students in their classrooms and realized that they needed to be more proactive in meeting these students' needs.

As one part of a comprehensive approach, they invented "make and take" science and play boxes with donated materials prepared by the children and family members. Their goal is to add another science play box each month so children have choices. A science book made by the class about a current class project is always included. Kara makes sure that the boxes have tops that work like trays so objects don't fall on hospital floors. Materials, like collections for sorting, are included so that children can do activities independently or with others. Other materials are provided that can be used for group games with other children or adults, such as science-themed game cards. The accompanying handout of ideas is not only translated into Spanish and Korean, but also includes photos so that the children themselves can "read ideas." Kara and the other teachers visited the nearby hospital, met the child life specialist, and made future plans to collaborate.

Play-Generated Science Curriculum

How can we extend opportunities for science and engineering? How can we decide if or how to intervene? What best supports children's learning of scientific and engineering practices, concepts, and content? The principles that guide orchestration constitute a continuum of intervention strategies that range from setting the stage to guided play to teacher-initiated play. When thinking about enriching the science curriculum, we consider strategies at all points along the play continuum and their implications for extending children's involvement with science.

Setting the Stage for Learning about the Physical World through Spontaneous Play   The basis for a play-centered curriculum is a well-planned environment that allows for multiple opportunities for spontaneous play. Developing an environment that is rich in opportunities for science is a creative challenge for educators. It takes careful planning to enable children to play with a wide variety of materials. Paints, clays, collage materials, blocks in different shapes and sizes, soil, sand and water, climbing structures, plants, animals, and collections of natural and manufactured objects are examples of the varied materials in play-centered programs.

The play-centered environment is flexible. Physical space and time are rearranged as interests change. Perhaps this week a group of children return each day to build complex constructions with large blocks. Their teacher might extend the time

Materials offer children opportunities for playful exploration of the physical world.

planned and space allotted for block activities as well as provide additional materials. Creative teachers and parents look for free and recycled materials. What might happen when a group of young engineers need more outdoor blocks for the huge bridge to connect two tall towers? We observed children in one class making additional blocks by fitting together milk cartons of different sizes.

Similarly, one fortunate class in a rural area had new possibilities open up when Russell's father brought in a truckload of coarse sand from the river, and the parent group built a sand and gravel pit that provided open-ended opportunities for imaginative activities. Some children spent weeks sifting, digging, and investigating the properties of wet and dry sand. Others became involved in engineering practices through large vehicle construction play.

Encouraging Further Exploration of the Indoor and Outdoor Environments

After initially developing the environment, teachers then observe children in their spontaneous play and modify the environment so that children can extend scientific dimensions of their play. Like a dance, this involves the teachers themselves in a creative and playful process.

> Based on her observations of Rosa at the water table, her teacher decided to place a box with an assortment of objects near the water table. She included some large wooden objects that floated and small metal objects that sank. Rosa's teacher understood that she was initiating greater opportunities for learning science for all the children as well as individualizing the curriculum for Rosa. ∅

Some children in the kindergarten classroom were using blocks to build towers. Perhaps placing a set of table blocks nearby would engage children in new engineering challenges to be solved. Jerry and Alicia demonstrated an extended interest in snails.

These vignettes show teachers observing children's spontaneous play, following the children's interests, thinking of possibilities related to these interests, and adding materials in thoughtful and sensitive ways. To engage children more deeply in science and engineering practices, teachers are engaged in an ongoing process of observing and reflecting.

Interacting with Children in Their Play   Taking the child's-eye view in science education often takes the form of wordless communication. A teacher's smile, returned to a child's questioning glance, is nonverbal communication. In the context of the child's attempt to balance one more block on a tower of blocks, it is a scientific conversation: "When you do it that way, they fall over." "Yes. I was surprised too."

During spontaneous play, teachers help children maintain their focus by assuming the role of the Artist Apprentice so that play areas remain less cluttered. In guided play, teachers might decide to take the role of parallel player, sitting side by side with children. If teachers enjoy exploring and playing with blocks or with sand or collage materials, their own sense of interest, wonder, and focused involvement through spontaneous play will be communicated. When teachers' own play reflects authentic interest and engagement, they avoid the trap of producing static models that children might copy.

Extending the Play-Generated Science Curriculum   The play-generated science curriculum moves back and forth along the continuum from spontaneous play to guided play to teacher-directed play.

In their play, Sarah, Dean, and Nellan expressed their interest in worms. John, their second-grade teacher, saw this as an opportunity for guided experiences involving worms. He encouraged further play and exploration by providing pieces of Plexiglas so the children could observe the movements of the worms in greater detail. When this proved a popular activity, John reflected on the children's interests and asked them if they could find other wormlike animals. Within a week, there was an exciting collection of caterpillars, several kinds of worms, and insect larvae that Nellan had brought in. This led to a conversation between Nellan and the other children about the differences between worms and insects, as well as the sequence of the insect life cycle. ⌀

One teacher in a school-age child-care program enjoyed the enthusiasm that the children brought to their play with light and shadows. She extended further play by showing them how to outline each other's shadows with chalk on the walkway. This led to the question, "How big can your shadow get?" In follow-up activities, they outlined their shadows on butcher paper several times during the day. The children and teachers had fun generating many researchable questions; for example, "Can you shake your shadow hand with someone else's?" "Can you get away from your shadow?" "Can you make your shadow stand on someone else's shadow's shoulders?" ♉

When a child is deeply involved in spontaneous play, teachers can find ways to extend and enrich play by turning to science resource materials and curriculum. After a windy week in which children ran and danced about the yard waving scarves, their teacher looked for resources on weather and wind, several of which included kite-making and parachute-making activities.

Teachers' decisions about extending play are driven by children's energy and current interests. Timing is everything. Extending the play-based science curriculum is informed but not driven by science frameworks and standards. The vignettes throughout this chapter illustrate how teachers support children's spontaneous play in ways that are recognized by society as "science and engineering."

For example, Shelley relates children's explorations with ice to the physical science strand of her state's frameworks that includes "states of matter" as an important concept. When John asks the children to collect other wormlike animals, he is thinking about his state's science frameworks that include a focus on living things, their life cycles, and their habitat for the primary level.

Science Curriculum–Generated Play

In a play-centered curriculum, teachers intentionally explore the ways in which the curriculum can promote play. The connection is seamless when the science curriculum emphasizes depth and is carefully planned and articulated throughout the year and across grades rather than simply a series of unrelated daily activities. Explorations of authentic questions are most likely to be replayed in children's subsequent spontaneous play. When science curricula are appropriate for the development levels and interests of the students, children replay what they are learning.

The following vignette describes an ongoing environmental education unit on arthropods and the continued exploration and play of Jenny's kindergarten and first-grade children.

> In September, Jenny teaches the children how to use bowls to collect insects and spiders in a wooded area near the kindergarten/first-grade classroom. She models tapping bushes or shrubs with a stick over a white plastic tub. Leaves, grit, dust, and small animals fall into the tub. Ned, Shawn, and Ashley crouch around the tubs eagerly narrating in careful detail the movements of the animals: "There's a tiny green spider. It's *so* small, wait, there's two. How many spiders do you have? Don't let it get out!"
>
> Children's interest in spiders continues. Several weeks later, Ashley, Yumi, Eric, and Ned are on their hands and knees, carefully using sticks to lift and adjust the position of a metal, wheeled object. Eric lifts the entire object

slowly, revealing mulch and many small arthropods. Suddenly Ashley yells, "Oh my gosh, a spider! A red spider! It has eggs." A large, rust-colored spider with a round, whitish abdomen is revealed. Quickly it burrows back into the litter and soil. Ned says quietly, "It's a mother spider. It's an egg sac. The white thing is an egg sac." Ashley declares, "It's red like the dirt." Over the next few weeks, the rust-colored spider appears in drawings in the children's science journals. The children return often to the area to seek the spider.

In January, the fourth and fifth graders join the kindergartners outdoors. Shawn walks to the white plastic tubs, chooses one from the wagon, and finds a large stick on the ground. He walks with his fourth-grade partner to a bush and gently taps the bushes. He stops, places the bowl on the ground, crouches and looks inside the bowl. His partner watches him. Shawn stands, takes a step back to the bush and taps again, carefully collecting more debris and animals. Again he places the bowl on the ground, squats and bends his head deeply over the bowl and looks. His fourth-grade partner adopts his stance. ✆

In this example, notice how technological tools were integral aspects of the teacher's thematic unit and the children's play. Teachers select or develop units that draw on children's interests and naturally lead back to spontaneous play.

ADDRESSING THE SCIENCE FRAMEWORK AND STANDARDS IN THE PLAY-CENTERED CURRICULUM

The 2012 *Framework for K–12 Science Education: Practices, Crosscutting Concepts, and Core Ideas* represents a major shift in recommendations for science education (National Research Council, 2012). It mandates the integration of the natural sciences, engineering, and technology in K–12 science education curriculum. Second, the framework requires the integration of scientific and engineering practices, crosscutting concepts, and content in science education. All early childhood educators should become familiar with the goals, principles, and conceptual framework. Despite the fact that the framework does not address science education for preschool children, it will certainly impact programs for all young children.

The goal of the framework is to ensure that by the end of 12th grade, students will have achieved goals related to the following dimensions:

- An emotional and intellectual appreciation for the wonder of science
- Content knowledge of science and engineering sufficient for them to become thoughtful consumers of everyday scientific and technological information, and participate in civic discussions about important current issues
- Sufficient knowledge and an interest in learning more about science throughout their lives
- The necessary scientific and engineering background to give them options in pursuing a career path, including careers in science and engineering

In efforts to achieve these goals, the framework describes aspirational principles to guide the development of science curriculum. The following principles are particularly relevant for early childhood educators:

- The science education curriculum should incorporate children's own dispositions to investigate.
- Children's understandings in science, engineering, and technology develop over time.
- Early childhood science curricula must incorporate children's interests and build upon their previous knowledge.
- All students must be provided with accessible, equitable opportunities.

The framework emphasizes coherence and depth of student understanding. Curricula are required to integrate three key dimensions of science education that we have discussed: practice, crosscutting concepts, and content:

1. Scientific and engineering practices are emphasized to ensure that students at all grade levels engage actively in direct experiences with objects, organisms, and systems.
2. Crosscutting concepts are emphasized so that students' experiences are coherent and integrated across scientific and engineering disciplines. The following crosscutting concepts are emphasized in kindergarten through second grade: pattern, cause and effect, structure and function, stability and change.
3. Core ideas or content knowledge relates to the natural sciences as well as to the relationships among science, engineering, and technology. The framework addresses fewer "big ideas of science" than previous frameworks so that students can develop greater depth of understanding.

At first glance, these aspirational goals and principles suggest that the corresponding standards might be developmentally and individually appropriate; however, a close examination of the standards raises serious questions. We are concerned that standards for kindergarten and primary grades as well as the process for their implementation are inconsistent and sometimes contradict these principles and aspirations. For example, will the state standards reflect an emphasis on active engagement with the practice of science? Will they drawing upon young students' interests and developmental abilities? Will they emphasize valuing students' cultures and experiences in their homes and communities?

Few early childhood educators were involved in developing the framework or writing the standards. Similarly, few early childhood educators responded to the calls for review and input. During the coming years, full participation in critical implementation decisions will require extensive study on the part of the entire early childhood education community. Implementation will impact most young children and teachers. It will involve major changes in curricula, teacher preparation, and changes to textbooks and instructional materials. (Note: The complete framework is available in electronic version without charge at the National Research Council's website: www.nationalacademies.org/nrc.)

Our review of science standards shows that though a science curriculum with play at its center does not address all standards, it can address those that are developmentally appropriate and draw on children's interests and prior experiences. In Table 9.1 we draw from vignettes in this chapter to illustrate how teachers develop play-based curriculum that address several Next Generation Science Standards (Achieve Inc., 2013).

TABLE 9.1 Addressing Next Generation Science Standards in the Play-Centered Curriculum

Vignettes	Next Generation Science Standards
At the water table, Rosa observes and interacts with objects. She explores what happens when she pushes wood chips below the surface of the water.	Disciplinary Core Ideas PS2.A: Forces and Motion Crosscutting Concepts: Cause and Effect
Mark and Gillian find answers to their question about the "lumps" on a worm. They use a magnifying lens to observe closely.	Science and Engineering Practices: With guidance, plan and carry out an investigation in collaboration with peers.
Ibrahim distinguishes the tomato leaf by its properties: shape, texture, and fragrance.	LS1.C: Organization for Matter and Energy Flow in Organisms Crosscutting Concepts: Patterns in the natural and human designed worlds can be observed and used as evidence (K-LS1-1)
As April and Tanisha roll toy cars down the bridge, they explore how incline and force affect speed.	PS2.A and B: Forces and Motion: Types of Interaction Crosscutting Concepts: Cause and Effect
Matt and Levi examine soil and rocks.	Disciplinary Core Ideas: PS3-B: Sunlight warms Earth's surface Crosscutting Concepts: Patterns in the natural world can be observed, used to describe phenomena, and used as evidence
Children in Janet's class in an urban area use blocks to build cityscapes.	ESS3.C: Human Impacts on Earth's Systems Crosscutting Concepts: Systems and System Models

Source: Achieve Inc. (2013). Next Generation Science Standards: For States, by States. Retrieved from http://www.nextgenscience.org/next-generation-science-standards.

DEVELOPING CONFIDENCE IN TEACHING SCIENCE

Many early childhood educators are concerned that they know too little about science to develop a rich play-centered science program. Unlike the scientists who toured the kindergarten classroom, many teachers are aware that they have little expertise in the natural sciences, engineering, and technology. How can teachers who feel insecure in this area develop a challenging, play-centered science curriculum?

View yourself and others as members of a community of playful investigators rather than as experts. Think about the science-related activities that you enjoy so that your students will observe your curiosity and your sense of wonder. Become knowledgeable about the science-related interests and abilities of your students and their families as well as others at school and in the community. By recognizing the scientific expertise of others, you are serving as a good role model for your students.

Vignettes such as the example of Bee's grandmother and the silkworm cocoons illustrate that teachers do not need to be scientific experts. Teachers can enrich their science programs by turning to local resources provided by children, their families, and community members. Think about the many possible classroom visitors: gardeners, scientists, engineers, farmers, physicians, veterinarians, high school science teachers, and bakers—this list goes on. Talk with colleagues to get their recommendations for visitors who are appropriately informative and interesting.

You can also find excellent resources to help you. The NSTA journal *Children and Science* includes articles especially for teachers of young children. Teachers share creative ideas for investigations of life science (e.g., Blackwell, 2008; McHenry & Buerk, 2008), earth and space science (e.g., Danisa et al., 2006; Ogu & Schmidt, 2009; Trundle, Willmore, & Smith, 2006), and physical science (e.g., Ashbrook, 2006; Longfield, 2007; Novakowski, 2009; Trundle & Smith, 2011) as well as engineering and technology (Ashbrook, 2012; Burton, 2012; Morgan & Ansberry, 2012).

Some education resource books and texts focus on science for young children. *Ramps & Pathways: A Constructivist Approach to Physics with Young Children* is an appealing and informative book in which DeVries and Sales (2011) examine how children mentally construct knowledge using their initiative. The book explores how children build ramps and pathways that answer the questions that arise: Can you build a ramp so a marble turns a corner? Can you build a ramp so that a ball hits one domino and sets off a chain reaction? Can you build a ramp where you use several fulcrums and drops to send a marble across a large area? *Ramps & Pathways* includes numerous large and detailed photos that portray children's deep involvement in scientific and engineering practices occurring over several years.

The Education Development Center's *Young Scientist Series* provides an integrated framework for science in early childhood education described in *Worms, Shadows, and Whirlpools: Science in the Early Childhood Classroom* (Worth & Grollman, 2004). A guiding principle is that "Children's science is about play: play with materials and objects and events" (p. 158). Open explorations are followed by more focused explorations and extension activities. The series includes the environmental education resource

Discovering Nature with Young Children (Chalufour & Worth, 2003) and the science and engineering resource *Building Structures with Young Children* (Chalufour & Worth, 2004).

The Full Option Science System (FOSS) is an articulated K–middle school curriculum. The modules for primary-grade students draw on the interests children reflect in their play. Co-director Larry Malone explains that "The challenge of curriculum development is to design opportunities for children to explore national phenomena . . . to create an engaging space . . . not to tell children what to do and what to think (Larry Malone, personal communication, January 25, 2013). For example, in the earth and space science unit *Air and Weather* (2012a) children construct and try out parachutes, make rocket systems with balloons, and build kites and pinwheels. During investigations, children discuss and evaluate their designs. In the *Balance and Motion* (2012b) investigations, we see children engrossed as they build toys that spin, construct mobiles, and build runways that control the motion of marbles. In other primary-grade modules, students further explore interests that are often shown in spontaneous play and explorations. These include *Insects and Plants* (2012c), *Solids and Liquids* (2012d), *and Pebbles, Silt, and Sand* (2012e).

All teachers can help children learn how scientists investigate and solve problems by surrounding children with science resources. By showing your students that you, yourself, turn to numerous science media including books, DVDs, and science websites you promote children's scientific literacy. In an environment rich in science resources and opportunities for play, children and teachers continually extend their knowledge of the physical world and their opportunities for exploring it.

SUMMARY

Young children are curious about the natural world. They are interested in finding out about their physical environment and finding out about how things work. A program based on children's interests therefore includes an emphasis on science.

- **Play supports development of scientific understandings.** As early childhood educators integrate the curriculum with children's play as the focal point, they see the great extent to which all children's activities involve science and engineering practices, concepts, and content. Like the scientists who toured the kindergarten class, teachers begin to "see science" everywhere.

- **The goals of a balanced early childhood science curriculum.** An essential goal of science education for early childhood education is to support and encourage dispositions such as curiosity and the drive to solve problems. Teachers support scientific literacy by observing children closely and developing an environment that invites children to explore their physical world through spontaneous play. Scientific literacy integrates practices with knowledge about concepts and content. Scientific literacy is developed over time and is greatly influenced by the social and cultural context.

■ **The nature of science.** Teachers' understanding of the goals of science education as well as their knowledge of scientific and engineering practices, the unifying concepts, and important "big" ideas of science guide their curriculum decisions.

■ **Science, play, and children's development.** Although children's abilities vary considerably and are often underestimated, the development of mature, sophisticated scientific understandings takes time. Children's understandings usually develop faster in areas in which they have greater social as well as physical experience.

■ **Nature and the environment: Developing a sense of place.** Early childhood educators and naturalists are concerned that so few children have opportunities to develop a deep sense of geographical place. Fortunately, in urban as well as rural environments educators find that neighborhood trees, gardens, schoolyards, and parks can provide opportunities (see the North American Association for Environmental Education).

■ **Promoting equity and excellence for all.** Teachers become aware of children's interests and strengths as well as their needs through their observations of play. Play promotes opportunities for all children to engage in science through engaging, low-stress activities.

■ **Play-generated science curriculum and science curriculum–generated play: Making connections.** Beginning with an environment rich in possibilities for engaging in science, engineering, and technology, thoughtful teachers balance child-initiated and teacher-planned activities. This balance changes from preschool through second grade. Teachers extend children's spontaneous play by guiding and directing play in which children deepen their understandings. This naturally leads to developmentally appropriate teacher-planned curriculum. Conversely, teacher-planned science activities that engage children's interests naturally lead to children's spontaneous play.

■ **Addressing the science framework and standards in the play-centered curriculum.** *A Framework for K–12 Science Education* (National Research Council, 2012), the newest framework for science education, emphasizes the integration of science, engineering, and technology. The framework points to the importance of the knowledge children bring to school as well as extensive explorations of familiar environments. The primary goal is for young children to develop a greater interest and deeper understandings. Many standards, however, seem inconsistent with guidelines about developmentally appropriate practice. Therefore, early childhood educators need to remain vigilant so that standards and their implementation are appropriate and increase students' enthusiasm and engagement with science. The science curriculum with play at its center can address those science standards that draw upon children's experiences and are geared to their interests and levels of development.

■ **Developing confidence in teaching science.** Many early childhood educators are concerned that they know too little about science to develop a rich play-centered science program. We suggest that you view yourself and others as members of a community of playful investigators rather than as experts. Think about the science-related activities that you enjoy so that your students will observe your curiosity and your sense of wonder. Become knowledgeable about the science-related interests and abilities of your students and their families as well as others at school and in the community. By recognizing the scientific expertise of others, you are serving as a good role model for your students.

The early childhood years provide a rich and perhaps critical opportunity to draw the natural power and direction of children's reasoning into the community of science. This is best accomplished by following children's own curiosity and interests in learning about the world. Play is central to young children's development of fundamental scientific interests and dispositions. As we incorporate these interests and energies into the early childhood education classroom, we promote equity for all children and promote a scientifically literate generation.

APPLYING YOUR KNOWLEDGE

1. Explain how spontaneous play deepens children's understandings of the physical world.
   a. Describe and draw a simple map of indoor and outdoor spaces to show how teachers can develop an environment for exploration of the physical world through spontaneous play for children with special needs and children who are dual language learners.

2. Discuss two goals of a balanced early childhood science curriculum; include examples related to science and engineering.
   a. If a scientist toured your program (or a program with which you are familiar), what would she or he find that promotes a balanced early childhood science curriculum? Draw a simple map of the environment and identify five or more opportunities for scientific learning.

3. Define and provide an example for terms relating to the nature of science: *scientific practice, scientific concepts, crosscutting scientific concepts,* and *scientific content.*
   a. As a teacher or future teacher, write or discuss a science-related activity you enjoy that might provide your students with opportunities to observe your own curiosity and sense of wonder. Use the above terms to analyze this activity.

4. Explain how constructivist theories can help us understand why young children do not carry out scientific and engineering practices the same way adults do.
   a. Use the vignettes from another chapter to explain why teachers who wish to promote a developmentally appropriate science education program must be knowledgeable about children's level of development.

5. Describe ways that teachers can foster an appreciation for nature and the environment.
   a. Increase your own observational abilities: Select a leaf that you find aesthetically pleasing. Observe it closely. What are its properties or attributes? Can you make a list naming more than 25 attributes? (For example, translucent, smooth, green, pointy.)
   b. Observe children playing outdoors in an environment of your choice. Describe how you, as an educator, might use their activity as an opportunity to foster their appreciation for nature.

6. Identify several ways that a teacher can build upon the strengths and address the needs of children who have special needs and children who are dual language learners.
   a. Describe an example that shows how teachers can include a child with a physical disability.
   b. Bee's grandmother demonstrates how to spin silk from cocoons into thread. Describe two or three specific activities familiar to young children from their families or communities that would promote science literacy.
   c. Share a website that early childhood educators can use as a resource to promote science understanding for students who are dual language learners.

7. Explain and provide examples that illustrate how curriculum-generated play and play-generated curriculum foster children's scientific literacy.
   a. Prepare and share an annotated bibliography with five nonfiction books related to science that you recommend for play-centered childhood programs for students in preschool or K–2.
   b. Using Table 9.1 as a model, develop a table that demonstrates how children's activities in a play-centered curriculum can address several science standards from your state or program.

8. Provide two examples from your observations showing that an integrated science curriculum with play at its center can address science standards.

9. Describe several strategies to help teachers gain confidence in teaching science.

CHAPTER 10

The Arts in the Play-Centered Curriculum

LEARNING OUTCOMES

- Discuss the ways that the four cornerstones of an arts curriculum—time, space, materials, and teacher know-how—support a viable arts program.

- Discuss the reasons to balance offerings in the arts curriculum across the continuum of spontaneous, guided, and directed play.

- Explain how knowledge of the stages observed in children's drawings provides a basis for understanding the trajectory of the children's development, interests, and competencies.

- Create some standards-based curricula that involve spontaneous and guided play in children's group projects and investigations.

As if in an opera, 4-year-old Noah stands at the easel, reflects, and then declaims in song what he has playfully discovered about color:

> There is some colors which are red, blue, yellow
> There is a lot of colors
> And there is aqua, aqua,
> And there is blue, blue, there is blue, blue . . .
> and white and aqua
> There is white and aqua

Now he contemplates his palette and sings, "There is some colors," and names the primaries, "Red, blue, and yellow." He dips his brush into the blue: "And there is blue, blue, there is blue, blue," emphasizing blue perhaps because it is basic to aqua. Noah intends to create aqua and knows that one does not do that by starting with white. Finally, the white is celebrated, "and white and aqua," and Noah closes softly, "There is white and aqua." ✆

This delightful image of a child singing while painting accompanies the closing credits of Thelma Harms's classic film, *My Art Is Me* (1969).

What does the image reveal? It reveals the creative transformations in the flow of play that lie at the heart of children's art making. It also tells a lot about what Noah knows about color, and about what he doesn't know about color—there is a bit of green in aqua. And, more importantly, it demonstrates how art (Noah's painting, poetry, and song) and problem solving (his creation of aqua) are intertwined in the context of play. Close observation of children playing within the arts gives teachers sound content for a developmental curriculum.

In this chapter, we stress that all curricula in the arts should encompass a balance of play options. These include opportunities to engage in directed and guided play in the arts, such as those that often occur at circle, project, and small-group time, but equally important, to assure there are ample time, space, and materials for children's spontaneous play as well.

The arts are indispensable to a successful developmental curriculum. This is because children spontaneously turn art into play, and play is the young child's principal means of learning. Indeed, the most successful curricula put art to use at every turn—and by art we mean graphic art, construction, poetry, storytelling, music, dance, and drama—so that play and the arts curriculum are indistinguishable from one another.

Now, the spontaneity with which children turn art into play does not mean that specific planning for art need not take place. Such planning embraces a number of considerations:

- When should arts activities be spontaneous? When should they be guided or directed?
- What can be learned from spontaneous engagement in the arts?
- What materials, tools, and resources do the children need?
- What technical homework should the teacher do?
- How can teachers and the environment encourage spontaneity?
- How should teachers provide guidance and direction?

Considerations such as these are discussed next with particular attention to graphic art and construction, but with references throughout to many of the other arts, such as music and drama.

A GUIDE FOR CURRICULUM DESIGN

An effective arts curriculum uses art to support children's play and uses play to support art. Because play occurs throughout the early childhood classroom, so too will the arts. Although we traditionally think that play serves the arts (Noah should discover that aqua has green in it), it is equally important in early childhood settings to ensure that the arts serve play. To see this happen, the teacher must often enter the children's world of play and bring into that world the basic materials and props of art (Edwards, 2010; Gee, 2000; Isenberg & Jalongo, 2014; Zimmerman & Zimmerman, 2000).

Entering the Child's World of Spontaneous Play

A teacher may enter the child's world of play by introducing a new material or a play prop or by modifying a play setting at points when play falters. Sometimes the teacher does this on his own initiative and sometimes at the children's need or request. Sometimes he discusses or demonstrates the new prop or setting directly, and sometimes he does not. Under what circumstances do these variations occur, and what, in the first place, impels the teacher to enter the children's play at all?

Drawing can be available at the easel as well as the worktables.

Spontaneous play is often of a "pretend" nature ("I'm the mommy, you be the baby," or "Look at me, I'm a puppy!"). Teachers may fear that entering the child's play requires drama skills in which they are unprepared to engage. The sensitive teacher, having observed children's play closely, knows that even simple modifications in props and settings will stimulate children to initiate more elaborate pretend play. She may pick up a play phone and, in a play voice, call for an "emergency crew." She may add to available props an armband with a red cross on it, a badge with "police" written on it, or a few chiffon scarves or transparent curtains. In these instances, little needs to be said to the children. They are likely to pick up the indirect cues instantaneously and create scripts to integrate those props into the ongoing play. British drama educator Dorothy Heathcote used this method of indirectly shaping the context to suggest new or elaborated avenues for drama or dramatic play (Bolton, 2003; Johnson & O'Neill, 1984; Lux, 1985; Wagner, 1999).

To stimulate playful engagement and focus in the graphic arts, the teacher might introduce novel painting tools. Sponges, for example, stimulate the creation of patterns and textures. Rollers invite children to paint over the entire surface of the paper rather than merely working in a cramped area in the middle. By demonstrating how the paintbrush can be used to apply paint to the sponge or roller, rather than dipping these tools directly into paint, the teacher helps children gain greater control and mastery over their productions. By modeling these somewhat sophisticated accessories and techniques, the teacher helps children create a new world of pretend.

In dramatic play, the teacher helps a child create his own superhero cape from paper, rather than pulling one from the costume box that he may have used before when he was 3. By bringing constructive art to dramatic play, the teacher engages the child anew. He makes sure that materials for drawing, cutting, and scribbling are near at hand so that accessories to complement dramatic and fantasy play can be created quickly.

Sometimes children engaged in dramatic play will seek the teacher's assistance, perhaps for new props: "We need things to make a hideout!" Blankets, old sheets, pieces of carpet, and large and small blocks will serve the purpose. Or it may be for technical help—say, to design a network of tunnels in the sand. Indeed, a young child's technical requirements can become quite elaborate. "There's buried treasure in the sand pit, we need a pirate's map," may signal a need for the teacher as "Artist Apprentice" to facilitate in constructing a network of lagoons, walkways, bridges, and highways, or to devise relevant graphics, such as a skull and crossbones, and DANGER, DETOUR, and other hazard signs.

Incorporating Artwork

Bringing artwork into the flow of play in the classroom environment is not difficult (Edwards, 2010; Isenberg & Jalongo, 2014). For example, on some bright, sunny day, we may want to trace around children's shadows with the fat chalks we made by mixing Plaster of Paris and powdered tempera with water in Dixie cups (remembering, of course, to pour the dry mixture into the water, as well as safety concerns about use of powdered media). Later the children will wonder why the chalk outlines of their shadows do not fit them when they return to capture them in the late afternoon.

Are the fat chalks still at hand for use on another day (wet and rainy this time) when there are no shadows at all? Then children can use them to create beautiful red, blue, and violet "expressionist" stains on the wet asphalt. Maybe this is the day that Noah will begin to construct his knowledge of color by discovering all the necessary pigments to make aqua. If the teacher is lucky, he may be able to share this epiphany by guiding Noah to notice the many tones of aqua on the pavement.

Abundant access to two-dimensional graphic arts, such as drawing, scribbling, and collage, lends itself to spontaneous exploration of the arts through play. These mediums are provocative adjuncts to children's fantasy play and make important contributions to the child's development of both literacy and small motor skills.

Monitoring the Quality and Challenge of Play: Tactile and Sensory Arts

Teachers know that tactile sensory play with mediums like water, finger painting, and play dough have universal appeal. Children find the tactile/sensory aspects engrossing, and knowledge of the physical properties of materials is acquired through free manipulation of such media. The ease with which finger paint and play dough can be transformed through manipulation also recommends them as valuable adjuncts to fantasy and functional play. Children frequently create songs and stories as they work with these materials. The following vignette illustrates how what begins as simple tactile/sensory play can bring greater challenge to an art activity. Guided by the teacher, it becomes more deeply complex, resulting in children's acquisition of a whole repertoire of art-making skills and engagement in reflection on what they have learned.

Six-year-old Jason attends a child art studio on Saturday mornings. One of the first activities involves finger painting to music and movement. Children begin by choosing two colors of finger paint. Jason and the other children are encouraged to spread the paint with hands and fingers as far as they can reach on the large sheet of paper that covers the whole table. Today, eight children, their teacher, and one parent volunteer are involved. Jason has been willing to don one of his father's old shirts with sleeves rolled, but is very tentative about touching the paint. However, when the music sets up a marching beat and children are encouraged to go around the table using fingers to draw lines, Jason falls in as all march around the table singing in time to the music.

Within a few minutes, the finger paint has covered most of the table. Special tools for making marks, such as twigs, old combs, and toothbrushes, are made available. The teacher announces, "We're making rivers and mountains and snakes that ripple and wiggle and squiggle around the table." Now a "snowstorm" comes as small scoops of dry tempera are sprinkled into the wet, and children use their hands to make beautiful, blended smudges.

But soon a rainstorm comes up. As mark-making tools are gathered, small brushes and trays of liquid tempera are introduced. As the rain comes faster and faster and faster, the adults and children create patterns of raindrops all over the table, with spatters and splashes. As trays of liquid are removed, seeds are sprouting, and plants are growing more lines.

By now the paper is quite wet. Torn and crushed strips and pieces of crepe paper and shiny pieces of giftwrap are distributed for children to press into the wetness to create textures and new patterns. The crepe paper makes multicolored stains, turning red and blue to violet. Finally, confetti is offered, and Jason delightedly integrates his bits into the group's composition.

The handsome piece is allowed to dry as the children clean up. Later it is hung, and at snack time they view their work. As they talk about their composition, they begin to learn the names of the processes they have used; color, line, texture, and space are just a few. Jason liked the bumpy parts the best (Scales, personal observation—Berkeley Child Art Studio). ✄

Manipulation of many **tactile/sensory materials** is intrinsically satisfying. In some classrooms these may be used in activities merely to keep children occupied, without asking how they can lead to more challenging experiences. The introduction by Jason's teacher of various new materials enhanced the children's acquisition of complex art-making skills. Her guidance of the children's reflective discussion of their finger-painting experience illustrates also how development can be enhanced around a relatively simple art activity. In the future, these children may use particular aspects of their experience, such as line and texture, in more deliberate creations.

With respect to tactile/sensory art activities, a number of questions can be raised:

- Does the activity have an educational rationale? How much learning does it really promote?
- Does it link with goals for the group curriculum or with a learning plan for individual children?
- Does it support extension into pretend play with peers?
- Does the activity have a balanced emphasis not only on aesthetics and the narrative aspects of sociodramatic play, but also on its potential to support children's growth in other areas, such as early math and science?
- Can we be sure that the components of the arts curriculum, particularly for the kindergartner and older child, are sufficiently challenging? Or are we "dumbing down" the curriculum for the older children?
- On the other hand, in mixed-age groupings, are too many aspects of the curriculum overly demanding for the youngest?

The Arts Enhance Knowledge in All Curriculum Domains

The arts, science, mathematics, and play merge when children work on the skeletons they will hang in the haunted house in October. This artful play with bones will get its scientific accuracy from a chart in the school's encyclopedia or, better yet, from a visit to the physiology department of a nearby college. Children may begin to get acquainted with their bodies: how they look and work and what's in them. In their art-making activities, children's use of resources drawn from language arts and math address the Common Core State Standard's emphasis on the informational content of literacy.

Are black paper and a clear plastic jar on hand to make a home for the worms dug up in the moist earth the day after it rained? In this seamless world, the teacher may wonder where art leaves off and science begins.

Constructive play with blocks involves art and math, often replicating architecture, whose interdisciplinary richness has earned it the title "queen of the arts." Blocks are a major accessory for pretend play, creating the context for elaborate fantasies for individuals, pairs, and groups of children. Blocks serve as an important adjunct to extend play. Shoebox houses furnished with fabric, wallpaper, and rug scraps and peopled by miniature clothespin dolls become a small city when blocks are laid end to end become "Main Street." Curved units define a small park and provide other needed structures. Here we see several guided play projects evolving and being integrated into the children's spontaneous block play, a sure validator of a play-generated curriculum.

Valuable insights into the child's developing intelligence, competence, and social awareness can be gained by teacher observations, notes, photos, or videotape recording of such play in block areas. (For a review of literature and new insights, see Frost, Wortham & Reifel, 2012, and Reifel & Yeatman, 1991.) Teachers will want to use other samples of children's artwork to make authentic assessments of development. What should they look for? Much information is available on universal features of the development of drawing schemas in such classic works as Lowenfeld (1947), Goodnow (1977), and Kellogg (1969).

Special Needs   Much less information is available on the features of development of drawing by children with emotional, perceptual, or developmental disabilities. Sara, an art therapist working on a kindergarten assessment team, noted that certain features of children's drawings offer early "warning signs." Some of these are a sudden regression to a **scribbling stage** in drawing schemes, drawings that show lesser competence in the execution of some features, the repetition of an obsessively recurring theme, or drawings with all lines leaning in one direction (S. Wasserman, personal communication, 2005). In the course of this discussion with the art therapist, a cautionary vignette was submitted by one of the teachers about a smaller-than-average child who consistently painted at the bottom edge of the paper at the easel. Teachers thought this child possibly had a perceptual problem. When they encouraged the child to elevate himself by standing on a large block while painting at the easel, his paintings began to fill the **pictorial space**.

Supporting Art and Play: Time, Space, Materials, and Teacher Know-How

An arts curriculum becomes established in the play-centered program through the modes of intervention described in Chapters 4 and 5. In the sections that follow, we illustrate how the establishment of a viable arts curriculum depends critically on specific forms of support. When adequate time, space, and well-managed materials are provided—and when teachers have done their technical and conceptual homework and strike an appropriate balance of spontaneous and guided play—engagement in the arts can be explored deeply.

Time   In ideal programs, ample time for spontaneous and guided play with arts materials is provided throughout the school day. A balance between the two is essential, however. Making spontaneous play the only mode leads to fragmentation and chaos; on the other hand, an overabundance of teacher-planned activities prevents children from integrating their knowledge by trying things out for themselves. A simple measure of the balance of play options can be achieved by examining the program's daily schedule and staffing pattern. This will allow the teacher to determine whether play options are sufficiently balanced and supported by adequate time and staff. If much of the day is devoted to teacher-directed group activity, it is likely that occasions for spontaneous play are reduced. Research indicates that in early childhood classrooms the most effective learning occurs in small groups (four to six children) engaged in either spontaneous or guided play activities.

Space   In well-planned programs, space is organized to encourage various configurations of children to engage in arts activities at multiple sites throughout the classroom and play yard:

- Clean, smooth work surfaces free of glue or paint residue from previous projects may be set up in several areas, with seating inviting the solitary play of an individual child or the collaborative or parallel play of pairs and groups. Small trays or Formica-backed blocks for individual work with clay and other wet mediums can be obtained (usually as scrap) from a local kitchen installer or lumber yard.
- Ideally, these areas will be relatively quiet and protected from the flow of fast-paced play, but at the same time be accessible to and visible from active play areas.
- Expectations for the kinds of play that will take place are clearly cued by furnishings and accessories, which will distinguish areas where free exploration of materials and resources is expected from those where teacher-planned activities or more structured projects will occur.

If monitored sensitively, both outdoor and indoor centers for drawing, scribbling, writing, dance, and music making can support engagement in the arts as an end in itself or as an adjunct to pretend play.

Pacific Oaks College has developed valuable guides for assessing the complexity of playground spaces. These guides provide a formula to be used to calculate the play potential of music- and art-making centers and help teachers achieve greater predictability in play patterns that occur in the classroom (Kritchevsky, Prescott, & Walling, 1977; Scales, Perry, and Tracy, 2010; Walsh, 2008).

How does the teacher know how many places to set up? One rule of thumb specifies setting up 1.5 play options per child, to allow for choice and variety. The teacher

Musical activities with multiple players need adult guidance.

organizes her setup to provide attractive play activities for children who may have to wait to exercise their first choice. In a classroom of 20 children, this implies the provision of about 30 play stations, for example:

4 places at the clay/art table

4 places at two easels (double-sided)

4 in the home-play area

3 places at the puzzle/manipulative table

4 children in the block area

4 in the book area/sofa

2 to 4 places at the writing center

3 in the science area with trays of shells or hermit crabs to be examined with a magnifying lens (Kritchevsky, Prescott, & Walling, 1977)

In this set-up strategy, the teacher uses the environment to offer children choices and redirects a child whose intentions cannot be accommodated in one area—for example, when the block area is full. These ratios can be modified for smaller or larger class enrollment (adapted from Scales, Perry, & Tracy, 2010).

Although management and predictability are important elements in any program, inflexible attempts to organize all aspects of arts activities lead to an inhibition and dwindling of children's creative expression. Conversely, too little organization in presentation and sequencing in arts activities can result in chaotic movement and environmental clutter. Both extremes undermine children's chances for mastery, competence, aesthetic development, and understanding.

Materials   Open-ended arts activities and construction materials ideally complement spontaneous play, providing the raw materials, resources, and accessories for the world of pretend. All the arts, including drama, song, and dance, often merge with and become indistinguishable from play. Not all materials, however, need to be open-ended. For example, older children can use templates for frequently called-on images—stars, various animals, dinosaurs, vehicles, geometric shapes, and even numerals and letters. The use of these materials should be couched, however, in an atmosphere of free exploration, creativity, and problem solving, and they should be well balanced with an abundance of open-ended materials. Music and rhythm instruments fall into a similar category and may need some preliminary introduction in their appropriate use to enhance the quality of spontaneous play.

At a drawing and scribbling table set up for guided play (e.g., with scissors, markers, and plastic templates set out), 4-year-old Toby uses the bus template turned on its side to represent a wind-filled flag fluttering from the main mast of his ship. By tracing the curved edges of the multiple wheels of the bus, he represents perfectly the rippling fabric. Several children immediately seize on the novel potential in the templates, creating flags for their own drawings. ✆

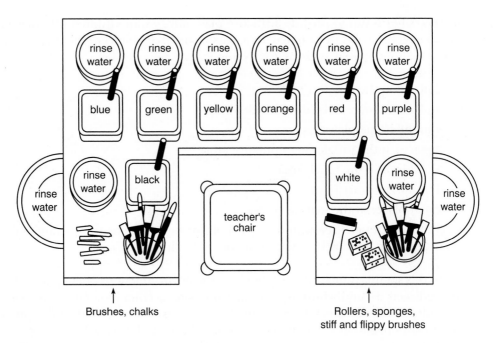

Figure 10.1
Berkeley Child Art Studio Group Palette for Painting Class

Teacher Know-How   In doing their homework, early childhood teachers will want to equip themselves with both technical and conceptual information. For example, on a technical level, What colors make pleasing blends? How do primary and secondary colors blend? Knowing this, the teacher can set up the palette at the easel, so that colors adjacent to each other blend pleasingly, as shown in Figure 10.1. Teachers should also be sufficiently familiar with art materials to be able to answer the following questions from their own experience:

- What are the characteristics of paint, paper, and clay?
- How much starch or extender should be added to the paint? The color should not look transparent, watery, and washed out. A creamy texture that flows off the brush pleasingly rather than clumping in globs is desired.
- What kind of clay would be best—a low-fire white clay that takes a glaze or acrylic paint nicely when it is fired, or a rich-toned red clay that is handsome in itself when fired but that might stain children's clothing if aprons are not worn?
- Have safety concerns for use of mediums such as glue, powdered pigments, wheat paste, and so on been addressed and children's allergies known to all staff (Isenberg & Jalongo, 2014)

Teachers will want to have a good understanding of the peer cultures that emerge in their classrooms. On another level, they will also want to know something about the cultural, historical, and aesthetic traditions of their own heritage and of other cultures. What kinds of folk art, music, dance, costumes, or use of color relate to the backgrounds of children in the classroom? What kinds of music or recorded materials are suitable for use with young children during active class time, in or out of doors? What about during naptime and during the late afternoon in afterschool care?

Presentation of Art Making and Constructive Play Materials

In addition to the nature and use of art resources and materials, we are concerned with their presentation, accessibility, maintenance, replenishment, and imaginative selection. Children do not use an item spontaneously if they cannot see it, if they do not have some basis for imagining its potential, or if it doesn't work. Therefore, the following should be instituted in the classroom:

- Items are displayed at eye level. If possible, use movable shelves as well as some storage units that are equipped with sturdy wheels; this provides flexibility to display materials where they will be used or needed. Musical instruments, movement accessories like scarves and headbands, and recorded music could be stored and displayed for use indoors or outdoors in such movable units.

- Crayons are kept clean and sorted by color with the paper peeled, so a real choice of color can be made.

- Tempera paint is of a good consistency, and tempera paint blocks are kept clean. Each medium is presented in a skill-appropriate choice of colors.

- Watercolor pans are clean, watercolors are set up in a skill-appropriate choice of colors and in a self-help setup.

- Paint setups will evolve, starting with (a) primaries, (b) secondaries and tertiaries, (c) black and white, and (d) tints.

- Brushes, rollers, and sponges are introduced as appropriate.

- Appropriate paper for each medium is available.

- Felt markers make a clean and clear mark, scissors cut with ease, and masking tape is readied for use in small strips on a block or two. All items are displayed in a self-help setup.

- Make sure that provocative new items are available from time to time, along with a continuous flow of novel "found" treasures and recyclables, such as the dots from the paper punch, various stickers, or old greeting card pictures and colorful paper scraps. Even the inevitable "anonymous" easel paintings can be recycled into beautiful collage material. Cut into strips or random shapes, they provide incentive for creating new inventions and accessories for fantasy play—headbands, bracelets, and belts—at spontaneous drawing and crafts tables.

- Both large and small unit blocks are made available indoors and outdoors, both with and without props. Block-shaped templates on shelves aid access and storage. Stacking blocks too neatly and storing them out of the way or in the same place at all times will diminish children's expressive use.

■ Heaping blocks in a box or basket is not recommended, because dumping them out can breed chaos rather than construction, as well as an indifference to the care of the environment.

Attention needs to be given to how different play materials are arranged relative to each other.

In one classroom, combative play that seemed to occur around dinosaurs located in the block area prompted teachers to relocate them to a carpeted area within the science center. The area included attractive books and materials that provided pictorial information on dinosaur habitats from the prehistoric age. In this way the science area was expanded and enriched, and the block area was liberated for constructive play. ✆

On another more general note, constant vigilance is needed to ensure that the children's display areas do not become usurped for teacher or project storage or become catchalls, thereby losing their effectiveness as a support for "choice." This is a particularly troublesome problem when there are multiple users, such as occurs in the necessary rotation of morning and afternoon staffs or when different age groups must be served.

In contemporary urban settings, with the exception of gardening, children have little opportunity to play with mud, even though this was a staple in the early days of preschool programs. Observing transformations in the properties of natural materials like this is an important benefit of play in natural settings, often severely restricted because of regulations about sanitation. One of the authors of this text developed a curriculum to recycle discarded, unfired clay pieces to replicate such experiences in a manageable form for a school setting.

Curriculum Goal: An ongoing project that enables children to experience the transformation of a natural material; a way for children not only to engage in sensory motor play, but to observe and learn about the properties of a natural substance, mud. All this by doing what they enjoy—that is, pounding, playing with water, and squishing and manipulating a nice cool substance.

Step 1.   Collect discarded and unfired clay pieces.

Step 2.   Break up the dried clay chunks with a wooden or rubber mallet.

(Tip: Place chunks of clay in a canvas bag before children pound them to keep bits from flying around. This step could be individualized so that each child recycles his or her own bit of clay.)

Step 3.   The first transformation created by pounding the dried chunks of clay produces a mixture called "grog," which can later be sprinkled or blended into clay that is over moistened. A small

Step 4.

portion of the grog can be moistened to become a more liquid, creamlike substance called "slip," with which children can later experiment to make their clay body moister or use like glue to stick pieces together or smooth the surface of a clay sculpture.

Step 4. The second transformation of the major portion of the dried clay involves adding water to the dried bits of clay and squishing and manipulating it to make sure all the particles of clay are thoroughly blended to make a thick, mud-like substance.

Step 5. For the next transformation, the thoroughly blended and moistened clay is spread on a plaster bat to draw out excess moisture. (Tip: Plaster bats can be made by pouring a few inches of a mixture of Plaster of Paris into the bottom of a square dish pan to dry—still another kind of transformation.)

Step 6. Transforming the recycled clay now simply involves wedging it into a nice, usable piece for the young sculptor. The teacher or an older child should do this since it may involve quite a lot of strength.

The teacher's respect for the child's expression is reflected in developmentally appropriate expectations as well as in the quality and appropriateness of materials available and the care taken in their presentation. For example, although newsprint or recycled computer paper may be adequate for the drawing and scribbling table, it is poor support for tempera applied with a young child's vigorous strokes. With the recycling of crayons and diligent scrounging of paper ends from local printers, perhaps a very good quality easel paper (ideally #80) could be affordable.

Standards for Competencies in the Arts   Teacher "know-how" includes a knowledge of standards of developmentally appropriate competencies in constructive arts, drama, music, and movement and dance, so all children's advances may be extended and supported through guided as well as spontaneous play. Teachers should acquaint themselves with the National Art Education Association's (1999) standards for the arts so that children in the classroom have opportunities to integrate their knowledge and express deep feelings and meaningful ideas through the arts (Edwards, 2010; Isenberg & Jalongo, 2014). See Table 10.1 for samples of standards and suggested curriculum in the arts.

Content

In the previous sections, we discussed how the classroom environment can be set up to enhance play, particularly spontaneous play, in the arts. In this section, we discuss various specific content that teachers will want to introduce to enhance children's knowledge. These curricula may involve a greater degree of preparation and guidance on the part of the teacher to ensure that much of the learning can occur in spontaneous engagement with the materials provided.

TABLE 10.1 Addressing Some Standards for Visual and Constructive Arts

Standards	Examples
Children will become responsible users of art media and tools.	Noah spontaneously experiments with mixing colors to make "aqua" at a well-organized painting center where he has learned routines for independent use of materials. Special tools, such as a paint roller, help him relate to the whole pictorial space rather than to only one small area.
Children should have opportunities to gain mastery of a variety of techniques and processes.	In guided play activities, Noah and his classmates begin to learn about volume by constructing tunnels out of clay for miniature animals.
Children will become aware of and be able to talk about line, texture, color, and space.	In a special multimedia finger -painting activity, Jason begins to learn about line, texture, space, and color. In a feedback session about the activity, the teacher guides the children in reflecting on what they have learned in the activity about line, texture, color, and space.
Children will be able to recognize their own work and that of peers.	At snack time, children discuss classmates' paintings that are on display for the monthly art show. Later they design invitations for parents and act as tour guides for an "opening" at "pickup" time later in the day.
Children will develop control and be able to dance and execute rhythmic movement in concert with music.	Masha's mother makes elastic head and waistbands for use in the movement and dance center. Tucking colorful scarves into the waistbands and headbands, Masha teaches other children her "Fly Horse" dance.
	At daily music time, some children learn and use a simple notational system to indicate a pattern of long and short accents and rests in a three-line composition for rhythmic hand clapping.
Children will become acquainted with and share in the classic genres of their own and other cultures.	Isabella interprets a Matisse painting in her own way in her K–1 art class. Matisse is her favorite painter. Her brother, Adrian, prefers the special African masks they have learned about in his second-grade class.

Sources: Information from National Art Education Association. (1999). *Purposes, Principles, and Standards for School Art Programs.* Reston, VA: Author; Seefeldt, C. (2005). *How to Work with Standards in the Early Childhood Classroom.* New York, NY: Teachers College Press; Isenberg, J. P., & Jalongo, M. R. (2014). *Creative Thinking and Arts-Based Learning.* Upper Saddle River, NJ: Pearson Education.

Cultural Enrichment in the Arts

In some school districts, primary-grade teachers and art specialists have adopted an arts curriculum that enhances cultural and aesthetic literacy. Children are introduced to the styles of artists from different periods and cultures and then invited to replicate a style in their own drawings or paintings. Isabella vividly emulates the style

Figure 10.2
Isabella's Matisse

of Matisse, who became her favorite artist, in a painting she made in her K–1 art class (Figure 10.2).

Through this same program, other older children noted parallels in the African masks they were making and the drawings they had rendered in the styles of Modigliani or Picasso. Some teachers use reproductions as a pivot to conversation with children about great works of modern and classical art forms.

Preschoolers at another school annually create and mount a spectacular display of African figures in what their teacher, Berta, describes as a Gallery of Cultures in their classroom. Berta assists them in preparing a support for each figure out of a wooden dowel or paper towel spool mounted on a base of heavy cardboard. The heads and hands of the figure are made of baker's clay. Pipe cleaners inserted into the spool provide flexible arms. An array of swatches of brightly colored African textiles, such as kente cloth along with ample amounts of tape and glue, is the inspiration for creating stunning costumes for the figures. Many books from the library with illustrations of traditional costumes influence the children's choices.

The cultural richness of children's communities is illustrated in the feature *Family Diversity: Family Members as Arts-Based Resources.*

FAMILY DIVERSITY
Family Members as Arts-Based Resources

Karen, an artist and parent who creates dolls depicting characters drawn from traditional African stories, began sharing her dolls and stories in her son's preschool class. She now shares them throughout the primary-grade school classrooms in her local school district. Other families also enjoy the presentation of her characters and storytelling through the education program at a major museum located in a nearby community. Think about family members in your classroom as resources for arts-based activities. The more you know the children and their families and what is going on in their lives, the better you will be able to draw them into the life of the school to participate and share their talents in the visual arts, music, dance, and drama.

Music and Movement in the Play-Centered Curriculum

As part of an arts program and each day's routine, teachers present a music and movement curriculum as a directed or guided experience for the whole group. New and traditional movement and music material, as well as ethnic songs and rhythms, can be introduced in this way (Edwards, 2013). One teacher discovered that the movement group became more cohesive and inclusive when she established a "boy/girl–boy/girl" seating arrangement in movement class. This made the option for cross-gender dancing possible when children paired for folk-dancing routines.

Sharing songs generated from children's own cultures can be an effective way to support spontaneous play involving music, and in one case enabled cross-gender play. When two 4-year-old girls, Yolanda and Shani, spontaneously demonstrated their knowledge of a superhero theme song, they were granted roles by a group of 4-year-old boys on the climbing structure in a previously gender-segregated game. Within the framework of guided musical play, the following are some other familiar possibilities.

Call and Response and Improvisational Routines   More formally, call-and-response routines, improvisation, **ensemble playing** with instruments, and voice enhance children's listening skills and perception of pattern and rhythm.

Alternating a single child's improvisation on instruments like a xylophone, drum, or triangle with ensemble playing and singing are illustrated in the next example, where the teacher rotates turns of improvisation by placing a baker's hat made of paper on the head of a child she selects to improvise after others sing and play:

Baker's hat, just your size,

When it's on your head you improvise.

Similar improvisation with instruments and singing can be used around traditional favorites with a strong, simple rhythm, such as "Noah's Ark." Perhaps one would alternate voice and instruments with the children singing unaccompanied at first:

Who built the ark, Noah, Noah.
Who built the ark, Noah did.

And then continue with both voice and rhythm instruments:

Here come the animals, two by two.
If I were there I'd come along too.

This is particularly effective when accompanied by various percussion instruments, such as those used in the Orff–Kodaly curriculum (Alper, 1987; Edwards, 2013; Isenberg & Jalongo, 2014). If the teacher has a piano and can play, this helps children maintain the rhythm and pitch.

Simple echo routines involving rhythmic patterns of hand clapping, finger snapping, knee slapping, and other sound making, with or without **rhythm instruments** to accompany patterned movement or dance, can be thoroughly satisfactory activities.

At the level of guided play, a well-organized listening center for two or more children, stocked with a diversity of recorded music, could be provided. These recordings can include cards with salient information about the music written out so that the guiding teacher can indicate aspects of it to the children. For older children who are beginning to read, the cards can be filed in the listening center for direct use. As many teachers know, children constantly create spontaneous songs and dances as they play, and these songs can be recorded and enjoyed at the listening center (Veldhuis, 1982).

Although much of this chapter deals with graphic and constructive play in the arts, music is an important avenue for the development of children's thinking and aesthetic sensibilities and, therefore, deserves to be carefully integrated into the curriculum.

Rhythmic Patterns and Tonal Discrimination Familiar songs and games can be integrated into a more systematic, guided play framework, as that developed in the Orff–Kodaly method (Alper, 1987; DeVries, Zan, Hildebrandt, Edmiaston, & Sales, 2002; Isenberg & Jalongo, 2014; Wheeler & Raebeck, 1985). The general objective of this approach is to refine the senses so that the child gains knowledge of and appreciation for various aspects of music, such as rhythmic patterns and tonal discrimination. Furthermore, because the emphasis is on making and enjoying music as a group activity rather than as an individual performance, the method has a positive social value and does not emphasize competitiveness.

Furth (1970) wrote,

The opportunity can be given to children to express facets of their personalities that go along with their developing intelligence in the medium of music. To play in rhythm, to control **intonation** and intensity of tone, to construct musical phrases over time, to symbolize all these things in **musical notation**, as well as to interact with others and submit one's activity to the group task—all this is part and parcel of human intelligence. It is for this reason the music teacher can justifiably rely on intrinsic motivation. His goal is musical thinking, with the accent on thinking. He is not concerned with turning every child into a professional . . . musician. (pp. 140–141)

To play and enjoy music together as a group without emphasizing competitiveness has a positive social value.

Counting and pattern-making skills can be developed in music activities when a notational system is used to mark accented beats and rests. One first-grade teacher encourages children to compose their own three-line songs in this way. Children then "read" and clap the simple pattern of fast and short beats and rests in unison as each child composer indicates them on a blackboard.

Music promotes **auditory discrimination** and phonemic awareness through rhyming words and segmentation (Genishi & Dyson, 2009; Seefeldt, 2005). Participating in music involves abstract thinking important to mathematics. Music contributes to social skills, and, of course, it can lighten a tense moment and ease transitions.

Diverse Musical Traditions Enrich the Classroom Culture

Teachers can use culturally and linguistically diverse selections of recorded music to accompany children's dance and movement. Parents are a rich resource for this diversity. In one class, a Chinese family provided a recording of popular contemporary Chinese children's songs. These became instant favorites because of their particularly catchy and appealing rhythm. In this same classroom, a Russian parent interested in dance provided accessories in the form of child-sized, elasticized headbands and waistbands decorated with bright ribbons and sequins. Children needed no teacher assistance to create their own dance costumes; they merely tucked brightly colored scarves into the headbands and waistbands. This mother's contribution helped her Russian-speaking daughter establish early communication with other children through dance and movement activities. Once such activities are launched with a small group of children, teachers may be able to withdraw but closely monitor from a distance. In this way, they can help ensure that such self-directed music and movement experiences will remain focused and evolve as musical play without being diverted into random tag or chasing games.

Music can enhance the affective tone of an environment. However, musical activities that merely distract or entertain, although possibly useful as "management strategies," cannot be justified as developmental curricula. In guided play in the arts, care should be taken to avoid undue focus on the virtuosity of a teacher rather than the particular needs of children. Such performances may well be enjoyed by and be interesting to children, but they fall into the category of directed play. As such, they should be carefully balanced with opportunities for free improvisation with music.

In addition—and this point is crucial—in high-quality programs, no teacher-directed play or planned circle time activity should be mere preparation for something else. Introduction of materials is important; however, nothing in the early childhood arts curriculum should be simply a "dry run," such as repetitive rehearsal for a play. Every single arts activity should make sense in the context of the children's lives at school, and each step in an art sequence should be intrinsically interesting.

Integrating All Dimensions of the Curriculum through the Arts   Art activities serve not only as aesthetic development, but also as an integral part of learning throughout the early childhood curriculum, for example, in mathematics and in development of logical and spatial knowledge. This is illustrated in the following example of curriculum-generating play.

> In a Head Start classroom, children were introduced to pattern duplication and pattern extension during small-group time. The teacher discussed and demonstrated the difference between patterns and designs. Later at the painting easel on the same day, one of the children spontaneously generated her own pattern sequence using geometric-shaped sponges to create a page full of small, multicolored triangles and circles arranged in an original pattern with accurate extensions. Other children followed suit, and the teacher created a display for the school corridor of the products the children created that involved the concept of patterning. These paintings also allowed the teacher to assess who was understanding the pattern concept. ✆

> In another case, a kindergarten teacher helped children learn the features of geometric figures—triangles, rectangles, and squares—through a guided play activity using toothpicks and clay balls to construct models of the figures. ✆

Intuitive math is going on "everywhere," including in arts activities. It is the teacher's responsibility to note and support these competencies when and where they occur (Scales, 2000).

Spontaneous play allowed Noah to integrate his new knowledge about colors—he used this growing grasp of color to start creating aqua. Such integration and recasting of experience and the application of knowledge in new contexts also can occur in guided play.

Integration of Children's Experiences and Feelings through Play in the Arts

A special dictated letter with a picture "for mom" or an e-mail may be called for when distressing experiences, such as the birth of a baby brother or Mom's too abrupt departure, occur.

> Lonnie, a formerly abused child currently healing in his adoptive home, needed to include multiple masking tape "band-aids" in the many self-portraits he produced. ✆

Jason's only painting for the monthly art show revealed much. His intense interest in depicting trains and the intersecting lines of railroad tracks revealed the cognitive and representational competence of a 5-year-old. Teachers were pleased to see that his mark making in art related to his new, spontaneous interest in writing his name and making signs to designate areas of play for himself and his younger friend, Wesley. Although Jason acted as a mentor to Wesley in many collaborative activities, his friend now felt left out because he did not share Jason's interest or capabilities in writing. The teacher was faced with a dilemma when Wesley's mother asked her "not to stress writing," especially because literacy through play was a centerpiece of the curriculum. ✐

As we can see, life in the zone of proximal development can be daunting. It does not always flow smoothly and presents challenges to both the children and their teachers.

A BALANCED ARTS CURRICULUM

Throughout this book and in this chapter, we stress the need to balance curriculum offerings across the continuum of spontaneous, guided, and directed play. When play is at the center, the arts as well as other options will be examined carefully to ensure that the balance between spontaneous and guided or directed play is optimal for the group served. In determining the appropriate balance of arts activities, we must always consider the following:

- The cultural, social, and developmental needs of both the group and individual children
- The dynamic of the group
- The quality and size of the physical environment
- The number of staff and length of the program day

As teachers plan curriculum, they will want to examine the types of activities they offer, along with the kinds of demands they make on resources available in their particular settings. Here is where a consideration for a balance of activities is needed. Too much spontaneous play at all sites can lead to chaos, whereas too much directed or guided activity can lead to the erosion of learning that occurs in spontaneous play. Some activities, such as painting, drawing, scribbling, and collage, can be monitored with minimal teacher intervention and so may be a staple offering most of the school day. The critical issue here is how well the children can read the cues the environment gives them about what they are expected to do with the available materials.

Establishing routines for using the available materials is essential. Caution must be exercised in the introduction of too many teacher-planned projects, as this not only stifles creativity on the part of children but ties up staff resources as well. In some primary classrooms, children select the centers they will go to at "choice time" during a morning meeting. Minimum and maximum numbers of children at a center can be adjusted as needed. This can work smoothly if centers are well set up and expectations are established.

The following is a discussion of some familiar activities with indications of their demand for teacher setup, monitoring, and guidance or direction. Some groups will need more structure and fewer options or more complexity with an increase in guided or even directed play; others will need less complexity with more opportunity for spontaneous play. In each case, the teacher will select from various curriculum offerings to create a menu of activities that enhances potential for playful engagement in the arts.

- Various kinds of drawing, scribbling, and collage activities have a high degree of potential for spontaneous and playful engagement. Attention to the setup of materials and space is important, and some degree of monitoring, if only to replenish and refresh supplies, is necessary.

- Many forms of sculpture and three-dimensional work also lend themselves to spontaneous play with materials offered. Clay, playdough, and wood gluing come to mind. Again, some degree of care in setup, introduction to routines, and monitoring is required.

- Printmaking, silkscreen, and projects involving precut elements, such as collage portraits, require a high degree of teacher guidance and direction, but some facets involve spontaneous and self-directed action. The process of selecting the textured elements for a relief print (**intaglio**) and placement of various facial features for a collage portrait involves creativity, challenge, and judgment for many young children. Coloring and rendering eyes, hair, complexion, and clothing in a painted self-portrait also involve creativity and critical thinking.

- Activities like story dictation, journal writing, music, and movement often fall into the category of more directed and guided play. However, these activities can become more spontaneous for children if the teacher creates a context in advance that clearly indicates expectations. For example, a music center can do much to enhance the development of musical sensitivity when routines for using instruments are established and the available number and kinds of instruments lend themselves to a harmonious, but not prescribed, sound.

- In the same sense, story dictation and journal writing should be collected by the teacher with minimal intervention as to content or demand for use of formal narrative conventions. The subsequent acting out of such stories may involve the teacher directly in reading the story and helping to guide an orderly selection of actors. Although these activities are generally guided and directed, the activity may lead to an enrichment of the content of children's subsequent spontaneous fantasy play.

Among all the numerous options available in the classroom, only one highly teacher directed project is recommended. If such projects are available each day for a week, then every child can participate in an unrushed and orderly way as their interest dictates. This will also avoid erosion of opportunities for self directed and spontaneous play.

KNOWLEDGE OF THE PATTERNS OF DEVELOPMENT IN CHILDREN'S ART MAKING

Being aware of evolving patterns in children's art can provide the teacher with a mirror to development and a guide for curriculum design. Like archaeological remains, children's paintings, constructions, block building, assemblage and collage, and recordings of songs, stories, and dances are a reflection of development and can be examined as documents of growth and development (DeVries et al., 2002; Griffin, 1998; Veldhuis, 1982). As such, they can be used to assess the effectiveness of the curriculum in supporting playful exploration of the arts.

Documenting Change and Growth: Heidi's Horses

Consider some of the drawings of horses made by one child over a period of about five years (Fein, 1984). Heidi's drawings, in Figure 10.3, reveal her interests and follow the general developmental sequence of drawing schemes (Gardner, 1993; Isenberg & Jalongo, 2014; Kellogg, 1969; Lowenfeld, 1947). Heidi was able to playfully explore her interest (indeed, passion) in a supportive environment that encouraged art making and allowed a free choice of subject matter. The drawings graphically illustrate that it is interest, intersecting with personality and intelligence, that fuels play and the development that results from play.

IMPORTANT CONSIDERATIONS

Guided play often provides opportunities for the teacher to observe closely and learn how the competencies, interests, and personality of a child complement or conflict with the social challenges of the group setting. For example, in a prekindergarten conference with a kindergarten assessment team, Sara, an art therapist, suggested that active and unfocused children often may be helped to gain control by working not with fluid materials, such as finger paints or water-based media, but with more resistant materials. Stitchery, when presented on a frame or an embroidery hoop, is an example of a material that can give structure and boundaries. Clearly defined patterns may be included as guidance. In addition, Sara noted that children with perceptual problems may need not only more form, but also activities that provide a calming effect derived from doing what they are good at. The issue here is to allow the child to experience control rather than lack of control (S. Wasserman, personal communication, 2005).

2 Years: ALL OVER
SCRIBBLES

Scribbles are scrubbed on,
off, and through paper.

2 Years / 6 months:

CLUSTERS

Lines are more controlled
and begin to be clustered
in center of paper.

3 Years:
DIRECTIONAL
MOVEMENT

Large arm movements
order themselves into a
circular mode around a
central mark.

3 Years / 6 months:

SPIRALS

Directional movement
develops to spiraling lines.

Spiraling lines separate
themselves into coils.

4 Years:
THE CIRCLE

Coiling lines become
deliberate circle
configurations, continuous
lines that start at one
point and return to that
point.

First Person;
Available Structures

Circle configurations are
elaborated with additional
circles and with lines
radiating to and from their
centers, creating a vertical-
horizontal relationship at
their intersection with the
perimeter. These become
representational: father,
mother, dog, cat, house,
birthday cake.

4 Years / 2 months:
THE FIRST HORSE:
RECTILINEAR
Multiple legs

The circular formation and
vertical-horizontal lines
permit formation of the
first horse.

Figure 10.3
Heidi's Horses

Source: From *Heidi's Horse* by Sylvia Fein, 1984, Exelrod Press. Reprinted with permission.

Breadth and width;
Four legs spaced

Refinement: the horse receives four legs—only four.

4 Years / 10 months:
DEVIATIONS FROM THE RECTILINEAR
Slanting legs; Curved back line

First deviations from the vertical-horizontal are used for ears and legs in opposing diagonal directions. The new diagonals immediately unify head and neck and create a new shape.

5 Years:
UNIFICATION OF HORSE PARTS

The unification of the head and neck is applied to contain the whole horse within one unbroken outline.

5 Years / 3 months:
DEVELOPMENT OF THE UNIFIED HORSE
Sturdy shape

Problems of leg-spacing and length are solved.

The new diagonal directions of line allow the horse to run.

Body markings: blazes and dapples

A learning plateau provides time to consolidate, and to enrich the horse's gear and markings.

Heidi's last major construction before her sixth birthday is to extend the horse's head toward the ground, "so he can eat."

6 Years: **THE HORSE MORE POWERFULLY CONSTRUCTED**
The boxy shape is rounded

The rigid, box-shaped horse is transformed by fluid, calligraphic outline into a powerful horse with flexible stride.

Figure 10.3
Heidi's Horses (*continued*)

7 Years: THE
HORSE IN ACTION
Cowboys and rodeo

Heidi shifts her interest to
action-packed
performances; the elegant
single horse recedes.

As storytelling becomes
more restrained, precision
returns to the drawings,
and the rider receives
artistic attention.

8 1/2 Years: HEIDI:
SELF-PORTRAITS
Queen Heidi, the very 1st

Heidi assumes importance
second to the horse, and
appears in favorable roles.
She thinks of herself as a
horse.

8 1/2 Years: TECHNICAL
TASKS: OVERLAPPING

The rider's body turns
partially to side view.

Overlapping begins. The
horse has two legs on one
side of his body, two on
the other.

8 Years / 11 months:
ADVANCES USING
OVERLAPPING
The rider in profile

Overlapping possibilities
are extended to arm and
stifle joints.

Problems appear when the
position of the horse's
hind legs are reversed.

Two horses side by side

One horse overlaps another
to show that they are
standing side by side.
Figure/ground relationships
have become more complex.

Figure 10.3
Heidi's Horses (*continued*)

Children with Special Needs: Guiding for Mastery and Competence

Consider Jerry, an active and often unfocused child:

> Four-year-old Jerry jumps from the jungle gym and dashes across the yard. yelling, "Rocket launch! Rocket launch!" Within seconds, he reaches the sand pit, jumps in, and plows through Andre's and Peter's sand towers. Taking Jerry gently by the hand, his teacher productively redirects this explosive energy. "You seem to know a lot about rockets," she says. "How about drawing one with me?" ⊘

Through drawing, she engages the child in a vivid and expressive rendering of his fantasy. The recognition Jerry may have been seeking in spontaneous play with peers might be accomplished more easily through guided, creative expression. Such expression will serve him better until linguistic ability and his competence in interacting with others advance to meet the need he feels to share his powerful fantasies.

Creating some segments of a cartoon strip about rockets might help Jerry. When the teacher labels aspects of his vigorous but seemingly meaningless scribbles by using words in bubbles and arrows that highlight and clarify important information—"here is the launching pad, here is the rocket's nose"—Jerry is led to experience himself as a more effective communicator.

More ambitiously, Jerry's drawings and words become a "movie" when taped together, attached, and wound onto take-up spindles of a paper movie machine a parent made for the classroom. As Jerry's movie is unreeled and narrated for the class, the teacher demonstrates sequence as a feature of a narrative while sharing Jerry's word images. Using today's digital camera and computer technology would allow Jerry's drawings to become an animated feature (e.g., a program like iStopMotion 2, www.boinx.com/istopmotion/education).

Enhancing Children's Membership in the Group   Guided play with art-making materials affords many opportunities for language use and social and cultural sharing and, again, gives the teacher an opportunity to observe quietly. Often the group project is stimulated directly by the children: "I want one like Martha has!" "So do I!" With the help of the teacher, the paper earrings that Martha just made are studied. The required materials are set up at a table so that Martha can teach the others to make earrings of their own.

In the primary grades in particular, projects that enhance group membership may sometimes be ongoing and involve long-range goals. Even so, every step toward the project goal is ideally play centered and **intrinsically satisfying**. Making a group book, a class poem, a quilt, a mural, or decorations for a school party can all support the child's growing ability to plan, to look forward, and to share socially.

Lisa frequently has difficulty sharing the available supply of playdough. With this knowledge, the teacher can ask her to assist in the preparation of a new batch of dough to be shared with others, thereby helping Lisa manage her needs, emotions, and impulses in the group setting. ✆

Let's look at some ways that group projects can enhance children's membership: Following an invasion of ants in the classroom, the children mounted a research project about ants. Two girls in a first-grade classroom sent a letter to the principal of their school requesting better pencils. Other children in this same first-grade classroom we discussed in Chapter 8 created a newspaper for all the members of the class. It involved several weeks of research and planning before the first and only edition was published. Group projects such as this one can provide valuable opportunities for children to learn about and participate in the cultural richness of many of today's classrooms.

Children's Play Interests Reflected in a Play-Centered Curriculum

Children's playful engagement in the arts is frequently the source for new and emergent curricula. This is reflected vividly in myriad ways. The monsters of one year's pretend play give way to Robin Hood in the next. The princes and princesses in this year's group book become the daddy and mommy dinosaur in next year's. The same is also true for the paintings and constructions. Musical interludes can become a part of children's spontaneous story-play dictation, or they can become part of an "author's theatre" in later elementary school. Once introduced as a genre, children will incorporate songs they know, such as nursery rhymes or contemporary media songs, into their plays. British drama educator Dorothy Heathcote (Bolton, 2003; Heathcote & Bolton, 1995) often used child-generated songs and chants in her drama work with children.

Guided and Directed Play in the Arts

Although we know that young children learn most effectively through play, educational strategies often rely solely on guided or directed play. Such play can become more spontaneous in some of the following ways. In the role of play tutor—for example, at the clay table—teachers can show children how to model basic clay shapes (as precursors to developing concepts of volume). After such modeling, the teacher can step back and allow the children to integrate their learning on their own. Often, other children will pick up the role of tutor in these instances.

To build the children's repertoire of three-dimensional forms, teachers can demonstrate to them how to hollow out a ball of clay to make a dinosaur's cave; or, more playfully, how to extend the hollow to make a tunnel where the hands of two friends meet; or how to make clay coils, slabs, and seriated balls. In one preschool program, Wade integrated knowledge about clay modeling when he added teeth to the jaws of his hollowed-out clay form. Sylvie, a second grader, using slabs of clay that she had rolled out smoothly, cut and shaped a beautiful rectangular jewelry box (complete with a fitted lid) for her grandmother's birthday.

A play-generating curriculum was introduced to children making their first transition from home to school. It involved creating a special room. To start, a shoe box is provided to each child, along with bits of wallpaper, tile, fabric, wood, and carpet pieces, with an invitation to create a replica of a room for themselves. Child-made models from previous years may be provided at the initiation of this project. Aurora is learning English in her bilingual classroom. Emulating labels on classroom furnishings, she asks that labels in both English and Spanish be placed on the items in her "room."

When guided or directed play in arts activities is linked in some relevant manner to children's fantasy play, or if the teacher can play parallel to children, then such play is protected from becoming merely work disguised as play. The teacher can then stay in touch with the children's developmental needs. In this manner, the teacher participates in what Vygotsky (1967) referred to as the zone of proximal development, that area where children experience their own future, more-advanced self through stimulation and challenge in the context of interactive play with peers or with an adult.

The Reggio Emilia and project-based curriculums referred to as **emergent curriculum**, are examples of the use of guided play. Many teachers who have adopted these approaches find that the knowledge and competencies set out in a standards-based curriculum can be readily achieved through child investigations and **documentation** inherent in the Reggio and **project approaches** (Bodrova & Leong, 2007; Katz & Chard, 2000; Wien, 2008, 2014).

In play, children recast their knowledge of the world in new ways.

SUMMARY

In this chapter our rationale for an arts-based curriculum in early childhood and the premises upon which it is based were discussed.

- **A guide for curriculum design.** A curriculum in the arts for early childhood at the preschool level and in the early elementary grades finds its center in the necessity for children to play. It encompasses not only graphic arts, but also drama, music, dance, movement, and all forms of constructive play. It can be an emergent, play-generating curriculum in which children's autonomy and interests are supported. It can take several forms, orchestrated along a continuum that supports both guided and spontaneous play.

    The effectiveness of an early childhood arts program will be measured by the degree to which we observe that children are able to enter into sustained, effective, self-directed play. Is guided or directed art the only form we see? Do we see knowledge gained in guided arts activities being integrated as it is reapplied in spontaneous play? In short, the major question to ask is, "What *are* the quality and quantity of children's spontaneous play within the arts curriculum?"

- **A balanced arts curriculum.** An important task for the teacher is to balance the options for kinds of play in the arts program. By ensuring the child's independent choices in play, the teacher supports development and engages the child's interests and authentic expression. Although implementation of developmentally appropriate standards is an important priority that provides equitable access to educational and cultural resources for all children, it is best to remember that children learn most effectively through play and are unable until middle childhood to perform work in the adult sense (Alward, 1995).

- **Knowledge of the patterns of development in children's art making.** Evolving patterns in children's art can provide the teacher with a guide for curriculum design, while children's products, like archeological remains, can be examined as evidence of change and growth in competence.

- **Important considerations.** Opportunities for both self-directed and guided play are important curriculum strategies in the play-based program. Play-generating curriculum as well as curriculum-generating play come to mind. Children with special needs may need the guidance of a directed play activity to productively share their ideas with peers. Guided group play activities, such as decorations for a party, a quilt project, or mural making, can enhance membership in the group.

    Much of children's development is revealed most vividly through the evolution of the documents they produce, which, when shared, allows them to gain self-esteem as they become witnesses to their advancing competence.

APPLYING YOUR KNOWLEDGE

1. Discuss the ways that the four cornerstones of an arts curriculum—time, space, materials, and teacher know-how—support a viable arts program.
   a. Draw a map of your own or a classroom you observe and label areas to illustrate how space is allocated for children to engage in self-directed or guided art-making activities.
   b. Create a daily schedule of routines for a full-day program that incorporates substantial amounts of time for art-making activities on a regular basis.
   c. Examine the self-directed art-making areas of the classroom and describe how the setup of the environment is developmentally appropriate and optimizes children's mastery and competence.

2. Discuss the reasons to balance offerings in the arts curriculum along the continuum of spontaneous, guided, and directed, play.
   a. Make a list of some self-directed activities that can be offered throughout the day.
   b. Describe the ways that the establishment of routines can be enhanced for using materials in a self-directed art center.
   c. Draw a table setup showing how materials and their presentation cue spontaneous, self-directed play, such as drawing and scribbling.
   d. Determine the maximum number of children expected, the materials they will use, and how these materials will be accessed.
   e. Consider how much teacher involvement will be required to handle replacement freshening of supplies, identification and storage of work children produce, and so on.
   f. Consider how the teacher's involvement affects total supervision of all centers in the classroom.

3. Explain how knowledge of the stages observed in most children's drawings provides a basis for understanding the trajectory of their development, interests, and competencies.
   a. Create an agenda for a parent conference around key items from a collection of their child's paintings and drawings.
   b. Consider what features you will want to point out that illustrate advances in development as well as mastery and competence.

4. Create some standards-based curricula that involve spontaneous and guided play in children's group projects and investigations.
   a. With a colleague, discuss some guided art-making activities to use in helping children manage their needs, emotions, and desires in a group setting.
   b. Describe some guided play projects that teachers can introduce to support children's membership in the group.
   c. Discuss how displaying children's art products in chronological order enables them as well as their teachers and parents to become witnesses to advances in their development.

APPENDIX

Table of Basic Art Activities for Early Learners

Below is a set of activities suitable for early childhood education settings that provide self-directed and guided experiences in a variety of simple drawing, painting, print-making, collage, and sculptural mediums. The purpose of these activities is to help children express their creativity and develop aesthetic and critical awareness, but these activities also can address the content of other curriculum areas such as math, science, language arts, and social studies. They can be adapted to many thematic approaches, such as culture and ethnicity in masks and fabric design, or context-specific concepts such as the creation of images of the seasons, nature and animal life, and habitats and homes of various creatures and cultures. Self-awareness and beginning knowledge of physiology are developed in family and self-portraits.

Activity	Setup	Teacher	Children
Drawing & Scribbling Center for preschool may be called a *Writing Center* for elementary-age children	Teacher sets up environment (cuing for number of users) and kinds of materials, such as pencils, chalk, crayons, scissors, punches, assorted papers, various templates. For example, two-dimensional geometric figures (circles, triangles, squares, and rectangles) or vehicle templates, and so on.	Monitors from a distance. Makes sure names are on children's work. Oil-based crayons are set out at four places to be used on black paper or with water based paint on white paper.	Free use of materials provides practice in small motor skills of writing, starting with early scribbles. Content can be introduced either by the children themselves or by their teachers.
	Resist drawing and painting with Cray-Pas.	Teacher provides a model to demonstrate effect.	
Collage	Teacher sets up materials and environment, providing seating for desired number of children. Provides materials, such as attractive paper scraps, construction paper, glue sticks, paper punch, and so on.	Monitors and helps with cutting and pasting as needed.	Select and arrange elements for their collage and learn from each other. Can lead to a study of the many uses of collage seen in children's books and art museums.

Activity	Setup	Teacher	Children
Painting at the Easels and at the Table	Teacher sets up the environment in a way that protects children's clothing and includes cleanup routines. Provides a varied palette of tempera paint, including black and white on occasion, good quality #80 paper, and color-coded brushes with rubber grips.	After routines are learned, monitors from a distance. Helps children put paintings on drying rack and assures names are on the work. Teacher available to discuss work.	Free to select content and apply paint to paper as they see fit. Content determined by children, but can be thematically cued by teachers, such as using pastel colors to depict spring blossoms or black and white to depict snowy scenes.
Group Palette	Sets up environment and presents palette; guides selection of paint and brushes and other implements. Assigns a large piece of paper, usually mounted on the wall, for each child. (See Figure 10.1)	Teacher monitors from a seat in front of the palette. May discuss children's color and brush choices with them. This form of painting is to provide direct instruction in the use of the brush or other implements to create a painting.	Children free to experiment with color and content and may use unusual implements, such as larger brushes, sponges, and rollers.
Watercolor Painting and Use of Payons	Sets up environment, cueing number of spaces by 4 trays with individual setups consisting of a 4 x 5½" sheet of good quality white paper, watercolor box, rinse water cup, dipping water in a small art dish, and one brush. May include a small folded cloth for absorbing excess water.	Introduces materials and demonstrates their use.	Free to experiment with color and content. Usually content free, but is an excellent way to learn about color.

Activity	Setup	Teacher	Children
Silk Screen (See also printmaking on page 287.)	Collects and sets up materials; water-based ink, small screen, hinged board, squeegee, suitable size of paper or fabric to be screened.	Presents materials and guides placement of elements to ensure registration on the paper. Directly assists in inking screen and drawing the squeegee across screen to create a print.	Involved in selecting elements to be torn or cut from paper. The particular value of this printmaking technique is that it allows very young children to see how the ink is transferred to the print.
Clay Sculpture (See page 278.)	Sets up environment with cueing for number of participants in activity—usually defines each space with a board in front of each chair—a small art dish containing slip and another containing powdered clay.	Directly instructs in initial steps, such as using a cutting wire to cut a piece of clay off a block of clay, use of slip and powdered clay. May model making slabs, balls, and coils after initial routines are explored and practiced.	Once routines are learned, provides free expression with ample amounts of clay. Decides when sculpture is finished and may obtain more clay for additional work with the medium. Both art and science are involved in the changes in the characteristics of the clay body as it is shaped and formed and with the addition of moisture or the drying ingredient of powdered clay.
Playdough or Baker's Clay	Sets up environment; prepares dough of good consistency, presents different types on various occasions.	Monitors from a distance. If child wishes to keep sculpture, incises name on the bottom and places in a drying space.	Free exploration with or without tools. Very inexpensive way to introduce sculptural concepts.
Wood Gluing	Collects and sets up materials, such as glue and wood scraps, and cues for optimal number of participants with trays for work.	Monitors from a distance once routines are learned; guides gluing as needed.	Once skills are learned and area is set up for use, can be self-directed. Another inexpensive form of sculpture.

CHAPTER 11
Play and Socialization

LEARNING OUTCOMES

▪ Discuss some family-life factors that can influence children's separation from parents at school entry.

▪ Consider some ways teachers can adapt to the challenge of classroom diversity in age, gender, inclusion, and culture.

▪ Describe some of the ways that observational research in the sociocultural tradition of Vygotsky has enhanced our understanding of how children's play interactions with peers contributes to socialization.

▪ Contrast some different forms of information that can be obtained from interpreting children's behavior from a classical constructivist point of view versus a sociocultural approach.

▪ Discuss how observational research of children's play communication and interactions can reveal how the environment provides implicit cues for children's behavior.

▪ Discuss how children do not use speech alone, but use all modalities of communication, such as gesture, rhythm, and intonation, to achieve their interactive goals.

▪ Consider some of the differences between children's early socialization and a formal social studies curriculum.

Andrew lopsidedly heads out the door of his preschool classroom with his mother's large leather briefcase slung over one shoulder. He insists on carrying it wherever he goes. Andrew's destination today is the swing at the rear of the play yard. Recently he has become willing to set the briefcase on a bench nearby when he uses the swing, but stormy protests can be expected if anyone goes near it.

Andrew is 3 years and 1 month old and a newcomer to this 4-hour program. Separation from his mother has been difficult. To ease his adjustment, his teacher invited Andrew's mother to remain at school until a reasonably amicable separation could be achieved. Andrew's mother was able to accommodate his need when she was on leave from her part-time job, and Andrew played happily when she was present. Although the teacher had anticipated that this period of accommodation would be brief, it stretched into weeks, and Andrew, even if engaged, continued to insist on leaving with his mother. With his mother's absence from her job nearly over, she and Andrew's teacher devised a strategy to allay his anxiety: His mother would leave her large leather briefcase on the bench near the door as a reminder that she would be returning at some predetermined time. First, she stayed away until snack time, then she was to return at story time, and so on for longer periods of time each day.

Andrew's mother was meticulous about returning at the promised times in the preschool day, and eventually Andrew was able to stay for the full

4 hours of the program—not without a catch, however; the briefcase had to stay behind to ensure his mother's return. It was many weeks before Andrew allowed his teacher to tuck the briefcase away safely into his cubby, and it was not until the second half of the school year that it did not come to school with Andrew at all. ✄

SAYING GOODBYE TO PARENTS

Some theorists consider **separation** from parents a major milestone for children, and research on this subject suggests that the character of this achievement is an important indicator of secure or insecure attachment to the parental figure. Attachment theorists assert that when unusual conflict or anxiety surrounds separation from the parent or caregiver, the child may also develop other significant problems in relating to others (Ainsworth, Bell, & Stayton, 1974; Balaban, 1985, 2006). Other studies indicate that such children may have difficulties in persevering or varying their attempts to initiate play with peers (Riley, San Juan, Kliner, & Ramminger, 2008; Tribble, 1996).

In this chapter we show how children's talk and interactive behavior are significant indicators of their social and communicative competence. Many of the illustrations

A comfortable transition from home is important to a child's school success.

presented are drawn from teacher observations, anecdotes, and research. They raise many questions, demonstrate some of the dilemmas teachers face, and suggest some solutions.

We recommend a sociocultural approach as an authentic way to examine the effects of social–emotional issues arising from attachment and separation from parents. Such an approach also illuminates cultural, ethnic, and linguistic diversities, as well as inequities due to gender differences and, of course, poverty. Many of the vignettes in this chapter present challenges that teachers and families face concerning some form of diversity in the classroom. The following vignette illustrates this approach, demonstrating how simply beginning school can itself be a complex social–emotional event that may affect a child's relations with peers and teachers.

From Separation to Integration: John's Fire Hydrants

John, 4-and-a-half-years-old, appears to teachers to be socially isolated from his peers (Scales, 2005). They believe this may have resulted from the intersection of several factors, which included a reluctance to separate from his father, a new baby brother in the home, and his first experience in a preschool class consisting of children with established relationships from the previous year.

In September, John arrived at school with his father, dressed in a long yellow raincoat, black boots, and a black fire helmet. Rain or shine, John wore this attire for the next 6 months. To help with John's transition, his father spent the better part of each morning at the school's drawing and writing center with his son and several girls. This pattern continued for many months.

John and his father studied the fire hydrants they saw on their walk to school. They took photographs and compiled many small books about fire hydrants. John's father drew many models of fire hydrants as he became a fixture with John at the drawing and writing table. John also drew and painted fire hydrants (Figure 11.1) and dictated stories about fire hydrants. John used

Figure 11.1
John's Earliest Fire Hydrant and One With a Loose Cap That Is Leaking

Figure 11.2
A "Walking, Talking" Fire
Hydrant

an adult-like style in his speech and storytelling and preferred the company of either his father or other adults, with whom he talked at length about fire hydrants. Shy offers of fire hydrant pictures by one of the girls at the drawing table were ignored. ⌀

Once established, this intense interest in fire hydrants continued relatively unchanged for many months. In enacting his stories at circle time, John always took the role of the fire hydrant and allotted few parts to others, except for the girls who were "regulars" at the drawing and writing table.

His teacher's analysis of his stories and paintings over time revealed that one major change occurred in December, when John depicted his fire hydrants with faces and introduced the character of a "walking, talking" fire hydrant. (Figure 11.2).

Here is a "walking, talking" fire hydrant story:

December 13 Story

Once there was a fire hydrant and it was a walking, talking fire hydrant. Then another hydrant came and it was the newest one that John, the walking, talking fire hydrant, had ever seen. The very new hydrant fell down and broke one of its caps!! The cap was made of cast iron; it was old but the model number was new. Then another hydrant came and another hydrant came and then another. Then the hydrants got broken. They did not put out water anymore. Then there was a very, very, very old fire hydrant that came and rewinded the camera that they were using. Then a ball popped out of a hose hookup. Then a block came out of the other hookup. ⌀

The fire hydrant pattern in painting, drawing, and storytelling persisted until spring. But, finally, in a story dictated in May, a major advance was made. This story indicated a shift in John's gradual socialization. He dictated a story about, and took the role of, a very silly firefighter. (There is no fire hydrant present in this story.) Here John abandoned his adult-like narrative style for what seemed to be "baby talk." The teachers wondered if John was emulating what he thought was the language of his peer group. Not accidentally, his awareness of the context of the classroom is indicated in his reference to the fence that surrounds the playground and is near where many of the more active boys congregate in the play yard.

May 1 Story

An Entire Fireman Once there was a fireman and he fell in a puddle and got his suit all wet. And then he got in front of the big hookup and the garbage truck went over his legs! And he went to the hospital and he got da-da yocky-not medicine. He felt much, much, much better. And then they went to the ba-ba fence and jumped in puddles [the ba-ba fence is the fence near the child-care center]. ℘

Additional evidence of John's growing interest in the classroom environment is seen in the paintings he produces around this same time (Figure 11.3).

Although John did not abandon the fire hydrant theme, he began to depict fire hydrants that had an Asian look, with pagoda-like appendages and Asian-looking calligraphy in the pictorial space. Is this a reflection of the Japanese calligraphy displayed on the walls of his classroom, or a response to the artwork created by his only friend, a Japanese girl who is also a "regular" at the drawing table?

But it was his final story, dictated in June, that revealed a great leap forward in socialization for John.

June 5 Story

Firefighters from all over the city came to a really big fire. There were not enough fireplugs close by. So the firefighters had to take their small hoses and hook them up to each truck. There were seven trucks. And then they got their monitors but there was not enough pressure! [Monitors are the big nozzles on top of the trucks.] They saved a very, very, very tall building from danger of the fire. The end. ℘

According to the teacher's field notes on the story-playing activity, in this story John created many roles—seven firefighters and seven fire trucks. Well over half

Figure 11.3
Fire Hydrants with Asian-Appearing Pagodas and Calligraphy

the class was included. He allocated the superordinate roles of firefighters to boys and the subordinate roles of trucks to girls. He did not place himself in a central role as a hydrant, and when asked about this, he replied, "I wanted to be among the firefighters."

John's integration into the classroom culture was facilitated by the storytelling, story-acting curriculum offered at his school. However, his integration came at a cost. In his selection of choice roles for boys and lesser roles for the girls, we see that John also incorporated stereotypical gender indicators of power that are often seen in group settings (Cook-Gumperz & Scales, 1996; Nicolopoulou, McDowell, & Brockmeyer, 2006; Nicolopoulou, Scales, & Weintraub, 1994; Reifel & Sutterby, 2009).

The sequence of stories and paintings in John's portfolio provides a vivid picture of his social adjustment and reveals the unique way in which John constructed his own form of social integration to the school culture over the school year. His stories illustrate how effective the story-play curriculum can be in facilitating socialization (Paley, 2004). The teachers' analysis of the stories over time gave them a grounded way to assess John's advances in social competence that were embedded in the culture of his classroom.

DIVERSITY CREATES SOCIAL ENRICHMENT FOR TODAY'S CLASSROOMS

Paley, as well as Genishi and Dyson (2009), Heath and Mangiola (1991), and many others, wrote extensively about how the culturally, linguistically, and ethnically diverse classrooms of today can provide great social enrichment for its members. They describe how such diversity expands the worldviews of both teachers and children.

Diversity Can Create Challenges for Teachers

While not all are contained within a box, most of the vignettes in this chapter involve diversity and its impact on children's socialization. The one that follows demonstrates the challenge diversity can present to teachers.

Along with the values of cultural and ethnic diversity, open play-based settings with mixed-age groups can also present a challenge to social integration, as the boxed feature *Family Diversity: Both a Gift and a Challenge* demonstrates.

Inclusion of Children with Special Needs

Teachers in play-centered classrooms must be realistic about the goals they set for all children, including those with special needs, and the availability of resources to implement them. Support for both inclusion as well as accommodation to special needs is a necessity; experience tells us that failure to establish agreement on goals and a time frame for their achievement with all concerned can hamper a successful inclusion program.

FAMILY DIVERSITY

Both a Gift and a Challenge

"Little Dragon"

After a celebration of the Chinese New Year as part of a multicultural program involving the children's astounding creation of a dragon, 3-year-old Christopher began emulating the actions of a dragon. He rigidly strode through the play yard, roaring and imaginatively breathing fire while stalking some of the older boys in the class. At about the same time, Christopher's mother began receiving an unusual number of "Ouch Reports" for Christopher (Alkon et al., 1994; see Figure 11.4).

She wondered what was going on. Christopher's descriptions of events in the "Ouch Reports" indicated that it was often Alex, the oldest, largest, and most popular child in the program, who had chased him. Was it possible that he, a Chinese American, was becoming a target of abuse for the "rough," older boys in the class? His mother began to wonder if she had made a mistake in enrolling Christopher in this integrated, university-based preschool. Perhaps she would have been wiser to place him in the new Chinese language school that was opening in a nearby community.

The teacher surveyed the file maintained by the school on "Ouch Reports" and found that Christopher did have a few more reports of bumps, falls, and scrapes than other children his age. The implications of these findings were discussed in a staff meeting. Teachers were also able to reference other observations that had been compiled for this child.

In the early days of the program, Christopher had spent most of his time near his early morning teacher, but now he had begun to spend more time in the active outdoor play areas of the school. Teachers noted that when Christopher pretended to be a dragon, the older boys chased him with cries, such as "Here comes the bad guy!" Teachers' attempts to reason with Christopher and the older boys about this pattern temporarily ended the chasing by the 4-year-old boys. Three-year-old Christopher, however, always tearfully insisted that he wished to continue to be a dragon. He seemed to have little interest in integrating himself by taking on a character from the play scenarios of the older boys. The moment the teacher's attention was averted, he approached the group again as a dragon, with the same consequences.

Christopher seemed enchanted with his ability to obtain the attention of the older boys. When conflict arose or when he fell while fleeing from the "superheroes," he seemed developmentally unable to comprehend the teacher's admonitions about the consequences of this entry strategy and the need to thematically coordinate his play with others. Developmentally, he did not yet have the perspective-taking skills to comprehend either the consequences of his own actions or to coordinate them with the interests of others (Espinosa, 2010; Gonzalez-Mena, 2010).

Luckily, around the time of spring break, another child about Christopher's age adopted the persona of Tyrannosaurus rex. Not surprisingly, the two formed a union and soon became the magnet for a small but cohesive group of younger children. When the teachers granted this group a special dragon territory on one of the smaller play structures, they were able to rant and rage with each other powerfully but be protected from forays by older "superheroes" in search of "bad guys." This teacher strategy allowed them to have a protected area within which they could engage in their dragon fantasy at their own developmental level.

OUCH REPORT

Child's Name: _John Doe_   Teacher's Name: _Jane Doe/Teacher_

Today's Date: _7 /25 /97_ Time of Accident _4 : 40_   a.m./(p.m.)

Location of Event: _Far yard_

Contributing Factors: _"I hurt myself right on the leg._
I was being chased and I bumped."

Type of Injury:

__ Cut
_✓_ Scrape
__ Bump or bruise
__ Mouth injury
__ Crush injury
__ Human bite
__ Insect bite/sting
__ Injury by foreign object
   (splinter, sand in eye, etc.)
__ Hair pulled
__ Other _____

Location of Injury:

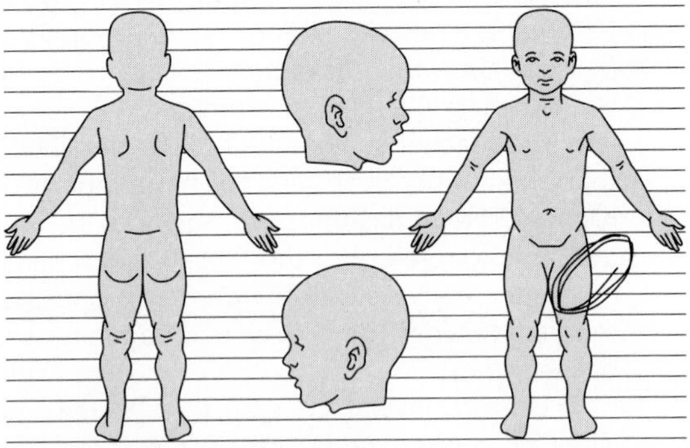

Type of Treatment Given:

— Cleaned injured site
_✓_ Ice pack applied
__ Band–Aid or dressing applied
_✓_ Child rested or laid down
_✓_ Given comfort
__ Antiseptic applied
__ Other _____
   _____

Recommended Follow-up:

He seems great - he was
a little shaken by
hurting himself.

Head Teacher (initial/date) _BJ_

Figure 11.4
Ouch Report

Source: Teacher designed form for class for classroom use.

Some of these diverse factors might have confounded support for successful inclusion in play of a child with a speech impairment in the vignette that follows. Not all teachers were in agreement about how to handle this child's efforts to socialize with younger children.

Matthew

Matthew, a large, slow-moving child (age 6 years and 5 months) with a severe speech impairment, has been retained for an additional year in the 4-year-old class. His parents and teachers believe that an extra year will help him make advances in social and interactive skills with peers who are a bit younger. ⌀

Previously, in the 4-year-old class, Matthew relied solely on the teachers to interpret his needs and support his efforts to socialize with peers. Recently he has been attempting to play and interact more frequently with other children. His teachers, however, still need to closely monitor his play with peers because of his limited speech and physical skills (Scales, 1989, 1996). In this, Matthew resembles many children with special needs, who rely greatly on adults to provide them with support in the interpretation of their needs (Erwin, 1993; Isenberg & Jalongo, 2014; Newcomer, 1993). According to van der Kooij (1989), some children with special needs respond to their environment in a single way, often nonverbally, making it difficult for them to effectively enter play situations. The following vignette is an example. Note the manner in which Matthew attempts to enter the play between Greg and François by kicking a tire as an initiating act.

"Quicksand"   The following excerpt from a longer text indicates what happens when Matthew attempts to enter into sand play with two boys. Greg, an unusually active child (5 years and 1 month), and François, a child of African American heritage (4 years and 9 months), have just negotiated a tenuous play interaction with one another. They are making "quicksand" by pouring water and sprinkling dry sand into a trench, which has been dug by the teacher.

Matthew jumps to a mound nearby the two boys and stands opposite Greg above the "quicksand." As they face each other, Matthew attempts to enter the play not by speaking, but by kicking a tire embedded in the sand above the trench. Greg responds by jumping across the trench to a sand mound near Matthew and shoves him over saying, "Take this, Matthew." Matthew responds by picking up a handful of sand and throwing it at Greg.

Greg shoves him over again and says, "Take this." He enlists François's help with a "Help me get him." Both boys are pulling and tugging on Matthew, and François asks, "Are we pushin' him in the quicksand?" Greg gives further directions to François as he points to the center of the quicksand: "No, push him right down there." François stands over Matthew and says, "Now you come here, Matthew, I've got something to show you."

Matthew points to François and says clearly, "I know what you're going to do. I saw it."

Greg and François continue to tug at Matthew, and François says, "Help me lift big boy up. Fat mouth."

Shortly after Greg begins to push Matthew, two teachers intervene. One attempts to encourage Matthew to use his language to tell Greg his objections to being pushed into the sand. A second teacher moves to assist and redirect Greg. She first acknowledges the good aspects of what Greg and François have made together, but also warns that it might need "special attention" because it could be "dangerous." Thus, she signals the boys that they can expect closer monitoring from teachers. Despite this warning, the two boys continue to attempt to push Matthew down into the sand.

The teacher returns to alter the direction this rough and tumble play has taken. "Are you playing the game with them, Matthew?" he asks. Without waiting for Matthew to respond, Greg and François chime in. They define the game as one that involves ". . . tryin' to push him [Matthew] down there." They say that Matthew has said, "Yes," he wishes to play the game. At this point Matthew speaks up quite clearly to say, "NO," indicating he does not wish to play. In some cases, teachers may tolerate what is known as rough and tumble play as an expression of affiliation if all the participants are willing to engage in it and it is not too rough (Bateson, 1976; Carlson, 2011a, 2011b).

Somewhat later, Matthew makes another attempt to enter the play with Greg and François. This time, he has modest success when he uses his language to assure the two boys relatively clearly, "I know what we can do, put sand on top." At this point François acknowledges Matthew's participation by saying, "You're right, Matthew. Then when people walk here, they'll sink in [and go in quicksand]. Kaboom!" Having affirmed the theme of the play, Matthew is not bothered further and appears to have succeeded in becoming a rather passive participant. ✄

While things turned out well in this episode, the teacher was wary about encouraging Matthew to enter this fast-paced, rough and tumble play with two unpredictable partners. This example illustrates the social difficulties that children with special needs may experience with peers during play and the dilemma it can create for teachers.

In the previous vignettes, we have illustrated the various factors that may impede children's ability to establish and maintain interactive play with peers in the classroom; the first two involve issues of separation, the third concerns the inability of a younger child to take the perspective of others, and the final episode involves three children attempting to play together. One of the three children, Matthew, is a child with special needs; the second is François, a child who is culturally different from his classmates; and the third is a child who often acts out aggressively. From these examples we see that it is not always easy to know precisely how to support play (Kaiser & Rasminsky, 2008).

TRADITIONAL RESEARCH AND PRACTICE

In the past, teachers who turned to research with questions related to play and socialization found relatively few answers. Researchers were sometimes uncertain that play was really taking place and were not always able even to identify its boundaries. This made it difficult to determine who was playing what and with whom, or how to intervene in a relevant way. Smilansky's (1968) recommendation (derived from her research) that intervention support elaborated dramatic play is one notable exception.

Various checklists and rating scales to assess environmental features, such as boundaries and links between areas, as well as level of play complexity, have been devised (Harms, Clifford, & Cryer, 1998; Kritchevsky, Prescott, & Walling, 1977; Scales, Perry, & Tracy, 2010; Walsh, 2008). These methods verify the presence or absence of desired features in classrooms and play yards, but do not reveal how these elements in themselves act to generate social and cooperative behavior.

CURRENT PRACTICE ILLUMINATED BY RESEARCH

Starting in the 1970s, play was studied in detail by a number of researchers influenced by Vygotsky and working in a sociocultural tradition (Cook-Gumperz & Corsaro, 1977; Dyson, 1997; Garvey, 1977/1990; Reed, 2005; Vygotsky, 1986). Many researchers collaborated closely with teachers or were teachers themselves (e.g., Cochran-Smith & Lytle, 1993; Cook-Gumperz & Scales, 1996; Corsaro, 1997, 2003; Erickson, 1993; Gallas, 1998; Perry, 2001; Qvortrup, Corsaro, & Sebastian-Honig, 2011; Reifel & Yeatman, 1991; Scales, 1996; Tribble, 1996). Drawing on this research, our knowledge of the specific ways that play interactions contribute to socialization has increased (Reifel, 2007; Sawyer, 2001).

Many of these were naturalistic, observational studies that looked at peer play and communication as it unfolded and demonstrated how children develop the skills to monitor varying social and cultural contexts. Some studies showed how school practice constrains or complements the development of essential features of social competence (Cook-Gumperz & Corsaro, 1977; Cook-Gumperz, Corsaro, & Streeck, 1996; Corsaro, 1985, 1997, 2003; Corsaro & Schwartz, 1991; Genishi & Dyson, 2009; Genishi, Huang, & Glupczynski, 2005; Qvortrup et al., 2011). Other research brought to light the complex issues involved in the gender socialization of boys and girls (Dyson, 1994; Goodwin, 1990; Nicolopoulou, McDowell, & Brockmeyer 2006; Nicolopoulou, Scales, & Weintraub, 1994; Scales & Cook-Gumperz, 1993).

Differences in Boys' and Girls' Play and Socialization

A year-long study of children's narratives by Nicolopoulou and Scales (1990) found that preschool boys' and girls' stories differed in both content and form (Nicolopoulou, McDowell, & Brockmeyer, 2006).

For girls, the family romance was paramount, with marriage, family relationships, or the frequent themes of arrival, losing, or finding babies. Boys, on the other hand,

Through interactions with playmates, children learn to negotiate roles with others.

rarely spoke of any relationship other than that of a "friend"—a friend with whom they more than likely battled as a culminating feature of their stories. These gender differences emerged early and persisted despite teachers' efforts to broaden the repertoires of both boys and girls.

"Tough Guys"   As we noticed in John's fire hydrant stories, the following vignette also reveals a previously hidden, gender-related social hierarchy in the allocation of roles in children's storytelling (Scales, 1996).

> Near the end of the day at a preschool, 28 children are seated around a square taped on the carpet. This is "the stage" where they enact stories that were dictated earlier to a teacher. At this particular moment the proceedings have stalled: the child-author's originally chosen actor for the part of a particular superhero has refused the role. The children are becoming restless and inattentive. The teacher, hoping to get things moving again, whispers a suggestion: "Why don't you pick Max? He really wants a part in your play!"
>
> "Oh no," responds the author. "He can't be it! It has to be one of the tough guys."
>
> The stalemate is resolved when it is suggested that Max can "pretend" to be a "tough" guy. ⌀

Suddenly, a previously unseen aspect of the social life of this classroom has become transparent. We knew that for the girls, "princess" roles were highly prized tokens of social favor, argued for and parceled out in play and story acting. Now, a hidden social hierarchy in the boys' world has been revealed as well.

When stories such as this and the power relationships they reveal are merely suppressed in "gender-neutral" classrooms, they go unnoted as a hidden curriculum. However, through story playing in preschool and an "author's theatre" in the primary-grade classroom, such issues can become accessible for negotiation and dialogue about who "gets in" and who "gets left out," who owns which social roles, and who has power in the play life of the classroom (Dyson, 1995, 2013; Scales, 1996, 2005).

As teachers and researchers are aware, not only do the themes and characteristics of boys' and girls' stories differ, but so too does their willingness to engage in play usually associated with members of the opposite sex. As far back as 1977, Garvey and Berndt noted that boys were reluctant to play roles such as a "prince" that are commonly associated with girls' stories or play. Teachers report that this is still the case in today's classroom.

Paley (1984), a teacher and writer, examined the differences in the play of preschool boys and girls. She found that when time for spontaneous play was lengthened, boys became more willing to engage in quiet table activities more typically favored by girls. She also recommended that teachers respect children's role choices, as they are an important part of their developing self-concept.

"Neighbors" An observational study of one classroom conducted by Cook-Gumperz and Scales (1996) revealed that the social dynamics of group settings alone may sometimes aggravate the occurrence of gender-stereotypic behaviors. Cook-Gumperz and Scales collected a set of observations of two groups playing adjacent to one another in the block area of the classroom. One group consisted of boys, the other of girls. When the group of boys moved to play more closely to the girls, the girls' interactive communication changed markedly. They began to enact roles of helpless mommies and babies who were in danger. Roles in their previous play had involved grooming and feeding miniature animals. In addition, during this time the boys' play became more assertively aggressive and "macho" as they circled around the girls, ostensibly to obtain blocks from a shelf to the rear of the girls (Cook-Gumperz & Scales, 1996).

At a brief interval midway through this long play event, the constellation of boys marched noisily out of the classroom. One boy remained behind and began inching near the girls' play space, making "strange clucking sounds." A brief conversation between the lone boy and one of the girls occurred when she commented on his strange noises. After this exchange, she turned to the girls and reassuringly said, "It's all right, he's just a neighbor." It was notable that no stereotypic forms were used as attempts were made to negotiate the lone boy's entrance into the girls' play space. However, the noisy return of the larger group of boys to the block area disrupted this negotiation, and the would-be "neighbor" was drawn back into the larger configuration. At this point, the assertive behavior accelerated and included loud singing and chanting. The noise finally aroused the attention of a teacher, who attempted to settle the matter by redirecting the children back into segregated groups to "share" the blocks. The attempt by the two groups to play together as "neighbors" (an inspired solution) went unnoticed (Cook-Gumperz & Scales, 1996). Had the teacher paused to discuss what was going on within the play frame of the girls' game, she might have discovered a way to make the play a bit more gender inclusive.

Instead, rather than make any attempt to scaffold possible cross-gender play, the teacher opted to merely "manage" the conflict. On the discourse boundaries between genders, teachers need to be alert to children's own efforts to define themselves and their relationships in new ways (Dyson, 1993, 2003; Tobin, 2000). In more structured ways, teachers might scaffold repertoires for cross-gender play by openly exploring with children at circle or small-group time some of the ways they think boys and girls can play together (Perry, 2001).

Children's Negotiations Create a Dynamic Context for Play

In studies of children's play communication, researchers have found that play interactions are shaped by and, in themselves, shape children's understanding of the **social and environmental expectations** of situations (Cook-Gumperz & Corsaro, 1977; Cook-Gumperz, Corsaro, & Streeck, 1996; Corsaro & Molinari, 2005). From such studies we find that children's lives in preschool are embedded in particular social contexts whose impact cannot be ignored without neglecting children's interest, self-direction, and motivation (Scales, 1997). The social work in which children engage as they play has been largely unexamined by practitioners whose valuing of play has its roots in early childhood's psychodynamic heritage.

Constructivists such as Piaget and Vygotsky have had an important impact on our view of children's development. Both researchers and teachers have been stimulated by Vygotsky's (1986) concept of the "zone of proximal development." Many recent articles have failed to note that Vygotsky also asserted that play in itself is the source of development and creates the zone of proximal development (Beck, 2013; Nicolopoulou, 1996; Nicolopoulou, McDowell, & Brockmeyer, 2006). The vignette about John and his fire hydrant persona is a vivid example of the way in which teachers create a **zone of proximal development** through the story-play curriculum, a guided play activity.

Consider the primary-school vignette in the next section, which also illustrates this possibility. Consider how an open activity period effectively creates a zone of proximal development for children. The play roles that four primary-school children set for themselves reflect their developing social competency (Vygotsky, 1986).

Newspapers

At midyear, 6-year-olds Clay, Zoe, Randall, and Michelle decide they will use their daily activity period to make a class newspaper. In this language- and literacy-rich first-grade classroom, they have many opportunities to generate their own literacy curriculum with different kinds of writing, such as letters, articles, books, lists, and signs. Their teacher, Harriet, wisely helps them develop traditional competencies in handwriting, spelling, and letter sounds on a daily basis. So Zoe, Clay, Randall, and Michelle have not come to their play project uninformed.

Their interest in the newspaper project extended over several weeks and involved much research and many revisions, additions, and reviews by their teacher and classmates. News articles as well as jokes and cartoons were collected and included in the final comprehensive version. Although only one "edition" was published, every child in the classroom received a copy (Morrison, 1985). In this primary-grade classroom, daily activity time, during which children have ample choices of things to do, provides a zone of proximal development, or what Newman, Griffin, and Cole (1989) call the "construction zone." The creation of such an activity period is similar to the project and Reggio Emilia approaches (Bodrova & Leong, 2006; Katz & Chard, 2000; Wien, 2008).

In the play that occurs in the free interaction among peers, children are provided with an opportunity to experience the "give and take," or reciprocity, that is a salient feature of effective social play, where shared needs, interests, and competencies and social and moral development can be mediated (Turner, 2009). "This reciprocity is rarely achieved between children and adults, but in play (among peers) it is the rule rather than the exception" (Alward, 2005, pp. 1–2).

Research on Play and Socialization within Special Education   Play in inclusive settings has the potential to enhance social competence for children with special needs. Researchers have focused on play and socialization within special education and inclusive classrooms (Hartmann & Rollett, 1994; McEvoy, Shores, Wehby, Johnson, & Fox, 1990; Ostrosky, Kaiser, & Odom, 1993). They have found that children with severe disabilities in integrated sites spent more time engaging in activities with their classmates than in unoccupied behavior, which broadened their base of social support (Erwin, 1993).

The vignette in this chapter about Matthew demonstrates in a realistic way that it is not an easy matter to support children with special needs as they attempt to participate in play with their classmates in inclusive classrooms. It often requires careful observation and sensitive intervention at the environmental level. New play designs for equipment and toys also enhance the potential of an inclusive classroom. For example, the acquisition of a wheelchair that is scaled to a height that enables eye contact with peers can contribute to enhancing communication for the child with special needs (Belkin, 2004). However, as Belkin found in his study of one child, such an acquisition may require considerable effort and expense on the part of the parents (Isenberg & Jalongo, 2014; Milligan, 2003). Research on patterns of socialization in inclusive classrooms can render more specific information on how the environment affects children with special needs and the dynamics of the classroom.

PLAY PROVIDES A BRIDGE BETWEEN THEORY AND PRACTICE

Our broad constructivist view of child development does not confine us to relying on any single, rigid theoretical approach. Classical Piagetian theory can serve us well in the study of individuals, but we also look to Vygotsky for a bridge to discover how the social dynamics of the classroom intersect with individual cognitive development (Genishi & Dyson, 2009).

Rather than taking a top-down approach—that is, bringing only a selected theory to bear—teachers might find greater explanatory power in analyzing their own records and observations from an **interpretive approach** (Corsaro & Molinari, 2005; Gaskins, Miller, & Corsaro, 1992).

Such an approach looks closely at specific play interaction and takes an insider's view rather than that of the detached outsider. It grounds these explanations in contexts well known to participants. By this means, findings can be corroborated and discrepant cases identified and explained (Cochran-Smith & Lytle, 1993; Erickson, 1993, 2004; Gaskins, Miller, & Corsaro, 1992; Perry, 2001; Sawyer, 2001).

The Interpretive Approach

The value of an interpretive approach, which draws on multiple theoretical perspectives, is demonstrated by the "tough guy" anecdote cited earlier in this chapter. Remember that the child-author first resisted letting Max play the role of a superhero in his play because he was not a "tough guy." Subsequently, he changed his mind when the teacher suggested that Max could *pretend* to be a tough guy.

The child-author's acquiescence to the teacher's suggestion might be analyzed from a number of perspectives. The classical Piagetian point of view might suggest that the issue simply involved a matter of relations between classes. In this case, for the child-author someone pretending to be a "tough guy" could be included in the class of "tough guys" and, therefore, be allowed to take such a part in his play.

Developmental and cognitive issues, such as a child's understanding of classification and the ability to conserve, certainly were involved. However, such an analysis does not account for all the child's reasoning or for his **agency** and **motivation**. Here an interpretive perspective, with its sociocultural orientation, broadens constructivist thinking to provide further explanatory power (Alward, 2005; Scales, 1996). From a sociocultural perspective, the context of the story-acting activity presented the child with a conflict and an ambiguity that needed to be resolved, and the teacher, as mentor, offered an alternative that helped him find a solution within the collaborative construction of the "play."

From a Piagetian perspective, this might be considered to be a **disequilibrating event** that possibly helped the child-author advance to a higher level of thinking. However, taking a broader sociocultural view, which encompasses the social dynamics of the classroom, this conflict could be seen as the kind of negotiation of power roles that Dyson (1995, 2013) referred to in her work on urban classrooms. When teachers take an interpretive approach, they discover that children actively contribute to their own socialization and a sense of themselves as social entities within the group, and to the production and reproduction of the children's culture (Corsaro, 1997; Gaskins et al., 1992; Qvortrup et al., 2011). In play-centered classrooms, teachers have a potent opportunity to observe how children insert elements from the larger culture into their play world. In so doing, they are forced, as was John in his fire hydrant persona, to make sense of both their real and fantasy worlds (Nicolopoulou, 1996; Reifel, 2007; Scales, 2005).

In discussing ethnographic and linguistic research on children's narratives, Dyson noted that individual children assume the voices of others, both past and present, as they use the linguistic forms they have appropriated from teachers, parents, and peers to construct a text (Dyson, 1995, 2003, 2013; Dyson & Genishi, 1994; Genishi & Dyson, 2009; Scales, 2005). Dyson also found, however, that when addressing present-day events, such as the ambiguity surrounding gender, the text is in and of itself transformative (Turner, 2009). That is, it transforms the child's perception of the past and the future.

For example, when today's child uses a past expression of gender (e.g., "princess"), she is not merely miming in some frozen way an outmoded social attitude. Rather, because the old-fashioned expression is now embedded in the different social context of today's world, it brings about change or transforms by giving rise to ambiguities the child must resolve through dialogue with others. If we merely drive gender expressions underground as a hidden curriculum, we fail to provide any occasion for this transformative mediation to occur as the child struggles to reconcile the tension between gender conventions of the past and emerging ones of the present (Dyson, 1995).

Teachers Take a Research Stance: Views from the Inside

Teachers can take a research stance by systematically observing play communication to see how the classroom social environment is being "read" by children. For example, the teachers' videotaped observation of the interactive strategies of the three children in the "quicksand" episode gave teachers important information about how to guide children's interactions and later modify the play environment of the sand pit to support more inclusive play (see Figure 11.5).

Figure 11.5

Children's Interactive Strategies

The interactive strategies that children use provide clues about their ability to understand the views of others. Situational strategies children employ also reveal how actions and speech are coordinated and synchronized to conform to a mutual understanding of the unfolding interaction. Such behaviors are essential to prosocial behavior. Children can be provided with opportunities to learn essential skills, such as "turn taking," in play interactions with peers. **Turn-taking skills** may be learned in play at the swings on the playground, or when children put their names or marks on a waiting list for a turn at the water table.

In many early childhood classrooms, turns at games start early in cooperative dyads. If groups are not too large or too formally structured, the understanding of a conversational turn can be demonstrated in talk at circle time. Games involving turns, such as lotto, and familiar songs with turns of a chorus or refrain can contribute as well. Children also need to be given ample opportunity to generate and practice their own turn-taking rules within the give-and-take of spontaneous play.

Central to this approach to understanding children's socialization is the notion that the play context is dynamic (Vygotsky, 1986). As they play, children develop their understanding of the unfolding activity (Cook-Gumperz & Gumperz, 1982). For example, when negotiating a theme, such as "home play," children come to understand that to successfully enter into play, one must be "**on topic**" (e.g., carrots are to be "cooked" and not used as guns).

Research tells us that to maintain social cooperation, children, like adults, constantly signal their mutual understanding of unfolding interactive themes. Mutual understanding is signaled when children initiate a play episode or topic or when a

Because play is inseparable from all facets of development, play itself must develop.

topic is changed; play partners will often be observed to affirm the change with a "right." "We're making soup, right?" "Right!" "And it'll have alphabets, OK?" "OK!" (Corsaro, 1979, 1997, 2003; Gumperz & Cook-Gumperz, 1982; Qvortrup et al., 2011; Sawyer, 2001). In the "quicksand" episode, Matthew acknowledged his understanding of the play theme with his "I know what we can do . . . put sand on top."

Although this is usually expressed in a co-player's "right" or an "OK," affirmation also can take a nonverbal form. For example, a co-player may express uptake of a cooking theme by an appropriate gesture, such as beginning to stir a bowl of "sand soup." Matthew's tire kicking was inappropriate as an entry strategy and, as we saw, was rejected.

Turn Taking and Children with Special Needs   The notion of turn taking is especially important for those with special needs who may have difficulty cooperating with peers. In general, we observe the mutual influence of individuals on one another. However, with regard to some children with special needs, "egocentrism" might block such "mutuality" (van der Kooij, 1989). Opportunities to practice turn-taking skills in the give-and-take of social play, as was provided to Matthew, are important for these children so that they can learn to interact effectively (Koplow, 1996; Odom, 2002; van der Kooij, 1989; Wolfberg, 1999).

STUDYING THE SOCIAL ECOLOGY OF A PRESCHOOL CLASSROOM

Most of the observational material cited in this chapter is drawn from naturalistic studies of preschool or early primary settings for 3- to 6-year-olds. The basic method of analysis was pioneered in conversational studies of adults conducted by such anthropologists as John Gumperz (Jaworski & Coupland, 1999, 2006). It was adapted for work with young children in preschools and primary grades by sociologists Corsaro and Cook-Gumperz (Cook-Gumperz & Corsaro, 1977; Corsaro, 2003; Corsaro & Molinari, 2005; Qvortrup et al., 2011).

Taking an Interpretive Approach to the Social Ecology of the Classroom

By using an interpretive approach to the analysis of their observations of children's interactions and communicative behavior, teachers and researchers can answer many questions. Dyson's interpretation of children's authoring in urban classrooms reveals the power of relationships operating within the social ecology of the classroom (Dyson, 2003, 2013). Studies of the play interactions of boys and girls have exposed vivid contrasts and demonstrate how children like John may adapt stereotypic forms from the wider culture to their own play relationships as they simultaneously advance in linguistic and social competence. Interpretation of the communicative styles of ethnically mixed play partners Greg and François reveals how the two boys creatively modify their speech style to establish a mutually agreed-on play scenario.

The research discussed in the following sections indicates how interpretative analysis of observations derived from site-specific interactive behaviors of children demonstrate that implied social expectations for play patterns are contained in the **social ecological elements** of various centers.

Contrasts in Social Ecologies

Researchers Cook-Gumperz and Corsaro (1977) analyzed four episodes that were drawn from videotapes of a preschool classroom. In this section, we discuss and contrast these episodes to demonstrate how the social and ecological cues of settings influence children's play and socialization.

In the Home Play Center: Rita and Bill   The first episode involves two children, Rita and Bill, playing husband and wife. It demonstrates how little negotiation is required to establish play themes in the home play center because children bring what the researchers call **conventionalized expectations** to this site.

For Rita and Bill, the most difficult portion of their interaction involves their attempt to ward off the incursion of two unruly "kitties" that attempt to enter the playhouse. Corsaro and Cook-Gumperz noted that once a play episode is underway, children are protective of their interactive space. We saw the same issue when Matthew attempted to engage in play with Greg and François, who vigorously resisted his attempt until he acknowledged that he understood their play theme.

Aware that children's interactions are fragile, teachers respect ongoing interactions by helping potential intruders like the "kitties" become established at a site nearby or involved with others who are not already engaged. In this case, Rita and Bill handle the problem themselves by dismissing the "kitties" to the "backyard." In the case of Matthew, discussed earlier in this chapter, the teachers were watchfully supportive of his efforts to enter an ongoing rough and tumble play event.

The Sand Table: Constructing a Play Fantasy   In the second episode, a four-sided sand tray is the site for more inventive and well-coordinated play themes. It challenges children's use of their linguistic and communicative skills to construct a unique collective play fantasy because at this site scenarios are not conventionalized as they are in home play centers. The collective fantasy opens with a "rainstorm." Then a small sand mound is elaborated into a "home for freezing bunnies." The players coordinate the changes of theme and do so again as the sand mound becomes a final safe haven from "lightning" in a "B . . . I . . . G steel home."

In contrast to the first episode, the children at the indoor sand tray are required to structure their activity creatively as it emerges. They cannot rely on conventional expectations, such as those in home play centers. Rather, they must depend on their own communication to collectively create and sustain the order of their talk about their spontaneous and novel fantasy (Turner, 2009).

Although the home play center is ideal for the beginner communicator, more open settings (such as the sand tray with miniatures) also are needed to provide challenge for older children. At such sites, children stretch their communicative strategies as they cue each other to the meaning of unfolding play events they collaboratively create. Such strategies include some of the following:

1. Using special **linguistic cues** to signify the fantasy (e.g., taking the role of the bunnies).

2. Using **repetition** to acknowledge some feature of a previous utterance (such as echoing and repeating key words and phrases like *freezing, rain,* and *lightning*).

3. **Tying** new material to previous thematic content. For example, using the word *and* plus a phrase containing new material allows an opening for another child to interact. In one episode, a child named Sabrina says, "I'll take the baby to the store." Her friend Sarah links her utterance by adding, ". . . and the big sister will drive the car; and I'll be the big sister."

4. Using an ongoing verbal description of behavior as it occurs; for example, saying, "Help, we're in the forest, and it's beginning to rain," while visually manipulating miniature toys.

Settings That Constrain Peer Talk and Interaction   Cook-Gumperz and Corsaro (1977) analyzed a third episode that occurred at a project table where the teacher inhibits the children's language use and development of interactive skills because she does most of the talking, controls the flow of talk, and initiates most topics.

With a greater awareness of the importance of the need for children to spontaneously exercise their interactive skills with peers, teachers might consider how they can support and maintain interactive talk during situations involving, for example, guided projects.

An Undefined Context   In a fourth episode, the setting involves an undefined context, where talk is also constrained. Here, conflict and confusion in play result from the ambiguous cues that are inadvertently created when the teacher moves a worktable from its usual place. Children do not know whether they are at a table for guided literacy play or spontaneous home-related play. Two of the three children try to establish a play scenario about being "teachers," and the other thinks he is playing "police." The play communication that results is marked by a singular lack of coordination in a short-lived attempt to interact.

Information about the subtle features of this breakdown in communication is derived from close observation of the uncoordinated features of communication and social ecological factors. An understanding of this event will not be revealed by observational schemes that merely code behavior into categories (e.g., solitary, parallel, or collaborative). Such categories give little information about how teachers can intervene in a way that will be relevant and make sense to children or support their play interaction. Teachers learned from this analysis that, although mixing environmental cues can sometimes produce interesting and positive transformations in children's play, it also can contribute to failed communication among participants, as it did in this case. Changing social ecological elements is more than merely "moving furniture" and can have unforeseen consequences.

KITCHEN PLAY REEXAMINED

We can also be misled about children's social skills when we classify play as fixed categories on the basis of one element of an interaction. For example, children do not place speech in the foreground of their communication. Instead, they use all **modalities of communication**, such as gesture, rhythm, and intonation, to achieve their interactive goals. This is demonstrated in the following example.

> Three children, Andrea (age 3 years and 2 months), Celine (age 3 years and 4 months), and Peter (age 3 years and 4 months) are playing with pots and pans at an outdoor sand table. Andrea and Celine are busy chatting about what the "baby" will eat for breakfast, while Peter silently stirs a bowl of sand nearby. ∅

Pam, their teacher, observes their play and assesses Peter's silent engagement as an example of solitary or parallel play. However, based on her later analysis of a videotape recording, this episode provides evidence of Peter's active participation in the group interaction.

Though close at hand, Pam fails to take note of the role that Peter has been assigned. Only at the end of the episode is she made aware that she and Peter have been filling the roles of "baby" and "babysitter," respectively. This is revealed to her when Andrea, the "mommy," emphatically points her finger at Pam and says, "Baby, you—I'm goin' out to the woods." Then with a gesture toward Peter, she says, "You stay here with the babysitter."

Whether Peter's play is solitary, parallel, or collaborative is not easily determined. However, close analysis of the videotape and Peter's affirmation of his role reveal that even without speech Peter is a significant participant in this interactive play, whereas Pam, the teacher, being the most passive, is of course the "baby" (Scales & Webster, 1976).

For older children, language plays a more important role, and they do not rely as heavily on environmental cues to guide understanding. With their increasing linguistic ability, they are able to detach play from its situational context and, should play be disrupted, are more capable of reestablishing it. As linguistic skills advance, children are also able to maintain interactive play across multiple sites (Scales, 1997).

Teacher Support for Play Interactions

In this chapter we show that initiating or entering play is a complex matter and involves more than mimicking adult formulas, such as "Hello, may I play with you?" Such an opening probably would be greeted with a resounding "No," particularly among 4-, 5-, and 6-year-olds. Within the children's culture, distinctive forms of communication are constructed.

Children develop their own particular strategies for making an entrance into an established play episode. One successful tactic involves circling about the site of the play event until the players make an overture to the newcomer (Corsaro, 1997,

2003). The teacher (in the role of **gatekeeper**), noting a child's desire to enter a play episode, can assist by helping the newcomer find an activity or role that complements the play event. The teacher also might set the newcomer up nearby with similar props.

An example of a unique solution to a gatekeeping problem occurred when two girls barred the entrance of a third to the playhouse. The teacher's repeated suggestions of possible roles for the entering child had been rejected again and again. Squabbling and howling ensued for some time until one of the rejecting pair had a marvelous idea: The newcomer could be the "door." This role eminently suited Mia, the newcomer, who often took the role of gatekeeper on other occasions, excluding others. She immediately barred the entrance with widespread arms and legs.

Children Grant Warrants for Play

Sometimes play is established around action alone, as in the game of tag. However, close observation of the natural history of an activity reveals that even such seemingly simple play involves what Cook-Gumperz and Corsaro (1977) called granting a **warrant**, or permission to establish or alter a play theme.

A typical example of granting a warrant occurred in connection with the quicksand segment presented earlier. Greg and François had agreed and established a warrant that an area in the sandpit was "quicksand." However, one of the pair at one point, seeing that the water poured into the sand created a froth, referred to it as "chocolate milk." This constituted an attempt to get a warrant for a new thematic direction and prompted his partner to respond, "You remember, we're makin' quicksand." This correction was quickly affirmed by a cheery, "Oh, right, right," and the previous warrant was reestablished.

Negotiations around granting warrants go on continuously in children's interactions. These warrants provide a thread to link sequences of activities. When a warrant is granted, close observation of the play interaction reveals this as a focal point where communicative modes, both verbal and nonverbal, converge. Teachers can observe that children's postures, rhythms, gestures, and actions are well coordinated. These focal points are evidence that a mutually satisfactory interaction is taking place.

On further observation, teachers also note sequences of maximal divergence or transition points. At these times, children do not share a mutual understanding of the context. They therefore have different views about the ongoing interaction. This lack of mutual understanding is even evident in lack of coordination in the children's body language and posture.

In the following segments of the "quicksand" interaction, because the event consists largely of rough and tumble play, most of the transition points involve a teacher intervention. Two of the boys, François and Greg, seem to want to engage in rough and tumble play and play fighting (as indicated by their laughter). The third child, Matthew, does not, signaled by the fact that he is not laughing (Bateson, 1976; Carlson, 2011a; Perry, 2001; Reed, 2005).

At such transition points, teachers may wish to intervene as Peacemakers to clarify and reorient the players to a mutually acceptable focus. However, if teachers are not observing closely, they may intervene at the wrong point or make an irrelevant suggestion, thereby disrupting rather than supporting the interaction. Even a teacher's well-meaning reinforcing behavior, such as registering approval of children's cooperative play, sometimes serves only to distract the players.

"Quicksand" Revisited   We return now to an earlier segment of the "quicksand" episode. Our purpose here is to consider in detail the initiating and sustaining of play. In this segment, we also learn about some of the problems that can arise in ethnically diverse play interactions. François, a child of African American heritage, speaks Black English as well as Standard English and a form of English one might hear a speaker use on TV. Unfortunately, most of François's teachers generally speak only Standard English. His play partner, Greg, uses Standard English and also a form of English used by TV speakers. At the beginning of the episode, Greg is in the center of the sandpit at the intersection of the three pathways teachers have configured. Greg stations himself there as soon as he arrives, at the beginning of the school day. Only three interactions occur in the sand on this day, and all involve the negotiation of a warrant with Greg to gain access to the sandpit (see Figure 11.5).

In environmental terms, an obvious feature of this particular sand "curriculum" is that the physical setup of the sandpit constrains play because the arrangement of intersecting passageways gives dominion over a large area to Greg, who stands at the center of the intersection. It also limits possibilities for the types of play interactions that might go on. The high mounds of sand, steep slopes, and narrow passages of the pathways invite very close physical contact. They tend to generate only a single possibility: rough and tumble play.

First Attempt to Establish a Warrant for Play

François enters the sandpit and addresses Greg with, "Hi ya, Greg."

Greg responds, "Hi ya, François." Then François jumps to a mound of sand near Greg as the episode begins:

François:	Let's see what time it is. Oh, yeah, it's time for one by two by two.	Speaks rapidly, using style, rhythm, and tone of Black English.
Greg:	No. No.	
François:	OK—well one by two by two, one by two, by two—ooda do da doo, one by two by two—me and my two by two—one by two by two—one by two by two is over.	François wrestles with Greg. Both boys are laughing.
Greg:	OK, François.	
François:	OK, Fatso.	François moves away.

| Greg: | Here you go. Take this! | Throws a handful of sand at François. Boys now begin to throw sand at each other. ⌀ |

In this sequence, François attempts to establish a warrant with Greg for a play-fighting game called "one by two by two." François addresses Greg in what is recognized by linguists as Black English because of its rhythm, intonation, and other features (Labov, 1972).

As the two children tussle about in the sand, François continues to address Greg in a distinct rhythm, saying, "Oh, I'm gonna catch you." The teacher begins to monitor more closely. As the children begin to throw sand at each other, the teacher moves in to intervene. The sand throwing, though a prohibited activity, is well coordinated and is not a transition point for the children since they are enjoying the activity. However, as a prohibited activity, the teacher cannot permit it. A transition that disrupts this interaction occurs when the teacher is required to enter.

Second Attempt to Establish a Warrant

François falls into the trench. Greg moves over and they tussle and toss sand about.

François:	Oh, oh, my goo goo.	
François	Why—I'll get rid of your shirt if you do that again. I'll take your shirt off and I'll tear your shirt right off. That's the first thing I'd do.	Greg moves on mound above trench; turns to look at François.
François:	Tear you [inaudible] come back.	Greg and François tussle about in the sand.
Greg:	(laughs) ⌀	

In this second attempt to establish a warrant, François again uses intimate Black English, addressing his friend as if Greg were a member of François's linguistic culture. The attempt ends with the boys tussling in the sand and the predictable entrance of the teacher.

At this point, Greg's complaint to the teacher, "I don't wanta play this," constitutes a rejection of François's second bid for a warrant for play. At this transition point, the teacher attempts to help the children find a more suitable focus.

Third Attempt to Establish a Warrant

Speaking in deeper tones and switching to a TV hero voice, François stands on the mound above Greg and initiates another warrant.

| François: | I'm at the cliff of the mountain. | François takes a new posture on the mound. |

| *Greg:* | You won't get me, François. | Greg moves from François and the intersection. |
| *François:* | You won't get me either. Try to tear me apart. | François moves out upper-left exit. Greg follows. ✍ |

This warrant is more to Greg's liking, and a well-coordinated game of tag is launched. The warrant attempt has succeeded. The play interaction, though primarily gross motor in nature at this point, is well coordinated and cohesive.

The episode just described is noteworthy because one of the children speaks Black and Standard English as well as TV English and shifts from one to the other midway through the episode. We see here that the demand is greater in this setting for the African American child to adapt his linguistic style to his play partner's speech style. François's initial overtures to establish a play warrant by using Black English are not successful (Labov, 1972; Reifel, 2007). However, because he speaks both standard and Black English, François is successful in communicating with Greg when he switches, first to a form of TV English and then to Standard English.

The challenge in this play episode for the three children is to find a common/mutually understood communicative style. Teachers, although remaining watchful, do not separate the two boys' from **play fighting**, but give them time to find a common focus for a play interaction on their own. Situations such as this provide an interesting challenge to the skills of teachers in creating a supportive play environment that responds to the diverse social needs of all children (Reifel, 2007).

Negotiation of multiple modes of communication in our increasingly diverse preschool and primary-grade classrooms can be viewed as a richness that expands children's worldviews (as seen by Genishi & Dyson, 2009.) As in the case with the three boys in the previous vignette, it also represents a challenge to children and teachers to interact effectively and to amicably share meaning with one another.

Supporting Interactive Play at the Environmental Level

Teachers facilitate cohesive interactive play by defining various areas in the classroom and play yard. Dividers and other spatial markings or arrangements protect interactive space so that players are not easily distracted and play is not disrupted. An example of this is seen when teachers arrange the environment so that block building or other floor play does not occur in the middle of pathways.

Teachers can establish spaces that bring children into proximity with one another, like around a rectangular sand tray or table. The visual array of toys shared by all informs an entering child about the play theme in progress and suggests a possible role to be taken. Such spaces also help establish "face engagement," where children are looking at each other across the rectangular table as well as at the toys.

In this case, the basics of communication are ensured, as is a shared understanding of the theme of the unfolding play (Goffman, 1974, 2000).

Such configurations provide what has been called "defensible space" (Cook-Gumperz, Gates, Scales, & Sanders, 1976). Each child has a territory (his or her side of the table) so that entry into interaction with another in this situation places everybody on equal footing. Such a space also provides for two pairs of children playing side by side in parallel play. This opens up the possibility that the play of two pairs may become socially more coordinated as a foursome.

PRECURSORS TO FORMAL SOCIAL STUDIES STANDARDS IN EARLY CHILDHOOD PROGRAMS

Although the activities we have been describing represent socialization to the classroom culture, teachers are feeling more and more pressure to place increasing emphasis on and assessment of formal academic curriculum standards. The broad area of **socialization** covers children's ability to interact with peers and dispositions to learn and what, in later schooling, is called social studies. As a discipline, **social studies** encompasses a wide array of subject areas representing content from a variety of academic fields of knowledge. A sampling of four of the ten areas of knowledge for social studies identified by the National Council for the Social Studies (1998) are as follows:

- Time, continuity, and change
- People, places, and environments
- Production, distribution, and consumption
- Civic ideals and practices

Social Science for Young Children

Many of the social studies content areas can be addressed in concrete ways in a play-centered curriculum grounded in children's day-to-day interactions with one another in the community life of the classroom. This community has its own culture and involves sharing social resources of the classroom by participants. In this sense, the classroom is a microcosm of the wider community of adults. Sharing, reciprocity, fairness, and democratic processes are necessities in the child's world as well as ours. Most standards relating to socialization involve dispositions, such as empathy for others, the ability to interact effectively with peers, and respect for the diversity of others. As this chapter amply illustrates, these attributes are best acquired by children as they engage in interactive play in the community of a caring classroom. Their assessment is best derived from systematic records of observations of the interactive behaviors of children engaged in guided and spontaneous play, as illustrated in Table 11.1.

Table 11.1 A Sample of Some Ways to Adapt the Social Studies Standards to the Early Childhood Curriculum.

Social Studies Strand	Curriculum/Teacher Examples	Children Learn and Experience
Time, continuity, and change	The marking of cyclical events, such as day and night, the rhythms of daily routines and the seasons, by special activities and projects (e.g., a mural of a winter scene); examining children's shadows at different times of the day	Children become aware of time, continuity, and change through the sequences and patterns of daily rituals, such as meeting time, choice time, small-group time, lunch, cleanup, etc.
People, places, and environments	Photographic displays of families illustrate diversity of peers and families; map making of the local environment, maps illustrating differing origins of our ancestors	Experiences in interacting with diverse others in the classroom. Noticing features of natural and human-made environments locally and in the wider community.
Production, distribution, and consumption	Classroom setup, where children play, learn, and participate, are defined areas in the inside and outside that are designated for production and use (the writing table, the art table, the ball area, the lunch tables); long- and short-term activities investigating where food comes from; making reports about a visit to a farm, a factory, or a supermarket, the port, an airport, the UPS store, or a construction site	Children begin to become aware that location is an essential feature of community. They share the resources of the classroom—toys, treats, and time—with teachers. Field trips and activities about them widen knowledge.
Civic ideals and practices	Provide guidance to children as they negotiate disputes, discuss differences, and generate and establish their own rules for how to make the classroom a more harmonious place; such rules become a part of the curriculum and relate to governance, civic ideals, and practices; provide games that build turn-taking skills; teachers model and scaffold ways to make requests in a diplomatic way; teachers intervene in play in a relevant way to help children find language that will enable them to amicably negotiate their needs and desires, for example, by finding a role for a newcomer: "Could Andrew be the grandfather coming to visit your house?"	Children begin to become aware of these concepts through day-to-day interactions with their peers and teachers in group situations like the classroom. Children adapt strategies modeled by teachers and their peers in interactions with each other in self-directed play. In play, they come to learn which strategies are effective and which are not. In play and guided activities they become aware of themselves as a community and gain confidence and poise as members of the classroom culture.

Information from National Council for the Social Studies (1998), *Curriculum Standards II. Thematic Strands.* Retrieved from www.socialstudies.org/standard/strands.

SUMMARY

This chapter assumes that a major way children develop socially is through the exercise of their communicative skills in play and interaction with peers. Adult modeling of verbal skills and interactive strategies is not enough. The child's application of given strategies is not only developmentally determined, but also requires the child to interpret meaning in unfolding play events. When teachers take over this interactive work, they rob children of opportunities to develop their own strategies. This makes close observation by teachers a critical factor in providing relevant support, particularly for mixed-age or inclusive groups, or in ethnically and linguistically diverse play settings. Such observation allows teachers to look first at issues surrounding the child's separation from parents on first entering school.

- **Saying goodbye to parents.** Separating from parents is a major milestone for children and is considered by theorists to be critical to their ability to relate to others and for future integration into the school culture.

- **Diversity creates social enrichment for today's classrooms.** The cultural diversity of today's classrooms expands the worldviews of both the teachers and children. It also can create challenges in open play settings for teachers as well as for the parents of children.

- **Traditional research and practice.** Traditional research has allowed us to assess the presence or absence of desired features of classrooms, but does not reveal how such features in themselves act to generate social and cooperative behavior.

- **Current practice illuminated by research.** The sociocultural tradition, deriving from the theories of Lev Vygotsky, has had a major influence on our thinking about research on children's behavior. Many of these studies look at children's communication and interaction as they unfold within the social context of play.

- **Play provides a bridge between theory and practice.** Our view of development does not rely on a single theory, but draws from a number of theories, including constructivists with a classic Piagetian orientation as well as those with a sociocultural viewpoint. We do not take a top-down approach, but rely on analysis of teachers' records and observations, thereby taking an "insider's" view rather than the detached view of an outsider.

- **Studying the social ecology of a preschool classroom.** A basic method of analysis of the child observations cited in this chapter is adapted from conversational studies of adults conducted largely by anthropologists and sociologists.

- **Kitchen play reexamined.** Using fixed categories to classify play can be misleading. Lack of speech may not be an indicator that interaction is not taking place. Young children do not give precedence to speech; they use all modalities of communication, including gesture and coordinated rhythm of action, to achieve their interactive goals.

■ **Precursors to formal social studies in early childhood programs.** The broad area of socialization in the early years covers children's dispositions to learn and ability to interact with peers. While objectives converge to some extent with what is called social studies, the emphasis in early childhood is on children's social–emotional development and interactive competence. A sampling of a few of the social studies standards with examples of adaptation to the early childhood classroom are offered.

Our heritage from the psychosocial and constructivist traditions in early childhood education has served us well. This heritage has been augmented by new technologies, analytic methods, and the theoretical orientations of the sociocultural school of Vygotsky and others, which are currently influencing our thinking on issues of identity, social equity, acquisition of cultural resources, and the impact of globalization in our classrooms (Anderson, 1995; Corsaro, 2003; Corsaro & Molinari, 2005; Jaworski & Coupland, 1999; Swartz, 1997).

Using these theoretical approaches, we can now design and implement curricula that support socialization in much more relevant and specific ways. Through observation and analysis of play in its sociocultural context, strategies for the assessment of the development of children can relate to the local context of the school and children's previous experiences, such as problems with separation, individual and special needs, and the cultural and linguistic diversity of their lives.

APPLYING YOUR KNOWLEDGE

1. Discuss some family-life factors that can influence children's separation from parents at school entry.
    a. Design a newsletter for families of newly entering preschool children that provides them with suggested strategies for leave-taking and returning that ease anxiety about the transition from home to school.

2. Consider some ways teachers can adapt to the challenge of classroom diversity in age, gender, inclusion, and culture.
    a. Conduct an observation in your own classroom or another of a diverse mixed-age program. Does children's age, gender or ethnicity appear to play a part in determining who plays with whom or which roles children take in play scenarios?

3. Describe some of the ways that observational research in the sociocultural tradition of Vygotsky has enhanced our understanding of how children's play interactions with peers contributes to socialization.
    a. Discuss what checklists and rating scales might miss that are captured by observational studies that include language and interactive behavior.

4. Contrast some different forms of information that can be obtained from interpreting a child's behavior, as manifested in the "Tough Guys" vignette

from page 312, from a classical Piagetian point of view versus a sociocultural approach.

    a. To obtain information on a child's ability to construct a series, would you observe them at play on the large climber outside or at play with manipulatives?

5. Discuss how observational research of children's play communication and interactions can reveal how the environment provides implicit cues for children's behavior.

    a. In a newsletter to families, define the meaning of social ecology and why teachers need to be aware of how it influences children's play and learning.

    b. Observe play patterns in two different activity centers in your classroom or one you observe. From children's language and behavior as they play, what can you say about how they are reading the expectations for play implied by the ecology?

6. Discuss how children do not use speech alone, but use all modalities of communication, such as gesture, rhythm, and intonation, to achieve their interactive goals.

    a. Collect a 10-minute video sample of two children playing together. Note the various communicative forms they use during their interaction.

7. Consider some of the differences between children's early socialization and a formal social studies curriculum.

    a. Use the social studies standards as a base for a field trip or other curriculum activity that is developmentally appropriate for preschool, kindergarten, or primary-grade children.

    b. Ask children to draw a picture, dictate or write a story about the activity.

CHAPTER 12

Outdoor Play

Jane P. Perry
University of California, Berkeley

LEARNING OUTCOMES

- Explain how physically active outdoor play, outdoor nature play, and child-initiated outdoor play contribute to children's healthy development. Compare the differences between the outdoor classroom and the inside classroom.

- Identify five goals for teachers in supporting outdoor play and explain how teaching goals in the outdoor classroom can be accomplished.

- Discuss best practices in planning outdoor play, including supporting children from diverse backgrounds and overcoming challenges to outdoor play.

- Name the three phases of children's peer play and explain how child-initiated play proceeds through this sequence. Review how to understand and support big body rough and tumble play and how to serve students with special needs.

- Discuss the three questions teachers ask themselves to help decide what strategies to use when supervising outdoor play.

- Contrast two different teaching styles that support outdoor play and compare child-initiated and teacher-planned outdoor activities.

- Define *inquiry* and review several guideposts for children's experience of inquiry during outdoor play.

- Describe the two ways teachers determine how their outdoor space supports play and provide examples of how assessment tools rate the outdoor environment.

- Discuss and provide examples of organizing efforts to enable and restore safe outdoor play space and time. Review recommendations for active, spontaneous outdoor play.

It is the first day of school in Rebecca's mixed-age preschool classroom. Children are indoors and outside during activity time. Gabrielle and Tomás, both 4-year-olds returning for a second year, take turns descending halfway down the extra-wide slide, stopping, and draping one leg off the lip of the slide. Other children slide past them, more or less deftly. Rebecca watches cautiously at some distance, looking to see how Tomás' and Gabrielle's co-ordination holds up to her anticipated fear: a flip off the slide at some distance. New children, a year younger, approach, see this game, and attempt to imitate it.

"Gabrielle and Tomás. Can you keep your legs inside the slide, please? I know you feel safe, but I'm not so sure kids who haven't had as much practice will be safe. They will see you dangling your leg and think it is OK, and they might flip off the slide and get hurt."

"But we are newts, and this is what they do," Tomás says.

"Newts! Of course." Rebecca pauses to gather her thoughts. "Say, newts? I want to help kids play and stay safe also. Would you mind enjoying your moist log with your legs inside the slide?"

Leah, a 4-year-old child with autism, slides down on her belly past Tomás, marking her descent by pressing her face to the slide.

Tomás returns his leg to the inside of the slide.

"Here comes Leah," Rebecca says, marking Leah's entrance into the play area. "Hi Leah. It's Gabrielle and Tomás. They are newts."

"We eat bugs and sleep," adds Gabrielle, lying on her belly midway down the slide. Tomás lays his head on her stomach and they descend the slide together.

Rebecca moves to closely shadow Leah as she attempts to climb up a challenging arched ladder.

"You might want to ask Leah if she wants to be a newt too," Rebecca suggests.

The next morning before school, Rebecca is preoccupied with the beauty of Tomás' and Gabrielle's physical re-creation of a newt. Setting up the playground, Rebecca pulls out two benches from under an overhanging roof. She places the benches next to a vine of wisteria. When Gabrielle and Tomás come running outside, Rebecca hears:

"We're newts, right?"

"Right."

Rebecca casually mentions, "There is a log for newts," pointing at the benches. Gabrielle and Tomás locate their game on the benches, lying face down and slinging one leg off, leaving the benches to explore the tan bark area, where trees offer shade as they dig for rolly-pollies. ✍

The newt game carries on for several months, including younger and older children. Rebecca checks out books about newts, salamanders, and forested areas from the library to enrich the children's interest. Some dictate stories about newts, which they act out in Rebecca's circle. Some draw pictures of different kinds of newts and salamanders. In her parent newsletter, she includes directions and hours for a local nature center, which features a display of newts found in the region. The class paints a mural of a forest with rocks, logs, and a stream, adding newts and other animals that share this habitat.

THE IMPORTANCE OF OUTDOOR PLAY

Play is central to children's healthy development (Pellegrini, 2009; Smith, 2010). Outdoor play is not merely a time to "get the wiggles out," let off some steam, and give teachers a break from classroom learning. Gabrielle's and Tomás' play shows us the multidimensional qualities of children's outdoor play (Pellegrini, 2005). Gabrielle and Tomás are understanding a sense of themselves as they physically act out being a newt. Their play is cognitive in that Gabrielle and Tomás are examining an interest

Social coordinations occur in outdoor play.

from their local region of nature by using their whole body to explore what it means to be a newt. They use language to communicate ideas with each other and to others. Gabrielle's and Tomás' play is physically driven and rigorous. They are using balance, timing, and upper-body strength to control their descent.

Leah also likes to climb. Her aide will help Leah abandon a self-stimulating behavior of going down the slide face first on her cheek and belly to sit up so she can see peers like Gabrielle and Tomás.

This vignette illustrates joyous, spontaneous, child-centered, rough and tumble outdoor play that is physically active, engaged with nature, and focused on a self-initiated interest from daily life. Rebecca acknowledges Gabrielle's and Tomás' interest, recognizes the social entry of Leah as another possible player, and keeps them safe with an enriched setup to promote their investigation. She supports and extends their play with teacher-planned aesthetic and cognitive enrichment that draws on their daily life.

Circumstances in the lives of families, education, communities, and society have led to a critical concern over children's loss of time outdoors. Louv (2010) makes the point that children are experiencing such a reduction in time out of doors that they run the risk of what he calls "nature deficit disorder." Louv initiated the Leave No Child

Inside campaign and the Children and Nature Network (www.childrenandnature. org), stressing not only the imperative of outdoor time for children, but also the importance of engaging in nature for the health of all ages and the planet as well.

Educational funding structures that tie continued funding to test achievement have led to some schools eliminating or severely curtailing recess and the essential experiences gained for children out of doors. Concerns for liability have led to playground designs that lack essential physical challenges. Family lifestyles involving parents working long hours or holding down several jobs leave less time for outdoor play. Commercial marketing has made children's free time into a commodity. Parents are susceptible to suggestions that they need to purchase packaged, learning-enhanced activities or that their children require organized activities to succeed. Neighborhood safety can be a very real obstacle to outdoor time, but media attention tends to fuel fear and misrepresent safe opportunities for children to explore and play outside.

In contrast to this dire picture are the benefits of outdoor play. Children who participate in daily outdoor play receive the following benefits:

1. They gain essential physical experiences that contribute to their strength and coordination.
2. They feel connected with and learn about the world of nature.
3. They use their own curiosities and interests during spontaneous peer play (American Academy of Pediatrics, 2007; Burdette & Whitaker, 2005; Jarrett, 2002; Frost, Brown, Sutterby, & Thornton, 2004; Oliver & Klugman, 2002; Pellegrini & Smith, 1998).

First graders Cella, Indi, and Jamila are on the tire swing, rain gear on, spinning and laughing as the moist, light air fills their mouths and mist blows about their faces and hands. These children are experiencing essential kinesthetic experiences that contribute to physical development. Cella, Indi, and Jamila are also practicing gross motor strength, balance, and coordination to successfully push the combined weight of themselves and the tire and mount the tire during a fast spin. They are rewarded by the sensory stimulation of being outside, especially in the light rain. Cella, Indi, and Jamila are also experiencing the pleasures of social affiliation. Having fun while experiencing the intimacy of face-to-face contact contributes to Cella's, Indi's, and Jamila's social development. ⌀

In addition to outdoor play being healthy on its own merits, without a recess break, children's attention to tasks decrease; after recess, children are significantly more attentive (Pellegrini, 2005).

The Importance of Outdoor Physically Active Play

Physically active play enhances growth by including a child's whole body in practice and skill development. Young children need to move: run, jump, hop, skip, gallop, climb, swing, skip, throw and catch, and push and pull heavy play props. The National Association for Sport and Physical Education (2004) provides six physical activity standards and guidelines that we use for young children:

1. Demonstrates competency in motor skills and movement patterns needed to perform a variety of physical activities
2. Demonstrates understanding of movement concepts, principles, strategies, and tactics as they apply to the learning and performance of physical activities
3. Participates regularly in physical activity
4. Achieves and maintains a health-enhancing level of physical fitness
5. Exhibits responsible personal and social behavior that respects self and others in physical activity settings
6. Values physical activity for health, enjoyment, challenge, self-expression, and/or social interaction

When we look at these standards, we see that Gabrielle's and Tomás' activity illustrates all six standards.

The National Association for Sport and Physical Education (NASPE) recommends that preschoolers have at least 60 minutes and up to several hours per day of **unstructured physical activity**. They recommend no more than 60 consecutive minutes of sedentary activity except for sleeping.

Children need to be physically active to establish endurance. In a study of children's physically active play outdoors, Perry and Branum (2009) introduce 4-year-old Mollie. Mollie is experiencing new coordination and balance after a period of tentativeness and several stumbles. She vocally expresses her displeasure and notes, coincident with her pace, "I'm very slow right now because I'm a turtle" (p. 204). When she picks up speed, notice how her new surety is linked to her imaginative thinking: "But right now I'm a lion" (p. 204). Mollie's physical movement is a companion in her spontaneous play. Running around the climber, she voices feelings of empowerment: "Sometimes I pounce on twigs because I'm a meat eater" (p. 205).

Developmental milestones in physical and motor competence include a continuum of abilities like traveling and changing direction quickly, throwing and catching a ball, and later, active play sequences that combine running, jumping, throwing, and catching. For example, Mollie's physical activity demonstrates competency in fast-paced movement across a rugged tanbark surface, her own understanding of her improved coordination, and her interest in physical activity.

Young children learn best when their whole body is engaged in active physical play. Gabrielle's and Tomás' newt play offered them the chance to move and refresh muscles that are not used as often when the children are inside. Their climbing and scampering increased blood flow to these muscles (Ayres, 1979). In a study of kindergarten children, Myers (1985) compared motor behaviors during a physical education class and during spontaneous play in a playground that provided lots of opportunities for a range of gross motor challenges. She found that children

Outdoor play provides opportunities for gross motor development.

engaged in more physically active behaviors during child-initiated play than during their regular physical education class.

Active outdoor play helps children integrate development and new learning (for example, see Frost, Wortham, & Reifel, 2008). Children experience cognitive and social demands to think, speak, and negotiate with playmates and teachers (Frost et al., 2004; Pellegrini & Holmes, 2006; Perry, 2001; Perry & Branum, 2009). The physicality of Gabrielle's and Tomás' newt game required that they talk with and negotiate proper safety expectations with Rebecca. They safely adjusted their balance and used upper-body endurance to share space with peers on the climber. Cella, Indi, and Jamila used refined turn-taking in trading off turns to physically push each other on the tire. Mollie expresses what her physical exertion means to her in vivid metaphors inspired by her natural surroundings.

The Importance of Outdoor Nature Play

Direct exposure to nature is essential for healthy development. Being outside in nature opens children's senses, enriching their play with sights, sounds, smells, touch, movement, and taste. Cella, Indi, and Jamila experience lively play precisely because their active play is outside, where the air is fresh and the precipitation enlivens their skin. Nature play, like Gabrielle's and Tomás' tanbark digging, which is described below, is intrinsically rewarding and offers children the chance to wonder, explore, observe, and investigate (Knight, 2011). Gabrielle's and Tomás' play is characteristic of the complexity, flexibility, and open-ended interpretation of materials found in nature play (Frost et al., 2004; Perry, 2001).

Gabrielle:	"We're digging for bugs, 'kay?" She uses a stick to turn over a layer of tanbark and dirt.
Tomás:	"Yeah. And I found three bugs." He shows Gabrielle his pail with three pill bugs inside.
Gabrielle:	"Three. That means we need enough dirt to cover the bottom. And some leaves for them to eat. No beetles, though." ✆

The newt game is an example of how a pretend game based on children's daily life experiences with nature turns children's attention to the process of **inquiry**. Gabrielle and Tomás use observation, exploration, and comparison to enrich their own play by collecting and caring for real bugs.

Play outdoors gives children the opportunity to experience and develop a relationship with nature. Louv (2010) argues that children's early experiences in nature establish a foundation for the attachment and compassion that builds feelings of stewardship and sustainability.

> When Calvert arrives as a transfer teacher to his new elementary school, he finds the playground empty of growing plants. After getting support at the next parent–teacher association meeting, Calvert secures the donation of four 3' by 5' planter boxes from the local nursery in exchange for a mention of their generosity in his first/second-grade combination classroom parent newsletter. He uses the newsletter to solicit help from parents in donating seeds, and Maurice's mom offers to build another planter box. Children from all grades water the seeds and tend to the weeds during recess because Calvert has sent a willing student into each classroom to talk about the garden. At first, either Calvert or another teacher supervises children's garden care, with children from his classroom teaching others on the playground how to tend the growing sprouts. Children make signs that guide care of the garden, and Calvert laminates the signs. After a rainstorm brings worms out onto the playground, Calvert helps children to nestle worms in the planter boxes. In 2 months' time, children are sampling two varieties of lettuce during recess, with descriptive language like "spicy" and "clean." The planter boxes become a gathering place, where kids go to hunt for bugs, make play plans, and reaffirm friendships. ✆

When teachers like Rebecca and Calvert include a nature-based educational component in the outdoor classroom, children experience a sense of wonder and connection with the natural world (Knight, 2011; Moore & Wong, 1997; Schultz, Shriver, Tabanico, & Khazian, 2004; Sobel, 2004; Wilson, 1997).

Caring and nurturing the health of the planet requires just such a relationship with nature. Play among living things engenders nurturance, as Gabrielle and Tomás show while tending to their pill bug collection. In one study, the power of this nurturance was so strong it fueled imaginative content as children searched on the playground for a missing classroom snail, experiencing affiliation not just with each other but also with the snail (Perry, 2008).

Play in nature allows children to share the habitats of outdoor living things like newts, pill bugs, and snails. Young children are readily empathic. Play in nature not only stimulates investigation and engenders feelings of nurturance, it offers children a place for feelings of settled calm and wonder as well.

> First-grader Maurice lays under the playground maple tree, watching puffy white clouds blowing across the sky and past the tree branches. He closes one eye, opens it, and closes it again, watching the tree branches shift position with his field of vision. One cloud is thick and dense. Maurice watches it as it spreads out and thins as it travels across the sky. He shifts his attention to the sound of the leaves rustling as a breeze moves across the yard. A crow catches the breeze and Maurice watches it sail in the wind with outstretched wings. ✆

Play in nature is compatible with Maurice's interests and abilities. As the experiences of Mollie, Cella, Indi, and Jamila show, play outdoors with nature complements children's healthy development with tactile, interactive, sensory-rich experiences (Knight, 2011; Moore & Wong, 1997). The science chapter complements this discussion of nature and an ecology component in a play-centered curriculum.

The Importance of Child-Initiated Play and Inquiry

Outdoor play offers children healthy developmental experiences in initiating activities and following their curiosity. Outdoor play that is directed by the children, rather than organized by adults, is just plain fun. It is also demanding—children work hard to talk and listen to each other and find language to express their curiosity.

When children play together with concentration, focus, and planning, they use inquiry to make sense of something they are curious about. Inquiry describes children's use of observation, comparison, exploration, and investigation in all aspects of their physical and social world. Gabrielle and Tomás explore and experiment with the physical feeling and skill of balance in being a newt on a branch, and their curiosity extends to observing and investigating bugs. The connections Gabrielle and Tomás experience with each other and with nature when they play outdoors contribute to social–emotional development because outdoor play helps children develop and establish relationships as they play, problem solve, and negotiate with fellow playmates (Moore & Wong, 1997; Perry, 2003, 2004; Thompson & Thompson, 2007).

Tomás: "Now let's say we were done, because a snake is coming to get us!"

Gabrielle: "But we don't get eaten, right?"

Tomás: "We *think* we are going to be eaten."

> *Gabrielle:*   "But not for real, right?"
>
> *Tomás:*   "Right, because we jump to a different branch, and the snake can only slither." ⌀

Here we see Tomás and Gabrielle establishing feelings of security as they imagine their independent survival in the wild. They are also gaining practice in using language to express their ideas and clarifying and negotiating the additions of new ideas. Their inquiry is a focus for their play on what it means to be a newt and what might be a predator. Tomás and Gabrielle experience the complexity of moving back and forth between the real and the imagined.

Spontaneous play outdoors enhances self-esteem and confidence in exploring different environments (Swarbrick, Eastwood, & Tutton, 2004; Thompson & Thompson, 2007). In Perry's and Branum's 2009 study, Mollie gained access to the fast-paced, vigorous peer play culture once she experienced confident mobility. She expresses her newly accomplished mobility by imagining herself as a lion, known for its dominance in the wild. Children seek out the playground because they see it as a time to make things happen and feel in control of their own curiosity, imagination, and expression. Where the indoor classroom tends to frame children's experiences with specific and fixed expectations, children experience more open-ended themes in their play and inquiry outside (Corsaro, 2011; Perry, 2001). The outdoor environment is flexible in noise, space, movement, and theme. Although children seek out this experience, they may also be hesitant.

> Five-year-old Portia is running with several children on the playground during recess. Everyone but Portia runs up a ladder to the upper deck of the climbing structure. Portia approaches her kindergarten teacher Aziza.
>
> "I can't go up the ladder and my friends are there."
>
> "Oh, let's try! I've seen you balance. Your legs are stable and strong," Aziza says matter of factly.
>
> "I want to be with my friends," Portia says.
>
> "Let's go then. I'll be there," Aziza offers.
>
> Portia and her teacher walk up to the climbing structure ladder. "Let's see if you can do this," Aziza says.
>
> Portia does climb up, proceeds down the slide, and climbs back up several times. Aziza moves away as Portia reunites with her playmates. At the end of the day, Aziza crouches down to speak with Portia. "Portia, you are learning a lot these few days. Today you found out you *do* know how to use the ladder." ⌀

We find that when outdoor play incorporates fast-paced routines, those fast-paced routines function to cement peer allegiance. Try to imagine Portia's friends running together, looking back and forth at each other, laughing, and feeling, with their fast movement, their zest, and spirit together. When a group of children can run together in a fun chase game, they feel connected.

The power of the peer group during outdoor play is that children can perform with greater competence than when they are alone. As Vygotsky emphasized, their abilities, buttressed by the collaborative efforts of the group, support what will be a next step on an individual level (Vygotsky, 1978). In the world of children's play with peers, active outdoor play helps children bond and feel affiliated (Pellegrini, 2005).

How the Outdoor Classroom Is Different from the Inside Classroom

In contrast to the inside classroom, the outdoor classroom can offer space and materials that can be used flexibly and with open-ended imaginative interpretation. Children invent their own themes and roles outside using natural materials that can be anything: a stick can be a screwdriver, an acorn cap can be a fairy cup, wood chips can be money, sand and water can be mixed into whatever their imagination calls forth. Outdoor environments like the ones Calvert, Aziza, and Rebecca designed invite exploration and experimentation. The outdoor environment is also one place where children are more involved in spontaneous play. Table 12.1 compares the differences in learning demands between inside and outdoor classroom.

Rebecca uses the outside classroom throughout the day because she has a classroom where children flow in and out at their inclination. Aziza uses the playground at recess for important healthy experiences. Calvert uses the outside for ecology activities during science and language arts and incorporates gardening and habitat activities into choices during recess.

TABLE 12.1   Comparing the Outdoor and Indoor Classroom

Outdoor Classroom	Classroom Component	Indoor Classroom
Loosely designed for movement and focus	**Space**	Defined, focused activity areas
Teacher arrangement of space to maximize active play *and* play with materials and accessories	**Organization of areas**	Teacher arrangement of space to maximize play with materials and accessories
Noisier, physically vigorous, child initiated, open ended, moving, exploring, experimenting, teacher facilitated	**Types of play**	Quieter, task oriented, exploring, experimenting, teacher generated as well as child initiated
Children invent themes and roles in open-ended, flexible activity areas as well as more guided thematic areas	**Play demands on children**	Children guided by explicit activity area cues

Based on information from *Outdoor Play: Teaching Strategies with Young Children* (p. 8), by J. P. Perry, 2001, New York, NY: Teachers College Press; and "Planning for Play in a Playground," by P. Walsh, 2008, *Exchange, 30*(5), 88–94.

TEACHING GOALS AND GUIDELINES
FOR THE OUTDOOR CLASSROOM

Teachers promote the same development through play in the outdoor classroom as they do indoors. Table 12.2 identifies five teacher goals that provide guidelines for maximizing outdoor play.

The teacher's first goal in the outdoor classroom is to promote child-initiated, spontaneous play by preparing spaces that suggest an activity and encouraging children to use those areas. Rebecca sets up benches and calls them a "log." Aziza supports Portia's practice in climbing and then moves away following Portia's wish to "be with her friends." When children see the playground as a place where they, rather than the teachers, define play and themes, then they receive social and cognitive benefits by initiating interactions ("We're newts, right?" "Right.") and verbally expressing their interests and plans ("Now let's say we were done, because a snake is coming to get us!").

The second goal in the outdoor classroom is to extend the duration of peer-guided interactive play by encouraging and facilitating child-directed negotiations. Cella, Indi, and Jamila are motivated to share pushing turns because the game is fun and their teacher has taken time to talk to them about their ideas for turn-taking. Children in self-directed outdoor play of long duration exercise demanding cognitive and social abilities in creative problem solving, organizing and remembering information, and attempting to regulate their impulses to keep the game going.

The teacher's third goal is to encourage imagination and creativity in the outdoor classroom by creating outdoor areas with natural materials and encouraging appropriate dress for play in a variety of weather. Gabrielle and Tomás benefit in their pretend play with tanbark ground cover. Cella's teacher wrote a letter to parents describing the benefits of outdoor play and the importance of appropriate-weather clothing. At a parent meeting her teacher played a six-minute *Video Presentation on Children and Nature* CD she received from the Children and Nature Network (www. childrenandnature.org). When teachers provide natural materials like sand, water, natural ground cover, and planted areas, they are supporting children's use of pretense. Pretend play encourages children to think flexibly, entertain multiple perspectives, collaborate, and increase their use of language literacy abilities and numeracy. With Rebecca's additional outdoor curriculum, Gabrielle and Tomás transfer their play into aesthetic and literary mediums.

The fourth goal of teachers in the outdoor classroom is to guide and enrich children's wonder, inquiry, connection to, and knowledge about nature by soliciting, verifying, reinforcing, and elaborating on children's focus in nature play.

Cella and Indi are on their hands and knees, nibbling at mature lettuce leaves from one of the planter boxes. A child-made sign in the planter box reads: "Ready to harvest."

Calvert: "Say, Cella, what is that you're eating?"
Cella: "Arugula! Me and Indi are horses."

TABLE 12.2 Teacher Guidelines for Maximizing Play in the Outdoor Classroom

Teaching Goal	Indirect Coordination of Play Areas	Direct Involvement as Player
1. Promote child-initiated spontaneous play	Prepare the following areas for children to initiate interactions, verbally communicate and listen, and negotiate with others • quiet focused concentration • open running and organized games • active, concentrated physical play	Use play voice, sound effects, modeling negotiating phrases inside child-initiated play theme. Step away to observe child direction through three phases of peer play.
2. Extend duration of play	Observe sequence of play progress. Restore clarity of play area cues as ideas/playgroups shift. Elaborate play theme with enriched materials based on theme. Refer to imaginative elements as if they were real.	Extend child-initiated play theme and language with • open-ended questions • reinforcing/elaborating on play theme and ideas When play group becomes too large for manageable exchanges, break into smaller groups with separate play spots.
3. Encourage imagination and creativity	Provide imaginary places with accessible natural materials, sand and water, loose parts. Reserve natural areas for unmanicured native grass, flowers, and plants	See above. Encourage play-appropriate dress.
4. Guide and enrich children's wonder, inquiry, connection, and knowledge about nature	Include designated nature area for exploring natural elements like water, soil, leaves, and trees. With children, prepare and sustain a garden.	Emphasize exploration, experimentation, comparison, and contrast with • open-ended questions • observation journals for drawings, computations, and information collection
5. Encourage reasonable risk	Physically close observation. Encourage small next steps in complexity of activity. Enrich complexity with loose parts. Maintain accessibility with • entrance/exit routes to play areas • ground-level play elements • use of ramps and transfer stations	Shadow during practice of new skills, then step back to observe. With children, generate safety rules and post. Confirm rules. Model appropriate rough and tumble play. Interrupt to ensure safety when immediate danger is present.

Based on information from *Outdoor Play: Teaching Strategies with Young Children* (p. 86), by J. P. Perry, 2001, New York, NY: Teachers College Press; "Planning for Play in a Playground," by P. Walsh, 2008, *Exchange, 30*(5), 88–94; and *The Developmental Benefits of Playgrounds,* by J. L. Frost, P.-S. Brown, J. A. Sutterby, and C. D. Thornton, 2004, Olney, MD: Association for Childhood International.

Indi:	"Horses eat only arugula."
Calvert:	"And how did you figure out which was arugula and which was kale? The greens are so bushy and close together now."
Cella:	"The arugula has light green leaves."
Indi:	"And they are smaller."
Cella:	"And wavy. See?" Cella gently brushes the lettuce leaves with her left hand. She is quiet as she looks at the sunlight shine through the leaves of lettuce.
Indi:	"Kale leaves are much longer and tougher and harder for horses to bite."
Calvert:	"The horses on your farm have pretty strong jaws. I remember we fed them carrots on our field trip." ✂

Calvert accepts the girls' imaginary game as the mode through which Cella and Indi closely observe, wonder about, ask questions, and communicate their ideas to others (Seefeldt, 2005).

The fifth important goal for teachers in the outdoor classroom is to support the development of the whole child by encouraging challenges defined as "reasonable risk" so that developmental trajectories proceed (Knight, 2011; Tovey, 2007). Aziza supports Portia to keep herself safe by taking a manageable risk in balance and upper body strength to satisfy her social need. During kindergarten recess, Aziza follows Portia's practice with close observation and firm encouragement. With a newly acquired large motor skill, Portia, like Mollie, could keep up physically with the other children's fast-paced play and experience the social and cognitive benefits of active peer play. Rebecca supports reasonable risk by recognizing Gabrielle's and Tomás' physically active needs. She negotiates safety standards while acknowledging the children's point of view and arranges an outdoor setup to support their interests.

BEST PRACTICES IN PLANNING FOR OUTDOOR PLAY

Active outdoor classrooms give teachers the chance to observe, reflect, and facilitate children's intentions as children direct their self-initiated play.

Serving Children from Diverse Backgrounds

Not everyone has grown up around nature and in the outdoors. This does not mean that children under adult care should be kept inside—far from it. What some may call "inclement weather" can, with the proper attire, offer unique experiences for children—for their senses and in the exploration and examination of the physical environment.

Fong teaches at an urban elementary school known for its outdoor environment. Her strategies are examples of how teachers can support children from diverse backgrounds in the outdoor classroom. Fong provides many opportunities for children to interact to make her outdoor classroom an essential component of all children's healthy development (Frost et al., 2004; Frost & Woods, 2006; Frost et al., 2008). Fong's school features an edible garden, outdoor art and music areas, a constructive sand and water area for digging and channeling, two planted trees, and one tree saved from excavation. Playground spaces reflect the educational traditions of Friedrich Froebel and John Dewey as well as current research and practice emphasizing the importance of children interacting with each other and of teachers following the children's own interests and inquiry using child observations guided by the Reggio Emilia and Project Approaches. Fong understands that children communicate best with playmates when they are in small groups of between two to five and where playmates can be heard and have opportunities for back-and-forth talk. She provides just enough tools, play props, and loose parts in each area to encourage small group play.

Fong uses the reflective self-study of NAEYC's Early Childhood Program Standards to assess her program. She rates her classroom yearly using the *School-Age Care Environmental Rating Scale* (Harms, Jacobs, & White, 1996). The playground encourages physically active play and helps children become connected to nature. The playground is on the same level as the ground-floor classroom, and doors remain open for children to flow indoors and outdoors much of the year based on their needs and interests. Fong has arranged a full range of developmentally appropriate activities outdoors, including four tone bars for music and space for movement next to a garden. Children have nature and art materials accessible throughout the day at two tables under an overhanging shelter space in the transition area between the outside and inside classroom. Both tables can seat between four to six children. Moving from the building out into the yard, children have separate areas for digging, climbing and running, and organized games.

With guidance from research on the importance of outdoor play, Fong organized several parent workdays to talk with parents about their developmental goals for their children. Fong shared her own beliefs about the value of outdoor play. Lashonda's mother heard about her daughter's accomplishments in language and literacy on the playground. That day, Lashonda's mother and other parents created landscaping that varied in terrain and elevation with a water zone, plantings, bark, and rises.

Fong and the other teachers encourage children's use of tools in activity areas with accessible shelves for working in the garden, sand, and water in a sand kitchen modeled after the indoor playhouse with loose parts that include dishes and cookware; in the digging area with shovels, gutters, and tubes for water channeling; and art and writing tools and constructive materials like glue, tape, and clay under the overhang. The nature area includes a garden with edible plants (a child-written sign in one pot reads "Our Pizza

Garden—thyme, basil, oregano, and sometimes tomatoes") and flowers that attract insects and butterflies for children to observe. Her school is lucky to have shade provided by trees. Two are in an area with tanbark ground cover and a climber. One is in the middle of the playground with a table underneath for focused nature observation, drawing and writing, and constructive manipulatives.

Fong keeps track of the range of materials she offers children outside, making sure they have materials found in nature such as sand, water, soil, rocks, and materials for stacking and constructing. Fong acquired a lockable storage bench and placed it under the overhang not just for children's daily use, but also for teachers to store extra tools, **loose parts**, and materials for aesthetic expression. Fong used several resources to help her place activity areas to ensure accessibility for all children while emphasizing places for all children to construct, tend and care, and be quiet (Dimensions Educational Research Foundation & Arbor Day Foundation, 2007; Frost et al., 2004; Kritchevsky & Prescott, 1977; Rui Olds, 2001; Walsh, 2008). Fong's outdoor classroom offers feelings of emotional attachment to special child-defined places. There are gardening and natural areas shared with plants and animals. The playground includes space for large and fine motor skill and strength development, semi-enclosed spaces for respite while maintaining safety and security, and open space for organized games (see Frost et al., 2008; Goodenough, 2003). ⌀

The feature *Family Diversity: A Closer Look at Outdoor Play* describes observing outdoor play with family and caretakers while the teacher interprets the play behavior in terms of educational and developmental goals.

FAMILY DIVERSITY

A Closer Look at Outdoor Play

Not all families may appreciate the developmental value of outdoor play. Cooper (1999) reflects on her strategies to gain the trust of adult family members and caregivers whose perspectives on play may be based on cultural norms and values and their own successful experiences with formal teacher-directed education. Cooper shares her observational skills with family members and caregivers as they mutually watch children in play. Cooper emphasizes the motor skills exhibited, the problem solving taking place, and the language development. Confidence in the value of outdoor play will be appreciated more readily from family members when, as Cooper says, "the trappings of school are present." The curriculum chapters in this book highlight the literacy, numeracy, art, and science possibilities for outdoor experiences, which Cooper says can be explained to adult family members. She suggests finding out adults' goals for their children and emphasizing those goals in conversations.

Teachers will encounter a diversity of play interactions and "ways of expending energy" based in ethnic heritage (Holmes, 2012, p. 332). Teachers support all children's outdoor play by doing the following:

1. Maximizing face-to-face engagement (having tire swings, extra-wide slides built into a hill, and tables with chairs that face each other)

2. Arranging activity areas to suggest places for imagination and concentration (including soft spots with cushions, use of light-weight cloth to mark a protected area, photographs of children using the areas in play, and signs written by children)

3. Protecting and defining play areas to draw children's attention (with low shelves or carts on wheels for child-accessible materials and props and spaces for one child to be alone, observe, or be quiet)

Sites with Outdoor Challenges

One study of outdoor recess play preferences in an urban primary school found that children spent most of their recess time talking and socializing, with this limiting caveat: "The playground consisted of an asphalt surface with little playground equipment except for a portable basketball court. The setting clearly drove the behavior that occurred within it" (Holmes, 2012, p. 347). Teachers with outdoor sites that are less than ideal can still cultivate children's physically active outdoor play, engagement with nature, and child-initiated play. The playground at Calvert's school is blacktop with one climber built on sand. Sometimes during recess and free play periods, Calvert turns the space under the active climber into a sand kitchen area using a portable, wheeled art cart supplied with loose parts for kitchen play that he stores in an outdoor shed. Calvert also stores a foldout table and a shade tent, which he uses for child-selected activities. Children can bring out Legos for assembly, a paper and drawing caddy with tape for 3-D constructions, play props to match imaginative play, nature specimens, and clipboards, magnifying glasses, and books from the shed as well.

Aziza takes children outside in her science and math periods because outdoor areas are integrated in her curriculum. She divides a large sand area with two hills, with shovels on both. She arranges a cart of kitchen play props in the sand under a shade tent made from draped cloth on a clothesline and a bench underneath. She positions a place for drawing for one so that a shy child can observe play in small groups as part of a next step in growth or just relax out of the fray of fast-paced play. Aziza stores the props and cart behind her classroom door for quick access when exiting.

Roxanne works in a preschool closed to neighborhood use, so some of her set-up props can be left outside overnight, whereas others she gathers from inside. She uses plastic storage crates instead of tables to balance old and outdated keyboards and office telephones, with a food container for paper and stubs of pencils to spark an array of fantasy play about work, connecting to a missing loved one, space travel, and so on. Roxanne tapes a large swatch of paper from a paper roll to the side of the building on the playground border, adds several containers of chalk, and thereby encourages children to express large motor coordination, strengthening, and balance in a cooperative mural. Roxanne presents music accessibly with a few drums on a rug for impromptu rhythm sessions, and Aziza uses professional paint buckets, large food tins, and cylindrical cardboard oatmeal containers for her outdoor music area.

Whether children are in cities or suburbs, teachers can cultivate nature appreciation with little expense. Inexpensive or free ideas to enrich the outdoor classroom are offered by the North Carolina Outdoor Learning Environment Alliance, which include creating an herb garden in planters, identifying a special place for digging, hanging a bird feeder, partnering with the U.S. Forest Service or community extension agencies for native trees, and using a log as a bench (Bradford, Easterling, Mengel, & Sullivan, 2010).

The Adult's Feelings about Being Outdoors

Best practices remind us of the importance of outdoor play in children's health. Recall when you were a young child. Did your childhood include playing outside? If so, where? What did you do? Were you alone or did you also play with others? Were you outside in all weather, or just some? What are your feelings about those times? If you did not play outside, why not? Was it a matter of safety?

Every child and adult needs to have safe, natural environments to explore, take care of, feel nurturance from, and be stimulated by. Some people, including many teachers, have not enjoyed such childhood opportunities. A teacher's readiness to develop children's opportunities for outdoor play directly relates to how comfortably and pleasurably that teacher feels about being outside.

Several organizations in this country, including the American Academy of Pediatrics, the Alliance for Childhood, the Arbor Day Foundation, the National Institute for Play, the Children and Nature Network, and the National Recreation and Park Association propose that being outdoors to play is a right of childhood. The UN Convention on the Rights of the Child recognizes the child's right to recreation.

Safety is also a basic right and necessity for everyone. Roxanne grew up in a neighborhood without access to safe play options. With child development coursework and a mentor teacher, she was able to take the extra step in imagining the invitation that the outdoors offers. Marisol wanted to do cartwheels and climb trees, but was not allowed to do so because her parents dressed her in skirts and dresses. In her student practicum training, she learned alongside the children about the benefits of active outdoor play in nature. As a child, Beth experienced admonishments about being dirty. We find that other teachers also recall causing adults extra work in managing cleanup after outdoor play when they were children. These teachers are challenged to consider experiences for children in their care that override past experiences.

If the school grounds are situated in a neighborhood that cannot reliably guarantee children's safety, teachers will not feel comfortable encouraging outdoor play. This means that children's right to be safe is compromised and needs immediate attention by creating safe play environments. City Repair (http://cityrepair.org) and KaBOOM! (http://kaboom.org) are both national organizations that provide guidelines to transform physical environments. (See their story in Wilson, Marshall, & Iserhott, 2011.)

Outdoor play is a right because outdoor play leads to good health. If teachers are in a position where they feel uncomfortable about outdoor play options, consider what contributes to this unease. If there is a real safety concern, than community action is necessary to ensure the health of children. If it is past personal experiences that do not offer instances of enrichment, pleasure, and nurturance from being outdoors, then the children and teachers like Roxanne will be exploring the wealth of the outdoors together.

OBSERVING AND INTERPRETING OUTDOOR PLAY

Spontaneous outdoor play allows the teacher to focus on children's development because the behavior is directed by the children: How well can Leah manage balance while using the ladder on the climber? Can Gabrielle stop herself in mid-descent if she scampers up onto the slide? It seems like she will need to learn to go down on her bottom so she can see her peers and be able to respond to their presence. Children establish familiar and particular play routines and habits in the company of each other. Teachers who understand children's peer play interactions can better appreciate what children are trying to do in the behavior they express.

Wintertime can offer unique outdoor play opportunities.

Understanding Children's Outdoor Peer Play

Outdoor spaces vividly invite the expression of peer play interactions. Children themselves see the playground as a place where they direct their own fun, energy, and interests. Corsaro (2011) identified the unique features of what it means to be children together. He described two major themes in young children's peer play: (a) a strong desire to play with others and (b) persistent attempts to challenge, make things happen, and direct their own actions. Children want to feel their own expertise.

When Gabrielle and Tomás scamper up the slide, Rebecca observes their enhanced gross motor and balance challenge. She recognizes the children's attention and focus to this managed risk and is ready to step in with a question to refocus concentration if necessary. Rebecca notices the children's broad smiles as they successfully manage this climbing challenge, as well as Leah's desire to be on the slide at the same time. All three children are feeling the pleasure of being in control, managing **big body play** amongst peers. Conversation and give-and-take comments indicate not only the physical, but also the social and cognitive experience as well.

Children interact during peer play in the following ways:

- Including others in their play based upon agreed imagined roles ("You have to be Rope Girl to be in our game.")
- Remembering past episodes of play, oftentimes in specific areas ("I know!" "Member we played horses and we cozied next to the garden?")
- Claiming territory ("This is our pirate ship!")
- Challenging adult authority ("Let's not get in line, 'kay?")
- Playing games of flee and chase
- Exhibiting rough and tumble, big body play
- Feigning fear and "playing dead"
- Using a singsong voice to accompany the game and its progression ("Nanny, nanny, boo, boo!")

The Phases of Peer Play

When left to their own devices, we find that children progress in their play interactions through a sequence of three phases. In the first phase, the *initiation phase,* children need to figure out who they are playing with. Sometimes this is easy when children have regular playmates. Children exchange mutual recognition with woops, face-to-face gestures like a smile, or a verbal invitation and acceptance like, "Let's play, OK?" "OK." Or "We're friends, right?" "Right." Some children, eager for interaction, will provoke peers and receive shrieks of irritation and anger, but still attention: "Quit it!" or "She wrecked our tunnel!" or "He stole our stuff!" Teachers can facilitate inexperienced children in making this first step in child-directed interactions with a comment like, "Gee, I think Portia wants to play with you," or coaching the inexperienced Portia with, "Say, 'What are you playing?'" as an initial entry strategy, or by commenting, "I think Tomás wants to play. What could he do instead of knocking your stuff down if he wants to play?"

The second phase of young children's peer play is the *negotiation phase*. Children decide on the theme of their game and perhaps their roles. Here again, children must agree to proceed: "Let's say we were dragons, 'kay?" "OK." Or "These [acorns] are for star power, right?" "Right." Each new idea involves a negotiation. Often children will need to be persistent: "We're playing freeze tag, right? Right?" "Yeah, and the slide is base. OK?" "'Kay." Notice how each new idea or proposal must be acknowledged for the interaction to proceed. Children often use higher-order cognitive and language functions during self-generated outdoor play. Here, too, teachers can help children by supporting pretend elements. Teachers can use sound effects to enrich the theme ("Dragons coming!"—teacher makes the sound of wind whooshing) and comments to support children's agreements ("OK, here is the rocket station place for your star power."). Teachers can offer a complementary idea, prop, or question to deepen the play ("Dragons! Where is your cloud for resting after flying?" or "Here is a keyboard for a control panel." or "Are you playing with them? Because they are playing *tag*, not wack, see?").

The third phase of peer play is the *enactment phase*, where children expand, develop, and transform the theme as play continues. Here, too, children mutually agree on the progression of ideas for the game to continue. Perry and Branum (2009) describe how Michael and his friends experiment with the mechanics of balance. Notice how they use agreement to proceed.

> Michael tried to balance his fulcrum so that the lower, inclined end of the board will be off the ground. He turned back and looked at Morgan, establishing facial engagement. "I think you're too heavy," he said, offering a hypothesis for the board's persistent downward angle.
>
> "Why don't you try me," suggested Emma. "I'm a little lighter than her," she added picking up on the element of weight as these children interpret Michael's arrangement.
>
> "'Kay," said Michael, accepting Emma's involvement in the interaction.
> Emma got into the crate. (p. 202) ✇

One way teachers support physically active play is by observing and following the sequence of children's play progression. The next section describes in more detail what physically active rough and tumble play is and is not, its value in children's early play experience, and how teachers can safely support children in rough and tumble play.

Supporting Big Body Rough and Tumble Outdoor Play

Rough and tumble play (RTP) is vigorous, intense, physical, big body play that children experience with pleasure: running, wrestling, climbing, fleeing, chasing, play fighting, open-palmed tagging, and jumping (Carlson, 2011a). Compared to real fighting, children in RTP voluntarily stay in the game rather than leave it or ask for a teacher's help. Look for a relaxed, smiling play face and laughing (Carlson, 2011b) compared to fighting, which includes tears, fists, slapping/grabbing with intent to harm, and tight, rigid facial muscles (Fry, 2005). RTP also involves self-handicapping, or disguising true skill level with a less skilled player to keep this fun game going (Flanders, Herman, & Paquette, 2013).

The NAEYC supports RTP because in it children experience developmental stimulation in physical control and coordination, perceive and recognize verbal and nonverbal language cues, understand cause and effect, and practice turn-taking, compromise, making and following rules, and negotiating social skills (Carlson, 2011a; NAEYC, 2012b). Children learn not to hurt each other and to recognize and monitor the emotions of others (Smith, Smees, & Pellegirni, 2004; Tannock, 2008). RTP also satisfies the need for touch (Carlson, 2006).

To support outdoor RTP, adult modeling is especially important in showing children appropriate big body play and helping children recognize how to control overtly aggressive impulses (Carlson, 2011a; Flanders, Leo, Paquette, Pihl, & Séguin, 2009). In addition, keep these points in mind:

- With children, designate and mark an outdoor area for RTP and facilitate child-generated rules for safe play (Carlson, 2011a; Perry, 2001). Post the rules.

- Prepare a space for safe, open, hazard-free play with 100 square feet per playing child and good ground cover under elevated play surfaces where children may jump (Carlson, 2011a).

- Inform parents. The NAEYC provides a "Message in a Backpack" for preschool (NAEYC, 2012b, p. 20) and a sample "Parent Handbook Policy for Big Body Play" for the parents of preschool and school-age children (Carlson, 2011a, pp. 87–88).

- Supervise by watching for gestures of pleasure or distress, verify children's intent when gestures are ambiguous ("Are you kids really fighting or are you just pretending?" or "Do you like it when she throws you to the ground? No? Ask her why she did that."), help interpret nonverbal cues ("They are chasing you because they want to play with you."), and support perspective-taking ("Look at his face. You have your whole body on top of him. Does he look happy or uncomfortable?").

- Gain cooperation from your program in receiving training in understanding and supporting RTP. Children supervised by teachers with such training play more actively and productively (Bower, Hales, Tate, Rubin, Benjamin, & Ward, 2008; Cardon, Van Cauwenberghe, Labarque, Haerens, & De Bourdeaudhulj, 2008).

The next section shows how the outdoor environment complements children's special needs with opportunities for safe, active play alongside playmates and the soothing effects of nature experiences.

Serving Students with Special Needs

Teachers accommodate the outdoor classroom to children's emerging physical and social capacities and special needs. Teachers adapt grounds and equipment for accessibility and use signs and photographs to encourage all children to be active and be with their peers. Teachers model and coach in language skills and play gestures with those less developed, supporting in close proximity to clarify the child's understanding.

Leah's Individual Educational Plan (IEP) includes an aide to facilitate her language and social interaction. Rebecca observes that Leah engages mostly with play props and equipment. When in the company of others, Leah may whimper or cry and is calmed with reassurance and physical closeness from a familiar adult. Leah's IEP includes practice playing alongside peers and encouragement to look at and notice what and how other children play. Today Leah is standing on the opposite side of a sand table from Gabrielle:

Leah:	"Help!"
Aide:	"Help me?"
Leah:	"Help me?"
Aide:	"Sure, I can help you." The aide holds down the block structure Leah is assembling vertically. Leah reaches for another block. She looks briefly at Gabrielle who is across the table.
Aide:	"You see Gabrielle building too? Gabrielle has built a top on her structure with long rectangle blocks. Oh look! There are many long blocks on the shelf, Leah."
Leah:	"Help me."
Aide:	"Help me build?"
Leah:	"Help me build."
Aide:	"Yes, I can help you build. Look, Leah. Get a long rectangle block to build. What are you building, Gabrielle?"
Gabrielle:	"I'm building a mall so we can go shopping." ✐

Outdoor play can also offer a calming experience when children play with natural materials (Kuo & Taylor, 2004) or simply take a break (Pellegrini & Pellegrini, 2013).

Seven-year-old Kendrick is trying hard to settle in Calvert's math activity involving the addition and subtraction of sets. After repeated encouragement to return to the dinosaur counters, Sonia, the librarian, invites Kendrick outside to look at the new corn growing. They weed together. Kendrick finds a ladybug and lets it crawl on his hand. Together they gather mint leaves and munch on them. They locate the gerber a daisies, some red, some yellow, and some orange. Kendrick adds, subtracts, and with Sonia's prompting, multiplies groups of flowers in this alternate and complementary environment. ✐

Later in this chapter we will address the special needs of children with impoverished outside space.

TEACHER DECISION MAKING DURING OUTDOOR PLAY

Teachers ask themselves three questions to help decide what strategies to use when supporting spontaneous outdoor play of long duration:

1. Can the child engage alone and with others independent of adults?
2. During peer play, is the interaction losing focus or becoming unsafe?
3. What is the purpose of the teacher's intervention?

Figure 12.1 reviews these teacher decisions during outdoor play, with a guide to accompanying strategies to use.

The feature *Advocacy in Action: Outdoor Play in Practice* provides a look at how Aziza applies this guide to her own classroom as well as how she informs parents of the developmental progression she sees in their children when outdoors.

When preschool children are not yet able to play independent of a teacher, Rebecca uses regularly set-up play spots to encourage adjacent play. Like the example of Leah building with blocks, the opportunity to play across from more experienced players gives most children the chance to recognize their next step. If outdoor play is not losing focus or becoming unsafe, the teacher continues to support children's experience by using play areas to encourage imagination,

Becoming an Informed Advocate for Play

ADVOCACY IN ACTION: OUTDOOR PLAY IN PRACTICE

Teachers encourage children to engage with each other because peer exchange and feedback is a powerful means for promoting development and because children naturally enjoy socializing with peers (Patte, 2010). Aziza arranges outdoor classroom areas so her kindergarten children have reliable spots to play repeatedly over days and weeks and months. She has several dual language learners in her classroom and consistently arranges several activities to promote peer talk, like wall ball games against the cafeteria wall after lunch is over, horses in a basket next to the garden, jump ropes on the blacktop, and a picnic table with paper, markers, tape, clipboards, and a few magnifying glasses. Just like the inside classroom, Aziza arranges outdoor areas so small groups of not more than two to five children can concentrate, talk, and listen, protected from interference of traffic and undue noise from other small groups. She uses identified play spots to support complex play interactions that encourage imagination, planning, and experimenting. Aziza eagerly interprets observations of outdoor play to her families at pick up and drop off. Her monthly parent newsletter provides examples of how and what children are learning in Aziza's outdoor areas across the year.

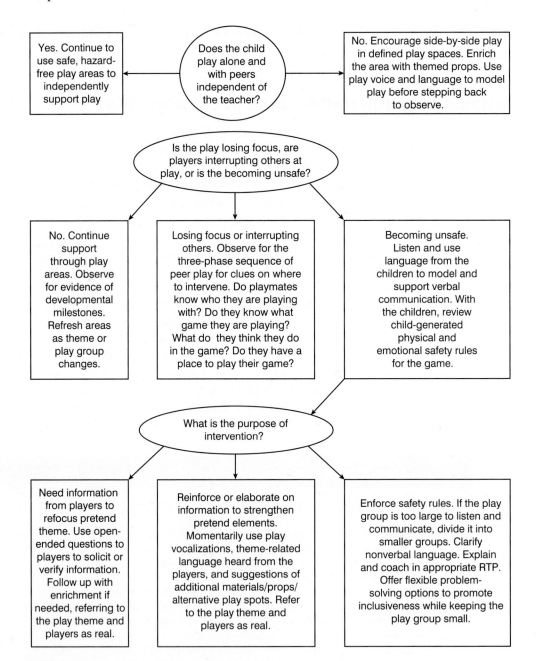

Figure 12.1
A Guide to Teacher Choices in Maximizing Spontaneous Outdoor Play.

Based on information from *Outdoor Play: Teaching Strategies with Young Children* (p. 85), by J. P. Perry, 2001, New York, NY: Teachers College Press; and *Big Body Play: Why Boisterous, Vigorous, and Very Physical Play Is Essential to Children's Development and Learning,* by F. M. Carlson, 2011, Washington DC: NAEYC.

planning, and problem solving. When outdoor play has lost focus or when physical or psychological safety is compromised, teachers must decide how best to intervene.

> Six- and 7-year-olds Cella, Kendrick, Eli, and Jamila are playing superheroes during recess. Calvert watches as the game escalates into pushing and wrestling.
>
> Calvert wonders: Have they all agreed to play together? Eli looks uncertain at times but also smiles. Do they know or have they agreed on what game they are playing? Are they managing turn-taking and playful restraint to keep the game safely going?
>
> Calvert watches Cella, Kendrick, Eli, and Jamila run gleefully throughout the playground but sees little verbal interchange. When he sees them running though spots where other playmate groups are concentrating on a different interest, he approaches them.
>
> Calvert wants to slow the group down to gather information and help them regain focus: "Say, kids, hold on a second, please. What game are you playing?" After hearing that they are "police" and they are "fighting bad guys," Calvert asks a clarifying question: "So who are the bad guys?" Kendrick points to two children on the tire swing. "Police, have you asked them if they want to be bad guys in your game?" Calvert asks. Cella runs off to ask, while Calvert arranges two telephones, keyboards, paper, and pencils on a table under an overhang. "Police: here's your police station," he says to the others. "Do you have a sign so people know this is the police station?" "I'm doing that," Jamila says. "This is where people call into when they need your help. The dispatchers can input the information into the computer and here is some squares of paper to write down who called, the time they called, and where they need help." ✄

Calvert's probing questions and prompts strengthen pretend elements and verbalizing. He hopes to extend the duration of the game by focusing on player roles and jobs. Calvert, like Rebecca, speaks to the children in their pretend roles to keep the game going.

TEACHING STYLES THAT SUPPORT OUTDOOR PLAY

In a year-long reflective study of how teachers support children's self-initiated play outside, Perry (2001) describes two equally valuable, effective teaching styles that support outdoor play: indirect coordination and direct involvement.

Indirect Coordination

One type of style involves the *indirect coordination* of play areas through preparation, observation of developmental progress, and refinement of the play space based on how children use the area. In this chapter's opening vignette, Rebecca uses this style when supervising Gabrielle, Tomás, and Leah.

> Roxanne intentionally provides sand and water in an outdoor sand kitchen because she knows children enjoy these materials and because the kitchen theme offers easy social and language possibilities by focusing on family life. Roxanne also knows that sand and water support the science of changing physical states and numeracy in categorization and counting when children "set the table." Here she offers further complexity:

> Roxanne: "So, you are making cake AND soup! Sounds like a café. Do you need menus? You can make them at the writing table." ⌀

Roxanne uses the sand kitchen to direct learning. She indirectly participates as an artist apprentice, observing the children's progress, noting their interests, and determining if enrichment is necessary in terms of additional materials like clipboards, pencils, and extra paper for taking orders.

Indirect coordination is especially effective when the teacher uses observation to "step into" the children's play, as we saw when Rebecca refers to Gabrielle and Tomás as newts. Roxanne uses open-ended questions to reveal how children are thinking and the intentions behind their actions: "Waiter? Can you tell me what types of soup you have today?" Roxanne observes and reflects as she follows the children's progress: Who makes pretend suggestions to move the game along? What vocabulary does she hear in her dual language learners? What instances of counting and one-to-one correspondence does she see? Even outdoors, observations during indirect involvement also facilitate assessments for Common Core standards.

Direct Involvement

Perry (2001) identifies a second style of *direct involvement* by the teacher as a player. Fong participates as a play organizer and promoter. She uses imaginative imagery to set up a play area as "a place where things can happen." Fong prepares a rocket ship, or a fire station, or a forest. She uses visual cues and play area adjustments like keyboards, milk crates, draped fabric, changes in elevation in sand areas with hills or trenches, and imaginative use of nature props like branches for trees, to suggest themes for interactive play. She uses play voice and sound effects, models language and negotiating phrases, and ensures mutual agreements with prompting words at the end of suggestions like, "Right?" and "OK?" Fong also provides verbal commentary as a means to cue inexperienced players.

> "Do you hear me, command central? We are ready for takeoff. Ten, nine, eight . . . "

Fong elaborates on the children's game to strengthen the meaning of their planning.

During lunch recess, Calvert recognizes several children who habitually sit off to the side of the playground talking. After lunch recess, Calvert begins his classroom meeting time by asking, "I'm curious. You are the experts here. What do you like about recess?" and "Besides the 45 minutes of time, how would you improve recess?" Calvert listens, rephrases, and summarizes the children's responses. He checks in with children "who have not yet had a turn to talk." In part, Calvert and the class learn that the children on the periphery want a place to play wallball. "What can we do about that?" Calvert asks. The children suggest several solutions, including moving a bench and some potted plants. The result is more active physical play from those previously sitting. ✁

Perry (2001) found that supporting outdoor play is almost always more effective when teachers take into account the children's play theme and intervene from inside that theme and include the children's play point of view. Table 12.2 provides suggestions for when and how to use both styles. With either style, teachers use direct involvement when play becomes unsafe.

FOSTERING INQUIRY IN THE OUTDOOR CLASSROOM

Inquiry describes children's use of observation, comparison, exploration, and investigation in all aspects of their physical and social world. Roxanne, Rebecca, Aziza, Calvert, and Fong foster inquiry outdoors by encouraging children's observation, exploration, and investigation. Teachers use their own skills of observation and reflection: Were Gabrielle and Tomás ready to take information from picture books and use it when painting a mural with other playmates? Cella is doing most of the pushing on the tire swing. Calvert asks her, "Cella, Jamila *loves* the tire swing. I wonder if you could show her the tricky part about jumping on after pushing?" Katz (2007) includes several guideposts for children's experience of inquiry during outdoor play, including that children

- be involved in sustained investigations of aspects of their own environment and experiences worthy of their interest, knowledge, and understanding
- experience the satisfaction that results from overcoming obstacles and setbacks and solving problems
- have confidence in their intellectual powers and questions
- help others to discover things and understand them better
- make suggestions to others and express appreciation of others' efforts for what is accomplished
- apply their developing literacy and numeracy abilities in purposeful ways
- feel that they belong to a group of their peers (pp. 94–95)

These guideposts show us that children's outdoor play can be purposeful and planned. The chapter on science elaborates on children's process of inquiry.

ASSESSING CHILDREN'S PLAY IN THE OUTDOOR CLASSROOM

Children engage in outdoor play behaviors guided in part by what the school setting supports. Teachers determine how their outdoor space supports play by observing the children using the space after it has been prepared and evaluating to improve the space. After engaging children in playground design plans, Calvert watches how Eli uses new sand and plantings independently. Calvert watches for behavioral evidence that children previously refraining from physical activity show interest in recess participation. Does Kendrick show pleasure and pride in accomplishments after respites in the garden? In staff meetings, Roxanne and her staff ask themselves if they have observed all children willingly spending time outside or do some need invitations and teacher facilitation? Aziza observes Portia. Can she play cooperatively and exhibit teamwork during investigative play? After children make "How We Care for Our Pizza Garden" signs in circle time, Fong observes how children demonstrate knowledge of how to care for outdoor classroom life. For example, can Anna look at the flowers in the garden and refrain from picking blossoms that will be turning into tomatoes? Does Maurice hold the class snake gently under the tree and refrain from taking it on the tire swing or in the sand?

Evaluating Outdoor Play Environments

Tools for assessing space for outdoor play are available to preschool, kindergarten, and primary-grade teachers. Most assessment tools begin with a plan or suggestions for outdoor design. Some have an explicit evaluative component. Others suggest that teachers follow a protocol of preparation, observation, refinement, and enriched direct interaction.

Frost (2007) offers "The Playground Checklist" to help in the design, use, and evaluation of school and community playgrounds for preschool, kindergarten, and primary settings. "The Playground Checklist" is a 60-item rating scale under three headings:

1. What does the playground contain?
2. Is the playground in good repair and relatively safe?
3. How should the playground and the play leader function?

The *Learning with Nature Idea Book: Creating Nurturing Outdoor Spaces for Children* (Dimensions Educational Research Foundation & Arbor Day Foundation, 2007) provides a research review for why young children need to connect with nature to be healthy and grow. The book provides 10 principles for outdoor classroom design, recommends activity areas, articulates appropriate natural materials, and emphasizes durability, low maintenance, beauty, visual clarity, and safety. It also offers problem-solving considerations based on the children's age, individual needs, and climate, as well as information on integrating with community resources.

The *Early Childhood Environment Rating Scale*—Revised Edition (Harms, Clifford, & Cryer, 2004) is an internationally used assessment of outdoor as well as indoor preschool environmental design features, materials, and routines. The *School-Age*

Care Environment Rating Scale (Harms et al., 1996) is a counterpart for kindergarten and primary grades. The 43-item assessment falls under seven subscales: space and furnishings, personal care routines, language reasoning, activities, teacher–child and child–child interactions, program schedule and structure, and provisions for parents and staff. Each item is rated on a seven-point continuum that offers next steps for quality improvement.

Preschool Outdoor Environment Measurement Scale (POEMS; DeBord, Hestenes, Moore, Cosco, & McGinnis, 2005) is a 56-item checklist for learning about, planning, evaluating, and conducting research on outdoor environments in preschool settings. POEMS groups items into five domains:

1. Physical environment
2. Child–environment interactions, teacher–child interactions, child–child interactions, and parent–child interactions
3. Materials and loose parts in the play settings
4. Program support features
5. The role of the teacher

Restoring outdoor play environments at school will involve both school and community effort. Teachers as advocates apply what they learn from assessments to ongoing conversations with families and the community to enrich outdoor play for the school.

ADVOCACY IN ACTION: OUTDOOR PLAY FOR ALL CHILDREN

As professional organizations and researchers highlight how critical outdoor play is for healthy development, at the same time outdoor play opportunities for children are being curtailed (Pellegrini & Pellegrini, 2013). The *Journal of the American Medical Association* reports that childhood obesity has more than tripled in the past 30 years (Ogden, Caroll, Curtin, Lamb, & Flegal, 2010). Others document both a sharp decline in the amount of free playtime for children and an increase in anxiety, depression, and other mental health issues later in childhood (Gray, 2011).

Here are some examples of community organizing efforts to enable and restore safe outdoor play space:

- Pogo Park (www.pogopark.org/Pogo_Park/home.html) is rebuilding a small city park and playground in a once-proud and vibrant inner-city neighborhood now devastated by violent crime, widespread blight, and deep poverty by focusing on child development, community development, and successful fundraising. Their story shows how the park is working now to provide a community experience where children experience safe, physically active, soulful play
- Design Your Own Park provides a case study model for collaboration between community groups, fundraising organizations, and municipalities to restore space for safe outdoor play (see Wilson, 2011).

- Hammond (2011) offers his personal account of mobilizing communities to create safe play spaces and founding KaBOOM!

- Aziza is concerned that some children on the playground are rarely active. Several children are obese. During recess and afterschool care they sit against the playground wall and trade cards. Aziza's district has mentioned a recess reduction to 10 minutes. Aziza contacts the Alliance for Childhood (www.allianceforchildhood.org), who sends her a free DVD copy of a documentary prepared by Michigan Television called *Where Do the Children Play?* She organizes a free screening of the movie for parents, teachers, and neighbors. An advocacy group forms after the movie to petition the school board to *increase* recess time and include a nature component in the elementary school curriculum that is consistent with Common Core standards.

- Calvert has planter boxes that attract butterflies and grow vegetables. The children run a small "farmer's market" on Fridays after school, where they sell greens, squash, cucumbers, beans, and tomatoes. With their money, the children start a collection to purchase "things to keep us strong and healthy," which include their ideas for active play: an A-frame climber and ladder, jump ropes, balls for organized games, and walking boards.

Restoring and enabling outdoor play for all children means creating play environments that encourage vigorous physical activity and a connection with nature while being safe and secure so that children receive the additional social and cognitive benefits of following their own curiosities and interests (Wilson et al., 2011). In conjunction with restoration efforts, we recommend several policy implications for enabling outdoor play for all children. Children need several periods each day of active, unstructured spontaneous play to be healthy. Teachers can do several things to encourage outdoor play:

- Ensure that outdoor spaces allow for children to use the props and tools of play and to run, jump, hop, skip, gallop, walk, climb, swing, skip, throw, and catch.
- Provide for nature and natural materials with water, sand, wood, sun, shade, height, slope, and growing plants.
- Create and maintain outdoor spaces to promote spontaneous play.
- Support outdoor play by providing child-accessible areas for the care of living things and the investigation of living creatures, including tactile experience as part of using materials, and engaging children in open-ended inquiry ("I wonder how . . .?").

We recommend that teachers receive professional training in using the outdoor classroom as part of their curriculum and reflectively address their own thoughts and feelings about being outdoors. Outdoor play happens in all weather because the classroom includes provisions for appropriate clothing and healthy options to explore and investigate the unique learning opportunities in nature.

SUMMARY

This chapter provides the background and clear rationale for the importance of outdoor play in early childhood curriculum. This chapter illustrates how joyous, spontaneous, child-centered outdoor play that is physically active, engaged with nature, and focused on a self-initiated interest in daily life can be part of the school experience.

- **The importance of outdoor play.** When children play outdoors daily, they gain essential experiences that contribute to their strength and coordination, feel connected with and learn about the world of nature, and use their own curiosities and interests during spontaneous peer play. Drawing upon research-based vignettes, the chapter follows several children to show how developmental milestones occur in the context of the outdoor classroom. In contrast to the inside classroom, the outdoor classroom can offer space and materials that can be used flexibly and invites exploration and experimentation. We introduce three teachers. Rebecca steps into the imaginary world of her preschoolers to enrich children's outdoor play with books, story dictations, art, and field trips. Calvert is a transfer teacher to his new elementary school who transforms the blacktop into spaces for gardening, art, and investigative inquiry. Aziza is a kindergarten teacher weaving challenges and achievements on the playground into her daily curriculum and later in the chapter will step into an advocacy role when recess time is threatened.

- **Teaching goals and guidelines for children in the outdoor classroom.** A play-centered outdoor curriculum is a balance that involves child-initiated and adult-initiated play as well as daily life activities and teacher-planned activities. This chapter articulates outdoor teaching goals matched with guidelines for how to promote them, emphasizing the promotion of spontaneous play of long duration involving imagination, creativity, and a sense of wonder, inquiry, connection, and knowledge about nature.

- **Best practices in planning for outdoor play.** We introduce two additional teachers alongside Rebecca, Calvert, and Aziza to show how to support children from diverse backgrounds in the outdoor classroom environment. The teachers exemplify choices in strategies and teaching styles that support outdoor play. Fong, in collaboration with family's goals for their children's schooling, provides a model of best teaching practices while maintaining safety and security. Roxanne, who grew up in a neighborhood without access to safe options for play, learns alongside her children and her mentor how to offer improved outdoor experiences in her playground. We emphasize the importance of gaining the trust of family members and caretakers by linking outdoor classroom practices to observations of children's skills. You will reflect on your own experiences and feelings about being outdoors and how teacher experiences as a child impact the advocacy for outdoor play. A practical section discusses ideas to improve sites with outdoor challenges.

- **Observing and interpreting outdoor play.** Active outdoor classrooms give teachers the chance to observe, reflect on, and facilitate children's intentions. This chapter provides a framework for observing and interpreting outdoor play based on understanding children's peer play interactions. A framework for appreciating the phases of peer play is presented so that teacher decisions for support and enrichment are based on children's intentions and frame of reference. This chapter highlights a discussion of rough and tumble play and the supervision strategies teachers can user to support big body peer play. Teachers can use the outdoor classroom to complement students with special needs, where the flexibility of space and the enrichment of the senses can guide children's emerging physical and social capacities.

- **Teacher decision making during outdoor play.** Teachers ask themselves three questions to help decide what strategies to use when supporting spontaneous outdoor play of long duration:
  1. Can the child engage alone and with others independent of adults?
  2. During peer play, is the interaction losing focus or becoming unsafe?
  3. What is the purpose of the teacher's intervention? You will see Aziza, Rebecca, and Calvert put their decision-making skills into practice on the playground.

- **Teaching styles that support outdoor play.** Two equally valuable and effective teaching styles support outdoor play: indirect coordination and direct involvement. Both Rebecca and a second teacher, Roxanna, model this indirect coordination by preparing play spaces, observing developmental progress, and refining play spaces based on how children use the area. Fong and Calvert model the strategies of direct involvement by organizing and promoting play that takes into account the children's play themes and point of view. You will see teachers encouraging development by supporting reasonable risk.

- **Fostering inquiry in the outdoor classroom.** The outdoor classroom can also be rich in the process of inquiry for both children and teachers, where inquiry involves using observation, comparison, exploration, and investigation.

- **Assessing children's play in the outdoor classroom.** A discussion of assessing and advocating for children's outdoor play offers useful quality improvement resources for students who will be working in a climate where teachers will need to demand outdoor play for their classrooms

- **Advocating for outdoor play for all children.** This chapter recognizes that part of being a teacher of young children includes active advocacy. Restoring outdoor play environments at school will involve both school and community-organizing efforts. You are provided with cases studies and online links that will support your professional development as an advocate, as well as policy recommendations we believe are essential in ensuring outdoor play for all children.

APPLYING YOUR KNOWLEDGE

1. Explain how physically active outdoor play, outdoor nature play, and child-initiated outdoor play contribute to children's healthy development. Compare the differences between the outdoor classroom and the inside classroom.
   a. Contrast characteristics of the outdoor classroom with the indoor classroom.
   b. Visit a playground with a classmate. Write a detailed observation of a young child engaged in outdoor play. What aspects of development did you observe? Compare your observation with your classmate's. Did you or your classmate find evidence of a connection/interest in nature, physical activity, or child-initiated activity? Did either of you observe any instances of big body rough and tumble play? If so, discuss what behaviors indicated it was play.

2. Identify five goals for teachers in supporting outdoor play and explain how teaching goals in the outdoor classroom can be accomplished
   a. Visit a school playground. What activities are set up for the children? Can you infer what the children are intended to do in these areas? Were there indicators of what kind of play is appropriate in different areas? If so, what were they? How many children were/could play in an area? What aspects of development do the areas support? Are there areas of development not included? What challenges would you expect the teachers to have supervising the children?

3. Discuss best practices in planning outdoor play, including supporting children from diverse backgrounds and overcoming challenges to outdoor play.
   a. Describe how Fong provides a model of best practices in planning for outdoor play, and apply some of her ideas and strategies to an outdoor site you are familiar with.
   b. Observe a real outdoor space and illustrate how you might maximize play opportunities based on observed limitations or other challenges. Discuss possible challenges *you* might face in implementing improvements to the space.
   c. Recall when you were a young child. Did you play outside? If so, where? What did you do? Were you alone or did you play with others? What kind of weather did you play in? What are your feelings about those times? If you did not play outside, why not?

4. Name the three phases of children's peer play and explain how child-initiated play proceeds through this sequence. Review how to understand and support big body rough and tumble play and how to serve students with special needs.
   a. With a classmate, separately write a detailed observation of the same child in peer play in an outdoor setting where you are familiar with the

children. Compare your observations and analyze the sequence of play progress in the play interaction. Did you observe any instances of rough and tumble play? What gestures and behaviors defined it? Did the child or teacher exhibit any behaviors that indicated an Individual Educational Plan was being followed?

   b. For further review of the sequence of peer play in an extended vignette on rough and tumble play including both girls and boys, download a free version of *Outdoor Play: Teaching Strategies with Young Children* (Perry, 2001; www.ebookweb.org/outdoor-play-pdf-download-free/1993583334), and read Chapter 5, "Two Guys." Apply some of the teaching strategies used in this vignette to a school setting you are familiar with.

5. Discuss the three questions teachers ask themselves to help decide what strategies to use when supervising outdoor play.

   a. Shadow a teacher supervising during lunch recess or while supervising recess yourself and use the three decision-making questions to decide what strategies you would adopt to facilitate child-initiated outdoor play of long duration.

6. Contrast two different teaching styles that support outdoor play and compare child-initiated and teacher-planned outdoor activities.

   a. Select one of the teachers presented in this chapter. List the important ways the teacher specifically encouraged outdoor play and identify the style or styles used.

7. Define *inquiry* and review several guideposts for children's experience of inquiry during outdoor play.

   a. Identify several of the guideposts that indicate that children are experiencing inquiry during outdoor play.

8. Describe the two ways teachers determine how their outdoor space supports play. Give an example of how one assessment tool rates the outdoor environment.

   a. Evaluate an outdoor space for children using one of the instruments mentioned in the chapter, and prepare a report of its strengths and next steps for improvement.

9. Discuss and provide examples of organizing efforts to enable and restore safe, outdoor play space and time. Review recommendations for active, spontaneous outdoor play.

   a. Interview a teacher in your area to learn more about the challenges in supporting several periods of outdoor play each day for children.

   b. Identify a community organizing story from online research into either Design Your Own Park, KaBOOM!, or Pogo Park. Identify what organizing efforts used or recommended sound like something you could try.

CHAPTER 13

Toys and Technology as Tools for Play

LEARNING OUTCOMES

- Discuss principles for considering toys and media technology as tools for play.
- Discuss the categories of toys that educators distinguish among and describe an example of each.
- Explain how children's use of toys relates to their development and individual differences.
- Discuss and provide examples of how some toys can limit children's development and undermine equity.
- Define the term *media technology* and summarize key research findings regarding the use of media technology in young children's lives.
- Summarize the recommendations for use of media technology in the play-centered curriculum.
- Describe an example of how educators can use media technology so that children's play leads to teacher-planned curriculum.
- Explain how play in early childhood programs can address standards for technology.

To begin their Night Sky project, kindergarten teachers Suzanne, Christa, and Margaret orchestrate their annual Friday night sleepover that is accompanied by sky watching through a telescope. How fortunate they are to live where the night sky is clear and young children see stars and planets throughout the year!

In this small town in the hills, everyone has been hearing about the Night Sky project. Children and families alike have been anticipating this fall event. All family members are invited to participate in the potluck and dusk to dark astronomy activities.

The teachers follow up this event with a mural that, over time, acquires children's renditions of objects that move in the night sky. This includes objects they've observed such as the moon, stars, planets, and aircraft as well as objects that they've heard about such as black holes and galaxies. The children also draw imaginary creatures such as unicorns, aliens, and fairies. They research their drawings and paintings using books from the library and resources contributed by families of children in all three classrooms. Mario's dad, who brought the telescope, comes to school to answer children's questions. He brings his laptop so children can see short videos of space explorations.

In the next phase, the children build a spaceship from a large cardboard box, complete with mission control. In the days that follow, they use blocks as walkie-talkies and pretend computers to orchestrate play landings on planets and moons. In a complementary teacher-planned activity, they construct a space ABC word wall that will later become a book for their kindergarten library. ∅

Throughout the world, young children have always employed the materials around them as tools to enrich their play. A 2-year-old folds up a small blanket and pretends it's a doll. A 3-year-old rolls a ball down a slope. Two 5-year-olds use acorns for cars and collect twigs to build roads and bridges. Seven-year-olds play tetherball, selecting teams and negotiating rules as they play.

The vignettes throughout this book show young children using a great variety of toys for play. Choices seem limitless:

- Objects and materials from the natural world, such as sand and water
- Manufactured objects found in everyday life
- Materials made especially for children's play, including toys and media technology

Choices for teachers also seem limitless. As they prepare the environment and interact with children, early childhood educators face constant decisions about selecting toys and technology as tools for play. For example, Andrea, a teacher in an afterschool program tells her co-teachers that she feels pressured to incorporate the latest commercial "educational materials" in much the same way that her students seem pressured to get the latest commercial toys and media technology. Other early childhood educators report that the advice they receive from professional organizations and colleagues sometimes seems conflicting. How do conscientious educators make informed decisions?

PRINCIPLES FOR CONSIDERING TOYS AND MEDIA TECHNOLOGY AS TOOLS FOR PLAY

We know that toys and media technology influence children's play. Educators who implement a play-centered curriculum assess how children in our care use toys and media technology as tools for play. All play is not equal. Although they may be promoted as educational, not all toys or media technology enrich children's play.

The first guiding principle for early childhood programs is to consider whether children use the objects, materials, or media technology as tools for rich and complex play. As potential tools of the imagination, good toys range from pebbles, sticks, and feathers found in nature to "classic" unstructured commercial toys such as balls, blocks, and clay. Toys that enrich play invite children to incorporate their own imagination, fantasies, images, roles, and scripts into their play.

The second guiding principle is to consider how the social contexts in which children use toys and media technology shape children's play in early childhood settings. The impact of media-based play and toy marketing on children and schools is an important social concern shared by parents, educators, and health professionals. What about the latest commercial toys on the market? What about the ever-increasing profusion of media technology, including tablets and smartphones? How can educators assess the multitude of toys and media technology promoted as educational and developmentally appropriate?

TYPES OF TOYS

Toys are the concrete objects that children use to fashion their experiences with sensorimotor play, constructive play, dramatic play, and games with rules. There are many ways to classify toys. Purely **sensorimotor toys** give rise to repetitive activity and the joy of making things happen with an object. Bouncing balls, shaking rattles, spinning tops, rocking horses, and monkey bars are a few familiar examples. **Representational toys** look like other objects in the culture or in nature. **Miniatures** of animals, vehicles, houses, utensils, furniture, and dolls are familiar examples. **Construction toys** can be manipulated and used to create new objects. Bristle blocks, wooden blocks, Lego blocks, and Keva planks are a few of the many examples we see in early childhood programs. **Locomotion toys** include trikes, bikes, scooters, and wagons.

Toys affect development in profound and sometimes subtle ways. For one thing, they orchestrate both individual and social activity. Toys have a "logic of action" that suggests how the toy is to be used. For example, a toy phone suggests or cues particular forms of motor, representational, and social behavior.

Some toys are specific in their cues. Lego and pattern blocks cue children for constructive play. Stuffed animals, dolls, action figures, and toy vehicles cue for dramatic play. Game boards suggest games with rules. Toys also cue teachers for specific play expectations. The toys that teachers designate as math **manipulatives** include collections of miniature animals, vehicles, or furniture for children to arrange in sets and thus construct logical–mathematical relationships. Manipulatives also include pattern blocks or Cuisenaire rods for similar purposes. In the case of miniature objects, experience with logical–mathematical thinking is linked to children's dramatic play accessories. In the case of patterning materials, these relationships are linked to constructive play.

Other common "teacher categories" for classroom toys are fine motor toys and gross motor toys. Pegboards, pattern boards, and puzzles aid in developing children's fine motor coordination. In contrast, trikes, scooters, swings, and playground climbers help children develop large muscle strength and coordination. Materials for sensorimotor play outside as well as in the classroom include raw materials for art and construction such as sand, water, paint, mud, and clay.

No matter how adults classify toys and raw materials for play, the key point is that children will use toys in their play in ways that suit their own agendas, not necessarily those of adults. The essential question is, "How does the child see the play potential of a given toy or material?"

Along these lines, Griffin (1988) suggests that teachers categorize toys by the effects they have on children's inner feelings and social interactions, rather than by the intellectual concepts and skills the toys are thought to develop. Some toys suggest active group play, such as blocks, housekeeping toys, and art materials. Others—such as pegboards, puzzles, miniature animals, and books—cue for quiet, solitary play. Griffin notes that toys that are self-correcting in nature, such as bead strings and pegboards, are soothing because they give children an opportunity to create order and control in their physical environments. They are calming in the same way that gardening might be for adults. Many of Montessori's self-correcting toys have long had this appeal for young children (Montessori, 1936).

In a solitary context, toys such as miniatures and books encourage children's flights of imagination without the challenge of negotiating pretend play with others. Children can use miniatures to represent emotionally laden experiences, thus allowing them to process confusing or troubling experiences at a more comfortable distance.

> Sean had trouble separating from his mother at the start of the preschool day. Each day for the first few weeks of school, after a tearful good-bye, Sean took out the tiny family dolls and a small, plastic playhouse. "Bye Mommy," he said as he walked the little boy doll into the house. "I love you," he whispered, as he put the Mommy doll into a toy car and "drove" it away. He then brought the Mommy doll back to the house and said, "It's time to go home now. Did you have a good day?" as he put the Mommy and little boy dolls into the car. ✿

This kind of play allows children to project their feelings onto toys without having to play just one role. It also allows them to control the situation from the outside. Accordingly, Griffin (1988) suggests that classrooms have an ample supply of toys that are potentially "charged" for children: baby bottles and high chairs, spiders, dragons, capes, magic wands, and hats. Teachers have long found that "raw" sensorimotor materials such as water, sand, mud, paint, glue, and collage materials are pleasing to the senses. They afford all children opportunities for mastery and control, and foster emotional equilibrium.

> It's a hot spring day in the desert, a day for outside adventures and quiet time beneath the shade tree. Three- and 4-year-old preschoolers move freely from outside to indoors. Low shelves, outdoors and inside, provide handy access for children to choose materials, toys, and equipment. A wide patio awning provides ample shade.
>
> Jasmine and Silas sit across from each other in the smaller sandbox. The nearby shelf has pails of different sizes, plastic shovels and scoops made from dried desert gourds, graduated measuring cups, and a collection of plastic food molds. They decide to make "wet, goopy sand." Each selects a large pail to fill with water from the nearby spigot and they run off. They trudge back and dump the water into the sand.
>
> *Silas:* "It's a pool. Wanna swim?"
>
> They laugh as they splash about in the small puddle they've made. It's so hot today that the water on their clothes dries in just a moment, leaving small spots of sand.
>
> *Silas:* "Let's get some divers!"
> *Jasmine:* ". . . from the blocks."

> She goes back inside the classroom and emerges carrying small plastic figures, a horse and cow as well as a few people. She tosses them into the puddle, announcing: "OK! Swim!"
>
> Then she notices how little water remains as a puddle. (Most has been absorbed into the sand, though a small amount has evaporated even in this short time).
>
> Jasmine: "Quick—the pool is draining. We've gotta fix it!"
>
> Wordlessly, they pick up the gourd scoops and begin to dig. ⌀

Special education teachers point out that sand, water, and other natural materials provide sensory experiences that meet the needs of many children with special needs, including children with autism spectrum disorder and attention-deficit/hyperactivity disorder.

> Three first graders have spent the last 30 minutes engrossed in making a collage, an extension of a science unit on the properties of material objects. Angelo searches through the collected objects for brightly colored feathers and beads. He and his peers negotiate the design details and assist each other as they place and paste. Children's individual needs are accommodated in this setting. Angelo, a child with cerebral palsy, participates fully in this social activity that promotes his fine motor coordination. ⌀

TOY USE AND CHILDREN'S DEVELOPMENT

As development proceeds, we see a change in children's uses of toys. The best toys for young children have flexible "**play-ability**," the quality that allows children to adapt the toy to their individual needs and stages of development over an extended period of time. Blocks are a good example of a toy with high play-ability. A 2-year-old might experiment with stacking and falling blocks, repeating the process over and over in sensorimotor play. Three- to 6-year-old children might use the blocks to build constructions they have seen ("This is the dolphin pool at Marine World") or as a prop in dramatic play ("Get the phone"). Finally, blocks can serve as the pieces for a game with rules as children stand blocks on end and "bowl" them down with a pitched tennis ball, giving points for each "hit."

In addition to providing highly flexible toys, teachers select toys that meet specific needs at particular developmental stages and for children with special needs. Teachers and researchers use the term **structure** to note the degree to which a toy or other object resembles the object that the child is symbolizing. Teachers need to be observant and sensitive to provide a good match between the structure of the toy and the child's developing symbolic abilities.

For example, to scaffold their play scripts, 2- and 3-year-olds might require high structure in their toys, such as replicas of tools, vehicles, or housekeeping accessories. Play may easily break down in disputes over who gets to talk on the toy phone or use the toy fire engine, so many teachers have multiple sets of realistic toys available.

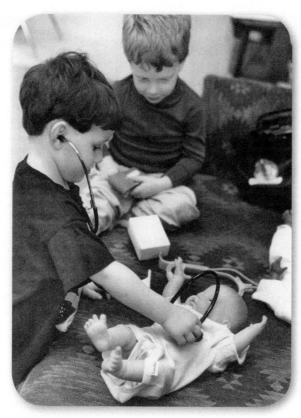

In pretend play, children explore technology from daily life.

Having multiple sets of replica toys also allows several younger children to explore similar interests or roles.

Older children, 4- to 8-year-olds, are more likely to use "unstructured" toys such as blocks, marbles, or sticks in their play. The representational abilities of older children have developed to the point that meaning exists in their own imaginations rather than depending primarily on the characteristics of the objects themselves. For example, an older child might appropriate a block to represent a sandwich or a helicopter or a wallet or a cup of coffee, all within the course of a single play episode.

Teachers who observe children's sociodramatic play carefully can ascertain the levels of symbolic distancing in play with objects. They are aware of the full range of children's abilities to use unstructured toys in pretend play. Then they can provide an array of toys for children ranging from structured replicas to unstructured objects as well as novel and familiar toys.

The feature *Advocating in Action: Families Share Traditional Toys and Games* describes how Sandra advocated for play as she turned to the children's families to share the cultural diversity of their play traditions.

Becoming an Informed Advocate for Play

ADVOCACY IN ACTION: FAMILIES SHARE TRADITIONAL TOYS AND GAMES

Sandra is a kindergarten teacher whose grandparents live in Mexico. Several years ago she began collecting traditional Mexican toys and games. Then she started inviting several parents to bring both traditional and nontraditional family toys and games to share with her kindergarten class. This was immediately popular. Family members came to school to watch the toys and games that the families of other children introduced. In a few weeks, the class had a growing collection of puppets, tops, dolls, balls, whistles, and carved animals. Sandra started a class photo book of traditional family toys and games from different countries.

Earlier this year, Sandra planned a family "traditional toy party" as a time for families and children to play together and even make a few homemade toys. She sent home an invitation in English, Spanish, Tagalog, and Chinese.

Everyone had such a great time playing together. The class book has chapters! There are all kinds of homemade and purchased spinners and tops, including trompos, bamboo spinning copters, and dreidels; all kinds of dolls, including rag dolls, dolls with heads make from dried apples, porcelain dolls, and yarn dolls; leather and cloth balls, cup and ball toys, and wire rollers; metal penny whistles and wooden flutes; animal and people puppets with different clothes; and kites that look like dragonflies and kites that look like birds.

Games with Rules

As children move from early childhood into middle childhood, games with rules become increasingly evident in their play. Board games and games of motor skill—such as hand games, jump rope, soccer, hopscotch, and four square—have long been favorite games with rules for children in primary grades. Many of us have vivid childhood memories of games passed down from one generation of children to the next that we played on school playgrounds or neighborhood streets.

Some games with rules, such as hopscotch or tic-tac-toe, require no special equipment and can be played in a variety of settings. Others, such as jump rope or soccer, require some purchased materials. In contemporary society, we have an increasing variety of commercial toys in the category of games with rules.

Planning for Development in Game Play   Playground games for kindergarteners, board games for first graders, soccer and baseball for second and third graders—whatever the game, teachers need to be sensitive to the cognitive leap represented by children's entry into the play stage of games with rules. This begins at about the age of 6, when we see a shift in the relationship of rules to fantasy. Now fantasy becomes implicit or taken for granted by the players, such as the "as-if" frame of reference for Candy Land or Monopoly. The rules are explicit and formulated by the manufacturer but can be negotiated further by the players before the play begins. Verbal discussion shifts from "Let's pretend . . ." to "The rule says . . ." to "Let's make a rule that . . ."

Games need to honor this developmental progression. Games with rules marketed for preschool and kindergarten children need to be used with caution and sensitivity by teachers. Board games and sports equipment have their place in the early childhood classroom but should not be used in place of the more appropriate constructive and dramatic play materials for this age group. Instead, sensitive teachers will encourage children who use balls and bats, jump ropes, card games, and board games to create their own rules and construct their own understandings of winning and losing (see DeVries, Zan, Hildebrandt, Edmiaston, & Sales, 2002).

Selecting Appropriate Games for All Young Children Understanding the development of play is only one aspect of selecting appropriate games for young children. Other features of game design are important when choosing games for children to play in early childhood classrooms. One important aspect of good games, whether traditional playground games or board games, is the social interaction among players. Good games have defined goals but uncertain outcomes. Levels of challenge escalate as children play repeated rounds and solve problems with more variables and create alternative strategies. These games engage children's minds and creative capacities.

CHILDREN UNDER SIEGE: TOYS AND THE MARKETPLACE

Children and parents are continually under siege from the toy industry to purchase toys and games that undermine imaginative play. Teachers are under siege as well. Even when teachers don't purchase them, these toys impact classrooms when children play out scripts suggested by these toys or bring them to show in school.

Teachers inform themselves about what play materials are most appropriate for their classrooms by considering developmental stages of play and the structure of children's games. Much of what is marketed to children is not only developmentally inappropriate but also exploits the very vulnerabilities of childhood, such as the desire to be more grown up, have more power, and have friends. Well-known early childhood educators such as Carlsson-Paige (2008), Levin (2011, 2013; Levin & Kilbourne, 2008), and Linn (2008) point out that this is not accidental.

Toy manufacturers rely heavily on the way that advertisers market childhood. Commercials and toy packaging promote socially constructed phenomena whereby children learn that there are certain toys to covet and accessories to buy that assure they will be seen as glamorous or "cool." See the TV commercial in which the preschool boy is looking longingly at the older boys playing happily with the set of racing cars. Notice the way that toys are packaged. See how the preschool girl is holding a post-pubescent doll with makeup and high heels.

Toys That Limit Development

The commercial exploitation of play is rapidly eclipsing the freedom inherent in many "classic" toys. To develop abstract concepts and the capacity for imagination, we have to give young children opportunities to apply their own meanings and actions to toys. A walk down the toy aisle in most stores, however, shows a profusion of single-use, electronic toys on the market. Toys that have only a single use do not provide children with the flexibility they need to use their imaginations in alternative ways.

The action figure whose role or behavior is narrowly defined by the toy's features or the doll whose body movements and talk are produced by its electronic technology, rather than by the child, restricts children's emerging imaginations. Such toys can interfere with the development of distancing strategies that underlie abstract thinking. These one-use-only toys make millions of dollars for toy manufacturers, but they are not conducive to children's development. In fact, the limiting characteristics of some toys not only negatively affect the development of cognition and imagination for young children, but also limit development in other areas. For example, media character dolls are often packaged to persuade children that each character performs only one role or function in play, often a gender-stereotyped role. Some action figures, even ones found in block areas, now suggest violent play.

Even "classic" constructive play toys such as Lincoln Logs, Legos, or animal action figures that once promoted unstructured play now come with templates for using the toys in specific arrangements. Many are marketed in specialized kits that have only the pieces for the particular model pictured on the package included. These marketing strategies affect the ways children use toys in schools when children imitate what they have seen in ads and toy packaging. Limited and stereotyped marketing stifles development as children grow accustomed to models to imitate rather than using toys to fulfill possibilities in their own imaginations. Teachers find that many children come to class with the notion that there is a right way to play and a "right script" to follow.

Toys That Undermine Gender Equity

Toys that are marketed in gender-stereotyped ways restrict gender equity in school and home settings. Many toys are marketed in dainty pastels for girls and bold primary colors for boys. The packaging shows gender-typed models for construction so that children get the message that there is an expected "right way for them to play."

As children construct ideas about gender, they sort information they learn from the people and popular media into categories of "boy behavior" and "girl behavior." Then their reasoning continues: "If I'm a boy, I must behave like a boy and play with boys' toys" or "If I'm a girl, I must behave like a girl and own girls' toys."

Like all stereotyping, gender stereotyping limits the range of experiences that children have in their play in all settings—including school—as well as the concepts and skills development associated with those experiences. Teachers report marked differences in the play of boys and girls in their classrooms and discuss the possible influences of "boy toys" and "girl toys," particularly those that represent media-themed characters such as Power Rangers, Star Wars, or Disney Princess dolls. Even when children don't have any of these toys at home or school, they learn these stereotypes from peers and the wider culture. Boys are more likely to dramatize play themes using toy weapons, vehicles, and superhero G.I. Joe and Transformer dolls. Girls are more apt to select Barbie or Disney Princess dolls, house accessories, and pretend cosmetics.

Has it always been like this? Yes and no. Before the 1960s and 1970s, toys were stereotyped according to the prevailing adult, gender-specific occupations of men and women. Boys might use toys as tools to play firemen or doctors; girls used toys as tools to play mothers or nurses. In the 1970s, parents and educators made concerted efforts to diminish the gender stereotypes promoted in children's literature, television, film, and toys. These efforts were somewhat successful. It became more acceptable for all children to use a wider range of toys in their play and for girls to be assertive and independent and for boys to be sensitive and nurturing.

In the 1980s, much of this ground was lost with the deregulation of TV. Newly permitted commercials shown during children's programming allowed toy manufacturers to specifically target children's interest in conforming to socially stereotyped perceptions of gender identity to sell more toys.

More stereotyped play reemerged. We still see this today. Messages regarding gender stereotyping are insidious. When we examine more structured toys such as dolls and "action figures," we find many that promote a restricted and dangerous gender identity. As Levin and Kilbourne emphasize in their book *So Sexy So Soon*, both boys and girls are learning that being a boy is linked to violent play and being a girl is linked to play characterized by precocious sexuality: " . . . they all learn damaging lessons about what to value in themselves and their own gender as well as about one another" (2008, p. 33).

Toys That Promote Early Sexualization   One of the marketing strategies to emerge in recent years involves the concept of "age compression," in which gender-related, sexualized products designed for older children or teens are heavily promoted for younger children (American Psychological Association, 2007; Levin & Kilbourne, 2008; Schor, 2004). For example, Barbie dolls are now more popular with preschool-age girls than with the older girls for whom they were originally designed. Popular dolls are marketed with names like "Barbie Fashion Designer" and advertised with glamorous fashions and colorful hair styling. Another marketing concept is the image of "edge," which Schor (2004) describes as a younger version of "coolness" with peers usually associated with teen music and sexuality. Marketing gives the message that fashionable clothing is the key to a girl's success. Teachers of young children witness the effects of this marketing message as girls check to see if they're wearing the "right clothes."

"Boy" Toys That Portray Power through Violence   Teachers are also concerned that many toys marketed to young boys have ratcheted up an ever-increasing focus on violence that can lead to bullying.

Four-year-old players Jeremy, Seth, and Mark are playing Teenage Mutant Ninja Turtles in and around the outdoor play structure. Though their topic involves the 25-year edition of the ever-popular ninjas, their play draws from a number of different cartoon action figures and video games marketed to younger children. They make swift martial arts moves like strikes and karate kicks interspersed with sounds like "Ooph!" and "Whaaa!" as they pretend to fight. Plant stalks used as swords supplement the fighting gear. Mark later points out the pinecone he wielded was "one of those spiky things" that kill the robots.

The robots in this scenario are the bad guys. Rough and tumble play fighting turns into real fighting. When Shane, their teacher, intervenes in their increasingly frenetic and violent moves, the children argue that "we aren't really hurting anyone. They are just machines!" Later, Shane remarked to his co-teachers that the most troublesome thing was that none of these children wanted to "be the bad guy," so the boys coerced younger, less-powerful players to be the robot victims of their violence. ∅

War-themed toys are examples of toys that promote violence and stereotypes. Today's young children, born since 9/11, have grown up during the wars in Afghanistan and Iraq. Popular war toys look like real weapons used in wars and school shootings—for example, the Nerf N-Strike Elite Retaliator blaster with its 18-dart reload automatic clip. These toys often come with warnings that they are not intended for children under 3, suggesting, in fact, that they are intentionally marketed to preschool and kindergarten children.

Teachers Respond to Gender Stereotyping   Early childhood educators can use the same repertoire of techniques to address all forms of stereotyping in classrooms with young children.

Leslie, a K–1 teacher, has purposely selected a wide range of play materials for her classroom. "I want both boys and girls to develop the fine motor skills, such as the cutting, pasting, and using a paintbrush, that accompany art play," she comments. "I want both genders to develop large motor skills in climbing, running, sliding, and riding. A wide range of toys helps both the boys and the girls in my group to develop spatial reasoning and the bodily kinesthetic intelligence associated with constructive play. Building a spaceship with Legos or a fort of blocks enhances these experiences for all children. To encourage this, we as teachers need to consciously arrange for children to move beyond stereotyped conventions of what boys and girls do and try new activities." ∅

There are numerous resources for teachers and parents concerned about children's frenzied, violent, and stereotyped play in school and at home. For several decades, Teachers Resisting Unhealthy Children's Entertainment (TRUCE) has distributed a toy guide for parents and teachers that highlights specific toys and commercial trends to avoid, strategies for how to respond, and recommendations for both new and classic toys (www.truceteachers.org).

MEDIA TECHNOLOGY IN THE LIVES OF CHILDREN

In the play-centered curriculum, educators evaluate media technology as tools to enhance play and development. They use the same guiding principles as they do to select toys. Will children use media technology as tools to promote rich and complex play? How will the social contexts in which children use media technology at home and in school affect their play, development, and learning?

The number and types of media technology have grown exponentially in the two decades since the first edition of *Play at the Center of the Curriculum* was published in 1993. At that time there was a lot of controversy about computer use in early childhood programs even though relatively few classrooms had computers. In the past two decades, the universe of media technology for children has grown exponentially to include thousands of products marketed to educators and families as "educational."

Early childhood educators face complex issues about whether or how to use media technology with children. What is the best use of a child's time in early education and child care? When might the use of media technology enrich play and promote learning? How can a teacher assess the multitude of programs and apps such as video games, videos, or e-books? These are challenging questions.

In the educational literature, **media technology** generally refers to **screen technology**. Most systems have screens—tablets, computers, smartphones, and smart boards—although some, like MP3 players, are audio only. This limited use of the term *media technology* contrasts with the broad meaning of the term *technology* as used by scientists, engineers, and mathematicians to refer to all systems and processes that result when people solve problems.

A Look at Research on Children's Use of Media Technology

Today, most young children's lives are media saturated with hours of screen time. Educators are concerned that children are spending less time interacting with peers and adults and less time playing outside. So what does the research show?

Zero to Eight: Children's Media Use in America (Common Sense Media & Rideout, 2011) presents the findings of a 2011 national survey of American children. Researchers report the average total screen time per day for children for the following age groups:

- Infants and toddlers (0–2 years)   53 minutes
- Children 2–4 years old   2 hours, 18 minutes
- Children 5–8 years old   2 hours, 50 minutes

These times include children's usage of all screen technologies but not time spent with audio-only technologies such as CDs and MP3 players. In recent years, young children's personal access to media technology has increased. More than 40% of young U.S. children have a TV in their bedroom. Roughly 50% have access to handheld mobile screen technologies such as tablets and smartphones.

Some national surveys of young children report even higher levels of screen time. For example, results from a 2009 Nielsen survey of TV screen viewing showed that American children 2–5 years old spent more than 32 hours in front of a TV screen watching TV, DVDs, or playing with game consoles (Nielsen Company & McDonough, 2009).

There is little scientific evidence that examines the effects on children who use media technology in early childhood programs. Despite claims that young children's early use promotes greater computer literacy, we found no empirical evidence that children who began using media technology in preschool had better educational outcomes than those who began using media technology later in primary or middle grades.

Most research on young children focuses on use in homes rather than early childhood or child-care settings. Few studies include large, diverse populations. Unfortunately, scientific bias remains an issue since much existing research is funded by media-related companies.

Fortunately, this research field is growing. In the next decade, we will have results from more studies about the consequences of the use of media technology in early childhood education settings. There will be more information about the effects of media technology on children's health including, for example, neuroscience research on brain development as well as physiological research on children's health (e.g., activity levels, rates of obesity, and vision). We will know more about the effects on young children's mental health, particularly children's emotional self-regulation and social competence. Within the next decade early childhood educators will be able to turn to considerably more scientific evidence on the effects of use of media technology to make informed program decisions.

Generation M2: Media in the Lives of 8- to 18-Year-Olds is the most recent report of a longitudinal survey research (Kaiser Family Foundation, 2010). These latest data show that nonschool-related use of media technology has increased. The average 8- to 18-year-old views an average of more than 7.5 hours of media technology each day, and more than 75 hours each week if we count the time that several technologies are used simultaneously (e.g., computer, TV, and smart phones). This significant increase is due mostly to the use of mobile media that can be used simultaneously and in combination with other screen technologies—for example, texting while using a computer and watching a video. Survey data show that higher rates of use were related to negative child outcomes such as decreased physical activity, higher rates of obesity, and lower measures of school performance.

A critical concern related to the high use of technologies is diminished self-regulation. Increasing numbers of children and adolescents as well as adults are concerned that they have difficulty limiting their screen time. In more extreme though not unusual cases, adolescents and adults describe feeling compulsions to check texts and e-mail. Others feel the need to always be connected and an intense sense of urgency when they're not. Powerful feelings of urgency and consequent loss of self-regulation are considered indicators of addictive behaviors such as smoking, drinking, or gambling. In the current psychological literature, there is controversy about whether people who exhibit these types of technology-related behaviors have an addiction or not. Whether or not these behaviors are true addictions, the challenge for educators is to promote students' wise practices and help students change unhealthy habits once formed such as overuse and dependence.

A related issue is the effect of screen usage in early childhood on later development. We do not yet know how different patterns of early use impact patterns of later use. Few studies consider the use of screen technologies within the longer arc of children's lives. For example, does increased screen time in early childhood relate to higher use among adolescents? What do higher levels mean for imaginative play, social relationships, and an active lifestyle?

Guidance from Professional Education and Public Health Associations

Early childhood educators recognize the enormous growth and development that occurs during the early years. They also recognize young children's vulnerabilities and turn to professional education and health associations to provide recommendations and standards for the use of media technology.

National Association for the Education of Young Children Recommendations   The NAEYC 2012 position statement "Technology and Interactive Media as Tools in Early Childhood Programs Serving Children from Birth through Age 8" was written jointly with the Fred Rogers Center for Early Learning and Children's Media. The statement recognizes the allure of media technology and the complexities educators face in making decisions about their use, particularly in view of conflicting empirical evidence. For example, the statement cites studies on the effects of media use on young children. It points to differences in access to technology as well both negative and positive outcomes associated with its use. The statement includes several key recommendations. The recommendations draw from the NAEYC's general guidelines for developmentally appropriate practice (Copple & Bredekamp, 2009). These guidelines emphasize that educators need to be intentional when choosing media technology and use it in developmentally appropriate ways.

The position statement emphasizes the vulnerabilities of infants and toddlers and underscores the importance of relationships with caregivers. The NAEYC recommends that, if used for children less than 2 years of age, technology should be used in ways that strengthen adult–child social interactions and relationships. The NAEYC emphasizes that passive use of technology should be prohibited for children less than 2 years of age and discouraged for all young children.

In keeping with their principles of developmentally appropriate practice, the NAEYC recommends that educators plan carefully to assure that programs for young children provide a balance of activities that emphasize children's "active, hands-on, creative, and authentic engagement with those around them and with their world." Within this balance, the NAEYC recommends that if educators use screen technology, it should be to support and extend children's active, playful engagement. Furthermore, the NAEYC recommends that educators "carefully consider" statements issued by public health associations calling for stricter limits on screen time.

Recommendations of Public Health Associations   For guidance from public health associations, we turned to the comprehensive *National Health and Safety Performance Standards: Guidelines for Early Care and Education Programs* (Third Edition) (American Public Health Association, American Academy of Pediatrics, & National Resource Center for Health and Safety in Child Care, 2011). This is a joint publication of the American Public Health Association (APHA), the American Academy of Pediatrics (AAP), and the National Resource Center for Health and Safety in Childcare and Early Education. (This publication is available without charge; go to www.nrckids.org.)

The specific guideline that addresses children and media technology is "Standard 2.2.0.3: Limiting Screen Time—Media, Computer Time." These public health associations emphasize that parents/guardians should always be informed if media technology is used. The standard states that programs serving children younger than 2 years of age should not allow children to view screen media such as televisions or use computers. Screen time in programs serving young children older than 2 years should be strictly limited. Viewing should not exceed 30 minutes once a week and only be for educational purposes, including physical activity. Viewing should not be permitted during meals or snacks. Children older than 2 may use computers if limited to 15 minutes per day. Computer use is permitted for children with special health needs who need to use adaptive screen technologies. School-age children may use computers to complete homework assignments.

The performance standard provides background information that underscores the importance of the early years for brain and physical development. Time for social interactions and play is essential. Time spent with media and computers leads to decreased social interactions. The performance standard summarizes important findings from the American Academy of Pediatrics' review of the research. This research shows that increases in young children's TV viewing time is associated with inactivity, obesity, decreased intake of fruits and vegetables, and increased intake of sugary drinks like those advertised on children's programming.

Use of Media Technology: Ethical Dimensions   The positions and recommendations of the health associations and the NAEYC differ. The public health organizations warn about serious negative health consequences and recommend definite limitations on young children's use of media technology in early care and education programs. In contrast, the NAEYC recommendations for educators are less restrictive.

How can educators resolve this apparent contradiction? As professionals, educators are bound by professional codes of ethics. We turned to the *NAEYC Code of Ethical Conduct and Statement of Commitment* (revised 2005) for guidance regarding ethical considerations inherent in making decisions about using screen technologies in early childhood education. Clearly, as early childhood educators, we wish to ensure that children use media technology in healthful ways. We developed our recommendations after consulting the NAEYC professional code of conduct.

The NAEYC Code of Conduct and Statement of Commitment states that:

"Above all, we shall not harm children." (NAEYC, 2005b)

The code states that this principle is paramount and, therefore, overrides all the other principles. Therefore, we decided that our recommendations should follow the more cautious practices recommended by the professional health associations.

RECOMMENDATIONS FOR THE USE OF MEDIA TECHNOLOGY IN A PLAY-CENTERED CURRICULUM

For this sixth edition of *Play at the Center of the Curriculum,* we revised our position on the use of media technology in programs for young children. After reviewing the research, professional literature, and the positions of professional organizations, we make the following recommendations based on the central role of play in development and the critical role of early childhood educators to safeguard the health and well-being of children.

The links between play and development are becoming increasingly well recognized. In their play, children interact directly with the complex social and physical dimensions of their environments. In play, children use all their senses as they interact directly with the social and physical dimensions of their environments. It is through spontaneous play and other direct experiences that young children build deepened personal relationships. It is through direct experiences such as play that young children develop a sense of place. Direct experiences with concrete objects provide grounding for increasingly abstract symbolic representations. Actual experiences rather than virtual ones are essential to provide children with a solid foundation for development throughout the life span.

In the United States and elsewhere, empirical research shows that children's home use of media technology exceeds the recommendations of professional health organizations and that many children do not have adequate time for social interactions and play. When early childhood educators make program decisions, they can promote a healthy balance if they consider the child's time in the early childhood setting within the fabric of the child's daily life. It is in this context that we advocate for play at the center of the early childhood curriculum.

How is children's time best spent in an early childhood classroom? In a play-centered curriculum, teachers promote direct experiences with the physical and social environment. When teachers plan the daily schedule, they question whether the time spent on technology-based experiences justifies any reduced time for direct experiences interacting with peers. A developmental approach recognizes that every child's time in early childhood programs is precious and that virtual experiences never replace direct experiences. (See, for example, Carlsson-Paige, 2012; Linn, 2012).

Table 13.1 presents our recommended guidelines for appropriate uses of media technology.

Table 13.1 Guidelines for Appropriate Uses of Media Technology in a Play-Centered Curriculum

- Early childhood programs serving children from birth through age 5 should be screen-free or have strict limits on children's screen use.

  - Programs serving children birth through age 2 should be screen-free.

  - Programs serving children 2–5 years of age should be screen-free or place strict limits on children' screen use.

- Early childhood programs serving children in kindergarten and grades 1 and 2 should be screen-free or limit screen time.

  - Time and range of screen technologies should increase only gradually from kindergarten through the primary grades.

- Adults who work with young children should model healthy, limited use of media technology.

- Children with special needs should have access to adaptive technologies and appropriate support to use these technologies.

- Early childhood programs should develop a written program policy for parents, staff, and administrators that includes a rationale and descriptive guidelines for the use of media technology.

Teachers Talk about Using Media Technology in a Play-Centered Curriculum

Our conversations with early childhood educators show the different ways in which they tailor guidelines to their specific program. Teachers talked about reasons for making as well as changing programmatic decisions.

We spoke with Elisa and Sheava, two family child-care providers who had screen-free policies for infants and toddlers. They explained that the biggest question for both of them is when to make a special exception.

> Elisa explained that two afternoons a week, she and the two preschool-age children watch and talk about a short video clip while the two toddlers nap. She pointed out that sometimes one or both of the toddlers doesn't nap. Usually she postpones showing the video in this situation, but sometimes she decides to make an exception.
>
> Sheava talked about a related example. Recently, she made a special exception when a mom brought a video of her child visiting with an aunt. Sheava knows the children and their families well. She and the mom used the video to talk with all five children about family visits with relatives. ∅

Our conversations with preschool teachers showed a wider range of practices, from no use to strictly limited use to more extensive use.

Trinity works in a preschool program based on Waldorf principles. One principle is that young children should not use screen technology. This agreement is clarified with families prior to enrollment. Throughout the year, Trinity sends home written articles about families and media technology, including recommendations from health and education organizations and research findings. ✆

Like many teachers, Lisa said that her program had a no-use policy for children as well as a policy for adult use. She explained that teachers and assistant teachers do use media technology in several ways. They take digital photos and videos of children, especially during spontaneous play. The children also see the adults using laptops and tablets to search the Web to answer children's questions or to find the title of particular book at the library. Lisa and the other teachers also use computers throughout the day to write observational records. ✆

Eric works in a full-day prekindergarten program with 4- and 5-year-old children. One of the program's key principles is equitable access to all aspects of education. Few children have access at home to computers or smartphones. After several months, families and school personnel decide to develop a written policy to promote all children's skills in using computers, cameras, and smart boards. In keeping with recommendations, total screen time is limited. Families are encouraged to reduce children's at-home screen time use by at least an hour each week so that teachers have more options to use technology in school.

Eric explains that each child's total use of computers is limited to 15 minutes per week, though he adds that the average use is about 10 minutes. The class usually spends another 15 to 30 minutes watching and discussing a video that relates to an aspect of their play or a current project. Eric keeps records of which children rotate through centers, including the center with the stationary computer. From time to time, with adult guidance, children get the chance to act as cinematographers, taking photos and videos of play projects and products. Eric points out that he's found it far more effective to work with children individually or in small groups rather than as a class when they talk about photos or use the Web for research. That way, he makes sure that each child sees the screen and can contribute to small-group discussions. ✆

Throughout our conversations, early childhood educators talked about the specific children and families in their programs, considerations of the families' uses of technology, and program policies about use of screen technology. There was great variability. Some teachers talked about how they were experimenting and using technologies in creative ways but emphasized that they had decided against daily use of media technology with students. Still other kindergarten and primary-grade teachers said that they decided to use media technology; they talked about the workshops they'd attended and the resources they use.

Many K–2 teachers pointed to financial support and professional training for the use of media technology, but some, particularly kindergarten teachers, mentioned the pressures they felt to use media technology in ways these teachers thought were not educationally sound and, possibly, were unhealthy. For example, one teacher explained that she felt pressured to increase students' computer time because her district's assessments of kindergarten as well as primary-grade students required that children use computers to answer the items.

In this chapter our emphasis is on media technology as tools for play. The early childhood educators we spoke with described a wide range of practices concerning not only play but all aspects of their program. They raised numerous, wide-ranging questions.

We recommend that educators turn to general resources on young children's use of media technology. *Facing the Screen Dilemma: Young Children, Technology and Early Education* provides a comprehensive but succinct exploration of multiple facets of these complex issues and cites scores of key resources (Campaign for a Commercial Free Childhood, Alliance for Childhood, and Teachers Resisting Unhealthy Children's Entertainment, 2012).

Numerous additional resources and articles are published by public health and education associations such as the American Academy of Pediatrics and the National Association for the Education of Young Children. *Young Children*, a journal published by the NAEYC, published a special 2012 issue on technology. The NAEYC's recently published book *Beyond Remote-Controlled Childhood: Teaching Young Children in The Media Age* provides a broad perspective on these issues (Levin, 2013).

Computers can support the learning of a diverse age range of children with special needs, but in general they should not be introduced before the primary grades.

Media Technology: Supporting Children with Special Needs

An important issue for all early childhood educators working with young children of all ages is to find technology resources that support children with special needs. Professional health and education associations recommend that children with special needs use assistive technologies that promote their independence and competencies. Limitations on children's use of media technology do not apply—these children should have access and sufficient support. The NAEYC recommends that teachers collaborate with families, work with other school personnel, and access numerous educational resources (see, for example, the Council for Exceptional Children and the National Early Childhood Technical Assistance Center). Many materials for educators are appropriate for parents and cross-age tutors as well. Technology recommendations and standards for technology emphasize the promotion of equity for all children in developing technology literacy.

> Maria is a fifth-grade mentor who helps in Andrea's kindergarten computer center twice a week. On this day, Joshua, a student with developmental delays, has been playing with a graphics program. He has made a line drawing of a bunny, and Maria guides him as he fills in the area with different colors. After several minutes, Josh frowns. "I don't want this bunny for my story. I want that bunny," he says, pointing to the painting he had made earlier. Maria, who recently learned to use a scanner for her own work, asks the teacher if she can take Joshua to the school library to scan his painting. Later, he dictates his story using the scanned image of his bunny. When Joshua's writing is printed with his scanned drawings, the result looks much like a printed book. ✆

Teachers promote inclusion when they arrange the environment to assure accessibility. It is particularly important to make sure that all children can see when teachers or other children use screen technology. Glare and size of pictures and text can be problems, especially on handheld devices such as tablets. Content is an important consideration. Teachers promote inclusion by reviewing photos and pictures with human characters to make certain that children with a range of special needs are included and their behaviors are not stereotyped.

Similarly, teachers must take care not to stereotype the interest and behaviors of children with special needs. Ella's parents pointed out to her teacher that they wanted to make sure there would be no assumptions that because of her physical disabilities she would be encouraged to use the computer inside rather than play actively outdoors.

Media Technology: Benefits and Challenges in Promoting Equity

Research and literature point to differences in children's use of media technology related to family income. Rich or poor, the average school-age child watches several hours of television each day. The discussion of the great media divide centers on kindergarten and primary-grade students and their access to computers, handheld mobile devices such as smartphones and tablets, and access to the Web.

We are concerned about these inequities. For example, we've observed some primary-grade classrooms and seen that the students who are more familiar with computers, digital cameras, and tablets assume control or direct the activity, leaving less time for other children. Therefore, we recommend that if media technology is used, early childhood educators keep observational records to make sure that all children have equitable opportunities.

Another aspect of the "digital divide" impacts communication with parents. Some educational materials urge teachers to use digital photos, e-mail, and social media to communicate with families. Considerate use of digital photos can indeed be an effective tool to build bridges between school and home, especially for parents who do not speak English fluently. But what about equity for families without access to computers, e-mail, or smartphones? How can we address this digital divide and ensure that all families receive important messages, photos of their children, and opportunities to build relationships with other parents?

While creating new challenges, educators use media technology to facilitate communication with families and children when educators don't speak the family's home language. In classrooms, media technology assists us in communicating with children who are dual language learners. Teachers and families turn to numerous programs that translate text or speech. However, translations are not always correct and may lead to misunderstandings. Therefore, we recommend that educators use these programs as a last resort.

MEDIA TECHNOLOGY: PLAY-GENERATED CURRICULUM AND CURRICULUM-GENERATED PLAY

We recommend that if educators choose to use screen technology with children 2 to 5 years old, they, not the children, use the technology. Adults can model healthy use and select technologies that enrich children's play and imagination. Used wisely,

FAMILY DIVERSITY

Communicating with Relatives at a Distance

Elijah and Zoë's grandparents live far away in the Netherlands. Since the children were babies, they have communicated weekly with their grandparents using Skype, an Internet service requiring a Web camera. They share family stories and sing together with lively communication in Dutch. The children show their *Oma* and *Opa* how they play, from clapping games when they were toddlers to tricycle rides when they were preschoolers to skateboarding when they were first-graders.

digital photos, videos, and apps such as Skype and FaceTime can be used to enrich children's understandings of their own play. The feature *Family Diversity: Communicating with Relatives at a Distance* illustrates how apps like Skype can enhance family ties and promote family understandings of the importance of play even for relatives who live far away.

> In the preschool morning program for 3-year-olds, Audrey takes photos of Jorge, Tanner, and Gabriela creating a block structure. By the next day, the photos are printed. The children look at the pictures of their block creation, talking excitedly. They arrange the photos in sequence and paste them on construction paper to share with the whole group. ✆

With children 5 to 8 years old, teachers may choose to incorporate a wider range of media technology and programs. Children can begin to take a more active role. From kindergarten through second grade, we recommend that teachers gradually increase the range of technologies used as well as the program time allotted.

> Nina is sitting at my Macintosh laptop computer in the library of her school. She is one of the youngest students in her kindergarten class. She types a string of letters and tells me that she is writing a story. I ask her if she would like the computer to read it to her. She watches me highlight the letters and select "speak selection" from the tools menu. She laughs with glee as the computer voice pronounces, "slifmefmaemf." (von Blanckensee, 1999, p. 52) ✆

Examples of Adult Use of Media Technology in Programs for Children 2–5 Years of Age

For decades, early childhood educators have used photos to display children's activities, create classroom books, and communicate with families about children's growth and development. In the past, film and processing was expensive and the time it took to develop the photos seemed especially long to young children. This changed dramatically with the availability of low-cost digital cameras. Educators use photos and videos to great advantage. Photos are easily enlarged to accommodate children with visual disabilities as well as group discussions. Books with photos and class displays can be created in a day. At the same time, teachers take a child's eye view to make sure that they don't remain hidden behind the eye of the camera. They remind themselves that eye-to-eye communication is primary and ensure that the convenience of digital cameras doesn't lead to less social interaction between children and teachers.

Many educators who are inspired by the philosophy and methods of Reggio Emilia employ photos as documentation to enable children to reflect more deeply and collaborate on ideas for enriching activities and projects. Videos of children's dramatic play, dances, music, and art encourage discussions and lead to new activities over weeks or months. Long-term projects foster young children's understandings of

Technology can aid discovery.

the concept of time, such as documenting the growth of bean plants or pumpkins planted and harvested in the school garden.

At the University of Toronto laboratory school, teacher-researchers Pelletier, Halewood, and Reeve (2005) enhanced their traditional journaling process with the use of digital photos. They combined the use of a database called Knowledge Forum with photo journals for kindergarten students. In one class, children kept electronic journals complete with digital photos as they were investigating the topic of simple machines.

> The students had been doing experiments in class with pulleys and levers. They were using Knowledge Forum to comment on photos of our experiments. At recess one day, the children became very excited when they discovered a shovel that had become wedged between the shed and the fence. They suggested that I could take a picture of it and to put it in our Machines view in Knowledge Forum. The children then decided that the question to go along with the photo would be, "How do we get it out?" The ensuing ideas and debate were quite lively—someone suggested putting tape on the end of a stick to retrieve the shovel. Someone else said that a lever might work. Yet another student wrote "uusrhns" (use your hands). Ultimately, the shovel came out in a river of water once the snow melted and the children had gone on to other investigations. It is still a lovely example of how children's ideas inform and direct the learning in a meaningful way. (C. Halewood, personal communication, October 8, 2005).

Examples of Children's Use of Media Technology in Kindergarten and Primary Grades

A prime consideration is creating an optimal environment for children's play with media technology in kindergarten, first grade, and second grade. To encourage peer interaction, we suggest a table large enough for two to three children with space on both sides of the computer or other screen for children to place materials related to their computer play. A printer should also be connected to a stationary computer so children can keep the products of their play.

Physical placement in the room is important. First, there are health and safety issues for the children and the technologies that may be stationary or handheld. All use of media technology needs to be far enough away from rigorous physical activity to avoid potential accidents. Avoid places where direct sunlight creates glare on the screen. Protect children's vision by making sure the screen is at an appropriate and comfortable distance. Remember that most young children are farsighted.

Stationary computers need to be placed near a grounded electrical outlet, away from water and other potential spills, and food. A surge protector is necessary to protect the hardware as well as to provide additional outlet space if necessary.

A Framework for Selecting Programs and Apps for Children 5–8 Years Old
Because new software becomes available constantly and existing software is upgraded frequently, we do not recommend specific software. Instead, teachers need a framework for judging software themselves or access to software reviews that share their point of view.

To help teachers choose instructional activities that are technology based, von Blanckensee designed and recently revised the "Choosing Technology-Based Activities for Young Children, Ages 5–8" scale (von Blanckensee, 1999; von Blanckensee, personal communication, April 23, 2013). The scale was developed for activities that use communication tools such as digital photography, audio and video recordings, and videoconferencing as well as electronic simulations, games, and books.

This rating scale includes three issues for teachers to consider when evaluating the appropriateness of an activity: (a) content/method, (b) technology design issues, and (c) computer software design issues. The items used for ratings help teachers ensure that they use technology in ways that reflect individual needs, promote gender equity, and respect cultural diversity (see Table 13.2). The scale takes technical and interface design into consideration. It provides an excellent framework for considering the many issues involved in selecting software that we have mentioned throughout this section (diversity, equity, and nonviolent content) and whether the software supports constructivist learning in ways that are age appropriate.

Evaluations of children's software are available through teacher resource websites, including those of various state departments of education. When choosing software rated by others, teachers will want to make sure that the criteria used for rating are philosophically consistent with their play-centered curriculum.

Children's Use of Graphics Programs in Kindergarten through Second Grade
Numerous graphics programs and multimedia programs that combine the

Table 13.2   Choosing Technology-Based Activities for Children 5–8 Years Old

Ratings: 0 = poor; 1 = adequate; 2 = good; 3 = excellent
Teachers may want to redesign or avoid activities that are poor on any criteria.

Content/Method

The activity supports learning objectives that are developmentally appropriate and consistent with the curriculum. The activity

- relates to the child's direct experiences at home, at school, and in the community
- is integrated into the curriculum through connections to other hands-on activities that support the same learning objectives
- is interesting and challenging to students at a wide range of ability and skill levels, including students with special needs
- is open-ended, allowing children to learn through their own playful investigation
- supports language development either directly, through interactive use by children in groups, or through extensions of the activity
- is appropriate to children with varied learning styles
- can involve two or more children working cooperatively
- positively addresses or is sensitive to issues of multiculturalism
- positively addresses or is sensitive to issues of linguistic diversity
- positively addresses or is sensitive to issues of gender equity
- positively addresses or is sensitive to issues of individual differences
- has nonviolent content, in the case of computer games and simulations

Technology Design Issues

- The child can learn to physically operate the technology independently.
- The technology is safe for the age level intended.
- The technology is chosen and set up to minimize the risk of breakage.
- The technology can be adapted, if necessary, for students with special needs.

Computer Software Design Issues

- The menu is uncluttered and uses picture clues with words for menu choices.
- The child can navigate through the software easily, go back to the main menu, or exit the software at any time.
- The program provides help. The child can escape or get help at any time.
- The design is attractive to children; it may include colorful graphics, sound, or animation.
- The program can be used in more than one language.
- The program can be used by students with special needs.
- Children can save and print their work so that it can be shared with family members who don't have e-mail access at home.

Source: Copyright 1997. Revised 2013 by Leni von Blanckensee (personal communication, April 23, 2013).

child's written words with images, sound, and sometimes animation are readily available. In the context of their play, children use these programs to create and illustrate stories; make books, greeting cards, and gifts of their creative work; or, in the same way as "real" drawings or paintings, to express their artistic inclinations. Children should be encouraged to create original artwork rather than rely on clip art or electronic coloring books. As educators, we focus our attention on the processes of children's play, not their products, but it is also important to think about both process and product from the child's view.

Children's Use of Simulations and Games in Kindergarten through Second Grade Good computer simulations and games are attractive to children because they offer opportunities to develop problem-solving strategies and creative thinking. In some programs and apps, children enter as characters into the play and control characters' actions on the screen. Others allow children to manipulate objects in interesting ways. One program, for example, allows children to create buildings and towns and then change their perspective gradually, as if they were able to fly overhead like a bird. Young children enjoy discussing their problem solving and their pretend landscapes. Teachers and researchers believe that peer-to-peer collaborations can enhance the cognitive and social value of electronic games (Kafai, 2006; Scarlett, Naudeau, Salonius-Pasternak, & Ponte, 2005; Singer & Singer, 2005; Silvern, 2006).

Children's Use of Media Technology as Tools to Promote Literacy For many years, some teachers have reported that when first- and second-grade students use computers, their work may be more complex and imaginative. One technology-based tool for literacy is text-to-speech. Programs have been around for years, but current ones have been greatly improved.

When using computers to write, some children seem more free to compose story lines and construct concepts about letter–sound relationships in invented spelling. The formation of letters no longer claims the lion's share of their attention.

E-mail can be a wonderful communication tool for primary-grade children. The speed of sending and receiving e-mail makes it especially exciting for children who have a hard time waiting for a response by "snail mail." Teachers often find that children write more, write in greater detail, and correct their writing more when they use computers to write for a real audience, as in using e-mail.

> In Nancy's first-grade class, students have same-age e-mail buddies at another school, adult e-mail buddies through a corporate partnership, and fifth-grade buddies at their own school. The children have partners in their class and, together, they write to their e-mail buddies. Nancy finds that the children not only benefit by helping each other, but also enjoy the social aspect of composing written language together.
>
> When the computer sounds to signify that a new e-mail message has arrived, a child rushes to the computer and announces that Lily and Brian have

e-mail. They head for the computer and find a message from their adult e-mail buddy. The children love getting mail and want to write back right away. In response to their question, their buddy has written about her pets and asks, "Do you have any pets?"

Twenty minutes later, Brian and Lily send off the following message:

1. I have a gol fis. My gol fis is bubbles.
2. I have a dog. My dog is very ol.
3. Do you like gol fis?
4. Do you like hres?
5. Do you like cows?
6. Do you have a cow?

Nancy finds that the students write differently to their different buddies. They write quickly and informally to their same-age buddies. They try hard to correct mistakes when they write to their adult buddies. Because their fifth-grade buddies come to class to read to them, they usually write with a purpose, asking for a particular book or commenting on a book that has been read. Although participating in e-mail is always a matter of choice, most children rush to answer their messages and wait with expectation for a response. ✍

Teachers exchange stories about how their classes are using e-mail to communicate with students and families around the country and around the globe. Salmon and Akaran (2006) write of their "cross-cultural e-mail connections" (p. 36) between Salmon's kindergarten students in urban New Jersey and Akaran's primary-grade students in Kotlik, Alaska, where her students live far from a large city and Native American families maintain a more traditional way of life.

MEDIA TECHNOLOGY, STANDARDS, AND PLAY

In the Night Sky project vignette that begins this chapter, the three kindergarten teachers embarked on a month-long project on space travel using sources on the Internet to view images of planets, stars, and space journeys. The ways that the media technology fits into the culture of the classroom and children's play within that culture become the important issues to consider.

In 2007, national educational technology standards for K–2 were adopted by the International Society for Technology in Education (see www.iste.org/standards). The society notes that early childhood educators can implement them in ways consistent with NAEYC guidelines for developmentally appropriate practice. The six standards are shown in Table 13.3. For each, a performance indicator relevant for play is illustrated with an example from the chapter.

Table 13.3	National Education Technology Standards for Students
Standard with Example of Performance Indicator	**Examples from the Chapter**
1. Creativity and Innovation	
Create original works as a means of personal or group expression.	Joshua dictates a story using a scanned image of the drawing he made using the computer.
2. Communicate and Collaborate	
Communicate information and ideas effectively to multiple audiences using a variety of media and formats.	Kindergarten students from Salmon's school in urban New Jersey and primary-grade students from Akaran's school in rural Alaska use e-mail to learn about each other's lives.
3. Research and Information Fluency	
Locate, organize, analyze, evaluate, synthesize, and ethically use information from a variety of sources and media.	Children in Halewood's class experiment with pulleys and levers. They use digital photos in their journals to document their findings.
4. Critical Thinking, Problem Solving, and Decision Making	
Identify and define authentic problems and significant questions for investigation.	As part of their Night Sky project, kindergartners use the Internet to find accurate information to inform their drawings and paintings.
5. Digital Citizenship	
Exhibit a positive attitude toward using technology that supports collaboration, learning, and production.	First graders in Nancy's class work together and use e-mail to communicate with children and adults.
6. Technology Operations and Concepts	
Understand and use technology systems.	With adult assistance, Nina uses text-to-speech tools. She types her name and is delighted to hear, "Nina."

Source: Based on ISTE. (2007). National Educational Technology Standards for K–2 adopted by the International Society for Technology in Education. Retrieved from www.iste.org/standards.

SUMMARY

Throughout the world, young children have always employed the materials around them as tools to enrich their sensorimotor play, constructive play, dramatic play, and games. As they prepare the environment and interact with children, early childhood educators face constant decisions about selecting toys and technology as tools for play.

- ■ **Principles for considering toys and media technology as tools for play.** One guiding principle for early childhood programs is to consider whether children use the objects, materials, or media technology as tools for rich and complex play. A second principle is to consider how various social contexts in which children use toys and media technology shape children's play in early childhood settings.

- **Types of toys.** Educators classify toys in many ways. Common classifications include sensorimotor toys, representational toys, toy miniatures, construction toys, manipulative toys, fine motor toys, and gross motor toys.

- **Toy use and children's development.** Educators provide toys that are flexible so children can use them for their own imaginative purposes. They also select toys that meet specific needs at particular developmental stages and for children with special needs. Teachers need to be observant and sensitive to provide a good match between the structure of the specific toy or game and the child's developing symbolic abilities.

- **Children under siege: Toys and the marketplace.** Much of what is marketed to children is not only developmentally inappropriate but also exploits the vulnerabilities of childhood, such as the desire to be more grown up, have more power, and have friends. Many toys are marketed in gender-stereotyped ways that restrict gender equity. Teachers discuss the possible influences of "boy toys" associated with more violent play and "girl toys" that lead to behaviors linked to early sexualization.

- **Media technology in the lives of children.** The term *media technology* refers to electronic technology used for viewing or listening. In general, media technology refers to screen technologies such as computers, tablets, and smartphones. Children's use of media technology has increased dramatically. There is little research that examines the results of use of technology in early childhood settings. In home settings, higher use among school-age children is associated with decreased physical activity, higher rates of obesity, and lower measures of school performance.

- **Recommendations for the use of media technology in a play-centered curriculum.** The following recommendations are based on the importance of play in development and the ethical injunction that educators "do no harm." Early childhood programs serving children from birth through age 5 should be screen-free or place strict limits on children's use of media technology: (a) Programs serving children birth through age 2 should be screen-free, and (b) programs serving preschool and kindergarten children should be screen-free or have limits placed on screen time. Children with special needs should have access to adaptive technology and appropriate support to use these technologies. All programs should develop a written program policy for parents, staff, and administrators that includes a rationale and descriptive guidelines for the use of media technology.

- **Media technology: Play-generated curriculum and curriculum-generated play.** In early child-care and education programs, educators are intentional in their selection of programs and apps as tools for play and learning. They use photos in numerous ways to document children's play to extend children's understandings and to communicate with parents about children's development. In kindergarten and the primary grades, children's knowledge and use of various media technology increases gradually. Throughout the early childhood years, teachers evaluate toys and media technology as tools that enrich play and lead to teacher-planned activities and, conversely, teacher-planned curriculum activities that generate play.

■ **Media Technology, Standards, and Play.** The ways that media technology fits into the culture of the classroom and children's play within that culture have become important issues to consider. In 2007, National Educational Technology Standards for K–2 were adopted by the International Society for Technology in Education. The society notes that early childhood educators can implement them in ways consistent with NAEYC guidelines for developmentally appropriate practice. The six standards for early childhood education and their relevancy for play are illustrated with examples from chapter vignettes.

Teachers can select classic and recent toys and media technology in developmentally appropriate ways as tools that support children's cognitive and social development. In play, children use tools to find ways to express themselves and communicate with others.

APPLYING YOUR KNOWLEDGE

1. Discuss principles for considering toys and media technology as tools for play.
   a. Bring in an object found in nature and explain how children might use it as a tool of the imagination.
   b. Bring in a "classic" unstructured children's toy and discuss how, as an adult, you might use it as a tool for play.

2. Discuss the categories of toys that educators distinguish among and describe an example of each.
   a. Compare and contrast two categories of toys.
   b. Observe an early childhood setting and discuss your observations of children's play with different categories of toys.

3. Explain how children's use of toys relates to their development and individual differences.
   a. Working individually or in a small group, play with a selection of toys and discuss how each toy might be used for different developmental levels or adapted for children with physical or mental disabilities.
   b. Visit a toy store or a toy aisle and describe toys you see that support development. Which ones have the highest "play-ability" over time? Explain.

    c. Develop a game or play experience designed for a specific stage of play development. If possible, field test with children and evaluate it.

4. Discuss and provide examples of how some toys can limit children's development and undermine equity.
    a. Discuss several ways in which teachers can respond to problems of inequity in their classrooms.
    b. Research the history of two popular toys that have become cultural icons, such as Barbie, G.I. Joe, and Disney characters. Have they changed over time? Describe any evidence you see of stereotypes.
    c. Reexamine the toy store or toy aisle (in question 3b above) and evaluate several toys in terms of gender, racial, and cultural stereotyping. What messages does the packaging convey about which children play with the toy and how they are supposed to play with it? Describe any evidence you found that toys for girls and boys were placed in different sections.

5. Define the term *media technology* and summarize key research findings regarding the use of media technology in young children's lives.
    a. Present an oral or written summary of a research article on young children's use of screen technology (e.g., *Zero to eight: Children's Media Use in America*).

6. Summarize the recommendations for use of media technology in the play-centered curriculum.
    a. Explain the rationale for the recommendations made by the NAYEC and public health associations.

7. Describe an example of how educators can use media technology intentionally so that children's play leads to teacher-planned curriculum.
    a. Describe an example of how teacher-planned curriculum can promote playful activities.
    b. Using the rating scale in Table 13.2, evaluate a program or app of your choice.

8. Explain how play in early childhood programs addresses standards for technology.
    a. Select one standard for technology usage, and based on your own observation in early childhood programs show how play can address this standard.

CHAPTER 14

Conclusion: Integrating Play, Development, and Practice

LEARNING OUTCOMES

▪ Discuss the relationship between constructivist theory and child development in a number of domains. Relate this discussion to the general framework of the coordination of means-ends relationships.

▪ Describe the developmental theories of Piaget and Vygotsky and explain how these theorists complement one another as well as relate to children's play.

▪ Discuss the central ideas of Piaget's theory of intelligence and its development.

▪ Discuss the role of social experience in the construction of reality.

▪ Discuss and define four areas of human development (intelligence, personality, competencies, and social consciousness or sense of self) and discuss how they are related to the coordination of means-ends relationships.

▪ Characterize the intersection between children's autonomy and the expectations of society. Include developmentally appropriate practice and standards in your discussion.

▪ Describe several ways that early childhood educators can advocate for play and give an example of a useful resource for each.

Two boys and a girl are walking up a hill. Four-year-old Charlie shudders and throws his arms up, making explosive sounds interrupted with calls for help. "I need your help; the bad guys are surrounding me."

Jerry, wearing a baseball cap, shouts acknowledgment and comes to the rescue. "It's OK, they're gone. Let's go." They link arms and descend.

Sheila follows. "I have to go to the bathroom."

The two boys look around. "The bathroom's over there," one says and points to a concrete building buried in the shadow of trees.

"Come with me." Her request is ignored, and the boys commence another episode. "I'll be Zelda," she says as she joins the play, but her body reminds her of other needs, and she descends toward the picnic tables. She later returns, holding her father's hand. They head toward the bathroom. Having addressed her own and her parent's concern for safety in unfamiliar places, she returns and reenters the play with an assertion of her competence: "I was right. That is the bathroom."

A few hours later, the children chase Jerry's father across the field. He turns and gently tosses his son to the ground. The chase continues, out past the concrete bathrooms, down to the beach, back up the hill. The two boys temporarily drop behind and plan their attack. "Listen, all we have to do is . . ."

As the chase ends, they huddle and plot the afternoon's play. Sheila is excluded. Some distance away she sits down on the hillside, pulling at weeds. Shortly afterward, she and Jerry begin walking together. She has a long face. "You weren't nice to me," she says.

> Charlie comes toward them, yelling, "Jerry, wait up! Wait up! There isn't a bee in it. I got it out (of the Coke can)." Sheila and Jerry wait for Charlie to catch up. The three old friends are again one. ᛳ

Look at all that is occurring in this simple vignette. These 4-year-olds are collaborating on common themes that are agreed to and adhered to. They are imitating and reproducing elements of their culture. They are using language to guide their play and to provide its content. They display practical knowledge, as in recognizing the bathroom, as well as understanding when parental protection is needed. Sheila is able to express her feelings of exclusion and to reinstate herself in the triad after her temporary absence. Finally, Charlie figured out how to get a bee out of a Coke can.

We see in play the expression of **intelligence**, the management of needs and emotions, the elaboration of common themes and efforts, and the reproduction of culture. We see the give-and-take of cooperation. The evolution of social consciousness and of sexual identity is also evident. The world of childhood and the world of play are inseparable. Play is evident from infancy through adulthood and unquestionably occupies a central role in human development. Our purpose is to put play at the center of classroom curriculum. In this concluding chapter, we revisit in somewhat broader terms the theoretical basis for our faith in the value of play as a focal point in curriculum planning and classroom management.

CONSTRUCTIVISM AND DEVELOPMENT

The term *constructivism* is used to express the belief that development is not simply maturation or biological unfolding, nor is it the result of the environment or experience imprinting itself on the developing mind through, for example, reinforcement. The term is derived from the word *construct* and is meant to suggest that the child plays an active role in constructing what is developed. Constructivism is a theme in education that resulted largely from an interpretation of Jean Piaget's work on child development.

What Is Developed?

Each of the main theorists who have written about child development could tell us something different about what is going on in the opening vignette. Jean Piaget could help us understand the representational methods and coordination of concepts used in the play. George Herbert Mead could help us understand the way in which this play affects the developing **sense of self** in these three children. Lev Vygotsky could show us how the collective activity of the children is creating a context for their own understanding. This context is a microculture developing among the children with its own history that intersects with the broader culture. Sigmund Freud could help us understand how the play addresses deeper emotional themes associated with the control of instinctive forces. Erik Erikson would show us the development of trust and autonomy represented in the play. For example, notice how Sheila asks the boys to escort her to the bathroom and how she comfortably tells Jerry he wasn't nice to her. John Dewey might point out the competence and industry represented here.

Even in the simplest scenes of spontaneous and unguided play, development is occurring in all areas of human growth. We identify these areas as intelligence, personality, competence, and social consciousness/sense of self. We believe that each is developed by the child through spontaneous and self-directed activity within social, cultural, and historical contexts. This is the meaning of the constructivist view of development. Development does not result from the unfolding of genetically predetermined potentials, nor as the direct result of social experience in the form of education or selective reinforcement. Intelligence, **personality**, competence, and sense of self are constructed by the child through self-regulated activity embedded in social, historical, and cultural contexts. We maintain that this view is consistent with the theorists just mentioned and believe that without play, no development would occur.

Our position can be summarized with five points:

1. Play is the primary context in which intelligence, personality, competencies, and social consciousness are developed and integrated.
2. These four domains are inseparable from social experience within cultural and historical contexts.
3. Self-directed activity is necessary for development in these domains and is aligned closely with play.

Props support symbolic play.

4. These four domains are functionally interdependent and are each involved in all forms of play.

5. Each domain is constructed through means-ends coordinations.

Means-Ends Coordinations and Development

Another way to view constructivism is to think about the ways in which the child constructs the means of achieving desired goals. This is called **means-ends coordinations** and it concerns, for example, how a reorganization of old means can be used to achieve new ends or, conversely, how new means can be constructed to reach old ends. This is similar to evolutionary biology, where old structures evolve to serve new functions and new structures evolve to serve old functions; that is, old means change to serve new ends, and old ends are met through new means. For example, early fish gills evolved to oxygenate fish blood. Eventually, lungs evolved to oxygenate the blood of land animals. The gill bone of early fish evolved into a middle ear bone in mammals, making modern hearing possible. Old means serve new ends, and new means serve old ends.

Intelligence is the area of development most closely associated with Piaget's means-ends analysis. The fact that intelligence develops through the dynamics of means-ends coordinations establishes the common tie between intelligence and constructivism. In Piaget's view, intelligence is not a measurable trait like IQ, but rather a process of adaptive understanding. Piaget perceived the development of reason to be an evolution in the child's adaptation to the environment that subsequently leads to understanding. This evolution occurs because early understandings ultimately are challenged by the environment. When new experiences are inconsistent or incompatible with earlier ways of understanding, change ultimately results. For example, basing an understanding of quantity on how things look will yield less consistent interpretations of the world than understanding that quantity is a composition of units. Knowing that rearranging objects does not change their cardinal number is universally understood by all children in all cultures, but takes most of early childhood to evolve. This evolution is a result of construction rather than learning, genetic unfolding, or social imitation and instruction.

Personality also entails means-ends relations and is constructed. Personality is each person's unique means of maintaining acceptable emotional states while at the same time satisfying goals. It's how we remain emotionally stable while carrying out daily goal-directed activity. In a sense, personality is the constructed means by which individuals develop emotional self-regulation. Everyday acts—such as playing with friends, doing what others expect of you, going to school, solving disputes, or negotiating turns on a swing—entail emotions. The way these emotions are managed is directed by personality.

Even at birth, some children are calm, some are more active, some accept changes in routines, and some do not. Although such temperaments occur early and sometimes remain into adulthood, the issue of personality is more complex and tied in direct and subtle ways to a child's experiences and to the deep emotional substrata that underlie all human activity. Personality, like intelligence, is constructed and not given at birth.

Competencies are the things that we can accomplish reliably—the abilities that allow us to function in the world. Competencies are largely fashioned through intelligence but cannot be separated from other areas of development. Like intelligence and personality, competencies also are tied to means-ends relationships because they are either the means of reaching goals or the goals themselves. A competency can be instrumental in achieving a goal, such as knowing how to play effectively with others, or a competency can be a goal itself, as when one tries to fashion the means of entering into play with others. Competencies always involve emotions because we always have feelings about what we do. Emotions also entail competencies in the sense of being able to relate our feelings to the feelings of others as well as in the competencies that allow us to regulate and control emotions.

Social consciousness refers to the child's evolving sense of self and how the self is related to the other "selves" it comes in contact with. Social consciousness is inseparable from intelligence, personality, and competency and, like these other areas, is constructed through the coordination of means-ends relations. Here, however, the means-ends coordinations are related to social causality, or how people affect one another.

The sense of self is fashioned through an understanding of two types of causality. One is linked to an objective understanding of ourselves, and the other is linked to understanding how we affect others and how social conditions, in turn, affect us. For example, a stable understanding of ourselves must take into account how we affect others and how others affect us. We are affected by the actions and perceptions of others, and we, in turn, create the same conditions for others. Understanding this requires a reflection on the means-ends relationships that occur in social causality; that is, how am I affecting others, and how do others affect me?

CONSTRUCTIVISM AND SOCIAL–CULTURAL THEORIES OF DEVELOPMENT

Two major developmental psychologists, Jean Piaget and Lev Vygotsky, were contemporaries and constructivists. However, they had differing views on childhood development. It's important that we understand some of the issues that divide and unite these important thinkers.

Jean Piaget (1896–1980)

People have posed the question of what it means to be human since the beginning of reflective thought. Historically, this question has been left to theology and philosophy, but in the 20th century it increasingly has become the province of developmental psychology. Jean Piaget, the Swiss biologist, is probably the single most recognized person in developmental psychology. His work spans a large part of the 20th century and transformed our understanding of human rationality and mental development.

Piaget, born in 1896, was a biologist interested in evolution. He made the startling discovery that some of the most basic of our understandings are not obtained or learned through cultural transmission or even by direct physical experience. The construction of knowledge, according to Piaget, occurs as a series of predictable and **universal stages** unfolding as a function of a slowly elaborated form of internal consistency in the means-ends coordination of actions that relate, first, to sensorimotor patterns of action and later to **internal mental representations** of actions. His theory assumes that this sequence of stages is universal, occurring in a similar way for all humans who are healthy and active.

Piaget's famous **conservation experiments** provide examples of predictable stages of understanding. The child first conserves number, understanding that rearranging a set of objects does not change the quantity of the set. This typically occurs toward the end of early childhood. It is years later before the child understands that changing the shape of something does not change its weight (i.e., the conservation of weight). It is later still that the child can understand conservation of volume, understanding that changing the shape of a substance does not change its volume.

Development was viewed by Piaget as changes in patterns of action within the individual, which result in increased **internal mental consistency**. This concept of development gives a completely new twist to the nature–nurture controversy. Piaget believed that developing children are not simply maturing according to a genetic program (nature) or the product of environmental influences (nurture), but rather are active constructors whose constructions evolve in a predictable pattern of stages. For Piaget, the child's development follows from the laws of activity and means-ends coordinations in the same way that thermodynamics or the movements of objects follow laws. The specific course of development is viewed as common to all people because the laws of activity and means-ends coordinations are common to all people, not because people share the same experiences or the same genetic makeup.

Teachers might find it difficult to derive practical curriculum from Piaget's theory because of his focus on autonomy and self-directed activity and because his theory says little about how social interactions affect development. In fact, Piaget did not address in depth the problems of education and curriculum. Despite this, educational theory throughout the world has been influenced by Piaget.

Lev Vygotsky (1896–1934)

The theories of Vygotsky, however, prompt us to think about what Piaget has left out of his formulations, and many educators today look to him for direction on how to structure the social elements of the classroom to achieve curriculum goals (Bodrova & Leong, 2007).

Lev Vygotsky was born in Russia in 1896, the same year Piaget was born in Switzerland. Both were part of the new modernism that was influencing thought throughout Europe at the time. Darwin's theory of evolution, Freud's theory of the unconscious, Einstein's theory of relativity, and Marx's theory of economics and social institutions were all part of the modernism of the late 19th and early 20th centuries. It was a time of great intellectual and social change and, in some instances, a time of revolutionary change.

Vygotsky was largely influenced by the social theory of his time and by the changes accompanying the Russian revolution. He was interested in how social interactions affect individuals, and how individuals and society are influenced by history and culture. Vygotsky greatly influenced Russian psychology and argued that conceptual activity cannot be separated from social experience. Further, this experience unfolds within a cultural–historical context. This was an extension of his belief that the regulation of conscious activity can take place only within a social context (Davydov, 1995).

Vygotsky believed that all activity happens in a social context and begins as social experience that is later internalized. Because Vygotsky died in 1934, before Piaget published his most significant works, we do not know how the two would have agreed or disagreed on the issue of individual development and social experience.

Connecting Piaget's and Vygotsky's Theories

Those who attempt to understand the relationship between development and education will benefit from understanding how Piaget's and Vygotsky's theories complement one another (Beck, 2013). Many assume that Piaget is an individualist, believing that development occurs independently of social experience, and that Vygotsky is an environmentalist, believing that learning occurs as a function of the social–cultural–historic environment. In fact, both Vygotsky and Piaget are constructivists, believing that learning is neither a direct function of social activity nor individual activity, but rather an interaction between both forces. For example, Piaget believed that true conceptual activity (by which he meant rational thought) cannot proceed without the use of a referential system that is tied to and dependent on social agreement. **Rationality** is impossible without language, words, and mathematical symbols embedded in social contexts, where people must coordinate their points of view with those of others and come to agreements and disagreements. Rationality is impossible when the world is viewed only from one's own perspective, because a single perspective cannot take into account all points of view (Piaget, 1954, 1962, 1995; Vygotsky, 1978).

Understanding this position is critical to understanding Piaget's work. He was concerned primarily with how humans establish logically necessary and objectively verifiable knowledge. **Objective knowledge** concerns our ability to think logically about spatial relationships; time; relationships among time, motion, and distance; geometric relationships; quantitative relationships such as number, volume, length, and weight; laws of causality; and chance. His theory holds that the attainment of objective knowledge is the result of a gradual "de-centering" process. This process involves a progressive development from a state in which the child's ability to represent is limited to what is immediately available or "presented" to the senses, to a later period in which "presentation" is still tied to the child's own experiences but less so than before. Eventually, after early childhood, the young adult can give a representation that is freed entirely from specific sensation and experience and is socially coordinated with others through the use of arbitrary signs such as words (Piaget, 1962).

A CLOSER LOOK AT PIAGET AND CONSTRUCTIVIST THEORY

Schemes: Assimilation, Accommodation, and Play

The concept of an **action scheme** is important to Piaget's theory. A scheme is a pattern for action that can be repeated, like a program in a computer. All of what a child knows about the world is tied to what the child can do in the world—to their action schemes. The reflexes of the newborn are the first schemes. Blinking, grasping, sucking, turning the head, moving the tongue, and opening and closing the mouth are examples. By 3 years of age, more elaborate schemes, such as chasing a ball or putting on a shirt, have evolved from a coordination of simpler schemes. This elaboration and **coordination of schemes** continues on a lawful course throughout development and yields at each stage the possibility of more complex and adaptive activity (Piaget, 1963).

The universal ways that children interpret experience are evidence that the construction of reality reflects developmental laws. For example, all children at some point overgeneralize language rules for marking time and number ("I played and I goed to the store" or "I put the shoes on my foots"). As another example, all children at some point in their development reason that a part is larger than the whole—that, for example, the vase contains more roses than flowers, even though only some of the flowers are roses. All children at some point believe that a quantity changes even if only its appearance has changed. They believe that pouring a liquid into a different-shaped container will change its amount, or that rearranging a pile of blocks will change the number of blocks. These ways of interpreting events are constructed and not copied from experience.

Human development is driven by adaptation to the environment and consists of the twin processes of assimilation and accommodation. *Assimilation* is an incorporation of the environment into the child's own patterns of action or schemes. In a sense, the child uses already-developed competencies to understand new events. *Accommodation* takes place when schemes or competencies are inadequate and create contradictory results. Accommodation is a change in schemes as they are modified to fit new circumstances and occurs as a result of interactions with the environment. For example, an amount can be changed by adding or subtracting substance. At some point in children's development, they sense the contradiction between this understanding and the belief that an amount can change even when no additions or subtractions have been made. This feeling of contradiction will contribute to the development of an understanding of conservation of quantities.

Assimilation distorts and changes things because it modifies the world according to the child's schemes. Accommodation, on the other hand, is a process of bending to the pressure of reality. Piaget identified play with assimilation. This reflects the link between assimilation and the distorting quality of play, where pretense and fantasy make the world what the child wishes it to be. When the child turns the living room furniture into a spaceship, the nature of the furniture has been distorted in the child's mind and turned, for the moment, into components of the rocket ship (Piaget, 1962).

Piaget identified accommodation with imitation because in reproducing reality (imitating), the child's action schemas are accommodated to reality. When a child imitates the sounds of a horse while pretending to be a horse, the child is accommodating to the sounds made by horses.

Although Piaget associated pure assimilation with play, assimilation and accommodation cannot be separated. Children's play develops from a coordination between assimilative and accommodative activity. As children develop, so does their play. Play themes become more elaborate, symbols become more evolved, and social coordinations become more complex and cooperative.

Stages of Development and Play

Because play is inseparable from all facets of development, play itself must develop. The first 2 years of life are called the sensorimotor period because during this phase, the child's understanding of the world is tied to physical behaviors and sensory experiences. Play consists of physical actions that are combined and repeated for the simple pleasure of mastering new combinations. During this period, the child gradually develops the ability to mentally represent the world. This development entails six distinct stages, beginning with birth and the exercise of sensorimotor reflexes and ending with the beginning of representational functions, such as imitation, pretense, and language, which emerge at around 2 years of age.

Sensorimotor play lacks the symbolic or pretend quality of later play because pretense requires representation, which is achieved only at the end of this period. During the early stages of this development, infants cannot construct the symbolism and imagery that are needed to support pretend activity, like picking up a piece of grass and pretending to eat it.

The second major developmental period, the preoperational period, begins with the onset of representation or the ability to form images of objects or events that are not immediately available to the senses. The emergence of representational thought is the result of an advance in the coordination of assimilation and accommodation. Assimilation and play are now capable of giving meaning to **symbols** produced by accommodation and imitation. The ability to create symbols has a profound effect on children's play in terms of its themes, the symbols used to support the play, and the means of communicating the purpose and manner of the play. The play of this period does not replace sensorimotor play, but rather joins sensorimotor play to create a more diverse palette of possible action (Piaget, 1962).

During the preoperational period, children form early concepts that are limited in stability. Comprehension of everything, from the concrete and familiar (e.g., mommies and daddies, brother and sister) to the abstract (e.g., number, time, movement, measurement), is unstable and in constant risk of contradiction because young children reason from particular to particular rather than understanding how particular cases relate to the whole set of possible cases. For example, at one moment mommies might be people who help you, even though not all who help you are mommies and not all mommies help. At another moment, a mommy might be anyone with a baby, even if the relationship is not maternal (Piaget, 1966).

Piaget elaborated on the fact that during the preconceptual stage, play is the primary and most suitable way for children to express themselves as well as modulate or understand their emotions. The medium of play allows a direct expression of emotions and allows the child to defuse and explore unpleasant emotional experiences, even to the point of changing reality to his or her liking (Piaget, 1962).

A third period, the concrete-operational period, begins at about the age of 6 or 7 and is characterized by the emergence of consistent concepts. The emergence of true conceptual reasoning is brought about by an increasingly reversible coordination between assimilation and accommodation. This, in turn, is facilitated by social coordinations made possible through language and other representational systems that allow for agreement and disagreement with others. These integrations allow the child to de-center from direct sensory data, such as imagery, perception, emotion, and practical behaviors. This de-centering allows the **formation of concepts** that go beyond individual experience and idiosyncratic symbols (Piaget, 1962, 1995).

Play is still necessary to development, but because of the achievements during this period the play of 6- and 7-year-olds is directed increasingly toward social coordinations and successful reproductions of reality. This might be seen in formal games with rules or an interest in constructing models.

Because of the new mental power provided by conceptual reasoning, the 7- to 8-year-old child is more easily able to express, regulate, and understand emotions through the use of words and concepts rather than pure play. However, play, pretense, and fantasy remain critical components of emotional self-regulation.

A fourth major period, the formal-operational period, begins with the elaboration of a **hypothetical possible**, or theoretically possible interpretations, and the elaboration of scientific or logical means of deciding between competing hypothetical propositions. All the earlier forms of play remain a part of the young adolescent's life, but during the formal operational period play also incorporates the complex refinements that characterize work. Youth group activities, with real tasks of working with others, and making things "that really work" are examples of play-related activity at this stage. Here emotions can become the focus of reflective activity with a gradual expanding of insight into the nature of human experience.

The Construction of Reality

The construction of reality entails gradual progress in the reliable and logical interpretation of experiences and their emotional content. This allows accurate predictions.

Emotions, intellect, and social life are drawn together in play.

For example, we know that pouring a liquid from one container into another does not change its amount. We know, without carrying out the activity, that if we were to pour the liquid back into the original container it would occupy the same amount of space.

As noted earlier, Piaget was interested in how we construct an objective or rational understanding of time (the temporal succession of events), objects (the differentiation of sensation into discrete entities), space (the relative movements and positions of objects), and causality (the attribution of necessary links between events). In each of these areas, human intelligence eventually fashions an objective understanding. Moreover, these understandings successively deepen from those of the infant to those of the most advanced scientific theorists. Modern science is, after all, a continuing quest to understand the nature of objects, time, space, and causality. This quest will never be finished, because each new understanding sets the conditions for further questions.

By 2 years of age, most children have constructed a limited yet reliable understanding that objects are permanent entities, organized in space and time, and linked in causal relationships. Even this seemingly simple understanding is constructed gradually. Imagine a child of 14 months sitting on the floor. His mother, whom he's been watching, approaches on his right and passes behind him. The infant turns to his left, anticipating seeing his mother reappear. This behavior suggests that objects, time, and space are becoming organized into a whole where objects continue to exist even though they appear and disappear over time; the child realizes that they exist in a space where, for example, the same target can be reached by different routes. He anticipated his mother's trajectory in space and intersected that point not by visually following her, but by taking an alternative route.

This simple understanding takes many months to develop and is a precursor to a more complex mental organization characterized by logical–mathematical coordinations. Finding objects hidden within or under other objects, finding one's way around the house, knowing that throwing the ball over the fence will be an obstacle to the dog with whom he's playing fetch, and being able to reach the same place by different routes all speak to a spatial understanding in which placements (position in space) are coordinated with displacements (changes in position). The ability to coordinate positions with changes in position is an early form of logical–mathematical thought. It makes possible the ability to problem solve in near space, which we observe in children toward the end of the sensorimotor period. Understanding that objects continue to exist as they appear and disappear marks the first conservations where, in the context of changing sensations, something remains unchanged. It is the reversible coordinations of sensorimotor actions that make the first constructions of space, time, causality, and object permanence possible (Piaget, 1954). This cognitive achievement has effects on the whole child and can be seen, for example, in the onset of separation anxiety, which coincides with the emergence of object permanence.

During the early school years, we see advances in the child's understanding of reality. Children begin to understand that reality can be ordered in a variety of ways; for example, things can be ordered in a series from least to most. This may be reflected in the understanding of time and numbers (e.g., history, age, the calendar). **Coordination of part–whole relations** is beginning, where the child understands that wholes are composed of parts, that a whole can be broken into parts, and that parts can be reassembled into wholes. This can be seen in the child's understanding of words ("There are more children in the classroom than there are boys, because some of the classmates are girls") and beginning arithmetic ("Seven is bigger than 4 because if you take 4 from 7, you have 3 left over").

As understanding becomes logically organized, we refer to the child's thinking as operational, meaning that the internal mental coordinations carried out by the child are organized in a system of **reversible operations** that allow concepts to remain stable and, further, to obtain the status of objective reasoning. An example of operations is seen in the reversible coordination of part–whole relations and in order relations. For example, two parts can be combined to yield a third ($A + B = C$), and a whole (C) can be divided into its parts (A and B).

SOCIAL EXPERIENCE AND THE CONSTRUCTION OF REALITY

As discussed earlier, Piaget endeavored to show that the construction of reality, expressed in what can be called objective knowledge, is constructed through the internal regulations of the child. Because the laws of these internal regulations are assumed to be universal, a communality of knowledge exists among all people. However, Vygotsky believed that all conceptual knowledge is encountered first in social interactions. If development is dependent on social experience, one might expect people from different cultures and different social experiences to develop differently. Piaget and Vygotsky complement one another by showing how inter- and intraindividual forces shape development.

Piaget believed that two developmental themes exist, each consisting of coordinations that eventually lead to stable concepts. One is the internal regulations of the child, and the other is cooperation with others. Social coordinations are essentially the conditions that allow us to agree or disagree with another person or to cooperate or compete with others. Piaget asserted that these two processes are inseparable and are simply different sides of assimilation and accommodation. Further, he believed that both aspects of development follow a lawful course. Social actions, like mental actions, tend to become organized in logical–operational systems. Social experience provides the possibility of differing points of view—agreeing and disagreeing, understanding and not understanding. Each of these affects the accommodations of our thinking. The corresponding and at times conflicting intelligence of others participates in the development of our own intelligence (Piaget, 1995).

The child's evolving ability to think rationally is tied to social life. The child's capacity for reason eventually must detach from the child's own perspective and incorporate the perspective of others. This process of agreeing and disagreeing with others depends on a means of representing reality that is free of the individual means of representation (practical knowledge, images, sensations, perceptions, emotions, dreams, and unconscious symbols). It depends on a socially agreed-on system of representation such as that provided by language (Piaget, 1962).

A child might have developed certain mental operations, but it does not follow that this same child is necessarily competent in the particular cultural forms of knowledge that require these operations. For example, most 8-year-olds throughout the world have developed the operations necessary for understanding simple addition. However, only some of these children know how to respond to the image $4 + 9 =$ ____. For individuals' intelligence to be applied or expressed in particular cultural forms, individuals must have experience in those forms and express their understanding as a competency in those forms. This is the job of schooling and other informal mechanisms of social transmission. The untutored mind can develop the intelligence to understand something, but without an encounter with the cultural expression of that understanding, the child will not be able to demonstrate or express the understanding in the language of the culture.

What we learn cannot be separated from social experience. Experience occurs only within the embrace of a particular historical–cultural moment; within the envelope of particular values and patterns for work and play; and with the use of particular, largely cultural, representational means. So although intelligence might proceed by a lawful coordination of schemes, what are coordinated are actions and representations, and these are inseparable from social experience. Thus, people in differing cultural and historical settings might develop through the same basic **developmental stages** and yet have different ways of expressing their intelligence in daily life. This is because the demands of daily life differ across cultures, societies, and periods in history. Furthermore, much of human knowledge is not subjected easily to the rigors of logically governed discourse and is, therefore, subject to complex disagreements. Science, for example, is an attempt to bring common interests into a discourse setting governed by laws of logic and mathematical reasoning, and even as such science proceeds through a complex process of argument, disagreement, critique, review, and revision.

PLAY AND DEVELOPMENT

In the following sections, we summarize the relationship between play and the four domains of development we've been exploring: intelligence, personality, competencies, and social consciousness.

Play and the Development of Intelligence

The natural activity of the child feeds the self-regulated development of intelligence. Natural activities in the early years are almost exclusively play-bound because the character of nonplay activity requires a way of understanding and a way of directing one's activity that has not yet developed in the young child. During the early childhood years, the child's intelligence is marked by a lack of coordination between assimilation and accommodation. The child's understanding of the world encompasses contradictions and fluctuations. The resulting modifications in understanding and behaviors are never complete enough to ward off continued uncertainties and contradictions. The ongoing and constant modification of the child's intellectual structures is marked by a progressive coordination, or **equilibrium**, among assimilation, accommodation, and social coordinations. However, it is not until the end of early childhood that this equilibrium is stable enough to yield a conceptually consistent and logically ordered world. Prior to this, the child is constantly processing contradictory information. A big block cannot fit into a small hole, but a big Santa Claus can fit down a small chimney. The examples are as numerous as the beliefs of children.

Until this equilibrium is achieved, the child's intellectual activity is always bound within the larger domain of play because, not being able to form an objective, reliable, and stable view of the world, there is always a subordination of the world to the child's immediate view. In a sense, because children make of the world what they wish, we say that children are bound by play, where work and practice are tied to pretense, fantasy, and imitation.

In short, intelligence develops through the child's self-directed and natural activities, which are always play-bound because all of a young child's activity tends toward the subordination of reality to the ego. Lacking the means of true work—where assimilation and accommodation are reliably coordinated, and where intelligence is coordinated with others—the child is forced into a playful mode. In this mode, goal-directed activity slips into fantasy, efforts to grasp reality give way to pretense, and attempts to reconcile diverse perspectives slip into a subordination of reality to the child's immediate interests or perspectives. Hence, it is a truth about intelligence that the child, of necessity, must play to one day be able to work. It is practice at play and not work that will one day produce the intelligent worker.

Play and the Development of Personality

The entire range of children's needs and emotions is arranged and expressed in play. Their play themes deal with abandonment, death, power, acceptance, and rejection. Emotions are practiced and linked to needs, but with pretense as a buffer between the real fear of abandonment, for example, and the fantasy expressed in the play, "Let's say our mothers died and we're all alone."

Play, personality, and intelligence all support each other; they are inseparable and are all related to emotions. Play is not simply one of the possible activities in which a child might engage—it is more accurate to say that play is an expression of the child's personality, intelligence, and feelings.

Personality and intelligence are similar in some ways, too, and it is here that we find the powerful relationship between the development of a healthy personality and the healthy expression of play. One of the tenets of constructivism is that as the child attempts to understand the world, intelligence becomes more structured, more consistent, better organized, and more powerful. However, sometimes personality and its regulation of emotions remains undeveloped, poorly formed, and maladaptive. For some, the process of living results in the development of adaptive, well-structured, healthy personalities; for others, the early and incomplete personality of childhood remains throughout life.

A process called **reflective abstraction** is inevitable and necessary in the case of intelligence, but not inevitable in the case of personality and the regulation of emotions. Piaget created the concept of reflective abstraction to describe the way in which intelligence bootstraps itself up the developmental ladder. In reflective abstraction, the child brings into recognized forms, through representational activity, the unrealized or unrecognized relationships that make practical behaviors possible. That is, a natural, regulative process advances intelligence simply through the activity of bringing unrealized ideas into representational focus (Piaget, 1977).

As adults we experience the power of reflective abstraction when, for example, we teach others. Teaching requires us to find a way of representing to others what we already know. The regulations underlying our practical knowledge are abstracted when we transform them into a representational form. In development, we might find a child, for example, who understands the conservation of discrete quantities (such as pennies) but who does not yet understand that pouring a liquid from a vessel into a different-shaped vessel does not change the amount of the liquid. Although still confused with the problem of conserving liquids, the child may be able to see that if a jar of pennies is poured into another jar, the number of pennies does not change. In this example, the child's ability to reflect on an earlier understanding assists the shift from the disequilibrium of an earlier stage to the relative equilibrium of a later stage resulting in understanding the conservation of liquids.

A process similar to reflective abstraction is necessary to the development of personality and its regulations of emotions. A child's personality develops toward an equilibrium between psychoemotional needs and possible interactions within the world. This process is furthered when the child can represent latent needs and emotions consciously. In the case of intelligence, reflective abstraction is inevitable because the child attempts to formulate goals and orchestrate means to reach those goals. It forces the child to represent goals and the links between possible actions and the realization of goals.

For example, in trying to put a necklace of beads into a paper cup, an 18-month-old child might imagine (represent) what is happening when the necklace, draped over the edge of the cup, knocks the cup over. The child might succeed by bunching the necklace into a ball and dropping it into the cup. In doing so, the child represents to himself the goal (getting the necklace into the cup), the obstacle (the necklace knocks the cup over), and the solution (bunching the necklace into a ball). In the case of personality, on the other hand, the inner self can remain unconscious, repressed, and fixated in patterns of action that can remain unconscious and not reflected on throughout life. For example, a child might develop a certain personality as a way of fitting into or resolving conflicts within the family. Although this development might be a coping mechanism, its origins can be repressed and unavailable to the child for reflection.

The parallel between intelligence and personality is established by the common process of means-ends coordination and reflective abstraction. For personality to continue to develop, it needs to be embedded constantly in reflective activity. Symbolic play is the way the child represents emotional needs and concerns, as well as how these needs and concerns are resolved. Adults might depend on therapy, analysis, ritual, art, or work, but the child depends on play for the development of personality. This points to the critical and necessary role that play occupies in the lives of children. Through the free and unconstrained process of play—unrestrained because it is freed from inhibition and bends the world to immediate needs and interests—the child brings into represented forms the unconscious and inner psychoemotional self.

Play and the Development of Competencies

During the early childhood years, children develop an astonishing array of intellectual, physical, social, and emotional competencies. The infant at birth is helpless, lacking in all but the most rudimentary reflexive sensorimotor competencies, such as sucking, grasping, or looking at objects. The simplest of human competencies, such as removing a blanket from the face or purposefully grasping an object, are not present at birth.

By the time they reach preschool, children have acquired control over their bodily functions; can feed themselves; can dress themselves; can jump, crawl, and run; and have acquired a language and a wide range of representational skills. They can initiate social interactions, have begun to learn how to regulate emotions and express needs and feelings, have learned something about what is acceptable and unacceptable behavior, and have developed a problem-solving intelligence. In short, the preschool child has developed the unmistakable qualities of being human. Older children are more competent in how they feed and dress themselves. They can skip as well as jump. They can use language not only to initiate, but also to sustain interactions and solve complex emotional issues with others. The origins and the continued development of these competencies are tied closely to play.

Many competencies are sensorimotor schemes, integrating the senses with the use of muscles. Obvious examples might be eating, dressing, running, and skipping, or even talking, which is a complex sensorimotor activity. Other competencies are not sensorimotor, but instead involve internal representations of possible actions and are representational and abstract. The ability of children to think, problem solve, and coordinate their play with others are examples. Whether the competencies are sensorimotor or representational, their development is dependent on play in a number of ways, the most obvious of which is functional practice. All acquired schemes, whether sensorimotor or not, are repeated. The repetition of newly acquired skills gives pleasure. Children play at making the sounds of their native language, play at gross and fine motor activities such as skipping or dressing, and in general enjoy exploring and practicing new intellectual powers.

Play, in addition to providing the functional practice for competencies, provides their contextualization and meanings. Children embed their emerging competencies in play activity, often with others, thereby refining not only their articulation but also their meaning. For example, doll play might contain maternal and family themes, or block play might contain themes of construction and destruction. Outdoor play might involve games that define conditions for running, jumping, and skipping. Much of this contextualized meaning making involves the fantasy and pretend elements of play and, therefore, might be thought of as symbolic play. In play, the child is either creating a symbol (e.g., by using a plate of sand to stand for a plate of food) or creating a tapestry of meaning in which a variety of symbols are woven into a meaningful whole.

Another role of play concerns the socialization of competencies. In some cases, they are themselves social, as in the ability to initiate and maintain interactions or a dramatic play theme. In other cases, the competencies are not in themselves social but can be brought together to meet social needs. For example, competencies for gross motor activity, language, problem solving, and considering the needs of others might be brought together in a playground chase game with hero figures taken from the culture.

The ability to form social relationships in which common goals can be established and activities between members of the group are coordinated to achieve these goals is an extremely complex competency and slow to unfold. It begins with children playing together in proximity only to eventually playing with each other but without common themes or purposes. Then it proceeds to attempt to establish and sustain common purposes, but with constant changes in direction, manner, and roles. Finally, social relationships develop into sustained and coordinated play with agreed-on purpose, direction, manner, roles, and sustained emotional compatibility. This broad competency is almost synonymous with socialization and is at its core an evolution of the child's play.

In summary, competencies are the manifestations of intelligence and personality in the presence of emotions. They represent children's ability to control means-ends relationships within the context of needs and emotions, and to develop the means of participation within their culture. Their development is from the beginning tied to play, which provides (a) functional practice, (b) contextualization and meaning, and (c) socialization.

Play and the Development of the Social Self

We are individuals from birth, and yet our identity—our sense of self—must be constructed, developing gradually and passing through many stages. During the first few months, infants cannot distinguish themselves from their surroundings because they lack the intentional ability to interact with the world. For example, infants are limited in their ability to purposely cause effects on objects or others because they cannot distinguish between what they are causing and what others are causing (Piaget, 1954). Without an awareness of what one causes, no real sense of self is possible. So the child will pass through the stages of intelligence, slowly moving from an undifferentiated beginning to a gradual recognition of the self as both the cause of effects and the effect of causes.

Because the awareness of self is, by necessity, tied to this reciprocal causality (the self being both a cause and an effect), its development takes two paths, each with its own ends—and yet, because of their common origin, ends that are inseparable. On the one hand is the developing sense of what one can do or who one is (i.e., an awareness of one's intelligence, personality, and competence). On the other hand is the gradual understanding of how the actions of others affect us and how we affect others. In the first, the end point of development is the objective self, a sense of self that progresses through a gradual shedding of its egocentric cloak, approaching an undistorted and objective stance where one's sense of self increasingly corresponds to how others see us. It is in the context of play that children learn to incorporate the viewpoints of others into their own sense of self. In the second, the end point of development is the generalized self, a sense of self as one social object among others where the reciprocities between "self" and other are understood such that what is true for one must be true for others, and vice versa (Mead, 1934).

The sense of self is perhaps the most interesting and profound aspect of human development because its end is not just the self but rather a social consciousness capable of generating the ethical, moral, and even spiritual conditions that make the human experience possible. It is because of the sense of self and its close tie to the development of a social conscience that we come to understand the necessary links between social experience and the conditions that foster healthy development and a healthy moral social order. The development of a sense of self is, from its inception, bound to play, where one's own efficacy is explored, where one's own view is coordinated with that of others, and where problems of social coordination are encountered and resolved every day. Play is at the foundation of humankind's most profound and necessary ability—the weaving of the individual spirit into a social fabric.

THE MEANING OF PLAY IN CHILDHOOD AND SOCIETY

How does play contribute to children eventually becoming full members of society? We believe that the world of childhood and the world of play are inseparable and that play is critical to social, emotional, and intellectual development. At the same time, we are aware that children would not develop the essential capacity to operate within the adult world if left solely to play. How is it that play rather than work—that play rather than conformity to adult models and that play rather than compliance with authority—is the major force in child development?

Play and the Work of Society

We distinguish between the work of childhood and the work of society. The first includes the many instances in which the child formulates ends and means, such as when an infant uses a stick to retrieve an object, when a toddler works at solving a puzzle, or when a school-age child works at understanding the rules of a game. The second consists of the many instances in which the purpose and desired ends, as well as the means and even the success of the work, are determined from outside.

Although both forms of work are important and often merge, they have different status in the child's development. Because we view children's work as self-directed activity, it is by definition **autotelic**, or containing within it its own direction and purpose. The work of society, which also must be faced by the child, is **heterotelic**, having a direction and purpose imposed from outside. Although the child might engage in both forms of work, autotelic activity is essential to development because the dynamics of development involve accommodations or modifications brought about by resistances that the world presents to the child's understanding. In a sense, the child treats the world according to what he or she knows; but since that is often inadequate, what the child knows must be modified. This is assimilation and accommodation. When, for example, children find their goal thwarted, it is within their inner experience that the goal, the obstacle, and the possible means of overcoming the obstacle are synthesized.

The dynamic interplay between the child's assimilations of the world and the corresponding accommodations is, by its very nature, autotelic because the understandings, the perceived sense of their inadequacy, and the willingness to make the necessary modifications are intrapersonal (within the child) rather than interpersonal (outside the child). We assert the primacy of play over work as a source of development because the development follows from the autotelic work of childhood, which in the early childhood years is bound to and subordinate to play.

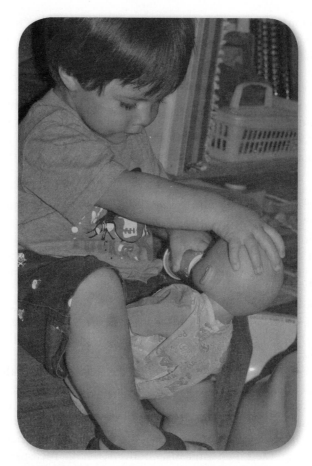

In playing with representational objects, children explore their culture.

In the schooling of children, we must seek a blend between the work of childhood and the work of society. We must find the balance that allows children to experience fully the inner tensions between what they presently know and the challenges of new experiences. We use the term *play* to characterize the context in which this balance is best achieved. This does not mean that we should not define the expected learning outcomes for the children in our care. It does, however, mean that in doing so we must never lose sight of the developmentally driven energies and interests of the child. Accordingly, we endeavor to place the issue of standards, for example, within the sphere of developmentally appropriate practice within integrated and holistic school environments.

Autonomy as the Context for Development

The child lives in two inseparable yet irreconcilable social worlds: the world of adults and the world of peers. The adult society imposes itself on youth, creating a **heteronomous** rather than **autonomous** condition, where codes of behavior are sanctioned by adults and derived by forces totally outside the child's control or comprehension. For example, an adult might tell a child to play fairly, but this does not mean that the child necessarily understands why being fair is important or how to be fair.

The social world of peers, on the other hand, constitutes a condition of autonomy rather than heteronomy. Here children create their own rules and codes for behavior, deciding among themselves what is fair, just, and appropriate to the immediate setting. In this world, they test the extension of their own wills and they orchestrate their campaigns against adult constraint.

Piaget made a strong argument that it is autonomy rather than heteronomy that creates the context for social, moral, and ethical development. Autonomy is essential to true social coordination—that is, the coordination of one's own activities and needs with those of others (Piaget, 1965c). Such coordinations require **reciprocity**, in which members of the social group are on an equal footing, addressing shared needs and shared frames of reference. The relationships between children and adults achieve this reciprocity only partially because children never can be on a truly equal footing with adults. We must wonder how it is that children, through their autonomous pursuits, eventually obtain the adult traits that now separate them from this world. We can offer three answers that support the belief that autonomy among children has an important place in curriculum.

First, children work and play at accomplishing what they believe they will (or must) become. The classroom constitutes a microculture that exemplifies a blend between the child's present level of development and the expectations of the adult world. Nothing is more important to children than participating in the adult world—of having its interest, attention, protection, and acceptance. Therefore, even when left to explore their own interests, children in large measure pursue the interests that correspond with our expectations.

Second, autonomy is necessary to development because social coordinations (and all shared knowledge is a social coordination) are in fact dependent on autonomy. Each party of the coordination must take the other party into account. They must operate under rules that are particular to their own purpose, understood by the participants and not imposed from without.

Finally, social autonomy creates the zone of proximal development (ZPD). We presented Vygotsky's concept of the zone of proximal development in Chapter 2. Vygotsky used the concept of the ZPD to characterize the social space where the disequilibrating social perpetrations of the world are close enough to the child's level of development that the child can profit developmentally from these disturbances. It is in the zone of proximal development that formal and informal teaching take place, because it is only within this zone that what takes place "out there" can affect what takes place "in here" (Vygotsky, 1967).

Autonomy in social relations creates a zone of proximal development. Peers share a common level of development, focus, and interest and, therefore, feed one another's development. The perpetrations that originate in peer relationships fit into the zone of proximal development, where problems and tasks that arise in activity between peers present appropriate stimuli to development.

Development, Developmentally Appropriate Practices, and Play

Historically, early childhood education in the United States has not been a universal experience. In the mid-1960s, the U.S. Congress determined that any national effort to break the cycle of poverty would be effective only if it included preschool education. This was the beginning of Head Start, which nearly half a century later continues to provide quality early childhood education to a diverse national population. Additional social forces such as an increase in the number of working mothers contributed to a push to introduce growing numbers of children to early educational experiences.

As part of the national move to provide early childhood education to increasing numbers of children, the National Association for the Education of Young Children (NAEYC) was founded. One of its early presidents, Millie Almy, was also one of the first U.S. educators to study with Piaget. Almy conducted studies with U.S. children replicating Piaget's work on Swiss children (Almy, 1967).

As the NAEYC took on an increasingly larger role in representing the educational needs of young children, it began to fashion the specifications for developmentally appropriate educational practices. It also defined "early childhood" as the period from birth to age 8. This was not an arbitrary choice. Piaget's work shows that even though schooling begins in many countries with children who are 6 or 7 years of age, children of this age are just beginning to reliably use conceptual reasoning to interpret experience. For example, the coordination of concepts such as "some and all," "more and less," "same and different" are still only partially formed in the early childhood years. Consequently, children of this age do not have a very clear understanding of numbers, time, space, causality, history, geometry, geography, classification, seriation, and so on. Although there are critics of Piaget's theories, there is no question about the universal difficulty that children have with these concepts in the early childhood years. The NAEYC believes, as do we, that the character of early childhood development requires specific concerns for the character of early childhood educational practices. These concerns are described by the NAEYC as developmentally appropriate practices.

We embrace developmentally appropriate practice but go further in expressing our belief that play is the central force in early childhood development and that play provides an ideal foundation for the articulation of an integrated and holistic early childhood curriculum. By "integrated" we mean a curriculum where learning outcomes, such as literacy, are embedded throughout the curriculum. By "holistic" we mean a curriculum that addresses the whole child in terms of social, emotional, and intellectual development and the development of competencies and sense of self. The fact that the early childhood years overlap with the early schooling years does not dissuade us from our belief in the placing of play at the center of the curriculum. We believe that spontaneous play and autonomous activity are critical in the preschool and kindergarten years. We believe that a blend of guided, spontaneous, and autonomous play is a valuable curriculum in the early primary grades.

Expectations for Ourselves and Our Children: Standards

Over the past two decades, there has been a nationwide effort to develop standards for prekindergarten to grade 12. The stated goal has been to provide quality educational experiences for all children. As such, it is a continuation of many of the same forces that ushered in Head Start and other early intervention programs. Standards are seen as a way of establishing clarity in curriculum content, raising expectations for the achievement of all children, and ensuring accountability for public education (Kendall & Marzano, 2004). From this perspective, the push for standards is part of the quest for quality education for all the children in our care.

However, as with any opportunity there are risks as well. The NAEYC pointed out such risks in their 2012 response to the adoption of Common Core State Standards. We agree that the biggest risk is that many in the educational community will find it challenging to maintain traditional early childhood educational values and at the same time be accountable for academic standards that do not align with what we know about young children's development and learning. In particular, how do educators who recognized the value of a play-centered curriculum assure the various stakeholders that they can also satisfy the attainment of academic expectations that are not developmentally appropriate? We are concerned about the lack of research and evidence to support the position that Early Learning Standards and Common Core State Standards lead to benefits for most young children. Honoring children's choices and interests in an integrated and holistic curriculum can be threatened by pressures on teachers to teach isolated facts and concepts. This threat can take on draconian proportions in settings where the allocation of resources and the possibilities of a job are tied to accountability in rigid and overdetermined terms. Research on classroom practices demonstrates the impact on students and teachers (e.g., Genishi, Dyson, & Russo, 2011; Wien, 2004). We are witnessing too many situations where individuals, schools, and even communities have not fared well under the academic standards movement.

We contend that it is our responsibility as early childhood educators to show that a play-centered curriculum can achieve the developmentally appropriate goals we set for our young children. We believe that this is the best articulation of the meaning of play in childhood and society. This responsibility leads us to advocate for play as the center of the curriculum in the broader society as well as for the children we serve in a particular program.

EARLY CHILDHOOD PROFESSIONALS AS ADVOCATES FOR PLAY

A central purpose of this text is to support early childhood educators who are effective, informed, and committed advocates for play. In the first chapter, we emphasized that advocacy is a dimension of professional practice and described the broad continuum of advocacy for play from small daily acts of advocacy at the personal level to the way we work to influence public policy. We suggested that a portfolio or "Toolkit for Play Advocacy" is a useful means to organize ideas, experiences, and resources. These are tools for advocacy in a real sense as well as a metaphorical sense. Each chapter included additional information, perspectives, resources, and vignettes about the central role of play in learning and development. We conclude with resources that you can use directly in your advocacy on behalf of children.

Resources for Action

Organizations   Many organizations have free materials and videos on the importance of play in children's development and learning. The following national organizations have resources for use with families, community members, the general public, and policymakers. The Alliance for Childhood and Defending the Early Years both have information on how to be an effective advocate as well resources for advocacy.

Alliance for Childhood

American Academy of Pediatrics (AAP)

Association of Children's Museums

Campaign for a Commercial Free Childhood (CCFC)

Defending the Early Years

National Association for the Education of Young Children (NAEYC)

Teachers Resisting Unhealthy Children's Entertainment (TRUCE)

Many local and state organizations host events and conferences on play. Advocate by volunteering your time and expertise. Create your own local play, advocacy, and action organization.

Books, Articles, and Blogs   A few of the best-selling books on the importance of children's play are written for a wider audience.

The Power of Play: Learning What Comes Naturally by David Elkind (2007)

Einstein Never Used Flashcards: How Our Children REALLY Learn—and Why They Need to Play More and Memorize Less by Kathy Hirsh-Pasek and Roberta M. Golinkoff, with Diane Eyers (2003)

Last Child in the Woods: Saving Our Children from Nature Deficit Disorder by Richard Luov (2008)

Taking Back Childhood: Helping Your Kids Thrive in a Fast-Paced, Media Saturated, Violence-Filled World by Nancy Carlsson-Paige (2008)

A Child's Work: The Importance of Fantasy Play by Vivian Gussin Paley (2004)

The authors of these and many other publications cited in this text have home pages with lists of publications and contact information. Some include links to videos, articles written for the general public, and blogs. (See, for example, Vivian Gussin Paley, Nancy Carlsson-Paige, Diane Levin, Richard Luov, Deborah Meier, Alison Gopnik, Kathy Hirsh-Pasek, and Roberta M. Golinkoff.)

The Washington Post's education column *The Answer Sheet* by Valerie Strauss features articles by preeminent early childhood educators addressing critical issues such as inequities in education, child poverty, assessments and the use of high-stakes testing, Common Core State Standards for K–2 students, and inadequate funding for education.

Sharing Our Advocacy Stories

Throughout this book, teachers have shared their stories about the ways that they advocate for play every day as they speak with families, colleagues, and administrators. Some explained how they participate in the committees that make policy at the school or district level. Across the country, early childhood educators are at the forefront of advocacy for policies that benefit children's lives.

One risk to children's development and health is reduced time for outdoor play. Many schools and districts have eliminated recess so that it no longer exists in many K–2 programs. In the feature *Advocacy in Action: Advocating for Recess,* Sandra Waite-Stupiansky, a co-author of the mathematics chapter, describes the successful actions she and others took to advocate for recess.

Advocating for Play through Play

Some of the liveliest stories we share about promoting a play-centered curriculum at the program level involve advocating for play through play. Teachers and administrators agree that the most successful workshops and open houses for families are playful and informative. Some of our favorites are workshops in which family members make toys and games to take home—along with informational handouts—as well as workshops to make games, puzzles, dress-up clothes, blocks, and other play materials for children to use at school. The workshop ideas in *From Play to Practice: Connecting Teachers' Play to Children's Learning* are excellent ways for family members to connect their play with engaging materials to children's learning (Nell & Drew, with D. E. Bush, 2013).

One local play coalition included members from community organizations, teachers, education administrators, health professionals, and coordinators from city parks and recreation centers. They began by identifying a need: to bring policymakers and the public together in an event that showed the importance of play in young children's development and learning. The coalition achieved great success by putting on a "community day-to-play" that was well attended by families with children, elected public officials, professionals that supervise programs for families, county and school district administrators, early childhood education college faculty, and students from nearby colleges.

Becoming an Informed Advocate for Play

ADVOCACY IN ACTION: ADVOCATING FOR RECESS

When our family moved to a new district, I was shocked to discover that my children's elementary school did not offer regular outdoor recess. I asked around and found several parents who were also concerned over the lack of outdoor play. About a dozen of us kept meeting on Saturday mornings over coffee to share ideas. Some of us interviewed school personnel to find out when and why recess was eliminated. Several scoured the professional literature to find studies on the effects of recess (positive and negative) on children's academic, social, physical, and emotional skills. One group enlisted other mothers to complete a quick survey every day asking their children if they went outside at all that day. They recorded their data on special calendars for 2 weeks so we could see patterns by school and by grade level. No information was recorded that could identify individual teachers or children.

Members of our group then fanned out and spoke to acquaintances and professionals who had an interest in children's health, such as doctors, psychologists, educators, parents, clergy, and others. We asked anyone who was willing to write a letter to the editor of the local newspaper about their perspectives on the value of recess for elementary-age children. The letters started arriving in droves; the newspaper printed several per week until the newspaper editor felt compelled to write an editorial pleading with the school board to "give the children back their recess."

When we were well informed on the issue, we asked to be put on the school board agenda. The school board agreed to allow only a 10-minute presentation. We felt the weight of all of the children in the district on our shoulders! We made our case using a PowerPoint presentation with a summary of the findings from the literature review, position statements, and our own data on the number of minutes that children spent outdoors during the 2-week study. The response of the school board was overwhelmingly positive, voting that evening to move toward reinstating recess for the next school year.

This happened over 10 years ago; I'm glad to report that the children still have recess every day in the elementary schools of the district. This experience of advocating to reinstate recess taught me that successful advocacy depends on connecting with others who have a stake in the cause, informing ourselves on the issues, enlisting the resources available to us, and persisting with patience over time.

Among early childhood educators and researchers, there is growing recognition that childhood should be playful and joyful and that learning must be engaging and benefit social, emotional, and physical development as well as cognitive development. This is mirrored in our advocacy efforts so that the adults who impact children's lives in such important ways will understand the central role of play in children's development and learning.

This does not mean, however, that adult guidance is not critical to the intellectual, emotional, and social development of the child. As we come to understand the constructivist point of view, we recognize that the guidance we provide must be a condition for growth, and growth in the early childhood years is indistinguishable from play itself.

SUMMARY

Play is a dominant activity from birth through early adolescence. It is part of all areas of social, emotional, and intellectual growth. Play is a way of understanding the world and of comforting the self. It takes its material from the social world of the child as well as from the child's inner emotional needs. When we acknowledge the primacy of play, we recognize the primary vehicle in the child's early development.

During the early childhood years, children develop in four important interrelated domains: intelligence, personality, competencies and sense of self or social consciousness. This development proceeds by a coordination of "ends" (the formation of goals) with "means" (the formation of ways to reach goals). The coordination of means and ends is a psychological constructive process and, in the early years, is inseparable from play.

- **Constructivism and development.** The constructivist thrust of developmental theory follows largely from the work of Jean Piaget and Lev Vygotsky. Piaget emphasized the self-regulatory dynamics of means-ends coordinations, whereas Vygotsky focused on the social and cultural–historical dynamics of development. Both theorists were constructivists and attributed equal importance to the child as an active participant in development within a context of social relationships embedded in history and culture.

- **Constructivism and social–cultural theories of development.** Both Piaget and Vygotsky are constructivists but with different orientations. Vygotsky focuses on the role of social–cultural forces in the constructive process, whereas Piaget focused on the coordination of actions. Where the two theorists come together is that for Piaget, the child's life is embedded in social action as well as sensorimotor action and the growing coordination of each and their internal representations are necessary for the full development of the human capacity for reason.

- **A closer look at Piaget and constructivist theory.** There are three central ideas in Piaget's theory:
  a. The child's understanding of the world is reflected in what the child can do and these abilities depend on schemes or action patterns.
  b. Through active interaction with the world, largely in the context of play, these action schemes change through a process of assimilation (understanding the world with existing schemes) and accommodation (a change of schemes and their coordination because of environmental pressures).
  c. Through the dynamics of assimilation and accommodation, the child's understanding of the world progresses through a universal series of stages as the child constructs an understanding of reality.

- **Social experience and the construction of reality.** There are three important ideas to keep in mind when thinking about social experience and the construction of reality; all three concern children's play.

a. Two interrelated developmental themes are the progression in the internal self-regulated schemes and the progression of social coordination with others.

b. Social actions, like all other actions, tend to become organized into logical–mathematical systems that provide the possibility of agreeing and disagreeing, understanding and not understanding.

c. For the child to become capable of rational thought, there must be a detachment from one's own view to an understanding and incorporation of the viewpoint of others.

- **Play and development.** Through a coordination of means-ends relationships in the context of play, the child constructs intelligence (understanding), personality (the means of maintaining acceptable emotional states while seeking to achieve ends), competencies (the forming of ends and means), and sense of self or social consciousness (an understanding of one's self as the cause of conditions for others and as vulnerable to the effects of others).

- **The meaning of play in childhood and society.** In the course of development and constructing a world for themselves, children must also develop the competencies and self-control that society expects. One of the ironies of development is that autonomy and freedom from constraint are critical to acquiring the abilities we, as educators, are required to enable. A privileged relationship exists between autonomy and development. Self-directed activity—as opposed to other-directed activity—is essential to development because development involves modifying existing ways of behaving or interpreting to adapt to new challenges. This process cannot take place outside the needs, tensions, and intuitively directed groping of the child. Hence, activity that is directed by the child is primary in development. The social conditions and regulations that children establish outside adult authority are also necessary conditions for social development. Social development is an evolution of social coordinations where children are increasingly able to align their individual goals to become partners in joint activity. This coordination and the ensuing reciprocities (how you treat me, I treat you) require autonomy rather than heteronomy (authority imposed from without) because reciprocity requires that the players be on an equal footing. The work of Vygotsky, Piaget, Erikson, and Mead make it clear that if children are not self-directed and engaged in autonomous social alliances, they will not develop into competent adults.

- **Early childhood professionals as advocates for play.** In this section we featured a story of an early childhood educator's successful advocacy for recess, a district policy that made a difference in children's opportunities to play. We discussed strategies and resources that you can use in your advocacy on behalf of children: (a) organizations that have free materials and videos on the importance of play in children's development and learning; (b) books, articles, and blogs that are resources for play advocacy; and (c) examples of ways to advocate for play through playful activities like workshops for families and the public.

We end with an optimistic belief that a play-centered curriculum is ultimately the best integrated curriculum for young children and that it can be articulated to meet whatever reasonable and developmentally based standards might be put forward for young children. We must ask ourselves whether we are truly engaging our students' intelligence, personality, emotions, competencies, and sense of self. If we are, we can be assured of success.

Teaching in a play-based and developmentally based curriculum requires knowing what the child knows, where the child's interests and energy lie, and where the child is going. It requires knowing how to engage the child so that the teacher's understanding of the child and the curriculum is developed along with the child's progress in understanding and acquiring skills. Entering into the child's play, by direct or indirect means, allows the teacher to see what the child knows and where the child is headed. Orchestrating play allows the teacher to support the child's progress through further manipulations of the play and nonplay environments. The teacher, rather than being the guardian and administrator of the curriculum, becomes the gardener and architect of the environment, using play as its nutrients and structure.

APPLYING YOUR KNOWLEDGE

1. Discuss the relationship between constructivist theory and child development in a number of domains. Relate this discussion to the general framework of the coordination of means-ends relationships.
   a. List the four domains of human development that are the focus of this chapter.
   b. Put in your own words your understanding of what is meant by *means-ends coordinations* and briefly describe the relationship of this concept to human development.
   c. Discuss your understanding of constructivism and how it differs from other ideas about human development.
2. Describe the developmental theories of Piaget and Vygotsky and explain how these theorists complement one another as well as relate to children's play.
   a. Discuss your understanding of universal stages and how this is illustrated by the development of children's understanding of conservation.
   b. In your own words, how does the idea of universal stages of development and the example of a developing understanding of conservation change your understanding of the nature–nurture discussion?
   c. How is Piaget's theory of development both helpful and unhelpful to teachers of young children?
   d. Discuss how constructivism and social–cultural theories of development support a play-based curriculum.

3. Discuss the central ideas of Piaget's theory of intelligence and its development.
   a. Give two examples that support the idea that the construction of reality reflects developmental laws.
   b. The child's intelligence, personality, competencies, and sense of self are reflected in action schemes that allow the child to act on the world. In general, how do these action schemes change with development? Give examples.

4. Discuss the role of social experience in the construction of reality.

5. Discuss and define four areas of human development (intelligence, personality, competencies, and social consciousness or sense of self) and discuss how they are related to the coordination of means-ends relationships.
   a. Explain in your own words why intelligence in the first 8 years of life is bound to play.
   b. How does play provide the context for the development of a healthy personality?
   c. How do means-ends relationships participate in the development of personality?

6. Characterize the intersection between children's autonomy and the expectations of society. Include developmentally appropriate practice and standards in your discussion.
   a. Elaborate on how heteronomy and autonomy relate to the work of society and the work of childhood and how autonomy is critical to development.
   b. This chapter proposes that autonomy operates in the pursuit of interests, in reciprocal coordination with others, and in the zone of proximal development. With this understanding, discuss how childhood autonomy participates in children's success at the work of society.
   c. Discuss your understanding of developmentally appropriate practices (DAP) and its relationship to standards and a play-based curriculum.

7. Describe several ways that early childhood educators can advocate for play and give an example of a useful resource for each.
   a. How might you advocate for play now or in the next year? Create a plan that includes your general goal and describes several actions you could carry out. Cite several useful resources for your advocacy.

GLOSSARY

Accessory boxes. Containers storing props and replicas of real objects that relate to familiar scripts like housekeeping and so on.

Action scheme. A scheme that specifically relates to an action of the muscles.

Activity areas. Designated spaces teachers set up in the classroom to engage children in play.

Adaptation. Modifying behavior to better align with the possibility of attaining goals in the real world.

Age-appropriate assessments. Assessments that are interpreted in ways that reflect and respond to the characteristics and abilities of a child of that age group.

Age-appropriate development. Development that falls within the range expected for a certain age group.

Agency. The capacity of a person to consciously act in the world or engage with the social structure. Agency for children is the ability to act within the school setting in a self-directed manner.

Artist Apprentice. A role in which the teacher helps to remove clutter in the physical space around an ongoing play episode or offers accessories for play, much like a set assistant in a theater.

Assimilation and accommodation. Critical concepts in Piaget's theory that account for how the child incorporates or assimilates the world into existing schemes and how these schemes undergo change or accommodation as children adapt to the world.

Auditory discrimination. The brain's ability to organize and differentiate between similar sounds or individual sounds used in speech.

Authentic assessments. Assessments based on knowledge of typical stages of child development and carried out in a manner that promotes children's learning and development.

Authentic questioning. Teacher questions asked when he or she does not already know the answer, which both acknowledges the children's play and adds to the teacher's information about them as individuals and as a group.

Author's chair. An opportunity for children to read or tell the class about what they have written or drawn. It is a social opportunity to share their stories with peers.

Author's theatre. Involves the stories written by children that are then performed by classmates of their choosing.

Autonomous. Being in control of oneself; self-directed.

Autonomy. Self-governed.

Autotelic. Activities that are self-motivating.

Benchmarks. See the definition for *standards*.

Big body play. Physically active play that can include running, throwing, jumping, wrestling, open-palmed tagging, chasing, and fleeing and is accompanied by relaxed facial features and often involves laughter, squealing, and/or exuberant screaming.

Cause-and-effect relationships. Understanding the relationship between a phenomenon (something observed) and the causes of what is observed.

Classification. Grouping objects according to one or more common properties.

Co-construction. When a pretend reality is jointly invented by the players, or, generally, when knowledge and understandings are jointly invented by two or more persons acting together.

Compensatory function. An action that can compensate for an emotional loss or other unpleasant experience.

Competencies. One's skills, abilities, and talents.

Concrete-operational period. A broad developmental period that begins with the onset of operations and true concepts that are, however, still tied to concrete physical reality and are not yet hypothetical in nature; usually starting around 6 years of age and ending around 13 years of age.

Concrete operational thought. A form of thinking that occurs in middle childhood that is logical and rational but still tied to the appearance of concrete objects and not yet hypothetical.

Conservation experiments. Experiments carried out with children generally between 4 and 13 years of age to explore their understanding that certain aspects of reality do not change even though their appearance changes.

Constructive play. Play in which children use materials to create or build new objects or models.

Construction toys. Toys used to create new objects or models (e.g., different kinds of blocks).

Constructivism. A view that in formulating and pursuing goals, individuals adapt to the world, thereby constructing an understanding of the world.

Conventionalized expectations. Standards of conduct or performance that belong to a common knowledge of behaviors or beliefs. For many children, play in the home center has many familiar expectations.

Coordination of part–whole relations. An understanding that wholes can be divided into parts and that parts can be combined into wholes and that there are certain logical relationships that hold between parts and wholes such that, for example, the whole is greater than the part.

Coordination of schemes. The theoretical assumptions that schemes are coordinated with each other to build more complex actions. By the second year of life, coordinated schemes can become abstracted representations of action schemes that are no longer sensorimotor and are now internal mental representations of possible actions.

Crosscutting concepts. Abstract ideas that can be applied across scientific disciplines or areas. Basic crosscutting scientific concepts include color and shape.

Cultural capital. A term used to refer to resources such as money, education, family, and social connections that lead to economic well-being, status, and power in life.

Curriculum-generated play. Refers to teacher-planned subject matter curriculum based on knowledge of children's experiences and interests reflected in their spontaneous play.

Daily life activities. Activities that are part of people's everyday behaviors (e.g., eating, sleeping, working).

Developmentally appropriate practice (DAP). A term defined by the NAEYC to describe practices grounded in knowledge of (a) young children's development and learning, (b) individual children's development and learning, and (c) children's social and cultural contexts.

Developmental stages. Periods in development that are distinct from both earlier and later periods. Stages contain elements of earlier periods and provide conditions for later periods.

Disequilibrating event. An event or situation that causes an imbalance, conflict, or ambiguity that needs to be resolved. Its resolution may lead to advances in development for the child.

Dispositions for learning. Personal attitudes, characteristics, or desires that support a student's learning (e.g., curiosity, imagination, creativity, persistence).

Dramatic play. Play that is organized around a narrative theme or story.

Drawing schemas. Markings and configurations in children's drawing and scribbling that are diagrammatic representations or patterns that evolve in a developmental way to more realistic forms.

Dual language learner. In this text, refers to students who are learning English in addition to their home languages.

Egocentric. An important concept in Piaget's theory that refers to the fact that the young child's thought is closely tied to immediate sensations and interests and not yet "de-centered."

Emergent curriculum. A way of planning curriculum based on students' expressed interests and engagement as well as teacher goals and expectations. It is never rigidly preplanned but flexible and continually developed.

Emergent literacy. The key features of this concept are that literacy begins to develop early, is ongoing and occurs in everyday contexts in interactions with others as well as in art, music, play, social studies, science.

Emotional development. The development of the ability to regulate and manage one's feelings or emotional states in the course of daily life.

Empirical evidence. Evidence based on observation, including results from experimental research.

Engineering. In science education, this term is used to describe people's systematic and persistent behaviors and practices carried out in attempts to solve problems.

Ensemble playing. Playing complementary parts as a unit or group that contribute to a single effect, such as musicians or actors who perform together.

Equilibrium. A central concept in Piaget's theory holding that stages of development represent a partial balance between assimilation and accommodation such that the child can effectively function within a certain domain of action.

Exploratory and self-correcting activity. Refers to play with materials that allow some experimentation in the discovery of the correct placement of pieces. Pegboards, form boards, miniatures, and picture lotto are examples.

Estimation. Refers to a judgment of the approximate quantity of a group of objects.

Expectations. See the definition for *standards*.

Fantasy play. Play in which children make up pretend stories that reflect issues that are emotionally important to them.

Focal points. Refers to core concepts or "big ideas" that the National Council of Teachers of Mathematics identifies as essential for mathematics education.

Formation of concepts. The formation of ideas that are capable of being shared.

Functional play. Play that is repetition of acquired abilities for the pleasure of repetition itself.

Games with rules. Play that entails the construction and/or following of rules that involve agreements and disagreements with others.

Gatekeeper. A teacher role in which he or she facilitates play by, for example, assisting a newcomer to enter a play event by finding an activity or role that complements the other children's play scenario.

Group glee. A phenomenon in which children respond to situations or activities such as coughing or snapping Velcro shoes with elated screaming, laughter, or intense physical acts. These responses may occur in coinciding bursts or spread from one child to another.

Group play. Play involving two or more children.

Guardian of the Gate. An indirect strategy that may be used by teachers to help a child make entry into an ongoing play group. Examples would include offering a relevant prop such as a similar toy already in use by the group or clarifying the context of the play to the newcomer.

Guided play. Children's play that adults purposely influence.

Heteronomy. Governed or controlled by others.

Heteronomous. Being controlled by outside forces; other directed.

Heterotelic. Activities that are motivated by outside forces.

Hypothetical possible. An ability to formulate ideas about what might be possible outside of any concrete evidence of those possibilities.

Hypothetical-deductive thinking. An advanced form of thinking that entails understanding the possible arguments that might be fashioned in solving a particular problem and deciding what evidence would support one argument over another.

Illicit play. This form of play in the classroom is not sanctioned by the teacher and is engaged in either behind the teacher's back or as a direct challenge to the teacher's authority.

Inclusive. The approach of including children with special needs in activities as a member of the classroom.

Inclusive environments. An environment that encourages a sense of belonging and attempts to foster respect and connection between children with special needs and their classmates, for example, through facilitating engagement with toys or materials that increase social interaction among children.

Individualized Education Plan (IEP). A plan for a student who has been identified with special needs that is developed by a team that includes the student's family member(s), teacher(s), and specialists. An IEP identifies specific goals and objectives as well as a plan for attaining the goals and providing needed services.

Individually appropriate assessments. Assessments that reflect the personal qualities and growth of a specific child, including the child's culture and language.

Individually appropriate development. Developmental characteristics and processes of a particular child.

Inquiry. A process of seeking information by observing, comparing, exploring, and investigating.

Instrumental play. In school settings, instrumental play is sanctioned and often employed by the teacher to meet goals consistent with school curriculum. Examples include play with blocks or teacher-initiated games with rules that promote the understanding of particular concepts or vocabulary, and dramatic play to promote peer interaction.

Intaglio. A relief print or design that is carved into or beneath a surface such as metal or stone.

Intellectual. Deriving from or engaging the act of thinking.

Intelligence. For constructivists, that which allows a person to function in the world.

Interactive space. Classroom arrangements and schedule of routines that help and support children to focus on their play and engagement with peers. For example, adult–child ratios are low and teachers provide environments that suggest interest areas and clear paths of movement between them.

Internal mental consistency. The organization of schemes such that, in assimilating the world, they do not produce contradictory outcomes. For example, a child may recognize that something is too big to fit in a hole but reach for a bigger object. In this instance, the schemes for placing objects in holes and the schemes associated with judgments about size are not coordinated and are inconsistent.

Internal mental representation. The ability to mentally represent events or objects to oneself when no longer in the presence of these events or objects.

Interpersonal. That which occurs within the individual.

Interpretive approach. This approach attempts to understand children's interactions and communicative behavior by analyzing the meanings that the children assign to them, for example, as when children's imaginative ideas are revealed through storytelling and narrative inquiry.

Intonation. The musician's awareness of pitch accuracy of one's voice or musical instrument. The intonation or pitch may be flat, sharp, or both.

Intrapersonal. That which occurs between individuals.

Intrinsically satisfying. Activities that produce an inherent feeling of fulfillment with a sense of accomplishment.

Intrinsic motivation. A drive that comes from inside an individual rather than from any external or outside rewards, such as money or grades. It can be described as an incentive to engage in activities that enhance or maintain one's self-concept.

Linguistic cues. Words that occur among other words within sentences that provide information about its meaning. For example, to signal agreement about an activity may be as simple as ending a sentence with a "right" or an "OK."

Liquidating function. A term used by Piaget referring to activities that can compensate for unpleasant feelings.

Literate behaviors. Behaviors that precede more specific literacy skills and have numerous forms of expression, both verbal and nonverbal, that fulfill the fundamental purpose of communicating the child's needs, interests, and desires. For the young child, these larger purposes of language provide the motivation and framework for later literacy development.

Locomotion toys. Toys that enable children to move themselves or materials from place to place (e.g., tricycles, scooters, wagons).

Logical–mathematical knowledge. A type of knowledge constructed by children that arises out of understanding the relationship between objects rather than the properties of objects (e.g., number, spatial logic, classification, seriation).

Loose parts. Easily moved play materials that can be carried, combined, taken apart, and reconfigured in multiple ways. Includes either natural materials such as sand, leaves, or logs, or provided materials such as boxes, planks, tubes, milk crates, reused tires, containers, trays, plates, or funnels.

Manipulatives. Toys that teachers use to support children's mathematical understandings or fine motor development (e.g., miniature animals and furniture, pattern blocks and other table blocks).

Mathematical concepts. Understandings of the world that individuals construct that relate to geometry, numbers and operations, and measurement.

Mathematical processes. How individuals develop mathematical understandings, for example, by solving problems.

Mathematize. How teachers understand and identify everyday routines, situations, and activities in mathematical terms.

Means-ends coordinations. The ability to fashion goals (ends) and construct the methods (means) of reaching those goals.

Media technology. Electronic visual and audio technologies. Generally refers to visual technologies that have a screen (screen technology) such as TVs, computers, tablets, or smartphones.

Mental representation. The way in which reality is "represented" to the self.

Mental tools. The cognitive processes that are socially shared by people in a culture that assist individual thinking, such as language, mathematics, or computer science.

Metacognitive. When a person thinks about their thinking.

Metacommunication. When used to describe certain play activities, refers to behaviors that are used to signal play such as winks or smiles, laughter, play voices, or exaggerated movements and verbal markers as such as, "Let's pretend that I'm the babysitter and you're the bad baby."

Miniatures. Toys that are small versions of common natural or manufactured objects or living things (e.g., animals, vehicles, furniture, dolls).

Modalities of communication. The many ways that children use to communicate or achieve their interactive goals, such as gestures, rhythm, and intonation.

Moral development. The developing ability of the child to consider the relationship between social actions and possible harm to self and others.

Motivation. The process that initiates, guides, or maintains one to act or behave in a particular way. In schooling it often refers to the desire to learn.

Musical notation. Symbols used to represent aural sounds.

Object transformations. Object transformations are a type of symbolic transformation where a child will attach imagined properties or identities to an object.

Objective knowledge. An expression that refers to logical or rational knowledge but further suggests a knowledge about the world "as the world really is."

On topic. Refers to the association of activities according to a theme. For example, to be on topic in home play, carrots are to be "cooked" and not used as guns.

Numerals. The symbols used to represent a number concept (e.g., 16).

One-to-one correspondence. Two sets can be put into one-to-one correspondence when for each element of one set there is a corresponding element in the other set; for example, four children and four chairs.

Onlooker behavior. When a child watches as others play, either not knowing how to join in or waiting for an opportunity to join the play.

Onsets. The part of the syllable that precedes the vowel of the syllable. Examples include "w" in will and "s" in still.

Parallel play. A form of play where children play adjacent to one another but do not appear to be interacting; however, this strategy is frequently used for entry into an ongoing play.

Peacemaker. A role teachers may take on the direct–indirect intervention continuum that may help children resolve conflicts that appear in their play in several ways.

Peer culture. A set of activities or routines, artifacts, values, and concerns that children produce and share in their interaction with their peers; it represents an alternative and, to some degree, a complement to the school culture.

Performance-based assessments. Assessments that provide information on children's behaviors as they engage in familiar activities in familiar settings.

Personality. The way an individual maintains acceptable emotional states while functioning in the world.

Phonemic awareness. An awareness that written symbols (letters) can represent sounds, that the same sounds can be represented by different phonemes, and that the same phoneme (letter) can represent different sounds.

Phonics. A method used to teach people to read by correlating sounds with letters or groups of letters in an alphabetic writing system.

Phonological awareness. An awareness of the relationship between symbols and sounds.

Phonological memory. Memorizing or recalling a sequence of unfamiliar sounds.

Physical knowledge. A type of knowledge that arises from the physical properties of objects that allows children to make generalizations about the general properties of objects.

Physically active play. Play that involves running, jumping, hopping, skipping, galloping, climbing, leaping, swinging, throwing, catching, pushing, and/or pulling.

Pivots. A term derived from Vygotsky's work that refers to a child's use of an object to represent other objects, concepts, or ideas; for example, using a book to represent a taco.

Play-ability. The quality that allows children to adapt the toy to their individual needs, purposes, and stage of development over an extended time period.

Play fighting. An activity in which children will pretend they are in combat without intending to harm their play partners. It is often signaled by a smiling face.

Play frame. A play frame refers to the imaginary boundaries in which a play scenario occurs. It is derived from studies of play therapy.

Play-generated curriculum. Refers to aspects of the curriculum that emerge directly from the interests of the children. Teachers draw on their observations of children's play to extend and elaborate on children's learning.

Preconceptual stage. A broad period in development, generally between 2 and 4 years of age, prior to the occurrence of "true concepts." This stage is also referred to as a preoperational period.

Preoperational intelligence. In Piaget's theory, "operations" are a kind of mental activity that is characterized by logical reasoning leading to logically necessary conclusions. Preoperational intelligence is a form of reasoning that lacks this operational quality.

Preoperational period. Generally refers to a broad period in development between the sensorimotor period and the onset of operational thought, which usually occurs around 7 years of age.

Pretend play. Play where a child is pretending to be something other than his or her self, or pretending to do something other than what he or she is actually doing.

Project approaches. An approach to curriculum that centers on an in-depth, extended investigation of a topic and incorporates children's developing competencies in language and literacy, art, science, social studies, and math.

Psychoanalytic theory. A theory of personality largely associated with Freud that assumes instinctual forces unconsciously exert influences on the lives of individuals in both development and daily life.

Psychosocial theory. The theory developed by Erikson to integrate the psychological dimensions and the social–cultural dimensions of development across the life span.

Rationality. A form of knowing that is closely aligned with logical necessity and can be reasoned about with others.

Reciprocal interactions. Interactions with others that are fair and equal.

Reciprocity. A social exchange of equal consequences; central to the concept of fairness.

Recreational play. This form of play is sanctioned by the teacher but often occurs outside the teacher's view. Playground play at recess and free play outdoors in some preschool and kindergarten settings are examples of this type of play.

Reflective abstraction. An aspect of Piaget's theory concerning how children advance their own level of development by understanding their own practical abilities or knowledge.

Reliability. The characteristic of an assessment that refers the degree to which the results of the assessment are consistent when administered repeatedly.

Repetition. As used in discourse with others, repetition, or doing something again, is a way to acknowledge some feature of a previous utterance (such as echoing and repeating key words and phrases).

Representational toys. Toys that look like other objects in nature or the culture.

Reversibility. The concept in Piaget's theory that operational thought (rational thought) is only possible because mental schemes are organized in systems such that the effects of one scheme can be reversed or undone by another in the system. For example, combining can be undone by decoupling (e.g., $7 + 2 = 9; 9 - 2 = 7$).

Reversible operations. Mental actions that are organized in a system of possible actions where one action can undo the effects of another action.

Rhythm instruments. Instruments such as percussion or piano whose prime functions are to supply rhythm rather than harmony or melody.

Rimes. Part of a syllable that consists of its vowel and any consonant sounds that come after it, such as *ack, ail, est, ice, ink,* and *ight.*

Role. A set of connected behaviors, characteristics, or norms assigned or assumed by an individual within a specific social situation, as when a child assumes a "baby" voice in a play scenario.

Rough and tumble play. Play that often involves wrestling or play fighting but may include behaviors such as running, chasing, pushing, or pulling for fun with loud voices or roaring sounds. Children initiate this type of play to establish affiliation, status, or dominance. It does not involve an intention to cause harm. See *big body play.*

Scaffold. An interactive strategy used by adults or more sophisticated peers that facilitate a deeper level of learning for the child and may entail the use of familiar cues or objects that assist the child in learning specific concepts or skills.

Schemes. The assumed underlying biological and psychological structures that make sensorimotor and mental actions possible.

School culture. The norms of school behavior commonly accepted in our society and shaped through teacher behavior.

Scientific concepts. The organizing principles of scientific knowledge (e.g., life cycle, climate, green, soft).

Scientific content. Factual subject-matter information relating to science, for example, to the life sciences, physical sciences, or earth sciences.

Scientific practices and processes. Those behaviors that are identified with scientific inquiry such as observing, communicating, problem solving, organizing information, and analyzing and interpreting results.

Screen technology. Generally refers to media technology such as TVs, computers, tablets, or smartphones.

Scribbling stage. This stage is made up of numerous developmental substages, including uncontrolled markings, controlled repetitions of motions, exploration of controlled motions, and storytelling.

Self-monitor. A trait that involves the child paying closer attention to a social situation so that he or she can change behaviors to fit that situation; it is a way an individual may regulate expressive controls.

Self-regulation. The ability to control oneself.

Sense of self. One's sense of being separate from others and from the environment and eventually taking into account how one affects others and is affected by others.

Sensorimotor intelligence. A way of understanding the world through the use of senses and muscles that does not depend on representational activity.

Sensorimotor period. A broad developmental period, generally in the first 2 years of life, preceding representational ability as expressed, for example, in pretend play, language, and imitation of past events.

Sensorimotor play. Play that uses the senses and muscles; generally implies the absence of representational activity.

Sensorimotor toys. Toys that promote the joy of making things happen and actions that are often repetitive (e.g., balls, rattles, tops, rocking horses).

Separation. Some theorists consider separation from parents a major milestone for children. Research on this subject suggests that the character of this achievement is an important indicator of secure or insecure attachment to the parental figure.

Seriation. Placing object in order according to a common property, such as length, size, shade of a color, etc.

Sideways glance. This term refers to an in-depth and holistic view of play that gives context to children's interactions.

Social and environmental expectations. Implicit classroom expectations that involve social values, beliefs, behaviors, or norms as well as features of the environment; for example, a small table with four chairs communicates that this is a place for four children.

Social consciousness. An awareness of one's self as a social object among others, as someone who is capable of having effects on others and who is affected by others.

Social ecological elements. Dynamic, interrelated factors that contribute to the relationships that exist between the child and his or her peers as well as the child and his or her environment, such as when relevant props generate a home play activity.

Social knowledge. Knowledge that is contained in the social world and imparted by other people (e.g., the names of things or particular cultural customs).

Socialization. The developmental processes by which individuals acquire the ability to function effectively with others. Socialization to school entails the children's ability to interact effectively with peers and teachers.

Social studies. A discipline that encompasses a wide variety of content areas that address social relationships and the functioning of society.

Socioecological. A context in which interactions between children are understood in relation to social and ecological (environmental) factors.

Sociocultural. Refers to combining social and cultural factors to understanding or analyzing a circumstance or phenomena.

Sociodramatic play. This form of play includes role-playing between peers; it helps children develop imaginative skills and learn social rules such as give and take, reciprocity, cooperation, and sharing.

Sociodramatic play training. A strategy of teacher intervention with preschool children whose dramatic play was believed to lack complexity.

Soft spaces. Areas within the classroom that are quiet and are defined by comforting materials, such as pillows and carpeting.

Solitary play. Play by one's self.

Special needs. A term used to describe individuals who require assistance for disabilities that may be mental, emotional, or physical in nature.

Spectator. The teacher can take the perspective of spectator or peripheral participant, which is an implicit and undefined onlooker to play.

Spiral curriculum. Curriculum that refers to the idea that, at many stages of their development, children may grasp basic concepts, each time returning to the same ideas at a more sophisticated level of understanding.

Spontaneous play. Play that children choose that expresses their own interests, motives, and behaviors.

Standards. Specifies the level of competence, knowledge, or skill that students in a program or grade level should demonstrate. The terms *standards*, *expectations*, and *benchmarks* are generally used synonymously.

Story play. An activity where a child dictates a narrative to a teacher that is later enacted by peers during circle time. Participation in the activity leads children to an early awareness that language contains within it the expectations of a responsive "other."

Structure. The degree to which a toy or other object resembles the object that the child is symbolizing.

Symbolic distancing. The use of symbols that do not share similarities to what they stand for; for example, a block of wood used to represent a phone is more symbolically distanced than a play phone.

Symbolic play. Another term for pretend play, where objects or people represent something other than what they are.

Symbolic role-play. Play in which the actors take on imaginary roles.

Symbols. An object, notation, or representation that stands for something other than itself.

Tactile/sensory materials. Materials that involve the sensation of touch and texture.

Teacher-directed play. Children's play that is organized and controlled by adults.

Technology. As it relates to science education, this term is used in the broad sense to describe the systems and processes that result when people solve problems.

Thematic curriculum. Curriculum that involves activities or projects that are planned around a particular idea or concept, which may be based on the children's and teacher's interests, children's families, past experiences, and resources.

Topic and sequence. These two terms represent the basic elements of written texts. In children's collaborative literate behaviors, a topic and an ordered sequence are coordinated with play partners, thereby successfully maintaining the narrative thread of a cohesive interaction.

Turn-taking skills. Interactive strategies that enable children to engage communicatively in the give-and-take process of social interaction. It is instrumental to how effectively children interact in play with peers.

Tying. To connect something together. In interactions with teachers and peers, children quickly learn that a turn of talk can be achieved by beginning an utterance with a conjunction, such as *and* to connect their utterances to a previous speaker's turn of talk.

Universal stages. Those stages of development that are thought to apply to all people.

Unstructured physical activity. Large muscle, gross motor play that is child directed rather than organized with rules by adults.

Validity. The characteristic of an assessment that refers to how well it measures what it intends to measure.

Warrant. The permission to establish or alter a play theme. It involves the agreement of the players to a mutual activity.

Zone of proximal development. A concept developed by Vygotsky to refer to the context in which the child's understanding is furthered as the result of social interaction; that is, a child learns to do certain tasks somewhat above his or her usual developmental level with the support of a more competent peer or adult.

REFERENCES

Achieve Inc. (2013). Next Generation Science Standards: For states, by states. Retrieved from http://www.nextgen-science.org/next-generation-science-standards.

Adams, S., & Wittmer, D. (2001). "I had it first": Teaching young children to solve problems peacefully. *Childhood Education, 78*(1), 10–16.

Ainsworth, M. D., Bell, S. M., & Stayton, D. J. (1974). Infant-mother attachment and social development: "Socialization" as a product of reciprocal responsiveness to signals. In M. M. Richards (Ed.), *The integration of a child into a social world.* London, UK: Cambridge University Press.

Alkon, A., Genevo, J. L., Kaiser, J., Tschann, J. M., Chesney, M. A., & Boyce, W. T. (1994). Injuries in child care centers: Rates, severity, and etiology. *Pediatrics, 94*(6), 1043–1046.

Alliance for Childhood. (2013). Joint statement of early childhood health and education professions on the common core initiative. Retrieved from http://www.allianceforchildhood.org/sites/allianceforchildhood.org/files/file/Joint%20Statement%20on%20Core%20Standards%20(with%20101%20names).pdf.

Allen, B. N., & Brown, C. R. (2002). Eddie goes to school: Facilitating play with a child with special needs. In C. R. Brown & C. Marchant (Eds.), *Play in practice: Case studies in young children's play* (pp. 123–132). St. Paul, MN: Redleaf Press.

Almy, M. (1967). *Young children's thinking: Studies of some aspects of Piaget's theory.* New York, NY: Teachers College Press.

Almy, M. (1975). *The early childhood educator at work.* New York, NY: McGraw-Hill.

Almy, M. (2000). What wisdom should we take with us as we enter the new century? *Young Children, 55*(1), 6–11.

Alper, C. D. (1987). Early childhood music education. In C. Seefeldt (Ed.), *The early childhood curriculum: A review of current research* (pp. 211–236). New York, NY: Teachers College Press.

Alward, K. R. (1995, June). *Play as a primary context for development: The integration of intelligence, personality, competencies, and social consciousness.* Poster presentation at the Annual Meeting of the Jean Piaget Society, Berkeley, CA.

Alward, K. R. (2005, June). *Construction of gender in the doll corner: Thoughts on Piaget's implicit social theory.* Paper for the Annual Meeting of the Jean Piaget Society, Montreal, QC, Canada.

Alward, K. R. (2012). The conservation of meaning as a function of constraints in the social context of puzzles: Piaget's social theory revisited. In L. E. Cohen & S. Waite-Stupiansky (Eds.), *Play: A polyphony of research, theories, and issues. Play and Culture Studies* (Vol. 12, pp. 121–132). New York, NY: University Press of America.

American Academy of Pediatrics. (2007). *The importance of play in promoting healthy child development and maintaining strong parent–child bonds.* Retrieved from http://www2.aap.org/pressroom/playfinal.pdf

American Psychological Association. (2007). *APA task force report on the sexualization of girls.* Retrieved from http://www.apa.org/pi/women/programs/girls/reportfull.pdf

American Public Health Association, American Academy of Pediatrics, & National Resource Center for Health and Safety in Child Care. (2011). *Caring for our children: National health and safety performance standards: Guidelines for early care and education programs* (3rd ed.). Elk Grove Village, IL: American Academy of Pediatrics.

Anderson, G. T., & Robinson, C. C. (2006). Rethinking the dynamics of young children's social play. *Dimensions of Early Childhood, 34*(1), 11–16.

Anderson, W. T. (Ed.). (1995). *The truth about truth.* New York, NY: Jeremy P. Tarcher/Putnam.

Arce, C. (2006). Molting mania: A kindergarten class learns about animals that shed their skin. *Science and Children, 43,* 28–31.

Ardley, J., & Ericson, L. (2002). "We don't play like that here!" Understanding aggressive expressions of play. In C. R. Brown & C. Marchant (Eds.), *Play in practice: Case studies in young children's play* (pp. 35–48). St. Paul, MN: Redleaf Press.

Ariel, S. (2002). *Children's imaginative play: A visit to Wonderland.* Westport, CT: Praeger.

Ashbrook, P. (2006). Roll with it. *Science and Children, 43,* 16.

Ashbrook, P. (2012). Drawing movement. *Science and Children, 50*(3), 30.

Ashton-Warner, S. (1963). *Teacher.* New York, NY: Simon & Schuster.

Axline, V. (1969). *Play therapy.* New York, NY: Ballantine.

Ayres, J. (1979). *Sensory integration and the child.* Los Angeles, CA: Western Psychological Services.

Bahktin, M. M. (2002). The problem of speech genres. In A. Jaworski & N. Coupland (Eds.), *The discourse reader* (pp. 121–132). London, UK: Routledge Press.

Balaban, N. (1985). *Starting school: From separation to independence.* New York, NY: Teachers College Press.

Balaban, N. (2006). *Everyday goodbyes: Starting school—a guide for the separation process.* New York, NY: Teachers College Press.

Barnes, E., & Lehr, R. (2005). Including everyone: A model preschool program for typical and special needs children. In J. P. Roopnarine & J. Johnson (Eds.), *Approaches to early childhood education* (4th ed., pp. 107–124). Upper Saddle River, NJ: Merrill/Prentice Hall.

Baroody, A. J. (2000). Research in review: Mathematics instruction for three- to five-year olds. *Young Children, 55*(4), 61–69.

Bartolini, V., & Lunn, K.). (2002). "Teacher, they won't let me play!" Strategies for improving inappropriate play behavior. In C. R. Brown & C. Marchant (Eds.), *Play in practice: Case studies in young children's play* (pp. 13–20). St. Paul, MN: Redleaf Press.

Bateson, G. A. (1976). A theory of play and fantasy. In J. S. Bruner, A. Jolly, & K. Sylva (Eds.), *Play: Its role in development and evolution* (pp. 119–129). New York, NY: Basic Books.

Beardsley, L. (1991). *Good day, bad day: The child's experience of child care.* New York, NY: Teachers College Press.

Beck, S. (2013). A critical-constructive discussion of Piaget and Vygotsky's theories of teaching and learning. Presentation at the 2013 meeting of the Jean Piaget Society, Chicago, IL.

Belkin, L. (2004, September). Is there a place in class for Thomas? What a year of "immersion" can do for a boy—and everyone around him. *New York Times Magazine, 40.*

Bellin, H. F., & Singer, D. G. (2006). My magic story car: Video-based intervention to strengthen emergent literacy of at-risk preschoolers. In D. Singer, R. M. Golinkoff, & K. Hirsh-Pasek (Eds.), *Play = learning: How play motivates and enhances children's cognitive and social emotional growth* (pp. 101–123). New York, NY: Oxford University Press.

Bennett, N., Wood, L., & Rogers, S. (1997). *Teaching through play: Teachers' thinking and classroom practice.* Philadelphia, PA: Open University Press.

Benson, J., & Miller, J. L. (2008). Experiences in nature: A pathway to standards. *Young Children, 63,* 22–28.

Bergen, D. (2002). The role of pretend play in children's cognitive development. *Early childhood research and practice, 4*(1), 2–15. Retrieved from http://ecrp.uiuc.edu/v4n1/bergen.html.

Bergen, D. (2003). Perspectives on inclusion in early childhood education. In J. P. Isenberg & M. R. Jalango (Eds.), *Major trends and issues in early childhood education* (2nd ed., pp. 47–68). New York, NY: Teachers College Press.

Bergen, D., & Fromberg, D. P. (2006). Epilogue: Emerging and future contexts, perspectives, and meanings for play. In D. P. Fromberg & D. Bergen (Eds.), *Play from birth to twelve* (2nd ed., pp. 417–425). New York, NY: Taylor & Francis Group.

Bergen, D., & Mauer, D. (2000). Symbolic play, phonological awareness, and literacy skills at three age levels. In K. Roskos & J. Christie (Eds.), *Play and literacy in early childhood: Research from multiple perspectives* (pp. 45–62). Mahwah, NJ: Erlbaum.

Bergeron, B. (1990). What does the term *whole language* mean? A definition from the literature. *Journal of Reading Behavior, 23,* 301–329.

Berk, L. E. (1994). Vygotsky's theory: The importance of make-believe play. *Young Children, 50*(1), 30–39.

Bettelheim, B. (1989). *The uses of enchantment.* New York, NY: Random House.

Blackwell, A. (2008). Worms out of this world! Earthworms excite young students to develop their observation skills. *Science and Children, 46,* 33–35.

Blurton-Jones, N. G. (1972). Categories of child–child interaction. In N. G. Blurton-Jones (Ed.), *Ethnological studies of child behavior* (pp. 97–129). New York, NY: Cambridge University Press.

Bodrova, E., & Leong, D. J. (2003). Chopsticks and counting chips: Do play and foundational skills need to compete for the teacher's attention in an early childhood classroom? *Young Children, 58*(3), 10–17.

Bodrova, E., & Leong, D. J. (2007) *Tools of the mind* (2nd ed.). Upper Saddle River, NJ: Pearson Education.

Bodrova, E., & Leong, D. (2007). *Tools of the mind: The Vygotskian approach to early childhood education.* Upper Saddle River, NJ: Pearson/Merrill Prentice Hall.

Bohart, H. (2012). Books count! Children's books with mathematics themes. In A. Shillady (Ed.), *Spotlight on young children: Exploring Math* (pp. 52–56). Washington, DC: NAEYC.

Bolton, G. (2003). *Dorothy Heathcote's story: The biography of a remarkable drama teacher.* Stoke-on-Trent, UK: Trentham Books.

Bourdieu, P. (2006). Language and symbolic power. In A. Jaworski & N. Coupland (Eds.), *The discourse reader* (2nd ed., pp. 480–490). New York, NY: Routledge.

Bower, J. K., Hales, D. P., Tate, D. F., Rubin, D. A., Benjamin, S. E., & Ward, D. F. (2008). The childcare environment and children's physical activity. *American Journal of Preventive Medicine, 34*(1), 23–29.

Bowman, B. (2005). Play in the multicultural world of children: Implications for adults. In E. Zigler, D. Singer, & S. Bishop-Josef (Eds.), *Children's play: The roots of reading* (pp. 125–142). Washington, DC: Zero to Three Press.

Bowman, B., & Moore, E. K. (Eds.). (2006). *School readiness and social-emotional development: Perspectives on cultural diversity.* Washington, DC: National Black Child Development Institute, Inc.

Bradford, M., Easterling, N., Mengel, T., & Sullivan, V. (2010). *Play outside! Getting started: Ten free or inexpensive ideas to enrich your outdoor learning environment today.* North Carolina Outdoor Learning Environment Alliance. Retrieved from http://www.earlylearning.nc.gov/OLE/pdf/Getting%20Started.pdf

Bredekamp, S. (2004). Play and school readiness. In E. Zigler, D. Singer, & S. Bishop-Josef (Eds.), *Children's play: The roots of reading* (pp. 159–174). Washington, DC: Zero to Three Press.

Broadhead, J.H., & Wood, E. (Eds.). (2010). *Play and learning in the early years: From research to practice.* London, UK: Sage.

Bronson, M. (2000). Research in review: Recognizing and supporting the development of self-regulation in young children. *Young Children, 55*(2), 32–37.

Bronson, W. (1995). *The right stuff for children from birth to 8: Selecting play materials to support development.* Washington, DC: NAEYC.

Brown, C. R., & Marchant, C. (Eds.). (2002). *Play in practice: Case studies in young children's play.* St. Paul, MN: Redleaf Press.

Brown, S. (2009). *Play: How it shapes the brain, opens the imagination, and invigorates the soul.* New York, NY: Penguin Group.

Brown, W. H., & Conroy, M. A. (2011). Social-emotional competency in young children with developmental delays: Our reflection and vision for the future. *Journal of Early Intervention, 33*(34), 310–320.

Bruder, M. B. (2010). Early childhood intervention: A promise to children and families for their future. *Exceptional Children 76*(3), 339–355.

Bruner, J. S. (1963). *The process of education.* Cambridge, MA: Harvard University Press.

Bruner, J. S. (1976). The nature and uses of immaturity. In J. S. Bruner, A. Jolly, & K. Sylva (Eds.), *Play: Its role in development and evolution* (pp. 28–64). New York, NY: Basic Books.

Bruner, J. S. (1986). *Actual minds, possible worlds.* Cambridge, MA: Harvard University Press.

Bruner, J. S. (1990). *Acts of meaning.* Cambridge, MA: Harvard University Press.

Buchannan, M., & Johnson, T. C. (2009). A second look at the play of young children with disabilities. *American Journal of Play, 2*(1), 41–59.

Burdette, H., & Whitaker, R. (2005). Resurrecting free play in young children: Looking beyond fitness and fatness to attention, affiliation, and affect. *Archives of Pediatrics & Adolescent Medicine, 159*(1), 46–50.

Burkhour, C. (2005). *Introduction to playground.* Chicago, IL: National Center on Physical Activity and Disability. Retrieved October 12, 2005, from http://www.ncpad.org/fun/fact_sheet.php?sheet=9&view=all.

Burton, B. (2012). Experiencing friction in first grade. *Science and Children, 50*(2), 68–72.

Burton, S. J., & Edwards, L. C. (2006). Creative play: Building connections with children who are learning English. *Dimensions of Early Childhood, 34*(2), 3–8.

Campaign for a Commercial-Free Childhood, Alliance for Childhood, & Teachers Resisting Unhealthy Children's Entertainment. (2012). *Facing the screen dilemma: Young children, technology and early learning.* Boston, MA: Campaign for a Commercial-Free Childhood; New York, NY: Alliance for Childhood. Retrieved from http://www.truceteachers.org/docs/facing_the_screen_dilemma.pdf.

Cardon, G., Van Cauwenberghe, E., Labarque, V., Haerens, L., & De Bourdeaudhulj, I. (2008). The contributions of preschool playground factors in explaining children's physical activity during recess. *International Journal of Behavioral Nutrition and Physical Activity, 5*(11), 1186–1192.

Carlson, F. M. (2006). *Essential touch: Meeting the needs of young children.* Washington, DC: NAEYC.

Carlson, F. M. (2011a). *Big body play: Why boisterous, vigorous, and very physical play is essential to children's development and learning.* Washington, DC: NAEYC.

Carlson, F. M. (2011b). Rough and tumble play: One of the most challenging behaviors. *Young Children, 66*(3), 18–25.

Carlsson-Paige, N. (2008). *Taking back childhood: Helping your kids thrive in a fast-paced, media-saturated, violence-filled world.* New York, NY: Hudson Street Press.

Carlsson-Paige, N., & Levin, D. E. (1990). *Who's calling the shots?* Santa Cruz, CA: New Society Publishers.

Carlsson-Paige, N., & Levin, D. E. (1998). *Before push comes to shove: Building conflict resolution skills with young children.* St. Paul, MN: Redleaf Press.

Caspe, M., Seltzer, A., Kennedy, J. L., Cappio, M., & DeLorenzo, C. (2013). Infants, toddlers, & preschool: Engaging families in the child assessment process. *Young Children, 68*(3), 8–15.

Cate, D., Diefendorf, M., McCullough, K., Peters, M., & Whaley, K. (Eds.). (2010). *Quality indicators of inclusive childhood programs/practices: A compilation of selected resources.* Chapel Hill, NC: FPG Child Development Institute, National Early Childhood Technical Assistance Center.

Cazden, C. B. (1983). Adult assistance to language development: Scaffolds, models and direct instruction. In R. P. Parker & F. A. Davis (Eds.), *Developing literacy: Young children's use of language* (pp. 3–18). Newark, DE: International Reading Association.

Chalufour, I., & Worth, K. (2003). *Discovering nature with young children.* St. Paul, MN: Readleaf Press.

Chalufour, I., & Worth, K. (2004). *Building structures with young children.* St. Paul, MN: Redleaf Press.

Chalufour, I., & Worth, K. (2006). Science in kindergarten. In D. Gullo (Ed.), *K today: Teaching and learning in the kindergarten year* (pp. 95–106). Washington, DC: NAEYC.

Chartrand, M. M., Frank, D. A., White, L. F., & Shope, T. R. (2008). Effect of parents' wartime deployment on the behavior of young children in military families. *Archives of Pediatric and Adolescent Medicine, 162*, 1009–1014.

Christie, D. J. (Ed.). (2011). *The encyclopedia of peace psychology.* Chichester, UK: Wiley-Blackwell.

Christie, D. J., Wagner, R. V., & Winter, D. D. (2001). *Peace, conflict, and violence: Peace psychology for the 21st century.* Upper Saddle River, NJ: Prentice Hall.

Christie, J. F. (2006). Play as a medium for literacy development. In D. P. Fromberg & D. Bergen (Eds.), *Play from birth to twelve* (2nd ed., pp. 181–186). New York, NY: Taylor & Francis Group.

Christie, J. F., & Roskos, K. A. (2006). Standards, science, and the role of play in early literacy education. In D. Singer, R. M. Golinkoff, & K. Hirsh-Pasek (Eds.), *Play = learning: How play motivates and enhances children's cognitive and social emotional growth* (pp. 57–73). New York, NY: Oxford University Press.

Clark, C. D. (2007). Therapeutic advantages of play. In A. Göncü & S. Gaskins (Eds.), *Play and development* (pp. 275–293). New York, NY: Erlbaum, Taylor & Francis Group.

Clawson, M. (2002). Play of language minority children in an early childhood setting. In J. L. Roopnarine (Ed.), *Conceptual, social-cognitive, and contextual issues in the fields of play: Play and culture studies* (Vol. 4, pp. 93–110). Westport, CT: Ablex Publishing.

Clay, M. (1966). *Emergent reading behaviors.* Unpublished doctoral dissertation. Auckland, New Zealand.

Clay, M. (2005). *Literacy lessons: Designed for individuals (Part 1: Why? When? And how?).* Portsmouth, NH: Heinemann.

Clayton, M., & Forton, M. B. (2001). *Classroom spaces that work.* Greenfield, MA: Northeast Foundation for Children.

Clements, D. H., & Sarama, J. (Eds.). (2004). *Engaging young children in mathematics: Standards for early childhood mathematics education.* Mahwah, NJ: Erlbaum.

Clements, D. H., & Sarama, J. (2009). *Learning and teaching early math: The learning trajectories approach.* New York, NY: Routledge.

Clements, R. (1990). *Counting on Frank.* Sydney, Australia: Collins.

Cochran-Smith, M., & Lytle, S. L. (1993). *Inside/outside: Teacher research and knowledge.* New York, NY: Teachers College Press.

Cohen, L. E., & Waite-Stupiansky, S. (2011). *Play: A polyphony of research, theories, and issues* (Vol. 12). Lanham, MD: University Press of America.

Common Sense Media, & Rideout, V. (2011). *Zero to eight: Children's media use in America.* San Francisco, CA: Common Sense Media.

Connery, M. P., John-Steiner, V. P., & Marjanovic-Shane, A. (2010). *Vygotsky and creativity: A cultural historical approach to play, meaning making and the arts.* New York, NY: Peter Lang.

Cook-Gumperz, J. (1986). *The social construction of literacy.* New York, NY: Cambridge University Press.

Cook-Gumperz, J., & Corsaro, W. (1977). Social-ecological constraints on children's communication strategies. *Sociology, 11,* 412–434.

Cook-Gumperz, J., Corsaro, W., & Streeck, J. (Eds.). (1996). *Children's worlds and children's language.* Berlin, DE: Mouton de Gruyter.

Cook-Gumperz, J., Gates, D., Scales, B., & Sanders, H. (1976). *Toward an understanding of angel's hair: Summary of a pilot study of a nursery play yard.* Unpublished manuscript, University of California, Berkeley, CA.

Cook-Gumperz, J., & Gumperz, J. (1982). Introduction: Language and social identity. In J. Gumperz (Ed.), *Language and social identity* (Vol. 2, pp. 1–2). Cambridge, UK: Cambridge University Press.

Cook-Gumperz, J., & Scales, B. (1982). *Toward an understanding of angel's hair: Report on a study of children's communication in sociodramatic play.* Unpublished manuscript.

Cook-Gumperz, J., & Scales, B. (1996). Girls, boys and just people: The interactional accomplishment of gender in the discourse of the nursery school. In D. Slobin, J. Gerhardt, A. Kyratzis, & J. Guo (Eds.), *Social interaction, social context, and language* (pp. 513–527). Mahwah, NJ: Erlbaum.

Cooney, M. (2004). Is play important? Guatemalan kindergartners' classroom experiences and their parents' and teachers' perceptions of learning through play. *Journal of Research in Childhood Education, 18*(4), 261–277.

Cooper, P. (2009). *The classrooms all young children need: Lessons in teaching from Vivian Paley.* Chicago, IL: University of Chicago Press.

Cooper, R. M. (1999, January/February). "But they are only playing": Interpreting play to parents. *Child Care Information Exchange.*

Coplan, R. J., Rubin, K. H., & Findlay, L. C. (2006). Social and nonsocial play. In D. P. Fromberg & D. Bergen (Eds.), *Play from birth to twelve* (2nd ed., pp. 75–86). New York, NY: Taylor & Francis Group.

Copley, J. V. (2000). *The young child and mathematics.* Washington, DC: National Council for the Education of Young Children; Reston, VA: National Council of Teachers of Mathematics.

Copley, J. V., Jones, C., & Dighe, J. (2007). *Mathematics: The creative curriculum approach.* Washington, DC: Teaching Strategies.

 pple, C., & Bredekamp, S. (Eds.). (2009). *Developmentally appropriate practice in early childhood programs: Serving children from birth through age 8* (3rd ed.). Washington, DC: NAEYC.

 aro, W. A. (1979). We're friends, right? Children's use of access rituals in a nursery school. *Language in Society, 8,* 315–336.

 ro, W. A. (1985). *Friendship and peer culture in the early ears.* Norwood, NJ: Ablex.

Corsaro, W. A. (1997). *The sociology of childhood.* Thousand Oaks, CA: Pine Forge Press.

Corsaro, W. A. (2003). *We're friends, right? Inside kids' culture.* Washington, DC: The Joseph Henry Press.

Corsaro, W. A. (2010) *The Sociology of Childhood.* Thousand Oaks, CA: Pine Forge Press

Corsaro, W. A. (2011). *The sociology of childhood.* (3rd ed.) Thousand Oaks, CA: Pine Forge Press.

Corsaro, W. A. (2012). Interpretive reproduction in children's play. *American Journal of Play, 4*(4), 488–504.

Corsaro, W. A., & Molinari, L. (2005). *I compagni: Understanding children's transition from preschool to elementary school.* New York, NY: Teachers College Press.

Corsaro, W. A., & Schwartz, K. (1991). Peer play and socialization in two cultures: Implications for research and practice. In B. Scales, M. Almy, A. Nicolopoulou, & S. Ervin-Tripp (Eds.), *Play and the social context of development in early care and education* (pp. 234–254). New York, NY: Teachers College Press.

Creasey, G. L., Jurvis, P. A., & Berk, L. E. (1998). Play and social competence. In O. N. Saracho & B. Spodek (Eds.), *Multiple perspectives on play in early childhood education* (pp. 116–143). Albany, NY: SUNY Press.

Cross, C. T., Woods, T. A., & Schweingruber, H. (Eds.). (2009). *Mathematics learning in early childhood: Paths toward excellence and equity.* Washington, DC: National Academies Press.

Cryer, D., Harms, T., & Riley, C. (2006). *All about the ECERS-R.* Lewisville, NC: Kaplan PACT House Publishing.

Csikszentmihalyi, M. (1993). *The evolving self: A psychology for the third millennium.* New York, NY: HarperCollins.

Curran, J. M. (1999). Constraints of pretend play: Implicit and explicit rules. *Journal of Research in Childhood Education, 14*(1), 47–55.

Curtis, D., & Carter, M. (2003). *Designs for living and learning: Transforming early childhood environments.* St. Paul, MN: Redleaf Press.

Danisa, D., Gentile, J., McNamara, K., Pinney, M., Ross, S., & Rule, A. (2006). Geoscience for preschoolers: These integrated math and science activities for young children really rock! *Science and Children, 44,* 30–33.

Davidson, J. I. F. (2006). Language and play: Natural partners. In D. P. Fromberg & D. Bergen (Eds.), *Play from birth to twelve* (2nd ed., pp. 31–40). New York, NY: Taylor & Francis Group.

Davydov, V. V. (1995). The influence of L. S. Vygotsky on education theory, research, and practice. *Educational Researcher, 24*(3), 12–21.

DeBey, M., & Bombard, D. (2007). Expanding children's boundaries: An approach to second-language learning and cultural understanding. *Young Children, 62*(2), 88–93.

DeBord, K., Hestenes, L., Moore, R., Cosco, N., & McGinnis, J. (2005). *Preschool outdoor environment measurement scale (POEMS).* Kaplan Early Learning Company. Retrieved from http://www.poemsnc.org/poems.html

DEC/NAEYC. (2009). *Early childhood inclusion: A joint position statement of the Division for Early Childhood (DEC) and the National Association for the Education of Young Children (NAEYC).* Chapel Hill, NC: The University of North Carolina, FPG Child Development Institute.

Derman-Sparks, L., & Edwards, J. O. (2010). *Anti-bias education for young children and ourselves.* Washington, DC: NAEYC.

Derman-Sparks, L., & Ramsey, P. (2005). A framework for culturally relevant, multicultural, and antibias education in the twenty-first century. In J. P. Roopnarine & J. Johnson (Eds.), *Approaches to early childhood education* (4th ed., pp. 107–124). Upper Saddle River, NJ: Merrill/Prentice Hall.

Desjean-Perotta, B., & Barbour, A. C. (2001). The prop box: Helping preservice teachers understand the value of dramatic play. *Journal of the National Forum of Teacher Education, 12*(1), 3–15.

DeVries, R. (2006). Games with rules. In D. P. Fromberg & D. Bergen (Eds.), *Play from birth to twelve* (2nd ed., pp. 119–125). New York, NY: Taylor & Francis Group.

DeVries, R., & Sales, C. (2011). *Ramps & pathways: A constructivist approach to physics with young children.* Washington, DC: NAEYC.

DeVries, R., & Zan, B. (2005). A constructivist perspective on the role of the sociomoral atmosphere in promoting children's development. In C. T. Fosnot (Ed.), *Constructivism: Theory, perspectives, and practice* (2nd ed., pp. 132–149). New York, NY: Teachers College Press.

DeVries, R., & Zan, B. S. (2012). *Moral classrooms, moral children: Creating a constructivist atmosphere in early education* (2nd ed.). New York, NY: Teachers College Press.

DeVries, R., Zan, B., Hildebrandt, C., Edmiaston, R., & Sales, C. (2002). *Developing constructivist early childhood curriculum: Practical principles and activities.* New York, NY: Teachers College Press.

Dewey, J. (1915). *The school and society.* Chicago, IL: The University of Chicago Press.

Dewey, J. (1998). *Experience and education: The 60th anniversary edition.* West Lafayette, IN: Kappa Delta Pi.

Dickinson, D. K., & Tabors, P. O. (2002, March). Fostering language and literacy in classrooms and homes. *Young Children, 57,* 10–18.

Dimensions Educational Research Foundation & Arbor Day Foundation. (2007). *Learning with nature idea book: Creating nurturing outdoor spaces for children, field-tested principles for effective outdoor learning environments.* Retrieved from http://issuu.com/arbordayfoundation/docs/lwnb_preview.

Drew, W. E., Christie, J., Johnson, J. E., Meckley, A. M., & Nell, M. L. (2008). Constructive play: A value-added strategy for meeting early learning standards. *Young Children, 63,* 38 44.

Duckworth, E. (2001). *"Tell me more": Listening to learners.* New York, NY: Teachers College Press.

Dunn, M. (2003). Getting along while getting ahead: Meeting children's social and emotional needs in a climate of academic accountability. *Dimensions of Early Childhood, 31*(3), 18–26.

Dyson, A. H. (1989). *Multiple worlds of child writers: Friends learning to write.* New York, NY: Teachers College Press.

Dyson, A. H. (1993). *Social worlds of children learning to write in an urban primary school.* New York, NY: Teachers College Press.

Dyson, A. H. (1994). *The ninjas, the X-men, and the ladies: Playing with power and identity in an urban primary school* (Technical Report No. 70). Berkeley, CA: University of California, National Center for the Study of Writing.

Dyson, A. H. (1995, April). *The courage to write: The ideological dimensions of child writing.* Paper presented at the Annual Meeting of the American Educational Research Association, San Francisco, CA.

Dyson, A. H. (1997). *Writing superheroes: Contemporary childhood, popular culture, and classroom literacy.* New York, NY: Teachers College Press.

Dyson, A. H. (2003). *The brothers and sisters learn to write: Popular literacies in childhood and school cultures.* New York, NY: Teachers College Press.

Dyson, A. H. (2013). *Rewriting the basics: Literacy learning in children's cultures.* New York, NY: Teachers College Press.

Dyson, A. H., & Genishi, C. (Eds.). (1994). *The need for story: Cultural diversity in classroom and community.* Urbana, IL: National Council of Teachers of English.

Edwards, C., Gandini, L., & Forman, G. (Eds.). (1993). *The hundred languages of children: The Reggio Emilia approach to early childhood education.* Norwood, NJ: Ablex.

Edwards, C., & Rinaldi, C. (Eds.). (2009). *The diary of Laura: Perspectives on a Reggio Emilia diary.* Italy: Reggio Children.

Edwards, L. C. (2010). *The creative arts: A process approach for teachers and children* (5th ed.). Upper Saddle River, NJ: Pearson Education.

Edwards, L. C. (2013). *Music and movement: A way of life for the young child.* Upper Saddle River, NJ: Pearson Education.

Egan, K. (1988). *Primary understanding: Education in early childhood.* New York, NY: Routledge.

Einarsdottir, J. (2000). Incorporating literacy resources into the play curriculum of two Icelandic preschools. In K. Roskos & J. Christie (Eds.), *Play and literacy in early childhood: Research from multiple perspectives* (pp. 77–90). Mahwah, NJ: Erlbaum.

Eisenhauer, M. J., & Feikes, D. (2009). Dolls, blocks, and puzzles: Playing with mathematical understandings. *Young Children, 64,* 18–24.

Elkind, D. (2003). Thanks for the memory: The lasting value of play. *Young Children, 58*(3), 46–51.

Elkind, D. (2007). *The power of play: Learning what comes naturally.* Philadelphia, PA: Da Capo Press.

Ellis, M. (1988). Play and the origin of species. In D. Bergen (Ed.), *Play as a medium for learning and development* (pp. 23–26). Portsmouth, NH: Heinemann.

English, A., & Stengel, B. (2010). Exploring fear: Rousseua, Dewey, and Freire on fear and learning. *Educational Theory, 60,* 521–542.

Ensign, J. (2003). Including culturally relevant math in an urban school. *Educational Studies, 34*(4), 414–423.

Erickson, F. (1993). Foreword. In M. Cochran-Smith & S. L. Lytle (Eds.), *Inside/outside: Teacher research and knowledge.* New York, NY: Teachers College Press.

Erickson, F. (2004). *Talk and social theory: Ecologies of speaking and listening in everyday life.* Malden, MA: Blackwell.

Erickson, F., & Schultz, J. (1982). *Counselor as gatekeeper: Social interaction in interviews.* New York, NY: Academic Press.

Erikson, E. (1950/1985). *Childhood and society.* New York, NY: Norton.

Erikson, E. (1977). *Toys and reasons.* New York, NY: Norton.

Erwin, E. J. (1993). Social participation of young children with visual impairments in specialized and integrated environments. *Journal of Visual Impairment & Blindness, 87*(5), 138–142.

Espinosa, L. M. (2010). *Getting it right for young children from diverse backgrounds: Applying research to improve practice.* Upper Saddle River, NJ: Pearson Education.

Falk, B. (2012). *Defending childhood: Keeping the promise of early education.* New York, NY: Teachers College Press.

Fantuzzo, J., Sutton-Smith, B., Coolahan, K. C., Manz, P. H., Canning, S., & Debnam, D. (1995). Assessment of preschool play interaction behaviors in low income children: Penn Interactive Peer Play Scale. *Early Childhood Research Quarterly, 10,* 105–120.

Farish, J. M. (2001) Helping children in frightening times. *Young Children, 59*(6), 6–7.

Fein, G. G. (1981). Pretend play in childhood: An integrative review. *Child Development, 52,* 1095–1118.

Fein, G. G., Ardeila-Ray, A., & Groth, L. (2000). The narrative connection: Stories and literacy. In K. Roskos & J. Christie (Eds.), *Play and literacy in early childhood: Research from multiple perspectives* (pp. 27–43). Mahwah, NJ: Erlbaum.

Fein, S. (1984). *Heidi's horse* (2nd ed.). Pleasant Hill, CA: Exelrod Press.

Fennimore, B. S., & Goodwin, A. L. (Eds.). (2011). *Promoting social justice for young children.* New York, NY: Springer.

Ferguson, C. (2001). Discovering, supporting, and promoting young children's passions and interests: One teacher's reflections. *Young Children, 56*(4), 6–11.

Fiorelli, J. A. & Russ, S. W. (2012). Pretend play, coping and subjective well-being in children. *American Journal of Play 5*(1) 81–103.

Fisman, L. (2001). *Child's play: An empirical study of the relationship between the physical form of school yards and children's behavior.* Retrieved from http://www.yale.edu/nixon/research/pdf/LFisman_Playgrounds.pdf.

Flanders, J., Leo, V., Paquette, D., Pihl, R. O., & Séguin, J. R. (2009). Rough-and-tumble play and the regulation of aggression: An observational study of father–child dyads. *Aggressive Behavior, 35*(4), 285–295.

Flanders, J. L., Herman, K. N., & Paquette, D. (2013). Rough-and-tumble play and the cooperation-competition dilemma: Evolutionary and developmental perspectives on the development of social competence. In D. Narvaez, J. Panksepp, A. N. Schore, & T. R. Gleason (Eds.), *Evolution, early experience and human development: From research to practice and policy* (pp. 371–387). New York, NY: Oxford University Press.

Forman, G. (2005). The project approach in Reggio Emilia. In C. T. Fosnot (Ed.). *Constructivism: Theory, perspectives, and practice* (2nd ed., pp. 212–221). New York, NY: Teachers College Press.

Forman, G. E., & Kaden, M. (1987). Research on science education for young children. In C. Seefeldt (Ed.), *The early childhood curriculum: A review of current research* (pp. 141–164). New York, NY: Teachers College Press.

⌐man, G. E., & Kuschner, D. S. (1977). *The child's construction of knowledge: Piaget for teaching children.* Belmont, CA: Wadsworth.

⌐ot, C. T., & Dolk, M. (2001). *Young mathematicians at work: Constructing number sense, addition, and subtraction.* Portsmouth, NH: Heinemann.

⌐erg, D. P. (2002). *Play and meaning in early childhood education.* Boston, MA: Allyn & Bacon.

Fromberg, D. P., & Bergen, D. (Eds.). (2006). *Play from birth to twelve: Contexts, perspectives, and meanings* (2nd ed.). New York, NY: Routledge.

Frost, J. L. (2007). Playground checklist. In J. L. Frost, S. Wortham, & S. Reifel (Eds.), *Play and child development* (3rd ed., pp. 394–398). Upper Saddle River, NJ: Pearson.

Frost, J. L., Brown, P., Sutterby, J. A., & Thornton, C. D. (2004). *The developmental benefits of playgrounds.* Olney, MD: Association for Childhood Education International.

Frost, J. L., & Woods, I. C. (2006). Perspectives on playgrounds. In D. P. Fromberg & D. Bergen (Eds.), *Play from birth to twelve* (2nd ed., pp. 331–342). New York, NY: Taylor & Francis Group.

Frost, J. L., Wortham, S. C., & Reifel, S. (2012). *Play and child development* (4th ed.). Upper Saddle River, NJ: Merrill/Prentice Hall.

Fry, D. (2005). Rough-and-tumble social play in humans. In A. D. Pellegrini & P. K. Smith (Eds.), *The nature of play: Great apes and humans* (pp. 54–85). New York, NY: Guilford Press.

Full Option Science System (FOSS). (2012a). *Air and weather.* Nashua, NH: Delta Education.

Full Option Science System (FOSS). (2012b). *Balance and Motion.* Nashua, NH: Delta Education.

Full Option Science System (FOSS). (2012c). *Insects and plants.* Nashua, NH: Delta Education.

Full Option Science System (FOSS). (2012d). *Solids and liquids.* Nashua, NH: Delta Education.

Full Option Science System (FOSS). (2012e). *Pebbles, silt, and sand.* Nashua, NH: Delta Education.

Furth, H. G. (1970). *Piaget for teachers.* Upper Saddle River, NJ: Prentice Hall.

Galinsky, E. (2010). *Mind in the making: The seven essential life skills every child needs.* New York, NY: Harper Collins.

Gallas, K. (1998). *Sometimes I can be anything: Power, gender, and identity in a primary classroom.* New York, NY: Teachers College Press.

Gallas, K. (2003). *Imagination and literacy: A teacher's search for the heart of meaning.* New York, NY: Teachers College Press.

Gandini, L., Hill, L., Cadwell, L., & Schwall, C. (2005). *In the spirit of the studio: Learning from the atelier of Reggio Emilia.* New York, NY: Teachers College Press.

Gardner, H. (1993). *Frames of mind: The theory of multiple intelligence.* New York, NY: Basic Books.

Gardner, H. (1999). *Intelligence reformed: Multiple intelligences for the 21st century.* New York, NY: Basic Books.

Gardner, H. (2011a). *Frames of mind: The theory of multiple intelligences* (2nd ed.). New York, NY: Basic Books.

Gardner, H. (2011b). *Creating minds: An anatomy of creativity seen through the lives of Freud, Einstein, Picasso, Stravinsky, Eliot, Graham, and Ghandi.* New York, NY: Basic Books.

Garvey, C. (1977/1990). *Play.* Cambridge, MA: Harvard University Press.

Garvey, C., & Berndt, R. (1977). *Organization of pretend play* (JSAS Catalogue of Selected Documents in Psychology, Manuscript 1589). Washington, DC: American Psychological Association.

Gaskins, S., Haight, W., & Lancy, D. F. (2007). The cultural construction of play. In A. Göncü & S. Gaskins (Eds.), *Play and development* (pp. 179–202). New York, NY: Erlbaum, Taylor & Francis Group.

Gaskins, S., Miller, P., & Corsaro, W. (1992). Theoretical and methodological perspectives in the interpretive study of children. *New Directions in Child Development, 58*, 5–23.

Gee, K. (2000). *Visual arts as a way of knowing.* York, ME: Stenhouse Publishers.

Genishi, C. (2002, July). Young English language learners: Resourceful in the classroom. *Young Children, 57*(4), 66–72.

Genishi, C., & DiPaolo, M. (1982). Learning through argument in preschool. In L. C. Wilkonson (Ed.), *Communicating in the classroom* (pp. 49–68). New York, NY: Academic Press.

Genishi, C., & Dyson, A. H. (1984). *Language assessment in the early years.* Norwood, NJ: Ablex.

Genishi, C., & Dyson, A. H. (2005). *On the case: Approaches to language and literacy research.* New York, NY: Teachers College Press and National Conference on Research in Language and Literacy.

Genishi, C., & Dyson, A. H. (Eds.). (2009). *Children, language and literacy: Diverse learners in diverse times.* New York, NY: Teachers College Press.

Genishi, C., Dyson, A. H., & Russo, L. (2011). Playful learning: Early education that makes sense to children. In B. S. Fennimore & A. L. Goodwin (Eds.), *Promoting social justice for young children* (pp. 59–70). New York, NY: Springer.

Genishi, C., & Goodwin, A. L. (2008). *Diversity in early childhood education: Rethinking and doing.* New York, NY: Routledge.

Genishi, C., Huang, S., & Glupczynski, T. (2005). Becoming early childhood teachers: Linking action research and postmodern theory in a language and literacy course. *Advances in Early Education and Day Care, 14*, 161–192.

Ghafouri, F., & Wien, C. A. (2005). Give us privacy: Play and social literacy in young children. *Journal of Research in Childhood Education, 19*(4), 279–291.

Giddens, A. (2000). *Runaway world: How globalization is reshaping our lives.* New York, NY: Routledge.

Ginsburg, H. P. (2006). Mathematical play and playful mathematics. In D. G. Singer, R. M. Golinkoff, & K. Hirsh-Pasek (Eds.). *Play = learning: How play motivates and enhances children's cognitive and social-emotional growth* (pp. 145–167). New York, NY: Oxford University Press.

Glod, M. (2008, July 17). Coping with their parents' war. *Washington Post*, A1, A9.

Goffman, E. (1974). *Frame analysis.* New York, NY: Harper & Row.

Goffman, E. (2000). On face-work: An analysis of ritual elements in social interaction. In A. Jaworski & N. Coupland (Eds.), *The discourse reader* (pp. 306–320). London, UK: Routledge.

Goleman, D. (1995). *Emotional intelligence.* New York, NY: Bantam Books.

Goleman, D. (2011). *The brain and emotional intelligence: New insights.* Northampton, MA: More Than Sound LLC.

Golomb, C., Gowing, E. D., & Friedman, L. (1982). Play and cognition: Studies of pretense play and conservation of quantity. *Journal of Experimental Child Psychology, 33*, 257–279.

Göncü, A. (1993). Development of intersubjectivity in the dyadic play of preschoolers. *Early Childhood Research Quarterly, 8*, 99–116.

Göncü, A., Jain, J., & Tuermer, U. (2007). Children's play as cultural interpretation. In A. Göncü & S. Gaskins (Eds.), *Play and development* (pp. 155–178). New York, NY: Erlbaum, Taylor & Francis Group.

Gonzalez-Mena, J. (1998). *The child in the family and the community.* Upper Saddle River, NJ: Merrill/Prentice Hall.

Gonzalez-Mena, J. (2008). *Diversity in early care and education: Honoring differences* (5th ed.). Washington, DC: NAEYC.

Gonzalez-Mena, J. (2010). *50 Strategies for communicating and working with diverse families* (2nd ed.). Upper Saddle River, NJ: Pearson Education.

Goodenough, E. (Ed.). (2003). *Secret spaces of childhood.* Ann Arbor, MI: University of Michigan Press.

Goodnow, J. (1977). *Children drawing.* Cambridge, MA: Harvard University Press.

Goodwin, M. (1990). *He-said-she-said: Talk as social organization among black children.* Bloomington, IN: Indiana University Press.

Gopnik, A. (2011, March). Why preschool shouldn't be like school: New research shows that teaching kids more and more, at ever-younger ages, may backfire. *Slate Magazine.* Retrieved from http://www.slate.com/articles/double_x/doublex/2011/03/why_preschool_shouldnt_be_like_school.html

Graves, D. (1983). *Writing: Teachers and children at work.* Exeter, NH: Heineman.

Gray, P. (2011). The decline of play and the rise of psychopathology in children and adolescents. *American Journal of Play, 3*(4), 443–463. Retrieved from http://www.journalofplay.org/sites/www.journalofplay.org/files/pdf-articles/3-4-article-gray-decline-of-play.pdf

Green, M. (2006). Social and emotional development in the zero-to-three child: A systems change approach. In B. Bowman & E. K. Moore (Eds.), *School readiness and social-emotional development: Perspectives on cultural diversity* (pp. 89–98). Washington, DC: National Black Child Development Institute, Inc.

Greenman, J. (2005, May). Places for childhood in the 21st century: A conceptual framework. *Beyond the Journal: Young Children on the Web.* Retrieved from http://www.naeyc.org/files/yc/file/200505/01Greenman.pdf.

Griffin, E. (1998). *Island of childhood: Education in the special world of the nursery school.* Troy, NY: Educators International Press.

Griffin, S. (2004). Number worlds: A research-based mathematics program for young children. In D. H. Clements & J. Sarama (Eds.), *Engaging young children in mathematics: Standards for early childhood mathematics education* (pp. 325–342). Mahwah, NJ: Erlbaum.

Gullo, D. (2006). Assessment in kindergarten. In D. Gullo (Ed.), *K today: Teaching and learning in the kindergarten year* (pp. 138–150). Washington, DC: NAEYC.

Gumperz, J. J., & Cook-Gumperz, J. (1982). Introduction: Language and the communication of social identity. In J. J. Gumperz & J. Cook-Gumperz (Eds.), *Language and social identity* (pp. 1–21). Cambridge, UK: Cambridge University Press.

Guralnick, M. J. (2010). Early intervention approaches to enhance the peer-related social competence of young children with developmental delays: A historical perspective. *Infants and Young Children, 23*(2), 73–83.

Gustafson, S. C. (2000). *Educating for peace and nonviolence in early childhood.* Unpublished manuscript.

Hachey, A. C., & Butler, D. L. (2009). Seeds in the window, soil in the sensory table: Science education through gardening and nature-based play. *Young Children, 64,* 42–48.

Haight, W., Black, J., Ostler, T., & Sheridan, K. (2006). Pretend play and emotion learning in traumatized mothers and children. In D. G. Singer, R. M. Golinkoff, & K. Hirsh-Pasek (Eds.), *Play = learning: How play motivates and enhances children's cognitive and social-emotional growth* (pp. 209–230). New York, NY: Oxford University Press.

Hamlin, M., & Wisneski, D. B. (2012). Supporting the scientific thinking and inquiry of toddlers and preschoolers through play. *Young Children, 67*(3), 82–88.

Hammond, D. (2011). *KaBOOM! How one man built a movement to save play.* New York, NY: Rodale Books.

Hand, H., & Nourot, P. M. (1999). *First class: Guide to early primary education.* Sacramento, CA: California Department of Education.

Hanline, M. F., & Fox, L. (1993). Learning within the context of play: Providing typical early childhood experiences for children with severe disabilities. *The Journal of the Association for Persons with Severe Handicaps, 18*(2), 121–129.

Harms, T. (1969). *My art is me* [Motion picture]. Berkeley, CA: University of California Extension Media Center.

Harms, T., Clifford, R. M., & Cryer, D. (1998). *Early childhood environment rating scale* (rev. ed.). New York, NY: Teachers College Press.

Harms, T., Jacobs, E. V., & White, D. R. (1996). *School-age care environment rating scale.* New York, NY: Teachers College Press.

Hartmann, W., & Rollett, B. (1994). Play: Positive intervention in the elementary school curriculum. In J. Hellendoorn, R. van der Kooij, & B. Sutton-Smith (Eds.), *Play and intervention* (pp. 195–202). Albany, NY: SUNY Press.

Heath, S. B. (1983). *Ways with words: Language, life and work in communities and classrooms.* New York, NY: Cambridge University Press.

Heath, S. B., & Mangiola, L. (1991). *Children of promise: Literate activity in linguistically and culturally diverse classrooms.* Washington, DC: National Education Association.

Heathcote, D. (1997). *Three looms waiting.* Berkeley, CA: University of California Media Center.

Heathcote, D., & Bolton, G. (1995). *Drama for learning: Dorothy Heathcote's mantle of the expert approach to education.* Portsmouth, NH: Heinemann.

Heathcote, D., & Herbert, P. (1985, Summer). A drama of meaning: Mantle of the expert. *Theory into Practice, 24*(3), 173–179.

Helm, J. H., & Beneke, S. (Eds.). (2003). *The power of projects: Meeting contemporary challenges in early childhood classroom—Strategies and solutions.* New York, NY: Teachers College Press.

Helm, J. H., & Katz, L. G. (2010). *Young Investigators: The Project Approach in the Early Years.* New York, NY: Teachers College Press.

Henderson, F., & Jones, E. (2002). "Everytime they get started, we interrupt them": Children with special needs at play. In C. R. Brown & C. Marchant (Eds.), *Play in practice: Case studies in young children's play* (pp. 133–146). St. Paul, MN: Redleaf Press.

Hendrickson, J. M., Strain, P. S., Trembley, A., & Shores, R. E. (1981). Relationship between a material use and the occurrence of social interactive behaviors by normally developing preschool children. *Psychology in the Schools, 18,* 500–504.

Hirsh-Pasek, K. & Golinkoff, R. M. with D. Eyers. (2003). Einstein never used flashcards: How our children really learn—and why they need to play more and memorize less.

Hirsh-Pasek, K., Golinkoff, R. M., Berk, L. E., & Singer, D. G. (2009). *A mandate for playful learning in preschool: Presenting the evidence.* New York, NY: Oxford University Press.

Holmes, R. M. (2012). The outdoor recess activities of children at an urban school: Longitudinal and intraperiod patterns. *American Journal of Play, 4*(3), 327–351. Retrieved from http://www.journalofplay.org/sites/www.journalofplay.org/files/pdf-articles/4-3-article-the-outdoor-recess-activites-of-children-at-an-urban-school.pdf

Holmes, R., & Geiger, C. (2002). The relationship between creativity and cognitive abilities in preschoolers. In J. L. Roopnarine (Ed.), *Conceptual, social-cognitive, and contextual issues in the fields of play* (pp. 127–148). *Play and Culture Studies* (Vol. 4). Westport, CT: Ablex.

Holton, D., Ahmed, A., Williams, H., & Hill, C. (2001). On the importance of mathematical play. *International Journal of Math Education in Science and Technology, 32*(3), 401–415.

Hong, M. (2011). Creating meaningful contexts in schools for English language learners. In B. S. Fennimore & A. L. Goodwin (Eds.), *Promoting social justice for young children* (pp. 125–134). New York, NY: Springer.

Honig, A. S. (2007). Ten power boosts for children's early learning. *Journal of the National Association for the Education of Young Children, 62*(5), 72–78.

Howard, J. (2010). The developmental and therapeutic value of children's play: Re-establishing teachers as play professionals. In J. Moyles (Ed.), *The excellence of play* (3rd ed.). Maidenhead, UK: Open University Press.

Howard, J., & Eisele, G. (2012). Exploring the presence of characteristics associated with play within the ritual repetitive behaviour of autistic children. *International Journal of Play, 1*(2), 139–150.

Howes, C. (with Unger, O., & Matheson, C.). (1992). *The collaborative construction of pretend: Social pretend play functions.* Albany, NY: SUNY Press.

Hughes, F. (2003). Sensitivity to the social and cultural contexts of the play of young children. In J. Isenberg & M. Jalongo (Eds.), *Major trends and issues in early childhood education: Challenges, controversies, and insights* (2nd ed., pp. 126–135). New York, NY: Teachers College Press.

Hutt, C. (1971). Exploration and play in children. In R. E. Herron & B. Sutton-Smith (Eds.), *Child's play* (pp. 231–251). New York, NY: Wiley.

Hyson, M. C. (2004). *The emotional development of young children: Building an emotion-centered curriculum.* New York, NY: Teachers College Press.

Hyson, M. (2008). *Enthusiastic and engaged learners: Approaches to learning in the early childhood classroom.* New York, NY: Teachers College Press.

International Reading Association & National Association for the Education of Young Children. (1998). Learning to read and write: Developmentally appropriate practices for young children: A joint position statement of the IRA and NAEYC. Washington, DC: NAEYC. Retrieved from http://oldweb.naeyc.org/about/positions/psread4.asp.

Isenberg, J. P., & Jalongo, M. R. (2001). *Creative expression and play in early childhood*. Upper Saddle River, NJ: Merrill/Prentice Hall.

Isenberg, J. P., & Jalongo, M. R. (2014). *Creative thinking and arts-based learning*. Upper Saddle River, NJ: Pearson Education, Inc.

Jablon, J. R., Dombro, A. L., & Ditchtelmiller, M. L. (2007). *The power of observation for birth through eight* (2nd ed.). Washington, DC: NAEYC.

Jacobs, G., & Crowley, K. (2010). *Reaching standards and beyond in kindergarten: Nurturing children's sense of wonder and joy in learning*. Thousand Oaks, CA: Corwin.

Jambor, T., & Palmer, S. D. (1991). *Playground safety manual*. Birmingham, AL: Injury Prevention Center, University of Alabama.

Jarrett, O. (2002). Recess in elementary school: What does the research say? *ERIC/EECE Digest Archive*, ED 466 331. Retrieved from http://ecap.crc.illinois.edu/eecearchive/digests/2002/jarrett02.html

Jarrett, O. S., & Waite-Stupiansky, S. (2009). Recess—It's indispensable! *Young Children, 64*(5), 66–69.

Jaworski, A., & Coupland, N. (Eds.). (1999). *The discourse reader*. London, UK: Routledge.

Jaworski, A., & Coupland, N. (Eds.). (2006). *The discourse reader* (2nd ed.). London, UK: Routledge.

Johnson, J. E. (2006). Play development from ages four to eight. In D. P. Fromberg & D. Bergen (Eds.), *Play from birth to twelve* (2nd ed., pp. 13–20). New York, NY: Taylor & Francis Group.

Johnson, L., & O'Neill, C. (Eds.). (1984). *Dorothy Heathcote's collected writings on drama and education*. London, UK: Hutchinson, Ltd.

Jones, E., & Cooper, R. (2006). *Playing to get smart*. New York, NY: Teachers College Press.

Jones, E., & Reynolds, G. (2011). *The play's the thing: Teachers' roles in children's play* (2nd ed.). New York, NY: Teacher's Press.

Joshi, A. (2005). Understanding Asian Indian families: Facilitating meaningful home-school relations. *Young Children, 60*, 75–79.

Kafai, Y. B. (2006). Play and technology: Revised realities and potential perspectives. In D. P. Fromberg & D. Bergen (Eds.), *Play from birth to twelve* (2nd ed., pp. 207–213). New York, NY: Taylor & Francis Group.

Kaiser, B., & Rasminsky, J. S. (2008). *Challenging behavior in elementary and middle school*. Upper Saddle River, NJ: Allyn & Bacon/Pearson.

Kaiser Family Foundation. (2010). *Generation M2: Media in the lives of 8- to 18-year-olds*. Retrieved http://kff.org/other/poll-finding/report-generation-m2-media-in-the-lives.

Kalmart, K. (2008). Let's give children something to talk about! Oral language and preschool literacy. *Young Children, 63*(1), 88–92.

Kamii, C. (1982). *Number in preschool and kindergarten: Educational implications of Piaget's theory*. Washington, DC: NAEYC.

Kamii, C. (Ed.). (1990). *No achievement testing in the early grades: The games grown-ups play*. Washington, DC: NAEYC.

Kamii, C. (with Housman, L. B.). (2000). *Young children reinvent arithmetic: Implications of Piaget's theory* (2nd ed.). New York, NY: Teachers College Press.

Kamii, C. (2013). Physical knowledge activities: Play before the differentiation of knowledge into subjects. In L. E. Cohen & S. Waite-Stupiansky (eds.), *Learning across the early childhood curriculum. Advances in Early Education and Day Care* (Vol. 17, pp. 57–72). London, UK: Emerald Press.

Kamii, C., & DeVries, R. (1993). *Physical knowledge in preschool education*. New York, NY: Teachers College Press. (Original work published in 1978).

Kamii, C., & Kato, Y. (2006). Play and mathematics at ages one to ten. In D. P. Fromberg & D. Bergen (Eds.), *Play from birth to twelve* (2nd ed., pp. 187–198). New York, NY: Taylor & Francis Group.

Kamii, C., Miyakawa, Y., & Kato, Y. (2004, September). The development of logico-mathematical thinking in a block building activity at ages 1–4. *Journal of Research in Childhood Education, 19*(1).

Katch, J. (2001). *Under deadman's skin: Discovering the meaning of children's violent play*. Boston, MA: Beacon Press.

Katch, J. (2003). *They don't like me: Lessons on bullying and teasing from a preschool classroom*. Boston, MA: Beacon Press.

Katz, L. (2007). Standards of experience. *Young Children, 62*(3), 94–95.

Katz, L., & Chard, S. (2000). *Engaging children's minds: The project approach* (2nd ed.). Stamford, CT: Ablex.

Katz, L., Evangelou, D., & Hartman, J. (1990). *The case for mixed age grouping in early education*. Washington, DC: NAEYC.

Kellogg, R. (1969). *Analyzing children's art*. Palo Alto, CA: National Press.

Kelly-Vance, L., & Ryalls, B. O. (2005). A systematic, reliable approach to play assessment in preschoolers. *School Psychology International, 26*(5), 398–412.

Kemple, K. M. (2004). *Let's be friends: Peer competence and social inclusion in early childhood programs*. New York, NY: Teachers College Press.

Kendall, J. S., & Marzano, R. J. (2004). *Content knowledge: A compendium of standards and benchmarks for K–12 education*. Aurora, CO: Mid-Continent Research for Education and Learning (McRel). Retrieved from http://www.mcrel.org/standards-benchmarks.

Kim, E. & Lim, J. (2007). Eco-early childhood education: A new paradigm of early childhood education in South Korea. *Young Children, 62*, 42–45.

Kirmani, M. H. (2007). Empowering culturally and linguistically diverse children and families. *Journal of the National Association for the Education of Young Children, 62*(6), 94–98.

Knight, S. (2011). *Risk and adventure in early years' outdoor play: Learning from Forest School*. London, UK: Sage Publications, Inc.

Koons, K. (1991). A center for writers. *First Teacher, 12*(7), 23.

Koplow, L. (Ed.). (1996). *Unsmiling faces: How preschools can heal*. New York, NY: Teachers College Press.

Kostelnik, M., Onaga, E., Rohde, B., & Whiren, A. (2002). *Children with special needs: Lessons for early childhood professionals*. New York, NY: Teachers College Press.

Kranor, L., & Kuschner, A. (Eds.). (1996). *Project exceptional: Exceptional children: Education in preschool techniques for inclusion, opportunity-building, nurturing, and learning*. Sacramento, CA: California Department of Education.

Kreidler, W., & Wittall, S. T. (1999). *Adventures in peacemaking* (2nd ed.). Cambridge, MA: Educators for Social Responsibility.

Kritchevsky, L., & Prescott, E. (1977). *Planning environments for young children: Physical space.* Washington, DC: NAEYC.

Kritchevsky, L., Prescott, E., & Walling, L. (1977). *Planning environments for young children: Physical space* (2nd ed.). Washington, DC: NAEYC.

Kuo, F., & Taylor, A. (2004, September). A potential natural treatment for attention-deficit/hyperactivity disorder: Evidence from a national study. *American Journal of Public Health, 94,* 9.

Kuschner, D. (2012). Play is natural to childhood but school is not: The problem of integrating play into the curriculum. *International Journal of Play 1*(3), 242–249.

Labov, W. (1972). *Language in the inner city: Studies in Black English vernacular.* Philadelphia, PA: Pennsylvania University Press.

Lancy, D. (2002). Cultural constraints on children's play. In J. L. Roopnarine (Ed.), *Conceptual, social-cognitive, and contextual issues in the fields of play* (pp. 53–62). *Play and Culture Studies* (Vol. 4). Westport, CT: Ablex.

Landreth, G., Homeyer, L., & Morrison, M. (2006). Play as the language of children's feelings. In D. P. Fromberg & D. Bergen (Eds.), *Play from birth to twelve* (2nd ed., pp. 47–52). New York, NY: Taylor & Francis Group.

Lantieri, L., & Goleman, D. (2008). *Building emotional intelligence: Techniques to cultivate inner strength in children.* Boulder, CO: Sounds True, Inc.

Laski, E. V. (2013). Portfolio picks: An approach for developing children's metacognition. *Young Children, 68*(3), 38–43.

Lederman, J. (1992). *In full glory early childhood: To play's the thing.* Unpublished manuscript.

Leong, D. J., & Bodrova, E. (2012). Assessing and scaffolding make-believe play. *Young Children, 67*(1), 28–34.

Levin, D. E. (2003a). Beyond banning war and superhero play: Meeting children's needs in violent times. *Young Children, 58*(3), 60–64.

Levin, D. E. (2003b). *Teaching children in violent times: Building a peaceable classroom* (2nd ed.). Cambridge, MA: Educators for Social Responsibility; Washington, DC: NAEYC.

Levin, D. E. (2006). Play and violence: Understanding and responding effectively. In D. P. Fromberg & D. Bergen (Eds.), *Play from birth to twelve* (2nd ed., pp. 395–404). New York, NY: Taylor & Francis Group.

Levin. D.E. (2011). Beyond remote-controlled teaching and learning: The special challenge of helping children construct knowledge today. *Exchange* (May/June), 59–62.

Levin, D. E. (2013). *Beyond remote-controlled childhood: Teaching young children in the media age.* Washington, DC: NAEYC.

Levin, D. E., & Carlsson-Paige, N. (2006). *The war play dilemma: What every parent and teacher needs to know* (2nd ed.). New York, NY: Teachers College Press.

Levin, D. E., Daynard, C., & Dexter, B. (2008). *The "so far" guide for helping children and youth cope with the deployment and return of a parent in the National Guard.* Retrieved from http://www.sofarusa.org/downloads/SOFAR_2008_Final.pdf.

Levin, D. E., & Kilbourne, J. (2008). *So sexy so soon: The new sexualized childhood and what parents can do to protect their kids.* New York, NY: Ballantine Books.

Linn, S. (2008). *The case for make believe: Saving play in a commercialized world.* New York, NY: The New Press.

Linn, S. (2012, June 1). About that app gap: Children, technology and the digital divide. *Huffington Post.*

Locke, P. A., & Levin, J. (1998). Creative play begins with fun objects, your imagination, and simple-to-use technology. *The Exceptional Parent, 28,* 36–40.

Longfield, J. (2007). A DASH of inspiration (Developmental Approaches in Science, Health and Technology). *Science and Young Children, 44*(5), 26–29.

Louv, R. (2008). *Last child in the woods: Saving our children from nature-deficit disorder* (2nd ed.). London, UK: Atlantic Books.

Lovsey, K. (2002). *Play entry strategies of autistic children* (unpublished Master of Arts thesis, Sonoma State University).

Lowenfeld, V. (1947). *Creative and mental growth.* New York, NY: Macmillan.

Lux, D. G. (Ed.). (1985, Summer). Educating through drama. *Theory into Practice, 24*(3).

Manning, K., & Sharp, A. (1977). *Structuring play in the early years at school.* London, UK: Ward Lock Educational.

Marvin, C., & Hunt-Berg, M. (1996). Let's pretend: A semantic analysis of preschool children's play. *Journal of Children's Communication Development, 17*(2), 1–10.

Mayer, K. (2007). Emerging knowledge about emergent writing. *Young Children, 62*(1), 34–40.

McCay, L., & Keyes, D. (2001). Developing social competence in the inclusive early childhood classroom. *Childhood Education, 78,* 70–78.

McCune, L. (1985). Play-language relationships and symbolic development. In L.C. Brown & A. Gottfried (Eds.) *Play interactions* (pp. 38–45). Skillman, NY: Johnson & Johnson.

McDonnough, J. T., & Cho, S. (2009). Making the connection. *Science Teacher, 76*(3), 34–37.

McEvoy, M., Shores, R., Wehby, J., Johnson, S., & Fox, J. (1990). Special education teachers' implementation of procedures to promote social interaction among children in integrated settings. *Education and Training in Mental Retardation, 25*(3), 267–276.

McEwan, H., & Egan, K. (Eds.). (1995). *Narrative in teaching, learning, and research.* New York, NY: Teachers College Press.

McGarvey, L. M. (2013). Is it a pattern? *Teaching Children Mathematics, 19*(9), 564–571.

McGhee, P. E. (2005). The importance of nurturing children's sense of humor. *Children Our Concern, 28*(1), 16–17.

McHenry, J. D., & Buerk, K. J. (2008). Infants and toddlers meet the natural world. *Beyond the journal: Young children on the Web.* Retrieved from http://www.naeyc.org/files/yc/file/200801/BTJNatureMcHenry.pdf.

McLloyd, V. (1983). The effects of the structure of play objects on the pretend play of low-income preschool children. *Child Development, 54,* 626–635.

McVicker, C. J. (2007). Young readers respond: The importance of child participation in emerging literacy. *Young Children, 62*(3), 18–22.

Mead, G. H. (1934). *Mind, self, and society.* Chicago, IL: University of Chicago Press.

Meisels, S. J. (2011, November 11). Common Core Standards pose dilemmas for early childhood. *Washington Post* [online]. Retrieved from http://www.washingtonpost.com/blogs/answer-sheet/post/common-core-standards-pose-dilemmas-for-early-childhood/2011/11/28/gIQAPs1X6N_blog.html.

Meisels, S. J., Marsden, D. B., Jablon, J. R., & Dichtelmiller, M. (2013). *The work sampling system* (5th ed.). Upper Saddle River, NJ: Pearson Education, Inc.

Meisels, S. J., Xue, Y., & Shamblott, M. (2008). Assessing language, literacy, and mathematics skills with Work Sampling for Head Start. *Early Education & Development, 19*, 963–981.

Melben, L. W. (2000). Nature in the city: Outdoor science projects for urban schools. *Science & Children, 37*(7), 18–21.

Miller, E., & Carlsson-Paige, N. (2013, January 29). A tough critique of Common Core on early childhood education. *Washington Post* [online]. Retrieved from http://www.washingtonpost.com/blogs/answer-sheet/wp/2013/01/29/a-tough-critique-of-common-core-on-early-childhood-education.

Miller, M. D., Linn, R. L., & Gronlund, N. E. (2013). *Measurement and assessment in teaching* (11th ed.). Upper Saddle River, NJ: Pearson Education.

Milligan, S. A. (2003, November). Assistive technologies: Supporting the participation of children with disabilities. *Young Children: Beyond the Journal.* Retrieved from http://www.journal.naeyc.org/btj/200311/assistive-technology.pdf.

Mindes, G. (2006). Can I play too? Reflections on the issues for children with disabilities. In D. P. Fromberg & D. Bergen (Eds.), *Play from birth to twelve* (2nd ed., pp. 289–296). New York, NY: Taylor & Francis Group.

Mitchell, G. (with Dewsnap, L.). (1993). *Help! What do I do about…? Biting, tantrums, and 47 other everyday problems.* New York, NY: Scholastic.

Monighan-Nourot, P., Scales, B., Van Hoorn, J., with Almy, M. (1987). *Looking at children's play: A bridge between theory and practice.* New York, NY: Teachers College Press.

Montessori, M. (1936). *The secret of childhood.* Bombay, India: Orient Longman.

Mooney, C.B. (2000). *Theories of childhood: An introduction to Dewey, Montessori, Erikson, Piaget, and Vygotsky.* St. Paul, MN: Redleaf Press.

Moore, R., & Wong, H. (1997). *Natural learning: Creating environments for rediscovering nature's way of teaching.* Berkeley, CA: MIG Communications.

Morgan, E., & Ansberry, K. (2012). Bridges and skyscrapers. *Science and Children, 50*(4), 22–27.

Morgenthaler, S. K. (2006). The meanings in play with objects. In D. P. Fromberg & D. Bergen (Eds.), *Play from birth to twelve* (2nd ed., pp. 65–74). New York, NY: Taylor & Francis Group.

Morrison, H. (1985). *Learning to see what I saw.* Unpublished report of a research project for the Bay Area Writing Project, Berkeley, CA: University of California.

Morrison, H., & Grossman, H. (1985). *Beginnings* [Videotape]. Produced for the Bay Area Writing Project, Berkeley, CA: University of California.

Morrow, L. M. (2009). *Literacy development in the early years: Helping children read and write.* Upper Saddle River, NJ: Pearson Education, Inc.

Murphey, D. A., & Burns, C. E. (2002). Development of a comprehensive community assessment of school readiness. *Early Childhood Research and Practice, 4*(2), 1–15.

Myers, G. D. (1985). Motor behavior of kindergartners during physical education and free play. In J. L. Frost & S. Sunderlin (Eds.), *When children play* (pp. 151–156). Wheaton, MD: Association for Childhood Education International.

Myhre, S. M. (1993). Enhancing your dramatic play area through the use of prop boxes. *Young Children, 48*(5), 6–11.

Nabhan, G. P., & Trimble, S. (1994). *The geography of childhood: Why children need wild places.* Boston, MA: Beacon Press.

Nachmanovitch, S. (1990). *Free play: The power of improvisation in life and the arts.* New York, NY: Putnam.

National Art Education Association. (1999). *Purposes, principles, and standards for school art programs.* Reston, VA: Author.

National Association for Sport and Physical Education. (2004). *Moving into the future: National standards for physical education* (2nd ed.). Reston, VA: Author.

National Association for the Education of Young Children. (2005a). Screening and assessment of young English-language learners. Retrieved from http://www.naeyc.org/files/naeyc/file/positions/ELL_Supplement_Shorter_Version.pdf.

National Association for the Education of Young Children. (2005b, April). *NAEYC Code of ethical conduct and statement of commitment.* Washington, DC. Retrieved from http://www.naeyc.org/files/naeyc/file/positions/PSETH05.pdf.

National Association for the Education of Young Children. (2012a). *The Common Core State Standards: Caution and opportunity for early childhood education.* Washington, DC: Author.

National Association for the Education of Young Children. (2012b). Message in a backpack: Rough and tumble play—A message from your child's teacher. *Teaching Young Children, 5*(4), 20. Retrieved from http://www.naeyc.org/tyc/files/tyc/file/V5N4/MIBP.%20Rough%20and%20Tumble%20Play.pdf

National Association for the Education of Young Children & Fred Rogers Center for Early Learning and Children's Media. (2012). Technology and interactive media as tools in early childhood programs serving children from birth through age 8. Retrieved from http://www.naeyc.org/files/naeyc/file/positions/PS_technology_WEB2.pdf.

National Association for the Education of Young Children & National Association of Early Childhood Specialists in State Departments of Education. (1991). Guidelines for appropriate curriculum content and assessment in programs serving children ages 3 through 8. *Young Children, 46*(3), 21–38.

National Association for the Education of Young Children & National Association of Early Childhood Specialists in State Departments of Education. (2002). Joint position statement: Early learning standards: Creating the conditions for success. Retrieved from http://www.naeyc.org/about/positions/early_learning_standards.asp.

National Association for the Education of Young Children & National Council of Teachers of Mathematics (2009).

Where we stand on early childhood mathematics. Joint position statement. Washington, DC: NAEYC.

National Association for the Education of Young Children & National Council of Teachers of Mathematics (2010). Early childhood mathematics: Promoting good beginnings. Joint position statement. Washington, DC: NAEYC.

National Association of Early Childhood Specialists in State Departments of Education. (2002). *Recess and the importance of play: A position statement on young children and recess.* Washington, DC: Author. Retrieved from http://naecscrc.uiuc.edu/position/recessplay.html.

National Council for the Social Studies. (1998). *Ten thematic strands in social studies.* Washington, DC: Author.

National Council of Teachers of Mathematics. (2000). *Principles and standards for school mathematics.* Reston, VA: Author.

National Council of Teachers of Mathematics. (2006). *Curriculum focal points for prekindergarten through grade 8 mathematics: A quest for coherence.* Reston, VA: Author.

National Council of Teachers of Mathematics. (2010). *Mathematics curriculum: Issues, trends, and future directions: 72nd NCTM yearbook.* Reston, VA: Author.

National Governors Association Center for Best Practices and Council of Chief State School Officers. (2010). *Common Core State Standards.* Washington, DC: Author.

National Research Council. (2012). *A framework for K–12 science education: Practices, crosscutting concepts, and core ideas.* Washington, DC: The National Academies Press.

National Science Teachers Association. (2009). NSTA position statement: Science for English language learners. Retrieved from http://www.nsta.org/about/positions/ell.aspx.

Neeley, P. M., Neeley, R. A., Justen, J. E., III, & Tipton-Sumner, C. (2001). Scripted play as a language intervention strategy for preschoolers with developmental disabilities. *Early Childhood Education Journal, 28*(4), 243–246.

Nel, E. (2000). Academics, literacy, and young children: A plea for a middle ground. *Childhood Education, 76*(3), 136–141.

Nell, M. L., & Drew, W. F. with D. E. Bush (2013). *From play to practice: Connecting teachers' play to children's learning.* Washington, DC: NAEYC.

Neves, P., & Reifel, S. (2002). The play of early writing. In J. L. Roopnarine (Ed.), *Conceptual, social-cognitive, and contextual issues in the fields of play* (pp. 149–164). *Play and culture studies* (Vol. 4). Westport, CT: Ablex.

New, R. (2005). The Reggio Emilia approach: Provocation and partnerships with U.S. early childhood educator. In J. P. Roopnarine & J. Johnson (Eds.), *Approaches to early childhood education* (4th ed., pp. 313–335). Upper Saddle River, NJ: Merrill/Prentice Hall.

Newcomer, P. (1993). *Understanding and teaching emotionally disturbed children and adolescents.* Austin, TX: PRO-ED.

Newman, D., Griffin, P., & Cole, M. (1989). *The construction zone: Working for cognitive change in school.* Cambridge, MA: Cambridge University Press.

Nicolopoulou, A. (1996). Narrative development in a social context. In D. Slobin, J. Gearhart, A. Kyratzis, & J. Guo (Eds.), *Social interaction, social context, and language* (pp. 369–390). Mahwah, NJ: Erlbaum.

Nicolopoulou, A. (2001). Peer-group culture and narrative development. In S. Blum-Kulka & C. Snow (Eds.), *Talking with adults.* Mahwah, NJ: Erlbaum.

Nicolopoulou, A. (2007). The interplay of play and narrative in children's development: Theoretical reflections and concrete examples. In A. Göncü, J. Jain, & U. Tuermer (Eds.), *Play and development* (pp. 247–273). New York, NY: Erlbaum, Taylor & Francis Group.

Nicolopoulou, A., McDowell, J., & Brockmeyer, C. (2006). Story reading and story acting meet journal writing. In D. Singer, R. M. Golinkoff, & K. Hirsh-Pasek (Eds.), *Play = learning: How play motivates and enhances children's cognitive and social emotional growth* (pp. 124–144). New York, NY: Oxford University Press.

Nicolopoulou, A., & Scales, B. (1990, March). *Teenage Mutant Ninja Turtles vs. the prince and the princess.* Paper presented at 11th Annual Meeting of the Pennsylvania Ethnography and Research Forum, Philadelphia.

Nicolopoulou, A., Scales, B., & Weintraub, J. (1994). Gender differences and symbolic imagination in the stories of 4-year-olds. In A. H. Dyson & C. Genishi (Eds.), *The need for story: Cultural diversity in classroom and community* (pp. 102–123). Urbana, IL: National Council of Teachers of English.

Nielsen Company & McDonough, P. (2009, October 26). TV viewing among kids at an eight-year high. The Nielsen Company. Retrieved from http://blog.nielsen.com/nielsenwire/media_entertainment/tv-viewing-among-kids-at-an-eight-year-high.

Nieto, S. (2012). Honoring the lives of all children: Identity, culture, and language. In B. Falk (Ed.), *Defending childhood: Keeping the promise of early education* (pp. 48–62). New York, NY: Teachers College Press.

Ninio, A., & Bruner, J. S. (1976). The achievement and antecedents of labeling. *Journal of Child Language, 5,* 1–15.

Nissen, H., & Hawkins, C. J. (2010). Promoting emotional competency in the preschool classroom. *Childhood Education, 86*(4), 255–259.

North American Association for Environmental Education. (2010). *Early childhood environmental education programs: Guidelines for excellence.* Washington, DC: Author.

Nourot, P. M. (1997). Playing with play in four dimensions. In J. Isenberg & M. Jalongo (Eds.), *Major trends and issues in early childhood education: Challenges, controversies and insights.* New York, NY: Teachers College Press.

Nourot, P. M. (2005). Historical perspectives on early childhood education. In J. P. Roopnarine & J. Johnson (Eds.), *Approaches to early childhood education* (4th ed., pp. 107–124). Upper Saddle River, NJ: Merrill/Prentice Hall.

Nourot, P. M. (2006). Sociodramatic play pretending together. In D. P. Fromberg & D. Bergen (Eds.), *Play from birth to twelve* (2nd ed., pp. 87–101). New York, NY: Taylor & Francis Group.

Nourot, P. M., Henry, J., & Scales, B. (1990, April). *A naturalistic study of story play in preschool and kindergarten.* Paper presented at the Annual Meeting of the American Educational Research Association, Boston.

Novakowski, J. (2009). Classifying classification: Teachers examine their practices to help first-grade students build a deeper understanding of how to categorize things. *Science and Children, 46,* 25–27.

O'Neill, B. E. (2013). Improvisational play interventions: Fostering social-emotional development in inclusive classrooms. *Young Children, 68*(3), 62–69.

Odom, S. (Ed.). (2002). *Widening the circle: Including children with disabilities in preschool programs*. New York, NY: Teachers College Press.

Ogden, C. L., Carroll, M. D., Curtin, L. R., Lamb, M. M., & Flegal, K. M. (2010). Prevalence of high body mass index in U.S. children and adolescents, 2007–2008. *Journal of the American Medical Association, 303*, 242–249.

Ogakaki, L., Diamond, K., Kontos, S., & Hestenes, L. (1998). Correlates of young children's interactions with classmates with disabilities. *Early Childhood Research Quarterly, 13*(1), 67–86.

Ogakaki, L., & Frensch, P. A. (1998). Parenting and children's school achievement: A multiethnic perspective. *American Educational Research Journal, 35*, 123–144.

Ogu, U., & Schmidt, S. R. (2009). Investigating rocks: Addressing multiple learning styles through and inquiry-based approach. *Young Children, 64*, 12–18.

Oliver, S., & Klugman, E. (2002, September). What we know about play. *Child Care Information Exchange*.

Opitz, M. F. (2000). *Rhymes and reasons: Literacy and language play for phonological awareness*. Portsmouth, NH: Heinemann.

Orellana, M. (1994). Appropriating the voice of the superheroes: Three preschoolers' bilingual language uses in play. *Early Childhood Research Quarterly, 9*(2), 171–193.

Ostrosky, M., Kaiser, A., & Odom, S. (1993). Facilitating children's social-communicative interactions through the use of peer-mediated interventions. In A. Kaiser & D. Gray (Eds.), *Enhancing children's communication* (pp. 159–185). Baltimore, MD: Brookes.

Otto, B. (2010). *Language development in early childhood*. Upper Saddle River, NJ: Merrill.

Owacki, G. (2001). *Make way for literacy! Teaching the way young children learn*. Washington, DC: NAEYC.

Paley, V. G. (1981). *Wally's stories*. Cambridge, MA: Harvard University Press.

Paley, V. G. (1984). *Boys & girls: Superheroes in the doll corner*. Chicago, IL: University of Chicago Press.

Paley, V. G. (1986). *Mollie is three*. Chicago, IL: University of Chicago Press. 1990,

Paley, V. G. (1988). *Bad guys don't have birthdays: Fantasy play at four*. Chicago, IL: University of Chicago Press.

Paley, V. G. (1990). *The boy who would be a helicopter*. Cambridge, MA: Harvard University Press.

Paley, V. G. (1992). *You can't say you can't play*. Cambridge, MA: Harvard University Press.

Paley, V. G. (1994). Princess Annabella and the black girls. In A. H. Dyson & C. Genishi (Eds.), *The need for story: Cultural diversity in classrooms and community* (pp. 145–154). Urbana, IL: National Council of Teachers of English.

Paley, V. G. (1995). *Kwanzaa and me: A teacher's story*. Cambridge, MA: Harvard University Press.

Paley, V. G. (1997). *The girl with the brown crayon*. Cambridge, MA: Harvard University Press.

Paley, V. G. (1999). *The kindness of children*. Cambridge, MA: Harvard University Press.

Paley, V. G. (2004). *A child's work: The importance of fantasy play*. Chicago, IL: University of Chicago Press.

Paley, V. G. (2010). *The boy on the beach: Building community through play*. Chicago, IL: University of Chicago Press.

Panksepp, J. (2008). Play, ADHD, and the construction of the social brain: Should the first class each day be recess? *American Journal of Play, 1*(1), 55–79.

Parten, M. B. (1932). Social participation among preschool children. *Journal of Abnormal Psychology, 27*, 243–269.

Patte, M. M. (2010). Can you imagine a world without recess? *Childhood Education, 87*(1), 62–63.

Pellegrini, A. D. (1984). The effects of exploration and play on young children's associative fluency: A review and extension in training studies. In T. D. Yawkey & A. D. Pellegrini (Eds.), *Child's play: Developmental and applied* (pp. 237–253). Hillsdale, NJ: Erlbaum.

Pellegrini, A. D. (1998). Play and the assessment of children. In O. Saracho & B. Spodek (Eds.), *Multiple perspectives on play in early childhood education* (pp. 220–239). Albany, NY: SUNY Press.

Pellegrini, A. D. (2005). *Recess: Its role in education and development*. Mahwah, NJ: Erlbaum.

Pellegrini, A. D. (2009). *The role of play in human development*. New York, NY: Oxford University Press.

Pellegrini, A. D., & Galda, L. (1993). Ten years after: A re-examination of play and literacy research. *Reading Research Quarterly, 28*(2), 163–175.

Pellegrini, A. D., & Holmes, R. M. (2006). The role of recess in primary school. In D. Singer, R. M. Golinkoff, & K. Hirsh-Pasek (Eds.). *Play learning: How play motivates and enhances children's cognitive and social-emotional growth* (pp. 36–53). New York, NY: Oxford University Press.

Pellegrini, A. D., & Pellegrini, A. F. A. (2013). Play, plasticity, and ontogeny in childhood. In D. Narvaez, J. Panksepp, A. N. Schore, & T. R. Gleason. (Eds.), *Evolution, early experience and human development: From research to practice and policy* (pp. 339–351). New York, NY: Oxford University Press.

Pellegrini, A. D., & Smith, P. K. (1998). Physical activity play: The nature and function of a neglected aspect of play. *Child Development, 69*(3).

Pelletier, J., Halewood, C., & Reeve, R. (2005). How knowledge forum contributes to new literacies in kindergarten. *Orbit, 10*(1), 30–33.

Perry, J. P. (2001). *Outdoor play: Teaching strategies with young children*. New York, NY: Teachers College Press.

Perry, J. P. (2003). Making sense of outdoor pretend play. *Young Children, 58*(3), 26–30.

Perry, J. P. (2004). Making sense of outdoor pretend play. In D. Koralek (Ed.), *Spotlight on young children and play* (pp. 17–21). Washington, DC: NAEYC.

Perry, J. P. (2008). Children's experience of security and mastery on the playground. In E. Goodenough (Ed.), *A place to play* (pp. 99–105). Detroit, MI: Wayne State University Press.

Perry, J. P. (2011). Outdoor play. In *Play at the center of the curriculum* (5th ed.). Upper Saddle River, NJ: Pearson Education.

Perry, J. P., & Branum, L. (2009). "Sometimes I pounce on twigs because I'm a meat eater": Supporting physically active play and outdoor learning. *American Journal of Play, 2*(2). Retrieved from http://www.journalofplay.org/sites/www.journalofplay.org/files/pdf-articles/2-2-article-pounce-on-twigs-because-im-a-meat-eater.pdf

Phillips, A. (2002). Roundabout we go: A playable moment with a child with autism. In C. R. Brown & C. Marchant

(Eds.), *Play in practice: Case studies in young children's play* (pp. 115–122). St. Paul, MN: Redleaf Press.

Piaget, J. (1947/2003). *The psychology of intelligence.* New York, NY: Routledge.

Piaget, J. (1954). *The construction of reality in the child.* New York, NY: Ballantine Books.

Piaget, J. (1962). *Play, dreams and imitation in childhood.* New York, NY: Norton.

Piaget, J. (1963). *The origins of intelligence in children.* New York, NY: Norton.

Piaget, J. (1965a). *The child's conception of number.* New York, NY: Norton.

Piaget, J. (1965b). *The child's conception of physical causality.* Totowa, NJ: Littlefield, Adams.

Piaget, J. (1965c). *The moral judgment of the child.* New York, NY: Free Press.

Piaget, J. (1966). *Judgment and reasoning in the child.* Totowa, NJ: Littlefield, Adams.

Piaget, J. (1977). *The development of thought: Equilibration of cognitive structures.* New York, NY: Viking.

Piaget, J. (1995). *Sociological studies.* New York, NY: Routledge.

Pincus, S. H., House, R., Christensen, J. & Adler, L.E. (2005). *The emotional cycle of deployment: A military family perspective.* Retrieved from http://4h.missouri.edu/programs/military/resources/manual/Deployment-Cycles.pdf.

Power, P. (2011). Playing with ideas: The affective dynamics of creative play. *American Journal of Play, 3,* 288–323.

Prairie, A. P. (2013). Supporting sociodramatic play in ways that enhance academic learning. *Young Children, 68*(2), 62–68.

Preissler, M. A. (2006). Play and autism: Facilitating symbolic understanding. In D. G. Singer, R. M. Golinkoff, & K. Hirsh-Pasek (Eds.), *Play = learning: How play motivates and enhances children's cognitive and social-emotional growth* (pp. 231–250). New York, NY: Oxford University Press.

Qvortrup, J., Corsaro, W. A., & Sebastian-Honig, M. S. (Eds.). (2011). *The Palgrave handbook of childhood studies.* Hampshire, UK: Macmillan Publishers Limited.

Ramsey, P. G. (2006). Influences of race, culture, social class, and gender: Diversity and play. In D. P. Fromberg & D. Bergen (Eds.), *Play from birth to twelve* (2nd ed., pp. 261–273). New York, NY: Taylor & Francis Group.

Ramsey, P. G., & Reid, R. (1988). Designing play environments for preschool and kindergarten children. In D. Bergen (Ed.), *Play as a medium for learning and development: A handbook of theory and practice* (pp. 213–240). Portsmouth, NH: Heinemann.

Ravitch, D. (2010). *The death and life of the great American school system: How testing and choice are undermining education.* New York, NY: Basic Books.

Ravitch, D. (2013). Why I cannot support the Common Core standards. Diane Ravitch's blog. Retrieved from http://dianeravitch.net/2013/02/26/why-i-cannot-support-the-common-core-standards/comment-page-7.

Reed, T. L. (2005). A qualitative approach to boys' rough and tumble play: There is more than meets the eye. In F. F. McMahon, E. E., Lytle, & B. Sutton-Smith (Eds.), *Play, an interdisciplinary synthesis. Play and Culture Studies* (Vol. 6). Lanham, MD: University Press of America.

Reifel, S. (2007). Hermeneutic text: Exploring meaningful classroom events. In J. A. Hatch (Ed.), *Early childhood qualitative research.* New York, NY: Routledge Press, Taylor & Francis Group.

Reifel, S., Hoke, P., Pape, D., & Wisneski, D. (2004). From context to texts: DAP, hermeneutics, and reading classroom play. In S. Reifel & M. Brown (Eds.). *Social contexts of early education, and reconceptualizing play (II): Advances in early education and day care* (Vol. 13, pp. 209–220). Oxford, UK: JAI/Elsevier Science.

Reifel, S., & Sutterby, J. A. (2009). Play theory and practice in contemporary classrooms. In S. Feeney, A. Galper, & C. Seefeldt (Eds.), *Continuing issues in early childhood education* (pp. 238–241). Upper Saddle River, NJ: Pearson Education.

Reifel, S., & Yeatman, J. (1991). Action, talk and thought in block play. In B. Scales, M. Almy, A. Nicolopoulou, & S. Ervin-Tripp (Eds.), *The social context of play and development in early care and education* (pp. 156–172). New York, NY: Teachers College Press.

Reifel, S., & Yeatman, J. (1993). From category to context: Reconsidering classroom play. *Early Childhood Research Quarterly, 8,* 347–367.

Reynolds, G. (2002). The welcoming place: Tungasuvvingat Inuit Head Start program. In C. R. Brown & C. Marchant (Eds.), *Play in practice: Case studies in young children's play* (pp. 87–104). St. Paul, MN: Redleaf Press.

Richner, E. S., & Nicolopoulou, A. (2001, April). The narrative construction of differing conceptions of the person in the development of young children's social understanding. *Early Education and Development, 12,* 393–432

Riley, D., San Juan, R. R., Klinkner, J., & Ramminger, A. (2008). *Social & emotional development: Connecting science and practice in early childhood settings.* St. Paul, MN: Redleaf Press.

Riojas-Cortez, M. (2001). It's all about talking: Oral language development in a bilingual classroom. *Dimensions of Early Childhood, 29*(1), 11–15.

Rivkin, M. S. (2006). Children's outdoor play: An endangered activity. In D. P. Fromberg & D. Bergen (Eds.), *Play from birth to twelve* (2nd ed., pp. 323–329). New York, NY: Taylor & Francis Group.

Robson, S. (2010). Self-regulation and metacognition in young children's self-initiated play and reflective dialogues. *International Journal of Early Years Education, 18*(3), 227–241.

Roopnarine, J. L., & Johnson, J. L. (2013). *Pathways to Cultural Competence Project in approaches to early childhood education* (6th ed.). Upper Saddle River, NJ: Pearson Education.

Roopnarine, J. L., Shin, M., Donovan, B., & Suppal, P. (2000). Sociocultural contexts of dramatic play: Implications for early education. In *Play and literacy in early childhood: Research from multiple perspectives* (pp. 205–220). Mahwah, NJ: Erlbaum.

Rosenow, N. (2008). Introduction: Learning to love the earth . . . and each other. *Young Children, 63,* 10–13.

Roskos, K. (2000). Through the bioecological lens: Some observations of literacy in play as a proximal process. In K. Roskos & J. Christie (Eds.), *Play and literacy in early childhood: Research from multiple perspectives* (pp. 125–138). Mahwah, NJ: Erlbaum.

Roskos, K., & Christie, J. (Eds.). (2000a). Afterword. In *Play and literacy in early childhood: Research from multiple perspectives* (pp. 231–240). Mahwah, NJ: Erlbaum.

Roskos, K., & Christie, J. (2001). On not pushing children too hard: A few cautionary remarks about literacy and play. *Young Children, 56*(3), 64–66.

Roskos, K., & Christie J. (2004). Examining the play-literacy interface: A critical review and future directions. In E. Zigler, D. Singer, & S. Bishop-Josef (Eds.), *Children's play: The roots of reading* (pp. 95–124). Washington, DC: Zero to Three Press.

Roskos, K., & Neuman, S. (1998). Play as an opportunity for literacy. In O. Saracho & B. Spodek (Eds.), *Multiple perspectives on play in early childhood education* (pp. 100–115). Albany, NY: SUNY Press.

Rowe, D. W. (1994). *Preschoolers as authors: Literacy learning in the social world of the classroom.* Creskill, NJ; Hampton Press.

Rubin, K. H., Fein, G., & Vandenberg, B. (1983). Play. In E. M. Hetherington (Ed.), *Handbook of child psychology: Volume IV: Socialization, personality and social development* (pp. 693–774). New York, NY: Wiley.

Rui Olds, A. (2001). *Child care design guide.* New York, NY: McGraw-Hill.

Salmon, M., & Akaran, S. E. (2001). Enrich your kindergarten program with a cross-cultural connection. *Young Children, 56*(4), 30–33.

Saltz, E., & Johnson, J. (1974). Training for thematic fantasy play in culturally disadvantaged children: Preliminary results. *Journal of Educational Psychology, 66,* 623–630.

Sammons, M. T., & Batten, S. V. (2008). Psychological services for returning veterans and their families: Evolving conceptualizations of the sequelae of war-zone experiences. *Journal of Clinical Psychology, 64*(8), 921–927.

Sandall, S. (2003). Play modifications for children with disabilities. *Young Children, 58*(3), 54–57.

Saracho, O. (2001). Teachers' perceptions of their roles in promoting literacy in the context of play in a Spanish-speaking kindergarten. *International Journal of Early Childhood, 33*(2), 18–32.

Sarama, J., & Clements, D. H. (2002). Learning and teaching with computers in early childhood education. In O. Saracho & B. Spodek (Eds.), *Contemporary perspectives on early childhood curriculum* (pp. 177–219). Greenwich, CT: Information Age Publishing.

Sarama, J., & Clements, D. H. (2006). Mathematics in kindergarten. In D. Gullo (Ed.), *K today: Teaching and learning in the kindergarten year* (pp. 85–94). Washington, DC: NAEYC.

Sarama, J., & Clements, D. H. (2009). Teaching math in the primary grades: The learning trajectories approach. *Young Children, 64,* 63–65.

Saunders, R., & Bingham-Newman, A.M. (1984). *Piagetian perspective for preschools: A thinking book for teachers.* Upper Saddle River, NJ: Merrell/Prentice Hall.

Sawyer, K. (2001). *Creating conversations: Performance in everyday life.* Creskill, NJ: Hampton Press.

Scales, B. (1989). Whoever gets to the bottom gets the soap, right? In *The Proceedings of the Annual Ethnography in Education Forum.* Philadelphia, PA: University of Pennsylvania.

Scales, B. (1996, April). *Researching play and the hidden curriculum.* Paper presented at the annual meeting of The Association for the Study of Play, Austin, TX.

Scales, B. (1997, April). *Play in the curriculum: A mirror of development and a catalyst for learning.* Paper presented at the annual meeting of The Association for the Study of Play, Washington, DC.

Scales, B. (2000, March). *Math: The missing learning center.* Sacramento, CA: California Association for the Education of Young Children.

Scales, B. (2004, November). *Standards? Not a problem.* Paper presented at the National Association for the Education of Young Children Annual Conference.

Scales, B. (2005, February). *Using technology to track the development of a socially isolated child.* Paper presented at the annual meeting of the Association for the Study of Play, Santa Fe, NM.

Scales, B., & Cook-Gumperz, J. (1993). Gender in narrative and play: A view from the frontier. In S. Reifel (Ed.), *Advances in early education and day care: Perspectives on developmentally appropriate practice* (Vol. 5, pp. 167–195). Greenwich, CT: JAI Press.

Scales, B., Perry, J. & Tracy, R. (2010). *Children making sense of their world,* unpublished manuscript.

Scales, B., & Webster, P. (1976). *Interactive cues in children's spontaneous play.* Unpublished manuscript.

Scarlett, W. G., Naudeau, S., Salonius-Pasternak, D., & Ponte, I. (2005). *Children's play.* Thousand Oaks, CA: Sage.

Schickedanz, J. A., & Collins, M. F. (2013). *So much more than the ABCs: The early phases of reading and writing.* Washington DC: NAEYC.

Schor, J. (2004). *Born to buy: The commercialized child and the new consumer culture.* New York, NY: Scribner.

Schultz, P.W., Shriver, C., Tabanico, J., & Khazian, A. (2004). Implicit connections with nature. *Journal of Environmental Psychology, 24,* 31–42.

Schwartzman, H. B. (1976). Children's play: A sideways glance at make-believe. In D. F. Laney & B. A. Tindall (Eds.), *The anthropological study of play: Problems and prospects* (pp. 208–215). Cornwall, NY: Leisure Press.

Seefeldt, C. (2005). *How to work with standards in the early childhood classroom.* New York, NY: Teachers College Press.

Seefeldt, C., & Galper, A. (2000). *Active experiences for active children: Social studies.* Upper Saddle River, NJ: Merrill/Prentice Hall.

Seefeldt, C., Galper, A., & Stevenson-Garcia. J. (2012). *Active experiences for active children: Mathematics* (3rd ed.). Columbus, OH: Pearson.

Segatti, L., Brown-DuPaul, J., & Keyes, T.L. (2003). Using everyday materials to promote problem-solving in toddlers. *Young Children, 58*(5), 12–18.

Seligman, M. (2009, May 4). One husband, two kids, three deployments. *New York Times,* p. A19.

Sennet, R. (2008). *The craftsman.* New Haven, CT: Yale University Press.

Seo, K-. H. (2003). What children's play tells us about teaching mathematics. *Young Children, 58*(1), 28–34.

Sheldon, A. (1992). Conflict talk: Sociolinguistic challenges to self-assertion and how young girls meet them. *Merrill-Palmer Quarterly, 38*(1), 95–117.

Shepard, L., Kagan, S. L., & Wurtz, E. (Eds.). (1998a). *Principles and recommendations for early childhood assessments.* Washington, DC: National Education Goals Panel.

(Adaptation). Retrieved from http://www.state.ia.us/educate/ecese/is/ecn/primaryse/tppse08.htm.

Shepard, L., Kagan, S. L., & Wurtz, E. (1998b). Public policy report: Goal 1, early childhood assessments resources group recommendations. *Young Children, 53*(3), 52–54.

Sheridan, M., Foley, G., & Radlinski, S. (1995). *Using the supportive play model: Individualized intervention in early childhood practice.* New York, NY: Teachers College Press.

Sherwood, S.A., & Reifel, S. (2013). Valuable and unessential: The paradox of preservice teacher's beliefs about the role of play in learning. *Journal of Research in Childhood Education, 27*(3), 267–282.

Shillady, A. (2012). Math is everywhere! Tips for mathematizing preschool settings. In A. Shillady (Ed.), *Spotlight on young children: Exploring Math* (pp. 34–35). Washington, DC: NAEYC.

Sigel, I. E. (1993). Educating the young thinker: A distancing model of preschool education. In J. L. Roopnarine & J. E. Johnson (Eds.), *Approaches to early childhood education* (pp. 179–193, 237–252). Upper Saddle River, NJ: Merrill/Prentice Hall.

Silvern, S. B. (2006). Educational implications of play with computers. In D. P. Fromberg & D. Bergen (Eds.), *Play from birth to twelve* (2nd ed., pp. 215–221). New York, NY: Taylor & Francis Group.

Simons, K. D., & Klein, J. D. (2007). The impact of scaffolding and student achievement levels in a problem-based learning environment. *Instructional Science, 35,* 41–72.

Singer, D. G., Golinkoff, R. M., & Hirsh-Pasek, K. (Eds.). (2006). *Play = learning: How play motivates and enhances children's cognitive and social emotional growth.* New York, NY: Oxford University Press.

Singer, D. G., & Singer, J. L. (1990). *The house of make believe.* Cambridge, MA: Harvard University Press.

Singer, D. G., & Singer, J. L. (2005). *Imagination and play in the electronic age.* Cambridge, MA: Harvard University Press.

Singer, D. G., & Singer, J. L. (2006). Fantasy and imagination. In D. P. Fromberg & D. Bergen (Eds.), *Play from birth to twelve* (2nd ed., pp. 371–378). New York, NY: Taylor & Francis Group.

Singer, J. L. (2006). Epilogue: Learning to play and learning through play. In D. G. Singer, R. M. Golinkoff, & K. Hirsh-Pasek (Eds.), *Play = learning: How play motivates and enhances children's cognitive and social-emotional growth* (pp. 251–262). New York, NY: Oxford University Press.

Singer, J. L., & Lythcott, M. (2004). Fostering school achievement and creativity through sociodramatic play in the classroom. In E. Zigler, D. Singer & S. Bishop-Josef (Eds.), *Children's play: The roots of reading* (pp. 77–94). Washington, DC: Zero to Three Press.

Sluss, D., & Stremmel, A. (2004). A sociocultural investigation of the effects of peer interaction on play. *Journal of Research in Childhood Education, 18*(4), 293–305.

Smilansky, S. (1968). *The effects of sociodramatic play on disadvantaged preschool children.* New York, NY: Wiley.

Smilansky, S. (1990). Sociodramatic play: Its relevance to behavior and achievement in school. In E. Klugman & S. Smilansky (Eds.), *Children's play and learning: Perspectives and policy implications* (pp. 18–42). New York, NY: Teachers College Press.

Smilansky, S., & Shefatya, L. (1990). *Facilitating play: A medium for promoting cognitive, socio-emotional and academic development in young children.* Gaithersburg, MD: Psychosocial and Educational Publications.

Smith, A. F. (2000). Reflective portfolios: Preschool possibilities. *Childhood Education, 76,* 204–208.

Smith, P.K. (2010). *Children and play.* Chichester, UK: John Wiley & Sons.

Smith, P. K., & Connolly, K. J. (1980). *The ecology of preschool behavior.* Cambridge, UK: Cambridge University Press.

Smith, P.K., & Gosso, Y. (2010). *Children and play.* Chichester, UK: Wiley-Blackwell.

Smith, P. K., Smees, R., & Pellegrini, A. J. (2004). Play fighting and real fighting: Using video playback methodology with young children. *Aggressive Behavior, 30,* 164–173.

Smith, S. S. (2009). *Early childhood mathematics* (4th ed.). Upper Saddle River, NJ: Pearson Education.

Sobel, D. (2004). *Place-based education: Connecting classrooms and communities.* Great Barrington, MA: The Orion Society.

Sobel, D. (2008). *Childhood and nature: Design principles for educators.* Portland, ME: Stenhouse Publishers.

Soderman, A. K., Clevenger, K. G., & Kent, I. G. (2013, March). Using stories to extinguish the hot spots in second language acquisition, preschool to grade 1. *Young Children, 68*(1).

Soundy, C. S., & Stout, N. L. (2002). Pillow talk: Fostering the emotional and language needs of young learners. *Young Children, 57*(2), 20–24.

Spivak, A., & Howes, C. (2011). Social and relational factors in early educational and pro-social actions of children of diverse ethnocultural communities. *Merrill Palmer Quarterly, 57*(1), 1–24.

Starbuck, S., Olthof, M., & Midden, K. (2002). *Hollyhocks and honeybees: Garden projects for young children.* St. Paul, MN: Redleaf Press.

Stegelin, D. (2005). Making the case for play policy: Research-based reasons to support play-based environments. *Young Children, 60*(2), 76–85.

Stewart, D. (2001). *Sophie the pig project.* Lafayette, CA: Old Firehouse School.

Stone, M., & Sagstetter, M. (1998). Simple technology: It's never too early to start. *The Exceptional Parent, 28,* 50–51.

Strickland, K., & Strickland, J. (2000). *Making assessment elementary.* Portsmouth, NJ: Heinemann.

Sutton-Smith, B. (1997). *The ambiguity of play.* Cambridge, MA: Harvard University Press.

Sutton-Smith, B., Meechling, J., Johnson, T. W., & McMahon, F. R. (1995). *Children's folklore: A source book.* New York, NY: Routledge.

Swarbrick, N., Eastwood, G., & Tutton, K. (2004). Self-esteem and successful interaction as part of the Forest School Project. *Support for Learning, 19*(3), 142–146.

Swartz, D. (1997). *Culture and power: The sociology of Pierre Bourdieu.* Chicago, IL: University of Chicago Press.

Swick, K. (2002). The dynamics of families who are homeless: Implications for early childhood educators. *Childhood Education, 80*(3), 116–120.

Sylva, K., Siraj-Blatchford, I., & Taggert, B. (2010). *ECERS-E: The Four curricular subscalese extensions to the Early Child-*

hood Environmental Rating Scales. New York, NY: Teachers College Press.

Tannock, M. (2008). Rough and tumble play: An investigation of the perceptions of educators and young children. *Early Childhood Education Journal, 35*(4), 357–361.

Thatcher, D. H. (2001). Reading in math class: Selecting and using picture books for math investigations. *Young Children, 56*(4), 20–26.

Thomas, K. (2005). Indian Island School, early childhood program, Old Town, Maine: Universal design. In S. Friedman (Ed.), *Environments that inspire. Young Children, 60*(3), 53–54.

Thompson, J. E., & Thompson, R. A. (2007). How connecting with nature supports children's social emotional growth. *Exchange, 178,* 46–49.

Thompson, R. (2013). How emotional development unfolds starting at birth. *Zero to Three 32*(3), 6–11.

Tobin, J. (2000). *"Good guys don't wear hats": Children's talk about the media.* New York, NY: Teachers College Press.

Tobin, J., Hsueh, Y., & and Karasawa, M. (2011). *1 preschool in three cultures revisited: China, Japan, and the United States.* Chicago, IL: University of Chicago Press

Topal, C. W. (2005). Bring the spirit of the studio into the classroom. In L. Gandini, L. Hill, L. Cadwell, & C. Schwall (Eds.), *In the spirit of the studio: Learning from the Atelier of Reggio Emilia* (pp. 119–124). New York, NY: Teachers College Press.

Torquati, J., & Barber, J. (2005). Dancing with trees: Infants and toddlers in the garden. *Young Children, 60*(3), 40–46.

Tovey, H. (2007). *Playing outdoors: Spaces and places, risk and challenge.* Maidenhead, UK: Open University.

The Toy Manufacturers of America guide to toys and play. (2005). Retrieved from http://www.kidsource.com/kidsource/content/toys_ply.html.

Trawick-Smith, J. (1992). A descriptive study of persuasive preschool children: How they get others to do what they want. *Early Childhood Research Quarterly, 7*(1), 95–114.

Trawick-Smith, J. (1994). *Interactions in the classroom: Facilitating play in the early years.* Upper Saddle River, NJ: Merrill/Prentice Hall.

Trawick-Smith, J. (1998). Why play training works: An integrated model for play intervention. *Journal of Research in Childhood Education, 12,* 117–129.

Trawick-Smith, J. (2001). Play and the curriculum. In J. Frost, S. Wortham, & S. Reifel (Eds.), *Play and child development* (pp. 294–339). Upper Saddle River, NJ: Merrill/Prentice Hall.

Trawick-Smith, J. (2010). *Early childhood development: A multicultural perspective.* Upper Saddle River, NJ: Pearson Education.

Trawick-Smith, J., & Dziurgot, T. (2010). Untangling teacher-child interactions: Do teacher education and experience influence "good fit" responses to children's play? *Journal of Early Childhood Teacher Education, 31,* 106–112.

Tribble, C. (1996). *Individual differences in children's entrance strategies into preschool peer groups as a function of the quality of the mother-child attachment relationship.* Unpublished dissertation, University of California, Berkeley, CA.

Trundle, K. C., & Smith, M. M. (2011). Let it roll: Exploring motion with young children. *Science and Children, 49*(2), 38.

Trundle, K. C., Willmore, S., & Smith, W. S. (2006). The moon project. *Science and Young Children, 43*(6), 52–55.

Turner, V. D. (2009). *Bridging Piaget and Vygotsky: Discourse between paradigms.* Paper presented at 2009 Annual Meeting of the Jean Piaget Society, Park City, UT.

Tyminski, A.M., & Linder, S.M. (2012). Encouraging preschoolers' emerging mathematics skills. In A. Shillady (Ed.), *Spotlight on young children: Exploring math* (pp. 28–33). Washington, DC: NAEYC.

United States Consumer Product Safety Commission For Kids' Sake: Think Toy Safety (2013) retrieved from http://www.cpsc.gov/en/Safety-Education/Safety-Guides/

Uren, N., & Stagnitti, K. (2009). Pretend play, social competence and involvement in children aged 5–7 years: The concurrent validity of the Child-Initiated Pretend Play Assessment. *Australian Occupational Therapy Journal, 56*(1), 33–40.

Uttal, D., Marzolf, D., Pierroutsakos, S., Smith, C., Troseth, G., Scudder, K., & DeLoache, J. (1998). Seeing through symbols: The development of children's understanding of symbolic relations. In O. Saracho & B. Spodek (Eds.), *Multiple perspectives on play in early childhood education* (pp. 59–79). Albany, NY: SUNY Press.

van der Kooij, R. (1989). Play and behavioral disorders in schoolchildren. *Play and Culture, 2*(1), 328–339.

VanderVen, K. (2006). Attaining the protean self in a rapidly changing world: Understanding chaos through play. In D. P. Fromberg & D. Bergen (Eds.), *Play from birth to twelve* (2nd ed., pp. 405–415). New York, NY: Taylor & Francis Group.

Van Hoorn, J., & Levin, D. (2011). In harms way? Or are they? War, young children in the United States and social justice. In B. S. Fennimore & A. L. Goodwin (Eds.), *Promoting social justice for young children* (pp. 47–58). New York, NY: Springer.

Van Hoorn, J. L., & McHargue, T. (1999, July). *Early childhood education for peace and nonviolence.* Paper presented at the International Union of Psychological Science: Sixth International Symposium on the Contribution of Psychology to Peace, San Juan, Costa Rica.

Van Thiel, L., & Putnam-Franklin, S. (2004). Standards and guidelines: Keeping play in professional practice and planning. *Play, Policy, and Practice Connections 8*(2), 16–19.

Vecchi, V. (2010). *Art and creativity in Reggio Emilia: Exploring the role and potential of ateliers in early childhood education.* London, UK: Routledge.

Veldhuis, H. A. (1982, May). *Spontaneous songs of preschool children.* Master's thesis, San Francisco State University, San Francisco, CA.

von Blanckensee, L. (1999). *Teaching tools for young learners.* Larchmont, NY: Eye on Education.

Vygotsky, L. S. (1962). *Thought and language.* Cambridge, MA: MIT Press.

Vygotsky, L. S. (1967). Play and its role in the mental development of the child. *Soviet Psychology, 12,* 62–76.

Vygotsky, L. S. (1976). Play and its role in the mental development of the child. In J. S. Bruner, A. Jolly, & K. Sylva (Eds.), *Play: Its role in development and evolution* (pp. 537–544). New York, NY: Basic Books.

Vygotsky, L. S. (1978). *Mind in society: The development of higher psychological processes.* Cambridge, MA: Harvard University Press.

Vygotsky, L. S. (1986). *Thought and language.* A. Kozulin (Ed. and Trans.). Cambridge, MA: MIT Press.

Wagner, B. J. (1999). *Dorothy Heathcote: Drama as a learning medium.* Portsmouth, NH: Heinemann.

Walker, S., & Berthelsen, D. C. (2008). Children with autistic spectrum disorder in early childhood education programs: A social constructivist perspective on inclusion. *International Journal of Early Childhood, 40*(1), 33–51.

Walsh, P. (2008, September/October). Planning for play in a playground. *Playground Planning Exchange,* 88–94.

Waniganayake, M. (2001). From playing with guns to playing with rice: The challenges of working with refugee children: An Australian perspective. *Childhood Education,* 77(5), 289–294.

Wasik, B. (2001). Phonemic awareness and young children. *Childhood Education, 77*(3), 128–133.

Wasserman, S. (2000). *Serious players in the primary classroom: Empowering children through active learning experiences* (2nd ed.). New York, NY: Teachers College Press.

Waters, A. (2008). *Edible schoolyard: A universal idea.* San Francisco, CA: Chronicle Books.

Weitzman, E., & Greenberg, J. (2002). *Learning language and loving it.* Toronto, ON: The Haner Centre.

Wertsch, J. V., & Stone, C. A. (1985). The concept of internalization in Vygotsky's account of the genesis of higher mental functions. In J. V. Wertsch (Ed.), *Culture, communication, and cognition: Vygotskian perspectives.* Cambridge, UK: Cambridge University Press.

Wheeler, L., & Raebeck, L. (1985). *Orff and Kodaly adapted for the elementary school* (3rd ed.). Dubuque, IA: Wm. C. Brown Publishers.

Wien, C. A. (2004). *Negotiating standards in the primary classroom: The teacher's dilemma.* New York, NY: Teachers College Press.

Wien, C. A. (2008). *Emergent curriculum in the primary classroom: Interpreting the Reggio Emilia approach in schools.* New York, NY: Teachers College Press.

Wien, C. A. (2014). *The power of emergent curriculum: Stories from early childhood settings.* Washington, DC: NAEYC

Williams, K. P. (2002). "But are they learning anything?" African American mothers, their children, and their play. In C. R. Brown & C. Marchant (Eds.), *Play in practice: Case studies in young children's play* (pp. 73–86). St. Paul, MN: Redleaf Press.

Wilson, D. S. (2011). The Design Your Own Park Competition: Empowering neighborhoods and restoring outdoor play on a citywide scale. *American Journal of Play, 3*(4), 538–550. Retrieved from http://www.journalofplay.org/sites/www.journalofplay.org/files/pdf-articles/3-4-article-wilson-design-park-competition.pdf

Wilson, D. S., Marshall, D., & Iserhott, H. (2011). Empowering groups that enable play. *American Journal of Play, 3*(4), 523–537. Retrieved from http://www.journalofplay.org/sites/www.journalofplay.org/files/pdf-articles/3-4-article-wilson-empowering-groups.pdf

Wilson, R. (1997). The wonders of nature: Honoring children's ways of knowing. *Early Childhood News, 6*(19).

Winnicott, D. W. (1971). *Playing and reality.* New York, NY: Basic Books.

Wohlwill, J. F. (1984). Relationships between exploration and play. In T. Yawkey & A. Pellegrini (Eds.), *Child's play: Developmental and applied* (pp. 143–201). Hillsdale, NJ: Erlbaum.

Wohlwend, K. (2011). *Playing their way into literacies: Reading, writing, and belonging in the early childhood curriculum.* New York, NY: Teachers College Press.

Wohlwend, K. (2013). *Literacy playshop: New literacies, popular media, and play in the early childhood classroom.* New York, NY: Teachers College Press.

Wolfberg, P. (1999). *Play and imagination in children with autism.* New York, NY: Teachers College Press.

Wolfberg, P. (2003). *Peer play and the autism spectrum: The art of guiding children's socialization and imagination.* Lenexa, KS: Autism Asperger Publishing Company.

Wolfberg, P. (2009). *Play and imagination in children with autism.* (2nd ed.). New York, NY: Teachers College Press.

Wolfe, C. R., Cummins, R. H., & Myers, C. A. (2006). Scientific inquiry and exploratory representational play. In D. P. Fromberg & D. Bergen (Eds.), *Play from birth to twelve* (2nd ed., pp. 199–206). New York, NY: Taylor & Francis Group.

Wolfe, J. (2002). *Learning from the past: Historical voices in early childhood education* (2nd ed.). Mayerthorpe, AB: Piney Branch Press.

Wood, E. (2010). Developing integrated pedagogical approaches to play and learning. In P. Broadhead, J. Howard, & E. Wood (Eds.), *Play and learning in the early years: From research to practice* (pp. 9–26). London, UK: Sage.

Worth, K., & Grollman, S. (2004). *Worms, shadows, and whirlpools: Science in the early childhood classroom.* Washington, DC: NAEYC.

Wortham, S. C. (2012). *Assessment in early childhood education* (6th ed.). Upper Saddle River, NJ: Pearson Education, Inc.

Wurm, J. P. (2005). *Working in the Reggio way: A beginner's guide for American teachers.* Washington, DC: NAEYC.

Yang, H., & McMullen, M. B. (2003). Understanding the relationships among American primary-grade teachers and Korean mothers: The role of communication and cultural sensitivity in the linguistically diverse classroom. *Early Childhood Research and Practice, 5*(1), 1–20.

Yopp, H. K. (1995). Read-aloud books for developing phonemic awareness: An annotated bibliography. *The Reading Teacher, 49,* 20–29.

Yopp, H. K., & Yopp, R. H. (2009, January). Phonological awareness in child's play. *Young Children, 64*(1).

Zapeda, M., Gonzalez-Mena, J., Rothstein-Fisch, C., & Trumbull, E. (2006). *Bridging cultures in early care and education: A training module.* Mahwah, NJ: Erlbaum.

Zimmerman, E., & Zimmerman, L. (2000). Art education and early childhood education: The young child as creator and meaning maker within a community context. *Young Children, 56*(6), 87–92.

AUTHOR INDEX

SUBJECT INDEX

459